TRAINING & REFERENCE

murach's
VB.NET
database programming with
ADO.NET

Anne Prince

Doug Lowe

MIKE MURACH & ASSOCIATES, INC.

2560 West Shaw Lane, Suite 101 • Fresno, CA 93711-2765
www.murach.com • murachbooks@murach.com

Authors:	Anne Prince
	Doug Lowe
Contributor:	Bryan Syverson
Copy editor:	Judy Taylor
Cover design:	Zylka Design
Production:	Karen Schletewitz
	Tom Murach

3 books for every VB.NET programmer

Murach's Beginning Visual Basic .NET
Murach's VB.NET Database Programming with ADO.NET
Murach's SQL for SQL Server

Other books in the Murach series

Murach's Beginning Java 2
Murach's Java Servlets and JSP

Murach's Visual Basic 6

Murach's Structured COBOL
Murach's OS/390 and z/OS JCL
Murach's CICS for the COBOL Programmer
Murach's CICS Desk Reference

Contents

Expanded contents

Section 3 Other database programming skills

Section 4 Database programming with ASP.NET

Introduction

Today, most of the critical Visual Basic applications in any company are database applications. Those are the applications that store, retrieve, and update the data in a database like a Microsoft SQL Server database. That's why you can't get far as a Visual Basic .NET programmer unless you know how to write database applications.

The trouble is that database programming is one of the most challenging aspects of .NET programming. To start, you have to get your mind around the new disconnected data architecture and the hundreds of classes, properties, methods, and events that are part of the new ADO.NET data access method. Then, for each database task, you have to figure out which of several possible programming techniques you should use.

To a large extent, that explains why it has been so difficult to learn database programming with ADO.NET. But now, if you already know the basics of VB.NET programming, this book will take you from beginner to database professional in a logical progression from the simple to the complex. When you're done, you'll be able to use VB.NET and ADO.NET to develop real-world Windows and web applications that make efficient use of databases.

What this book does

To present all the database programming skills in a manageable progression, this book is divided into five sections.

- In section 1, chapter 1 introduces you to the database concepts and terms that you need to know, and chapter 2 gives you your first look at the classes of ADO.NET. Then, chapter 3 shows you how to develop your first complete database application. When you're done, you'll know how to use the disconnected data architecture and the basic ADO.NET classes, and you'll be well prepared for all that follows.

- In section 2, you'll learn how to use the ADO.NET classes and techniques that every database programmer should know. That includes the use of typed and untyped datasets, bound and unbound controls, data views, parameterized queries, and relationships. When you're done, you'll be well on your way to becoming an accomplished database programmer.

- In section 3, you'll raise your skills to another level. In chapters 8 and 9, you'll learn how to work with data commands directly and you'll learn three more ways to create the schemas that define the tables in a dataset. Then, chapter 10 shows you how to create and use database classes so you can separate the database layer from the business and presentation layers of an application. Last, to show you how the skills of the first 10 chapters are used in the real world, chapter 11 presents a complete order entry application that updates 9 different tables.

- In section 4, you'll learn the database programming skills that you need as you develop web applications with ASP.NET. In particular, you'll learn three programming techniques that are commonly used with web applications that use databases, and you'll learn how to use two Web Server controls that are specifically designed for working with databases.

- Finally, section 5 completes the set of skills that every .NET database programmer should have. Here, chapter 15 introduces you to ADO.NET's XML features. Chapter 16 shows how to use Crystal Reports to generate reports from a database. And chapter 17 shows how to use the Server Explorer to perform common database tasks like managing the database objects that you work with.

Why you'll learn faster and better with this book

Like all our books, this one has features that you won't find in competing books. That's why we believe you'll learn faster and better with our book than with any other. Here are just a few of those features.

- This book presents everything you need to know to develop VB.NET database applications at a professional level. That sounds simple. But to get all of this information from other sources would take you 3 or 4 other books plus the Microsoft documentation…and you'd still have to figure out how it all worked together!

- To show you how all of the pieces of a database application interact, this book presents 21 complete applications ranging from the simple to the complex. This includes the forms, the code, and the property settings. As we see it, the only way to master database programming is to study applications like these. And yet, you won't find them in other books.

- If you page through this book, you'll see that all of the information is presented in "paired pages," with the essential syntax, guidelines, and examples on the right page and the perspective and extra explanation on the left page. This helps you learn faster by reading less...and this is the ideal reference format when you need to refresh your memory about how to do something.

Two companion books that will enhance your skills

If you have basic VB.NET programming skills, the kind you should get from any beginning book, you're ready for this book. The trouble is that too many beginning books trivialize VB.NET programming so you don't learn all of the basics that you need for developing real-world applications.

So, if you don't know all of the basics or if you're new to VB.NET, we would like to recommend *Murach's Beginning Visual Basic .NET*. This book will quickly get you up-to-speed on the basic VB.NET skills, and it's a terrific reference book that you can use whenever you need to refresh those skills. If, for example, you don't know how to use a multiple-document interface like the one that's used in the order entry application or if you don't know how to use constructors or how overloaded methods work, this book will fix that fast. It also has a section on ASP.NET web programming, which is all that you need for getting the most from section 4 of this book.

The second book that we recommend for all database programmers is *Murach's SQL for SQL Server*. To start, it shows you how to write SQL statements in all their variations so you can code the right statements for your ADO.NET command objects. This often gives you the option of having Microsoft SQL Server do more so your VB.NET application does less. Beyond that, this book shows you how to design and implement databases and how to use advanced features like stored procedures and triggers. In short, we believe that our SQL book is the perfect companion to this ADO.NET book for any VB.NET database programmer who uses Microsoft SQL Server.

What software you need for developing VB.NET database applications

Most likely, you already have the software for Visual Basic .NET installed on your PC. But here's a quick summary of what you need for developing and running VB.NET database applications on your own PC.

First, to develop any VB.NET application, you need to be running Windows 2000 or Windows XP on your PC. You also need to install either Visual Studio .NET or Visual Basic .NET. Although Visual Studio .NET includes other languages and features, you can do almost everything that this book requires with the Standard Edition of Visual Basic .NET, which sells for around $110. In contrast, the Professional Edition of Visual Studio .NET sells for about $1,080 and the Upgrade version sells for about $550.

There are a few limitations to using the Standard Edition of VB.NET with this book, however. To be specific, it doesn't include the following: the XML Designer that can be used to define dataset schemas as described in parts of chapters 7 and 9; Crystal Reports, which is covered in chapter 16; and the tools for designing SQL Server databases that are shown in chapter 17. So if you need any of these features, you'll have to use the Professional Edition of Visual Studio .NET.

If you want to run database and web applications on your PC (as opposed to using a database or web server on a network), you also need to install MSDE and IIS on your PC. MSDE is Microsoft's desktop database engine that's available from Microsoft free of charge. IIS is the web server that comes with Windows, except for Windows XP Home Edition (if you're using that version of Windows, you can't create or run web applications from your own PC). To learn how to install these products as well as Visual Studio or Visual Basic, please refer to appendix A in this book. *But please do this before you start the installations, because it's likely to save you some time.* If you don't install the products in the right order, you'll have to re-install some of them.

Downloadable files that can help you learn

If you go to our web site at www.murach.com, you can download the source code and databases for all of the applications presented in this book. Then, you can test and review these applications on your own PC to see exactly how they work. We recommend this for anyone who is using this book.

You can also download instructional aids like chapter summaries, learning objectives, review questions, exercises, and projects. These files, though, are designed primarily for students or trainees who are using this book for a class. As a result, your instructor can direct your use of these materials.

Support materials for trainers and instructors

If you're a trainer or instructor who would like to use this book for a course, we offer an Instructor's Guide on CD that includes everything that you need for an effective course. Besides the student downloadables that are listed above, this CD includes a complete set of PowerPoint slides, solutions to the downloadable exercises and projects, and short-answer and multiple-choice tests.

To download a sample of this Instructor's Guide and to find out how to get the complete Guide, please go to our web site at www.murach.com and click on the Instructors link. Or, if you prefer, you can call Kelly at 1-800-221-5528 or email kelly@murach.com.

Please let us know how this book works for you

When we started working with VB.NET, we found database programming with ADO.NET to be extremely frustrating for several reasons: the disconnected data architecture added a new level of complexity; there were numerous classes, properties, methods, and events to learn about; there were too many ways to get the same task done; and none of the available books or tutorials made the job much easier. Eventually, though, we got our minds around ADO.NET and realized that it could be presented in a way that would be much easier for our readers than it was for us.

Now that we're done, we hope that the many months we put into the development of this book will mean that you can become a proficient VB.NET database programmer in just a few weeks. So, if you have any comments about this book, we would appreciate hearing from you. And we thank you for buying it.

Anne Prince, Author
anne@murach.com

Doug Lowe, Author
doug@murach.com

Section 1

An introduction to database programming and ADO.NET

Before you can learn the details of developing database programs using Visual Basic .NET and ADO.NET, you need to understand the basic concepts and terms of ADO.NET database programming. That's the purpose of the three chapters in this section. Chapter 1 introduces you to the basics of relational databases and SQL. Then, chapter 2 gives you an overview of the ADO.NET classes you use to develop database programs in Visual Basic .NET. Finally, chapter 3 shows you how to develop a simple database program. When you finish these chapters, you'll be ready to learn the more complex database programming techniques presented in the rest of this book.

1

An introduction to database programming

This chapter introduces you to the basic concepts and terms that apply to database applications. In particular, it explains what a relational database is and how you work with it using SQL, the industry-standard language for accessing data in relational databases.

To illustrate these concepts and terms, this chapter presents examples that use the *Microsoft SQL Server 2000 Desktop Engine* (*MSDE*). MSDE, which comes with Visual Basic .NET, is a scaled-back version of Microsoft *SQL Server 2000*. And SQL Server 2000 is the database you're most likely to use as you develop database applications with Visual Basic .NET. However, the concepts and terms you'll learn in this chapter apply to other databases as well.

An introduction to client/server systems

In case you aren't familiar with client/server systems, this topic introduces you to their essential hardware and software components. Then, the rest of this chapter presents additional information on these components and how you can use them in database applications.

The hardware components of a client/server system

Figure 1-1 presents the three hardware components of a client/server system: the clients, the network, and the server. The *clients* are usually the PCs that are already available on the desktops throughout a company. And the *network* is made up of the cabling, communication lines, network interface cards, hubs, routers, and other components that connect the clients and the server.

The *server*, commonly referred to as a *database server*, is a computer that has enough processor speed, internal memory (RAM), and disk storage to store the files and databases of the system and provide services to the clients of the system. This computer is usually a high-powered PC, but it can also be a midrange system like an AS/400 or Unix system, or even a mainframe system. When a system consists of networks, midrange systems, and mainframe systems, often spread throughout the country or world, it is commonly referred to as an *enterprise system*.

To back up the files of a client/server system, a server usually has a tape drive or some other form of offline storage. It often has one or more printers or specialized devices that can be shared by the users of the system. And it can provide programs or services like email that can be accessed by all the users of the system. In larger networks, however, features such as backup, printing, and email are provided by a separate server. That way, the database server can be dedicated to the task of handling database requests.

In a simple client/server system, the clients and the server are part of a *local area network* (*LAN*). However, two or more LANs that reside at separate geographical locations can be connected as part of a larger network such as a *wide area network* (*WAN*). In addition, individual systems or networks can be connected over the Internet.

A simple client/server system

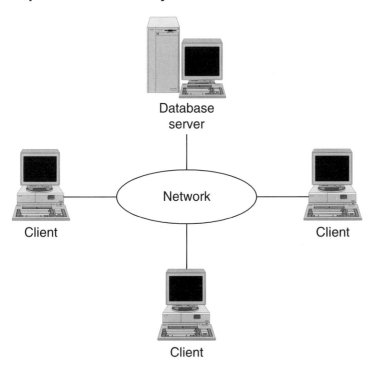

The three hardware components of a client/server system

- The *clients* are the PCs, Macintoshes, or workstations of the system.
- The *server* is a computer that stores the files and databases of the system and provides services to the clients. When it stores databases, it's often referred to as a *database server*.
- The *network* consists of the cabling, communication lines, and other components that connect the clients and the servers of the system.

Client/server system implementations

- In a simple *client/server system* like the one shown above, the server is typically a high-powered PC that communicates with the clients over a *local area network* (*LAN*).
- The server can also be a midrange system, like an AS/400 or a Unix system, or it can be a mainframe system. Then, special hardware and software components are required to make it possible for the clients to communicate with the midrange and mainframe systems.
- A client/server system can also consist of one or more PC-based systems, one or more midrange systems, and a mainframe system in dispersed geographical locations. This type of system is commonly referred to as an *enterprise system*.
- Individual systems and LANs can be connected and share data over larger private networks, such as a *wide area network* (*WAN*), or a public network like the Internet.

Figure 1-1   The hardware components of a client/server system

The software components of a client/server system

Figure 1-2 presents the software components of a typical client/server system. In addition to a *network operating system* that manages the functions of the network, the server requires a *database management system* (*DBMS*) like Microsoft SQL Server, Oracle, or MySQL. This DBMS manages the databases that are stored on the server.

In contrast to a server, each client requires *application software* to perform useful work. This can be a purchased software package like a financial accounting package, or it can be custom software that's developed for a specific application. This book, of course, shows you how to use Visual Basic .NET for developing custom software for database applications.

Although the application software is run on the client, it uses data that's stored on the server. To make this communication between the client and the *data source* possible when a Visual Basic .NET application is being used, the client accesses the database via a *data access API* such as ADO.NET.

Once the software for both client and server is installed, the client communicates with the server by passing *SQL queries* (or just *queries*) to the DBMS through the data access API. These queries are written in a standard language called *SQL*, which stands for *Structured Query Language*. SQL lets any application communicate with any DBMS. After the client sends a query to the DBMS, the DBMS interprets the query and sends the results back to the client. (In conversation, SQL is pronounced as either *S-Q-L* or *sequel*.)

As you can see in this figure, the processing done by a client/server system is divided between the clients and the server. In this case, the DBMS on the server is processing requests made by the application running on the client. Theoretically, at least, this balances the workload between the clients and the server so the system works more efficiently. In contrast, in a file-handling system, the clients do all of the work because the server is used only to store the files that are used by the clients.

Client software, server software, and the SQL interface

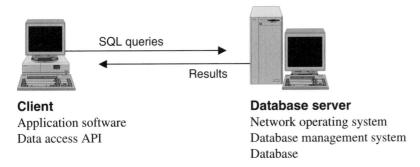

Client
Application software
Data access API

Database server
Network operating system
Database management system
Database

Server software

- To manage the network, the server runs a *network operating system* such as Windows 2000 Server.

- To store and manage the databases of the client/server system, each server requires a *database management system (DBMS)* such as Microsoft SQL Server.

- The processing that's done by the DBMS is typically referred to as *back-end processing*, and the database server is referred to as the *back end*.

Client software

- The *application software* does the work that the user wants to do. This type of software can be purchased or developed.

- The *data access API (application programming interface)* provides the interface between the application program and the DBMS. The newest data access API is ADO.NET, which is a part of Microsoft's .NET Framework.

- The processing that's done by the client software is typically referred to as *front-end processing*, and the client is typically referred to as the *front end*.

The SQL interface

- The application software communicates with the DBMS by sending *SQL queries* through the data access API. When the DBMS receives a query, it provides a service like returning the requested data (the *query results*) to the client.

- *SQL,* which stands for *Structured Query Language*, is the standard language for working with a relational database.

Client/server versus file-handling systems

- In a client/server system, the processing done by an application is typically divided between the client and the server.

- In a file-handling system, all of the processing is done on the clients. Although the clients may access data that's stored in files on the server, none of the processing is done by the server. As a result, a file-handling system isn't a client/server system.

Figure 1-2   The software components of a client/server system

Other client/server system architectures

In its simplest form, a client/server system consists of a single database server and one or more clients. Many client/server systems today, though, include additional servers. In figure 1-3, for example, you can see two client/server systems that include an additional server between the clients and the database server.

The first illustration is for a Windows-based system. With this system, only the user interface for an application runs on the client. The rest of the processing that's done by the application is stored in one or more *business components* on the *application server*. Then, the client sends requests to the application server for processing. If the request involves accessing data in a database, the application server formulates the appropriate query and passes it on to the database server. The results of the query are then sent back to the application server, which processes the results and sends the appropriate response back to the client.

Web-based applications use a similar type of architecture, as illustrated by the second example in this figure. In a web application, a *web browser* running on the client is used to send requests to a *web application* running on a *web server* somewhere on the Internet. The web application, in turn, can use *web services* to perform some of its processing. Then, the web application or web service can pass requests for data on to the database server.

Although this figure gives you an idea of how client/server systems can be configured, you should realize that they can be much more complicated than what's shown here. In a Windows-based system, for example, business components can be distributed over any number of application servers, and those components can communicate with databases on any number of database servers. Similarly, the web applications and services in a web-based system can be distributed over numerous web servers that access numerous database servers.

A Windows-based system that uses an application server

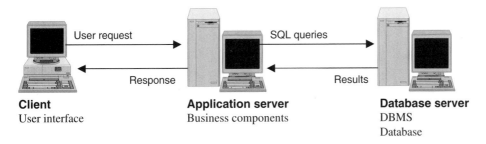

Client
User interface

Application server
Business components

Database server
DBMS
Database

A simple web-based system

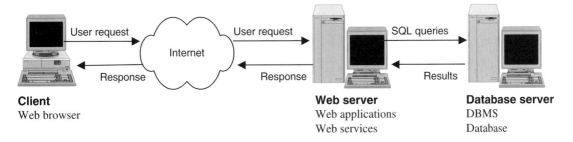

Client
Web browser

Web server
Web applications
Web services

Database server
DBMS
Database

Description

- In addition to a database server and clients, a client/server system can include additional servers, such as *application servers* and *web servers*.

- Application servers are typically used to store *business components* that do part of the processing of the application. In particular, these components are used to process database requests from the user interface running on the client.

- Web servers are typically used to store *web applications* and *web services*. Web applications are applications that are designed to run on a web server. Web services are like business components, except that, like web applications, they are designed to run on a web server.

- In a web-based system, a *web browser* running on a client sends a request to a web server over the Internet. Then, the web server processes the request and passes any requests for data on to the database server.

- More complex system architectures can include two or more application servers, web servers, and database servers.

Figure 1-3   Other client/server system architectures

An introduction to relational databases

In 1970, Dr. E. F. Codd developed a model for what was then a new and revolutionary type of database called a *relational database.* This type of database eliminated some of the problems that were associated with standard files and other database designs. By using the relational model, you can reduce data redundancy, which saves disk storage and leads to efficient data retrieval. You can also view and manipulate data in a way that is both intuitive and efficient. Today, relational databases are the de facto standard for database applications.

How a table is organized

The model for a relational database states that data is stored in one or more *tables.* It also states that each table can be viewed as a two-dimensional matrix consisting of *rows* and *columns.* This is illustrated by the relational table in figure 1-4. Each row in this table contains information about a single vendor.

In practice, the rows and columns of a relational database table are sometimes referred to by the more traditional terms, *records* and *fields.* In fact, some software packages use one set of terms, some use the other, and some use a combination. In this book, we've used the terms *rows* and *columns* for consistency.

If a table contains one or more columns that uniquely identify each row in the table, you can define these columns as the *primary key* of the table. For instance, the primary key of the Vendors table in this figure is the VendorID column. In this example, the primary key consists of a single column. However, a primary key can also consist of two or more columns, in which case it's called a *composite primary key.*

In addition to primary keys, some database management systems let you define additional keys that uniquely identify each row in a table. If, for example, the VendorName column in the Vendors table contains a unique name for each vendor, it can be defined as a *non-primary key.* In SQL Server, this is called a *unique key,* and it's implemented by defining a *unique key constraint* (also known simply as a *unique constraint*). The only difference between a unique key and a primary key is that a unique key can contain a null value and a primary key can't.

Indexes provide an efficient way to access the rows in a table based on the values in one or more columns. Because applications typically access the rows in a table by referring to their key values, an index is automatically created for each key you define. However, you can define indexes for other columns as well. If, for example, you frequently need to sort the Vendor rows by zip code, you can set up an index for that column. Like a key, an index can include one or more columns.

The Vendors table in a Payables database

Primary key   Columns

VendorID	VendorName	VendorAddress1	VendorAddress2
1	US Postal Service	Attn: Supt. Window Services	PO Box 7005
2	National Information Data Ctr	PO Box 96621	
3	Register of Copyrights	Library Of Congress	
4	Jobtrak	1990 Westwood Blvd Ste 260	
5	Newbrige Book Clubs	3000 Cindel Drive	
6	California Chamber Of Commerce	3255 Ramos Cir	
7	Towne Advertiser's Mailing Svcs	Kevin Minder	3441 W Macarthur Blvd
8	BFI Industries	PO Box 9369	
9	Pacific Gas & Electric	Box 52001	
10	Robbins Mobile Lock And Key	4669 N Fresno	
12	City Of Fresno	PO Box 2069	
13	Golden Eagle Insurance Co	PO Box 85826	
15	ASC Signs	1528 N Sierra Vista	
16	Internal Revenue Service		

Rows

Concepts

- A *relational database* uses *tables* to store and manipulate data. Each table consists of one or more *records*, or *rows*, that contain the data for a single entry. Each row contains one or more *fields*, or *columns*, with each column representing a single item of data.

- Most tables contain a *primary key* that uniquely identifies each row in the table. The primary key often consists of a single column, but it can also consist of two or more columns. If a primary key uses two or more columns, it's called a *composite primary key*.

- In addition to primary keys, some database management systems let you define one or more *non-primary keys*. In SQL Server, these keys are called *unique keys*, and they're implemented using *unique key constraints*. Like a primary key, a non-primary key uniquely identifies each row in the table.

- A table can also be defined with one or more *indexes*. An index provides an efficient way to access data from a table based on the values in specific columns. An index is automatically created for a table's primary and non-primary keys.

Figure 1-4   How a table is organized

How the tables in a database are related

The tables in a relational database can be related to other tables by values in specific columns. The two tables shown in figure 1-5 illustrate this concept. Here, each row in the Vendors table is related to one or more rows in the Invoices table. This is called a *one-to-many relationship*.

Typically, relationships exist between the primary key in one table and the *foreign key* in another table. The foreign key is simply one or more columns in a table that refer to a primary key in another table. In SQL Server, relationships can also exist between a unique key in one table and a foreign key in another table. For simplicity, though, I'll assume relationships are based on primary keys.

Although one-to-many relationships are the most common, two tables can also have a one-to-one or many-to-many relationship. If a table has a *one-to-one relationship* with another table, the data in the two tables could be stored in a single table. Because of that, one-to-one relationships are used infrequently.

In contrast, a *many-to-many relationship* is usually implemented by using an intermediate table, called a *linking table*, that has a one-to-many relationship with the two tables in the many-to-many relationship. In other words, a many-to-many relationship can usually be broken down into two one-to-many relationships.

The relationship between the Vendors and Invoices tables in the database

Primary key

VendorID	VendorName	VendorAddress1	VendorAddress2	VendorCity
114	Postmaster	Postage Due Technician	1900 E Street	Fresno
115	Roadway Package System, Inc	Dept La 21095	<NULL>	Pasadena
116	State of California	Employment Development Dept	PO Box 826276	Sacramento
117	Suburban Propane	2874 S Cherry Ave	<NULL>	Fresno
118	Unocal	P.O. Box 860070	<NULL>	Pasadena
119	Yesmed, Inc	PO Box 2061	<NULL>	Fresno
120	Dataforms/West	1617 W. Shaw Avenue	Suite F	Fresno
121	Zylka Design	3467 W Shaw Ave #103	<NULL>	Fresno
122	United Parcel Service	P.O. Box 505820	<NULL>	Reno
123	Federal Express Corporation	P.O. Box 1140	Dept A	Memphis

InvoiceID	VendorID	InvoiceNumber	InvoiceDate	InvoiceTotal
29	123	4-314-3057	5/2/2002	13.75
30	94	203339-13	5/2/2002	17.5
31	123	2-000-2993	5/3/2002	144.7
32	89	125520-1	5/5/2002	95
33	123	1-202-2978	5/6/2002	33
34	110	0-2436	5/7/2002	10976.06
35	123	1-200-5164	5/7/2002	63.4
36	110	0-2060	5/8/2002	23517.58
37	110	0-2058	5/8/2002	37966.19
38	123	963253272	5/9/2002	61.5

Foreign key

Concepts

- The tables in a relational database are related to each other through their key columns. For example, the VendorID column is used to relate the Vendors and Invoices tables above. The VendorID column in the Invoices table is called a *foreign key* because it identifies a related row in the Vendors table.

- Usually, a foreign key corresponds to the primary key in the related table. In SQL Server, however, a foreign key can also correspond to a unique key in the related table.

- When two tables are related via a foreign key, the table with the foreign key is referred to as the *foreign key table* and the table with the primary key is referred to as the *primary key table*.

- The relationships between the tables in a database correspond to the relationships between the entities they represent. The most common type of relationship is a *one-to-many relationship* as illustrated by the Vendors and Invoices table. A table can also have a *one-to-one relationship* or a *many-to-many relationship* with another table.

Figure 1-5   How the tables in a database are related

How to enforce referential integrity

Although the primary keys and foreign keys indicate how the tables in a database are related, those relationships aren't enforced automatically. To enforce relationships, you use *referential integrity* features like the ones described in figure 1-6. Although the features covered here are for SQL Server 2000, most database systems have similar features.

To understand why referential integrity is important, consider what would happen if you deleted a row from the Vendors table and referential integrity wasn't in effect. Then, if the Invoices table contained any rows for that vendor, those rows would be *orphaned*. Similar problems could occur if you inserted a row into the foreign key table or updated a primary key or foreign key value.

To avoid these problems and maintain the referential integrity of the tables, you can use one of two features: foreign key constraints or triggers. A *foreign key constraint* defines how referential integrity should be enforced when a row in a primary key table is updated or deleted. The options are to raise an error if the primary key row has corresponding rows in the foreign key table or to *cascade* the update or delete operation to the foreign key table.

For example, suppose a user attempts to delete a vendor that has invoices in the Invoices table. In that case, the foreign key constraint can be configured to either raise an error or automatically delete the vendor's invoices along with the vendor. Which option is best depends on the requirements of the application.

Triggers are special procedures that can be executed automatically when an insert, update, or delete operation is executed on a table. A trigger can determine whether an operation would violate referential integrity. If so, the trigger can either cancel the operation or perform additional actions to ensure that referential integrity is maintained.

Although most database servers provide for foreign key constraints, triggers, or both, not all databases take advantage of these features. In that case, it's up to the application programmer to enforce referential integrity. For example, before deleting a vendor, your application would have to query the Invoices table to make sure the vendor has no invoices. Whenever you develop an application that modifies database information, you need to find out what the application's referential integrity requirements are, whether those requirements are implemented in the database by constraints or triggers, and which referential integrity requirements must be implemented in the application's code.

The dialog box for defining foreign key constraints in SQL Server 2000

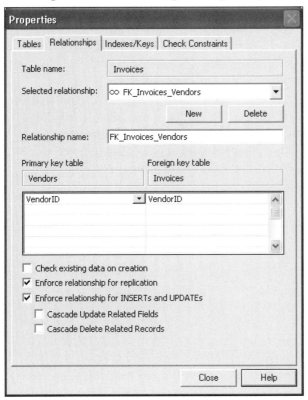

Description

- *Referential integrity* means that the relationships between tables are maintained correctly. That means that the foreign key values in a table with a foreign key must have matching primary key values in the related table.

- In SQL Server 2000, you can enforce referential integrity by using foreign key constraints or triggers.

- A *foreign key constraint* tells SQL Server what to do when a row is updated or deleted from a primary key table if a foreign key table has related rows. The options are to return an error or *cascade* the update or delete operation to all related rows in the foreign key table.

- A *trigger* is a SQL procedure that's defined in the database and executed automatically whenever an insert, update, or delete operation is performed on a table. A trigger can determine if a referential integrity violation has occurred and then handle it accordingly.

- If referential integrity isn't enforced and a row is deleted from the primary key table that has related rows in the foreign key table, the rows in the foreign key table are said to be *orphaned*.

Figure 1-6   How SQL Server enforces referential integrity

How the columns in a table are defined

When you define a column in a table, you assign properties to it as indicated by the design of the Invoices table in figure 1-7. The two most important properties for a column are Column Name, which provides an identifying name for the column, and Data Type, which specifies the type of information that can be stored in the column. With SQL Server 2000, you can choose from *system data types* like the ones in this figure, and you can define your own data types that are based on the system data types. As you define each column in a table, you generally try to assign the data type that will minimize the use of disk storage because that will improve the performance of the queries later.

In addition to a data type, you must identify whether the column can store a *null value*. A null represents a value that's unknown, unavailable, or not applicable. As you'll learn later in this book, columns that allow nulls often require additional programming.

You can also assign a *default value* to each column. Then, that value is assigned to the column if another value isn't provided. If a column doesn't allow nulls and doesn't have a default value, you must supply a value for the column when you add a new row to the table. Otherwise, an error will occur.

Each table can also contain a numeric column whose value is generated automatically by the DBMS. In SQL Server, a column like this is called an *identity column*, and you establish it using the Identity, Identity Seed, and Identity Increment properties. An identity column is often used as the primary key for a table.

A *check constraint* defines the acceptable values for a column. For example, you can define a check constraint for the Invoices table in this figure to make sure that the InvoiceTotal column is greater than zero. A check constraint like this can be defined at the column level because it refers only to the column it constrains. If the check constraint for a column needs to refer to other columns in the table, however, it can be defined at the table level.

After you define the constraints for a database, they're managed by the DBMS. If, for example, a user tries to add a row with data that violates a constraint, the DBMS sends an appropriate error code back to the application without adding the row to the database. The application can then respond to the error code.

Another alternative is to validate the data that is going to be added to a database before the program tries to add it. That way, the constraints shouldn't be needed and the program should run more efficiently. In many cases, both data validation and constraints are used. That way, the programs run more efficiently if the data validation routines work, but the constraints are there in case the data validation routines don't work or aren't coded.

The Server Explorer design view window for the Invoices table

Column Name	Data Type	Length	Allow Nulls	
InvoiceID	int	4		
VendorID	int	4		
InvoiceNumber	varchar	50		
InvoiceDate	smalldatetime	4		
InvoiceTotal	money	8		
PaymentTotal	money	8		
CreditTotal	money	8		
TermsID	int	4		
InvoiceDueDate	smalldatetime	4		
PaymentDate	smalldatetime	4	✓	

Columns

Description	
Default Value	
Precision	10
Scale	0
Identity	Yes
Identity Seed	1
Identity Increment	1
Is RowGuid	No
Formula	
Collation	

Common SQL Server data types

Type	Description
bit	A value of 1 or 0 that represents a True or False value.
char, varchar, text	Any combination of letters, symbols, and numbers.
datetime, smalldatetime	Alphanumeric data that represents a date and time. Various formats are acceptable.
decimal, numeric	Numeric data that is accurate to the least significant digit. The data can contain an integer and a fractional portion.
float, real	Floating-point values that contain an approximation of a decimal value.
bigint, int, smallint, tinyint	Numeric data that contains only an integer portion.
money, smallmoney	Monetary values that are accurate to four decimal places.

Description

- The *data type* that's assigned to a column determines the type of information that can be stored in the column. Depending on the data type, the column definition can also include its length, precision, and scale.

- Each column definition also indicates whether or not the column can contain *null values*. A null value indicates that the value of the column is not known.

- A column can be defined with a *default value*. Then, that value is used for the column if another value isn't provided when a row is added to the table.

- A column can also be defined as an *identity column*. An identity column is a numeric column whose value is generated automatically when a row is added to the table.

- To restrict the values that a column can hold, you define *check constraints*. Check constraints can be defined at either the column level or the table level.

Figure 1-7   How the columns in a table are defined

The design of the Payables database

Now that you've seen how the basic elements of a relational database work, figure 1-8 shows the design of the Payables database that we'll use in the programming examples throughout this book. Although this database may seem complicated, its design is actually much simpler than most databases you'll encounter when you work on actual database applications.

The purpose of the Payables database is to track vendors and their invoices for the payables department of a small business. The top-level table in this database is the Vendors table, which contains one row for each of the vendors the company purchases from. For each vendor, this table records the vendor's name, address, phone number, and other information. The primary key for the Vendors table is the VendorID column. This column is an identity column, so SQL Server automatically generates its value whenever a new vendor is created.

Information for each invoice received from a vendor is stored in the Invoices table. Like the Vendors table, the primary key for this table, InvoiceID, is an identity column. To relate each invoice to a vendor, the Invoices table includes a VendorID column. A foreign key constraint is used to enforce this relationship. That way, an invoice can't be added for a vendor that doesn't exist, and vendors with outstanding invoices can't be deleted.

The InvoiceLineItems table contains the line item details for each invoice. The primary key for this table is a combination of the InvoiceID and InvoiceSequence columns. The InvoiceID column relates each line item to an invoice, and a foreign key constraint that cascades updates and deletes from the Invoices table is defined to enforce this relationship. The InvoiceSequence column gives each line item a unique primary key value. Note, however, that this column is not an identity column. As a result, the application programs that create line items must calculate appropriate values for this column.

The other three tables in the Payables database—States, Terms, and GLAccounts—provide reference information for the Vendors, Invoices, and InvoiceLineItems tables. The States table has a row for each state in the U.S. It provides a state code, which is the primary key, as well as each state's full name and its starting and ending zip codes. Each Vendor has a VendorState column that relates the vendor to a row in the States table.

The Terms table records invoice terms, such as "Net Due 10 Days" or "Net Due 90 Days." The primary key of this table is TermsID, which is an identity column. Each invoice also has a TermsID column that relates the invoice to a row in the Terms table. In addition, each Vendor has a DefaultTermsID column that provides the default terms for new invoices for that vendor.

Finally, the GLAccounts table provides general-ledger account information. The primary key of this table is AccountNo. Each line item also includes an AccountNo column that specifies which account the purchase is charged to, and each Vendor has a DefaultAccountNo column that provides a default value for new invoices. The foreign key constraints that enforce the relationships between the GLAccounts table and the Vendors and InvoiceLineItems tables are defined so that updates are cascaded to those tables. That way, if an account number changes, that change is reflected in the related vendors and invoices.

The tables that make up the Payables database

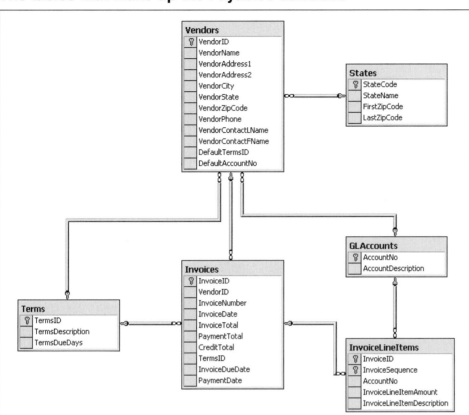

Description

- The Vendors table contains one row for each vendor. Its primary key is VendorID, which is an identity column that's generated automatically by SQL Server whenever a new vendor is added.

- The Invoices table contains one row for each invoice. Its primary key is InvoiceID, which is an identity column that's generated automatically whenever a new invoice is added. VendorID is a foreign key that relates each invoice to a vendor. TermsID is a foreign key that relates each invoice to a row in the Terms table.

- The InvoiceLineItems table contains one row for each line item of each invoice. Its primary key is a combination of InvoiceID and InvoiceSequence. InvoiceID is also a foreign key that relates the line item to an invoice.

- States, Terms, and GLAccounts are simple reference tables that are related to the Vendors, Invoices, and InvoiceLineItems tables by foreign keys.

- The relationships between the tables in this diagram appear as links, where the endpoints indicate the type of relationship. A key indicates the "one" side of a relationship, and the infinity symbol (∞) indicates the "many" side.

Figure 1-8   The design of the Payables database

How to use SQL to work with the data in a relational database

In the topics that follow, you'll learn about the four SQL statements that you can use to manipulate the data in a database: Select, Insert, Update, and Delete. As you'll learn later in this book, you can often let Visual Basic generate the Insert, Update, and Delete statements for you based on the Select statement you specify. To master the material in this book, however, you need to understand what these statements do and how they're coded.

Although you'll learn the basics of coding these statements in the topics that follow, you may want to know more than what's presented here. In that case, we recommend our book, *Murach's SQL for SQL Server*. In addition to the Select, Insert, Update, and Delete statements, this book teaches you how to code the statements you use to define the data in a database, and it teaches you how to use other features of SQL Server that the top professionals use.

Although SQL is a standard language, each DBMS is likely to have its own *SQL dialect*, which includes extensions to the standard language. So when you use SQL, you need to make sure that you're using the dialect that's supported by your DBMS. In this chapter and throughout this book, all of the SQL examples are for Microsoft SQL Server's dialect, which is called *Transact-SQL*.

How to query a single table

Figure 1-9 shows how to use a Select statement to query a single table in a database. In the syntax summary at the top of this figure, you can see that the Select clause names the columns to be retrieved and the From clause names the table that contains the columns. You can also code a Where clause that gives criteria for the rows to be selected. And you can code an Order By clause that names one or more columns that the results should be sorted by and indicates whether each column should be sorted in ascending or descending sequence.

If you study the Select statement below the syntax summary, you can see how this works. Here, the Select statement retrieves columns from the Invoices table. It selects a row only if the row has a balance due that's greater than zero. And it sorts the returned rows by invoice date in ascending sequence (the default).

Please note in this Select statement that the last column in the query, BalanceDue, is calculated by subtracting PaymentTotal and CreditTotal from InvoiceTotal. In other words, a column by the name of BalanceDue doesn't actually exist in the database. This type of column is called a *calculated column*, and it exists only in the results of the query.

This figure also shows the *result table*, or *result set*, that's returned by the Select statement. A result set is a logical table that's created temporarily within the database. When an application requests data from a database, it receives a result set.

Simplified syntax of the Select statement

```
Select column-1 [, column-2]...
From table-1
[Where selection-criteria]
[Order By column-1 [Asc|Desc] [, column-2 [Asc|Desc]]...]
```

A Select statement that retrieves and sorts selected columns and rows from the Invoices table

```
Select InvoiceNumber, InvoiceDate, InvoiceTotal,
    PaymentTotal, CreditTotal,
    InvoiceTotal - PaymentTotal - CreditTotal As BalanceDue
From Invoices
Where InvoiceTotal - PaymentTotal - CreditTotal > 0
Order By InvoiceDate
```

The result set defined by the Select statement

InvoiceNumber	InvoiceDate	InvoiceTotal	PaymentTotal	CreditTotal	BalanceDue
P-0608	8/7/2002	20551.18	0	1200	19351.18
989319-497	8/13/2002	2312.2	0	0	2312.2
989319-487	8/14/2002	1927.54	0	0	1927.54
97/553B	8/22/2002	313.55	0	0	313.55
97/553	8/23/2002	904.14	0	0	904.14
97/522	8/26/2002	1962.13	0	200	1762.13
203339-13	8/28/2002	17.5	0	0	17.5
0-2436	9/2/2002	10976.06	0	0	10976.06
963253272	9/4/2002	61.5	0	0	61.5
963253271	9/4/2002	158	0	0	158
963253269	9/4/2002	26.75	0	0	26.75
963253267	9/4/2002	23.5	0	0	23.5

Concepts

- The result of a Select statement is a *result table,* or *result set,* like the one shown above. A result set is a logical set of rows that consists of all of the columns and rows requested by the Select statement.

- A result set can include *calculated columns* that are calculated from other columns in the table.

- To select all of the columns in a table, you can code an asterisk (*) in place of the column names. For example, this statement will select all of the columns from the Invoices table:

```
Select * From Invoices
```

Figure 1-9   How to query a single table

How to join data from two or more tables

Figure 1-10 presents the syntax of the Select statement for retrieving data from two tables. This type of operation is called a *join* because the data from the two tables is joined together into a single result set. For example, the Select statement in this figure joins data from the Invoices and Vendors table into a single result set.

An *inner join* is the most common type of join. When you use an inner join, rows from the two tables in the join are included in the result set only if their related columns match. These matching columns are specified in the From clause of the Select statement. In the Select statement in this figure, for example, rows from the Invoices and Vendors tables are included only if the value of the VendorID column in the Vendors table matches the value of the VendorID column in one or more rows in the Invoices table. If there aren't any invoices for a particular vendor, that vendor won't be included in the result set.

Although this figure shows how to join data from two tables, you should know that you can extend this syntax to join data from additional tables. If, for example, you want to include data from the InvoiceLineItems table in the results shown in this figure, you can code the From clause of the Select statement like this:

```
From Vendors
    Inner Join Invoices
        On Vendors.VendorID = Invoices.VendorID
    Inner Join InvoiceLineItems
        On Invoices.InvoiceID = InvoiceLineItems.InvoiceID
```

Then, in the column list of the Select statement, you can include any of the columns in the InvoiceLineItems table.

The syntax of the Select statement for joining two tables

```
Select column-list
From table-1
    [Inner] Join table-2
    On table-1.column-1 {=|<|>|<=|>=|<>} table-2.column-2
[Where selection-criteria]
[Order By column-list]
```

A Select statement that joins data from the Vendors and Invoices tables

```
Select VendorName, InvoiceNumber, InvoiceDate, InvoiceTotal
From Vendors Inner Join Invoices
    On Vendors.VendorID = Invoices.VendorID
Where InvoiceTotal >= 500
Order By VendorName, InvoiceTotal Desc
```

The result set defined by the Select statement

VendorName	InvoiceNumber	InvoiceDate	InvoiceTotal
IBM	Q545443	7/10/2002	1083.58
Ingram	31359783	9/18/2002	1575
Ingram	31361833	9/18/2002	579.42
Malloy Lithographing Inc	0-2058	9/3/2002	37966.19
Malloy Lithographing Inc	P-0259	8/12/2002	26881.4
Malloy Lithographing Inc	0-2060	9/3/2002	23517.58
Malloy Lithographing Inc	P-0608	8/7/2002	20551.18
Malloy Lithographing Inc	0-2436	9/2/2002	10976.06
Pollstar	77290	9/30/2002	1750
Reiter's Scientific & Pro Books	C73-24	8/13/2002	600
United Parcel Service	989319-457	8/20/2002	3813.33

Concepts

- A *join* lets you combine data from two or more tables into a single result set.

- The most common type of join is an *inner join*. This type of join returns rows from both tables only if their related columns match.

Figure 1-10   How to join data from two or more tables

How to add, update, and delete data in a table

Figure 1-11 presents the basic syntax of the SQL Insert, Update, and Delete statements. You use the Insert statement to insert one or more rows into a table. As you can see, the syntax of this statement is different depending on whether you're adding a single row or selected rows.

To add a single row to a table, you specify the name of the table you want to add the row to, the names of the columns you're supplying data for, and the values for those columns. The example in this figure adds a row to the Terms table. Because the value of the TermsID column is generated automatically, though, it's not included in the Insert statement. If you're going to supply values for all the columns in a table, you can omit the column names, but then you must be sure to specify the values in the same order as the columns appear in the table.

To add selected rows to a table, you include a Select statement within the Insert statement. Then, the Select statement retrieves data from one or more tables based on the conditions you specify, and the Insert statement adds rows with that data to another table. In the example in this figure, the Select statement selects all the columns from the rows in the Invoices table that have been paid in full and inserts them into a table named InvoiceArchive.

To change the values of one or more columns in a table, you use the Update statement. On this statement, you specify the name of the table you want to update, expressions that indicate the columns you want to change and how you want to change them, and a condition that identifies the rows you want to change. In the example in this figure, the Update statement changes the TermsID value to 4 for each row in the Invoices table that has a TermsID value of 1.

To delete rows from a table, you use the Delete statement. On this statement, you specify the table you want to delete rows from and a condition that indicates the rows you want to delete. The Delete statement in this figure deletes all the rows from the Invoices table that have been paid in full.

How to add a single row

The syntax of the Insert statement for adding a single row

```
Insert [Into] table-name [(column-list)]
    Values (value-list)
```

A statement that adds a single row to a table

```
Insert Into Terms (TermsDescription, TermsDueDays)
    Values ("Net due 90 days", 90)
```

How to add selected rows

The syntax of the Insert statement for adding selected rows

```
Insert [Into] table-name [(column-list)]
    Select-statement
```

A statement that adds selected rows from one table to another table

```
Insert Into InvoiceArchive
    Select * From Invoices
    Where InvoiceTotal - PaymentTotal - CreditTotal = 0
```

How to update rows

The syntax of the Update statement

```
Update table-name
    Set expression-1 [, expression-2]...
    [Where selection-criteria]
```

A statement that changes the value of the TermsID field for selected rows

```
Update Invoices
    Set TermsID = 4
    Where TermsID = 1
```

How to delete rows

The syntax of the Delete statement

```
Delete [From] table-name
    [Where selection-criteria]
```

A statement that deletes all paid invoices

```
Delete From Invoices
    Where InvoiceTotal - PaymentTotal - CreditTotal = 0
```

Note

- In many cases, Visual Basic can generate Insert, Update, and Delete statements for you based on the Select statement you supply. For more information, see chapters 3 and 6.

Figure 1-11   How to add, update, and delete data in a table

Perspective

As a Visual Basic programmer, you don't need to be a expert in client/server architecture, database design, or SQL programming. But you do need to know something about all of these subjects because they underlie your application code. So if you understand the information presented in this chapter, you're ready to learn about the classes that make up ADO.NET. As you'll see in chapter 2, you use these classes to access and process the data stored in the relational databases of a client/server system.

Terms

Microsoft SQL Server 2000 Desktop Engine (MSDE)	field
	column
SQL Server 2000	primary key
client	composite primary key
server	non-primary key
database server	unique key
network	unique key constraint
client/server system	unique constraint
enterprise system	index
local area network (LAN)	foreign key
wide area network (WAN)	foreign key table
network operating system	primary key table
database management system (DBMS)	one-to-many relationship
back-end processing	one-to-one relationship
back end	many-to-many relationship
application software	linking table
data source	referential integrity
data access API	foreign key constraint
application programming interface	cascaded update
front-end processing	cascaded delete
front end	trigger
SQL query	orphaned row
query	data type
SQL (Structured Query Language)	system data type
query results	null value
application server	default value
web server	identity column
business component	check constraint
web application	SQL dialect
web service	Transact-SQL
web browser	result table
relational database	result set
table	calculated column
record	join
row	inner join

2

An introduction to ADO.NET

ADO.NET consists of a set of classes defined by the .NET Framework that you can use to access the data in a database. This chapter presents a brief introduction to these classes. Here, you'll learn what classes are available, how they fit together in the overall architecture of ADO.NET, and what they offer. That will prepare you for learning the details of ADO.NET programming that are presented in the chapters that follow.

An overview of ADO.NET

ADO.NET (*ActiveX Data Objects .NET*) is the primary data access API for the .NET Framework. It provides the classes that you use as you develop database applications with Visual Basic .NET as well as other .NET languages. In the two topics that follow, you'll learn about how ADO.NET uses these classes to provide access to the data in a database and the two ways you can create ADO.NET objects in your Visual Basic programs.

How ADO.NET works

To work with data using ADO.NET, you use a variety of ADO.NET objects. Figure 2-1 shows the primary objects you'll use to develop Windows-based ADO.NET applications in Visual Basic.

To start, the data used by an application is stored in a *dataset* that contains one or more *data tables*. To load data into a data table, you use a *data adapter*. The main function of the data adapter is to manage the flow of data between a dataset and a database. To do that, it uses *commands* that define the SQL statements to be issued. The command for retrieving data, for example, typically defines a Select statement. Then, the command connects to the database using a *connection* and passes the Select statement to the database. After the Select statement is executed, the result set it produces is sent back to the data adapter, which stores the results in the data table.

To update the data in a database, the data adapter uses a command that defines an Insert, Update, or Delete statement for a data table. Then, the command connects to the database and performs the requested operation.

Although it's not apparent in this figure, the data in a dataset is independent of the database that the data was retrieved from. In fact, the connection to the database is typically closed after the data is retrieved from the database. Then, the connection is opened again when it's needed. Because of that, the application must work with the copy of the data that's stored in the dataset. The architecture that's used to implement this type of data processing is referred to as a *disconnected data architecture*. Although this is more complicated than a connected architecture, the advantages offset the complexity.

One of the advantages of using a disconnected data architecture is improved system performance due to the use of fewer system resources for maintaining connections. Another advantage is that it makes ADO.NET compatible with ASP.NET web applications, which are inherently disconnected. You'll learn more about developing ASP.NET web applications that use ADO.NET in chapters 12 through 14 of this book.

The ADO.NET classes that are responsible for working directly with a database are provided by the *.NET data providers*. These data providers include the classes you use to create data adapters, commands, and connections. As you'll learn later in this chapter, the .NET Framework currently includes two different data providers, but additional providers are available from Microsoft and other third-party vendors such as IBM and Oracle.

Basic ADO.NET objects

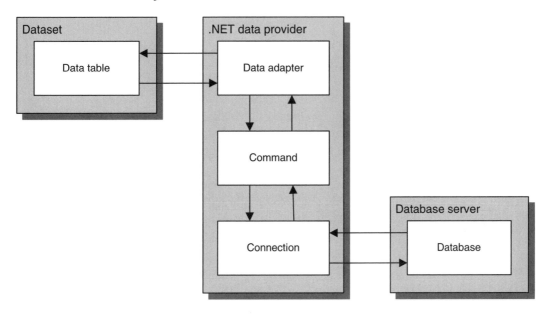

Description

- ADO.NET uses two types of objects to access the data in a database: *datasets*, which can contain one or more *data tables*, and *.NET data provider* objects, which include data adapters, commands, and connections.

- A dataset stores data from the database so that it can be accessed by the application. The .NET data provider objects retrieve data from and update data in the database.

- To retrieve data from a database and store it in a data table, a *data adapter* object issues a Select statement that's stored in a *command* object. Next, the command object uses a *connection* object to connect to the database and retrieve the data. Then, the data is passed back to the data adapter, which stores the data in the dataset.

- To update the data in a database based on the data in a data table, the data adapter object issues an Insert, Update, or Delete statement that's stored in a command object. Then, the command object uses a connection to connect to the database and update the data.

- The data provider remains connected to the database only long enough to retrieve or update the specified data. Then, it disconnects from the database and the application works with the data via the dataset object. This is referred to as a *disconnected data architecture.*

- All of the ADO.NET objects are implemented by classes in the System.Data namespace of the .NET Framework. However, the specific classes used to implement the connection, command, and data adapter objects depend on the .NET data provider you use.

Figure 2-1   How ADO.NET works

Two ways to create ADO.NET objects

Figure 2-2 shows two basic techniques you can use to create the ADO.NET objects you need as you develop database applications. First, you can use the components in the Data tab of the Toolbox to create ADO.NET objects by dragging and dropping them onto a form. Notice that the names of most of the components in the Data tab are prefixed with either "OleDb" or "Sql." As you'll learn in the next figure, these prefixes identify the data provider that these components are associated with.

Before I go on, you should realize that when you drag one of the data adapter components onto a form, Visual Studio starts the Data Adapter Configuration Wizard. This wizard gathers information about the data you want to retrieve and then generates code to create the required ADO.NET objects. You'll learn how to use the Data Adapter Configuration Wizard in the next chapter.

The Visual Basic project shown in this figure contains four ADO.NET objects: two data adapters named daVendors and daStates, a connection named conPayables, and a dataset named DsPayables1. Because these objects don't have a visual interface like the controls that you add to a form, they don't appear on the form itself. Instead, they appear in the *Component Designer tray* below the form. Then, when you select one of these objects, its properties appear in the Properties window and you can work with them from there.

The second technique for creating ADO.NET objects is to write the code yourself. The code shown in this figure, for example, creates three objects: a connection named conPayables, a data adapter named daVendors, and a dataset named dsPayables. It also uses the Fill method of the data adapter to retrieve data from the database identified by the connection and load it into the dataset. (Don't worry if you don't understand all of this code. You'll learn more about coding these types of statements throughout this book.)

Although creating ADO.NET objects through code is more time-consuming than using the components and wizards, it can result in more compact and efficient code. In addition, because the components and wizards have limitations, there are times when you'll need to write your own code. You'll learn more about how you do that in chapter 6.

For now, you should realize that whether you create ADO.NET objects using the components in the Toolbox or using code, you need to be familiar with object-oriented programming techniques such as constructors and overloaded methods. For example, when you use the Fill method of a data adapter to retrieve data from a database and store it in a dataset, you'll need to know which of the eight overloaded methods to use. And when you create ADO.NET objects like connections and data adapters through code, you'll need to know which of the overloaded constructors to use. If you're not familiar with these basic object-oriented programming techniques, we recommend that you review chapters 6 and 15 of our book, *Murach's Beginning Visual Basic .NET*.

ADO.NET objects created using components in the Toolbox

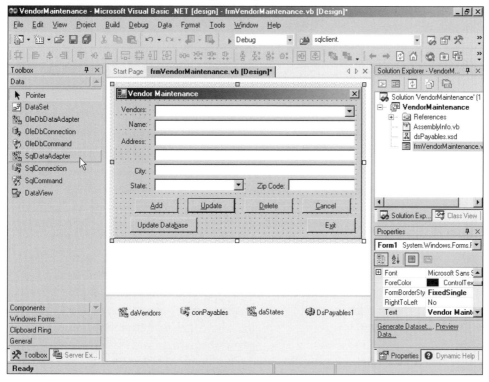

ADO.NET objects created using code

```
Dim sConnectionString As String = "data source=DOUG\VSdotNET;"& _
        "initial catalog=Payables;integrated security=SSPI;"& _
        "persist security info=False;workstation id=DOUG;packet size=4096"
Dim conPayables As New SqlConnection(sConnectionString)
Dim sVendorSelect = "Select * From Vendors"
Dim daVendors As New SqlDataAdapter(sVendorSelect, conPayables)
Dim dsPayables As New DataSet()
daVendors.Fill(dsPayables, "Vendors")
```

Description

- You can use the ADO.NET components in the Data tab of the Toolbox to add ADO.NET objects to a form. Then, you can set the properties of the objects using the Properties window.

- If you add a data adapter from the Toolbox, the Data Adapter Configuration Wizard is started. This wizard helps you create the data adapter and the related connection and command objects. See chapter 3 for details.

- To create ADO.NET objects in code, you use Dim statements that identify the class that each object is created from. This method requires more coding than using the components but is more flexible.

Figure 2-2   Two ways to create ADO.NET objects

ADO.NET data providers

To access a database, you use an ADO.NET data provider. In the topics that follow, you'll learn more about the classes that make up a data provider. First, you'll learn about the two data providers that come with the .NET Framework. Then, you'll learn what each of the core data provider classes does.

The SQL Server and OLE DB data providers

All .NET data providers must include core classes for creating the four types of objects listed in the first table in figure 2-3. You've already learned the basic functions of the connection, command, and data adapter objects. In addition to these, you can use a data reader object to access the data in a database in a read-only, forward-only manner.

The second table in this figure lists the two data providers that come with the .NET Framework. The SQL Server data provider is designed to provide efficient access to a Microsoft SQL Server database. The OLE DB data provider is a generic data provider that can access any database that supports the industry standard OLE DB interface, such as Oracle or MySQL. Although you can use the OLE DB data provider to access a SQL Server database, you shouldn't do that unless you plan on migrating the data to another database since the SQL Server data provider is optimized for accessing SQL Server data.

In addition to the .NET data providers, you should also know that several database vendors have developed .NET data providers that are optimized for use with their databases. For example, .NET data providers are available for the popular MySQL database as well as for Oracle and SQL Anywhere. Before you develop an application using the OLE DB provider, then, you should check with your database vendor to see if a specialized .NET data provider is available.

The third table in this figure lists the names of the classes you use to create objects using the SQL Server and OLE DB providers. Notice that like the components you saw in the Toolbox in figure 2-2, all of the SQL Server classes are prefixed with "Sql" and all of the OLE DB classes are prefixed with "OleDb." That way, it's easy to tell which data provider you're using in your applications.

When you develop a Visual Basic application that uses ADO.NET, you may want to add an Imports statement for the namespace that contains the data provider classes at the beginning of each source file that uses those classes. These namespaces are listed in the second table in this figure. If you include an Imports statement, you can then use the data provider classes without having to qualify them with the name of the namespace. The code shown in this figure illustrates how this works.

Now that you're familiar with the core classes of the two .NET data providers, the next two topics will describe the classes of the SQL Server data provider in more detail. You should realize, though, that the information presented in these topics applies to the classes of the OLE DB data provider as well. In later chapters, you'll learn some of the differences between these classes.

.NET data provider core objects

Object	Description
Connection	Establishes a connection to a database.
Command	Represents an individual SQL statement that can be executed against the database.
Data reader	Provides read-only, forward-only access to the data in a database.
Data adapter	Provides the link between the command and connection objects and a dataset object.

Data providers included with the .NET framework

Provider	Namespace	Description
SQL Server	System.Data.SqlClient	Lets you connect to a SQL Server database.
OLE DB	System.Data.OleDb	Lets you connect to any database that supports OLE DB.

Class names for the SQL Server and OLE DB data providers

Object	SQL Server provider class	OLE DB provider class
Connection	SqlConnection	OleDbConnection
Command	SqlCommand	OleDbCommand
Data reader	SqlDataReader	OleDbDataReader
Data adapter	SqlDataAdapter	OleDbDataAdapter

Code that uses qualification to identify the data provider namespace

```
Dim conPayables As New SqlClient.SqlConnection()
```

Code that uses an Imports statement to identify the data provider namespace

```
Imports System.Data.SqlClient
.
.
Dim conPayables As New SqlConnection()
```

Description

- In addition to the core classes shown above, classes are provided for other functions such as passing parameters to commands or working with transactions.

- To use a .NET data provider in a program, you should add an Imports statement for the appropriate namespace at the beginning of the source file. Otherwise, you'll have to qualify each class you refer to with the SqlClient or OleDb namespace since these namespaces aren't included as references by default.

- Other .NET data providers are available to provide efficient access to non-Microsoft databases such as Oracle, MySQL, and SQL Anywhere.

Note

- Version 1.1 of the .NET Framework, which comes with Visual Studio and Visual Basic 2003, includes Oracle and ODBC data providers. Although these data providers aren't presented in this book, they work like the SQL Server and OLE DB data providers.

Figure 2-3   The .NET data providers

The SqlConnection class

Before you can access the data in a database, you have to create a connection object that defines the connection to the database. To do that, you use the SqlConnection class presented in figure 2-4.

The most important property of the SqlConnection class is ConnectionString. A *connection string* is a text string that provides the information necessary to establish a connection to a database. That means it includes information such as the name of the database you want to access and the database server that contains it. It can also contain authentication information such as a user-id and password. You'll learn more about coding connection strings in chapter 6.

The two methods of the SqlConnection class shown in this figure let you open and close the connection. In general, you should leave a connection open only while data is being retrieved or updated. That's why when you use a data adapter, the connection is opened and closed for you. In that case, you don't need to use the Open and Close methods.

The SqlCommand class

To execute a SQL statement against a SQL Server database, you create a SqlCommand object that contains the statement. Figure 2-4 presents the SqlCommand class you use to create this object. Notice that the Connection property of this class associates the command with a SqlConnection object, and the CommandText property contains the SQL statement to be executed.

The CommandType property indicates how the command object should interpret the value of the CommandText property. Instead of specifying a SQL statement for the CommandText property, for example, you can specify the name of a stored procedure, which consists of one or more SQL statements that have been compiled and stored with the database (see chapter 8 for details). Or you can specify the name of a table. If you specify a SQL statement, you set the value of the CommandType property to CommandType.Text. If you specify the name of a stored procedure, you set it to CommandType.StoredProcedure. And if you specify the name of a table, you set it to CommandType.TableDirect. Then, a Select * statement will be executed on the table.

Earlier in this chapter, you learned that you can use a data adapter to execute command objects. In addition, you can execute a command object directly using one of the three Execute methods shown in this figure. If the command contains a Select statement, for example, you can execute it using either ExecuteReader or ExecuteScalar. If you use ExecuteReader, the results are returned as a DataReader object. If you use ExecuteScalar, only the value in the first column and row of the query results is returned. You're most likely to use this method with a Select statement that returns a single summary value.

If the command contains an Insert, Update, or Delete statement, you'll use the ExecuteNonQuery method to execute it. This method returns an integer value that indicates the number of rows that were affected by the command. For example, if the command deletes a single row, the ExecuteNonQuery method returns 1.

Common properties and methods of the SqlConnection class

Property	Description
ConnectionString	Contains information that lets you connect to a SQL Server database. The connection string includes information such as the name of the server, the name of the database, and login information.

Method	Description
Open	Opens a connection to a database.
Close	Closes a connection to a database.

Common properties and methods of the SqlCommand class

Property	Description
Connection	The SqlConnection object that's used by the command to connect to the database.
CommandText	The text of the SQL command or the name of a stored procedure or database table.
CommandType	A constant in the CommandType enumeration that indicates whether the CommandText property contains a SQL statement (Text), the name of a stored procedure (StoredProcedure), or the name of a database table (TableDirect).
Parameters	The collection of parameters used by the command.

Method	Description
ExecuteReader	Executes a query and returns the result as a SqlDataReader object.
ExecuteNonQuery	Executes the command and returns an integer representing the number of rows affected.
ExecuteScalar	Executes a query and returns the first column of the first row returned by the query.

Description

- Each command object is associated with a connection object through the command's Connection property. When a command is executed, the information in the ConnectionString property of the connection object is used to connect to the database.

- When you use a data adapter to work with a database, the connection is opened and closed automatically. If that's not what you want, you can use the Open and Close methods of the connection object to open and close the connection.

- You can use the three Execute methods of a command object to execute the SQL statement it contains. You can also execute the SQL statement in a command object using methods of the data adapter. See figure 2-5 for more information.

Figure 2-4   The SqlConnection and SqlCommand classes

The SqlDataReader class

A data reader provides an efficient way of reading the rows in a result set returned by a database query. In fact, when you use a data adapter to retrieve data, the data adapter uses a data reader to read through the rows in the result set and store them in a dataset.

A data reader is similar to other types of readers you may have encountered in the .NET Framework, such as a TextReader, a StreamReader, or an XMLReader. Like these other readers, a data reader lets you read rows but not modify them. In other words, a data reader is read-only. In addition, it only lets you read rows in a forward direction. Once you read the next row, the previous row is unavailable.

Figure 2-5 lists the most important properties and methods of the SqlDataReader class. You use the Read method to read the next row of data in the result set. In most cases, you'll code the Read method in a loop that reads and processes rows until the end of the data reader is reached.

To access a column of data from the current row of a data reader, you use the Item property. To identify the column, you can use either its index value like this:

```
drVendors.Item(0)
```

or its name like this:

```
drVendors.Item("VendorName")
```

Since Item is the default property, you can also omit it like this:

```
drVendors("VendorName")
```

The SqlDataAdapter class

As you know, the job of a data adapter is to provide a link between a database and a dataset. The four properties of the SqlDataAdapter class listed in figure 2-5 identify the four SQL commands that the data adapter uses to transfer data from the database to the dataset and vice versa. The SelectCommand property identifies the command object that's used to retrieve data from the database. And the DeleteCommand, InsertCommand, and UpdateCommand properties identify the commands that are used to update the database based on changes made to the data in the dataset.

To execute the command identified by the SelectCommand property and place the data that's retrieved in a dataset, you use the Fill method. Then, the application can work with the data in the dataset without affecting the data in the database. If the application makes changes to the data in the dataset, it can use the data adapter's Update method to execute the commands identified by the DeleteCommand, InsertCommand, and UpdateCommand properties and post the changes back to the database.

Common properties and methods of the SqlDataReader class

Property	Description
Item	Accesses the column with the specified index or name from the current row.
FieldCount	The number of columns in the current row.

Method	Description
Read	Reads the next row. Returns True if there are more rows. Otherwise, returns False.
Close	Closes the data reader.

Common properties and methods of the SqlDataAdapter class

Property	Description
SelectCommand	A SqlCommand object representing the Select statement used to query the database.
DeleteCommand	A SqlCommand object representing the Delete statement used to delete a row from the database.
InsertCommand	A SqlCommand object representing the Insert statement used to add a row to the database.
UpdateCommand	A SqlCommand object representing the Update statement used to update a row in the database.

Method	Description
Fill	Executes the command identified by the SelectCommand property and loads the result into a dataset object.
Update	Executes the commands identified by the DeleteCommand, InsertCommand, and UpdateCommand properties for each row in the dataset that was deleted, added, or updated.

Description

- A data reader provides read-only, forward-only access to the data in a database. Because it doesn't require the overhead of a dataset, it's more efficient than using a data adapter. However, it can't be used to update data.

- When the Fill method of a data adapter is used to retrieve data from a database, the data adapter uses a data reader to load the results into a dataset.

Figure 2-5   The SqlDataReader and SqlDataAdapter classes

ADO.NET datasets

Now that you have a general idea of how the data provider classes provide access to a database, you need to learn more about the disconnected part of ADO.NET processing: the ADO.NET dataset. So in the topics that follow, you'll first learn how a dataset is organized. Then, you'll see an overview of the classes you use to define dataset objects. Finally, you'll learn how ADO.NET handles concurrency issues that arise when you work with disconnected data.

How a dataset is organized

Figure 2-6 illustrates the basic organization of an ADO.NET dataset. The first thing you should notice in this figure is that a dataset is structured much like a relational database. It can contain one or more tables, and each table can contain one or more columns and rows. In addition, each table can contain one or more constraints that can define a unique key within the table or a foreign key of another table in the dataset. If a dataset contains two or more tables, the dataset can also define the relationships between those tables.

Although a dataset is structured much like a relational database, it's important to realize that each table in a dataset corresponds to the result set that's returned from a Select statement, not necessarily to an actual table in a database. For example, a Select statement may join data from several tables in a database to produce a single result set. In this case, the table in the dataset would represent data from each of the tables involved in the join.

You should also know that each group of objects in the diagram in this figure is stored in a collection. All of the columns in a table, for example, are stored in a collection of columns, and all of the rows are stored in a collection of rows. You'll learn more about these collections in the next figure and in later chapters.

The basic dataset object hierarchy

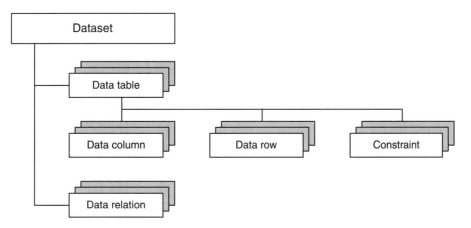

Description

- A dataset object consists of a hierarchy of one or more data table and *data relation* objects.

- A data table object consists of one or more *data column* objects and one or more *data row* objects. The data column objects define the data in each column of the table, including its name, data type, and so on, and the data row objects contain the data for each row in the table.

- A data table can also contain one or more *constraint* objects that are used to maintain the integrity of the data in the table. A unique key constraint ensures that the values in a column, such as the primary key column, are unique. And a foreign key constraint determines how the rows in one table are affected when corresponding rows in a related table are updated or deleted.

- The data relation objects define how the tables in the dataset are related. They are used to manage constraints and to simplify the navigation between related tables.

- All of the objects in a dataset are stored in collections. For example, the data table objects are stored in a data table collection, and the data row objects are stored in a data row collection. You can refer to these collections through properties of the containing objects.

Figure 2-6   How a dataset is organized

The dataset classes

Figure 2-7 presents some of the properties and methods of the four main classes that you use to work with a dataset: DataSet, DataTable, DataColumn, and DataRow. As you saw in the previous figure, the objects you create from these classes form a hierarchy where each dataset can contain one or more tables and each table can contain one or more rows and one or more columns. Because of that, a dataset contains a Tables property that provides access to the collection of tables in the dataset. Similarly, a data table contains a Columns property and a Rows property that provide access to the collections of columns and rows in the table. These are the properties you're most likely to use as you work with these objects.

Although they're not shown in this figure, the collections you refer to through the Tables property of a dataset and the Columns and Rows properties of a data table have properties and methods of their own. For instance, each collection has a Count property that you can use to determine how many items are in the collection. To get the number of tables in a dataset named dsPayables, for example, you could use code like this:

```
dsPayables.Tables.Count()
```

To access a specific item in a collection, you use the Item property. On that property, you specify the index value or name of the item you want to access. To access the Vendors table in the dsPayables dataset, for example, you can use code like this:

```
dsPayables.Tables.Item("Vendors")
```

Since Item is the default property of the collection class, however, you typically omit it like this:

```
dsPayables.Tables("Vendors")
```

The code in this figure shows how you can use a For Each...Next statement to loop through the items in a collection. Here, the statement loops through the rows in the Vendors table. To do that, it uses a variable that's declared as a DataRow object. Then, the For Each...Next statement uses this variable to retrieve the value of the VendorName column in each row. You can use similar code to loop through the columns in a table or the tables in a dataset.

Common properties and methods of the DataSet class

Property	Description
DataSetName	The name of the dataset.
Tables	A collection of the DataTable objects contained in the dataset.
Relations	A collection of the DataRelation objects contained in the dataset.

Common properties and methods of the DataTable class

Property	Description
TableName	The name of the table.
Columns	A collection of the DataColumn objects contained in the data table.
Rows	A collection of the DataRow objects contained in the data table.
Constraints	A collection of the Constraint objects contained in the data table.

Method	Description
NewRow	Creates a new row in the table.

Common properties and methods of the DataColumn class

Property	Description
ColumnName	The name of the column.
AllowDBNull	Indicates whether the column allows null values.
AutoIncrement	Indicates whether the column is an auto-increment column, which is similar to an identity column in SQL Server.

Common properties and methods of the DataRow class

Property	Description
Item	Accesses the specified column of the row.
IsNull	Indicates whether the specified column contains a null value.

Method	Description
Delete	Deletes a row.

Code that refers to the rows collection in the tables collection of a dataset

```
Dim sMsg As String, dr As DataRow
For Each dr In dsVendors.Tables("Vendors").Rows
    sMsg &= dr.Item("VendorName") & ControlChars.CrLf
Next
MessageBox.Show(sMsg)
```

Description

- You'll use the properties and methods of the dataset classes most often when you work with ADO.NET objects through code, as described in chapter 6.

- Each collection of objects has properties and methods that you can use to work with the collection.

Figure 2-7   The DataSet, DataTable, DataColumn, and DataRow classes

Concurrency and the disconnected data architecture

Although the disconnected data architecture has advantages, it also has some disadvantages. One of those is the conflict that can occur when two or more users retrieve and then try to update data in the same row of a table. This is called a *concurrency* problem. This is possible because once a program retrieves data from a database, the connection to that database is dropped. As a result, the database management system can't manage the update process.

To illustrate, consider the situation shown in figure 2-8. Here, two users have retrieved the Vendors table from a database, so a copy of the Vendors table is stored on each user's PC. These users could be using the same program or two different programs. Now, suppose that user 1 modifies the address in the row for vendor 123 and updates the Vendors table in the database. And suppose that user 2 modifies the phone number in the row for vendor 123 and then tries to update the Vendors table in the database. What will happen? That will depend on the *concurrency control* that's used by the programs.

When you use ADO.NET, you have two choices for concurrency control. By default, a program uses *optimistic concurrency*, which checks whether a row has been changed since it was retrieved. If it has, the update or deletion will be refused and a *concurrency exception* will be thrown. Then, the program should handle the error. For example, it could display an error message that tells the user that the row could not be updated and then retrieve the updated row so the user can make the change again.

In contrast, the *"last in wins"* technique works the way its name implies. Since no checking is done with this technique, the row that's updated by the last user overwrites any changes made to the row by a previous user. For the example above, the row updated by user 2 will overwrite changes made by user 1, which means that the phone number will be right but the address will be wrong. Since errors like this corrupt the data in a database, optimistic concurrency is used by most programs, which means that your programs have to handle the concurrency exceptions that are thrown.

If you know that concurrency will be a problem, you can use a couple of programming techniques to limit concurrency exceptions. If a program uses a dataset, one technique is to update the database frequently so other programs can retrieve the current data. The program should also refresh its dataset frequently so it contains the recent changes made by other programs.

Another way to avoid concurrency exceptions is to retrieve and work with just one row at a time. That way, it's less likely that two programs will update the same row at the same time. In contrast, if two programs retrieve the same table, they will of course retrieve the same rows. Then, if they both update the same row in the table, even though it may not be at the same time, a concurrency exception will occur when they try to update the database.

Of course, you will understand and appreciate this more as you learn how to develop your own database applications. As you develop them, though, keep in mind that most applications are multi-user applications. That's why you have to be aware of concurrency problems.

Two users who are working with copies of the same data

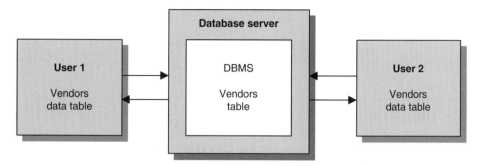

What happens when two users try to update the same row

- When two or more users retrieve the data in the same row of a database table at the same time, it is called *concurrency*. Because ADO.NET uses a disconnected data architecture, the database management system can't prevent this from happening.

- If two users try to update the same row in a database table at the same time, the second user's changes could overwrite the changes made by the first user. Whether or not that happens, though, depends on the *concurrency control* that the programs use.

- By default, ADO.NET uses *optimistic concurrency*. This means that the program checks to see whether the database row that's going to be updated or deleted has been changed since it was retrieved. If it has, a *concurrency exception* occurs and the update or deletion is refused. Then, the program should handle the exception.

- If optimistic concurrency isn't in effect, the program doesn't check to see whether a row has been changed before an update or deletion takes place. Instead, the operation proceeds without throwing an exception. This is referred to as *"last in wins"* because the last update overwrites any previous update. And this leads to errors in the database.

How to avoid concurrency errors

- For many applications, concurrency errors rarely occur. As a result, optimistic concurrency is adequate because the users will rarely have to resubmit an update or deletion that is refused.

- If concurrency is likely to be a problem, a program that uses a dataset can be designed so it updates the database and refreshes the dataset frequently. That way, concurrency errors are less likely to occur.

- Another way to avoid concurrency errors is to design a program so it retrieves and updates just one row at a time. That way, there's less chance that two users will retrieve and update the same row at the same time.

Figure 2-8   Concurrency and the disconnected data architecture

Perspective

As you've seen in this chapter, you can use standard Visual Basic statements like Dim and For Each...Next to work with ADO.NET objects. In addition, you can work with many of the ADO.NET objects through collections. If you're familiar with basic VB coding features like these, you're ready to go on to the next chapter where you'll learn how to develop a simple database application. If you aren't familiar with the basic features of VB.NET, though, you may want to refer to our book, *Murach's Beginning Visual Basic .NET,* before you continue.

Terms

ADO.NET
ActiveX Data Objects .NET
dataset
data table
.NET data provider
data adapter
command
connection
disconnected data architecture
Component Designer tray
connection string
data relation
data column
data row
constraint
concurrency
concurrency control
optimistic concurrency
concurrency exception
"last in wins"

3

How to develop a simple database application

Now that you know the concepts and terms that you need for developing database applications with ADO.NET, this chapter shows you how to develop simple database applications of your own. First, you'll learn how to use the Data Adapter Configuration Wizard to create the data adapter, command, and connection objects. Then, you'll learn how to create and work with a dataset and how to use a data grid control to work with the data in the dataset.

How to use the Data Adapter Configuration Wizard

The easiest way to create the components you need to work with a database is to use the Data Adapter Configuration Wizard. The topics that follow lead you step-by-step through the process of using this wizard. When you're done, you'll have the data adapter, command, and connection objects you need for developing a database application.

How to start the wizard

To start the Data Adapter Configuration Wizard, display the Toolbox, click on the Data tab to display the data components, and then double-click on the data adapter component you want to use. When you do that, the first dialog box of the wizard is displayed as shown in figure 3-1. This dialog box describes the function of the wizard.

This also adds a data adapter to the Component Designer tray at the bottom of the designer window. Then, as you proceed through the wizard's dialog boxes, the data adapter is configured depending on the information you provide. To proceed with the configuration, you can click on the Next button.

If you want to define the data adapter and the other data components without using the wizard, you can click on the Cancel button from this dialog box. Then, you can use the Properties window to set the properties for the data adapter, and you can use the Data tab of the Toolbox to create the other ADO.NET components. Because the wizard quickly and easily creates all the components you need, however, I recommend that you use it whenever possible.

The dialog box that's displayed when you start the Data Adapter Configuration Wizard

Description

- The Data Adapter Configuration Wizard helps you create the data adapter, connection, and command objects for working with a database.

- To start the wizard, simply double-click on the OleDbDataAdapter or SqlDataAdapter component in the Data tab of the Toolbox. The data adapter is then added to the Component Designer tray at the bottom of the designer window, and the first dialog box of the wizard is displayed.

- The first dialog box displays a welcome message and describes the function of the wizard. To continue with the wizard, click on the Next button.

- If you click on the Cancel button from the wizard's Welcome dialog box, the wizard is canceled. Then, you can set the properties of the data adapter from the Properties window, and you can create the other ADO.NET objects using the components in the Data tab of the Toolbox.

Figure 3-1   How to start the wizard

How to define the connection

The next dialog box helps you define the connection object as illustrated in figure 3-2. From this dialog box, you can select an existing connection (one you've used previously), or you can click on the New Connection button to display the Data Link Properties dialog box shown here. This dialog box helps you identify the database that you want to access and provides the information you need to access it.

When the Data Link Properties dialog box is first displayed, the Connection tab is visible. In this tab, you select the name of the server that contains the database you want to access; enter the information that's required to log on to the server; and select the name of the database you want to access. How you do that, though, varies depending on whether you're using MSDE on your own PC or whether you're using a database on your company's or school's computer.

If you're using MSDE on your own PC and you've installed MSDE and attached the Payables database to it as described in Appendix A, the server name should be the name of your computer followed by \VSdotNet. On my computer, for example, the server name is ANNE\VSdotNet. Next, for the logon information, you should click on the Use Windows NT Integrated security button. Then, MSDE will use the login name and password that you use for your computer as the name and password for the database too. As a result, you won't need to provide a separate user name and password in this dialog box. Last, you select the name of the database that you want to connect to. When you're done, you can click on the Test Connection button to be sure that the connection works.

In contrast, if you're using a database that's on your company's or school's server, you need to get the connection information from the network administrator, the database administrator, or your instructor. That will include the server name, logon information, and database name. Once you establish a connection to a database, you can use that connection for all of the other applications that use that database.

If you use the Data Adapter Configuration Wizard to create a SQL Server or OLE DB data adapter, the wizard configures the data adapter to use the SQL Server provider. Although that's what you want for a SQL Server data adapter, that's probably not what you want for an OLE DB data adapter. Then, to change the provider, you can click the Provider tab of the Data Link Properties dialog box and select a provider from the list that's displayed. The default provider is the OLE DB provider for SQL Server.

The dialog boxes for defining a connection

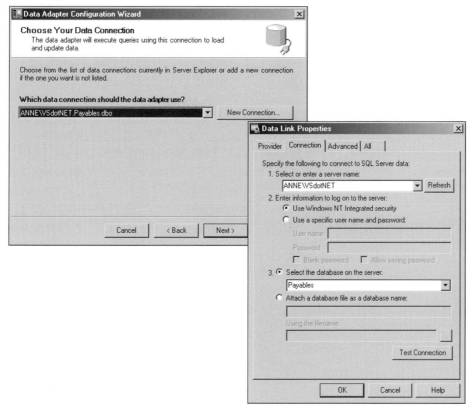

Description

- The Choose Your Data Connection dialog box asks you to identify the data connection you want to use. If you've already defined a data connection, you can select it from the drop-down list. Otherwise, you can click on the New Connection button to create a connection.

- When you click the New Connection button, the Connection tab of the Data Link Properties dialog box is displayed. You use this dialog box to provide the information that's needed to connect to the database.

- If you're creating an OleDbDataAdapter, the default is to use the OLE DB provider for SQL Server. If that's not what you want, you can select a different OLE DB provider from the Provider tab. The information that's required on the Connection tab will vary depending on the provider you choose.

- To be sure that the connection is configured properly, you can click on the Test Connection button. Then, click on the OK button to return to the wizard.

Figure 3-2   How to define the connection

How to define the SQL statements

The next two dialog boxes let you define the SQL statements that your program will use to work with the database. The three options in the first dialog box let you use SQL statements, create new stored procedures, and use existing stored procedures. For now, you'll learn how to use SQL statements. You'll learn more about working with stored procedures in chapter 8.

If you select the Use SQL statements option and click on the Next button, the wizard displays the second dialog box in this figure. This dialog box lets you enter the Select statement you want to use to retrieve data. Alternatively, you can click on the Query Builder button to use the Query Builder to build the Select statement as described in the next figure. Because that's the easiest way to create the Select statements that you need, that's what you'll usually do.

The Select statement in this figure selects several columns from a table named Vendors, and it sorts the rows by the VendorName column. You saw this table in chapter 1. Notice that the primary key column, VendorID, isn't included in this query. Because the primary key is needed to perform update and delete operations, however, the wizard will add it for you.

Before I go on, you should realize that Select queries can have a significant effect on the performance of a client/server application. The more columns and rows that are returned by a query, the more traffic the network has to bear. When you design a query, then, you should try to keep the number of columns and rows to the minimum required by the form.

The dialog boxes for defining the SQL statements

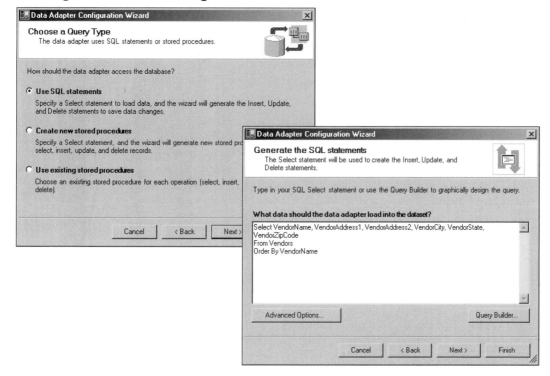

Description

- You use the Choose a Query Type dialog box to specify whether the database will be accessed using SQL statements, new stored procedures, or existing stored procedures.

- If you choose to use SQL statements, the Generate the SQL statements dialog box is displayed when you click on the Next button. This dialog box lets you enter the Select statement that will be used to retrieve the data. You can also click on the Query Builder button from this dialog box to build the Select statement interactively (see figure 3-4).

- If you don't include a table's primary key in the Select statement, the wizard adds it for you. Then, it generates Insert, Update, and Delete statements based on the Select statement. If that's not what you want, you can change the advanced options as described in figure 3-5.

- If you choose to create new stored procedures, a dialog box is displayed that lets you enter a Select statement. Then, after you enter the names you want to use for the stored procedures, the wizard generates those stored procedures with the appropriate Select, Insert, Update, and Delete statements.

- If you choose to use existing stored procedures, the wizard displays a dialog box that lets you select the stored procedures to use for select, insert, update, and delete operations.

Figure 3-3   How to define the SQL statements

How to use the Query Builder

Figure 3-4 shows the *Query Builder* window you can use to build a Select statement. You can use this graphical interface to create a Select statement without even knowing the proper syntax for it. Then, when you get the query the way you want it, you can click on the OK button to return to the wizard and the Select statement will be entered for you. This is usually easier and more accurate than entering the code for the statement directly into the wizard dialog box.

When the Query Builder window first opens up, the Add Table dialog box is displayed. This dialog box lists all of the tables in the database you selected. Then, you can use it to add one or more tables to the *diagram pane* of the Query Builder window so you can use them in your query. In this figure, for example, you can see that the Vendors table has been added to the diagram pane.

In the *grid pane*, you can see the columns that are going to be included in the query. To add columns to this pane, you just check the boxes before the column names that are shown in the diagram pane. You can also enter an expression in the Column column to create a calculated column, and you can enter a name in the Alias column to give the calculated column a name.

Once the columns have been added to the grid pane, you can use the Sort Type column to identify any columns that should be used to sort the returned rows and the Sort Order column to give the order of precedence for the sort if more than one column is identified. Here, for example, the rows will be sorted in ascending sequence by the VendorName column. Similarly, you can use the Criteria column to establish the criteria to be used to select the rows that will be retrieved by the query. For example, to retrieve only the rows for California vendors, you can specify "CA" in the Criteria column for the VendorState column. Since no criteria are specified in this query, all of the rows will be retrieved.

As you create the query, the *SQL pane* shows the current version of the resulting Select statement. You can also run this query at any time to display the selected rows in the *results pane*. That way, you can be sure that the query works the way you want it to.

The Query Builder window

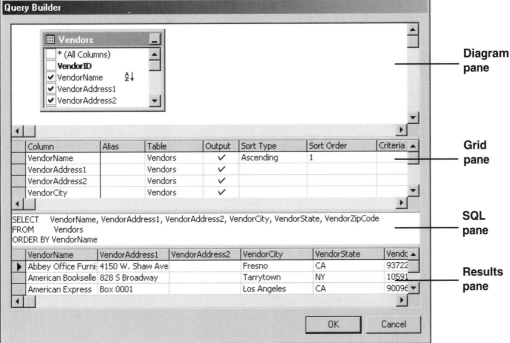

Description

- When you first start the *Query Builder*, the Add Table dialog box is displayed. You can use this dialog box to select the tables you want to include in the query. Then, those tables are displayed in the *diagram pane*.

- To include a column from a table in the query, click on the box to its left. Then, that column is added to the *grid pane*. You can also select all the columns at once by checking the * (All Columns) item.

- To create a calculated column, enter an expression in the Column column and then enter the name you want to use for the column in the Alias column.

- To sort the returned rows by one or more columns, select the Ascending or Descending option from the Sort Type column for those columns in the sequence you want them sorted. You can also use the Sort Order column to set the sort sequence directly.

- To specify selection criteria (like a specific value that the column must contain to be selected), enter the criteria in the Criteria column.

- To use a column for sorting or for specifying criteria without including it in the query results, remove the check mark from the Output column.

- As you select columns and specify sort and selection criteria, the Query Builder builds the Select statement and displays it in the *SQL pane*.

- You can also use the Query Builder shortcut menu to work with a query. To display the results of a query, for example, select the Run command from this menu. The results are displayed in the *results pane*.

Figure 3-4   How to use the Query Builder

How to control the Insert, Update, and Delete statements that are generated

If you click on the Next or Finish button from the Generate the SQL Statements dialog box, the wizard completes the configuration. That includes using the Select statement you specified as the basis for generating Insert, Update, and Delete statements that can be used to modify the database when changes are made to the dataset. If the program you're developing won't allow for data modification, however, you won't need the Insert, Update, and Delete statements. In that case, you should click on the Advanced Options button to display the dialog box shown in figure 3-5. Then, click on the first check box to turn this option off so the extra statements aren't generated.

If you leave the first option checked, which is the default, you can use the second option to provide for optimistic concurrency. And you can use the third option to determine if the dataset will be refreshed after each insert or update operation. These options are also on by default and the simplest solution is to accept the defaults.

As you should remember from the last chapter, *optimistic concurrency* applies to updates and deletions. If this option is on, the wizard adds code to the Update and Delete statements that checks the data in the database rows that are going to be updated or deleted against the original values in these rows. Then, if the data has changed, the update or deletion is refused and a concurrency exception is thrown. That way, one user can't make changes to rows that have been changed by another user and thus write over those changes. For that reason, you almost always use optimistic concurrency for multi-user applications that insert, update, and delete rows.

When you choose the Refresh the Dataset option, the wizard generates two additional Select statements. One comes after the Insert statement that's used to add a new row to the database, and it retrieves the new row into the dataset. This is useful if you add rows to a table that contains an identity column, columns with default values, or columns whose values are calculated from other columns. That way, the information that's generated for these columns by the database is available from the dataset. Similarly, the wizard adds a Select statement after the Update statement that's used to modify a row so any column values that are calculated by the database will be available from the dataset.

Of course, if the values that are generated by the database aren't used by your application, it isn't necessary to refresh the dataset with this information. In fact, it would be inefficient to do that. In some cases, though, you need to refresh the dataset for your application if you want it to work properly.

The dialog box for setting advanced SQL generation options

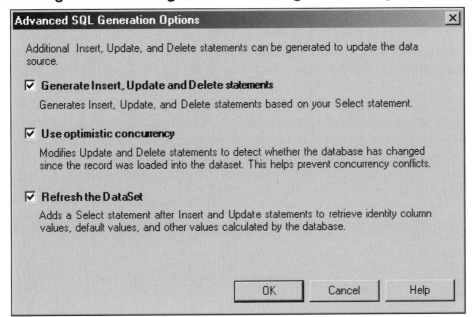

Description

- If you click on the Advanced Options button from the Generate the SQL statements dialog box, the Advanced SQL Generation Options dialog box is displayed. This dialog box lets you set the options related to the generation of the Insert, Update, and Delete statements that will be used to update the database.

- If your application doesn't need to add, change, or delete rows in the database, you should remove the check mark from the Generate option. Then, the other options become unavailable.

- The Use optimistic concurrency option determines whether or not the program checks to be sure that the rows that are updated or deleted haven't been changed by another user since they were retrieved. If this option is checked, the wizard adds code to the Update and Delete statements to provide for this checking.

- If you remove the check mark from the Use optimistic concurrency option, rows are updated and deleted whether or not they've been changed by another user since they were retrieved.

- The Refresh the DataSet option determines whether or not the dataset is refreshed after an insert or update operation. If this option is selected, a Select statement that retrieves the affected row is executed after each Insert and Update statement.

Figure 3-5   How to control the Insert, Update, and Delete statements that are generated

How to complete the configuration

After it generates the SQL statements, the wizard displays the dialog box shown in figure 3-6. This dialog box lists the SQL statements that were generated so you can be sure that you selected the correct options. If not, you can use the Back button to return to the appropriate dialog box and make corrections.

The Results dialog box also indicates that it generated *table mappings*. Table mappings are what the data adapter uses to map the data in the database to a data table in a dataset. For example, the table mappings for the data adapter created in this chapter indicate that the source table identified by the Select statement will be mapped to a data table named Vendors. And the columns within the source table will be mapped to columns in the dataset with the same names. Although you can change the name of the data table or any of the data columns and even the way the columns are mapped, you don't usually need to do that.

The dialog box that displays the configuration results

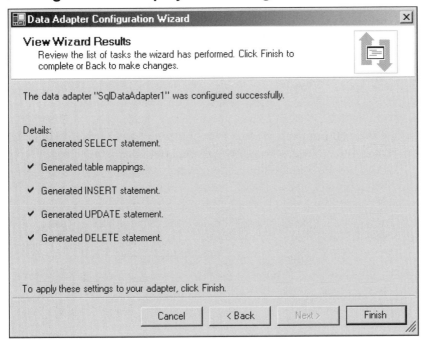

Description

- When you click on the Next button from the Generate the SQL statements dialog box, the wizard completes the configuration and displays the results in the View Wizard Results dialog box. To create the adapter with this configuration, click on the Finish button.

- In addition to Select, Insert, Update, and Delete statements, the wizard generates *table mappings*. The table mappings map the columns in the source table with columns in the data table that's created when you generate a dataset from the data adapter (see figure 3-8).

- Although you can use the TableMappings property of the data adapter to change the table mappings, you shouldn't need to do that.

Figure 3-6   How to complete the configuration

The objects created by the Configuration Wizard

When you click on the Finish button in one of the Configuration Wizard dialog boxes, the wizard creates data adapter and connection objects based on the information you specified. These objects are displayed in the Component Designer tray as you can see in figure 3-7. Then, you can click on either of these objects to display and work with its properties in the Properties window.

When you select the data adapter object, three links appear at the bottom of the Properties windows. You can use the first link, Configure Data Adapter, to redisplay the dialog boxes of the Configuration Wizard so you can change the configuration. You can use the second link to generate a dataset from the data adapter as you'll see in the next figure. And you can use the third link to preview the data that's defined by a data adapter as you'll see later in this chapter.

In addition to the data adapter and connection objects, the wizard also creates one or more command objects. At the least, it creates a command object that defines the Select statement that will be used to retrieve data. In addition, if you indicated that you wanted the wizard to generate Insert, Update, and Delete statements, a command object is created for each of these statements. Although you might think that these objects would be displayed in the Component Designer tray, they usually aren't. My guess is that this is a bug in Visual Basic.

Even if the command objects don't appear in the Component Designer tray, you can still review their properties by selecting them from the list of objects at the top of the Properties window. You can also access these objects through the data adapter object. In the Properties window in this figure, for example, you can see the property of the data adapter that refers to the Select command: SelectCommand. If you scroll down this window, you can see the properties for the Insert, Update, and Delete commands too. You'll learn more about working with these properties later in this chapter. For now, just realize that if you expand the property for one of these commands by clicking on the plus button next to the property, you can work with the properties of the command object it defines.

The objects created by the Data Adapter Configuration Wizard

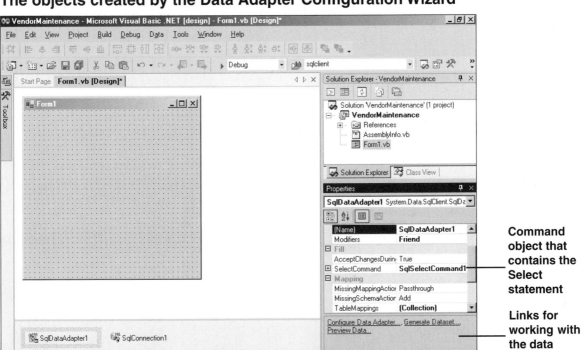

Command object that contains the Select statement

Links for working with the data adapter

Data adapter object

Connection object

Description

- When the configuration is complete, the data adapter and connection objects created by the wizard are displayed in the Component Designer tray. To display the properties for either object, just click on it.

- The wizard also creates the command objects that will be used to execute the Select, Insert, Update, and Delete statements against the database. You can access these objects through properties of the data adapter as shown above. Or, you can select the object from the drop-down list at the top of the Properties window.

- You can use the links that are displayed in the Properties window or the commands in the Data menu to work with the data adapter.

Visual Basic bug

- Occasionally, the command objects created by the Configuration Wizard appear in the Component Designer tray, but most of the time they don't.

Figure 3-7   The objects created by the Configuration Wizard

How to work with a dataset

Each data adapter defines a single result table that can be used in an application. Before you can use the result table, though, you have to load the data for it into a dataset. So in the topics that follow, you'll learn how to generate a dataset for an application and load data into it. Then, for applications that make changes to the data in a dataset, you'll learn how to write those changes back to the original database.

How to generate a dataset

Figure 3-8 shows you how to generate a dataset. When the Generate Dataset dialog box is first displayed, the New option is selected so you can create a new dataset with the default name or the name you supply. Then, you can choose the tables to be included in the dataset from the list of tables in this dialog box. In this example, only one data adapter was created, so only one table is listed. If you create more than one data adapter for a form, though, there will be one table for each adapter listed in this dialog box. Then, you can include more than one table in the dataset.

When you complete the Generate Dataset dialog box, Visual Basic generates a custom dataset class that defines the data to be stored in the dataset. In addition, if the Add this dataset to the designer option is selected, Visual Basic creates a dataset object based on the class. If that's not what you want, you can remove the check mark from this option so only the class is generated. If you do that, though, you have to create a dataset object through code or by using the DataSet component in the Toolbox (see chapter 9). In most cases, then, you'll leave this option checked so the dataset object is created for you.

You can also use this dialog box to modify an existing dataset. To do that, select the dataset you want to modify from the Existing combo box. Then, you can add or remove tables from the dataset by checking or unchecking the appropriate tables. If you do that, though, keep in mind that Visual Basic changes the original dataset class, but not the dataset object that was created from it. Because of that, you'll need to create a new dataset object as well.

The dialog box for generating a dataset

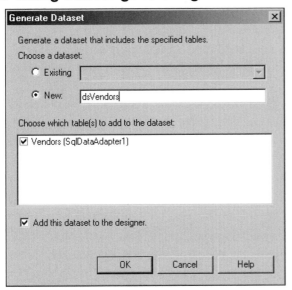

Description

- A dataset lets you work with the data defined by the Select statements in one or more data adapters. To generate a dataset, select the data adapter or the form it's associated with, and then choose the Data→Generate Dataset command from the menu bar or click on the Generate Dataset link that's displayed in the Properties window.

- In the Generate Dataset dialog box that's displayed, select the New option and enter the name you want to use for the dataset class that will be created. Then, select the tables you want to include in the dataset from the list that's provided.

- The list of tables that's displayed in this dialog box includes the result tables defined by the data adapters in the project (each data adapter defines a single result table). A dataset can include any or all of the tables in the list.

- The name for each table in the list is taken from the name of the source table in the Select statement for the data adapter. If the Select statement defines a join, the name of the first source table in the statement is used.

- To add an instance of the dataset class that's created to the application, select the Add this dataset to the designer option (this is the default). If you don't select this option, you can create an instance of the dataset class in the code for the application or by using the Dataset component in the Toolbox.

- You can also use the Generate Dataset dialog box to change an existing dataset. If you've already defined one or more datasets, the Existing option will be selected when you display this dialog box and you can select the dataset you want to change from the drop-down list. Then, you can add or delete tables from the dataset.

Figure 3-8   How to generate a dataset

The dataset schema file, class, and object

Figure 3-9 shows the dataset schema file, class, and object that are created when you generate a dataset. The *schema file* defines the structure of the dataset, including the tables it contains, the columns that are included in each table, the data types of each column, and the constraints that are defined for each table. The schema is then used by the dataset class to implement the dataset.

A dataset object that's created from a custom dataset class, like the one shown in this figure, is called a *typed dataset*. You'll learn more about how typed datasets work in the next chapter. For now, just realize that the code in the dataset class makes it possible for you to refer to the tables, rows, and columns in the typed dataset using the simplified syntax that you'll see in this chapter.

Like the other ADO.NET objects you've seen, dataset objects are displayed in the Component Designer tray since they don't have a visual interface. By default, a dataset object is given the same name as the class it's created from with a number added to the end. For example, the dataset class in this figure is named dsVendors and the dataset object is named DsVendors1. If you created another dataset from the same class, it would be named DsVendors2. And so on.

A dataset schema file, class, and object

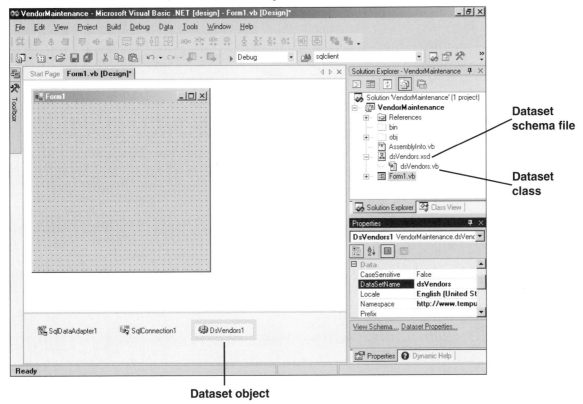

Dataset object

Description

- When you generate a dataset, Visual Basic creates a dataset *schema file* that defines the structure of the dataset. This file is listed in the Solution Explorer and is given the name you specify in the Generate Dataset dialog box with a file extension of *xsd*.

- The dataset generator also creates a custom dataset class. By default, this class isn't displayed in the Solution Explorer. To display it, click on the Show All Files button at the top of the Solution Explorer and then expand the schema file for the dataset. The dataset class will appear below the schema file.

- If you selected the option in the Generate Dataset dialog box to add the dataset to the designer, a dataset object is created from the dataset class and added to the Component Designer tray. This object is given the same name as the dataset class, but with a numeric suffix.

Common dataset properties

Property	Description
Name	The name of the dataset object.
DataSetName	The name of the class that the dataset is derived from.

Figure 3-9   The dataset schema file, class, and object

How to load and unload a dataset

Before you can work with a dataset, you have to load data into it. To do that, you use the Fill method of the data adapter as shown in figure 3-10. The first statement in this figure, for example, loads the data defined by a data adapter named SqlDataAdapter1 into a dataset named DsVendors1. Notice that only the name of the dataset, and not the name of the data table, is used in this method. That's because a data adapter defines a single table even though a dataset can contain more than one data table. So this Fill method stores the data it retrieves in the table identified by the TableMappings property of the data adapter.

If you want to name the table for clarity, though, you can do that as illustrated by the second statement in this figure. This assumes that the dataset name is DsPayables1 and the table name is Vendors.

If you want to know how many rows were loaded into a dataset, you can retrieve the return value of the Fill method as illustrated in the third statement in this figure. Here, the return value is assigned to an integer variable. Then, you can use this variable any way you like within your program. For example, you might want to use it to keep a count of the number of rows in the dataset as the user adds, modifies, and deletes rows.

You can also use the Fill method to refresh the contents of a dataset during the execution of a program. To do that, you can use one of two techniques. First, you can use the Clear method of the dataset or a data table within the dataset to remove all the rows from that dataset or data table as illustrated in the last two statements in this figure. Then, you can use the Fill method to load the table with new data. This is the preferred method, and it's usually the most efficient.

Second, you can use the Fill method without clearing the dataset or data table. Then, if the table being refreshed is defined with a primary key, the rows in the existing table are updated by the rows in the database table. That, however, can be a time-consuming process if the table contains a large number of rows. In addition, rows that have been deleted from the database table by other users will still be included in the table in the dataset. That's why we recommend that you clear the table first. If the table isn't defined with a primary key, the newly retrieved rows are appended to the existing rows, which isn't usually what you want. In that case, you'll want to be sure to clear the dataset or data table before executing the Fill method.

Another way to refresh a dataset is to refresh each row as it's added or updated within the application. You already learned how to use the Data Adapter Configuration Wizard to provide for that, and you'll learn more about how that works later in this chapter. This technique is usually more efficient than refreshing the entire data table or dataset because only new or modified rows are refreshed. On the other hand, if other users will be modifying the same database data at the same time, you may want to refresh the entire data table periodically so it reflects the changes made by other users.

How to load a data table

The basic syntax of the Fill method for a data adapter
```
dataAdapter.Fill(dataSet[.dataTable])
```

A statement that loads the data table defined by a data adapter into a dataset
```
SqlDataAdapter1.Fill(DsVendors1)
```

A statement that names the data table to be loaded
```
SqlDataAdapter1.Fill(DsPayables1.Vendors)
```

A statement that retrieves the return value from a Fill method
```
iRowCount = SqlDataAdapter1.Fill(DsVendors1)
```

How to unload a dataset or data table

The syntax of the Clear method for a dataset or data table
```
dataset[.datatable].Clear()
```

A statement that clears all the tables in a dataset
```
DsVendors1.Clear()
```

A statement that clears a single data table
```
DsPayables1.Vendors.Clear()
```

Description

- The Fill method retrieves rows from the database using the Select statement specified by the SelectCommand property of the data adapter. The rows are stored in a data table within the dataset you specify.

- In most cases, you don't need to specify the name of the table where you want the results stored. Instead, the table is identified by the data adapter. However, you may want to code the table name for clarity.

- When the Fill method is executed, the connection object that's associated with the SelectCommand object is opened automatically. After the dataset is loaded, the connection object is closed.

- If you use the Fill method to refresh a table that already contains data, it will merge the rows retrieved from the database with the existing rows in the dataset based on the table's primary key. If the table isn't defined with a primary key, the Fill method appends the rows to the end of the table.

- The Fill method is implemented as a function that returns an integer value with the number of rows that were added or refreshed, as shown by the third Fill example above.

- The Clear method removes all the data from the data table or dataset you specify. You can use this method to clear the data from a table that isn't defined with a primary key before you refresh that table. You can also use it to improve the efficiency of a retrieval operation for a table with a primary key.

Figure 3-10   How to load and unload a dataset

How to update the database with changes made to a dataset

Figure 3-11 shows how to use the Update method of a data adapter to update a database with the changes made to a dataset. Notice in the syntax of this method that, just like the Fill method, you can specify the name of a dataset or a data table within a dataset. In most cases, though, you'll just name the dataset as shown in the first statement in this figure. Then, the table identified by the data adapter is used to update the database.

When you execute the Update method, Visual Basic checks the RowState property of each row in the table to determine if it's a new row, a modified row, or a row that should be deleted. If it's a new row, the Insert statement identified by the InsertCommand property of the data adapter is used to add the row to the table in the database. Similarly, the Update statement identified by the UpdateCommand property is used to update a modified row, and the Delete statement identified by the DeleteCommand property is used to delete a row. After each Insert or Update statement is executed, the RowState property of the affected row is updated to reflect that it has not changed. After a Delete statement is executed, the row is simply deleted from the dataset.

If you want to know how many rows were updated, you can retrieve the return value of the Update method as illustrated by the second example in this figure. You might want to use this value to display a message to the user that indicates the number of rows that were updated. Or, you might want to use it to determine if the update completed successfully. In the next chapter, though, you'll learn other ways to test for the successful completion of an update operation.

To be sure that changes have been made to a dataset before executing the Update method, you can use the HasChanges method of the dataset. This method returns True if the dataset has been updated and False if it hasn't. You can see how this method is used in the third example in this figure.

The syntax of the Update method for a data adapter

```
dataAdapter.Update(dataSet[.dataTable])
```

A statement that updates a database with the data in a dataset

```
SqlDataAdapter1.Update(DsVendors1)
```

A statement that retrieves the return value from an Update method

```
iUpdateCount = SqlDataAdapter1.Update(DsVendors1)
```

Code that checks for changes to the dataset before updating the database

```
If DsVendors1.HasChanges Then
    SqlDataAdapter1.Update(DsVendors1)
End If
```

Constants in the DataRowState enumeration

Constant	Description
Added	The row has been added to the dataset.
Deleted	The row has been deleted from the dataset.
Modified	The row has been changed.
Unchanged	The row has not changed.

Description

- The Update method saves changes made in the data table to the database that the data was retrieved from. To do that, it checks the RowState property of each row in the data table to determine if the row has changed. This property contains one of the constants in the DataRowState enumeration shown above.

- If the RowState property of a row indicates that the row has been deleted, the SQL Delete statement for the data adapter is executed for the row. If it indicates that the row has been modified, the SQL Update statement is executed. And if it indicates that the row has been added, the SQL Insert statement is executed.

- Before you execute the Update method, you should check if any changes have been made to the dataset. To do that, you can use the HasChanges method of the dataset. This method checks the RowState property of each row in the dataset to determine if changes have been made and returns a True or False value.

- When the Update method is executed, a connection to the database is opened automatically. The connection is closed when the update is complete.

- The Update method is implemented as a function that returns an integer value with the number of rows that were updated.

Figure 3-11   How to update the database with changes made to a dataset

How to use a data grid control with a dataset

Now that you've learned how to create and work with a dataset, you're ready to learn how to display the data it contains on a form so the user can work with it. In this chapter, you'll learn how to use a data grid control to display all of the rows and columns in a dataset at once. Then, in the next chapter, you'll learn how to use text boxes and combo boxes to display the data in individual columns of a single row.

A Vendor Maintenance form that uses a bound data grid control

Figure 3-12 presents a Vendor Maintenance form that displays the contents of the Vendors dataset that was created from the Select statement shown in figure 3-3. The *data grid control* on this form lets the user add, modify, and delete rows from the dataset. To do that, the control is *bound* to the dataset. You'll learn how to bind a data grid to a dataset in just a moment.

For now, just realize that when a data grid is bound to a dataset, it automatically displays the data in that dataset. Likewise, it automatically updates the dataset when the user adds, modifies, or deletes a row. That means that the only code that's required is the code that loads the dataset and updates the database. Because of that, using a data grid control is the quickest and easiest way to provide access to a dataset.

The design of the Vendor Maintenance form

Description

- The Vendor Maintenance form lets the user view, add, modify, and delete rows in the Vendors table. To do that, it uses a *data grid control*, which displays data in a row and column format.

- The data grid control provides built-in functionality for maintaining the data in a data table. Because of that, no code is required to display the data or to implement the add, modify, and delete operations.

- When this form is first loaded, it retrieves data from the database and stores it in the data table used by the data grid.

- When the user clicks on the Update Database button, the database is updated with changes made to the dataset. The user can click on this button after one row or a group of rows have been added, changed, or deleted.

- To use the built-in functionality of a data grid control, you must *bind* it to a data table as described in figure 3-13. Then, you can work with the data as described in figure 3-15.

Figure 3-12   A Vendor Maintenance form that uses a bound data grid control

How to bind a data grid control to a dataset

Figure 3-13 shows the data grid control on the Vendor Maintenance form in design view. Here, you can see the two properties for binding a data grid control to a dataset in the Properties window. The DataSource property identifies the dataset, and the DataMember property identifies the data table within the dataset that the control is bound to.

The technique that's used to bind a data grid control to a dataset is called *complex data binding*. With this type of binding, a control can be bound to more than one element of a data table. When you use complex data binding with a data grid, for example, the grid is bound to the entire table.

Incidentally, when you drop down the list for the DataSource property, you'll see that you can select a dataset or a table within a dataset. If you select a table, you don't need to set the DataMember property. Either way, the result is the same, so the technique you use is a matter of preference.

A data grid control that's bound to a Vendors table

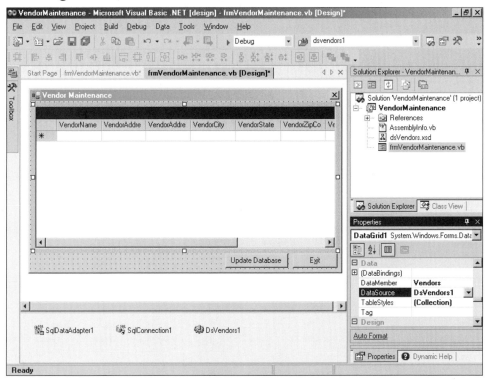

The properties for binding a data grid control to a dataset

Property	Description
DataSource	The name of a data source, such as a dataset.
DataMember	The name of a data table associated with the data source.

Description

- You bind a data grid control to a dataset using a technique called *complex data binding*. This just means that the control is bound to more than one data element. A data grid control, for example, is bound to an entire table.

- To bind a data grid control, you set its DataSource and DataMember properties as indicated above. Then, all of the rows and columns in the table you specify are displayed in the data grid.

Note

- You can also set the DataSource property so it points to a specific data table. In that case, you set the DataMember property to (none).

Figure 3-13   How to bind a data grid control to a dataset

The code for the Vendor Maintenance form

Figure 3-14 presents the code for the Vendor Maintenance form. As you can see, two procedures provide all of the code that's required for working with the dataset. The Fill method in the Load event procedure retrieves the data from the database into the dataset, which loads the data grid. And the Update method in the Click event procedure for the Update Database button updates the database with the changes that have been made to the dataset, but only if any changes have been made.

Of course, we've deliberately kept this application as simple as possible so you can focus on the basic skills for creating and working with ADO.NET objects. In practice, you usually won't use a data grid control to manage the maintenance functions of a dataset. And you usually will have to handle any concurrency exceptions that are thrown by an application. As you will see in the next chapter, then, database programming can get complicated in a hurry.

The Visual Basic code for the Vendor Maintenance form

```
Public Class Form1
    Inherits System.Windows.Forms.Form

    Private Sub Form1_Load(ByVal sender As System.Object, _
            ByVal e As System.EventArgs) Handles MyBase.Load

        SqlDataAdapter1.Fill(DsVendors1)

    End Sub

    Private Sub btnUpdate_Click(ByVal sender As System.Object, _
            ByVal e As System.EventArgs) Handles btnUpdate.Click

        If DsVendors1.HasChanges Then
            SqlDataAdapter1.Update(DsVendors1)
        End If

    End Sub

    Private Sub btnExit_Click(ByVal sender As System.Object, _
            ByVal e As System.EventArgs) Handles btnExit.Click

        Me.Close()

    End Sub

End Class
```

Description

- The dataset that contains the vendor rows is loaded in the procedure for the Load event of the form so this data is available when the form is first displayed.

- Because the user can click on the Update Database button without having made any changes to the dataset, the code for the Click event procedure for this button checks for changes before performing the update.

Figure 3-14   The code for the Vendor Maintenance form

How to work with the data in a data grid control

If you haven't used a data grid control before, you may be wondering how to work with the data it displays. So figure 3-15 summarizes the techniques for doing that. In addition, it presents some basic properties you can use to control the appearance and operation of a data grid control. Since these properties are self-explanatory, I'll focus on the operational techniques here.

First, to modify an existing row, you simply click in the column whose value you want to change and enter the change. Then, the change is saved to the dataset when you press the Tab key to move to the next column or the Enter key to move to the next row. The change is also saved if you click anywhere else in the data grid.

To delete a row, you start by clicking on the row header to the left of the row to select it. Then, you press the Delete key to delete it. Note that the row is deleted immediately without any confirmation.

To add a new row, you scroll to the last row in the data grid. This row has an asterisk in the row header and the value (null) in each column. Then, you can enter the appropriate value in each column as shown in the form at the top of this figure. Note that as soon as you begin entering a new row, a pencil appears in the row header and another blank row is added at the bottom of the control.

If you realize that you've made a mistake as you enter a value in a column, you can press the Esc key to cancel the change. Then, the column returns to its original value. You can also return the values in all of the columns in a row to their original values by pressing the Esc key twice. Note, however, that this works only if you don't have the CancelButton property of the form set to a button control. If you do, the Click event of that button is executed the second time you press the Esc key.

The Vendor Maintenance form with a row being added to the data grid

Basic properties for controlling the appearance and operation of a data grid control

Property	Description
AllowSorting	Determines whether the rows in the grid can be sorted by any column. By default, the rows are sorted in the order specified by the Select statement. If no order is specified, the rows are displayed in the same order that they're retrieved from the database.
ReadOnly	Determines whether rows can be added, changed, and deleted. The default is False, which means that the rows can be modified.
PreferredColumnWidth	The default width of each column in the control. This property must be set before the control is bound.

Basic techniques for working with the data in a data grid

- To add a row, scroll to the bottom of the dataset, click in the row that has an asterisk (*) in the row header, and enter the data for each column. By default, the columns in a new row contain null values.

- To change the value of a column, just click in the column and enter the change. A pencil appears in the row header to indicate that the row is being changed. When you press the Tab key to move to the next column, the change is saved to the dataset.

- To delete a row, click on the row header to select the row and then press the Delete key.

- To cancel a change to a column, press the Esc key. To cancel all the changes made to a row, press the Esc key twice.

- If the AllowSorting property is set to True (the default), you can click on a column header to sort by that column. The first time you click the header, the rows are sorted in ascending sequence. The second time, they're sorted in descending sequence.

- To change the width of individual columns at run time, drag the line to the right of the column header to the desired width. You can also double-click on this line to change the column width so it accommodates the widest value in the column.

Figure 3-15   How to work with the data in a data grid control

How to customize a data grid control

If you look back at the data grid control in figure 3-12, you'll see that the data in some of the columns would be easier to work with if the columns were wider so you could see more data at one time. In addition, the column headings would be easier to read if they were simplified. In the topics that follow, you'll learn how to make simple changes like these. In addition, you'll learn how to change the overall appearance of a data grid control.

Basic properties for customizing a data grid

Figure 3-16 presents some basic properties for changing the overall appearance of a data grid control. To set these properties automatically, you can select one of the *auto formats* that are available from the Auto Format dialog box. These auto formats also set some of the color properties of a data grid control that aren't listed in this figure.

You can also create your own custom format by setting the appearance and display properties manually. For example, you can change the appearance of the text in a data grid by changing the Font, HeaderFont, and CaptionFont properties. And you can change the appearance of the row headers by changing the RowHeaderWidth and RowHeadersVisible properties. If you experiment with these properties, you shouldn't have any trouble figuring out how they work.

The dialog box for selecting an auto format

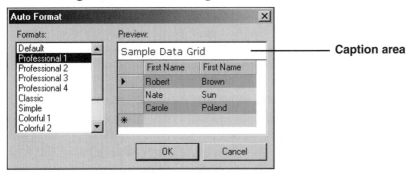

Caption area

Some of the appearance and display properties of the data grid control

Property	Description
BorderStyle	Determines the appearance of the data grid border.
FlatMode	Determines whether or not the grid has a flat appearance.
Font	The font that's used to display the text in the data grid.
GridLineStyle	Determines whether a solid line or no line is displayed between rows in the grid.
HeaderFont	The font that's used to display the text in the row and column headers.
CaptionFont	The font that's used to display the text in the caption area.
CaptionText	The text that's displayed in the caption area.
CaptionVisible	Determines whether or not the caption area is displayed.
ColumnHeadersVisible	Determines whether or not the column headers are displayed.
RowHeadersVisible	Determines whether or not the row headers are displayed.
RowHeaderWidth	The width of the row header.

Description

- To customize the appearance of a data grid, you can set the data grid properties manually, or you can select an *auto format* and the properties will be set for you. You can also define table styles and column styles as described in figures 3-17 and 3-18.

- Several of the data grid properties allow you to format the *caption area*. This is the title area across the top of the data grid, immediately above the column headers.

- In addition to the appearance and display properties shown above, you can set a variety of color properties for various parts of a data grid.

- To display the Auto Format dialog box, click on the Auto Format link that appears at the bottom of the Properties window for the data grid.

Figure 3-16   Basic properties for customizing a data grid

How to use table styles to customize a data grid

If the properties in figure 3-16 don't give you the flexibility you need, you can also customize a data grid control using *table styles*. To do that, you use the DataGridTableStyle Collection Editor to create a table style as shown in figure 3-17. Then, to identify the data that the style will be mapped to, you select a data table from the list that drops down from the MappingName property. In most cases, this will be the table identified by the DataMember property of the data grid control. In chapter 7, though, you'll see how you can create two or more table styles to work with the data in related tables within the same data grid.

You can also change any of the other table style properties so that the data grid looks and works the way you want it to. Since many of these properties are the same as the properties that you saw in the last figure, though, you usually won't create a table style just so you can change these properties. Instead, you'll create a table style so that you can change the style of each individual column in the data grid. To do that, you use the GridColumnStyles property of the table style.

The DataGridTableStyle Collection Editor

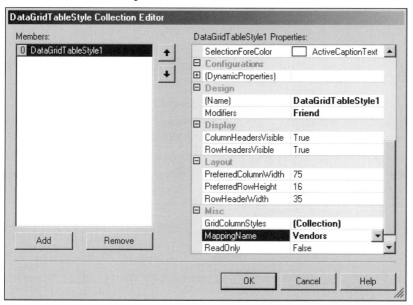

Description

- You can use the DataGridTableStyle Collection Editor to create one or more *table styles* to customize the appearance of a data grid. To display the Collection Editor, click on the TableStyles property of the data grid control, then click on the ellipsis (...) that appears for the property.

- To add a new table style, click on the Add button. Then, set the properties the way you want them.

- To identify the data that the style will be mapped to, select the name of a data table from the MappingName property. Then, that style will be used any time that data table is displayed in the grid.

- To modify a style, highlight it in the Members list and then change its properties. To delete a style, highlight it and then click on the Remove button.

- You can use the GridColumnStyles property to customize the appearance of individual columns as described in figure 3-18.

Figure 3-17   How to use table styles to customize a data grid

How to use column styles to customize a data grid

To create custom styles for the columns in a data grid, you use the DataGridColumnStyle Collection Editor shown in figure 3-18. This editor lets you display the data in each column of the data table in a text box or, if a column contains Boolean data, in a check box. In this example, all of the data will be displayed in text boxes. Note that when you create *column styles*, you don't have to include all of the columns in the underlying table. For example, you may want to omit an identity column so the user doesn't try to modify it.

After you create a column style, you identify its data source by selecting a column name from the list that drops down from the MappingName property. This list includes all of the columns in the data source that's specified by the MappingName property of the table style. In this case, it's all of the columns in the Vendors table.

Some of the other properties you'll use frequently are Alignment, which specifies the alignment of the data within a column; HeaderText, which specifies the text that's displayed in the column header; and Width, which determines the width of the column. You can also use the NullText property to indicate what value you want displayed if the column contains a null value. The default is (null), but you may want to delete this default as shown in this figure so that the column appears blank. Finally, you can use the Format property to specify how the data in the column should be formatted when it's displayed. When you format columns, you can use any of the standard formatting codes provided by the .NET Framework.

The DataGridColumnStyle Collection Editor

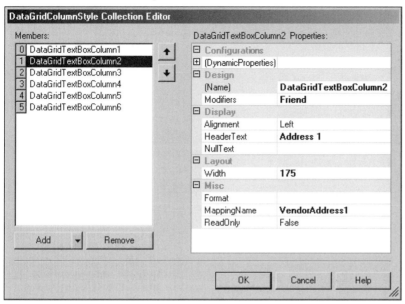

Description

- You can use the DataGridColumnStyle Collection Editor to create one or more *column styles* to customize the appearance of individual columns in a data grid. To display the Collection Editor, click on the GridColumnStyles property of a table style, and then click on the ellipsis that appears for the property.

- You can add two types of columns to a data grid. A text box column displays the value from a column in the data source and lets you edit that value. A Boolean column displays a True or False value from a Boolean column in the data source as a check box.

- To add a text box column, click on the Add button and then set the properties the way you want them. To add a Boolean column, click on the drop-down arrow to the right of the Add button and select DataGridBoolColumn from the list that's displayed.

- To identify the source of data for a column, select a column name from the list that drops down from the MappingName property. This list includes all of the columns in the data table for the table style.

- To remove a column so it doesn't appear in the data grid, highlight it in the Members list and then click on the Remove button.

- To modify an existing column, highlight it in the Members list and then change its properties.

- The Format property determines how a value is formatted when it's displayed. You can specify any of the standard .NET codes for formatting numbers, dates, and times.

- The other properties for a data grid column let you control the alignment of the data in the column, the text that's displayed in the column header, the text that's displayed for a null value, the width of the column in pixels, and whether the data can be edited.

Figure 3-18   How to use column styles to customize a data grid

Other skills for working with ADO.NET objects

The last four topics of this chapter present some additional skills for working with ADO.NET objects. These skills will help you understand the ADO.NET objects better and work with them more efficiently.

How to preview the data in a data adapter

Before you create a dataset from a data adapter, you may want to be sure that the data adapter retrieves the correct data. To do that, you can preview the data as shown in figure 3-19. Here, you can see the data that's retrieved and used by the Vendor Maintenance form.

When you first display the Data Adapter Preview dialog box, the Results box will be empty. Then, you can click on the Fill Dataset button to retrieve the data defined by the data adapter in the Data adapters combo box. If more than one data adapter is defined, you can select the one you want to use from this combo box. When you make a selection and click on the Fill Dataset button, the results are displayed in the Results box.

Notice that the value of the Target dataset combo box in this example is Untyped Dataset. That means that no dataset has been generated from the data adapter. Because of that, no structural information about the data is available. If you preview the data in a data adapter after creating a dataset for it, however, you can select the dataset from this combo box. Then, the names of the columns in the dataset are displayed in the Results box even before the data is retrieved. In addition, if the dataset contains two or more tables, those tables are listed in the Data tables list, and you can select the table that holds the data you want to display.

Keep in mind, though, that the main reason for previewing the data in a data adapter is to be sure it's what you want *before* you generate a dataset for it. Because of that, you'll typically work with an *untyped dataset* as shown in this figure.

The dialog box for previewing the data in a data adapter

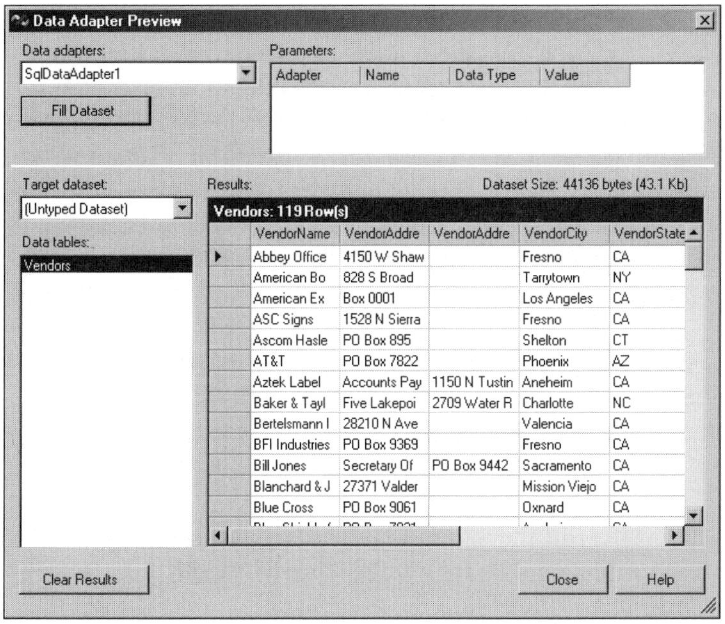

Description

- To preview the data in a data adapter, select the Data→Preview Data command or click on the Preview Data link that's displayed in the Properties window for the data adapter. This displays the Data Adapter Preview dialog box.

- To display the data specified by a data adapter, select the data adapter from the combo box at the top of the dialog box and then click on the Fill Dataset button. The results are displayed in the Results box.

- You can sort the results by clicking on the header for the column you want to sort by. Click once to sort in ascending sequence. Click again to sort in descending sequence.

- You can change the width of a column by dragging the line to the right of its column header or by double-clicking on this line to change the column width so it accommodates the values in all the rows.

- If you've already created a dataset from a data adapter, you can select the dataset from the Target dataset list. Then, the column headers for the columns in that dataset are displayed in the Results box before the results are retrieved. Otherwise, the results are saved in an *untyped dataset* whose structure is unknown until the data is retrieved.

- If the dataset you select contains two or more tables, you can select the table you want to display by highlighting it in the Data tables list.

Figure 3-19   How to preview the data in a data adapter

How to view the dataset schema

When you generate a dataset, Visual Basic creates a schema file that defines the structure of the dataset. To view this schema, you can use the *XML Designer* shown in figure 3-20.

By default, the XML Designer displays the schema in *schema view*. In this view, the schema is represented graphically as shown in this figure. Here, you can see that the Vendors dataset consists of a single table: Vendors. You can also see the names and data types of each of the columns in this table. Notice the key symbol to the left of the VendorID column. This symbol identifies the primary key of the table.

As the name of the XML Designer implies, the schema for a dataset is defined using *XML*, the *Extensible Markup Language*. If you want to display the XML that's generated, you can do that by clicking on the XML tab at the bottom of the designer window. Then, the schema is displayed in *XML view*. Although you can modify the code that's displayed in this window, I don't recommend you do that. Instead, you should modify the schema from schema view. You'll learn how to do that in chapter 9.

The schema for the Vendors dataset

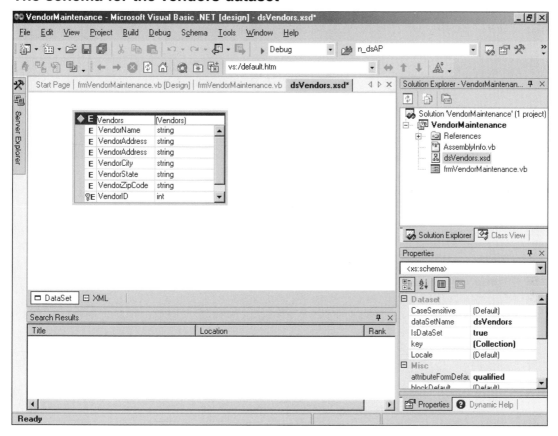

Description

- You can view the schema that's created for a dataset in the *XML Designer*. To do that, double-click on the schema file in the Solution Explorer.

- The XML Designer displays the tables in a dataset, along with the names and data types of the columns in each table. If a table is defined with a primary key, each key column is identified by a key symbol as shown above.

- The schema for a dataset is defined using the *Extensible Markup Language*, or *XML*. To display the XML that's generated for a dataset, click on the XML tab at the bottom of the XML Designer window.

- You can also use the XML Designer to define or modify the schema for a dataset. For more information, see chapter 9.

Figure 3-20   How to view the dataset schema

How to review the properties for generated ADO.NET objects

Figure 3-21 shows how you can review the properties that are generated for the data adapter, command, and connection objects. As you know, the data adapter includes properties that refer to the related Select, Insert, Update, and Delete commands. If you expand the property for one of these command objects, you can see the properties of that object. In this figure, for example, you can see the properties of the Update command object used by the Vendor Maintenance form.

The command object property you're most likely to review is the CommandText property. As you know, this property contains the SQL statement that's issued when the Update method is executed to update the database. In this case, the CommandText property contains the Update statement that's used to update the database with changes made to a row in the dataset. I'll have more to say about this statement and the Insert and Delete statements in the next figure. For now, just realize that you can display the full text of the CommandText property in a ToolTip by pointing to the property with the mouse. Or you can click on the ellipsis button that appears when you select the property to display the statement in the Query Builder window.

In addition to the CommandText property, you can review the Connection property of a command object. If you expand the Connection property, you can see the properties of the connection object as shown in this figure. Specifically, you can see the value of the ConnectionString property, which provides the information that the command object will use to connect to the database. The connection string in this figure, for example, can be used to connect to a database named Payables in a data source named ANNE\VSdotNET. Although this string contains other information, you don't need to worry about it when you use the Configuration Wizard since it's generated for you based on the information you supply.

Each ADO.NET object also has a Name property. When the Configuration Wizard creates an object, it gives it a generic name like SqlDataAdapter1, SqlConnection1, or SqlSelectCommand1. In most cases, you'll want to change the names of these objects to reflect their contents and make them easier to work with.

If you change the name of one of these objects, you should know that the properties in related objects are changed automatically. If you change the name of the connection object, for example, the Connection properties in all of the related command objects are changed. And if you change the name of a command object, the related property in the data adapter object is changed.

The UpdateCommand property for a data adapter

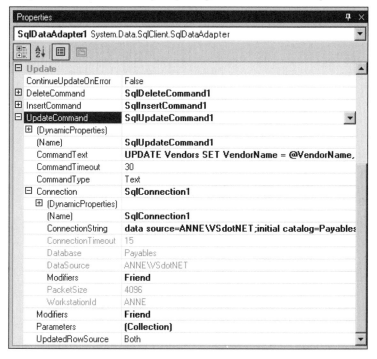

Description

- You can use the Properties window to review the properties that are generated by the Configuration Wizard for the data adapter, command, and connection objects.

- The properties in the Update group for a data adapter include the insert, update, and delete command objects. You can expand these objects to see their properties, and you can expand the connection object within each command object to see its properties.

- To work with the SQL statement in a CommandText property, you can click on the ellipsis button that appears when that property is selected. This displays the statement in the Query Builder window.

Figure 3-21   How to review the properties for generated ADO.NET objects

How to interpret the generated SQL statements

When you execute the Update method of a data adapter to update a database, Visual Basic issues the SQL statements associated with the data adapter's Insert, Update, and Delete statements. To help you understand what these statements do, figure 3-22 presents the statements that were generated for the Vendor Maintenance form. Although these statements may look complicated, the information presented here will give you a good idea of how they work.

To start, notice that the Insert statement in the first example is followed by a Select statement. This statement retrieves the row that was just added to the database and uses it to update the row in the dataset. That way, the VendorID column in the dataset is set to the value of the VendorID column that's generated by the database. You may remember that this Select statement is added if you select the Refresh the DataSet option when you configure the data adapter.

A Select statement is also added after the Update statement, as shown in the second example. It retrieves the database row that was just updated and uses it to refresh the row in the dataset. In this case, though, this statement isn't necessary because none of the data for a changed row is generated by the database. As a result, you could delete this statement to improve the efficiency of the operation.

Another option that affects the SQL statements that are generated is the Use optimistic concurrency option. If you select this option, code is added to the Where clauses of the Update and Delete statements to check whether any of the columns have changed since they were retrieved from the database. You can see this code in the second and third examples in this figure. It compares the current value of each column in the database against the original value of the column, which is stored in the dataset. If none of the values have changed, the operation is performed. Otherwise, it's not.

Most of the statements in this figure use one or more *parameters*, variables whose names start with an at sign (@). For example, parameters are used in the Values clause of the Insert statement and the Set clause of the Update statement to refer to the current values of the columns in the dataset. They're used in the Where clauses of the Update and Delete statements to refer to the original values of the columns in the dataset. And one is used in the Where clause of the Select statement after the Update statement to refer to the current row. In addition, the Where clause of the Select statement after the Insert statement includes a *system function* named @@IDENTITY. This function is used throughout SQL Server to refer to the most recent value generated for an identity column. The wizard inserts parameters and system functions when it creates the command objects for a data adapter. Then, before each statement is executed, Visual Basic substitutes the appropriate value for each variable.

This should give you more perspective on how the dataset is refreshed and how optimistic concurrency is provided when you use ADO.NET. Because of the disconnected data architecture, these features can't be provided by the database management system or by ADO.NET. Instead, they are provided by the SQL statements that are generated by the Configuration Wizard.

SQL that inserts a vendor row and refreshes the row in the dataset

```
INSERT INTO Vendors (VendorName, VendorAddress1, VendorAddress2,
                     VendorCity, VendorState, VendorZipCode)
VALUES (@VendorName, @VendorAddress1, @VendorAddress2,
        @VendorCity, @VendorState, @VendorZipCode);
SELECT VendorName, VendorAddress1, VendorAddress2,
       VendorCity, VendorState, VendorZipCode, VendorID
FROM Vendors WHERE (VendorID = @@IDENTITY) ORDER BY VendorName
```

SQL that updates a vendor row and refreshes the row in the dataset

```
UPDATE Vendors
SET VendorName = @VendorName, VendorAddress1 = @VendorAddress1,
    VendorAddress2 = @VendorAddress2, VendorCity = @VendorCity,
    VendorState = @VendorState, VendorZipCode = @VendorZipCode
WHERE    (VendorID = @Original_VendorID)
    AND (VendorAddress1 = @Original_VendorAddress1
     OR @Original_VendorAddress1 IS NULL AND VendorAddress1 IS NULL)
    AND (VendorAddress2 = @Original_VendorAddress2
     OR @Original_VendorAddress2 IS NULL AND VendorAddress2 IS NULL)
    AND (VendorCity = @Original_VendorCity)
    AND (VendorName = @Original_VendorName)
    AND (VendorState = @Original_VendorState)
    AND (VendorZipCode = @Original_VendorZipCode);
SELECT VendorName, VendorAddress1, VendorAddress2, VendorCity,
       VendorState, VendorZipCode, VendorID
FROM Vendors WHERE (VendorID = @VendorID) ORDER BY VendorName
```

A SQL Delete statement that deletes a vendor row

```
DELETE FROM Vendors
WHERE    (VendorID = @Original_VendorID)
    AND (VendorAddress1 = @Original_VendorAddress1
     OR @Original_VendorAddress1 IS NULL AND VendorAddress1 IS NULL)
    AND (VendorAddress2 = @Original_VendorAddress2
     OR @Original_VendorAddress2 IS NULL AND VendorAddress2 IS NULL)
    AND (VendorCity = @Original_VendorCity)
    AND (VendorName = @Original_VendorName)
    AND (VendorState = @Original_VendorState)
    AND (VendorZipCode = @Original_VendorZipCode)
```

Description

- If you select the Use optimistic concurrency option when you create a data adapter, the wizard adds code to the Update and Delete statements that checks that the data hasn't changed since it was retrieved.

- If you select the Refresh the DataSet option, the wizard adds a Select statement after the Insert and Update statements that refreshes the new or modified row in the dataset.

- The SQL statements use *parameters* to identify the new values for an insert or update operation. Parameters are also used for the original column values, which are used to check that a row hasn't changed for an update or delete operation. The values for these parameters are stored in and retrieved from the dataset.

- If a table contains an identity column, the *system function* named @@IDENTITY is used to get the value that's generated for a new row so the row in the dataset can be refreshed.

Figure 3-22   How to interpret the generated SQL statements

Perspective

Now that you've completed the chapters in the first section of this book, you should have a basic understanding of how you use SQL and ADO.NET to work with a relational database. In addition, you should be able to develop simple database applications of your own. With that as background, you're ready to go on to the next section of this book. The chapters in that section will teach you the database programming skills you need to develop professional applications.

Terms

Query Builder
diagram pane
grid pane
SQL pane
results pane
optimistic concurrency
table mappings
schema file
typed dataset
data grid control
bound control
complex data binding
auto format
caption area
table style
column style
untyped dataset
XML Designer
XML (Extensible Markup Language)
schema view
XML view
parameter
system function

Before you do the following exercise...

The exercise that follows lets you practice the introductory skills you've learned in this chapter. If you're going to use MSDE on your own PC to do this exercise, you need to install MSDE and attach the Payables database to it. If you haven't already done that, please refer to Appendix A. Similarly, if the Payables database is going to be on the server at your company or school, you need to find out what information you need for establishing a connection to the database.

Exercise: Create the Vendor Maintenance form

In this exercise, you'll create the Vendor Maintenance form that was presented in this chapter. That will help you understand how data adapter, connection, and command objects work together to access the data in a database. It will also help you understand how you use a dataset to work with the data retrieved from a database. And that will help prepare you to learn the skills presented in the rest of this book.

Start a new project and create the ADO.NET objects

1. Start a new project named VendorMaintenance in the C:\ADO.NET\Chapter 3 folder.

2. Open the Toolbox, click on the Data tab, and then double-click on the SqlDataAdapter component to start the Data Adapter Configuration Wizard.

3. Complete each dialog box that's displayed to create a data adapter you can use to access the name and address data in the Vendors table of the Payables database. The data adapter should use SQL statements to access the table, and it should provide for retrieving, inserting, updating, and deleting data. Refer to figures 3-1 through 3-6 if you need any help.

Review the properties of the ADO.NET objects and preview the data

4. Display the properties for the data adapter object generated by the wizard. Then, expand the SelectCommand group to display and review the properties for the command object that contains the Select statement. Next, expand the Connection group to display and review the properties for this object.

5. Expand the InsertCommand group for the data adapter, click on the CommandText property, and then click on the ellipsis button (...) that's displayed. The Insert and Select statements that are executed when a row is added to the database will be displayed in the Query Builder window. Review these statements, and then close this window. Repeat this procedure for the UpdateCommand and DeleteCommand groups.

6. With the data adapter still selected, click on the Preview Data link at the bottom of the Properties window to display the Data Adapter Preview dialog box. Click on the Fill Dataset button to display the results of the Select statement. Review the results and then close the dialog box.

7.   Click on the Generate Dataset link at the bottom of the Properties window to display the Generate Dataset dialog box, and create a new dataset named dsVendors that contains the Vendors table. Make sure that the option to add an instance of the dataset to the form is selected.

8.   A dataset schema file named dsVendors.xsd should appear in the Solution Explorer. Double-click on this file to display the dataset schema in the XML Designer. Notice that a VendorID column is included in the schema and that this column is identified as the primary key. When you're done reviewing the schema, close the XML Designer window.

Design and code the form

9.   Add two button controls to the default form, name them btnUpdate and btnExit, and change their Text properties so they look like the buttons shown in figure 3-13. Then, change the properties of the form so it looks like the one in this figure.

10. Add code to the form that fills the dataset when the form is loaded, updates the database when the user clicks on the Update Database button, and closes the form when the user clicks on the Exit button. Make sure that the database is updated only if changes have been made to the dataset.

11. Add a data grid control to the form and size and position the form and its controls so it looks like the one shown in figure 3-13. Then, set the DataSource and DataMember properties of the data grid so they refer to the Vendors table in the dataset you created.

Build and test the form

12. Run the project to display the form. Change the data in any row and column of the data grid, and notice that a pencil icon appears in the row header to indicate that the row is being changed. Now, press the Tab key to move to the next column and notice that the pencil icon disappears, indicating that the row has been updated in the dataset.

13. Scroll to the bottom of the data in the data grid, and add the data for a new row. Notice that a value is generated for the VendorID column and you can't change it. When you press the Tab key from this column, the new row is added to the dataset.

14. Click on the Update Database button to apply the changes to the database. Then, click on the column header for the VendorName column to sort the vendors by vendor name. This will move the vendor you just added to the appropriate position in the data grid.

15. Locate the row you just added and click on its row header. Then, press the Delete key to delete it from the dataset, and click on the Update Database button to delete it from the database.

16. Continue experimenting with the form. When you're done, close the form and then close the solution.

Section 2

Database programming essentials

The chapters in this section present the essential skills for developing database programs using Visual Basic .NET and ADO.NET. You'll begin in chapter 4 by learning how to work with typed datasets and bound controls. Then, in chapter 5, you'll learn how to work with typed datasets and unbound controls. In chapter 6, you'll learn how to work with untyped datasets with both bound and unbound controls. And in chapter 7, you'll learn how to use data views to sort and filter the data in a data table; how to use parameterized queries to select just the data you need; and how to work with related tables. When you finish these chapters, you'll have the skills you need to start developing database applications at a professional level.

4

How to work with typed datasets and bound controls

In the last chapter, you learned how to use the Data Adapter Configuration Wizard to generate a schema file and a typed dataset. You also learned how to create an instance of a typed dataset and use a data grid control that's bound to that dataset to work with its data. In this chapter, you'll learn more about how typed datasets work and how you can bind other controls like text boxes and combo boxes to them.

How to create and work with a typed dataset

To create and work with a typed dataset, you start by creating the class that defines it. Then, you can create a dataset object based on that class, and you can work with the dataset object using the properties and methods defined by the class.

How to create a typed dataset class

Figure 4-1 describes two ways that you can create a typed dataset class. First, you can generate it from a data adapter as you saw in the last chapter. When you use this technique, the schema file that the dataset class is based on is generated for you. Second, you can create the dataset class using the XML Designer. When you use this technique, the dataset class is generated based on the schema you define using the designer. You'll learn how to use the XML Designer in chapter 9.

How to create an instance of a typed dataset class

After you generate the class for a typed dataset, you can use one of the three techniques in figure 4-1 to create an instance of that class. First, you can create it when you generate the schema file and typed dataset class from a data adapter as you saw in the last chapter. Second, you can create it using the DataSet component in the Toolbox. You'll learn more about how to do that in chapter 9. When you use either of these techniques, the dataset object is added to the Component Designer tray. That way, you can work with it as you design the form. For example, you can refer to the dataset from the Properties window so you can bind a control to it.

Instead of adding a typed dataset to the Component Designer tray, you can define it through code. Note that when you use this third technique, you don't have access to the dataset as you design the form, which means that you can't refer to it from the Properties window. Because of that, you have to set the values of any control properties that bind the control to the dataset through code.

The code in this figure illustrates how this works. Here, the first statement creates a dataset named DsPayables1 from a typed dataset class named dsPayables. Then, the second statement sets the DataSource property of a data grid to the name of the dataset, and the third statement sets the DataMember property to the name of a table in that dataset.

Two ways to create a typed dataset class

- Generate it from a data adapter. This creates a schema file based on the data defined by the data adapter and a typed dataset class that's based on the schema file.
- Create it using the XML Designer. When you use this technique, the typed dataset class is generated as you define the schema of the dataset.

Three ways to create an instance of a typed dataset class

- Create it when you generate the typed dataset class from a data adapter. When you use this technique, the dataset object appears in the Component Designer tray and you can use it as you design the form.
- Create it using the DataSet component in the Data tab of the Toolbox. This technique also places the dataset object in the Component Designer tray.
- Create it in code. When you use this technique, the dataset is only available from the Code Editor window.

Code that creates an instance of a typed dataset class and binds a control to it

```
Dim DsPayables1 As New dsPayables
grdVendors.DataSource = DsPayables1
grdVendors.DataMember = Vendors
```

Description

- The class that defines a typed dataset is generated from the schema file for the dataset. You can use one of the two techniques listed above to create a typed dataset class.
- After you create a typed dataset class, you can create an instance of it using one of the three techniques listed above.

Figure 4-1   How to create a typed dataset

How to work with a typed dataset

A typed dataset class includes definitions for several classes. In addition to the dataset class itself, three classes are generated for each table in the dataset. Figure 4-2 lists these classes and some of the properties and methods they provide. For example, the dataset class includes a property that lets you retrieve a table from the dataset, the data table class includes a property that lets you retrieve a row from the table, and the data row class includes a property that lets you retrieve a column value from a row.

Notice that the names of some of the classes, properties, and methods depend on the name of the table or a column in the table. For example, the name of the class that defines a row in the Vendors table is named VendorsRow. Similarly, the name of the property that lets you retrieve the Vendors table from the dataset is Vendors, and the name of the property that lets you retrieve the value of the VendorName column from a row in the Vendors table is VendorName.

The code example in this figure illustrates how this works. Here, the first statement declares a variable named drVendor as a VendorsRow. Then, the next statement retrieves the first row in the Vendors table and assigns it to that variable. To do that, it uses the Vendors property of the DsPayables1 dataset to retrieve the Vendors table. It also uses the Item property of the Vendors table to retrieve the first row in the table, which has an index value of 0. Finally, the last statement in this example uses the VendorName property of the row to retrieve the value of the VendorName column and assign it to the Text property of a text box.

Although it's not necessary for you to understand the details of how a typed dataset is implemented, you do need to be aware of the properties and methods that are provided by a typed dataset so that you can use them when necessary. As you'll see in this chapter, you'll use basic properties like the ones shown in the example in this figure when you work with bound controls. When you work with unbound controls, however, you'll use some of the other properties and methods listed in this figure. You'll learn more about these in the next chapter.

In addition to the properties and methods shown in this figure, you should know that each class that's defined by a typed dataset inherits properties and methods from another class. Specifically, the dataset class inherits the DataSet class, the data table class inherits the DataTable class, the data row class inherits the DataRow class, and the row change event class inherits the EventArgs class. Because of that, you can use the properties and methods defined by those classes in addition to the ones defined by the typed dataset. You'll see how some of these properties and methods are used in chapter 6.

Classes defined by a typed dataset

Class	Description	Example
Dataset	The dataset itself.	dsPayables
Data table	A table in the dataset.	VendorsDataTable
Data row	A row in the data table.	VendorsRow
Row change event	Arguments for a data table event.	VendorsRowChangeEvent

Property defined by the dataset class

Property	Description	Example
tablename	Gets a table.	Vendors

Properties and methods defined by the data table class

Property	Description	
Count	Gets the number of rows in the table.	
Item	Gets the row with the specified index.	

Method	Description	Example
Add*tablename*Row	Adds the specified data row to the table, or adds a row with the specified values to the table.	AddVendorsRow
FindBy*columnname*	Finds a row based on the specified key value.	FindByVendorID
New*tablename*Row	Creates a new row based on the table definition.	NewVendorsRow
Remove*tablename*Row	Removes the specified data row from the table.	RemoveVendorsRow

Properties and methods defined by the data row class

Property	Description	Example
columnname	Gets or sets the value of a column.	VendorName
Is*columnname*Null	Determines whether a column contains a null.	IsVendorAddress1Null

Method	Description	Example
Set*columnname*Null	Sets the value of a column to null.	SetVendorAddress1Null

Code that retrieves a data row and the value of a column in that row

```
Dim drVendor As dsPayables.VendorsRow
drVendor = DsPayables1.Vendors.Item(0)
txtName.Text = drVendor.VendorName
```

Description

- When you create a typed dataset, you can use the classes, properties, and methods it defines to work with the dataset.

- The names of some of the classes, properties, and methods depend on the names of the tables and columns.

- The dataset, data table, and data row classes of a typed dataset inherit the DataSet, DataTable, and DataRow classes respectively. That means that they can use the properties and methods defined by those classes.

Figure 4-2   How to work with a typed dataset

How to use bound controls to display individual data columns

In the topics that follow, you'll learn how use bound text box controls to display the data in individual columns of a data table. When you bind controls to individual data columns, the data in the current row of the table is displayed in those controls. Then, you can navigate through the other rows to display the data they contain.

A Vendor Display form that uses bound controls

To illustrate the basic skills for working with bound controls, I'll use the Vendor Display form shown in figure 4-3. This form lets the user display the data in a table of Vendors. To do that, each text box on this form is bound to an individual column in the Vendors table. Then, the user can click on the navigation buttons that are provided to move from one row in this table to another.

Notice that the number of the current row and the total number of rows in the table are displayed in a label between the navigation buttons. That helps give the users a feel for where they are in the table. Keep in mind, though, that if the table is large, you'll want to provide a way for the user to access a row directly rather than having to scroll through hundreds of rows to get to a specific one. You'll learn one way to do that later in this chapter.

Before I go on, you should notice that this form doesn't display the two-character state code from the VendorState column in the State text box. Instead, it uses the StateName column from a States table to display the full state name. Although this may not be realistic (most applications would just display the state code), it will illustrate the use of a join in a data adapter. You'll see the Select statement that includes this join when I present the property settings for this form.

The Vendor Display form

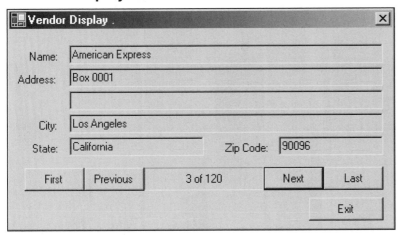

Description

- The Vendor Display form lets you display the data in a single row of the Vendors data table. To do that, each of the text boxes on this form is bound to an individual column in the table.

- When this form is first displayed, it contains the data from the first row in the Vendors table. To navigate to another row, the user can click on the First, Previous, Next, or Last button.

- To give users an idea of where they are in the table, this form includes a label control that indicates the position of the row that's currently displayed and the total number of rows in the table.

- Instead of displaying the VendorState column from the Vendors table in the States text box, this form displays the StateName column from a table named States. That means that the data adapter has to get data from two tables.

- Although the navigation provided by this form is acceptable for a dataset that contains a small number of rows, it isn't acceptable for datasets that contain more than a few dozen rows.

The data adapter used by this form

- This form uses a data adapter that joins selected columns from the Vendors and States tables in the database. See figure 4-6 for details.

Figure 4-3   A Vendor Display form that uses bound controls

How to bind text box controls

Figure 4-4 shows how to bind a text box control to a data column. To do that, you expand the DataBindings group for the control in the Properties window and then select the appropriate column from the drop-down list for the Text property. In this case, the Name text box is being bound to the VendorName column of the Vendors table. This type of binding is called *simple data binding* because the control is bound to a single data element.

When you run a form with bound text box controls, the values in the bound columns of the current row are automatically assigned to the Text properties of the controls. That, of course, means that the values are displayed in the text boxes. Then, as you move from one row to another, the data in the controls changes to reflect the data in the current row. In addition, if you change the data in one or more of the bound controls, those changes are saved to the row when you move to another row. (Although the Vendor Display form doesn't provide for modifications, it could easily be changed to do so.) One of the keys to using bound controls, then, is knowing how to navigate through the rows in a data table.

A text box that's bound to a column in the Vendors data table

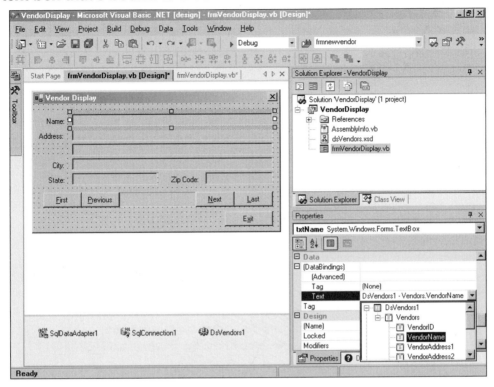

How to bind a text box control to a data column

- To bind a text box control to a data column, set the Text property in the DataBindings group to the name of the data column. This type of binding is called *simple data binding* because the control is bound to a single data element, in this case, a single column value.

- When a text box is bound to a data column, the value of that column in the current row is displayed in the control as the program executes. In addition, if the value of the control changes, that value is saved in the data table.

- The drop-down list that's available for the Text property lists all of the datasets, data tables, and data columns that are available to the project, so you can navigate through this list to locate the column you want.

Figure 4-4   How to bind text box controls

How to navigate through the rows in a data table

By default, when you display a form that contains bound controls, the controls reflect the data in the first row of the table they're bound to. Then, to move to other rows in the table, you use a BindingManagerBase object as described in figure 4-5. This object lets you manage all of the controls on the form that are bound to the same table.

To create a BindingManagerBase object, you use the syntax shown at the top of this figure. As you can see, you use the BindingContext property of the form (Me) to refer to its BindingContext object. This object contains information about the bound controls on the form. When you refer to this object, you specify the name of the dataset and data table to which the controls you want to work are bound. Then, a BindingManagerBase object is created for those controls, and you can use this object to navigate through the rows in the data table.

The first coding example in this figure shows how you can create a binding manager base for the Vendors table. Here, the first statement declares the variable that will hold the reference to the binding manager base, and the second statement uses the BindingContext property of the form to create the binding manager base. Notice that you must pass both the dataset and the data table names to the BindingContext property even if the dataset contains a single table.

The second coding example shows how to use the binding manager base to navigate through the rows in the data table. Notice that the Handles clause of this event procedure has been modified so it handles the Click event of four buttons. These buttons let the user move to the first row, the next row, the previous row, and the last row in the data table. To determine which button was clicked, this procedure uses a Select Case statement that checks the Name property of the sender argument that's passed to the procedure. This property contains the name of the button that was clicked. If, for example, the Name property contains the value "btnFirst," you know that the user clicked the First button. Then, the code should move to the first row in the data table so its data is displayed.

To move to a specific row in a data table, you set the Position property of the binding manager base. To move to the first row, for example, you set the Position property to 0 since the collection of rows in a table is zero-based. To move to the next row in a table, you add 1 to the Position property. To move to the previous row, you subtract 1 from the Position property. And to move to the last row, you set the Position property to the value of the Count property minus 1. (Since the Count property indicates the number of rows in the table, you must subtract 1 to convert this number to the index value of the last row.)

Notice that the code for moving to the previous row works even if the first row is already displayed. That's because the binding manager won't let you set the Position property to a value less than 0. So if the value of this property is 0, subtracting 1 from it has no effect. Similarly, the binding manager won't let you set the Position property to a value greater than the Count property minus 1. So you don't need to check whether the last row is displayed before adding 1 to the Position property.

The syntax for creating a BindingManagerBase object

```
bindingManagerBase = Me.BindingContext(dataSet, tablename)
```

Common BindingManagerBase properties

Property	Description
Position	A zero-based index that indicates the current position in the data table.
Count	The number of rows in the data table.

Code that creates a BindingManagerBase object

```
Dim bmbVendors As BindingManagerBase
bmbVendors = Me.BindingContext(DsVendors1, "Vendors")
```

Code that provides for navigating through the rows in a data table

```
Private Sub NavigationButtons_Click(ByVal sender As System.Object, _
        ByVal e As System.EventArgs) Handles btnFirst.Click, _
        btnPrevious.Click, btnNext.Click, btnLast.Click
    Select Case sender.Name
        Case "btnFirst"
            bmbVendors.Position = 0
        Case "btnPrevious"
            bmbVendors.Position -= 1
        Case "btnNext"
            bmbVendors.Position += 1
        Case "btnLast"
            bmbVendors.Position = bmbVendors.Count - 1
    End Select
End Sub
```

Description

- You use the BindingManagerBase object to manage all of the controls on a form that are bound to the same data table.

- To create a BindingManagerBase object, you use the BindingContext property of the form. This property contains a reference to the form's BindingContext object, which is created automatically when controls on the form are bound to the columns in a data table.

- The BindingManagerBase object ensures that all controls that are bound to the same data table are synchronized. That way, when you move to another row, the data-bound controls will display the values in that row.

- If the form provides for updating the rows in a data table, moving from one row to another causes any changes made to the current row to be saved to the data table.

Figure 4-5   How to navigate through the rows in a data table

The property settings for the Vendor Display form

Figure 4-6 presents some of the property settings for the Vendor Display form. Before you look at those, though, look at the Select statement that's used by the Vendors data adapter for the form. This statement uses a join to combine information from the Vendors and States tables into a single data table. In this case, the join is based on the VendorState and StateCode columns in the joined tables, and the StateName column in the States table is included in the result table. That way, the state name rather than the state code can be displayed in the form.

The property settings for the data-bound text boxes should be easy to understand. The Text property of each of these controls is bound to the appropriate data column of the Vendors table in the dataset named DsVendors1. The Name text box, for example, is bound to the VendorName column, and the States text box is bound to the StateName column. Notice that when you join data from two or more tables, the result table is given the name of the first table specified on the From clause of the Select statement. In this example, then, the table is named Vendors.

The other property settings shown here are for the label that displays the number of the current row and the total number of rows in the table. It's displayed with a fixed, three-dimensional border, and the text it contains will be centered in the control. In a moment, you'll see how the contents of this control change as the program executes.

Because this form doesn't provide for data modification, the ReadOnly properties of all of the text boxes have been changed to True and the TabStop properties have been set to False. In addition, no Insert, Update, or Delete statements were generated when the data adapter was created. In fact, the wizard couldn't generate these statements from the Select statement. That's because the Select statement joins data from two tables, but only one table can be updated at a time. Since the wizard would have no way of knowing which table you want to update, it's not possible for it to generate the appropriate statements. Because of that, you would have to make some changes to this form before you could use it to maintain the vendor data. You'll see one way to do that later in this chapter.

The Select statement for the Vendors data adapter

```
Select VendorID, VendorName, VendorAddress1, VendorAddress2,
    VendorCity, VendorZipCode, StateName
From Vendors
Inner Join States On VendorState = StateCode
Order By VendorName
```

Property settings for the data-bound text boxes

Name	Text (DataBindings) as shown in the Properties window
txtName	DsVendors1 - Vendors.VendorName
txtAddressLine1	DsVendors1 - Vendors.VendorAddress1
txtAddressLine2	DsVendors1 - Vendors.VendorAddress2
txtCity	DsVendors1 - Vendors.VendorCity
txtState	DsVendors1 - Vendors.StateName
txtZipCode	DsVendors1 - Vendors.VendorZipCode

Property settings for the row position label

Property	Setting
Name	lblPosition
BorderStyle	Fixed3D
TextAlign	MiddleCenter

Description

- The Select statement that's used to retrieve the data that's displayed on the form joins data from the Vendors and States tables. That way, the form can display the StateName column from the States table instead of the state code that's stored in the VendorState column of the Vendors table.

- Because this form doesn't provide for updating data, Insert, Update, and Delete statements aren't generated. In addition, the ReadOnly property of each text box is set to True so the data in the controls can't be modified, and the TabStop property of each text box is set to False so the focus doesn't move to those controls when the user presses the Tab key.

- The dataset class is given the name dsVendors, and the dataset object is generated with the name DsVendors1.

Figure 4-6   The property settings for the Vendor Display form

The code for the Vendor Display form

Figure 4-7 presents the Visual Basic code for the Vendor Display form. To start, this code declares a variable that will hold a reference to the binding manager base for the bound controls on the form. Then, the Load event procedure for the form is executed.

In the Load event procedure, the first statement uses the Fill method of the data adapter to load the data into the DsVendors1 dataset. Then, the second statement creates the BindingManagerBase object for the Vendors table of that dataset. And the third statement calls the DisplayPosition procedure to format the label so it indicates the current position in the table.

The DisplayPosition procedure uses both the Position and Count properties of the binding manager base to display the appropriate information. Because the Position property hasn't been set explicitly at this point, it defaults to 0. Because of that, the first row in the table is displayed on the form after the Load procedure has been executed.

When the user clicks on one of the navigation buttons to display another row, the event procedure that's executed sets the Position property so the requested row is displayed on the form. This is the key to this program, and you already saw how this code works. Then, after the new position is established, the DisplayPosition procedure is called to format the position label so it reflects the new position.

The Visual Basic code for the Vendor Display form

```
Public Class frmVendorDisplay
    Inherits System.Windows.Forms.Form

    Dim bmbVendors As BindingManagerBase

    Private Sub frmVendorDisplay_Load(ByVal sender As System.Object, _
            ByVal e As System.EventArgs) Handles MyBase.Load
        SqlDataAdapter1.Fill(DsVendors1)
        bmbVendors = Me.BindingContext(DsVendors1, "Vendors")
        Me.DisplayPosition()
    End Sub

    Private Sub DisplayPosition()
        lblPosition.Text = bmbVendors.Position + 1 & " of " _
                        & bmbVendors.Count
    End Sub

    Private Sub NavigationButtons_Click(ByVal sender As System.Object, _
            ByVal e As System.EventArgs) Handles btnFirst.Click, _
            btnPrevious.Click, btnNext.Click, btnLast.Click
        Select Case sender.Name
            Case "btnFirst"
                bmbVendors.Position = 0
            Case "btnPrevious"
                bmbVendors.Position -= 1
            Case "btnNext"
                bmbVendors.Position += 1
            Case "btnLast"
                bmbVendors.Position = bmbVendors.Count - 1
        End Select
        Me.DisplayPosition()
    End Sub

    Private Sub btnExit_Click(ByVal sender As System.Object, _
            ByVal e As System.EventArgs) Handles btnExit.Click
        Me.Close()
    End Sub

End Class
```

Figure 4-7   The code for the Vendor Display form

How to use bound controls to add, update, and delete data rows

Once you understand how the binding manager base works, you shouldn't have any trouble using it to navigate through the rows in a data table as illustrated by the Vendor Display form. But you can use the binding manager base for more than just navigation. You can also use it to add, update, and delete rows from a table. You'll learn how to do that in the topics that follow.

A Vendor Maintenance form that uses bound controls

Figure 4-8 presents a Vendor Maintenance form that lets the user add, modify, and delete rows from a table of vendors. When this application first starts, the data for the first vendor in the table is displayed just as it is on the Vendor Display form. Instead of providing navigation buttons that let the user move to another vendor, though, the Vendor Maintenance form lists all of the existing vendors in a combo box at the top of the form. Then, the user can select a vendor to display its data, which is clearly more efficient than using the controls shown in figure 4-3.

Once the data for a vendor is displayed, the user can modify that data or delete the vendor. Alternatively, the user can click on the Add button to add a new vendor.

In addition to the combo box that lists the vendors, this form uses a combo box that lists the state names from the States table. When the user selects a state from this list, the state code in the current row is updated. You'll see how that's accomplished in a minute. For now, just realize that I included this combo box to illustrate how you can use a combo box to update data as well as to illustrate the use of two data adapters with a single form. In this case, one data adapter is used to retrieve data from the Vendors table, and one is used to retrieve data from the States table.

When the Vendor Maintenance form is first displayed and each time a different vendor is selected, the Update and Cancel buttons on the form are disabled. But the program enables these controls if the user changes any of the data on the form. Then, the user can click on the Update button to save the changes or on the Cancel button to cancel the changes. In contrast, the Add and Delete buttons are enabled when the form is first displayed and each time a different vendor is selected, but they're disabled when the user changes the data in the current row. The program enables these buttons again when the user accepts or cancels the changes.

The Update Database button is also disabled when this form is first displayed. It's enabled after the user clicks on the Update button to save changes to the Vendors table or on the Delete button to delete a vendor. Then, the user can click on this button to save all the changes made to the Vendors table to the Payables database.

The Vendor Maintenance form

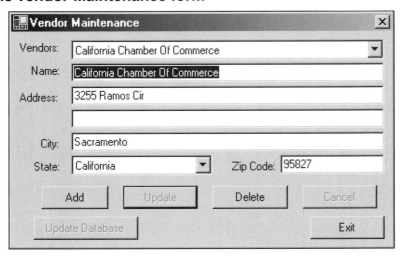

Description

- The Vendors combo box at the top of this form lists the names of all of the vendors in the Vendors table. To modify or delete a vendor, the user selects that vendor from the combo box to display its information on the form.

- To delete the current row from the dataset, the user can click on the Delete button. Before the row is deleted, a confirmation message is displayed.

- To modify the current row, the user can type over the existing data. Then, the Update and Cancel buttons are enabled. To save the changes to the dataset, the user can click on the Update button. To cancel the changes, the user can click on the Cancel button.

- To add a new row, the user can click on the Add button. Then, the controls on the form are cleared so the user can enter the data for the new row. To save the changes to the dataset, the user can click on the Update button. To cancel the changes, the user can click on the Cancel button.

- To update the database with the changes made to the dataset, the user can click on the Update Database button. This button becomes available when a row is added, changed, or deleted.

The two data adapters used by this form

- The first data adapter retrieves data from the Vendors table. This data is used to display the list of vendors in the Vendors combo box and to display the information for a selected vendor.

- The second data adapter retrieves data from the States table. This data is used to display a list of the state names in the States combo box, associate a state name with a state code in a Vendors row, and check that a zip code is valid for a state.

Figure 4-8   A Vendor Maintenance form that uses bound controls

How to bind combo box and list box controls

Figure 4-9 shows how to bind combo box controls like the ones used on the Vendor Maintenance form. To do that, you use both complex data binding and simple data binding. The complex data binding provides for displaying all of the values in one column of a table in the list portion of the control. And the simple data binding provides for displaying and updating a single value in a single data column. These techniques also work with list box controls.

To complex-bind a combo box control, you use the DataSource and DisplayMember properties. The DataSource property identifies the table the control is bound to, and the DisplayMember property identifies the column whose values are displayed in the list portion of the control. In this figure, for example, the DataSource property of the States combo box is set to the States table, and the DisplayMember property is set to the StateName column. That way, this combo box will list all of the state names in the States table so the user can select one of them.

The Vendors combo box for this application is also bound with complex binding so all of the vendor names in the Vendors table are displayed in the combo box list. In this case, the DataSource property is set to the Vendors table, and the DisplayMember property is set to the VendorName column.

In contrast, you use the SelectedValue and ValueMember properties to simple-bind a combo box control. You do that when you want to use the combo box selection as the basis for updating a column in a row of a related data table. The SelectedValue property identifies the data table and column that should be updated. For instance, the States combo box in this figure is simple-bound to the VendorState column in the Vendors table, which contains the state code for the vendor. In this case, though, the state code isn't the value that's displayed in the combo box. So for this to work, the ValueMember property must be set to the StateCode column in the States table. Then, when the user selects a state name in the States combo box list, the related StateCode value from the States table is stored in the VendorState column of the current row in the Vendors table.

Although the DisplayMember and ValueMember properties are different in this example, you should realize that they don't have to be. In other words, the values that are displayed in the combo box list can be the same as the values that are stored in the list. If, for example, you display the state codes in the States combo box list instead of the state names, you can set the DisplayMember property to StateCode. Then, when the user selects a state code from the combo box, that value is stored in the VendorState column of the current row in the Vendors table.

Although this may seem complicated at first, you'll soon be able to get the result you want by using the four properties that are summarized in this figure. With complex data binding, you can display all the values of a specified column in a combo box list or list box. With simple data binding, you can update a column in another data table with a value taken from the first data table.

A combo box that uses simple and complex binding

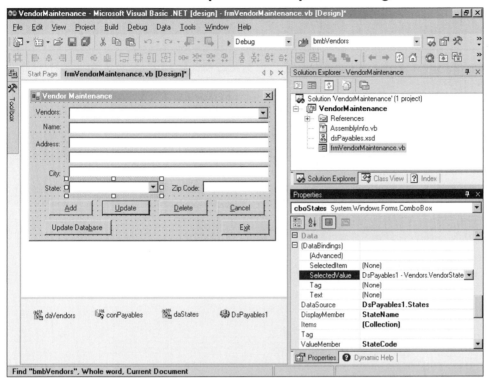

Combo box and list box properties for binding

Property	Description
DataSource	The name of the data table that contains the data displayed in the list.
DisplayMember	The name of the data column whose data is displayed in the list.
SelectedValue	The name of the data column that the control is bound to.
ValueMember	The name of the data column whose value is stored in the list. This value is used to update the value of the data column specified by the SelectedValue property of the control.

Description

- To complex-bind a combo box or list box to a data table so all the values in a column of a data table are included in the list, use the DataSource and DisplayMember properties.

- To simple-bind a combo box or list box to a data column so the value of that column changes when the user selects an entry from the list, use the SelectedValue and ValueMember properties. Then, the value of the data column specified by the ValueMember property is used to update the data column specified by the SelectedValue property.

Figure 4-9   How to bind combo box and list box controls

How to add, update, and delete data rows

To add, update, and delete rows using the binding manager base, you use the methods shown in figure 4-10. To add a new blank row, for example, you use the AddNew method. Then, after the user enters the data for the row, you use the EndCurrentEdit method to save the row to the data table. Alternatively, you can use the CancelCurrentEdit method to remove the new row from the table.

You also use the EndCurrentEdit and CancelCurrentEdit methods to save and cancel changes made to an existing row. Note that you don't explicitly start the edit of an existing row. Instead, that happens automatically when the user changes the data in a bound control.

Finally, you use the RemoveAt method to delete a specific row. Notice that you identify the row to be deleted by specifying its index value. If you want to delete the current row, for example, you can specify the index value using the Position property of the binding manager base as shown in the example in this figure.

Common BindingManagerBase methods

Method	Description
AddNew	Adds a new blank row to a data table.
RemoveAt(index)	Deletes the row with the specified index from a data table.
EndCurrentEdit	Ends the edit by saving the changes to the current row.
CancelCurrentEdit	Reverses the changes made to the current row.

A statement that adds a new row to a dataset

```
bmbVendors.AddNew()
```

A statement that removes the current row from a dataset

```
bmbVendors.RemoveAt(bmbVendors.Position)
```

A statement that saves the changes to the current row and ends the edit operation

```
bmbVendors.EndCurrentEdit()
```

A statement that cancels the changes to the current row

```
bmbVendors.CancelCurrentEdit()
```

Description

- When you add a new row using the AddNew method, the Position property of the binding manager base is set to one more than the position of the last row in the data table.
- You can use the EndCurrentEdit and CancelCurrentEdit methods to cancel or save the changes to an existing row or a new row that was added using the AddNew method.

Figure 4-10   How to add, update, and delete data rows

The property settings for the Vendor Maintenance form

Figure 4-11 presents some of the property settings for the Vendor Maintenance form. The first thing you should notice is that this form uses two data adapters: one for the Vendors table and one for the States table. However, both tables are stored in the same dataset, which is named DsPayables1.

Like the text boxes on the Vendor Display form, the Text property of each text box on the Vendor Maintenance form is bound to a column in the Vendors table. In addition, the SelectedValue property of the States combo box is bound to the VendorState column of the Vendors table. Then, this combo box is complex-bound to the States table so it contains a list of the state names associated with the state codes. That way, the user can select a state from the combo box list rather than having to enter a state name manually.

The Vendors combo box is also complex-bound to the VendorName column of the Vendors table. That way, the user can select a vendor from the list instead of having to navigate through the rows to find the one to be modified or deleted. You'll see how this lookup operation is implemented in a minute when I show you the code for this form. For now, notice that because this combo box isn't used to update a column in the Vendors table, its SelectedValue property is left at (None) and its ValueMember property isn't specified.

In addition to the StateCode and StateName columns, the States data adapter retrieves the FirstZipCode and LastZipCode columns. These columns contain the range of zip codes that are valid for the state. As you'll see in a moment, they're used to validate the zip code entered by the user.

Before I go on, you should notice that the MaxLength property of each text box on this form has been changed from the default. When you use the data in a text box to update a column in a table, you'll want to be sure that the user doesn't enter more characters than are allowed by the column definition. In this case, you want to be sure that the user doesn't enter more than 50 characters into the VendorName, VendorAddress1, VendorAddress2, and VendorCity columns or more than 10 characters into the VendorZipCode column. The easiest way to do that is to set the MaxLength property, which specifies the maximum number of characters the user can enter into the control.

The Select statements for the data adapters

Data adapter	Select statement

daVendors	`Select VendorID, VendorName, VendorAddress1,`
	`        VendorAddress2, VendorCity, VendorState,`
	`        VendorZipCode`
	`From Vendors`
	`Order By VendorName`

daStates	`Select StateCode, StateName, FirstZipCode, LastZipCode`
	`From States`
	`Order By StateName`

Property settings for the data-bound text boxes

Name	Text (DataBindings) as shown in the Properties window	MaxLength
txtName	DsPayables1 - Vendors.VendorName	50
txtAddressLine1	DsPayables1 - Vendors.VendorAddress1	50
txtAddressLine2	DsPayables1 - Vendors.VendorAddress2	50
txtCity	DsPayables1 - Vendors.VendorCity	50
txtZipCode	DsPayables1 - Vendors.VendorZipCode	10

Property settings for the data-bound combo boxes

Property	Vendors	States
Name	cboVendors	cboStates
DropDownStyle	DropDownList	DropDownList
DataSource	DsPayables1.Vendors	DsPayables1.States
DisplayMember	VendorName	StateName
SelectedValue (DataBindings)	(None)	DsPayables1 - Vendors.VendorState
ValueMember		StateCode

Notes

- Because the data in the States table will not be updated, Insert, Update, and Delete statements aren't generated for it.

- The dataset class is given the name dsPayables, and the dataset object is generated with the name DsPayables1. This dataset includes the two tables defined by the Vendors and States data adapters.

- The MaxLength properties of the text boxes are set so that the user can't enter more characters than are allowed by the columns they're bound to.

Figure 4-11   The property settings for the Vendor Maintenance form

The code for the Vendor Maintenance form

Figure 4-12 presents the code for the Vendor Maintenance form. It starts by defining three public variables used by the form. The first two will hold Boolean values that will determine when certain processing is done, and the third one will hold a reference to the binding manager base.

When the form is first loaded, both the States and Vendors tables are populated. But first, the bLoading variable is set to True. That way, the code in the cboVendors_SelectedIndexChanged and Control_DataChanged procedures isn't executed during the loading process. This variable is changed back to False after the tables are loaded.

Notice in this procedure that the Vendors table is loaded after the States table. That's necessary because the States combo box associates the VendorState column in the Vendors table with a column in the States table. But if the States table hasn't been loaded, this association can't be applied for the first Vendor that's displayed.

Next, the Load procedure calls the SetMaintenanceButtons procedure, which sets the Enabled property of the Add, Update, Delete, and Cancel buttons. In this case, a value of True is passed to this procedure, so the Add and Delete buttons are enabled and the Update and Cancel buttons are disabled. Finally, the Load procedure disables the Update Database button to indicate that no changes have been made to the dataset, and it creates the BindingManagerBase object.

When the user selects a vendor from the Vendors combo box, the SelectedIndexChanged event procedure is executed. After it checks the bLoading variable, it sets the Position property of the binding manager base to the SelectedIndex property of the combo box. In other words, it positions the binding manager base to the selected row. This works because the items in the combo box are in the same sequence as the rows in the Vendors table, and both use a zero-based index. Note that if the user makes any changes to the current row before selecting another vendor, those changes are automatically saved when the binding manager base is repositioned.

After the binding manager base is repositioned, the SetMaintenanceButtons procedure is called to enable the Add and Delete buttons and disable the Update and Cancel buttons. Next, the Enabled property of the Update Database button is set to the value of the HasChanges property of the dataset. That way, if any changes have been made to the dataset, the Update Database button is enabled. This code is necessary because when the user changes the data in a row, the Update Database button is disabled so the user can't click on it until the changes are accepted or canceled. So using the HasChanges property is the easiest way to reset the Enabled property of this control.

The next procedure is executed when the user clicks on the Add button. This procedure starts by executing the AddNew method to add a new row to the Vendors table. Then, it calls the SetMaintenanceButtons procedure to disable the Add and Delete buttons and enable the Update and Cancel buttons. To do that, a value of False is passed to the procedure. It also disables the Update Database button so the user can't click on it until the new row is accepted or canceled.

The Visual Basic code for the Vendor Maintenance program   Page 1

```vb
Public Class Form1
    Inherits System.Windows.Forms.Form

    Dim bLoading As Boolean
    Dim bNewRow As Boolean
    Dim bmbVendors As BindingManagerBase

    Private Sub Form1_Load(ByVal sender As System.Object, _
            ByVal e As System.EventArgs) Handles MyBase.Load
        bLoading = True
        daStates.Fill(DsPayables1)
        daVendors.Fill(DsPayables1)
        bLoading = False
        Me.SetMaintenanceButtons(True)
        btnUpdateDB.Enabled = False
        bmbVendors = Me.BindingContext(DsPayables1, "Vendors")
    End Sub

    Private Sub SetMaintenanceButtons(ByVal bAddDeleteMode As Boolean)
        btnAdd.Enabled = bAddDeleteMode
        btnUpdate.Enabled = Not bAddDeleteMode
        btnDelete.Enabled = bAddDeleteMode
        btnCancel.Enabled = Not bAddDeleteMode
    End Sub

    Private Sub cboVendors_SelectedIndexChanged(ByVal sender As System.Object, _
            ByVal e As System.EventArgs) Handles cboVendors.SelectedIndexChanged
        If Not bLoading Then
            bmbVendors.Position = cboVendors.SelectedIndex
            Me.SetMaintenanceButtons(True)
            btnUpdateDB.Enabled = DsPayables1.HasChanges
            txtName.Focus()
        End If
    End Sub

    Private Sub btnAdd_Click(ByVal sender As System.Object, _
            ByVal e As System.EventArgs) Handles btnAdd.Click
        bmbVendors.AddNew()
        Me.SetMaintenanceButtons(False)
        btnUpdateDB.Enabled = False
        cboStates.SelectedIndex = -1
        bNewRow = True
        txtName.Focus()
    End Sub

    Private Sub Control_DataChanged(ByVal sender As System.Object, _
            ByVal e As System.EventArgs) Handles txtName.TextChanged, _
            txtAddressLine1.TextChanged, txtAddressLine2.TextChanged, _
            txtCity.TextChanged, txtZipCode.TextChanged, _
            cboStates.SelectedIndexChanged
        If Not bLoading Then
            Me.SetMaintenanceButtons(False)
            btnUpdateDB.Enabled = False
        End If
    End Sub
```

Figure 4-12   The code for the Vendor Maintenance form (part 1 of 3)

Next, the Add procedure sets the SelectedIndex property of the States combo box to -1 so no value is selected in this combo box. Then, it sets the bNewRow variable to True to indicate that a new row is being added. Finally, it moves the focus to the Name text box so the user can begin entering the data for the new vendor.

The last procedure on the first page of this listing is executed when the user changes the data in the current row. Notice that a single procedure handles the TextChanged event for all the text boxes as well as the SelectedIndexChanged event for the States combo box. Within this procedure, the SetMaintenanceButtons procedure is called to enable the Update and Cancel buttons and to disable the Add and Delete buttons. Then, the Update Database button is disabled so the user can't click on it until the changes are updated or canceled. Notice that this code isn't executed when the form is loaded.

If the user changes the data in a row and then clicks on the Update button, the Update procedure on page 2 of this listing starts by executing a procedure named ValidData. This procedure checks that the user has entered data for the required columns. In this case, it checks the Name, City, and ZipCode text boxes and the States combo box. It also checks to be sure that the zip code is within the valid range identified by the FirstZipCode and LastZipCode columns in the row for the state. To do that, it uses the index of the States combo box to identify the row in the States table that contains the selected state.

If invalid data is detected, an error message is displayed and the return value of the ValidData function is set to False. Otherwise, the return value is set to True so the Update procedure will continue with the update operation.

To save the changes to the current row, the Update procedure issues an EndCurrentEdit method. Then, if the current row is a new row, this procedure sets the SelectedIndex property of the Vendors combo box to the position of the last row in the table, which is the position of the new row. That way, the name of the new vendor is displayed in the combo box. It also sets the bNewRow variable to False so the program is ready for the next operation. The last three statements in this procedure call the SetMaintenanceButtons procedure to disable the Update and Cancel buttons and enable the Add and Delete buttons, enable the Update Database button, and set the focus to the Vendors combo box so the user can select the next vendor to be processed.

Similar code is included in the Click event procedure for the Cancel button. Instead of issuing an EndCurrentEdit method, however, this procedure issues a CancelCurrentEdit method to reverse the changes made to the current row. And instead of setting the Enabled property of the Update Database button to True, this procedure sets it to the HasChanges property of the dataset. That way, if this button was enabled before the current row was changed and the changes were canceled, it will be enabled again. Otherwise, it will be disabled. In addition, if the user canceled the addition of a new row, this procedure sets the Position property of the binding manager base to the SelectedIndex property of the Vendors combo box. That causes the data for the vendor that was selected before the user clicked on the Add button to be displayed on the form, since this vendor is still selected in the combo box.

The Visual Basic code for the Vendor Maintenance program Page 2

```vb
Private Sub btnUpdate_Click(ByVal sender As System.Object, _
        ByVal e As System.EventArgs) Handles btnUpdate.Click
    If ValidData() Then
        bmbVendors.EndCurrentEdit()
        If bNewRow Then
            cboVendors.SelectedIndex = bmbVendors.Count - 1
            bNewRow = False
        End If
        Me.SetMaintenanceButtons(True)
        btnUpdateDB.Enabled = True
        cboVendors.Focus()
    End If
End Sub

Private Function ValidData() As Boolean
    Dim sErrorMessage As String
    If txtName.Text = "" Then
        sErrorMessage = "Name required."
        txtName.Focus()
    ElseIf txtCity.Text = "" Then
        sErrorMessage = "City required."
        txtCity.Focus()
    ElseIf cboStates.SelectedIndex = -1 Then
        sErrorMessage = "State required."
        cboStates.Focus()
    ElseIf txtZipCode.Text = "" Then
        sErrorMessage = "Zip code required."
        txtZipCode.Focus()
    ElseIf txtZipCode.Text < DsPayables1.States.Rows _
            (cboStates.SelectedIndex).Item("FirstZipCode") _
        Or txtZipCode.Text > DsPayables1.States.Rows _
            (cboStates.SelectedIndex).Item("LastZipCode") Then
        sErrorMessage = "The zip code is invalid."
        txtZipCode.Focus()
    End If
    If sErrorMessage = "" Then
        ValidData = True
    Else
        ValidData = False
        MessageBox.Show(sErrorMessage, "Data entry error", _
            MessageBoxButtons.OK, MessageBoxIcon.Error)
    End If
End Function

Private Sub btnCancel_Click(ByVal sender As System.Object, _
        ByVal e As System.EventArgs) Handles btnCancel.Click
    bmbVendors.CancelCurrentEdit()
    If bNewRow Then
        bmbVendors.Position = cboVendors.SelectedIndex
        bNewRow = False
    End If
    Me.SetMaintenanceButtons(True)
    btnUpdateDB.Enabled = DsPayables1.HasChanges
    cboVendors.Focus()
End Sub
```

Figure 4-12 The code for the Vendor Maintenance form (part 2 of 3)

The first procedure on page 3 of this listing is executed when the user clicks on the Delete button. This procedure starts by displaying a message box to confirm that the user wants to delete the row. If the user responds by clicking on the Yes button, a RemoveAt method is executed to remove the current row. Then, the SetMaintenanceButtons procedure is called to reset the Add, Update, Cancel, and Delete buttons, and the focus is moved to the Vendors combo box.

The next procedure is the event procedure that's executed when the user clicks on the Update Database button to apply the changes that have been made to the Vendors table to the database. It starts by issuing an Update method to perform this update. Notice that this procedure doesn't check if changes have been made to the dataset before issuing this method. That's because this procedure can be executed only if the Update Database button is enabled, and this button is enabled only if changes have been made to the dataset.

After the database is updated, this procedure sets the bLoading variable to True. That way, the code in the Data_Changed procedure isn't executed when the Clear and Fill methods that follow are executed. These methods are included so that the dataset is refreshed with the current data in the database. After these two methods are executed, the bLoading variable is set to False. Then, the Enabled property of the Update Database button is set to False to indicate that no changes have been made to the dataset, and the focus is moved to the Vendors combo box.

The next to last procedure is executed when the user clicks on the Exit button. This procedure simply closes the form, which causes the Closing event of the form to fire. The last procedure for this form handles this event. Note that this procedure also fires if the user clicks on the close button in the upper right corner of the form.

The procedure for the Closing event starts by checking if any changes have been made to the dataset that haven't been saved to the database. If so, a message box is displayed to ask the user if the form should be closed without saving the changes. If the user responds by clicking on the No button, the Cancel property of the e argument that's passed to this procedure is set to True so that the form remains open. Otherwise, it's closed. If no changes have been made to the dataset, the form is closed without displaying a message box.

* * *

If the coding for this form seems complicated, you should know that this is typical of database programs when insertions, updates, and deletions are made to a dataset and to the related database tables. Remember, too, that this is a simple application with limited data validation and no exception handling. So a production program is likely to be far more complicated.

Aside from the database handling elements, the Visual Basic code in this program should be familiar to you. So if you've had any trouble understanding it, you can quickly review the basics by using *Murach's Beginning Visual Basic .NET*. It covers all the VB skills that you'll need for working with this book.

The Visual Basic code for the Vendor Maintenance program   Page 3

```vb
    Private Sub btnDelete_Click(ByVal sender As System.Object, _
            ByVal e As System.EventArgs) Handles btnDelete.Click
        Dim iResult As DialogResult _
            = MessageBox.Show("Delete " & cboVendors.Text & "?", _
              "Confirm Delete", MessageBoxButtons.YesNo, _
              MessageBoxIcon.Question)
        If iResult = DialogResult.Yes Then
            bmbVendors.RemoveAt(bmbVendors.Position)
            cboVendors.Focus()
        End If
    End Sub

    Private Sub btnUpdateDB_Click(ByVal sender As System.Object, _
            ByVal e As System.EventArgs) Handles btnUpdateDB.Click
        daVendors.Update(DsPayables1.Vendors)
        bLoading = True
        DsPayables1.Vendors.Clear()
        daVendors.Fill(DsPayables1)
        bLoading = False
        btnUpdateDB.Enabled = False
        cboVendors.Focus()
    End Sub

    Private Sub btnExit_Click(ByVal sender As System.Object, _
            ByVal e As System.EventArgs) Handles btnExit.Click
        Me.Close()
    End Sub

    Private Sub Form1_Closing(ByVal sender As Object, _
            ByVal e As System.ComponentModel.CancelEventArgs) _
            Handles MyBase.Closing
        If DsPayables1.HasChanges Then
            Dim iResult As DialogResult _
                = MessageBox.Show("You have made changes that have not " _
                & "been saved to the database. " & ControlChars.CrLf _
                & "If you continue, these changes will be lost." _
                & ControlChars.CrLf & "Continue?", "Confirm Exit", _
                MessageBoxButtons.YesNo, MessageBoxIcon.Question)
            If iResult = DialogResult.No Then
                e.Cancel = True
            End If
        End If
    End Sub

End Class
```

Figure 4-12   The code for the Vendor Maintenance form (part 3 of 3)

How to handle data exceptions

Both ADO.NET and the .NET data providers have specific classes you can use to catch the data exceptions that may occur as your database applications are running. You'll learn how to work with these classes in the topics that follow. In addition, you'll learn some specific procedures for handling update errors.

How to handle ADO.NET errors

Even if you check bound controls for valid data, ADO.NET errors can occur when you operate on ADO.NET objects. Figure 4-13 presents some of the most common of those errors. As you can see, you can catch any ADO.NET error using the DataException class. In addition, you can catch specific errors using the other classes shown here. All of these classes are members of the System.Data namespace.

Like other exception classes provided by the .NET Framework, each ADO.NET exception class has a Message and Source property that you can use to display information about the error. The error-handling code shown in this figure, for example, catches errors caused by the EndCurrentEdit method and then uses a message box to display the Message property of the exception object. Notice that the first Catch clause catches constraint exceptions, the second Catch clause catches null exceptions, and the third Catch clause catches any other data exceptions. The last Catch clause is included to catch any other exceptions that might occur.

One of the data exception classes that isn't illustrated by this example is the DbConcurrencyException class. This is the exception you use to catch concurrency exceptions, which you learned about in chapter 2. This exception can occur when you execute the Update method of a data adapter. Although you might think that this error would be generated by the database rather than ADO.NET, it's not. To understand why, you need to remember that the SQL statements that are executed for an update or delete operation contain code that checks that a row hasn't changed since it was retrieved. But if the row has changed, the row with the specified criteria won't be found and the SQL statement won't be executed. When the data adapter discovers that the row wasn't updated or deleted, however, it realizes there was a concurrency error and throws an exception. You'll learn more about how and when to handle this exception later in this chapter.

Common ADO.NET exception classes

Name	Description
DataException	The general exception that's thrown when an ADO.NET error occurs.
DbConcurrencyException	The exception that's thrown if the number of rows affected by an Insert, Update, or Delete operation is zero. This exception is typically caused by a concurrency violation.
ConstraintException	The exception that's thrown if an operation violates a constraint.
NoNullAllowedException	The exception that's thrown when an add or update operation attempts to save a null value in a column that doesn't allow nulls.

Common properties of the ADO.NET exception classes

Property	Description
Message	A message that describes the exception.
Source	The name of the object that caused the exception.

Error-handling code for the EndCurrentEdit method

```
Try
    bmbVendors.EndCurrentEdit()
Catch eConstraint As ConstraintException
    MessageBox.Show(eConstraint.Message, "Constraint error")
Catch eNull As NoNullAllowedException
    MessageBox.Show(eNull.Message, "Null error")
Catch eData As DataException
    MessageBox.Show(eData.Message, "ADO.NET error")
Catch eSystem As Exception
    MessageBox.Show(eSystem.Message, "System error")
End Try
```

Description

- An ADO.NET exception is an exception that occurs on any ADO.NET object. All of these exceptions are members of the System.Data namespace.

- In most cases, you'll include validation code in your programs to make sure that exceptions like ConstraintException and NoNullAllowedException don't occur. Then, you can just use the DataException class to catch any unexpected ADO.NET exceptions.

- A DbConcurrencyException occurs if the return value of an Insert, Update, or Delete statement that's issued by the Update method of a data adapter indicates that the row wasn't processed. That's typically the result of an operation that tries to modify or delete a row that has been changed by another user. It can also be the result of an operation that tries to add a row with a unique constraint that already exists in the table.

Figure 4-13   How to handle ADO.NET errors

How to handle data provider errors

Figure 4-14 describes the two exception classes you can use to catch errors encountered by a data provider. As you can see, there's one class for each of the two data providers supported by the .NET Framework. You use the SqlException class to catch errors encountered by the SQL Server data provider, and you use the OleDbException class to catch errors encountered by the OLE DB data provider.

Unlike the other types of exceptions, the SQL and OLE DB exceptions include a collection of one or more error objects. You can refer to this collection through the Errors property of the exception object. Then, you can loop through this collection to display information about each of the errors.

The code in this figure shows how this works. Here, a Fill method that retrieves data from the Vendors table of a SQL Server database is executed within the Try clause of a Try...Catch statement. The first Catch clause in this statement catches any ADO.NET error that occurs as described in the previous figure. Then, the second Catch clause catches any error that occurs on the SQL Server data provider and assigns the exception object to a variable named eSql.

The code within this Catch clause starts by declaring three variables. The first one is an integer variable named iError that will be used to loop through the errors in the error collection. The second variable, named SqlErrors, is declared as an SqlErrorCollection object. The value that's assigned to this variable is the Errors property of the SqlException object, which contains a reference to the error collection of that object. Finally, the third one is a string variable named sErrorSummary that will be used to format the errors for display.

Next, this code uses a For...Next loop to get information about each of the errors and format it in the error summary variable. Like other collections, the error collection is zero-based. So this loop starts with the error item that has an index value of zero. Then, it continues through the last item in the collection, whose index value is identified by the Count property of the collection minus one. When the loop ends, the error summary is displayed in a message box.

Notice in this code that two properties of each error object are included in the error message: Number and Message. A third property you might want to use is Source, which contains the name of the provider that generated the error. In addition to the properties of the individual error objects, the exception object itself has Number, Message, and Source properties that you can use to get information about the error. In fact, in many cases, these properties will provide all the information you need.

.NET data provider exception classes

Name	Description
SqlException	The exception that is thrown when a warning or error is returned by SQL Server. This class can be found in the System.Data.SqlClient namespace.
OleDbException	The exception that is thrown when a warning or error is returned by an OLE DB data source. This class can be found in the System.Data.OleDb namespace.

Error-handling code for the Fill method of a SQL Server data adapter

```
Try
    daVendors.Fill(DsPayables1)
Catch eData As DataException
    MessageBox.Show(eData.Message, "ADO.NET error")
Catch eSql As SqlException
    Dim iError As Integer
    Dim SqlErrors As SqlErrorCollection = eSql.Errors
    Dim sErrorSummary As String
    For iError = 0 To SqlErrors.Count - 1
        sErrorSummary = sErrorSummary & SqlErrors(iError).Number & " - " _
                                      & SqlErrors(iError).Message _
                                      & ControlChars.CrLf
    Next iError
    MessageBox.Show(sErrorSummary, "SQL Server error")
Catch eSystem As Exception
    MessageBox.Show(eSystem.Message, "System error")
End Try
```

Common properties of data provider exception and error objects

Property	Description
Number	An error number that identifies the type of error.
Message	Text that describes the error.
Source	The name of the provider that generated the error.

Description

- Whenever the data provider (SQL Server or OLE DB) encounters a situation it can't handle, an exception object (SqlException or OleDbException) is created.

- The exception object contains a collection of error objects (SqlErrorCollection or OleDbErrorCollection) that contain information about the error. You can use the Errors property of the exception object to loop through the errors in this collection.

- You can also use the Number, Message, and Source properties of the exception object to determine the cause of an error. The Number and Source properties contain the same information as the first error object, and the Message property contains a concatenation of the messages in all the error objects.

Figure 4-14   How to handle data provider errors

How to handle update errors

When you update multiple rows, you can use a technique like the one shown in figure 4-15 to handle any errors that might occur. To use this technique, you must set the ContinueUpdateOnError property of the data adapter to True. Then if an error occurs during the update, the data adapter doesn't throw an exception. Instead, it flags the row to indicate that it has an error, and it continues the update operation until all of the rows in the data table have been processed.

To flag an error, the data adapter sets the HasErrors property of the row to True, and it sets the RowError property of the row to a description of the error. It also sets the HasErrors property of the table and dataset to True. That way, you can use these properties to check for errors before checking each individual row.

The example in this figure shows one way you can use this update technique. The first thing you should notice here is that the Update method isn't coded within a Try...Catch statement. That's because no exception will be thrown when an error occurs.

After the Update method is executed, this code checks the HasErrors property of the dataset to determine if any errors were encountered. If so, this code loops through the rows in the Vendors table to locate the ones with errors. To do that, it starts by declaring an object variable as a data row. Then, it uses that variable in a For Each...Next statement that checks the HasErrors property of each row in the table. If it finds an error, it formats a message string so it includes the name of the vendor and the description of the error that's stored in the RowError property. After it locates all of the rows in error, this code displays a message box that lists all the vendors that weren't updated.

In a production program, of course, you would want to include some additional processing for each error. For example, you might want to retrieve the rows in error and let the user modify and update them again. Because the processing that's performed will vary from one shop to another, however, I haven't included it here.

Common properties for working with update errors

Object	Property	Description
Data adapter	ContinueUpateOnError	Determines whether processing continues when an error occurs during an update operation. The default is False, which causes an exception to be thrown and the update to end.
Dataset, data table, and data row	HasErrors	Indicates whether errors were encountered during the update of the dataset, data table, or data row. These properties are automatically set to True if an error is encountered and the ContinueUpdateOnError property of the data adapter is set to True.
Data row	RowError	Contains a description of the error that occurred.

Code that handles a multi-row update

```
daVendors.Update(DsPayables1.Vendors)
If DsPayables1.HasErrors Then
    Dim VendorRow As DataRow
    Dim sMessage As String
    sMessage = "The following rows were not updated:" _
        & ControlChars.CrLf & ControlChars.CrLf
    For Each VendorRow In DsPayables1.Vendors
        If VendorRow.HasErrors Then
            sMessage &= VendorRow("VendorName") & ": " _
                    & VendorRow.RowError & ControlChars.CrLf
        End If
    Next
    MessageBox.Show(sMessage, "Update errors")
End If
```

Description

- When you perform a multi-row update, an exception will be thrown and the update operation will end if a concurrency error (or any other error) occurs on a row. To avoid that, you can set the ContinueUpdateOnError property of the data adapter to True. Then, no exception is thrown and the update operation will process the remaining rows.

- If the ContinueUpdateOnError property is set to True and an error occurs on the update of a row, the HasErrors properties of the row, table, and dataset are set to True. In addition, the RowError property of the row is set to a description of the error. You can use these properties to identify the rows in error and process them appropriately.

Figure 4-15   How to handle update errors

How to use data table events

The Vendor Maintenance program presented earlier in this chapter uses a function named ValidData to validate the data the user enters into the bound controls before it's saved to the data table. Another way to validate data is to use the events that are available for a data table. You'll learn how to use these events in the two topics that follow.

How to provide for data table events

Figure 4-16 lists six events that can occur on a data table when you add, change, or delete data. The first event, ColumnChanging, occurs just before the data in a bound column is changed. That happens when the focus leaves the control that's bound to the column and the CausesValidation property of the control that receives the focus is set to True (the default). You can use this event to validate the data in each bound control as it's entered by the user.

The RowChanging event occurs just before the data in a row is saved to the dataset. That happens when you issue the EndCurrentEdit method of the binding manager base. You can use this event to validate all of the data in a row at once. This is particularly useful if two or more column values are related in some way. For example, you could use this event to check that the zip code the user enters is valid for the state code. This is the event that's used most frequently to validate the data in bound controls.

Although four other data table events are listed in this figure, you won't typically use them for data validation. However, you might use them for some other common purposes. For example, you could use the RowDeleting event to let the user confirm the delete operation, and you could use the RowChanged and RowDeleted events to confirm that the operations completed successfully.

Unfortunately, the data table events aren't available by default. That's because the declaration for a data table within the dataset class doesn't include the WithEvents keyword. To make these events available, then, you need to declare a module-level variable for the table that includes this keyword. This is illustrated by the first statement in this figure. It creates a variable named VendorsTable that refers to the Vendors data table defined by the dataset class named dsPayables. Notice that the object type that's specified is the name of the class that defines the table in the typed dataset.

After you declare a table variable with the WithEvents keyword, you need to assign the appropriate table to it, as illustrated by the second statement in this figure. Here, the Vendors table in the DsPayables1 dataset is assigned to the VendorsTable variable. At this point, you're ready to use this variable to work with the events of the Vendors table.

Data table events

Event	Description
ColumnChanging	This event occurs when the focus moves out of a bound control whose value has changed. The CausesValidation property of the control that the focus is moved to must be set to True for this event to occur. This is the default for all controls.
ColumnChanged	This event occurs after a value in a data column has been updated with the value in a bound control.
RowChanging	This event occurs when the EndCurrentEdit method of the binding manager base is executed.
RowChanged	This event occurs after the changes to a data row have been saved.
RowDeleting	This event occurs when the RemoveAt method of the binding manager base is executed.
RowDeleted	This event occurs after a data row is deleted.

A statement that declares a data table variable with events

```
Dim WithEvents VendorsTable As dsPayables.VendorsDataTable
```

A statement that assigns the table to the data table variable

```
VendorsTable = DsPayables1.Vendors
```

Description

- To make the events for a data table available to your program, you declare a module-level variable for the table that includes the WithEvents keyword. The object type you specify on this statement must be the name of the class for the table in the typed dataset, which is the name of the table followed by "DataTable."

- After you declare the table object, you assign the appropriate table to it. In most cases, you include this assignment statement in the Load procedure for the form.

- You can use the RowChanging event to check the values of all of the controls at once. Then, you can also check that the values of related columns, like state and zip code, are consistent.

Figure 4-16   How to provide for data table events

How to use the RowChanging event

Figure 4-17 presents code that uses the RowChanging event of the Vendors table. The first procedure is executed when the RowChanging event occurs. Notice that the code in this procedure isn't executed as the form is being loaded. If it was, it would be executed each time a row was loaded into the table, which would be inefficient.

If the form isn't being loaded, the code in this procedure checks the values in the Name, City, and Zip Code text boxes to be sure that the user entered a value into each of these controls. If not, an appropriate error message is assigned to an error message variable and the focus is moved to the control so the user can enter a value.

After all the columns are validated, this procedure checks the error message variable to see if any errors were detected. If so, a Throw statement is issued. This statement not only causes an error to be thrown, but it also causes the RowChanging event to be canceled, which is what you want. Notice that this statement also passes the error message to the procedure that catches the exception.

The procedure that catches the exception is the one that issued the EndCurrentEdit method that caused the RowChanging event to occur. As you can see, this statement is coded within the Try clause of a Try...Catch statement. That way, if the EndCurrentEdit method, or any other code that's executed as a result of this method, throws an error, it's displayed by the code in one of the Catch clauses of this statement. In this case, the error that's thrown within the RowChanging event procedure is a system exception, so it's caught by the second Catch clause.

Code that validates data using the RowChanging event

```
Private Sub VendorsTable_RowChanging(ByVal sender As Object, _
        ByVal e As System.Data.DataRowChangeEventArgs) _
        Handles VendorsTable.RowChanging
    If Not bLoading Then
        Dim sErrorMessage As String
        If txtName.Text = "" Then
            sErrorMessage = "Name required."
            txtName.Focus()
        ElseIf txtCity.Text = "" Then
            sErrorMessage = "City required."
            txtCity.Focus()
        ElseIf txtZipCode.Text = "" Then
            sErrorMessage = "Zip code required."
            txtZipCode.Focus()
        End If
        If sErrorMessage <> "" Then
            Throw New System.Exception(sErrorMessage)
        End If
    End If
End Sub
```

Code that causes the RowChanging event to occur and catches the thrown exception

```
Private Sub btnUpdate_Click(ByVal sender As System.Object, _
        ByVal e As System.EventArgs) Handles btnUpdate.Click
    Try
        bmbVendors.EndCurrentEdit()
        Me.SetMaintenanceButtons(True)
        btnUpdateDB.Enabled = True
        cboVendors.Focus()
    Catch eData As DataException
        MessageBox.Show(eData.Message, "ADO.NET error")
    Catch eSystem As Exception
        MessageBox.Show(eSystem.Message, "System error")
    End Try
End Sub
```

Description

- You can use the RowChanging event to check the values in one or more of the controls on a bound form to be sure they're valid.

- The RowChanging event will occur as each row is loaded into a table. To prevent this, you can set a Boolean variable in the Load procedure of the form and then test it in the RowChanging event procedure.

- When an error is detected, your code should display an error message and move the focus to the control that contains the invalid data.

- To cancel a row change operation, use the Throw statement to throw an exception. Then, you can catch the exception in the procedure that executes the EndCurrentEdit method. If you include an error message on the Throw statement, that message is used for the Message property of the exception.

Figure 4-17   How to use the RowChanging event

Perspective

One goal of this chapter has been to introduce you to typed datasets. Another goal has been to teach you the skills you need for developing database programs in the real world when using bound controls. Finally, a third goal has been to introduce you to the complexity of this type of programming. If you understand the techniques and code presented in this chapter, you're ready to learn the skills in the chapters that follow.

Term

simple data binding

5

How to work with typed datasets and unbound controls

When you use bound controls as described in the last chapter, you can display and update data quickly and easily. In many cases, though, you won't have as much control over how the data is processed as you would like. Because of that, professional programmers frequently use unbound controls in their applications. So in this chapter, you'll learn how to use unbound controls with typed datasets.

Keep in mind as you read this chapter that although unbound controls aren't simple-bound to the data source that contains the data to be displayed or updated, they may be complex-bound to other data sources. For example, you could complex-bind a combo box or a list box so that it displays a list of all the possible values for the control. You'll see how that works in the program example in this chapter.

How to work with unbound controls

In the Vendor Maintenance program you saw in the last chapter, the controls were bound to the Vendors data table. Because of that, you worked with this table through a binding manager base object. When you work with unbound controls, however, you work directly with the data table. You'll learn how to do that in the topics that follow.

How to process unbound data

Figure 5-1 summarizes the functions of the binding manager base that you must provide for when you work with unbound controls. As you can see, some of these functions are provided by properties and methods of the binding manager base that you learned about in the last chapter. Others, such as moving data from a data column to a form control and vice versa, are provided automatically by the binding manager base.

When you use unbound controls, you must provide for all of these functions explicitly using the methods, properties, and statements indicated in this figure. You'll learn how to code these in the figures that follow. You'll also see how to use many of them in a complete application when I present an unbound version of the Vendor Maintenance program.

This figure also indicates when each of the methods, properties, and statements needs to be performed. For the most part, you shouldn't have any trouble understanding this information. Notice, however, that a new row isn't added to a data table until the user accepts the data for the new row. Although you might think that you would add a row as soon as the user indicates that he wants to add a new row, that's not necessary since the controls on the form aren't bound to the underlying data table. If you don't understand this now, it'll make more sense when you see the complete code for the Vendor Maintenance program.

BindingManagerBase functions that must be provided through code

Function	Method, property, or statement	When it should be executed
Retrieve a row and move values from columns in the row to controls	Item property or FindBy… method of the data table and assignment statements that use data row properties	When the form is first loaded, when the user selects another row to be displayed, when a row is deleted, when the addition of a new row or changes to an existing row are canceled, and when the data table is refreshed.
Clear control values	Assignment statements	When the user indicates that he or she wants to add a new row.
Create a new data row	New…Row method of the data table	When the user indicates that the dataset should be updated with the data for a new row.
Move values from controls to the selected row or a new row	Assignment statements that use data row properties	When the user indicates that the dataset should be updated with the data for a new row or the changes to an existing row.
Add a row to the table	Add...Row method of the data table	When the user indicates that the dataset should be updated with the data for a new row. This is done after the new row is created and values are assigned to its columns.
Delete a row from the table	Delete method of a data row	When the user indicates that a row should be deleted from the dataset.
Begin an edit operation	BeginEdit method of a data row	When the user changes the data in an existing row.
End an edit operation	EndEdit method of a data row	When the user indicates that the dataset should be updated with the changes to an existing row.
Cancel an edit operation	CancelEdit method of a data row	When the user indicates that the changes to an existing row should be canceled.
Keep track of the current row	Assignment statements	When the form is first loaded, when the user selects another row to be displayed, when the user indicates that the dataset should be updated with the data for a new row, when a row is deleted, and when the data table is refreshed.

Description

- When you process data that's not bound to controls on a form, you must provide the same functions that are provided by the BindingManagerBase object of the form. That includes displaying the rows in the data table, adding new rows to the data table, and updating and deleting existing rows.

Figure 5-1   How to process unbound data

How to retrieve and work with a data row

Before you can work with the data in a data row, you have to retrieve the row. Figure 5-2 shows you how to do that. To start, you declare a variable that will hold the row as illustrated by all three examples in this figure. In the first two examples, a variable named drVendor is declared with a type of dsPayables.VendorsRow. That way, you can use the properties defined by the VendorsRow class to get and set the value of each column in a row as you'll see in a moment. Similarly, the third example declares a variable named drLineItem with a type of dsPayables.InvoiceLineItemsRow.

After you declare a variable to hold a row, you can retrieve a row and assign it to that variable. This figure shows two ways to do that. First, you can retrieve a row using its index as illustrated in the first example. Here, the Item property of the table is used to retrieve the row with the specified index. Because the Item property is the default property of a table, however, it can be omitted as shown.

The rest of the code in this example retrieves values from individual columns of the row and assigns them to the appropriate properties of controls on a form. Here, you can see that the value of each column is retrieved using a property of the row. To retrieve the value of the VendorName column, for example, the VendorName property is used.

If a table is defined with a primary key, you can also use the technique illustrated in the second example to retrieve a row from the table. This example uses the FindBy... method that's generated for the table to retrieve a row by its key value. In this case, the table is the Vendors table and the primary key is the VendorID column. Notice that the name of the method includes the name of this column. To retrieve a row from this table based on its key value, you pass the key value as an argument to the FindByVendorID method. In this example, the SelectedValue property of a combo box is used to identify the key value.

Before I go on, you should realize that to use the SelectedValue property of a combo box or a list box this way, you have to set the DataSource, DisplayMember, and ValueMember properties of the control. You'll remember from chapter 4 that the DataSource and DisplayMember properties complex-bind the control to the data source, which populates the list portion of the control. The ValueMember property, on the other hand, names the column in the data source whose value is stored in the list. Then, when you select an item from the list, you can use the SelectedValue property to get the value of this column. You'll see how this technique is used in the program that's presented later in this chapter.

You can also use the FindBy... method with a primary key that consists of two or more columns. In that case, the name of the FindBy... method includes the names of all the key columns in sequence, as you can see in the third example in this figure. Then, the arguments that contain the values for these columns are coded in the same sequence.

Code that retrieves a row using its index and assigns column values to form controls

```
Dim drVendor As dsPayables.VendorsRow
Dim iCurrentRow As Integer
    .
    .
    .
drVendor = DsPayables1.Vendors(iCurrentRow)
txtName.Text = drVendor.VendorName
txtAddressLine1.Text = drVendor.VendorAddress1
txtAddressLine2.Text = drVendor.VendorAddress2
txtCity.Text = drVendor.VendorCity
    .
    .
    .
```

Code that uses the FindBy… method to retrieve a row with the selected key value

```
Dim drVendor As dsPayables.VendorsRow
drVendor = DsPayables1.Vendors.FindByVendorID(cboVendors.SelectedValue)
```

Code that uses the FindBy… method to retrieve a row with a composite key

```
Dim drLineItem As dsPayables.InvoiceLineItemsRow
Dim iInvoiceID As Integer
Dim sInvoiceSequence As Short
drLineItem = DsPayables1.InvoiceLineItems.FindByInvoiceIDInvoiceSequence _
    (iInvoiceID, sInvoiceSequence)
```

Description

- To declare a variable for a row in a data table, you use the class for the data row that's defined by the typed dataset.

- To retrieve a row from a data table, you can use the Item property of the table and the index of the row. Since Item is the default property of a table, you can omit it as shown above.

- To get the values of the columns in a row, use the properties of the row that have the same names as the columns in the data table.

- You can use the FindBy… method of a data table to retrieve the row with the specified key value. If the row doesn't exist, this method returns Nothing.

- The FindBy… method is defined for the primary key of a table. The name of this method includes the name of the key column. If the key consists of two or more columns, the names are appended to each other to form the name of the method.

- The FindBy… method accepts one argument for each column of the primary key. The columns must be specified in the same sequence that they appear in the key.

- To use the FindBy… method with a combo box or a list box that's complex-bound to a data table, the ValueMember property of the control must be set to the column that contains the key value. That way, the SelectedValue property can be used to retrieve the value of a selected item.

Figure 5-2   How to retrieve and work with a data row

How to modify or delete an existing data row

Figure 5-3 illustrates how you modify or delete an existing data row. Note that the examples in this figure assume that you have already retrieved a row as described in the previous figure. Then, you can modify the data in the row using code like that shown in the first example.

This code starts by executing a BeginEdit method, which places the row in *edit mode*. While in this mode, the RowChanging event isn't fired if the user changes the data in the row. If you code a procedure for the RowChanging event in a program, you'll want to be sure to use the BeginEdit method. You'll also want to use this method if you need to work with the proposed values in the row before they're saved, since these values are available only while a row is in edit mode. You'll learn more about working with the RowChanging event and proposed values later in this chapter. If you won't use the RowChanging event or proposed values, you probably won't use BeginEdit.

After the edit is started, the statements that follow assign new values to the columns in the row. Like the statements in the previous figure that assigned column values to form controls, the statements in this example use the properties of the data row to assign values to the columns. Once the new values have been assigned, the EndEdit method is executed to commit the changes. This method also causes the RowChanging event to fire. If you code a procedure for this event, you can validate the data before the changes are committed.

You can use two different techniques to delete a row from a data table. First, you can use the Delete method of the data row to mark the row as deleted, as shown in the second example in this figure. Then, the row isn't deleted permanently until you issue the Update method of the data adapter. Second, you can use the Remove…Row method of the table to permanently remove the row from the table as illustrated in the third example. Since the row is removed permanently when you use this method, issuing an Update method later will have no effect on the database. Because of that, you should use the Delete method if you want to delete the row from the database.

Code that modifies the values in the data row

```
drVendor.BeginEdit()
drVendor.VendorName = txtName.Text
drVendor.VendorAddress1 = txtAddressLine1.Text
drVendor.VendorAddress2 = txtAddressLine2.Text
drVendor.VendorCity = txtCity.Text
drVendor.VendorState = cboStates.SelectedValue
drVendor.VendorZipCode = txtZipCode.Text
drVendor.EndEdit()
```

A statement that uses the Delete method to mark the row as deleted

```
drVendor.Delete()
```

A statement that uses the Remove method to delete the row

```
DsPayables1.Vendors.RemoveVendorsRow(drVendor)
```

Description

- The BeginEdit method of a data row places the row in *edit mode*. In this mode, the RowChanging event of the data table isn't fired. See figure 5-7 for more information on using this event.

- To set the values of the columns in a row, you use the properties of the data row.

- After you assign new values to the columns in a row, you can use the EndEdit method to commit the changes and fire the RowChanging event. To cancel the changes, you can use the CancelEdit method.

- During the time that a row is in edit mode, a version of the row that contains its proposed values is available. You can use this version to determine if the edit should be committed or canceled. See figure 5-9 for more information on row versions.

- The Delete method of a row marks the row for deletion. The row isn't actually deleted until the Update method of the data adapter is executed.

- The Remove…Row method permanently removes a row from the table. To identify the row to be deleted, you code it as an argument on this method. You should use the Remove…Row method only if you don't need to delete the related row in the database.

- If you issue the Update method of a data adapter and the row is updated successfully in the database, the changes are committed to the dataset. That means that the proposed values of a modified row become the current values, and rows that are marked as deleted are permanently deleted from the data table.

Figure 5-3   How to modify or delete an existing data row

How to add a data row

Figure 5-4 shows how you add new rows to a data table. To do that, you use the New...Row method of the table, and you assign the result to a data row variable as shown in the first example in this figure. Then, you assign values to the columns in the row just as you do for an existing row. When you're done, you use the Add...Row method of the table to add the new row to the table.

When you add new rows to a data table, they're added to the end of the table. If you add a new row to the Vendors table using the Vendor Maintenance program, for example, you'll notice that the vendor appears at the end of the list in the Vendors combo box. If that's not what you want, you can update the database and then refresh the dataset as shown in the second example in this figure. Then, the rows will be displayed in the sequence that's specified by the Select statement that retrieves them.

Code that creates a new row, assigns values to it, and adds it to the dataset

```
Dim drVendor As dsPayables.VendorsRow
drVendor = DsPayables1.Vendors.NewVendorsRow
drVendor.VendorName = txtName.Text
drVendor.VendorAddress1 = txtAddressLine1.Text
drVendor.VendorAddress2 = txtAddressLine2.Text
drVendor.VendorCity = txtCity.Text
drVendor.VendorState = cboStates.SelectedValue
drVendor.VendorZipCode = txtZipCode.Text
DsPayables1.Vendors.AddVendorsRow(drVendor)
```

Code that updates the database and refreshes the dataset

```
daVendors.Update(DsPayables1.Vendors)
DsPayables1.Vendors.Clear()
daVendors.Fill(DsPayables1)
```

Description

- To create a new row based on the schema of a table, you use the New…Row method of the table and assign the result to a data row variable.

- To set the values of the columns in a new row, you use the properties of the data row just as you do when you're working with an existing row.

- After you assign values to the columns in the row, you use the Add…Row method of the table to add the row to the table.

- When you add new rows to a table, they're added to the end of the table. Then, after you update the database with the new rows, you can refresh the table using the Clear and Fill methods so that the new rows are in the correct sequence.

Figure 5-4   How to add a data row

How to work with data columns that allow nulls

When you work with the data that's retrieved from a database, you need to know which columns allow nulls so you can provide for them in your code. For example, the Vendors table in the Payables database allows nulls in the VendorAddress1 and VendorAddress2 columns. Because of that, you can't just assign the value of one of these columns to the Text property of a text box control because this property requires a string value. Similarly, you don't want to just assign the value of the Text property of a text box control to a column that allows nulls. Instead, you want to check for and handle the nulls appropriately.

Figure 5-5 presents two methods of a typed dataset that you can use to work with nulls. To check for a null in a column, you use the Is...Null method that's provided for that column in the data row class. The code in this figure, for example, uses a function named IsVendorAddress1Null to check if the column named VendorAddress1 is null. If it is, an empty string (**""**) is assigned to the Text property of a text box. Otherwise, the value of the column is assigned to this property.

To assign a null to a column, you use the Set...Null method for the column. In the second example in this figure, you can see how this method is used to set the value of the VendorAddress1 column to null. Notice that this column is set to null only if the text box contains an empty string. Otherwise, the value of the Text property is assigned to the column.

Code that uses the Is...Null method to test for a null column value

```
If drVendor.IsVendorAddress1Null() Then
    txtAddressLine1.Text = ""
Else
    txtAddressLine1.Text = drVendor.VendorAddress1
End If
```

Code that uses the Set...Null method to assign a null value to a column

```
If txtAddressLine1.Text = "" Then
    drVendor.SetVendorAddress1Null()
Else
    drVendor.VendorAddress1 = txtAddressLine1.Text
End If
```

Description

- If a data column allows nulls, you'll need to provide additional code to display the column values in a control and to save the value of a control to the column. That's because most form controls don't allow nulls.

- To test a data column for a null, you can use the Is...Null method of the data row for that column. This method returns a True or False value that indicates whether the column contains a null.

- To set the value of a data column to null, you can use the Set...Null method of the data row for that column. This method uses the DBNull field of the System.Convert class. This field is a static field that contains a null.

Figure 5-5   How to work with data columns that allow nulls

A Vendor Maintenance program that uses unbound controls

Now that you've seen the basic techniques for working with unbound data, you're ready to see a program that uses unbound controls. The program I'll present here is another version of the Vendor Maintenance program you saw in chapter 4. Because it looks and works just like the program in that chapter, I won't show you the design of the program again here. You should realize, however, that although most of the controls in this version are unbound, the Vendors and States combo boxes are still complex-bound to the Vendors and States tables. That way, they'll automatically reflect all the vendors and states currently in those tables so that the user can make the appropriate selections.

The code for this version of the Vendor Maintenance program is presented in figure 5-6. To start, it declares variables named bLoading and bNewRow just like the program in chapter 4. Instead of declaring a variable for the binding manager base, however, it declares a variable named drVendor. As you'll see in a moment, this variable will be used to hold the current row in the Vendors table.

The Load procedure starts by setting the bLoading variable to True. Then, it calls a procedure named FillTables to load the Vendors and States data tables. This procedure includes a Try...Catch statement that will catch any SQL Server exceptions. Within the Try clause, the connection is opened, the Vendors and States tables are loaded, and the connection is closed. Note that the statements that open and close the connection aren't required, since the Fill methods take care of that automatically. By coding these statements, however, the connection is opened and closed only once.

After the tables are loaded, the Load procedure assigns the first row in the Vendors table to the drVendor variable. To do that, it simply retrieves the row with an index value of zero. Then, the Load procedure calls a procedure named FillControls. This procedure moves the values of the columns in the current row to the appropriate controls on the form. Notice that the Is...Null method is used to test the VendorAddress1 and VendorAddress2 columns for nulls before their values are assigned to the controls. If either of these columns contains a null, an empty string is assigned to the control instead. Also notice that the bLoading variable is set to True at the beginning of this procedure. That way, the code in the Control_DataChanged event won't be executed as the controls are filled. (Although this isn't necessary when the controls are first loaded since the Load procedure has already set this variable to True, it is necessary for other procedures that call the FillControls procedure.)

The rest of the Load procedure works like the one in the program in chapter 4. It calls a procedure named SetMaintenanceButtons to enable the Add and Delete buttons on the form and disable the Update and Cancel buttons. Then, it sets the Enabled property of the Update Database button to False so that this control isn't available. And it sets the bLoading variable to False.

The Vendor Maintenance program with unbound controls   Page 1

```vb
Imports System.Data.SqlClient
Public Class Form1
    Inherits System.Windows.Forms.Form

    Dim bLoading As Boolean
    Dim bNewRow As Boolean
    Dim drVendor As dsPayables.VendorsRow

    Private Sub Form1_Load(ByVal sender As System.Object, _
            ByVal e As System.EventArgs) Handles MyBase.Load
        bLoading = True
        Me.FillTables()
        drVendor = DsPayables1.Vendors(0)
        Me.FillControls()
        Me.SetMaintenanceButtons(True)
        btnUpdateDB.Enabled = False
        bLoading = False
    End Sub

    Private Sub FillTables()
        Try
            conPayables.Open()
            daStates.Fill(DsPayables1)
            daVendors.Fill(DsPayables1)
            conPayables.Close()
        Catch eSql As SqlException
            MessageBox.Show(eSql.Message, "SQL Server error")
        End Try
    End Sub

    Private Sub FillControls()
        bLoading = True
        txtName.Text = drVendor.VendorName
        If drVendor.IsVendorAddress1Null Then
            txtAddressLine1.Text = ""
        Else
            txtAddressLine1.Text = drVendor.VendorAddress1
        End If
        If drVendor.IsVendorAddress2Null Then
            txtAddressLine2.Text = ""
        Else
            txtAddressLine2.Text = drVendor.VendorAddress2
        End If
        txtCity.Text = drVendor.VendorCity
        cboStates.SelectedValue = drVendor.VendorState
        txtZipCode.Text = drVendor.VendorZipCode
        bLoading = False
    End Sub

    Private Sub SetMaintenanceButtons(ByVal bAddDeleteMode As Boolean)
        btnAdd.Enabled = bAddDeleteMode
        btnUpdate.Enabled = Not bAddDeleteMode
        btnDelete.Enabled = bAddDeleteMode
        btnCancel.Enabled = Not bAddDeleteMode
    End Sub
```

Figure 5-6   A Vendor Maintenance program that uses unbound controls (part 1 of 5)

When the user selects a vendor from the Vendors combo box, the SelectedIndexChanged procedure starts by getting the selected row. To do that, it uses the FindByVendorID method of the Vendors table. The argument that's specified on this method is the SelectedValue property of the Vendors combo box, which gets the value of the column specified by the ValueMember property. In this case, you want to get the value of the VendorID column, so the ValueMember property must be set to this column for this to work. After the row is retrieved, the FillControls procedure is called to assign the column values in this row to the controls on the form.

When the user clicks on the Add button, the Add procedure starts by calling the ClearControls procedure. Like the FillControls procedure, this procedure starts by setting the bLoading variable to True so that the Control_DataChanged procedure doesn't fire as the controls are cleared. Then, it moves empty strings to all the text boxes. It also moves -1 to the SelectedIndex property of the States combo box twice so that a state isn't selected. This statement must be executed twice because the first time, it causes the SelectedIndex property to be set to zero. This is a known bug that you'll need to provide for until it's fixed.

After the controls are cleared, the Add procedure calls the SetMaintenanceButtons procedure to enable the Update and Cancel buttons and disable the Add and Delete buttons. Then, it disables the Update Database button, sets the bNewRow variable to True to indicate that a new row is being added, and moves the focus to the Name text box so the user can start entering the data for the new vendor.

When the user clicks on the Update button, the Update procedure starts by calling the ValidData procedure to validate the data just like the bound program in chapter 4. If the data is valid, the procedure continues by setting the bLoading variable to True. If you don't set this variable, the code in the procedure for the SelectedIndexChanged event of the Vendors combo box will execute when you assign a value to the VendorName column of the row since the combo box is bound to this column. You'll see the code that assigns this value in a moment.

If a new row is being added to the Vendors table, the Update procedure continues by executing the NewVendorsRow method of the table to create the row. Then, it executes a procedure named FillRow. You can see this procedure on page 3 of this listing. It moves the values in the form controls to the columns in the new row. Notice that it uses the Set…Null method to set the VendorAddress1 and VendorAddress2 columns to null if the text boxes for those controls contain empty strings.

After the data is assigned to the new row, the Update procedure adds the new row to the table using the AddVendorsRow method of the table. Then, it sets the SelectedIndex property of the Vendors combo box to the number of items in the combo box list, minus 1. Since the new vendor is added to the end of the Vendors table, it will appear at the end of the combo box list. So this statement causes the name of the new vendor to be displayed in the combo box.

If an existing row is being updated, the Update procedure simply calls the FillRow procedure to move the new values to that row. Then, it sets the bLoading variable to False, it calls the SetMaintenanceButtons procedure to

The Vendor Maintenance program with unbound controls   Page 2

```
Private Sub cboVendors_SelectedIndexChanged(ByVal sender As System.Object, _
        ByVal e As System.EventArgs) Handles cboVendors.SelectedIndexChanged
    If Not bLoading Then
        drVendor = DsPayables1.Vendors.FindByVendorID _
            (cboVendors.SelectedValue)
        Me.FillControls()
        Me.SetMaintenanceButtons(True)
        btnUpdateDB.Enabled = DsPayables1.HasChanges
        txtName.Focus()
    End If
End Sub

Private Sub btnAdd_Click(ByVal sender As System.Object, _
        ByVal e As System.EventArgs) Handles btnAdd.Click
    Me.ClearControls()
    Me.SetMaintenanceButtons(False)
    btnUpdateDB.Enabled = False
    bNewRow = True
    txtName.Focus()
End Sub

Private Sub ClearControls()
    bLoading = True
    txtName.Text = ""
    txtAddressLine1.Text = ""
    txtAddressLine2.Text = ""
    txtCity.Text = ""
    cboStates.SelectedIndex = -1
    cboStates.SelectedIndex = -1
    txtZipCode.Text = ""
    bLoading = False
End Sub

Private Sub Control_DataChanged(ByVal sender As System.Object, _
        ByVal e As System.EventArgs) Handles txtName.TextChanged, _
        txtAddressLine1.TextChanged, txtAddressLine2.TextChanged, _
        txtCity.TextChanged, txtZipCode.TextChanged, _
        cboStates.SelectedIndexChanged
    If Not bLoading Then
        Me.SetMaintenanceButtons(False)
        btnUpdateDB.Enabled = False
    End If
End Sub

Private Sub btnUpdate_Click(ByVal sender As System.Object, _
        ByVal e As System.EventArgs) Handles btnUpdate.Click
    If ValidData() Then
        bLoading = True
        If bNewRow Then
            drVendor = DsPayables1.Vendors.NewVendorsRow
            Me.FillRow()
            DsPayables1.Vendors.AddVendorsRow(drVendor)
            cboVendors.SelectedIndex = cboVendors.Items.Count - 1
            bNewRow = False
        Else
            Me.FillRow()
```

Figure 5-6   A Vendor Maintenance program that uses unbound controls (part 2 of 5)

reset the Add, Update, Delete, and Cancel buttons, it sets the Enabled property of the Update Database button to True so the user can update the database with the changes, and it moves the focus to the Vendors combo box.

On page 3 of this listing, you can see the ValidData procedure that's executed when the user clicks on the Update button. Notice that this procedure uses a different technique to check that the zip code is valid for the selected state. Here, the FindByStateCode method of the States table is used to get the row for the selected state. Then, the FirstZipCode column in that row is compared with the zip code entered by the user to be sure that it's not greater than that value. Similarly, the value in the LastZipCode column is compared with the zip code entered by the user to be sure it's not less than that value.

If the user clicks on the Cancel button, the Cancel procedure on page 4 of this listing is executed. This procedure checks if a new row was being added and then sets the bNewRow variable to False if it was. Then, it calls the FillControls procedure to assign the values in the drVendor row to the form controls. Note that because this row isn't modified until the user clicks the Update button, it still contains the original values for a row that's being modified or the values for the row that was previously displayed if a row is being added. The remaining code in this procedure resets the buttons on the form and moves the focus to the Vendors combo box.

If the user clicks on the Delete button, the Delete procedure starts by displaying a message box to confirm the deletion. If the deletion is confirmed, the procedure executes the Delete method of the data row to delete it. That, in turn, causes the SelectedIndexChanged event of the Vendors combo box to fire since the vendor that's currently displayed in this control is no longer valid. As you saw earlier, the code for this procedure locates the selected vendor, which in this case is the vendor that follows the deleted vendor. It also calls the FillControls procedure so that the data for this vendor is displayed on the form. After this procedure completes, the Delete procedure moves the focus to the Vendors combo box.

If the user clicks on the Update Database button, the UpdateDB procedure sets the bLoading variable to true and then calls the UpdateDatabase procedure. This procedure updates the database and then clears and reloads the Vendors table. That way, any rows that were added to the table will appear in the correct sequence and any changes made by other users will be reflected. The rest of the UpdateDB procedure gets the row for the first vendor, calls the FillControls procedure to display the data for that row on the form, sets the bLoading variable to False, disables the Update Database button, and moves the focus to the Vendors combo box.

The last two procedures, shown on page 5 of this listing, work just like the ones you saw in the last chapter. They handle the processing for closing the form when the user clicks on the Exit button or on the close button of the form.

Although this program requires a few more lines of code than the program you saw in the last chapter that uses bound controls, it shouldn't be any more difficult for you to understand. In general, when you don't bind controls to a dataset, you just work directly with the dataset instead of working with it through the binding manager. In most cases, this is the preferred technique because it gives you more control over how the data is processed.

The Vendor Maintenance program with unbound controls   Page 3

```vbnet
            End If
            bLoading = False
            Me.SetMaintenanceButtons(True)
            btnUpdateDB.Enabled = True
            cboVendors.Focus()
        End If
End Sub

Private Function ValidData() As Boolean
    Dim sErrorMessage As String
    If txtName.Text = "" Then
        sErrorMessage = "Name required."
        txtName.Focus()
    ElseIf txtCity.Text = "" Then
        sErrorMessage = "City required."
        txtCity.Focus()
    ElseIf cboStates.SelectedIndex = -1 Then
        sErrorMessage = "State required."
        cboStates.Focus()
    ElseIf txtZipCode.Text = "" Then
        sErrorMessage = "Zip code required."
        txtZipCode.Focus()
    ElseIf txtZipCode.Text < DsPayables1.States.FindByStateCode _
            (cboStates.SelectedValue).FirstZipCode _
        Or txtZipCode.Text > DsPayables1.States.FindByStateCode _
            (cboStates.SelectedValue).LastZipCode Then
        sErrorMessage = "The zip code is invalid."
        txtZipCode.Focus()
    End If
    If sErrorMessage = "" Then
        ValidData = True
    Else
        ValidData = False
        MessageBox.Show(sErrorMessage, "Data entry error", _
            MessageBoxButtons.OK, MessageBoxIcon.Error)
    End If
End Function

Private Sub FillRow()
    drVendor.VendorName = txtName.Text
    If txtAddressLine1.Text = "" Then
        drVendor.SetVendorAddress1Null()
    Else
        drVendor.VendorAddress1 = txtAddressLine1.Text
    End If
    If txtAddressLine2.Text = "" Then
        drVendor.SetVendorAddress2Null()
    Else
        drVendor.VendorAddress2 = txtAddressLine2.Text
    End If
    drVendor.VendorCity = txtCity.Text
    drVendor.VendorState = cboStates.SelectedValue
    drVendor.VendorZipCode = txtZipCode.Text
End Sub
```

Figure 5-6   A Vendor Maintenance program that uses unbound controls (part 3 of 5)

The Vendor Maintenance program with unbound controls   Page 4

```
Private Sub btnCancel_Click(ByVal sender As System.Object, _
        ByVal e As System.EventArgs) Handles btnCancel.Click
    If bNewRow Then
        bNewRow = False
    End If
    Me.FillControls()
    Me.SetMaintenanceButtons(True)
    btnUpdateDB.Enabled = DsPayables1.HasChanges
    cboVendors.Focus()
End Sub

Private Sub btnDelete_Click(ByVal sender As System.Object, _
        ByVal e As System.EventArgs) Handles btnDelete.Click
    Dim iResult As DialogResult _
        = MessageBox.Show("Delete " & cboVendors.Text & "?", _
            "Confirm Delete", MessageBoxButtons.YesNo, _
            MessageBoxIcon.Question)
    If iResult = DialogResult.Yes Then
        drVendor.Delete()
        cboVendors.Focus()
    End If
End Sub

Private Sub btnUpdateDB_Click(ByVal sender As System.Object, _
        ByVal e As System.EventArgs) Handles btnUpdateDB.Click
    bLoading = True
    Me.UpdateDatabase()
    drVendor = DsPayables1.Vendors(0)
    Me.FillControls()
    bLoading = False
    btnUpdateDB.Enabled = False
    cboVendors.Focus()
End Sub

Public Sub UpdateDatabase()
    Try
        daVendors.Update(DsPayables1.Vendors)
        DsPayables1.Vendors.Clear()
        daVendors.Fill(DsPayables1)
    Catch eData As DataException
        MessageBox.Show("An error occured during the database update. " _
            & ControlChars.CrLf & "Not all rows were updated.", _
            "ADO.NET error")
    Catch eSql As SqlException
        MessageBox.Show(eSql.Message, "SQL Server error")
    End Try
End Sub
```

Figure 5-6   A Vendor Maintenance program that uses unbound controls (part 4 of 5)

The Vendor Maintenance program with unbound controls   **Page 5**

```
Private Sub btnExit_Click(ByVal sender As System.Object, _
    ByVal e As System.EventArgs) Handles btnExit.Click
    Me.Close()
End Sub

Private Sub Form1_Closing(ByVal sender As Object, _
        ByVal e As System.ComponentModel.CancelEventArgs) _
        Handles MyBase.Closing
    If DsPayables1.HasChanges Then
        Dim iResult As DialogResult _
            = MessageBox.Show("You have made changes that have not " _
            & "been saved to the database. " & ControlChars.CrLf _
            & "If you continue, these changes will be lost." _
            & ControlChars.CrLf & "Continue?", "Confirm Exit", _
            MessageBoxButtons.YesNo, MessageBoxIcon.Question)
        If iResult = DialogResult.No Then
            e.Cancel = True
        End If
    End If
End Sub

End Class
```

Figure 5-6   A Vendor Maintenance program that uses unbound controls (part 5 of 5)

Additional skills for validating and updating data

In the remaining topics of this chapter, you'll learn some additional skills for working with the data in a maintenance program. Specifically, you'll learn additional techniques for validating data entered by users and for handling errors. In addition, you'll learn how to accept or reject changes made to a data row, a data table, or an entire dataset. As you learn about these techniques, be aware that the properties and methods covered here aren't specific to typed datasets because a typed dataset inherits them from other classes. Because of that, you can also use them with untyped datasets, which you'll learn about in the next chapter.

How to use the RowChanging event

In the last chapter, you learned how to use the RowChanging event to validate the data in a bound form. The technique for using this event with an unbound form is similar. To suspend the RowChanging event during an edit operation, however, you have to execute the BeginEdit method of the data row as shown in figure 5-7. Here, the BeginEdit method is executed when the user changes the data in a form control. This code is taken from a variation of the Vendor Maintenance program you just saw.

To end the edit operation and fire the RowChanging event, you execute the EndEdit method of the row. In this example, this method is included in the procedure that's executed when the user clicks on the Update button. Notice that the procedure for the RowChanging event is identical to the one you saw in the last chapter. It checks the value of each control and, if an error is detected, it throws an exception. Because the EndEdit method is coded within a Try...Catch statement, that exception is then caught by the second Catch clause.

Code that suspends the RowChanging event during editing

```
Private Sub Control_DataChanged(ByVal sender As System.Object, _
        ByVal e As System.EventArgs) Handles txtName.TextChanged, ...
    If Not bLoading Then
        drVendor.BeginEdit()
        Me.SetMaintenanceButtons(False)
        btnUpdateDB.Enabled = False
    End If
End Sub
    .
    .
Private Sub btnUpdate_Click(ByVal sender As System.Object, _
        ByVal e As System.EventArgs) Handles btnUpdate.Click
    Try
        Me.FillRow
        drVendor.EndEdit()
        Me.SetMaintenanceButtons(True)
        btnUpdateDB.Enabled = True
        cboVendors.Focus()
    Catch eData As DataException
        MessageBox.Show(eData.Message, "ADO.NET error")
    Catch eSystem As Exception
        MessageBox.Show(eSystem.Message, "System error")
    End Try
End Sub
```

The code for the RowChanging event

```
Private Sub VendorsTable_RowChanging(ByVal sender As Object, _
        ByVal e As System.Data.DataRowChangeEventArgs) _
        Handles VendorsTable.RowChanging
    If Not bLoading Then
        Dim sErrorMessage As String
        If txtName.Text = "" Then
            sErrorMessage = "Name required."
            txtName.Focus()
            .
            .
        ElseIf txtZipCode.Text = "" Then
            sErrorMessage = "Zip code required."
            txtZipCode.Focus()
        End If
        If sErrorMessage <> "" Then
            Throw New System.Exception(sErrorMessage)
        End If
    End If
End Sub
```

Description

- To suspend the firing of the RowChanging event for a row, execute the BeginEdit method of the row. Then, the RowChanging event isn't fired until you execute the EndEdit method.

- To cancel a row change operation, use the Throw statement to throw an exception. Then, you can catch the exception in the procedure that executes the EndEdit method.

Figure 5-7   How to use the RowChanging event

How to work with row states

The RowState property of a row indicates the current state of a row. If no changes have been made to a row, for example, it has a row state of Unchanged. Similarly, if a row has been modified, it has a state of Modified. Figure 5-8 illustrates how you can work with row states.

To refer to a row state, you use the members of the DataRowState enumeration. The two examples in this figure show you how this works. The first example simply checks the RowState property of a row to determine if the row has been modified.

The second example in this figure starts by declaring two variables. The first one will hold a count of the number of rows that are inserted into a database table when the database is updated. The second one, named dtInserted, will hold rows from the Vendors table. Specifically, it will hold all of the rows that have been added to the Vendors table. To get those rows, the next statement uses a GetChanges method with the DataRowState.Added argument. Note that you can also code this method without an argument, in which case all added, modified, and deleted rows are returned.

After the GetChanges method is executed, an If statement is used to check that one or more rows were returned. If not, the dtInserted variable will have a value of Nothing. Otherwise, an Update statement is executed to add the new rows to the database and return a count of the number of rows that were added. Finally, a message is displayed that indicates the number of rows that were added.

Before I go on, you should realize that when you issue the Update method, the row state of any inserted or modified row that was updated is changed to Unchanged. In addition, any rows that were marked for deletion are permanently removed from the table. In other words, the changes are committed to the data table and can't be reversed.

DataRowState enumeration members

Member	Description
Unchanged	No changes have been made to the row.
Added	The row has been added to the table.
Modified	One or more column values in the row have been changed.
Deleted	The row has been marked for deletion.
Detached	The row has been deleted or removed from the collection of rows, or a new row has been created using the New...Row method but not added to the table.

Code that checks the current state of a row

```
If drVendor.RowState = DataRowState.Modified Then ...
```

Code that updates the database with new rows

```
Dim iInsertCount As Integer
Dim dtInserted As dsPayables.VendorsDataTable
dtInserted = DsPayables1.Vendors.GetChanges(DataRowState.Added)
If Not dtInserted Is Nothing Then
    iInsertCount = daVendors.Update(dtInserted)
End If
MessageBox.Show("Rows inserted: " & iInsertCount, "Update results")
```

Description

- The state of a data row depends on the operations that have been performed on the row and whether or not the operations have been committed.

- To determine if a row has a given state, use the RowState property of the row. To refer to a row state, use the members of the DataRowState enumeration.

- The GetChanges method of a data table gets a copy of the table that contains just the rows that have been changed. If you don't specify an argument on this method, all the changed rows are returned. If you specify a row state, only the changed rows with the given state are returned.

- When you execute the Update method of a data adapter, all of the rows with a state of Deleted are removed from the data table. All other rows are given a row state of Unchanged.

Figure 5-8 How to work with row states

How to work with row versions

In addition to maintaining a RowState property, Visual Basic maintains one or more versions of each row. For example, each row except rows that have been added has an Original version that contains the original values for the row. Then, if a row is changed, a Current version exists that contains the current values for the row. Figure 5-9 lists all the possible versions for a row.

To check if a particular version of a row exists, you use the HasVersion method of the row. On this method, you specify the member of the DataRowVersion enumeration for the version you want. The statement shown in this figure, for example, checks whether a row contains an Original version.

The code example in this figure shows one way to use the Proposed version of a row. This code is taken from a modified version of the Vendor Maintenance program. In this example, you can assume that the row that's being processed is in edit mode so that the Proposed version is available. Then, when the user clicks on the Update button to save the changes to the row, the Update procedure starts by executing the FillRow procedure to move the values in the form controls to the columns in the data row. Note that at this point, the data the user entered hasn't been validated. Instead, it's validated after the new values are moved into the row.

To validate the data, the Update procedure calls a procedure named ValidateData. As you can see, this procedure tests the Proposed value of each column to see if it contains valid data. To do that, it specifies this version following the name of the column. Notice that this code doesn't use the column name properties to refer to the columns in the row. That's because this property doesn't accept a data row version as an argument. So, instead, you have to refer to its name in quotes. As you'll see in the next chapter, this is the technique you use when you work with untyped datasets.

If the data in a column isn't valid, the ValidateData procedure assigns an appropriate value to an error message variable and sets a variable named bValidData to False. (These variables are defined at the module level.) The bValidData variable is then tested in the Update procedure to determine if the data was valid. If so, the EndEdit method is executed to end the edit of the row. This method causes the values in the Proposed version of the row to be saved in the Current version. Then, the Proposed version is omitted.

The code in this figure shows just one way you can use the data row versions, but you can probably think of others. For example, you might use the Original version to handle concurrency errors. Suppose, for instance, that a concurrency error occurs when you try to update a row that's been modified. Then, you could compare the data in the Original version of the row with the values in the current row of the database and let the user know what values had changed.

By the way, you should know that if you access a row without specifying a version, the Default version is accessed. In most cases, the Default version of a row contains the same values as the Current version. If a row has been deleted, however, the Default version contains the same values as the Original version.

DataRowVersion enumeration members

Member	Description
Original	Contains the original values for the row that were retrieved from the database. This version doesn't exist for a row that's been added to the table.
Current	Contains the current values for the row. This is the same as the Original version for an existing row if the row hasn't changed. A row that's marked for deletion doesn't have a Current version. A row that's been added to the table has only a Current version.
Proposed	Contains the proposed values for the row. This version exists during the time that a row is in edit mode. To place a row in edit mode, issue the BeginEdit method.
Default	Contains the values in the default row version. The default row version for a deleted row is Original. The default row version for a row that's been added or modified or a row that hasn't been changed is Current. And the default version for a detached row is Proposed.

A statement that checks if the Original version of a row exists

```
If drVendor.HasVersion(DataRowVersion.Original) Then ...
```

Code that uses the Proposed version to validate the data in a row

```
Private Sub btnUpdate_Click(ByVal sender As System.Object, _
        ByVal e As System.EventArgs) Handles btnUpdate.Click
    Me.FillRow()
    Me.ValidateData()
    If bValidData Then
        drVendor.EndEdit()
        ...
    End If
End Sub

Private Sub ValidateData()
    bValidData = True
    If drVendor("VendorName", DataRowVersion.Proposed) = "" Then
        sErrorMessage = "Name required."
        bValidData = False
        txtName.Focus()
    ElseIf drVendor("VendorCity", DataRowVersion.Proposed) = "" Then
    ...
    End If
End Sub
```

Description

- One or more versions of the data in a data row are available depending on the operations that have been performed on the row. You can use the HasVersion method of a data row along with the DataRowVersion enumeration to test if a version of a row exists.

- If you issue the EndEdit method for a row in edit mode, the Current version is updated with the values in the Proposed version and the Proposed version is omitted. If you issue the CancelEdit method, the Proposed version is omitted without updating the Current version.

- When you execute the Update method of a data adapter, the values in the Original version of the row are overwritten with the values in the Current version, and rows that are marked for deletion are removed.

Figure 5-9   How to work with row versions

How to save and work with table and row errors

Figure 5-10 presents some properties and methods you can use to work with errors in data rows, data tables, and datasets. To check if a data row, data table, or dataset has errors, for example, you test its HasErrors property. Note, however, that you don't set this property directly. Instead, to indicate that a column has an error, you use its SetColumnError method to specify an error description. To indicate that a row has an error, you use its RowError property to specify an error description. In either case, the HasErrors properties of the row, table, and dataset are set to True automatically.

The other methods in this figure let you work with the errors in a table or row. You can see how some of them are used in the code example in this figure. This code validates the data in the proposed version of a data row just like the code in the previous figure. Instead of assigning an error message to a string variable for each column in error, however, the ValidateData procedure uses the SetColumnError method to assign an error message to each column in error. Then, the Update procedure tests the HasErrors property of the row to determine if any errors were detected. If so, a procedure named DisplayErrors is executed. This procedure uses the GetColumnsInError method of the row to get the columns in error. Then, it loops through those columns and uses the GetColumnError method to get the error description for each column and append it to an error message variable. Then, all of the errors are displayed in a message box.

Properties and methods for working with errors

Object	Property	Description
Dataset, data table, or data row	HasErrors	Gets a Boolean value that indicates whether or not there are errors in the dataset, data table, or data row.
Data row	RowError	Gets or sets a custom error description for a row.

Object	Method	Description
Data table	GetErrors	Returns an array of the data rows in a data table that contain errors.
Data row	ClearErrors	Clears all errors from the row.
Data row	GetColumnError	Returns the error description for a column.
Data row	GetColumnsInError	Gets an array of the data columns in a data row that contain errors.
Data row	SetColumnError	Sets a custom error description for a column.

Code that sets and displays column and row errors

```
Private Sub btnUpdate_Click(ByVal sender As System.Object, _
        ByVal e As System.EventArgs) Handles btnUpdate.Click
    Me.FillRow()
    Me.ValidateData()
    If drVendor.HasErrors Then
        DisplayErrors()
    Else
        drVendor.EndEdit()
        .
        .
    End If
End Sub

Private Sub ValidateData()
    drVendor.ClearErrors()
    If drVendor("VendorName", DataRowVersion.Proposed) = "" Then
        drVendor.SetColumnError("VendorName", "A vendor name is required.")
    End If
    .
    .
End Sub

Private Sub DisplayErrors()
    Dim sErrorMessage As String
    Dim dcVendor As DataColumn
    For Each dcVendor In drVendor.GetColumnsInError
        sErrorMessage &= drVendor.GetColumnError(dcVendor) _
                    & ControlChars.CrLf
    Next
    MessageBox.Show(sErrorMessage, "Data validation errors")
End Sub
```

Description

- You'll typically use the properties and methods for working with errors to store error information to be used later on.

Figure 5-10   How to save and work with table and row errors

How to accept or reject changes to a dataset

Figure 5-11 presents two methods you can use to accept or reject all the changes that have been made to a data row, a data table, or an entire dataset. To accept the changes, you use the AcceptChanges method. Note, however, that this method is executed automatically when you update the database with the changes using the Update method of the data adapter. Because of that, you're not likely to use the AcceptChanges method in a typical database application. However, you may occasionally need to reverse all the changes that have been made to a data row, data table, or dataset. To do that, you use the RejectChanges method.

The code in this figure presents a simple example that uses the AcceptChanges and RejectChanges methods. Here, the ValidateData procedure you saw in the previous figure is executed to assign an error message to each column of a row that isn't valid. Then, the HasErrors method of the row is used to determine whether any errors were detected. If so, the RejectChanges method is executed to reverse the changes. Otherwise, the AcceptChanges method is executed to accept the changes.

Note that when you execute AcceptChanges, the changes are committed to the dataset. That means that you can't update the database with the changes after executing this method. Because of that, you won't usually use this method unless you want to save changes to the dataset without updating the database.

Methods for accepting and rejecting changes

Object	Method	Description
Dataset, data table, or data row	AcceptChanges	Commits all changes made to the dataset, data table, or data row since the dataset was filled or since the AcceptChanges method was last executed.
Dataset, data table, or data row	RejectChanges	Reverses all changes made to the dataset, data table, or data row since the dataset was filled or since the AcceptChanges method was executed.

Code that accepts or rejects changes to a row

```
Private Sub btnUpdate_Click(ByVal sender As System.Object, _
        ByVal e As System.EventArgs) Handles btnUpdate.Click
    Me.FillRow(drVendor)
    Me.ValidateData(drVendor)
    If drVendor.HasErrors Then
        drVendor.RejectChanges
        .
        .
    Else
        drVendor.AcceptChanges
        .
        .
    End If
End Sub
```

Description

- The AcceptChanges method is executed automatically when you execute the Update method of a data adapter. Because of that, you won't usually execute this method explicitly.

- The EndEdit method is executed automatically for any row in edit mode when the AcceptChanges method is executed. That means that any Proposed row values are saved to the dataset.

- When the AcceptChanges method commits changes, any rows with a row state of Deleted are removed and all other rows are given a row state of Unchanged. Because of that, you can't use the Update method to update the database after using AcceptChanges.

- The CancelEdit method is executed automatically for any row in edit mode when the RejectChanges method is executed. That means that the Current and Proposed versions of the rows are discarded. In addition, all rows are given a row state of Unchanged.

Figure 5-11   How to accept or reject changes to a dataset

Perspective

Now that you know how to use both bound and unbound controls with typed datasets, you may want to look at how a typed dataset is defined. To do that, you can double-click on the dsPayables.vb class file in the Solution Explorer. Then, the Visual Basic code that defines the dataset is displayed in the Code Editor window.

As you review the code, you may notice that many of the methods presented in this chapter are inherited from other classes, as I mentioned earlier. For example, the BeginEdit method is inherited from the DataRow class, and the Add...Row method is implemented using the Add method of the data rows collection, which is inherited from the DataTable class. Although you may not understand all of the code, you should understand enough to get a good feel for how a typed dataset lets you work with data using the techniques you've seen in the last two chapters. Then, you can compare that to the techniques you'll learn in the next chapter for working with untyped datasets.

Term

edit mode

6

How to work with untyped datasets

If a dataset schema for the data used by an application is available as you design the application, you can use the techniques you learned in the last two chapters to work with the data using a typed dataset. If you don't have access to a dataset schema at design time, however, you'll have to work with the data using an untyped dataset. You'll learn how to do that in this chapter. In addition, you'll learn how to create and work with data provider objects through code. Although you can use this technique with typed as well as untyped datasets, you're more likely to use it with untyped datasets since they're created through code as well.

An introduction to untyped datasets

An *untyped dataset* is one that isn't based on a dataset schema and a custom dataset class. Instead, it's based on the generic ADO.NET DataSet class. In the two topics that follow, you'll learn the basic skills for creating and working with untyped datasets and some of the disadvantages of using them.

How to create and work with untyped datasets

Figure 6-1 presents the basic skills for creating and working with an untyped dataset. To create an untyped dataset, you use the New keyword and specify DataSet as the type. When you do that, the constructor for the DataSet class is executed, which causes the object to be created and assigned to the variable you name. The first statement in this figure, for example, creates an untyped dataset and assigns it to a variable named dsPayables. As you can see in the syntax at the top of this figure, you can also assign a name to the dataset when you create it. In most cases, though, you won't need to do that.

To work with an untyped dataset, you use the properties and methods of the DataSet class. You'll learn about some of these properties and methods in this chapter. Right now, I want to focus on the properties you use to access the collections of objects contained within a dataset. This figure lists some of those properties and describes the collections they access. To access the collection of tables in a dataset, for example, you use the Tables property of the dataset. To access the collection of rows in a table, you use the Rows property of the table.

The second and third statements in this figure help illustrate how this works. Both statements access a table in the dsPayables dataset. The second statement accesses a table by name. To do that, it passes a string that contains the table name to the Tables property. The second statement accesses a table by index. In this case, an index value of 0 is specified, so the first table is retrieved. You use similar techniques to refer to items in other collections.

The disadvantages of untyped datasets

This figure also lists some of the disadvantages of using untyped datasets. Most important, untyped datasets make applications more difficult to develop. If you compare the code shown in this figure with the same code for working with a typed dataset, for example, you'll see that the code for working with a typed dataset is simpler and more direct. In addition, you can't use the Intellisense feature of Visual Studio to work with untyped datasets, so you can't be sure that the names you're using for tables, columns, and other objects, are correct. Untyped datasets are also less efficient than typed datasets because the program can't determine until runtime what needs to be accessed. For these reasons, you should use typed datasets whenever possible.

Two ways to create an untyped dataset

```
dataset = New DataSet()
dataset = New DataSet(dataSetName)
```

Common properties used to access data collections

Object	Property	Description
Dataset	Tables	A collection of the tables in the dataset.
Data table	Rows	A collection of the rows in a data table.
	Columns	A collection of the columns in a data table.

A statement that creates an untyped dataset

```
Dim dsPayables As New DataSet()
```

A statement that refers to a table in the dataset by name

```
cboVendors.DataSource = dsPayables.Tables("Vendors")
```

A statement that refers to a table in the dataset by index

```
cboVendors.DataSource = dsPayables.Tables(0)
```

Description

- An *untyped dataset* is one that's created from the generic ADO.NET DataSet class. You use the properties and methods of this class to work with an untyped dataset and the objects it contains.

- The information within a dataset is stored in collections. To refer to a collection, you can use a property of the parent object. To refer to the collection of tables in a dataset, for example, you use the Tables property of the dataset as shown above.

- To refer to a specific object in a collection, you can use a string with the object's name or its index value. All of the ADO.NET collections are zero-based.

Disadvantages of untyped datasets

- Untyped datasets can't take advantage of the IntelliSense feature of Visual Studio, which makes it more difficult to develop the code for working with the datasets.

- Code that refers to an untyped dataset isn't checked at compile time, which can increase the possibility of errors in assigning values to dataset members.

- Access to the members of an untyped dataset isn't determined until runtime. In contrast, access to the members of a typed dataset is determined at compile time so they can be accessed more quickly at runtime.

Figure 6-1   An introduction to untyped datasets

How to create and work with data provider objects

Before you can retrieve data into a dataset, you have to create the data provider objects. In the topics that follow, you'll learn how to create and work with connection, command, and data adapter objects through code. In addition, you'll learn how to use a command builder object to generate Insert, Update, and Delete statements from the Select statement that's associated with a data adapter.

How to create and work with connections

Figure 6-2 shows how you create and work with a connection for a SQL Server database. As you can see from the syntax at the top of this figure, you can specify a connection string when you create the connection. If you do, this string is assigned to the ConnectionString property. Otherwise, you have to assign a value to this property after you create the connection object. This is illustrated by the first two examples in this figure.

The first example also shows how you can use the Open and Close methods to open and close a connection. Remember, though, that a data adapter automatically opens and closes the connection when it needs to access the database. Because of that, you don't need to use the Open and Close methods when you use a data adapter. As you saw in the last chapter, however, you may not always want a connection to be opened and closed automatically.

This figure also shows some of the common values that you specify in a connection string. For a SQL Server database, for example, you typically specify the name of the server where the database resides, the name of the database, the type of security to be used, and the name of the workstation that will attach to the connection. You can also specify the additional values shown in this figure, as well as others. For more information on these values, see online help.

To create a connection for an OLE DB provider, you use code similar to that shown in this figure. The main difference is the information you provide for the connection string. The connection string for a Jet (Access) OLE DB provider, for example, must include the name of the provider and the location of the database as shown in the last example in this figure. Because the requirements for each provider differ, you may need to consult the documentation for that provider to determine what values to specify.

Before I go on, you should realize that the connection strings for production programs are frequently stored in configuration files outside the program rather than in the program itself. That way, they can be accessed by any program that needs them, and they can be modified without having to modify each program that uses them. How a program actually retrieves the connection string depends on how it's stored. If it's stored in a text file, for example, the program can use a text reader; if it's stored in an XML file, the program can use an XML reader. You'll see an example of a connection string that's stored in an XML file in chapter 10.

Two ways to create a SqlConnection object

```
connection = New SqlConnection()
connection = New SqlConnection(connectionString)
```

Common properties and methods of a connection

Property	Description
ConnectionString	Provides information for accessing a SQL Server database.

Method	Description
Open	Opens the connection using the specified connection string.
Close	Closes the connection.

Common values used in the ConnectionString property

Name	Description
Data source/Server	The name of the instance of SQL Server you want to connect to.
Database/Initial catalog	The name of the database you want to access.
Integrated security	Determines whether the connection is secure. Valid values are True, False, and SSPI. SSPI uses Windows integrated security and is equivalent to True.
Persist security info	Determines whether sensitive information, such as the password, is returned as part of the connection. The default is False.
Packet size	The number of bytes in the packets used to communicate with SQL Server. The default is 8192, but the Configuration Wizard sets this value to 4096.
User id	The user id that's used to log in to SQL Server.
Password/Pwd	The password that's used to log in to SQL Server.
Workstation ID	The name of the workstation that's connecting to SQL Server.

Code that creates, opens, and closes a SQL connection

```
Dim sConnection As String = "server=ANNE\VSdotNET;database=Payables;" _
    & "integrated security=SSPI;workstation id=ANNE"
Dim conPayables As New SqlConnection()
conPayables.ConnectionString = sConnection
conPayables.Open
...
conPayables.Close
```

Another way to create a SqlConnection object

```
Dim conPayables As New SqlConnection(sConnection)
```

A connection string for the Jet OLE DB provider

```
Provider=Microsoft.Jet.OLEDB.4.0;Data Source=C:\Databases\Payables.mdb
```

Description

- You can set the ConnectionString property after you create a connection or as you create it by passing the string to the constructor of the connection class.

- The values you specify for the ConnectionString property depend on the type of database you're connecting to.

Figure 6-2   How to create and work with connections

How to create and work with commands

Figure 6-3 shows three ways you can create a command object using the SqlCommand class. First, you can create it without specifying any arguments. Then, you must set the Connection property to identify the connection to be used by the command, and you must set the CommandText property to specify the text of the statement to be executed. This is illustrated by the first example in this figure. Second, you can set the CommandText property by specifying the statement to be executed when you create the object. In that case, you still have to set the Connection property after you create the object. Third, you can specify both the connection and the statement when you create the object. This is illustrated by the second example in this figure.

Another property you may need to set is the CommandType property. This property determines how the value of the CommandText property is interpreted. The values you can specify for this property are members of the CommandType enumeration that's shown in this figure. The default value is Text, which causes the value of the CommandText property to be interpreted as a SQL statement. If the CommandText property contains the name of a stored procedure, however, you'll need to set this property to StoredProcedure. And if the CommandText property contains the name of a table, you'll need to set this property to TableDirect. Then, all the rows and columns will be retrieved from the table.

The last property that's shown in this figure, Parameters, lets you work with the collection of parameters for a command. As you'll see in chapter 7, you can use parameters to restrict the data that's retrieved by a command. That's important when you're developing client/server applications.

In addition to the properties shown in this figure, you can also use the Execute methods of a command object to execute the statement it contains. If you're using a data adapter, however, you don't need to use these methods. Instead, you'll use the Fill method of the data adapter to execute a command that retrieves rows, and you'll use the Update method to execute commands that insert, update, and delete rows. Because of that, you won't learn how to use the Execute methods in this chapter. Instead, you'll learn about them in chapter 8 when I present some additional skills for working with command objects.

Three ways to create a SqlCommand object

```
command = New SqlCommand()
command = New SqlCommand(cmdText)
command = New SqlCommand(cmdText, connection)
```

Common properties of a command

Property	Description
Connection	The connection used to connect to the database.
CommandText	A SQL statement, the name of a stored procedure, or the name of a table.
CommandType	A member of the CommandType enumeration that determines how the value in the CommandText property is interpreted.
Parameters	The collection of parameters for the command (see chapter 7 for details).

CommandType enumeration members

Member	Description
Text	The CommandText property contains a SQL statement. This is the default.
StoredProcedure	The CommandText property contains the name of a stored procedure.
TableDirect	The CommandText property contains the name of a table (OleDb only).

Code that creates a SqlCommand object that executes a Select statement

```
Dim sVenderSelect As String = "Select VendorID, VendorName, " _
    & "VendorAddress1, VendorAddress2, VendorCity, VendorState, " _
    & "VendorZipCode From Vendors Order By VendorName"
Dim cmdVendors As New SqlCommand()
With cmdVendors
    .Connection = conPayables
    .CommandText = sVendorSelect
End With
```

Another way to create a SqlCommand object

```
Dim cmdVendors As New SqlCommand(sVendorSelect, conPayables)
```

Description

- The CommandText and Connection properties are set to the values you pass to the constructor of the command class. If you don't pass these values to the constructor, you must set the CommandText and Connection properties after you create the command object.

- If you set the CommandText property to the name of a stored procedure or table, you must also set the CommandType property.

Figure 6-3   How to create and work with commands

How to create and work with data adapters

You can use two techniques to create SqlDataAdapter objects, as illustrated by the syntax diagrams at the top of figure 6-4. If you use the first technique, you don't pass an argument to the constructor. In that case, you have to set the value of the SelectCommand property after you create the object. This property identifies the command object that will be used to retrieve data when the Fill method of the data adapter is executed. If you use the second format, you can pass the value of the SelectCommand property to the constructor.

If you will be updating the data that's retrieved by a data adapter, you'll need to create command objects that contain Insert, Update, and Delete statements and assign them to the InsertCommand, UpdateCommand, and DeleteCommand properties of the data adapter. Although you can create these objects yourself, ADO.NET provides a command builder object to do it for you. You'll learn how to use this object in the next figure.

This figure also presents the three methods of a data adapter that you're most likely to use. You're already familiar with the Fill and Update methods: You use the Fill method to load a data table with data from a database, and you use the Update method to update a database with changes made to a data table. Notice in the code in this figure, though, that a second argument is included on the Fill method when you're working with an untyped dataset. This argument names the data table where the data that's retrieved from the data source is stored. In other words, it identifies the table mapping for the source data. If the table you specify doesn't already exist, it's created when you execute the Fill method. Otherwise, the data in the table that's named is refreshed. Note that if you don't include a table name on the Fill method, the data is placed in a table named "Table," which usually isn't what you want.

The third method presented in this figure, FillSchema, retrieves the schema of the source data and uses it to define the schema of a data table. Although the schema is also retrieved when you use the Fill method, FillSchema doesn't retrieve any data. You probably won't use this method often, and you won't see it used in this book.

When you retrieve the schema of the source data using the Fill or FillSchema method, the value of the MissingSchemaAction property determines what happens if the schema doesn't match the schema of a table in the dataset. To set the value of this property, you use the members of the MissingSchemaAction enumeration shown in this figure. The default is MissingSchemaAction.Add, which causes the schema of the data table to be defined based on the columns in the source table. If you need to include a primary key in the data table, however, you can specify the MissingSchemaAction.AddWithKey constant for this property. Later in this chapter, for example, you'll learn about two methods you can use to search for key data in a table. To use these methods, the table you're searching must have a primary key.

Two ways to create a SqlDataAdapter object

```
dataAdapter = New SqlDataAdapter()
dataAdapter = New SqlDataAdapter(selectCommand)
```

Common properties and methods of a data adapter

Property	Description
SelectCommand	The command object used to retrieve data from the database.
InsertCommand	The command object used to insert new rows into the database.
UpdateCommand	The command object used to update rows in the database.
DeleteCommand	The command object used to delete rows from the database.
MissingSchemaAction	A member of the MissingSchemaAction enumeration that determines the action that's taken when the data retrieved by a Fill method doesn't match the schema of a table in the dataset.

Method	Description
Fill	Retrieves rows from the database using the command specified by the SelectCommand property and stores them in a data table.
FillSchema	Retrieves the schema of the data specified by the SelectCommand property and uses it to define the schema of a data table.
Update	Saves changes made in the data table to the database using the commands specified by the InsertCommand, UpdateCommand, and DeleteCommand properties.

MissingSchemaAction enumeration members

Member	Description
Add	Adds the columns in the source table to the schema. This is the default.
AddWithKey	Adds the columns and primary key in the source table to the schema.
Error	A SystemException is generated.
Ignore	The columns that don't match the schema are ignored.

Code that creates a SqlDataAdapter object and then loads the dataset

```
Dim daVendors As New SqlDataAdapter()
daVendors.SelectCommand = cmdVendors
daVendors.Fill(dsPayables, "Vendors")
```

Description

- The SelectCommand property is set to the value you pass to the constructor of the data adapter. If you don't pass a Select command to the constructor, you must set this property after you create the data adapter.

- Although you can set the InsertCommand, UpdateCommand, and DeleteCommand properties directly, you can also use a command builder to build these commands for you. See figure 6-5 for more information.

- By default, the Fill method maps the data in the source table to a data table named "Table." Since that's usually not what you want, you should include the name of the data table as the second argument of the Fill method.

Figure 6-4   How to create and work with data adapters

How to create and work with command builders

A command builder is an ADO.NET object that lets you create command objects for a data adapter's Insert, Update, and Delete statements, based on the adapter's Select statement. That way, you don't have to worry about coding these statements and creating these commands yourself. In particular, you don't have to worry about writing code like the code you saw in chapter 3 for implementing optimistic concurrency. Instead, the command builder generates this code for you.

Figure 6-5 shows the two ways you can create a SQL Server command builder. In the first example, you can see that no arguments are passed to the constructor of the SqlCommandBuilder class. Because of that, you must set the DataAdapter property of the command builder after you create it. In the second example, the data adapter is passed to the constructor of the command builder. Then, when an Update method is executed on the data adapter, the Insert, Update, and Delete statements are generated and executed.

The method shown in this figure, RefreshSchema, refreshes the schema that the command builder uses to generate the Insert, Update, and Delete statements. You'll want to use this method if you change the Select statement associated with the data adapter as a program executes. Then, if the program issues another Update statement, the command builder will generate new Insert, Update, and Delete statements based on the new Select statement.

Although a command builder can save you some coding effort, you can't always use one. Specifically, you can't use a command builder if the Select command for the data adapter contains the name of a stored procedure or if it contains a Select statement that retrieves data from more than one table. In those cases, you'll have to create the Insert, Update, and Delete commands yourself. In addition, you'll want to create your own commands if you want to use a method of concurrency checking other than the one that's used by the command builder.

Two ways to create a SqlCommandBuilder object

```
commandBuilder = New SqlCommandBuilder()
commandBuilder = New SqlCommandBuilder(dataAdapter)
```

Common properties and methods of a command builder

Property	Description
DataAdapter	The data adapter that contains the Select statement that will be used to generate Insert, Update, and Delete statements.

Method	Description
RefreshSchema	Refreshes the schema information that's used to generate the Insert, Update, and Delete statements.

Code that creates a SqlCommandBuilder object

```
Dim cbVendors As New SqlCommandBuilder()
cbVendors.DataAdapter = daVendors
```

Another way to create a SqlCommandBuilder object

```
Dim cbVendors As New SqlCommandBuilder(daVendors)
```

Description

- You can use a command builder to generate Insert, Update, and Delete commands for a data adapter from the Select command for the data adapter. For this to work, the Select command must contain a Select statement.

- The DataAdapter property is set to the value that you pass to the constructor of the command builder. If you don't pass a value, you must set the DataAdapter property after you create the command builder.

- The Insert, Update, and Delete commands are generated when you execute the Update method of the data adapter. If you change the Select statement for the data adapter after these statements are generated, you should execute the RefreshSchema method of the command builder before you execute another Update method.

Notes

- A command builder can't be used with a Select command that contains the name of a stored procedure or a Select statement that retrieves data from more than one table.

- The Select statement associated with the data adapter must include a primary key or a unique column from that table.

Figure 6-5   How to create and work with command builders

How to work with bound controls

As with a typed dataset, you can bind controls to an untyped dataset. The difference is that you have to use code to bind the controls since an untyped dataset isn't available at design time. You'll learn how to bind controls to a data source in the topic that follows. Then, you'll see a program that uses bound controls with an untyped dataset.

How to bind controls to a data source

Figure 6-6 shows how you can use code to bind controls to a data source. As you can see, the technique you use depends on whether you're using simple binding or complex binding. To complex-bind a control, you just set the values of the appropriate properties. To complex-bind a combo box control, for example, you set the DataSource and DisplayMember properties as shown in the first example in this figure. Here, the combo box named cboStates is complex-bound to the States table. That way, all of the values of the StateName column are displayed in the combo box list so the user can select from these values.

To simple-bind a control, you add a binding object to the collection of binding objects for the control. You refer to this collection using the DataBindings property of the control as shown at the top of this figure. Because the DataBindings property refers to a collection, you can use the Add method to add an item to the collection. In this case, the item is a binding object that's identified by the name of the property you want to bind, along with the data source and the data member you want to bind to. The second example in this figure should help you understand how this works.

First, notice that this code creates a binding manager base and assigns a value to it. Then, the next statement binds the Text property of a control named txtName to the VendorName column of the Vendors table in the dsPayables dataset. The statement that follows is similar, but it binds the SelectedValue property of a combo box named cboStates to the VendorState column. Then, the last statement sets the ValueMember property of the combo box to the StateCode column in the States table. That way, if the user selects a different value from this combo box, the value of the StateCode column is saved to the VendorState column in the Vendors table.

Notice in the syntax and in the second example in this figure that a binding object isn't created explicitly. Instead, it's created by the Add method of the DataBindings collection using the arguments you specify. You should realize, however, that you could create a binding object and then add it to the data bindings collection using code like this:

```
Dim bdgName As New Binding("Text",dsPayables,"Vendors.VendorName")
txtName.DataBindings.Add(bdgName)
```

Unless you use the binding object elsewhere in your code, though, there's no reason to use this technique.

The syntax for simple-binding a control to a data source

```
control.DataBindings.Add(propertyName, dataSource, dataMember)
```

Argument	Description
propertyName	The name of the control property to be bound.
dataSource	The data source for the control. Can be a dataset, a data table, or a data view.
dataMember	The member of the data source that the control will be bound to.

Code that complex-binds a combo box control

```
cboStates.DataSource = dsPayables.Tables("States")
cboStates.DisplayMember = "StateName"
```

Code that creates a BindingManagerBase object and simple-binds a text box control and a combo box control

```
Dim bmbVendors As BindingManagerBase
bmbVendors = Me.BindingContext(dsPayables,"Vendors")
txtName.DataBindings.Add("Text",dsPayables,"Vendors.VendorName")
cboStates.DataBindings.Add("SelectedValue",dsPayables,"Vendors.VendorState")
cboStates.ValueMember = "StateCode"
```

Description

- To simple-bind a control to a data source, you use the Add method of the data bindings collection of the control to add a binding object to the collection. To refer to the data bindings collection, you use the DataBindings property of the control.

- Before you can use the binding objects that you add to the controls on the form, you must create a binding manager base object that names the data source that the controls are bound to. You can do that using the same technique you learned in chapter 4.

- You can also complex-bind a control to a data source by setting the appropriate properties as described in chapter 4. For a combo box control, for example, you set the DataSource and DisplayMember properties as shown above.

Figure 6-6   How to bind controls to a data source

A Vendor Maintenance program that uses bound controls

Figure 6-7 presents the code for another version of the Vendor Maintenance program. In this version, all the ADO.NET objects are created through code. As you'll see, however, once these objects are created, the dataset is filled, and the controls are bound, this program works much like the one in chapter 4 that used a typed dataset. Because of that, I'll just focus on the new code here.

On page 1 of the code listing, you can see that four additional variables are declared at the module level. The first one is for a dataset object named dsPayables that's created from the DataSet class. The next two are for data adapters named daVendors and daStates that are created from the SqlDataAdapter class. And the fourth one is for a connection named conPayables that's created from the SqlConnection class.

The procedure for the Load event of the form starts by setting the bLoading variable to True just like the program in chapter 4. Then, it calls a procedure named CreateADONETObjects. This procedure sets the ConnectionString property of the Connection object. In addition, it creates the command objects that define the Select statements for retrieving data from the Vendors and States tables, and it sets the SelectCommand properties of the data adapters to these commands. It also creates a command builder object and associates it with the Vendors data adapter so that the appropriate Insert, Update, and Delete statements will be generated.

After it creates the ADO.NET objects, the Load procedure calls the FillTables procedure to load the Vendors and States data tables. Then, it calls the BindControls procedure to bind the text box and combo box controls on the form to the dataset. You can see this procedure on the second page of this listing. It starts by complex-binding the Vendors combo box to the Vendors table so that the names of all the vendors are displayed in the combo box list. Then, it adds a binding object to the data bindings collection of each text box control to simple-bind the Text property of the control to the appropriate column in the Vendors table. Finally, it complex-binds the States combo box to the StateName column of the States table, and it simple-binds the SelectedValue property of that control to the VendorState column of the Vendors table.

If you look at the rest of the code for this program, you'll see that it's almost identical to the code for the Vendor Maintenance program you saw in chapter 4. In fact, the only differences are in the procedure for the Click event of the Update Database button. Like the Vendor Maintenance program in chapter 5, this procedure calls another procedure named UpdateDatabase that updates the database and then refreshes the Vendors data table.

The code for the Vendor Maintenance program   **Page 1**

```
Imports System.Data.SqlClient
Public Class Form1
    Inherits System.Windows.Forms.Form

    Dim bLoading As Boolean
    Dim bNewRow As Boolean
    Dim bmbVendors As BindingManagerBase
    Dim dsPayables As New DataSet()
    Dim daVendors As New SqlDataAdapter()
    Dim daStates As New SqlDataAdapter()
    Dim conPayables As New SqlConnection()

    Private Sub Form1_Load(ByVal sender As System.Object, _
            ByVal e As System.EventArgs) Handles MyBase.Load
        bLoading = True
        Me.CreateADONETObjects()
        Me.FillTables()
        Me.BindControls()
        bLoading = False
        Me.SetMaintenanceButtons(True)
        btnUpdateDB.Enabled = False
        bmbVendors = Me.BindingContext(dsPayables, "Vendors")
    End Sub

    Public Sub CreateADONETObjects()
        Dim sPayablesConnection As String _
            = "server=Anne\VSdotNET;" _
            & "database=Payables;" _
            & "integrated security=SSPI;" _
            & "workstation id=ANNE"
        conPayables.ConnectionString = sPayablesConnection

        Dim cmdVendors As New SqlCommand()
        cmdVendors.Connection = conPayables
        Dim sVendorSelect As String _
            = "Select VendorID, VendorName, VendorAddress1, " _
            & "VendorAddress2, VendorCity, VendorState, VendorZipCode " _
            & "From Vendors Order By VendorName"
        cmdVendors.CommandText = sVendorSelect
        daVendors.SelectCommand = cmdVendors
        Dim cbVendors As New SqlCommandBuilder()
        cbVendors.DataAdapter = daVendors

        Dim cmdStates As New SqlCommand()
        cmdStates.Connection = conPayables
        Dim sStateSelect As String _
            = "Select * From States Order By StateCode"
        cmdStates.CommandText = sStateSelect
        daStates.SelectCommand = cmdStates
    End Sub
```

Figure 6-7   A Vendor Maintenance program that uses bound controls (part 1 of 5)

The code for the Vendor Maintenance program   **Page 2**

```vb
Private Sub FillTables()
    Try
        conPayables.Open()
        daVendors.Fill(dsPayables, "Vendors")
        daStates.Fill(dsPayables, "States")
        conPayables.Close()
    Catch eSql As SqlException
        MessageBox.Show(eSql.Message, "SQL Server error")
    End Try
End Sub

Private Sub BindControls()
    With cboVendors
        .DataSource = dsPayables.Tables("Vendors")
        .DisplayMember = "VendorName"
    End With
    txtName.DataBindings.Add("Text", dsPayables, "Vendors.VendorName")
    txtAddressLine1.DataBindings.Add("Text", dsPayables, _
        "Vendors.VendorAddress1")
    txtAddressLine2.DataBindings.Add("Text", dsPayables, _
        "Vendors.VendorAddress2")
    txtCity.DataBindings.Add("Text", dsPayables, "Vendors.VendorCity")
    txtZipCode.DataBindings.Add("Text", dsPayables, _
        "Vendors.VendorZipCode")
    With cboStates
        .DataSource = dsPayables.Tables("States")
        .DisplayMember = "StateName"
        .ValueMember = "StateCode"
        .DataBindings.Add("SelectedValue", dsPayables, _
            "Vendors.VendorState")
    End With
End Sub

Private Sub SetMaintenanceButtons(ByVal bAddDeleteMode As Boolean)
    btnAdd.Enabled = bAddDeleteMode
    btnUpdate.Enabled = Not bAddDeleteMode
    btnDelete.Enabled = bAddDeleteMode
    btnCancel.Enabled = Not bAddDeleteMode
End Sub

Private Sub cboVendors_SelectedIndexChanged _
        (ByVal sender As System.Object, ByVal e As System.EventArgs) _
        Handles cboVendors.SelectedIndexChanged
    If Not bLoading Then
        bmbVendors.Position = cboVendors.SelectedIndex
        Me.SetMaintenanceButtons(True)
        btnUpdateDB.Enabled = dsPayables.HasChanges
        txtName.Focus()
    End If
End Sub
```

Figure 6-7   A Vendor Maintenance program that uses bound controls (part 2 of 5)

The code for the Vendor Maintenance program

Page 3

```
Private Sub btnAdd_Click(ByVal sender As System.Object, _
        ByVal e As System.EventArgs) Handles btnAdd.Click
    bmbVendors.AddNew()
    Me.SetMaintenanceButtons(False)
    btnUpdateDB.Enabled = False
    cboStates.SelectedIndex = -1
    bNewRow = True
    txtName.Focus()
End Sub

Private Sub Control_DataChanged(ByVal sender As System.Object, _
        ByVal e As System.EventArgs) Handles txtName.TextChanged, _
        txtAddressLine1.TextChanged, txtAddressLine2.TextChanged, _
        txtCity.TextChanged, txtZipCode.TextChanged, _
        cboStates.SelectedIndexChanged
    If Not bLoading Then
        Me.SetMaintenanceButtons(False)
        btnUpdateDB.Enabled = False
    End If
End Sub

Private Sub btnUpdate_Click(ByVal sender As System.Object, _
        ByVal e As System.EventArgs) Handles btnUpdate.Click
    If ValidData() Then
        bmbVendors.EndCurrentEdit()
        If bNewRow Then
            cboVendors.SelectedIndex = bmbVendors.Count - 1
            bNewRow = False
        End If
        Me.SetMaintenanceButtons(True)
        btnUpdateDB.Enabled = True
        cboVendors.Focus()
    End If
End Sub

Private Function ValidData() As Boolean
    Dim sErrorMessage As String
    If txtName.Text = "" Then
        sErrorMessage = "Name required."
        txtName.Focus()
    ElseIf txtCity.Text = "" Then
        sErrorMessage = "City required."
        txtCity.Focus()
    ElseIf cboStates.SelectedIndex = -1 Then
        sErrorMessage = "State required."
        cboStates.Focus()
    ElseIf txtZipCode.Text = "" Then
        sErrorMessage = "Zip code required."
        txtZipCode.Focus()
    ElseIf txtZipCode.Text < dsPayables.Tables("States").Rows _
            (cboStates.SelectedIndex).Item("FirstZipCode") _
        Or txtZipCode.Text > dsPayables.Tables("States").Rows _
            (cboStates.SelectedIndex).Item("LastZipCode") Then
        sErrorMessage = "The zip code is invalid."
        txtZipCode.Focus()
    End If
```

Figure 6-7   A Vendor Maintenance program that uses bound controls (part 3 of 5)

The code for the Vendor Maintenance program   **Page 4**

```
        If sErrorMessage = "" Then
            ValidData = True
        Else
            ValidData = False
            MessageBox.Show(sErrorMessage, "Data entry error", _
                MessageBoxButtons.OK, MessageBoxIcon.Error)
        End If
    End Function

    Private Sub btnCancel_Click(ByVal sender As System.Object, _
            ByVal e As System.EventArgs) Handles btnCancel.Click
        bmbVendors.CancelCurrentEdit()
        If bNewRow Then
            bmbVendors.Position = cboVendors.SelectedIndex
            bNewRow = False
        End If
        Me.SetMaintenanceButtons(True)
        btnUpdateDB.Enabled = dsPayables.HasChanges
        cboVendors.Focus()
    End Sub

    Private Sub btnDelete_Click(ByVal sender As System.Object, _
            ByVal e As System.EventArgs) Handles btnDelete.Click
        Dim iResult As DialogResult _
            = MessageBox.Show("Delete " & cboVendors.Text & "?", _
                "Confirm Delete", MessageBoxButtons.YesNo, _
                MessageBoxIcon.Question)
        If iResult = DialogResult.Yes Then
            bmbVendors.RemoveAt(bmbVendors.Position)
            cboVendors.Focus()
        End If
    End Sub

    Private Sub btnUpdateDB_Click(ByVal sender As System.Object, _
            ByVal e As System.EventArgs) Handles btnUpdateDB.Click
        bLoading = True
        Me.UpdateDatabase()
        bLoading = False
        btnUpdateDB.Enabled = False
        cboVendors.Focus()
    End Sub
```

Figure 6-7   A Vendor Maintenance program that uses bound controls (part 4 of 5)

The code for the Vendor Maintenance program | Page 5

```
Public Sub UpdateDatabase()
    Try
        daVendors.Update(dsPayables.Tables("Vendors"))
        dsPayables.Tables("Vendors").Clear()
        daVendors.Fill(dsPayables, "Vendors")
    Catch eData As DataException
        MessageBox.Show _
            ("An error occurred during the database update. " _
            & ControlChars.CrLf & "Not all rows were updated.", _
            "ADO.NET error")
    Catch eSql As SqlException
        MessageBox.Show(eSql.Message, "SQL Server error")
    End Try
End Sub

Private Sub btnExit_Click(ByVal sender As System.Object, _
        ByVal e As System.EventArgs) Handles btnExit.Click
    Me.Close()
End Sub

Private Sub Form1_Closing(ByVal sender As Object, _
        ByVal e As System.ComponentModel.CancelEventArgs) _
        Handles MyBase.Closing
    If dsPayables.HasChanges Then
        Dim iResult As DialogResult _
            = MessageBox.Show("You have made changes that have not " _
            & "been saved to the database. " & ControlChars.CrLf _
            & "If you continue, these changes will be lost." _
            & ControlChars.CrLf & "Continue?", "Confirm Exit", _
            MessageBoxButtons.YesNo, MessageBoxIcon.Question)
        If iResult = DialogResult.No Then
            e.Cancel = True
        End If
    End If
End Sub

End Class
```

Figure 6-7   A Vendor Maintenance program that uses bound controls (part 5 of 5)

How to work with unbound controls

The remaining topics of this chapter show you how to use unbound controls with an untyped dataset. Because the techniques are similar to those that you use with a typed dataset, I won't present a complete application here. Instead, I'll just show you how to perform the same functions you learned in the last chapter for working with unbound controls.

How to retrieve and work with a data row

Figure 6-8 illustrates how you retrieve and modify the data in a data row. To start, you declare a variable that will hold the data row as illustrated by all three examples in this figure. Notice that the data row is declared using the generic DataRow type. That's because a custom data row class isn't available for an untyped dataset like it is for a typed dataset. That also means that you can't use properties of the data row to refer to its columns, as you'll see in a moment.

After you declare a variable to hold a row, you can retrieve a row and assign it to that variable. This figure shows two ways to do that. First, you can retrieve a row using its index as illustrated in the first example. Here, the Tables property of the dataset is used to get the table that contains the row, and the Rows property of the table is used to get the row with the specified index.

The rest of the code in this example retrieves values from individual columns of the row and assigns them to the appropriate properties of controls on a form. To do that, it uses the Item property of the data row and specifies the name of the column as an argument. Note that because the Item property is the default property of a row, it can be omitted as shown in this figure.

If the primary key for a table is included in the table's schema, you can also use the Find method of the data rows collection to get a row with the key you specify. If the key contains a single column, you can simply specify the key value on this method as illustrated by the second example in this figure.

In contrast, if the key contains two or more columns, you specify the key as an array. The third example illustrates how this works. Here, after a data row object is declared, an array that will hold two elements is declared. Then, the first element in the array is set to a value of 15, which represents the value of the first column in the key, and the second element in the array is set to a value of 1, which represents the value of the second column in the key. Finally, the Find method is used to retrieve the row with the key specified by the array. In this case, it returns a row in the InvoiceLineItems table.

In this example, you can see that the array that holds the key values is declared with type Object. That's necessary because the two columns in the key have different data types. If both of the columns had the same data type, however, the array could have been defined with that data type instead.

Code that retrieves a row using its index and assigns column values to form controls

```
Dim drVendor As DataRow
Dim iCurrentRow As Integer
    .
    .
    .
drVendor = dsPayables.Tables("Vendors").Rows(iCurrentRow)
txtName.Text = drVendor("VendorName")
txtAddressLine1.Text = drVendor("VendorAddress1")
txtAddressLine2.Text = drVendor("VendorAddress2")
txtCity.Text = drVendor("VendorCity")
cboStates.SelectedValue = drVendor("VendorState")
txtZipCode.Text = drVendor("VendorZipCode")
```

Code that retrieves a row with the selected key value

```
Dim drVendor As DataRow
drVendor = dsPayables.Tables("Vendors").Rows.Find(cboVendors.SelectedValue)
```

Code that retrieves a row with a composite key

```
Dim drLineItem As DataRow
Dim objValues(1) As Object
objValues(0) = "15"
objValues(1) = "1"
drLineItem = dsPayables.Tables("InvoiceLineItems").Rows.Find(objValues)
```

Description

- You can use the Rows property of a data table to retrieve a row using its index. Then, you can assign that row to a variable that's declared with the DataRow type.

- To get the value of a column in a row, use the Item property of the row and specify the name of the column as the argument. Since Item is the default property of a data row, you can omit it as shown above.

- You can use the Find method of a data rows collection to get the row with the specified key. If the row doesn't exist, this method returns a null.

- To use the Find method, a primary key must be defined for the data table. To retrieve the primary key from the database, set the MissingSchemaAction property of the data adapter to MissingSchemaAction.AddWithKey.

- To use the Find method with a table that has a composite key, you code an array for the argument. If the columns in a composite key have different data types, you must declare the array as an object variable so the items in the array can accommodate any data type. Otherwise, you can declare the array with the appropriate data type.

Note

- You can use another method of a data rows collection, Contains, to determine if a row with the specified key exists. You code this method just like the Find method. This method returns a Boolean value that you can use to test for the existence of a row.

Figure 6-8   How to retrieve and work with a data row

How to modify or delete an existing data row

Figure 6-9 illustrates how you modify or delete an existing data row. Note that the examples in this figure assume that you have already retrieved a row as described in the previous figure. Then, you can modify the data using code like that shown in the first example in this figure. This code starts by executing a BeginEdit method. As you know, this method places the row in edit mode, which suspends the firing of the RowChanging event. It's typically used if the program includes a procedure for the RowChanging event of the table or if the program needs to use the Proposed version of a row.

The statements that follow the BeginEdit method assign new values to the columns in the row. As in the previous figure, the statements in this example use the Item property of the data row to identify each column by its name. The last statement in this example executes the EndEdit method, which ends the edit operation and causes the RowChanging event to fire.

As with typed datasets, you can use two different techniques to delete a row from a data table in an untyped dataset. First, you can use the Delete method of the data row to mark the row as deleted, as shown in the second example in this figure. Then, the row isn't deleted permanently until you issue the Update method of the data adapter. Second, you can use the Remove method of the data rows collection to permanently remove a row from the table as illustrated in the third example. You should use this technique only if you don't need to delete the row from the database.

Code that modifies the values in the data row

```
drVendor.BeginEdit()
drVendor("VendorName") = txtName.Text
drVendor("VendorAddress1") = txtAddressLine1.Text
drVendor("VendorAddress2") = txtAddressLine2.Text
drVendor("VendorCity") = txtCity.Text
drVendor("VendorState") = cboStates.SelectedValue
drVendor("VendorZipCode") = txtZipCode.Text
drVendor.EndEdit()
```

A statement that uses the Delete method to mark the row as deleted

```
drVendor.Delete()
```

A statement that uses the Remove method to delete the row

```
dsPayables.Tables("Vendors").Rows.Remove(drVendor)
```

Description

- You can use the BeginEdit method of a data row to suspend the RowChanging event of a table just as you can when you work with typed datasets. Then, you can use the EndEdit method to end the edit operation and fire the RowChanging event, or you can use the CancelEdit method to cancel the edit operation.

- To set the value of a column in a data row, you use the Item property of the row and specify the column name as the argument. Since Item is the default property, you can omit it as shown above.

- The Delete method of a row marks the row for deletion. The row isn't actually deleted until the Update method of the data adapter is executed.

- The Remove method of the data rows collection of a table permanently removes a row from the table. To identify the row to be deleted, you code it as an argument on this method. You should use the Remove method only if you don't need to delete the related row in the database.

- If you issue the Update method of a data adapter and the row is updated successfully in the database, the changes are committed to the dataset.

Figure 6-9   How to modify or delete an existing data row

How to add a data row

Figure 6-10 shows how you add new rows to a data table. To do that, you use the NewRow method of the table, and you assign the result to a data row variable as shown in the first example in this figure. The NewRow method creates a row based on the schema of the data table you specify. In this case, it's based on the schema of the Vendors table. Because of that, you can refer to the columns in the row by name as illustrated by the assignment statements in this example. After you assign values to the columns of the new row, you use the Add method of the data rows collection of the table to add the new row to the table.

The second example shows how you can refresh a dataset after updating the database. You might want to do that if you add rows to a data table, since the new rows are added to the end of the table. You might also want to do that so that changes made to the data in the database by other users are included in the dataset.

Code that creates a new row, assigns values to it, and adds it to the dataset

```
Dim drVendor As DataRow
drVendor = dsPayables.Tables("Vendors").NewRow
drVendor("VendorName") = txtName.Text
drVendor("VendorAddress1") = txtAddressLine1.Text
drVendor("VendorAddress2") = txtAddressLine2.Text
drVendor("VendorCity") = txtCity.Text
drVendor("VendorState") = cboStates.SelectedValue
drVendor("VendorZipCode") = txtZipCode.Text
dsPayables.Tables("Vendors").Rows.Add(drVendor)
```

Code that updates the database and refreshes the dataset

```
daVendors.Update(dsPayables)
dsPayables.Tables("Vendors").Clear()
daVendors.Fill(dsPayables)
```

Description

- To create a new row based on the schema of a table, use the NewRow method of the table and assign the result to a data row variable. Because the new row is based on the schema of the table, you can refer to the columns in the table by name as shown above.

- To set the value of a column in a new row, use the Item property of the row and the column name just as you do when you're working with an existing row.

- After you assign values to the columns in the row, you use the Add method of the data rows collection for the table to add the row to the table.

- Because new rows are added to the end of a table, you may want to refresh the table using the Clear and Fill methods after updating the database. That way, the new rows will be in the correct sequence.

Figure 6-10   How to add a data row

How to work with data columns that allow nulls

As with a typed dataset, you need to know which columns in an untyped dataset allow nulls so you can provide for them in your code. Figure 6-11 presents some techniques you can use to work with nulls in untyped datasets. To check for a null, you can use either the IsNull method of a data row or the Visual Basic IsDBNull function.

When you use the IsNull method, you specify the column you want to check as shown in the first example in this figure. This code checks the VendorAddress1 column of a data row named drVendor, which contains a row from the Vendors table. If this row contains a null, an empty string ("") is assigned to the Text property of a text box. Otherwise, the value of the column is assigned to this property.

The IsDBNull function is similar, but it can be used to check for a null in any expression. To check for a null value in a column, you specify the column and its table in the expression, as shown in the second example. The code in this example has the same effect as the code in the first example.

Instead of checking for a null before you assign a column value to the Text property of a control, you can simply convert the value of the column to a string. To do that, you use the ToString method as illustrated by the third example in this figure. Then, if the column contains a null, it's converted to an empty string.

The last example in this figure shows how you can assign a null to a column. This example uses the Value field of the DBNull class. In this case, a null is assigned to a column if the Text property of the related control contains an empty string. Note that because Value is a static field, you can use it without creating an instance of the DBNull class. You can also use the DBNull field of the System.Convert class to accomplish the same thing. Like the Value field, the DBNull field is a static field that you can use without creating an instance of the class.

How to use the IsNull method

The syntax of the IsNull method

```
dataRow.IsNull(dataColumn)
```

Code that uses the IsNull method to test for a null value

```
If drVendor.IsNull("VendorAddress1") Then
    txtAddressLine1.Text = ""
Else
    txtAddressLine1.Text = drVendor("VendorAddress1")
End If
```

How to use the IsDBNull function

The syntax of the IsDBNull function

```
IsDBNull(expression)
```

Code that uses the IsDBNull function to test for a null value

```
If IsDBNull(drVendor("VendorAddress1")) Then
    txtAddressLine1.Text = ""
Else
    txtAddressLine1.Text = drVendor("VendorAddress1")
End If
```

Code that uses the ToString method to convert a null value to a string

```
txtAddressLine1.Text = drVendor("VendorAddress1").ToString
```

Code that uses the Value field of the DBNull class to assign a null value

```
If txtAddressLine1.Text = "" Then
    drVendor("VendorAddress1") = DBNull.Value
Else
    drVendor("VendorAddress1") = txtAddressLine1.Text
End If
```

Description

- If a data column allows nulls, you'll need to provide additional code to display the column values in a control and to save the value of a control to the column. That's because most form controls don't allow null values.

- You can use the IsNull method of a data row to test a column in that row for a null. This method returns a Boolean value that indicates whether the column contains a null.

- You can use the IsDBNull function to test the expression you specify for a null. To use this function with a data column, you specify the column name for the expression. Then, the function returns a Boolean value that indicates whether the column contains a null.

- You can also use the ToString method to convert the value of a data column to a string. If the data column contains a null, this method returns an empty string ("").

- To set the value of a data column to null, you can use the Value field of the DBNull class. This is a static field that you can use without creating an instance of the class.

- You can also use the DBNull field of the System.Convert class to set the value of a data column to null. This too is a static field.

Figure 6-11   How to work with data columns that allow nulls

How to create and use event handlers with data table events

In chapter 4, you learned how to use data table events with typed datasets. You may recall from that chapter that to use a table event, you have to declare a table object that's based on the table class. When you use untyped datasets, however, you don't have a table class to work with. Because of that, you have to use the technique shown in figure 6-12.

To start, you code an AddHandler statement that associates an event with an *event handler*, which is simply the name of the procedure that will respond to the event. The first statement shown in this figure, for example, associates the RowChanging event of the Vendors table with a procedure named VendorsTable_RowChanging. To do this, the AddHandler statement creates a *delegate* for the specified procedure. A delegate is an object that holds a reference to a method of another object. In this case, the delegate holds a reference to the VendorsTable_RowChanging procedure, which is a method of the form class. Then, the AddressOf operator in the AddHandler statement tells Visual Basic to create an instance of the procedure delegate.

The code for the procedure that's associated with the RowChanging event is also shown in this figure. If you compare it with the procedure you saw back in figure 4-17, you'll see that it's almost identical. The main difference is that the Sub statement doesn't include a Handles clause. That's because the procedure is associated with an event through the AddHandler statement. The other difference is that the bLoading variable isn't checked at the beginning of the procedure.

Before you can code an event handler, you need to know what arguments the event passes to it. All event procedures include an argument named *sender* that identifies the object that fired the event. In addition, every event includes an argument named *e* that provides access to any other arguments passed by the event. The class that this argument is created from depends on the event. The e argument of the RowChanging event, for example, is created from the DataRowChangeEventArgs class. To find out what class to use for a particular event, you can refer to the online help topic for the event.

After you associate an event with an event handler, you can use the RemoveHandler statement to remove the association. You might want to do that, for example, to suspend data table events while a user is editing the data in a row. Then, you can execute the AddHandler statement again to reestablish the association when the edit is complete.

You should also know that you can use the AddHandler and RemoveHandler statements with objects other than data tables. In addition, you can use them with typed as well as untyped datasets. That makes it possible to code more than one event handler for an event and change the association between an event and its event handler dynamically as a program executes. As you can imagine, that makes event handling more flexible than using the Handles clause.

The syntax of the AddHandler and RemoveHandler statements

```
{AddHandler|RemoveHandler} event, AddressOf eventhandler
```

An AddHandler statement that associates the RowChanging event with an event handler

```
AddHandler dsPayables.Tables("Vendors").RowChanging, _
    AddressOf VendorsTable_RowChanging
```

A RemoveHandler statement that removes the association

```
RemoveHandler dsPayables.Tables("Vendors").RowChanging, _
    AddressOf VendorsTable_RowChanging
```

The event handler for a RowChanging event

```
Private Sub VendorsTable_RowChanging(ByVal sender As Object, _
        ByVal e As System.Data.DataRowChangeEventArgs)
    Dim sErrorMessage As String
    If txtName.Text = "" Then
        sErrorMessage = "Name required."
        txtName.Focus()
    ElseIf txtCity.Text = "" Then
        sErrorMessage = "City required."
        txtCity.Focus()
        .
        .
        .
    End If
    If sErrorMessage <> "" Then
        Throw New System.Exception(sErrorMessage)
    End If
End Sub
```

Description

- The AddHandler statement associates an event with an *event handler*. Because an untyped dataset doesn't have a class that defines it, you have to use the AddHandler statement to associate data table events with event handlers.

- The AddHandler statement creates a *delegate* that refers to the event handler in an instance of the form class. Then, the AddressOf operator creates an instance of this delegate.

- An event handler requires an argument named *sender* that's created from the Object class and an argument named *e* that's created from a class that's specific to the event. To find out what class to use for a specific event, refer to the help topic for that event.

- The RemoveHandler statement removes the association between an event and an event handler. You can use this statement to suspend event processing.

- You can also use the AddHandler and RemoveHandler statements with typed datasets and with objects other than data tables. Then, you can code more than one event handler for an event, and you can change the event handler dynamically at runtime.

Figure 6-12   How to create and use event handlers with data table events

Perspective

In this chapter, you've learned more than how to use untyped datasets. You've also learned how to work directly with ADO.NET's data provider classes to create connection, command, and data adapter objects without using the Data Adapter Configuration Wizard.

Although the Configuration Wizard can help you develop database applications rapidly, many developers avoid it for several reasons. One is that Visual Studio occasionally loses track of a database component. Then, the component simply disappears from the Component Designer tray and you have to recreate it manually. That can be a tricky task because some of the code that the wizard generated for the missing component may still be present in your code. In fact, this happened while I was developing the Order Entry application that's shown in chapter 11. This is undoubtedly due to a bug in Visual Studio that may be corrected in a future release.

Beyond that, the Configuration Wizard typically generates more code for the data provider components than you actually need for the application. Another reason to create data provider objects in code, then, is so that you can include just the features you need. This also gives you more precise control over how these objects work. And it makes it easier to separate the database code from the rest of the application by placing it in a database class. You'll learn more about this in chapter 10.

As for untyped datasets, you need to know about them for a couple of reasons. First, typed datasets are derived from untyped datasets, so knowing how untyped datasets work will help you better understand how typed datasets work. Second, you'll occasionally encounter situations where you don't know at design time what tables and columns the dataset will need to have. For example, an untyped dataset may be best in an application that includes an ad hoc query feature that lets the user select the columns to be displayed. Beyond that, if you've already decided that you don't want to use the Configuration Wizard, you may prefer to use an untyped dataset rather than create a typed dataset without using the wizard as described in chapter 9.

Keep in mind, too, that you can create and use data provider classes in code with typed datasets as well as with untyped datasets. Then, you can take advantage of the features of typed datasets at the same time that you take advantage of the benefits of creating the data provider objects through code.

Terms

untyped dataset
event handler
delegate

7

How to work with data views, parameterized queries, and relationships

In this chapter, you'll learn about three different ways to work with the data in a dataset. First, you'll learn how to use data views to filter and sort the data in a data table. Second, you'll learn how to use parameterized queries to restrict the data that's retrieved from a database and stored in a dataset. And third, you'll learn how to use relationships to work with two or more related tables in a dataset. These are essential skills that you'll need to have as a professional programmer.

How to use data views

When you retrieve data from a database using a Select statement, you can specify a filter expression on the Where clause that restricts the rows that are retrieved. In addition, you can specify a sort expression on the Order By clause that returns the rows in the specified sequence. If you want to filter the rows further as a program executes, however, or you want to sort the rows in a different sequence, you can do that using a *data view*. In the topics that follow, you'll learn how to create and use data views in your applications.

An introduction to data views

Figure 7-1 illustrates how a data view works. At the top of this figure, you can see a Select statement that retrieves data from the Invoices table. Notice that this statement doesn't include a Where clause, which means that all of the rows in the table will be retrieved. Also notice that the Order By clause indicates that the rows will be sorted by the VendorID column. You can see the results in the data table that follows the Select statement.

After you retrieve rows into a data table, you can use a data view to sort and filter those rows. The two statements in this figure, for example, filter and sort the rows in the Invoices data table. The first statement filters the invoices so that only those for Vendor ID 110 with a balance due greater than zero are displayed. The second statement sorts the invoices by balance due. The result is shown in the table that follows.

When you use a data view, you should realize that it doesn't affect the data in the table in any way. Instead, it simply determines the rows that are available and the sequence in which they're retrieved. To do that, it uses a set of indexes to point to the rows that are included in the view.

In the next figure, you'll learn how to create a data view. Once you do that, you can use it much as you would a data table. In particular, you can bind controls to it and then use a binding manager base to work with the data in those controls. You'll see how that works in the Invoice Display program that's presented later in this chapter.

A Select statement that retrieves data from the Invoices table

```
Select VendorID, InvoiceNumber, InvoiceDate, InvoiceTotal, InvoiceDueDate,
    InvoiceTotal - PaymentTotal - CreditTotal As BalanceDue
From Invoices
Order By VendorID
```

The data that's stored in the Invoices data table

VendorID	InvoiceNumber	InvoiceDate	InvoiceTotal	InvoiceDueDate	BalanceDue	
104	P02-3772	9/29/2002	7125.34	10/14/2002	0	
105	94007005	9/18/2002	220	9/25/2002	0	
106	9982771	9/29/2002	503.2	10/14/2002	503.2	
107	RTR-72-3662-X	9/30/2002	1600	10/14/2002	0	
108	121897	9/27/2002	450	10/15/2002	0	
110	0-2436	9/2/2002	10976.06	11/12/2002	10976.06	
110	0-2060	9/3/2002	23517.58	10/5/2002	0	
110	0-2058	9/3/2002	37966.19	10/5/2002	0	
110	P-0608	8/7/2002	20551.18	10/26/2002	19351.18	
110	P-0259	8/12/2002	26881.4	9/11/2002	0	
113	77290	9/30/2002	1750	10/14/2002	0	
114	CBM9920-M-T7710	10/3/2002	290	10/8/2002	0	
115	24780512	9/24/2002	6	9/26/2002	0	
115	25022117	9/19/2002	6	10/17/2002	6	

The row filter and sort settings for the Invoices data view

```
dvInvoices.RowFilter = "VendorID = 110 And BalanceDue > 0"
dvInvoices.Sort = "BalanceDue"
```

The rows retrieved by the Invoices data view

VendorID	InvoiceNumber	InvoiceDate	InvoiceTotal	InvoiceDueDate	BalanceDue
110	0-2436	9/2/2002	10976.06	11/12/2002	10976.06
110	P-0608	8/7/2002	20551.18	10/26/2002	19351.18

Description

- A *data view* provides a customized view of the data in a data table. Data views are typically used to sort or filter the rows in a data table.

- You can use a data view in much the same way that you use a data table. You can bind controls to a data view, and you can use it with a binding manager base to perform add, update, and delete operations.

- Unlike a view in a database, you can't use a data view to exclude or add columns to a table. The data view simply contains a set of indexes that point to the rows in the data table that are included in the view.

Figure 7-1   An introduction to data views

How to create and work with data views

Now that you have a general idea of how data views work, you're ready to learn how to create and work with them. Figure 7-2 presents the basic skills.

The easiest way to create a data view is to use the DataView component in the Data tab of the Toolbox. When you use this technique, the data view object appears in the Component Designer tray. Then, you can select it and work with its properties in the Properties window. Before you can bind controls to the data view, for example, you'll need to set the Table property. This is the property that associates the data view with a table. Although you can also set the sort and filter properties of the data view from the Properties window, you're not likely to do that. Instead, you'll set these properties as the program executes based on selections made by the user.

Like other ADO.NET objects, you can also create a data view through code. To do that, you can use one of the three formats shown at the top of this figure. The first format simply creates the data view with its default settings. The second format sets the Table property of the data view to the data table you specify. The first statement shown in this figure, for example, creates a data view named dvInvoices and sets its Table property to Invoices. The third format sets the Table, RowFilter, Sort, and RowStateFilter properties.

You saw examples of the RowFilter and Sort properties in the previous figure, and you'll see additional examples in the next figure. For now, I want you to focus on the RowStateFilter property. This property determines the state and version of the rows that are included in the data view. You can set this property to any of the values in the DataViewRowState enumeration shown in this figure. The second statement in this figure, for example, sets this property to Added so that the data view includes only those rows that have been added to the table. The default setting for the RowStateFilter property is CurrentRows, which is usually what you want. With this setting, all of the changed, unchanged, and added rows are included in the view, but not deleted rows.

Before I go on, you should know that each data table has a default data view that you can use to specify sort and filter criteria. This data view isn't available at design time, though, so it can only be accessed through code. To access the default view of a table, you use its DefaultView property. The third statement in this figure, for example, sets the RowStateFilter property of the default data view for the Invoices table.

Although you should be aware of a table's default view, you usually won't use it. That's particularly true if you're developing a form with bound controls. In that case, you'll want to create a view using the DataView component so you can bind the controls at design time. In addition, when you use the default view, you're limited to working with just that view. In contrast, when you use custom views, you can define two or more views for the same table.

Three ways to create a data view in code

```
dataView = New DataView()
dataView = New DataView(table)
dataView = New DataView(table, rowFilter, sort, rowState)
```

Common data view properties

Property	Description
Table	The table that the view is associated with.
Sort	An expression that determines the order of the rows in the view.
RowFilter	An expression that determines the rows that are included in the view.
RowStateFilter	A member of the DataViewRowState enumeration that determines the state and version of the rows that are included in the view.
Count	The number of rows in the view.

DataViewRowState enumeration members

Member	Description
Added	Includes all rows that have been added to the table.
CurrentRows	Includes all rows with a current version.
Deleted	Includes all rows that have been deleted.
ModifiedCurrent	Includes the current version of all rows that have been modified.
ModifiedOriginal	Includes the original version of all rows that have been modified.
None	No filter.
OriginalRows	Includes all rows with an Original version.
Unchanged	Includes all unchanged rows.

A statement that creates a data view and sets its Table property

```
Dim dvInvoices As New DataView(DsPayables1.Invoices)
```

A statement that filters a table so that only new rows are displayed

```
dvInvoices.RowStateFilter = DataViewRowState.Added
```

A statement that uses the default data view to filter the table

```
DsPayables1.Invoices.DefaultView.RowStateFilter = DataViewRowState.Added
```

Description

- If you want to bind controls to a data view at design time, you must create it using the DataView component in the Toolbox's Data tab. Then, a data view object is added to the Component Designer tray, and you can use the Properties window to set its properties.

- You can also create a data view object through code and set its properties at runtime.

- Each data table has a default data view that you can use to sort and filter the data in the table. To access this view, you use the DefaultView property of the table. Because this data view is only available at runtime, its properties must be set through code and controls can only be bound to it through code.

Figure 7-2   How to create and work with a data view

How to code sort and filter expressions

To help you understand how you can sort and filter a data table using a data view, figure 7-3 presents some typical expressions you can code for the Sort and RowFilter properties. As you can see, both sort expressions and filter expressions are specified as string values.

To code a *sort expression*, you list one or more column names separated by commas. After each column name, you can code Asc or Desc to indicate whether the column values should be sorted in ascending or descending sequence. If you omit these keywords, the column values are sorted in ascending sequence.

The first three sort expressions in this figure illustrate how this works. Here, the first sort expression consists of a single column name, so the data view will be sorted by that column in ascending sequence. The second expression consists of a single column name followed by Desc, so the data view will be sorted by that column in descending sequence. The third sort expression names two columns. In this case, the data view will be sorted by the first column in ascending sequence. Then, within that sequence, the data view will be sorted by the second column in descending sequence.

You can also code sort expressions that include calculated values. This is illustrated by the fourth expression in this figure. Here, the data view will be sorted by the balance due for an invoice, which is calculated by subtracting the PaymentTotal and CreditTotal columns from the InvoiceTotal column.

A *filter expression* is a conditional expression that returns a True or False value. The first filter expression in this figure, for example, tests that the VendorState column is equal to CA. Notice that because the entire filter expression is enclosed in double quotes, the string literal within this expression must be enclosed in single quotes.

To include a date literal in a filter expression, you enclose it in pound signs (#). This is illustrated by the second filter expression in this figure. This expression tests that the invoice date is greater than 01/01/2003.

The third filter expression shown here simply tests that the VendorID column is equal to a specific value. Then, the fourth expression specifies a compound condition. In this case, the VendorID column must be equal to a specific value and the balance due must be greater than zero.

The last three filter expressions show how to use the Like keyword and *wildcards*. A wildcard represents one or more characters within a string. For example, the fifth filter expression tests the VendorName column for values that start with Fresno, the sixth expression tests for values that end with Fresno, and the last expression tests for values that have Fresno anywhere in them.

Although most of the values used in the RowFilter expressions shown here are coded as literals, you'll typically specify these values based on selections made by the user. To do that, you use code like that shown in the code example in this figure. Here, the RowFilter property is set to an expression that's similar to the second one in this figure that filters for all invoices after a given date. In this case, though, the date is taken from a text box. Notice, however, that the date must still be enclosed in pound signs within the filter expression.

Typical expressions for the Sort property of a data view

```
"InvoiceDate"
"InvoiceTotal Desc"
"InvoiceDate Asc, InvoiceTotal Desc"
"InvoiceTotal - PaymentTotal - CreditTotal"
```

Typical expressions for the RowFilter property of a data view

```
"VendorState = 'CA'"
"InvoiceDate > #01/01/2003#"
"VendorID = 123"
"VendorID = 123 And InvoiceTotal - PaymentTotal - CreditTotal > 0"
"VendorName Like 'Fresno*'"
"VendorName Like '*Fresno'"
"VendorName Like '*Fresno*'"
```

Code that sets the RowFilter property of a data view

```
Private Sub btnGetInvoices_Click(ByVal sender As System.Object, _
        ByVal e As System.EventArgs) Handles btnGetInvoices.Click
    dvInvoices.RowFilter = "InvoiceDate > #" & txtInvoiceDate.Text & "#"
End Sub
```

Description

- A *sort expression* is a string value that consists of the names of one or more data columns or calculated values that refer to one or more data columns, separated by commas.

- If you don't specify a sort sequence, the rows are sorted in ascending sequence. To sort in descending sequence, include the Desc keyword.

- A *filter expression* is a string value that consists of a conditional expression that evaluates to True or False. The expression can refer to one or more columns in the data table.

- If you include a string in a filter expression, it must be enclosed in single quotes. If you include a date, it must be enclosed in pound signs (#).

- You can use the Like keyword along with the * and % *wildcards* in a filter expression. The wildcards are interchangeable and represent one or more characters.

- By default, string comparisons are not case-sensitive. To make them case-sensitive, you can set the CaseSensitive property of the dataset or the data table to True.

Figure 7-3   How to code sort and filter expressions

How to work with the rows in a data view

Figure 7-4 presents some techniques you can use to work with the rows in a data view. To start, you should know that each row in a data view is retrieved as a DataRowView object. This object represents the version of the data row that's specified by the RowStateFilter property.

You can work with a data row view in much the same way that you work with a data row. For example, you can use the BeginEdit, EndEdit, and CancelEdit methods of a data row view to edit the row, and you can use the Delete method to delete the row. You can also use the Item property to get the value of a column in the row. This is illustrated by the first example in figure 7-4. Here, a view is used to filter the Vendors table by a state selected by the user. Then, a For Each…Next statement is used to loop through the rows in the view and add each vendor name to a list box.

You should realize that even though a data row view points to a data row, you can't use properties to refer to columns in the data row view even if the data row is defined by a typed dataset. For example, you couldn't refer to the VendorName column in this example like this:

```
drvVendor.VendorName
```

That's because the data view, and therefore the data row view, isn't part of the typed dataset.

If the table that a data view is associated with has a *sort key*, you can use the FindRows method to locate the rows with a specified key. A sort key is defined by the Sort property of the data view. If a value isn't assigned to this property, you can also use the primary key of the table as the sort key. To do that, you set the ApplyDefaultSort property of the data view to True.

The FindRows method returns an array of DataRowView objects with the key you specify. Notice that you can use this method regardless of how many columns are included in the sort key. To use it with a sort key that has two or more columns, you pass the columns as an array of objects.

The second code example in this figure illustrates how the FindRows method works. Here, this method is used to get all of the rows in a view named dvVendors that have the city that's selected by the user. Notice that before the FindRows method is executed, the RowFilter property of the data view is set to a state selected by the user. In addition, the Sort property is set to the VendorCity column. That way, this column can be used as the sort key in the FindRows method.

You can also use the Find method of a data view that's defined with a sort key. This method finds the first row with the specified sort key and returns the index of that row. The last statement in this figure illustrates how you might use this method. Here, the Find method is used to get the index of the row that has the key value selected from a combo box. Then, this index is assigned to the Position property of the binding manager base so that the data in that row is displayed on the form.

How to retrieve rows from a view

```
Dim dvVendors As New DataView(DsPayables1.Vendors)
dvVendors.RowFilter = "VendorState = '" & cboStates.SelectedValue & "'"
Dim drvVendor As DataRowView
For Each drvVendor in dvVendors
    lstVendors.Items.Add(drvVendor("VendorName"))
Next
```

How to retrieve rows with a specified key

The syntax of the FindRows method

```
dataRowView() = dataView.FindRows(key|key())
```

Code that uses the FindRows method to get the specified rows from a view

```
Dim dvVendors As New DataView(DsPayables1.Vendors)
dvVendors.RowFilter = "VendorState = '" & cboStates.SelectedValue & "'"
dvVendors.Sort = "VendorCity"
Dim drvVendor As DataRowView
For Each drvVendor In dvVendors.FindRows(cboCities.SelectedValue)
    lstVendors.Items.Add(drvVendor("VendorName"))
Next
```

How to get the index of a row with a specified key

The syntax of the Find method

```
integer = dataView.Find(key|key())
```

A statement that uses the Find method to locate a vendor row

```
bmbVendors.Position = dvVendors.Find(cboVendors.SelectedValue)
```

Description

- When you retrieve a row from a data view, it's returned as a DataRowView object. A DataRowView object represents the version of a data row that's determined by the RowStateFilter property of the data view.

- You can work with a data row view in much the same way that you work with a data row. To refer to a column in a data row view, for example, you use the Item property (the default) and either the column name or its index.

- You use the FindRows method of a data view to get the rows with the specified sort key. The rows are returned in an array of DataRowView objects.

- If form controls are bound to a data view, you can use the Find method to get the index of a row in the view with the specified sort key. Then, you can position the binding manager base to that row so it's displayed on the form.

- If more than one row exists with the key you specify on a Find method, only the index of the first row is returned. If no rows have the specified key, this method returns -1.

- To use the Find or FindRows method, a *sort key* must be defined for the view. To define a sort key, you can specify a value for the Sort property of the view, or you can set the ApplyDefaultSort property to True to use the primary key of the table as the sort key.

- To use the Find or the FindRows method with a sort key that contains two or more columns, specify the key as an array of objects.

Figure 7-4   How to work with the rows in a data view

The design and property settings for the Invoice Display form

Figure 7-5 presents an Invoice Display form that uses a data view. As you can see, this form lets the user select a vendor from a combo box. This combo box is bound to the Vendors table, which includes the VendorID and VendorName for each vendor. Because the ValueMember property of the combo box is set to the VendorID column, the program will be able to use the value of this column to get the invoices for the selected vendor. You'll see how that works in a minute.

After the user selects a vendor, all of the invoices for that vendor are displayed in a data grid. To do that, the program filters the rows in the Invoices table. As you can see by the property settings for this form, the data grid is bound to a data view that will provide for this filtering. Also notice that as the invoices are filtered, a count of the current number of rows in the data view is displayed in the caption bar of the data grid.

By default, all of the invoices for a vendor are displayed and the invoices are sorted in ascending sequence by invoice date. If the user selects the Unpaid invoices only check box, however, only the invoices with a balance due are displayed. In that case, the invoices are sorted by due date. As you can see, then, the Sort and Filter properties of the data view must change as the program executes based on the user selections.

The design of the Invoice Display form

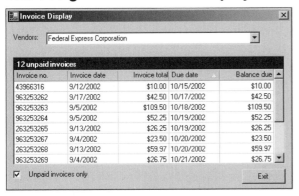

The Select statements for the data adapters

Data adapter	Select statement
daVendors	Select VendorID, VendorName From Vendors Order By VendorName
daInvoices	Select InvoiceID, VendorID, InvoiceNumber, InvoiceDate, InvoiceTotal, InvoiceDueDate, InvoiceTotal - PaymentTotal - CreditTotal As BalanceDue From Invoices

Property settings for the data view

Property	Setting
Name	dvInvoices
Table	DsPayables1.Invoices

Property settings for the combo box and data grid

Property	Combo box	Data grid
Name	cboVendors	grdInvoices
DataSource	DsPayables1.Vendors	dvInvoices
DisplayMember	VendorName	n/a
ValueMember	VendorID	n/a

Description

- When the user selects a vendor from the Vendors combo box, the invoices are filtered so that only the invoices for that vendor are displayed in the data grid on the form. If the user checks the Unpaid invoices only check box, the invoices are further filtered so that only those with a balance due are displayed.

- If the Unpaid check box is selected, the invoices are sorted by due date. If this box isn't selected, the invoices are sorted by invoice date.

- Because this is a simple display program, it uses a typed dataset named dsPayables and bound controls.

Figure 7-5   The design and property settings for the Invoice Display form

The code for the Invoice Display program

Figure 7-6 presents the code for the Invoice Display program. To start, you can see that the procedure for the Load event of the form fills the Vendors and Invoices tables. Notice that the Invoices table is filled before the Vendors table. That way, the invoice count that's displayed for the first vendor will be correct. In contrast, if the Invoices table were loaded after the Vendors table, the invoice count would be zero.

To understand why that is, remember that the Vendors combo box is bound to the Vendors table. Then, when the Vendors table is filled, the event procedure for the SelectedIndexChanged event of the Vendors combo box is fired. As you'll see in a moment, this procedure calls another procedure that gets a count of the number of invoices in the data view. If the Invoices table hasn't been filled when this procedure is executed, though, the count will be zero.

The main processing for this program occurs in a procedure named GetInvoices. This procedure is called when the user selects a vendor from the Vendors combo box or checks or unchecks the Unpaid check box. It consists of a Select Case statement that tests the status of the check box and then sets the RowFilter and Sort properties of the data view accordingly. If you study this code, you shouldn't have any trouble figuring out how it works.

The GetInvoices procedure also sets the CaptionText property of the data grid to indicate the number of invoices that are displayed and whether all invoices or just unpaid invoices are displayed. Notice that the statements that set this property use the IIf function. In case you're not familiar with this function, it evaluates the expression that's specified as the first argument. Then, if the expression is true, the value of the second argument is returned. Otherwise, the value of the third argument is returned.

An Invoice Display program that uses a data view

```
Imports System.Data.SqlClient
Public Class Form1
    Inherits System.Windows.Forms.Form

    Private Sub Form1_Load(ByVal sender As System.Object, _
            ByVal e As System.EventArgs) Handles MyBase.Load
        Try
            conPayables.Open()
            daInvoices.Fill(DsPayables1)
            daVendors.Fill(DsPayables1)
        Catch eSql As SqlException
            MessageBox.Show(eSql.Message, "SQL Server error")
        Finally
            conPayables.Close()
        End Try
    End Sub

    Private Sub cboVendors_SelectedIndexChanged _
            (ByVal sender As System.Object, ByVal e As System.EventArgs) _
            Handles cboVendors.SelectedIndexChanged
        Me.GetInvoices()
    End Sub

    Private Sub GetInvoices()
        Select Case chkUnpaidInvoices.Checked
            Case False
                dvInvoices.RowFilter = "VendorID = " _
                    & cboVendors.SelectedValue
                dvInvoices.Sort = "InvoiceDate"
                grdInvoices.CaptionText = dvInvoices.Count _
                    & " invoice" & IIf(dvInvoices.Count = 1, "", "s")
            Case True
                dvInvoices.RowFilter = "VendorID = " _
                    & cboVendors.SelectedValue & " And BalanceDue > 0"
                dvInvoices.Sort = "InvoiceDueDate"
                grdInvoices.CaptionText = dvInvoices.Count _
                    & " unpaid invoice" & IIf(dvInvoices.Count = 1, "", "s")
        End Select
    End Sub

    Private Sub chkUnpaidInvoices_CheckedChanged _
            (ByVal sender As System.Object, ByVal e As System.EventArgs) _
            Handles chkUnpaidInvoices.CheckedChanged
        Me.GetInvoices()
    End Sub

    Private Sub btnExit_Click(ByVal sender As System.Object, _
            ByVal e As System.EventArgs) Handles btnExit.Click
        Me.Close()
    End Sub

End Class
```

Figure 7-6   The code for the Invoice Display program

How to use parameterized queries

The database applications you've seen so far have retrieved all of the rows from the Vendors and Invoices tables when they start. That works because these tables contain a manageable number of rows. But what if you need to work with tables that contain hundreds or even thousands of rows? In that case, you need to restrict the number of rows that are retrieved at any one time. In addition to making your program more efficient, this helps reduce concurrency errors. That's because the less data you retrieve, the less likely it is that another user will retrieve and change the same data.

To reduce the number of rows a program retrieves, you can use a variety of techniques. One technique is to filter the rows based on one or more columns in the table. To filter a table of customers, for example, you could let the user enter a last name and state. Then, the program could retrieve and display all the customers that meet those criteria, and the user could select from those customers. Another technique is to retrieve a single row based on a unique value entered by the user, like a vendor number or customer number.

To implement either of these techniques, you use *parameterized queries*. With this type of query, you retrieve just the rows you want each time the query is executed.

A Vendor Maintenance form that uses a parameterized query

Figure 7-7 presents the design of a Vendor Maintenance form that uses a parameterized query. The main difference between this form and the Vendor Maintenance forms presented earlier in this book is that this form doesn't retrieve all the vendor rows when it starts. Because of that, the user can't select a vendor from a combo box to display the data for that vendor. Instead, the user must enter a Vendor ID and then click on the Get Vendor button to retrieve an existing vendor row. Or, the user can click on the Add button to add a new row. Note that the user doesn't enter a Vendor ID for a new row. That's because it's an identity column, so its value is generated by the database when the row is added.

Like the Vendor Maintenance forms presented earlier, this form also provides Update, Delete, and Cancel buttons that the user can use to work with the rows in the Vendors table. Notice, however, that this form doesn't include an Update Database button. Instead, each time the user clicks on the Update button to add or modify a row or on the Delete button to delete a row, both the dataset and database are updated. That makes sense because this program is designed to work with only one row at a time. In addition, because the program updates the database immediately, the most current information will always be available to other users.

A Vendor Maintenance form that uses a parameterized query

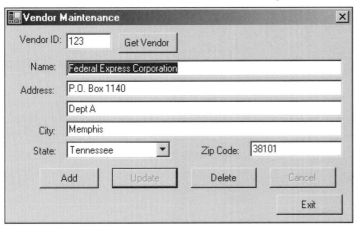

Description

- This Vendor Maintenance form is designed so it retrieves only one vendor row at a time. That's more efficient for working with tables that contain a large number of rows. That also makes sense if concurrency is an issue because the program only holds one row at a time and the data it retrieves is always current.

- To retrieve a vendor, the user enters a Vendor ID and clicks on the Get Vendor button. Then, if a row is found with that Vendor ID, the row is retrieved and its data is displayed on the form.

- After a row is retrieved, the user can modify it by entering the changes in the text boxes and then clicking on the Update button that becomes available. This saves the changes to the dataset and updates the row in the database.

- The user can also delete an existing row by clicking on the Delete button. Then, the row is deleted from the dataset and the database.

- To add a new row, the user can click on the Add button and then enter the data for the new vendor. To save the data to the dataset and add the new row to the database, the user can click on the Update button.

- This form uses a typed dataset and unbound controls.

Figure 7-7   A Vendor Maintenance form that uses a parameterized query

How to create a parameterized query

A parameterized query is a query that depends on the value of one or more *parameters*. For example, the parameterized query that will be used by the Vendor Maintenance form in figure 7-7 will depend on the value of a parameter that holds the Vendor ID. This parameterized query is shown in the first example in figure 7-8. Here, the parameter is identified by a placeholder named @VendorID.

When you use parameters in a SQL statement for a SQL Server command, you use *named variables* for placeholders like the one shown in this example. Note that the variable name must begin with an at sign (@) and is usually given the same name as the column it's associated with. In contrast, the placeholder for a parameter in a SQL statement for an OLE DB command is a question mark, as illustrated by the second example in this figure.

After you define the SQL statement, you create the parameter objects that will hold the values that are substituted for the placeholders. If you use the Data Adapter Configuration Wizard to create the data adapter and its related components, the parameter objects are created for you. In that case, the parameters for a SQL Server command are given the names specified in the SQL statement, and the parameters for an OLE DB command are given the names of the columns they're associated with. The parameter used by the second Select statement in this figure, for example, would be given the name VendorID. Then, you can refer to the parameters by name when you set their values.

If you don't use the Data Adapter Configuration Wizard, you can define the parameters using code. I'll show you how to do that in just a moment. But first, I want to show you how to work with parameters that are created by the wizard.

A parameterized query for a SQL Server command

```
Select VendorID, VendorName, VendorAddress1, VendorAddress2,
    VendorCity, VendorState, VendorZipCode
From Vendors
Where VendorID = @VendorID
```

A parameterized query for an OLE DB command

```
Select VendorID, VendorName, VendorAddress1, VendorAddress2,
    VendorCity, VendorState, VendorZipCode
From Vendors
Where VendorID = ?
```

Description

- A *parameterized query* is a query that depends on the values of one or more *parameters*. In most cases, you'll use parameters in the Where clause of a Select statement to identify the rows to be retrieved.

- To create a parameterized query, you code a SQL statement with placeholders for the parameters. Then, you create a parameter object that defines the parameter, and you add it to the parameters collection of the command object that contains the SQL statement.

- The placeholder for a parameter in a SQL Server command is a *named variable* whose name begins with an at sign (@). In most cases, you'll give the variable the same name as the column it's associated with.

- The placeholder for a parameter in an OLE DB command is a question mark. The question mark simply indicates the position of the parameter.

- If you define a parameterized query using the Data Adapter Configuration Wizard, the parameter objects are created for you and added to the parameters collection of the command.

- The Configuration Wizard gives SQL Server parameters the names you specify in the SQL statement. Each parameter name must be unique.

- The Configuration Wizard gives OLE DB parameters the names of the columns they're associated with. If two or more OLE DB parameters are specified for the same column, the first parameter is given the name of the column, the second parameter is given the name of the column with the number 1 appended to it, and so on.

Note

- To include a placeholder in a Select statement using the Query Builder, type a variable name or a question mark into the Criteria column.

Figure 7-8   How to create a parameterized query

How to work with parameters created by the Configuration Wizard

In most cases, the Data Adapter Configuration Wizard generates parameters so they work the way you want them to. If you want to view the definition of a parameter, however, or you want to change any of its properties, you can do that using the dialog box shown at the top of figure 7-9. Here, you can see the definition for the @VendorID parameter that was included in the first Select statement in the previous figure.

If you review the properties that are available for a parameter, I don't think you'll have any trouble understanding what they do. If you're unclear about any of these properties, though, you can refer to the topic that follows.

Although you can set the initial value of a parameter from the Collection Editor dialog box, you'll typically want to change its value as the program executes depending on selections or entries made by the user. When the user enters a Vendor ID into the Vendor Maintenance form, for example, you'll want to change the value of the @VendorID parameter so you can retrieve the row for that vendor. To do that, you use code like that shown in this figure.

As you can tell from the name of the Collection Editor dialog box, the parameters for a command are stored in a collection. To refer to this collection, you use the Parameters property of the command. The first statement in this figure, for example, refers to the @VendorID parameter in the parameters collection for the Select command of the daVendors data adapter. It sets the Value property of this parameter to the Text property of the txtVendorID text box.

When the Select statement that refers to this parameter is executed, the value that's assigned to the parameter is substituted for the placeholder. For example, if a value of 94 is assigned to the parameter, the Select statement that's executed will look like this:

```
Select VendorID, VendorName, VendorAddress1, VendorAddress2,
    VendorCity, VendorState, VendorZipCode
From Vendors
Where VendorID = 94
```

That way, only the vendor with a Vendor ID of 94 will be retrieved.

You can also refer to a parameter in the parameters collection by its index value. This is illustrated by the second assignment statement in this figure, which refers to the parameter with an index value of zero. If the Select statement contains two or more parameters, however, you should use names instead of index values so you can be sure you're referring to the appropriate parameter.

The dialog box for working with a collection of parameters

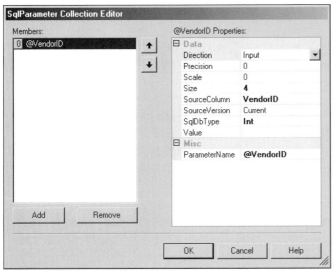

A statement that assigns a value to a parameter by name

```
daVendors.SelectCommand.Parameters("@VendorID").Value _
    = txtVendorID.Text
```

A statement that assigns a value to a parameter by index

```
daVendors.SelectCommand.Parameters(0).Value _
    = txtVendorID.Text
```

Description

- If you use the Data Adapter Configuration Wizard to create a command object with a Select statement that includes parameters, you can use the Collection Editor dialog box to work with those parameters.

- To display this dialog box, select the data adapter to display its properties in the Properties window. Then, expand the SelectCommand property of the data adapter, click on the Parameters property, and then click on the ellipsis that's displayed.

- To display or change the properties for a parameter, select the parameter in the Members list. See figure 7-10 for a description of these properties.

- Before you can execute a parameterized query, you must set the values of the parameters. You can set initial values from the Collection Editor dialog box, but you'll want to use code to change these values as the program executes.

- To refer to a parameter through code, use the Parameters property of the command object to access the parameters collection of the command. Then, use the parameter name or index to identify the parameter, and use the Value property to set its value.

Note

- You can also use the Collection Editor dialog box to add and delete parameters. You're not likely to do that if the parameters are created by the Configuration Wizard, though.

Figure 7-9   How to work with parameters created by the Configuration Wizard

How to create and work with parameters using code

Figure 7-10 shows you how to create and work with parameters using code. Here, you can see three formats for creating a SQL Server parameter. Although there are others, these are the three you're most likely to use. You create a parameter for the OLE DB command using similar techniques.

Before you can use a parameter, you must assign a name, a data type, and a value to it. If you don't assign these values when you create the object, you can do that using some of the properties shown in this figure. Notice that you can specify the data type using either the DbType or SqlDbType property (OleDbType for an OLE DB parameter.)

The first example in this figure shows how to create a parameter and add it to the collection of parameters for a command. This code creates the parameter named @VendorID that's used by the Select statement you saw in figure 7-8. Like the VendorID column in the Vendors table, this parameter is assigned a data type of Int. Then, the Add method of the parameters collection is used to add the parameter to the collection of parameters for a command named cmdVendors. Although it's not shown in this figure, this is the command that contains the Select statement.

In most cases, you'll create a parameter object, assign it to a variable, set its properties, and add it to the parameters collection as shown in this example. You should know, however, that you can also add a parameter to the parameters collection without creating a parameter variable. For example, to create the parameter shown in this figure and add it to the parameters collection, you could use a statement like this:

```
cmdVendors.Parameters.Add("@VendorID", SqlDbType.Int)
```

If you do that, of course, you won't be able to refer to the parameter using a variable. So if you need to set additional properties of the parameter, you'll have to access the parameter through the command object.

The second example in this figure shows one way to set the Value property of a parameter. To do that, you use the Parameters property of the command to access the parameters collection and you identify the parameter by name or by index. If the command is associated with a data adapter, you can also use the technique shown in the previous figure to set its parameter value. And if the parameter is assigned to a variable, you can use that variable to set its Value property as shown in the third example in this figure. To do that, of course, the variable must be within the scope of the procedure that sets its value, which usually means that it's defined at the module level.

When you assign a name to a SQL Server parameter, you should realize that it must be the same name that's specified in the SQL statement. That's because ADO.NET associates the parameters with the placeholders by name. Because of that, if a statement uses two or more parameters, you can add them to the parameters collection in any sequence. In contrast, OLE DB parameters must be added to the collection in the same order that they appear in the SQL statement.

Three ways to create a SqlParameter object

```
sqlParameter = New SqlParameter()
sqlParameter = New SqlParameter(parameterName, value)
sqlParameter = New SqlParameter(parameterName, dbType)
```

Common properties of a SQL Server parameter

Property	Description
DbType	A member of the DbType enumeration that determines the type of data that the parameter can hold.
Direction	A member of the ParameterDirection enumeration that determines if the parameter will be used for input, output, both input or output, or to hold the return value from a stored procedure or function. The default is Input.
IsNullable	A Boolean value that indicates if the parameter accepts nulls. The default is False.
ParameterName	The name of the parameter.
Size	The maximum size of the value that the parameter can hold.
SourceColumn	A data column that's used to set the value of an input parameter or receive the value of an output parameter.
SourceVersion	The data row version to be used when loading a parameter value.
SqlDbType	A member of the SqlDbType enumeration that determines the type of data that the parameter can hold. This property is synchronized with the DbType property.
Value	The value of the parameter.

Code that creates a parameter and adds it to a parameters collection

```
Dim prmVendorID As New SqlParameter()
prmVendorID.ParameterName = "@VendorID"
prmVendorID.SqlDbType = SqlDbType.Int
cmdVendors.Parameters.Add(prmVendorID)
```

A statement that sets the value of the parameter

```
cmdVendors.Parameters("@VendorID").Value = txtVendorID.Text
```

Another way to set the value of the parameter

```
prmVendorID.Value = txtVendorID.Text
```

Description

- When you create a parameter, you can specify the parameter name along with a value or a data type. If you don't specify these values, you can set the values of the associated properties after you create the parameter.

- When you create parameters for a SQL Server command, you must give them the same names you used in the SQL statement. Then, you can add the parameters to the parameters collection in any order you want since ADO.NET refers to them by name.

- Because the parameters for an OLE DB command aren't named in the SQL statement, they can be given any name you want, but they must be added to the parameters collection in the same order that they appear in the statement.

- You can refer to a parameter through the parameters collection of the command or through the variable that the parameter is assigned to.

Figure 7-10   How to create and work with parameters using code

In that case, ADO.NET associates the parameters with the placeholders in the SQL statement by sequence since the placeholders aren't named.

By default, the Direction property for a parameter is set to Input, which means that it will be used to provide input to the command object. If you execute a command object directly rather than through a data adapter, though, you can use the other options for this property. You'll learn how to do that in the next chapter when I present some additional skills for working with commands.

Instead of assigning the value of a parameter through code, you can assign the value automatically by setting the SourceColumn and SourceVersion properties to a data column and a row version. These properties are particularly useful when you add, update, or delete rows. To help you understand how this works, you can display the properties for the parameters in an Update statement that's generated by the Configuration Wizard. If you do, you'll see that the current version of each column is used to update the data in the database, and the original version of each column is used to perform concurrency checking. Then, you can display the Update statement to see how these parameters are used.

The code for the Vendor Maintenance program

Figure 7-11 presents the code for the Vendor Maintenance program. Before I describe this code, you should know that this program uses a typed dataset with unbound controls like the program in chapter 5. Because of that, some of the basic procedures in this program are similar or identical to the procedures in the program in that chapter.

The Load procedure for the form is somewhat different than the Load procedure for the program in chapter 5. First, because it doesn't use a Vendors combo box and because it won't retrieve a vendor until the user enters a Vendor ID, it's not necessary to set the bLoading variable to True before the rest of the code in the procedure is executed. In addition, it doesn't fill the Vendors table, get the first vendor row, or fill the form controls. Instead, it just calls a procedure named FillStatesTable to fill the States table. Then, it calls the ClearControls procedure to clear the form controls, and it calls the SetMaintenanceButtons procedure to enable the Add and Delete buttons and disable the Update and Cancel buttons. Notice that the SetMaintenanceButtons procedure also sets the Enabled property of the Vendor ID text box and the Get Vendor button. Since a value of True is passed to this procedure when the program first starts, these controls are both enabled.

The last statement in the Load procedure calls another procedure named SetEntryControls. Depending on the Boolean value that's passed to it, this procedure enables or disables the Delete button along with the five text boxes and the combo box that are used to enter vendor data. In this case, a value of False is passed to the procedure so the controls are disabled. That way, the user won't be able to enter any data without first retrieving a vendor or clicking on the Add button to add a new vendor. Notice that the Enabled property of the Delete button is set only if a new row isn't being added. That way, this button will be disabled while a new row is being added.

The Vendor Maintenance program with a parameterized query   Page 1

```
Imports System.Data.SqlClient
Public Class Form1
    Inherits System.Windows.Forms.Form

    Dim bLoading As Boolean
    Dim bNewRow As Boolean
    Dim drVendor As dsPayables.VendorsRow

    Private Sub Form1_Load(ByVal sender As System.Object, _
            ByVal e As System.EventArgs) Handles MyBase.Load
        Me.FillStatesTable()
        Me.ClearControls()
        Me.SetMaintenanceButtons(True)
        Me.SetEntryControls(False)
    End Sub

    Private Sub FillStatesTable()
        Try
            daStates.Fill(DsPayables1)
        Catch eSql As SqlException
            MessageBox.Show(eSql.Message, "SQL Server error")
        End Try
    End Sub

    Private Sub ClearControls()
        bLoading = True
        txtName.Text = ""
        txtAddressLine1.Text = ""
        txtAddressLine2.Text = ""
        txtCity.Text = ""
        cboStates.SelectedIndex = -1
        cboStates.SelectedIndex = -1
        txtZipCode.Text = ""
        bLoading = False
    End Sub

    Private Sub SetMaintenanceButtons(ByVal bAddDeleteMode As Boolean)
        btnAdd.Enabled = bAddDeleteMode
        btnUpdate.Enabled = Not bAddDeleteMode
        btnDelete.Enabled = bAddDeleteMode
        btnCancel.Enabled = Not bAddDeleteMode
        txtVendorID.Enabled = bAddDeleteMode
        btnGetVendor.Enabled = bAddDeleteMode
    End Sub

    Private Sub SetEntryControls(ByVal bEditMode As Boolean)
        txtName.Enabled = bEditMode
        txtAddressLine1.Enabled = bEditMode
        txtAddressLine2.Enabled = bEditMode
        txtCity.Enabled = bEditMode
        cboStates.Enabled = bEditMode
        txtZipCode.Enabled = bEditMode
        If Not bNewRow Then
            btnDelete.Enabled = bEditMode
        End If
    End Sub
```

Figure 7-11   The code for the Vendor Maintenance program (part 1 of 5)

To restrict the characters that the user can enter into the Vendor ID text box, this program includes a procedure for the KeyPress event of that control. This procedure uses a Select Case statement to test the value of the KeyChar property of the e argument that's passed to the procedure. This property contains the ASCII character associated with the key. To make it easier to work with keys for non-displayable characters such as the backspace, this ASCII character is converted to an integer value using the Visual Basic Asc function. In this case, the user can use the backspace key (integer value 8) or enter a number from 0 through 9 (integer values 48 through 57) in this text box.

The key to using the KeyPress event is setting the Handled property of the e argument properly. This property indicates whether the event procedure handled the event. If it didn't (False), the default Windows processing is performed. That's what you want if the user presses a valid key. If the user presses any of the numeric keys listed in the first Case clause in this figure, for example, the default processing will cause the character to be added to the text box. And if the user presses the backspace key, the default processing will cause the last character that was entered to be erased. However, if the user presses any other key, the Handled property is set to True so no processing takes place. In other words, the key is ignored. That way, the Vendor ID will always be an integer.

When the user clicks on the Get Vendor button to retrieve a vendor, the Click event procedure for this button is executed. It starts by checking that the user entered a Vendor ID. If not, an error message is displayed and the focus is moved back to the Vendor ID text box. If so, the parameter in the Select statement for the Vendors data adapter is set to the value of the Vendor ID text box. Then, the Vendors table is cleared so it no longer contains any row that was retrieved previously, and the FillVendorsTable procedure is called to retrieve the row for the selected vendor.

After the Fill method is executed, the Get Vendor procedure checks the Count property of the data rows collection of the Vendors table to determine if a row with the specified Vendor ID was found. If the value of this property is zero, which means that the Vendor ID wasn't found, the ClearControls procedure is called to clear any data that was previously displayed, the SetEntryControls procedure is called to disable the entry controls, an error message is displayed, and the focus is moved back to the Vendor ID text box. Otherwise, the entry controls are enabled, the vendor row is assigned to the drVendor variable, the FillControls procedure is called to display the vendor data on the form, and the focus is moved to the Name text box.

The Vendor Maintenance program with a parameterized query   Page 2

```vb
Private Sub txtVendorID_KeyPress(ByVal sender As Object, _
        ByVal e As System.Windows.Forms.KeyPressEventArgs) _
        Handles txtVendorID.KeyPress
    Select Case Asc(e.KeyChar)
        Case 8, 48 To 57
            e.Handled = False
        Case Else
            e.Handled = True
    End Select
End Sub

Private Sub btnGetVendor_Click(ByVal sender As System.Object, _
        ByVal e As System.EventArgs) Handles btnGetVendor.Click
    If txtVendorID.Text <> "" Then
        daVendors.SelectCommand.Parameters("@VendorID").Value _
            = txtVendorID.Text
        DsPayables1.Vendors.Clear()
        Me.FillVendorsTable()
        If DsPayables1.Vendors.Rows.Count = 0 Then
            Me.ClearControls()
            Me.SetEntryControls(False)
            MessageBox.Show("Vendor row not found.", "Entry error")
            txtVendorID.Focus()
        Else
            Me.SetEntryControls(True)
            drVendor = DsPayables1.Vendors(0)
            Me.FillControls()
            txtName.Focus()
        End If
    Else
        MessageBox.Show("You must enter a Vendor ID.", "Entry error")
        txtVendorID.Focus()
    End If
End Sub

Private Sub FillVendorsTable()
    Try
        daVendors.Fill(DsPayables1)
    Catch eSql As SqlException
        MessageBox.Show(eSql.Message, "SQL Server error")
    End Try
End Sub

Private Sub FillControls()
    bLoading = True
    txtName.Text = drVendor.VendorName
    If drVendor.IsVendorAddress1Null Then
        txtAddressLine1.Text = ""
    Else
        txtAddressLine1.Text = drVendor.VendorAddress1
    End If
    If drVendor.IsVendorAddress2Null Then
        txtAddressLine2.Text = ""
    Else
        txtAddressLine2.Text = drVendor.VendorAddress2
    End If
```

Figure 7-11   The code for the Vendor Maintenance program (part 2 of 5)

When the user clicks on the Add button, the Click event procedure of this button starts by blanking out the Vendor ID text box, clearing the Vendors table to remove the current row, and setting the bNewRow variable to True to indicate that a row is being added. Then, it clears the controls, sets the maintenance buttons and entry controls appropriately, and moves the focus to the Name text box so the user can begin entering the data for the new vendor.

When the user clicks on the Update button, the Update procedure starts by checking for valid data. If the data is valid and a new row is being added, the procedure creates a new row, calls the FillRow procedure to fill the row with the data the user entered, and adds the row to the Vendors table. Then, it calls the UpdateDatabase procedure to add the new row to the database. Next, it sets the Vendor ID text box to the Vendor ID that was generated by the database. That's possible because, as you may recall from chapter 3, an Insert statement that's generated by the Configuration Wizard is followed by a Select statement that refreshes the row in the dataset. That way, any data that's generated by the database is available to the program. The last statement that's executed for an add operation sets the bNewRow variable to False to indicate that the operation is complete.

If an existing row is being updated, the Update procedure calls the FillRow procedure to fill the row with the updated data. Then, it calls the UpdateDatabase procedure to update the row in the database.

If the user cancels out of an add or update operation, the Cancel procedure shown on page 5 of the program listing starts by resetting the maintenance buttons. Then, if a new row was being added, the bNewRow variable is set to False and the controls are cleared and disabled. Note that you can't redisplay the previous vendor at this point because the Vendors table was cleared when the user first clicked on the Add button. If you wanted to, though, you could modify this program so that the Vendors table isn't cleared until the user clicks on the Update button. Then, you could redisplay the previous row if the user cancels out of an add operation. If the user cancels out of an update operation, the Cancel procedure simply calls the FillControls procedure to redisplay the original row values.

Finally, if the user clicks on the Delete button, the Delete procedure confirms the delete operation and then deletes the row and updates the database. Then, it clears the controls, resets the maintenance buttons and the entry controls, and moves the focus to the Vendor ID text box so the user can retrieve another vendor.

Although the logic of this program is different from the logic of the Vendor Maintenance program in chapter 5, you can see that it isn't any more difficult to code. In fact, I think the code is more straightforward because you're never dealing with more than one vendor row at a time. What's most important, though, is that by restricting the program to work with a single vendor at a time, only the rows that the user requests during each execution of the program are retrieved from the database. And that can improve the overall performance of the application. In addition, it can reduce concurrency errors because it's less likely that another user will request the same row at the same time.

The Vendor Maintenance program with a parameterized query   **Page 3**

```vb
        txtCity.Text = drVendor.VendorCity
        cboStates.SelectedValue = drVendor.VendorState
        txtZipCode.Text = drVendor.VendorZipCode
        bLoading = False
    End Sub

    Private Sub btnAdd_Click(ByVal sender As System.Object, _
            ByVal e As System.EventArgs) Handles btnAdd.Click
        txtVendorID.Text = ""
        DsPayables1.Vendors.Clear()
        bNewRow = True
        Me.ClearControls()
        Me.SetMaintenanceButtons(False)
        Me.SetEntryControls(True)
        txtName.Focus()
    End Sub

    Private Sub Control_DataChanged(ByVal sender As System.Object, _
            ByVal e As System.EventArgs) Handles txtName.TextChanged, _
            txtAddressLine1.TextChanged, txtAddressLine2.TextChanged, _
            txtCity.TextChanged, txtZipCode.TextChanged, _
            cboStates.SelectedIndexChanged
        If Not bLoading Then
            Me.SetMaintenanceButtons(False)
        End If
    End Sub

    Private Sub btnUpdate_Click(ByVal sender As System.Object, _
            ByVal e As System.EventArgs) Handles btnUpdate.Click
        If ValidData() Then
            If bNewRow Then
                drVendor = DsPayables1.Vendors.NewVendorsRow
                Me.FillRow()
                DsPayables1.Vendors.AddVendorsRow(drVendor)
                Me.UpdateDatabase()
                txtVendorID.Text = drVendor.VendorID
                bNewRow = False
            Else
                Me.FillRow()
                Me.UpdateDatabase()
            End If
            Me.SetMaintenanceButtons(True)
            txtVendorID.Focus()
        End If
    End Sub

    Public Sub UpdateDatabase()
        Try
            daVendors.Update(DsPayables1.Vendors)
        Catch eConcurrency As DBConcurrencyException
            MessageBox.Show("This row has been changed by another user. " _
                & ControlChars.CrLf & "The row has not been processed.", _
                "Concurrency error")
        Catch eSql As SqlException
            MessageBox.Show(eSql.Message, "SQL Server error")
        End Try
    End Sub
```

Figure 7-11   The code for the Vendor Maintenance program (part 3 of 5)

The Vendor Maintenance program with a parameterized query   Page 4

```
Private Function ValidData() As Boolean
    Dim sErrorMessage As String
    If txtName.Text = "" Then
        sErrorMessage = "Name required."
        txtName.Focus()
    ElseIf txtCity.Text = "" Then
        sErrorMessage = "City required."
        txtCity.Focus()
    ElseIf cboStates.SelectedIndex = -1 Then
        sErrorMessage = "State required."
        cboStates.Focus()
    ElseIf txtZipCode.Text = "" Then
        sErrorMessage = "Zip code required."
        txtZipCode.Focus()
    ElseIf txtZipCode.Text < DsPayables1.States.FindByStateCode _
            (cboStates.SelectedValue).FirstZipCode _
        Or txtZipCode.Text > DsPayables1.States.FindByStateCode _
            (cboStates.SelectedValue).LastZipCode Then
        sErrorMessage = "The zip code is invalid."
        txtZipCode.Focus()
    End If
    If sErrorMessage = "" Then
        ValidData = True
    Else
        ValidData = False
        MessageBox.Show(sErrorMessage, "Data entry error", _
            MessageBoxButtons.OK, MessageBoxIcon.Error)
    End If
End Function

Private Sub FillRow()
    drVendor.VendorName = txtName.Text
    If txtAddressLine1.Text = "" Then
        drVendor.SetVendorAddress1Null()
    Else
        drVendor.VendorAddress1 = txtAddressLine1.Text
    End If
    If txtAddressLine2.Text = "" Then
        drVendor.SetVendorAddress2Null()
    Else
        drVendor.VendorAddress2 = txtAddressLine2.Text
    End If
    drVendor.VendorCity = txtCity.Text
    drVendor.VendorState = cboStates.SelectedValue
    drVendor.VendorZipCode = txtZipCode.Text
End Sub
```

Figure 7-11   The code for the Vendor Maintenance program (part 4 of 5)

The Vendor Maintenance program with a parameterized query   **Page 5**

```
Private Sub btnCancel_Click(ByVal sender As System.Object, _
        ByVal e As System.EventArgs) Handles btnCancel.Click
    Me.SetMaintenanceButtons(True)
    If bNewRow Then
        bNewRow = False
        Me.ClearControls()
        Me.SetEntryControls(False)
    Else
        Me.FillControls()
    End If
    txtVendorID.Focus()
End Sub

Private Sub btnDelete_Click(ByVal sender As System.Object, _
        ByVal e As System.EventArgs) Handles btnDelete.Click
    Dim iResult As DialogResult _
        = MessageBox.Show("Delete " & txtName.Text & "?", _
          "Confirm Delete", MessageBoxButtons.YesNo, _
          MessageBoxIcon.Question)
    If iResult = DialogResult.Yes Then
        drVendor.Delete()
        Me.UpdateDatabase()
        txtVendorID.Text = ""
        Me.ClearControls()
        Me.SetMaintenanceButtons(True)
        Me.SetEntryControls(False)
        txtVendorID.Focus()
    End If
End Sub

Private Sub btnExit_Click(ByVal sender As System.Object, _
    ByVal e As System.EventArgs) Handles btnExit.Click
    Me.Close()
End Sub

Private Sub Form1_Closing(ByVal sender As Object, _
        ByVal e As System.ComponentModel.CancelEventArgs) _
        Handles MyBase.Closing
    If btnUpdate.Enabled Then
        Dim iResult As DialogResult _
            = MessageBox.Show("You have made changes that have not " _
            & "been saved to the database. " & ControlChars.CrLf _
            & "If you continue, these changes will be lost." _
            & ControlChars.CrLf & "Continue?", "Confirm Exit", _
              MessageBoxButtons.YesNo, MessageBoxIcon.Question)
        If iResult = DialogResult.No Then
            e.Cancel = True
        End If
    End If
End Sub

End Class
```

Figure 7-11   The code for the Vendor Maintenance program (part 5 of 5)

How to use relationships

If a dataset contains two or more tables, you can define relationships between those tables by creating data relation objects. Then, the data relations can be used to work with the rows in the related tables. In the topics that follow, you'll learn how to define and work with relationships.

How to define a relationship

You define a relationship between a unique key in one table and a foreign key in another table. The table with the unique key is called the *parent table* or *master table*, and the table with the foreign key is called the *child table* or *detail table*. The relationship itself is called a *parent/child relationship*.

As its name implies, a parent/child relationship typically identifies all of the rows in the child table that are related to a single row in the parent table. This is similar to the one-to-many relationships you learned about in chapter 1 that are supported by relational databases, and it's the type of relationship I'll focus on in this chapter. You should know, however, that ADO.NET also lets you create the equivalent of many-to-many relationships. You'll learn more about that in chapter 9.

Chapter 9 also presents three different techniques you can use to define a relationship. In this chapter, I'll show you just one of those techniques, which is to use the XML Designer. Figure 7-12 presents this designer and the dialog box that's displayed for defining a relationship.

To display the XML Designer for a dataset, you can double-click on the schema file for the dataset in the Solution Explorer. When you do, the definitions of all of the tables in the dataset are displayed in the designer window. Then, to create a relationship between two tables, you can drag from the bar at the left side of the parent table to the child table to display the Edit Relation dialog box.

If you display the Edit Relation dialog box using this technique, most of the settings should be the way you want them. If the parent table has more than one unique key, however, you may have to select the correct key from the Key drop-down list. When you select a key, the key fields are displayed in the left side of the Fields box. Then, you can select the correct foreign key fields from the drop-down lists in the right side of this box. You can also create a new unique key by clicking on the New button.

When you create a data relation using the Edit Relation dialog box, a foreign key constraint is created in the child table if it doesn't already exist. The dataset properties at the bottom of this dialog box determine how this constraint works. You'll learn more about these properties in chapter 9.

The XML Designer with a relationship between Vendors and Invoices

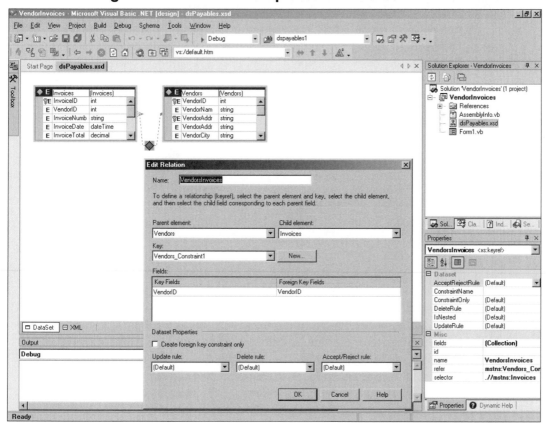

Concepts

- A data relation object represents a relationship between a *parent table*, also called a *master table*, and a *child table*, also called a *detail table*. A *parent/child relationship* is based on a unique key in the parent table and a foreign key in the child table.

- If the unique key and foreign key identified by a relationship don't already exist, they're created automatically when the data relation object is created.

How to define a relationship using the XML Designer

- Double-click on the schema file for the dataset in the Solution Explorer to display the XML Designer. Then, drag from the left side of the parent table to the child table to display the Edit Relation dialog box.

- Check that the parent and child tables, the unique key, and the key fields are correct and the relation name is what you want. Then, click the OK button to create the relationship.

Note

- See chapter 9 for more information on defining relationships.

Figure 7-12   How to define a relationship

How to use a relationship with a data grid

After you define a relationship, you can use it within a data grid to display parent and child rows. After I defined the relationship between the Vendors and Invoices tables in figure 7-12, for example, I used it to create the form shown in figure 7-13. As you can see, this form contains a data grid that displays the names of all of the vendors in the Vendors table. It also provides for displaying information about the invoices for each vendor. Note that this feature is provided automatically by the data grid when its source of data is a parent table. In this case, the source of data is the Vendors table.

When this form is first displayed, all of the Vendors are listed in the data grid and a plus sign appears in the row header of each row. If you click on one of these plus signs, a link appears that identifies the available relationship. This is illustrated by the first form shown in this figure. Then, you can click on this link to display the child rows for that parent row as illustrated by the second form.

To customize the display for the parent and child rows in a data table, you can define a separate table style for each table. The data grid in this figure, for example, has one table style that defines the layout of the data in the Vendors table and one that defines the layout of the data in the Invoices table. Note that the DataMember property of each table style should be set to the name of the table, not the name of the relationship. The DataMember properties for the styles in this figure, for example, are set to Vendors and Invoices.

You should notice in the second form that when the child rows are displayed, the information from the parent row is displayed above the column headers for the child rows, which is usually what you want. If you want to hide this information, however, you can click on the rightmost icon in the data grid's caption bar. You can return to the display of the parent rows by clicking on the leftmost icon in the caption bar.

You can also set the source of data for a data grid to a data relation. Then, you can display the parent rows in another control and display just the child rows in the data grid. For example, suppose I used a combo box to list the vendor names instead of including them in the data grid in this figure. Then, I could display the invoices for a selected vendor in the data grid by setting its DataMember property to the VendorsInvoices data relation. Note that this relation is listed under the Vendors table, so the property would be set as Vendors.VendorsInvoices. You'll see a program that uses this technique in just a moment. But first, I want to present some of the properties and methods of data relations that you can use to work with relationships through code.

A data grid that displays rows from a parent table

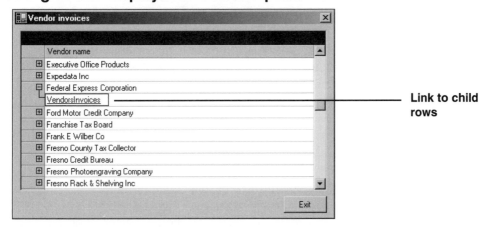

Link to child rows

The same data grid displays child rows for a parent row

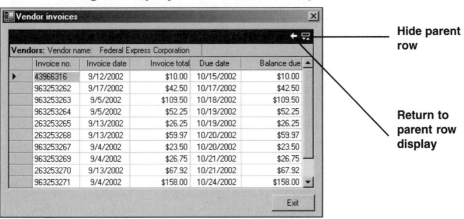

Hide parent row

Return to parent row display

Description

- If the source of data for a data grid is the parent table in a parent/child relationship, the data grid automatically provides for displaying the child rows in that relationship.

- To display the child rows for a parent row, click on the plus sign to the left of the parent row, then click on the relationship link that's displayed.

- When child rows are displayed, you can use the icons at the right side of the caption bar to return to the parent row display and to hide or show the data in the parent row.

- When a data grid displays both parent and child rows, you can define separate styles for each table. The DataMember property for each style should be set to the name of the table, not the name of the relationship.

- You can also display child rows in a data grid whose parent row is determined by another control, such as a combo box control. To do that, set the DataMember property to the name of the relationship that identifies the child rows.

Figure 7-13   How to use a relationship with a data grid

How to work with relationships through code

When you use a relationship within a data grid as shown in the previous figure, the data grid handles the details of working with the relationship. If you want to use a relationship with other controls, however, you'll have to work with the data relation object that defines it. Figure 7-14 presents some of the properties you can use to do that. It also presents the methods of a data row that you can use to get the rows related to a parent or child row.

The data relation objects defined for a dataset are stored in a collection within the dataset. To access this collection, you use the Relations property of the dataset. This is illustrated by the first example in this figure. Here, a For Each...Next statement is used to loop through the data relations in the DsPayables1 dataset. Then, for each data relation, the ParentTable and ChildTable properties are used to get these tables, and the TableName property of each table is used to get the table name. These names are then formatted and added to a list box. The result is a list box that displays all the relationships in the dataset.

The second example shows how you can use the GetChildRows method of a data row to get the child rows for a parent row. This is the method you'll use most often when you work with relationships through code. Notice that it returns the child rows in an array. Then, you can use a loop like the one in this example to work with the items in that array. Although this illustration is simple, it should help you understand the basic technique for working with related tables through code.

In this case, a relationship exists between the Vendors and Invoices tables as in previous examples. Then, when the user selects a vendor from a combo box, the GetChildRows method is used to get the invoices for that vendor. Notice that the name of the relationship is passed as an argument to this method. After the child rows are retrieved, a loop is used to add the invoice number for each invoice to a list box.

Common properties of a DataRelation object

Property	Description
ChildColumns	Gets an array of data column objects that includes the child columns in the relationship.
ChildTable	Gets the child table for the relationship.
DataSet	Gets the dataset that the relation belongs to.
ParentColumns	Gets an array of data column objects that includes the parent columns in the relationship.
ParentTable	Gets the parent table for the relationship.
RelationName	Gets or sets the name of the relationship.

DataRow methods for working with relationships

Method	Description
GetChildRows	Returns an array of data rows that contains the child rows for a parent row.
GetParentRow	Returns the data row that is the parent row of a child row.
GetParentRows	Returns an array of data rows that contains the parent rows for a child row.

Code that lists the data relations in a dataset

```
Dim drRelation As DataRelation
For Each drRelation In DsPayables1.Relations
    lstRelations.Items.Add(drRelation.ParentTable.TableName _
        & " to " & drRelation.ChildTable.TableName)
Next
```

Code that adds the invoice numbers for a vendor to a list box

```
Private Sub cboVendors_SelectedIndexChanged _
        (ByVal sender As System.Object, ByVal e As System.EventArgs) _
        Handles cboVendors.SelectedIndexChanged
    Dim drVendor As dsPayables.VendorsRow
    drVendor = DsPayables1.Vendors.FindByVendorID(cboVendors.SelectedValue)
    lstInvoices.Items.Clear()
    Dim drInvoice As dsPayables.InvoicesRow
    For Each drInvoice In drVendor.GetChildRows("VendorsInvoices")
        lstInvoices.Items.Add(drInvoice.InvoiceNumber)
    Next
End Sub
```

Description

- To refer to the collection of data relations in a dataset, use the Relations property of the dataset. To refer to a specific relation within the collection, use the relation name or its index number.

- You can specify a relationship on the GetChildRows, GetParentRow, or GetParentRows methods using either the relationship name as shown above or a data relation object.

Figure 7-14   How to work with relationships through code

An Invoice Display form that uses relationships

Figure 7-15 presents another form that uses relationships. Like the form you saw in figure 7-13, this form uses a relationship between the Vendors and Invoices tables that's based on the VendorID columns in those tables. In addition, it uses a relationship between the Invoices and InvoiceLineItems tables that's based on the InvoiceID columns in those tables.

As you can see, this form lets the user select a vendor from a combo box at the top of the form. Then, it displays the invoices for that vendor in a data grid. The data grid, in turn, lets the user display the line items for each invoice.

Because this form uses bound controls, it's relatively easy to develop. In fact, the hardest part of developing this form is defining the table and column styles for the Invoices and InvoiceLineItems tables. In contrast, little code is required to implement this form, as you'll see next.

The design of the Invoice Display form

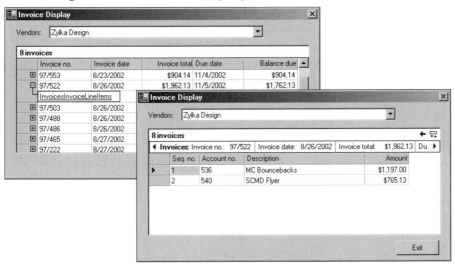

The Select statements for the data adapters

Data adapter	Select statement
daVendors	`Select VendorID, VendorName From Vendors` `Order By VendorName`

daInvoices	`Select InvoiceID, VendorID, InvoiceNumber,`
	`    InvoiceDate, InvoiceTotal, InvoiceDueDate,`
	`    InvoiceTotal - PaymentTotal - CreditTotal As BalanceDue`
	`From Invoices Order By InvoiceDate`

daLineItems	`Select InvoiceID, InvoiceSequence, AccountNo,`
	`    InvoiceLineItemAmount, InvoiceLineItemDescription`
	`From InvoiceLineItems Order By InvoiceID`

Property settings for the combo box and data grid

Property	Combo box	Data grid
Name	cboVendors	grdInvoices
DataSource	DsPayables1.Vendors	DsPayables1
DisplayMember	VendorName	n/a
DataMember	n/a	VendorsInvoices

Description

- Two relationships are defined for this program. The Vendors and Invoices tables are related by their VendorID columns, and the Invoices and InvoiceLineItems tables are related by their InvoiceID columns.

- When the user selects a vendor from the combo box, the invoices for that vendor are displayed in the data grid. The user can click on the plus sign to the left of an invoice and then on the link that's displayed to display the line items for that invoice.

Figure 7-15   An Invoice Display form that uses relationships

The code for the Invoice Display program

Figure 7-16 presents the code for the Invoice Display program. When this program first starts, the Load procedure fills the Vendors, Invoices, and InvoiceLineItems tables. Note that because relationships, and thus foreign key constraints, are defined between these tables, the parent tables must be filled before the child tables. Otherwise, an error will occur when the program tries to store a row in a child table that doesn't have a row in the parent table.

Next, the Load procedure sets the binding manager base to the Vendors table. Then, it calls a procedure named DisplayInvoiceCount. This procedure determines how many rows are related to the current vendor and displays the count in the caption bar of the data grid. To do that, it uses the GetChildRows method of the vendor row to get an array of invoice rows. Notice that the vendor row is identified by the SelectedIndex property of the Vendors combo box. When the form is first loaded, this property will have a value of zero, so the first row in the Vendors table will be retrieved. Once the child rows are retrieved, the GetUpperBound method of the array is used to determine the size of the array, and 1 is added to the size to determine the number of items it contains. Notice that this is all done in a single statement, and the result is assigned to an integer variable. Although you could define variables to hold the vendors row and the invoices array, that's not necessary since these variables aren't used anywhere else in the program.

When the user selects a vendor from the Vendors combo box, the procedure that responds to this event starts by positioning the Vendors table to that vendor. That causes the invoices for the selected vendor to be displayed automatically in the data grid. Then, the user can display the line items for those invoices using the links that are provided by the data grid. This procedure also calls the DisplayInvoiceCount procedure to display a count of those invoices.

An Invoice Display program with relationships

```
Imports System.Data.SqlClient
Public Class Form1
    Inherits System.Windows.Forms.Form

    Dim bmbVendors As BindingManagerBase

    Private Sub Form1_Load(ByVal sender As System.Object, _
            ByVal e As System.EventArgs) Handles MyBase.Load
        Me.FillTables()
        bmbVendors = Me.BindingContext(DsPayables1, "Vendors")
        Me.DisplayInvoiceCount()
    End Sub

    Private Sub FillTables()
        Try
            conPayables.Open()
            daVendors.Fill(DsPayables1)
            daInvoices.Fill(DsPayables1)
            daLineItems.Fill(DsPayables1)
        Catch eSql As SqlException
            MessageBox.Show(eSql.Message, "SQL Server error")
        Finally
            conPayables.Close()
        End Try
    End Sub

    Private Sub cboVendors_SelectedIndexChanged _
            (ByVal sender As System.Object, ByVal e As System.EventArgs) _
            Handles cboVendors.SelectedIndexChanged
        bmbVendors.Position = cboVendors.SelectedIndex
        Me.DisplayInvoiceCount()
    End Sub

    Private Sub DisplayInvoiceCount()
        Dim iInvoiceCount As Integer
        iInvoiceCount = DsPayables1.Vendors(cboVendors.SelectedIndex). _
            GetChildRows("VendorsInvoices").GetUpperBound(0) + 1
        grdInvoices.CaptionText = iInvoiceCount _
            & " invoice" & IIf(iInvoiceCount = 1, "", "s")
    End Sub

    Private Sub btnExit_Click(ByVal sender As System.Object, _
            ByVal e As System.EventArgs) Handles btnExit.Click
        Me.Close()
    End Sub

End Class
```

Figure 7-16   The code for the Invoice Display program

Perspective

The skills you've learned in this chapter are skills that you'll use frequently as you develop professional business applications. With these skills, you now have additional options for handling various application requirements. The technique you choose for a specific application often depends on a variety of factors, including system efficiency, ease of use, and number of users. Before you begin developing an application, then, you should consider your choices carefully to be sure you're using the technique that's most appropriate for the situation.

Terms

data view
sort expression
filter expression
wildcard
sort key
parameterized query
parameter
named variable
parent table
master table
child table
detail table
parent/child relationship

Section 3

Other database programming skills

With the basic skills you now have, the chapters in this section take you deeper into the programming for database objects so you can handle more demanding program requirements and produce more professional applications. To start, chapter 8 teaches you how to create command objects to execute SQL statements and stored procedures. It also teaches you how to work with command objects within transactions. Then, chapter 9 shows three ways you can create dataset schemas other than using the Data Adapter Configuration Wizard.

Chapter 10 shows you how you can develop and use database classes. When you use database classes, all of the code for handling the database operations for an application is separated from the code that handles the user interface. This technique is particularly useful for developing web applications, as you'll see in chapter 13, but it can also be used to develop Windows applications.

Finally, chapter 11 shows you the code for a complete order entry application that is similar to those you'll find in many businesses. This application will illustrate how you can combine many of the techniques you've learned into a single application. It will also give you a greater understanding of the complexities involved in developing database applications with ADO.NET.

8

How to work with data commands

When you use a data adapter to work with the data in a dataset, the data adapter handles the transfer of data to and from the database. To do that, it uses data commands that contain Select, Insert, Update, and Delete statements. In some cases, though, it doesn't make sense to use a dataset or a data adapter. Then, you'll need to know how to work with data commands directly to retrieve and update data. That's what you'll learn in this chapter.

How to work with queries that return a result set

When you execute a command object that contains a Select statement, the command object returns the result set in a data reader object. Then, to work with that result set, you use properties and methods of the data reader object. You'll learn how to do that in the topics that follow.

How to create and work with a data reader

Figure 8-1 presents the basic skills for creating and working with a data reader. To create a data reader, you use the ExecuteReader method of a command object that contains a Select statement. Notice that when you execute this method, you can specify a behavior. The behavior you specify must be a member of the CommandBehavior enumeration. Some of the most common members of this enumeration are listed in this figure. You can use these members to simplify your code or to improve the efficiency of your application.

After you create a data reader, you can use the properties and methods shown in this figure to work with it. To retrieve the next row of data in the result set, for example, you use the Read method. Note that you must execute the Read method to retrieve the first row of data. It's not retrieved automatically when the data reader is created.

To retrieve a column from a data reader, you use the Item property. Like many of the other objects you've seen previously, the Item property is the default property of a data reader. Because of that, you can omit it.

The code example in this figure illustrates how you use a data reader. For the purpose of this example, you can assume that the data command contains a Select statement that retrieves data from the Invoices table. Then, this code creates a data reader object and opens the connection used by the data command. Next, it executes the ExecuteReader method of the command to retrieve the data specified by the Select statement. Because the CloseConnection behavior is included on this method, the connection will be closed automatically when the data reader is closed. The ExecuteReader method also opens the data reader and positions it before the first row in the result set.

Next, a Do loop is used to loop through the rows in the result set. The condition on this statement executes the Read method of the data reader. This works because the Read method returns a Boolean value that indicates whether the result set contains additional rows. As long as this condition is true, the program processes the row that was retrieved. In this case, the program gets the value of the InvoiceNumber column and adds it to the list of items in a list box. After all of the rows have been processed, the data reader is closed.

Although most data commands execute a single Select statement and return a single result set, a command can also execute two or more Select statements and return two or more result sets. To combine two or more Select statements,

Two ways to create a SqlDataReader object

```
sqlDataReader = sqlCommand.ExecuteReader()
sqlDataReader = sqlCommand.ExecuteReader(behavior)
```

Common CommandBehavior enumeration members

Member	Description
CloseConnection	Closes the connection when the data reader is closed.
Default	Equivalent to specifying no command behavior.
SingleResult	Only a single result set is returned.
SingleRow	Only a single row is returned.

Common properties and methods of a SqlDataReader object

Property	Description
IsClosed	Gets a value that indicates if the data reader is closed.
Item	Gets the value of the column with the specified name or position in the row.

Method	Description
Close	Closes the data reader. If the command executed a stored procedure that included output parameters or a return value, this method also sets these values.
NextResult	Advances the data reader to the next result set and returns a Boolean value that indicates whether there are additional result sets. Can be used when a command executes two or more Select statements.
Read	Retrieves the next row and returns a Boolean value that indicates whether there are additional rows.

Code that uses a data reader to populate a list box with invoice numbers

```
Dim rdrInvoices As SqlDataReader
conPayables.Open()
rdrInvoices = cmdInvoices.ExecuteReader(CommandBehavior.CloseConnection)
Do While rdrInvoices.Read()
    lstInvoices.Items.Add(rdrInvoices("InvoiceNumber"))
Loop
rdrInvoices.Close()
```

Description

- A data reader lets you read rows from the result set defined by a command object. To create a data reader object, you use the ExecuteReader method of the command. Before you execute this method, you must open the connection that's used by the data reader.

- The data reader is opened automatically when it's created. While it's open, no other data readers can be opened on the same connection.

- When you first create a data reader, it's positioned before the first row in the result set. To retrieve the first row, you have to execute the Read method.

- You can specify two or more command behavior members by combining them using the And operator.

Figure 8-1   How to create and work with a data reader

you code a semicolon between them. For example, suppose you want to retrieve both vendor and invoice information for a selected vendor. To do that, you could code two Select statements in a single command like this:

```
Select VendorName, VendorAddress1, VendorAddress2, VendorCity,
VendorState, VendorZipCode From Vendors Where VendorID = @VendorID1;
Select InvoiceNumber, InvoiceDate, InvoiceTotal From Invoices
Where VendorID = @VendorID2
```

To process the two result sets returned by these statements, you would read the vendor row in the first result set. Then, you would use the NextResult method to move to the result set that contains the invoices, and you would read the rows in that result set. Of course, you could also store the two Select statements in separate commands and process them separately.

How to improve the efficiency of column lookups

When you retrieve a column from a data reader using the column name as shown in the previous figure, the data reader has to search for the appropriate column. To make the retrieval operation more efficient, you can specify the position of the column instead of its name. One way to do that is to use a literal value. For example, you can use a statement like this to retrieve the value of the first column in the Invoices data reader:

```
sInvoiceNumber = rdrInvoices(0)
```

This technique is errorprone, though, because you can easily specify the wrong position for a column. In addition, if the columns that are retrieved change, you may have to modify your code to accommodate the new column positions.

An alternative is to use the GetOrdinal method of the data reader to get the position, or *ordinal*, of a column with the specified name. Then, you can assign the result of that method to a variable and use the variable to refer to the column. To understand how this works, take a look at the code example in figure 8-2. Here, the command contains a Select statement that will return a result set with two columns. The first column will contain a vendor name, and the second column will contain the sum of the balances due for all of the vendor's invoices.

After the connection is opened and the ExecuteReader method is executed, the GetOrdinal method is used to get the position of each of the columns. Notice that this method must locate the column using its name just as the statement in the previous figure did. In this case, though, the column is looked up by name only once. Then, within the Do loop that processes the rows in the result set, the columns' ordinals are used.

When you refer to a column using its ordinal, you can also use the other methods listed in this figure. These methods let you specify the type of data that's retrieved. The two columns in the code in this figure, for example, are retrieved using the GetString and GetDecimal methods. This can improve the efficiency of the operation by eliminating unnecessary data conversion.

Common methods for improving the efficiency of column lookups

Method	Description
GetOrdinal	Gets the position of the column with the specified name. The position is zero-based.
GetBoolean	Gets the value of the column at the specified position as a Boolean.
GetDateTime	Gets the value of the column at the specified position as a date and time.
GetDecimal	Gets the value of the column at the specified position as a decimal.
GetInt16	Gets the value of the column at the specified position as a 16-bit signed integer.
GetInt32	Gets the value of the column at the specified position as a 32-bit signed integer.
GetInt64	Gets the value of the column at the specified position as a 64-bit signed integer.
GetString	Gets the value of the column at the specified position as a string.

Code that uses type-specific Get methods and ordinals

```
Dim sCommandText As String = "Select VendorName, " _
    & "Sum(InvoiceTotal - PaymentTotal - CreditTotal) " _
    & "As BalanceDue From Vendors Join Invoices " _
    & "On Vendors.VendorID = Invoices.VendorID " _
    & "Group By VendorName Order By BalanceDue Desc"
Dim cmdInvoices As New SqlCommand(sCommandText, conPayables)

conPayables.Open()
Dim rdrInvoices As SqlDataReader = cmdInvoices.ExecuteReader()
Dim iNameOrd As Integer = rdrInvoices.GetOrdinal("VendorName")
Dim iBalDueOrd As Integer = rdrInvoices.GetOrdinal("BalanceDue")
Do While rdrInvoices.Read()
    sListItem = rdrInvoices.GetString(iNameOrd).PadRight(40) _
            & FormatCurrency _
                (rdrInvoices.GetDecimal(iBalDueOrd)).PadLeft(11)
    lstInvoices.Items.Add(sListItem)
Loop
rdrInvoices.Close()
conPayables.Close()
```

Description

- Instead of retrieving a column by name, you can retrieve it by its position, or *ordinal*, in the row. That improves the efficiency of the retrieval operation because the data reader can retrieve the column directly rather than looking for it by name.

- If you know that the position of a column won't change, you can specify the position as a literal value. Otherwise, you can use the GetOrdinal method to get its position.

- When you use the Item property to get the value of a column, the value is returned with the Object data type. To improve efficiency, you can use one of the type-specific Get methods to retrieve a column value with the appropriate type.

Figure 8-2   How to improve the efficiency of column lookups

A Vendor Invoices form that uses a data reader

Figure 8-3 presents the design and property settings for a form that uses a data reader. This form lets the user select a vendor name from a combo box and then displays information about the invoices for that vendor in a list box. To get the invoice information, it uses a data reader. In contrast, the vendor information is retrieved using a data adapter. That way, the Vendors combo box can be bound to the Vendors table to make lookup operations easier to perform.

The code for the Vendor Invoices program

Figure 8-4 presents the code for the Vendor Invoices program. If you study this code, you'll see that the difficult part isn't using the data reader; it's formatting the invoice data for display in the list box. If you need more information on the string-handling functions and methods that are used in this program, you can refer to online help or to *Murach's Beginning Visual Basic .NET*.

When this program starts, the Load procedure fills the Vendors table, creates the command that will be used to retrieve invoices, and then displays the invoices for the first vendor. The DisplayInvoices procedure is also executed each time the user selects a different vendor. It starts by calling a procedure named FormatHeadings, which clears the list box and adds the column headings you saw in the previous figure. Then, it sets the VendorID parameter of the Invoices command to the Vendor ID of the selected vendor. Finally, it executes the GetInvoices procedure, which contains the main processing for this program.

The GetInvoices procedure, shown on page 2 of this listing, starts by opening the connection and creating the data reader. Then, it uses a Do loop to retrieve and format the rows in the result set. Notice that I used the PadRight and PadLeft methods to align the columns in the list box. Also notice that, for simplicity, I used column names to retrieve the value of each column. To make this program more efficient, though, you could use ordinals as described in figure 8-2.

After all of the rows are processed, the data reader and connection are closed. Because the CloseConnection behavior wasn't specified on the ExecuteReader method, the connection must be closed explicitly. That's done in the Finally clause of the Try...Catch statement. That way, if an error occurs during the processing of the data reader, the connection will still be closed. This also closes the data reader if it's still open.

The design of the Vendor Invoices form

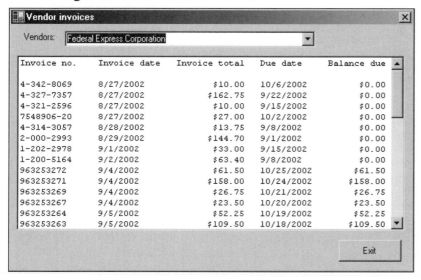

The Select statement for the Vendors data adapter

```
Select VendorID, VendorName From Vendors Order By VendorName
```

The Select statement for the Invoices command

```
Select InvoiceNumber, InvoiceDate, InvoiceTotal, InvoiceDueDate,
    InvoiceTotal - PaymentTotal - CreditTotal As BalanceDue
From Invoices
Where VendorID = @VendorID Order By InvoiceDate
```

The property settings for the Vendors combo box

Property	Description
DataSource	DsPayables1.Vendors
DisplayMember	VendorName
ValueMember	VendorID

Description

- The Vendor Invoices form lets the user select a vendor from a combo box and then formats and displays the invoices for that vendor in a list box.

- The Vendors combo box is bound to the Vendors table that's defined by the Vendors data adapter. That way, the value of the VendorID column can be used to look up the invoices for a vendor.

- A data reader is used to process the rows in the result set retrieved by the Invoices command. The Select statement for this command includes a parameter that identifies the vendor whose invoices are to be retrieved.

Figure 8-3   A Vendor Invoices form that uses a data reader

A Vendor Invoices program that uses a data reader Page 1

```
Imports System.Data.SqlClient
Public Class Form1
    Inherits System.Windows.Forms.Form

    Dim sListItem As String
    Dim cmdInvoices As New SqlCommand()

    Private Sub Form1_Load(ByVal sender As Object, _
            ByVal e As System.EventArgs) Handles MyBase.Load
        Me.FillVendorsTable()
        Me.CreateInvoiceCommand()
        Me.DisplayInvoices()
    End Sub

    Private Sub FillVendorsTable()
        Try
            daVendors.Fill(DsPayables1)
        Catch eSql As SqlException
            MessageBox.Show(eSql.Message, "SQL Server error")
        End Try
    End Sub

    Private Sub CreateInvoiceCommand()
        cmdInvoices.Connection = conPayables
        cmdInvoices.CommandText = "Select InvoiceNumber, InvoiceDate, " _
            & "InvoiceTotal, InvoiceDueDate, InvoiceTotal - PaymentTotal " _
            & "- CreditTotal As BalanceDue From Invoices " _
            & "Where VendorID = @VendorID Order By InvoiceDate"
        Dim prmVendorID As New SqlParameter("@VendorID", SqlDbType.Int)
        cmdInvoices.Parameters.Add(prmVendorID)
    End Sub

    Private Sub cboVendors_SelectedIndexChanged _
            (ByVal sender As System.Object, ByVal e As System.EventArgs) _
            Handles cboVendors.SelectedIndexChanged
        Me.DisplayInvoices()
    End Sub

    Private Sub DisplayInvoices()
        Me.FormatHeadings()
        cmdInvoices.Parameters("@VendorID").Value = cboVendors.SelectedValue
        Me.GetInvoices()
    End Sub

    Private Sub FormatHeadings()
        lstInvoices.Items.Clear()
        sListItem = "Invoice no." & Space(4) _
                & "Invoice date" & Space(3) & "Invoice total" & Space(3) _
                & "Due date" & Space(5) & "Balance due"
        Me.AddListItem()
        sListItem = ""
        Me.AddListItem()
    End Sub
```

Figure 8-4 The code for the Vendor Invoices program (part 1 of 2)

A Vendor Invoices program that uses a data reader   **Page 2**

```
Private Sub AddListItem()
    lstInvoices.Items.Add(sListItem)
End Sub

Private Sub GetInvoices()
    Try
        conPayables.Open()
        Dim rdrInvoices As SqlDataReader = cmdInvoices.ExecuteReader()
        Do While rdrInvoices.Read()
            sListItem _
                = rdrInvoices("InvoiceNumber").PadRight(15) _
                & FormatDateTime(rdrInvoices("InvoiceDate"), _
                  DateFormat.ShortDate).PadRight(13) _
                & FormatCurrency(rdrInvoices("InvoiceTotal")).PadLeft(15) _
                & Space(3) _
                & FormatDateTime(rdrInvoices("InvoiceDueDate"), _
                  DateFormat.ShortDate).PadRight(12) _
                & FormatCurrency(rdrInvoices("BalanceDue")).PadLeft(12)
            Me.AddListItem()
        Loop
        rdrInvoices.Close()
    Catch eData As DataException
        MessageBox.Show(eData.Message, "ADO.NET error")
    Catch eSql As SqlException
        MessageBox.Show(eSql.Message, "SQL Server error")
    Finally
        conPayables.Close()
    End Try
End Sub

Private Sub btnExit_Click(ByVal sender As System.Object, _
        ByVal e As System.EventArgs) Handles btnExit.Click
    Me.Close()
End Sub

End Class
```

Figure 8-4   The code for the Vendor Invoices program (part 2 of 2)

How to work with queries that don't return a result set

In addition to executing queries that return result sets, you can use a data command to execute queries that return a single value or that perform an action against the database. In the first topic that follows, you'll learn how to use commands for these two purposes. Then, you'll see another version of the Vendor Maintenance program that uses these techniques.

How to execute queries that don't return a result set

The first code example in figure 8-5 shows you how to execute a command that returns a single value, called a *scalar value*. To do that, you execute the ExecuteScalar method of the command. In this case, the command contains a Select statement that retrieves the total balance due for a selected vendor by adding up the balances due of all the vendor's invoices. This type of summary value is often called an *aggregate value*. A scalar value can also be the value of a single column, a calculated value, or any other value that can be retrieved from the database. In the program that follows, for example, you'll see how the ExecuteScalar method is used to retrieve the value of an identity column that's generated for a row that's added to a database.

Before I go on, you should realize that you can use the ExecuteScalar method with a Select statement that retrieves more than one value. In that case, though, the ExecuteScalar method returns only the first value and the others are discarded.

As you know, you can use an Insert, Update, or Delete statement to perform actions against a database. For that reason, these statements are often referred to as *action queries*. To execute an action query, you use the ExecuteNonQuery method of a data command as shown in the second code example in this figure. In this case, the command contains a Delete statement that will delete all of the invoices in the Invoices table that have a balance due of zero. Notice that the ExecuteNonQuery method returns an integer that indicates the number of rows in the database that were affected by the operation. In this case, the value is used to display a message to the user. In other cases, you can use it to check if the operation was successful as you'll see in the program that follows.

Code that creates and executes a command that returns an aggregate value

```
Dim cmdInvoices As New SqlCommand()
cmdInvoices.Connection = conPayables
cmdInvoices.CommandText _
    = "Select Sum(InvoiceTotal - PaymentTotal - CreditTotal) " _
    & "As BalanceDue From Invoices " _
    & "Where VendorID = @VendorID " _
    & "Group By VendorID"
Dim prmVendorID As New SqlParameter("@VendorID", SqlDbType.Int)
cmdInvoices.Parameters.Add(prmVendorID)
.
.
cmdInvoices.Parameters("@VendorID").Value = cboVendors.SelectedValue
conPayables.Open()
Dim dBalanceDue As Decimal = cmdInvoices.ExecuteScalar
conPayables.Close()
```

Code that creates and executes a command that deletes rows

```
Dim iRowCount As Integer
Dim cmdInvoices As New SqlCommand()
cmdInvoices.Connection = conPayables
cmdInvoices.CommandText = "Delete From Invoices " _
    & "Where InvoiceTotal - PaymentTotal - CreditTotal = 0"
conPayables.Open()
Try
    iRowCount = cmdInvoices.ExecuteNonQuery()
    MessageBox.Show(iRowCount & " rows deleted")
Catch eSql As SqlException
    MessageBox.Show(eSql.Message, "SQL Server error")
Finally
    conPayables.Close()
End Try
```

Description

- You use the ExecuteScalar method of a command object to retrieve a single value, called a *scalar value*.

- The value that's returned can be the value of a single column and row in the database, a calculated value, an *aggregate value* that summarizes data in the database, or any other value that can be retrieved from the database.

- If the Select statement returns more than one column or row, only the value in the first column and row is retrieved by the ExecuteScalar method.

- You use the ExecuteNonQuery method of a command object to execute an Insert, Update, or Delete statement, called an *action query*. This method returns an integer that indicates the number of rows that were affected by the query.

- You can also use the ExecuteNonQuery method to execute statements that affect the structure of a database object. For more information, see the documentation for your database management system.

Figure 8-5   How to execute queries that don't return a result set

The code for a Vendor Maintenance program that uses action queries

Figure 8-6 presents another version of the Vendor Maintenance program. Like the program you saw in the last chapter, this program accepts a Vendor ID from the user and then uses a parameterized query to get the data for that vendor. However, this program doesn't store the data in a dataset. Instead, it uses a data reader to read the data into variables. Then, it uses action queries to insert, update, and delete vendor rows. It also uses a query that returns a scalar value to get the Vendor ID for a new vendor. As you can see in this figure, the variables for all of the commands used by this program as well as the variables for the vendor data are defined at the module level.

The Load procedure for the Vendor Maintenance form starts by creating the ADO.NET objects used by the program. I'll describe this code in a moment. Then, it fills the States table, clears the controls on the forms, sets the maintenance buttons, and sets the entry controls. Because you've seen all four of these procedures before, I've omitted them from this listing. If you want to see the code for these procedures and the others that have been omitted, you can refer to figure 7-11.

The procedure that creates the ADO.NET objects starts by setting the Connection and CommandText properties of the command that will be used to retrieve the data for a vendor. Because the Vendor ID will be entered by a user, the Select statement includes a placeholder for a parameter named @VendorID. Then, a parameter object with this name is added to the parameters collection of the command.

The next group of statements sets the properties for the command that will be used to insert a new vendor row. Notice that the Insert statement for this command will include values for each column in the Vendors table that doesn't allow nulls or that doesn't have a default value. The exception is the VendorID column, which will be generated by the database. Because the required values will be entered by the user, the Insert statement will use parameters to provide their values, as you can see here.

The last two statements on the first page of this listing set the Connection and CommandText properties of the command that will be used to retrieve the Vendor ID when a new vendor is added to the database. The Select statement for this command simply returns the value of the @@Identity function. @@Identity is a SQL Server system function that returns the last value that was generated for an identity column on the server.

A Vendor Maintenance program that uses action queries   Page 1

```
Imports System.Data.SqlClient
Public Class Form1
    Inherits System.Windows.Forms.Form

    Dim bLoading As Boolean
    Dim bNewRow As Boolean
    Dim cmdVendorSelect As New SqlCommand()
    Dim cmdVendorInsert As New SqlCommand()
    Dim cmdVendorUpdate As New SqlCommand()
    Dim cmdVendorDelete As New SqlCommand()
    Dim cmdVendorID As New SqlCommand()
    Dim iVendorID As Integer
    Dim sVendorName As String
    Dim sAddress1 As String
    Dim sAddress2 As String
    Dim sCity As String
    Dim sState As String
    Dim sZipCode As String

    Private Sub Form1_Load(ByVal sender As System.Object, _
            ByVal e As System.EventArgs) Handles MyBase.Load
        Me.CreateADONETObjects()
        Me.FillStatesTable()
        Me.ClearControls()
        Me.SetMaintenanceButtons(True)
        Me.SetEntryControls(False)
    End Sub

    Private Sub CreateADONETObjects()
        cmdVendorSelect.Connection = conPayables
        cmdVendorSelect.CommandText _
            = "Select VendorID, VendorName, VendorAddress1, " _
            & "VendorAddress2, VendorCity, VendorState, VendorZipCode " _
            & "From Vendors " _
            & "Where VendorID = @VendorID"
        cmdVendorSelect.Parameters.Add("@VendorID", SqlDbType.Int)

        cmdVendorInsert.Connection = conPayables
        cmdVendorInsert.CommandText _
            = "Insert Into Vendors " _
            & "(VendorName, VendorAddress1, VendorAddress2, " _
            & "VendorCity, VendorState, VendorZipCode) " _
            & "Values (@NewName, @NewAddress1, @NewAddress2, " _
            & "@NewCity, @NewState, @NewZipCode)"
        With cmdVendorInsert.Parameters
            .Add("@NewName", SqlDbType.VarChar)
            .Add("@NewAddress1", SqlDbType.VarChar)
            .Add("@NewAddress2", SqlDbType.VarChar)
            .Add("@NewCity", SqlDbType.VarChar)
            .Add("@NewState", SqlDbType.Char)
            .Add("@NewZipCode", SqlDbType.Char)
        End With

        cmdVendorID.Connection = conPayables
        cmdVendorID.CommandText = "Select @@Identity"
```

Figure 8-6   The code for the Vendor Maintenance program (part 1 of 6)

The next group of statements in this procedure sets the properties for the command that will be used to update a vendor row. As you can see, the Set clause of the Update statement assigns new values to each of the columns in the vendor row using parameters. Then, the Where clause starts by specifying the Vendor ID for the vendor to be updated. Next, it checks that none of the columns that are being updated have changed since the row was retrieved. In other words, this statement provides for concurrency checking. To do that, it uses parameters that will be assigned the original values of the columns. Finally, all of the parameters used by this statement are added to the parameters collection of the command.

The last group of statements in this procedure sets the properties for the command that will be used to delete a vendor row. Like the Update statement, this Delete statement provides for concurrency checking.

A Vendor Maintenance program that uses action queries   Page 2

```
        cmdVendorUpdate.Connection = conPayables
        cmdVendorUpdate.CommandText _
            = "Update Vendors " _
            & "Set VendorName = @NewName, " _
            & "VendorAddress1 = @NewAddress1, " _
            & "VendorAddress2 = @NewAddress2, " _
            & "VendorCity = @NewCity, " _
            & "VendorState = @NewState, " _
            & "VendorZipCode = @NewZipCode " _
            & "Where VendorID = @VendorID " _
            & "And VendorName = @OldName " _
            & "And (VendorAddress1 = @OldAddress1 " _
            & "Or (@OldAddress1 = '' And VendorAddress1 Is Null)) " _
            & "And (VendorAddress2 = @OldAddress2 " _
            & "Or (@OldAddress2 = '' And VendorAddress2 Is Null)) " _
            & "And VendorCity = @OldCity " _
            & "And VendorState = @OldState " _
            & "And VendorZipCode = @OldZipCode "
        With cmdVendorUpdate.Parameters
            .Add("@NewName", SqlDbType.VarChar)
            .Add("@NewAddress1", SqlDbType.VarChar)
            .Add("@NewAddress2", SqlDbType.VarChar)
            .Add("@NewCity", SqlDbType.VarChar)
            .Add("@NewState", SqlDbType.Char)
            .Add("@NewZipCode", SqlDbType.Char)
            .Add("@VendorID", SqlDbType.Int)
            .Add("@OldName", SqlDbType.VarChar)
            .Add("@OldAddress1", SqlDbType.VarChar)
            .Add("@OldAddress2", SqlDbType.VarChar)
            .Add("@OldCity", SqlDbType.VarChar)
            .Add("@OldState", SqlDbType.Char)
            .Add("@OldZipCode", SqlDbType.Char)
        End With

        cmdVendorDelete.Connection = conPayables
        cmdVendorDelete.CommandText _
            = "Delete From Vendors " _
            & "Where VendorID = @VendorID " _
            & "And VendorName = @OldName " _
            & "And (VendorAddress1 = @OldAddress1 " _
            & "Or (@OldAddress1 = '' And VendorAddress1 Is Null)) " _
            & "And (VendorAddress2 = @OldAddress2 " _
            & "Or (@OldAddress2 = '' And VendorAddress2 Is Null)) " _
            & "And VendorCity = @OldCity " _
            & "And VendorState = @OldState " _
            & "And VendorZipCode = @OldZipCode "
        With cmdVendorDelete.Parameters
            .Add("@VendorID", SqlDbType.Int)
            .Add("@OldName", SqlDbType.VarChar)
            .Add("@OldAddress1", SqlDbType.VarChar)
            .Add("@OldAddress2", SqlDbType.VarChar)
            .Add("@OldCity", SqlDbType.VarChar)
            .Add("@OldState", SqlDbType.Char)
            .Add("@OldZipCode", SqlDbType.Char)
        End With
    End Sub
```

Figure 8-6   The code for the Vendor Maintenance program (part 2 of 6)

When the user clicks on the Get Vendor button, the Click event procedure for that button starts by checking that the user entered a Vendor ID. If so, the @VendorID parameter of the Select command is set to that value. Then, the connection is opened and the ExecuteReader method of the Select command is used to retrieve the vendor data into a data reader. Notice that this method specifies the SingleRow behavior since the Select statement will return at most one row.

Next, the Read method of the data reader is used as the condition on an If statement to determine if a row was returned. If so, the GetVendorData procedure is called. This procedure gets the data from the data reader and stores it in the module-level variables. Then, the SetEntryControls procedure is called to enable the entry controls so the user can modify the vendor data, and the FillControls procedure is called to assign the values in the module-level variables to the form controls. Finally, the focus is moved to the Name text box. If a vendor row was not returned, the procedure clears the controls, disables the entry controls, displays an error message, and moves the focus to the Vendor ID text box so the user can enter another Vendor ID. In either case, the data reader and the connection are closed.

A Vendor Maintenance program that uses action queries   **Page 3**

```
Private Sub btnGetVendor_Click(ByVal sender As System.Object, _
        ByVal e As System.EventArgs) Handles btnGetVendor.Click
    If txtVendorID.Text <> "" Then
        cmdVendorSelect.Parameters("@VendorID").Value = txtVendorID.Text
        Try
            conPayables.Open()
            Dim rdrVendor As SqlDataReader _
                = cmdVendorSelect.ExecuteReader(CommandBehavior.SingleRow)
            If rdrVendor.Read Then
                Me.GetVendorData(rdrVendor)
                Me.SetEntryControls(True)
                Me.FillControls()
                txtName.Focus()
            Else
                Me.ClearControls()
                Me.SetEntryControls(False)
                MessageBox.Show("Vendor row not found.", "Entry error")
                txtVendorID.Focus()
            End If
            rdrVendor.Close()
        Catch eData As DataException
            MessageBox.Show(eData.Message, "ADO.NET error")
        Catch eSql As SqlException
            MessageBox.Show(eSql.Message, "SQL Server error")
        Finally
            conPayables.Close()
        End Try
    Else
        MessageBox.Show("You must enter a Vendor ID.", "Entry error")
        txtVendorID.Focus()
    End If
End Sub

Private Sub GetVendorData(ByVal rdr As SqlDataReader)
    iVendorID = rdr("VendorID")
    sVendorName = rdr("VendorName")
    sAddress1 = rdr("VendorAddress1").ToString
    sAddress2 = rdr("VendorAddress2").ToString
    sCity = rdr("VendorCity")
    sState = rdr("VendorState")
    sZipCode = rdr("VendorZipCode")
End Sub

Private Sub FillControls()
    bLoading = True
    txtName.Text = sVendorName
    txtAddressLine1.Text = sAddress1
    txtAddressLine2.Text = sAddress2
    txtCity.Text = sCity
    cboStates.SelectedValue = sState
    txtZipCode.Text = sZipCode
    bLoading = False
End Sub
```

Figure 8-6   The code for the Vendor Maintenance program (part 3 of 6)

The procedure that's executed when the user clicks on the Add button is similar to the procedure you saw in the last chapter. The only difference is that this procedure doesn't clear the dataset, since the dataset isn't used to store the vendor row in this program.

When the user clicks on the Update button, the Update procedure starts by checking that the data is valid. Then, it checks if a new row is being added. If so, it calls the SetNewValues procedure. This procedure assigns values to the parameters used by the Insert command. I'll describe it in a moment. Notice that the Insert command is passed as an argument to this procedure. That way, the procedure can also be used to set the parameters for an update operation, as you'll see in a moment.

After the parameter values are assigned, the Update procedure opens the connection and uses the ExecuteNonQuery method to execute the Insert command. In addition, it uses the ExecuteScalar method to execute the command that returns the value of the Vendor ID column for the new vendor. This value is assigned to the Vendor ID text box so that it's displayed on the form.

Next, the procedure closes the connection and sets the bNewRow variable to False. Then, it calls the SaveNewData procedure to save the data for the new vendor. I'll describe this procedure and explain why it's necessary to save this data in a moment.

If a row is being modified, the Update procedure starts by calling the SetNewValues procedure to set the values of the parameters that will be used to update the vendor data. Then, it calls the SetOldValues procedure. This procedure sets the values of the parameters that will be used for concurrency checking. Like the SetNewValues procedure, this procedure accepts a command as an argument. That way, it can be used by the Delete command, which also provides for concurrency checking.

Next, the connection is opened, the query is executed, and the connection is closed. Then, the value that's returned by the ExecuteNonQuery method, which is stored in the iRowCount variable, is tested to see if it's equal to zero. If it is, it means that the concurrency checking failed and the row wasn't updated. In that case, an error message is displayed and the form is set for the user to retrieve another vendor. Of course, this is just one way you can handle a concurrency error. Another way would be to automatically retrieve the row again so that the user can reapply the changes.

If the row was updated, the procedure continues by setting the maintenance buttons so that the user can perform additional operations. Then, the SaveNewData procedure is called to save the updated data for the vendor in the module-level variables.

A Vendor Maintenance program that uses action queries   Page 4

```
Private Sub btnAdd_Click(ByVal sender As System.Object, _
        ByVal e As System.EventArgs) Handles btnAdd.Click
    txtVendorID.Text = ""
    bNewRow = True
    Me.ClearControls()
    Me.SetMaintenanceButtons(False)
    Me.SetEntryControls(True)
    txtName.Focus()
End Sub

Private Sub btnUpdate_Click(ByVal sender As System.Object, _
        ByVal e As System.EventArgs) Handles btnUpdate.Click
    If ValidData() Then
        If bNewRow Then
            Me.SetNewValues(cmdVendorInsert)
            Try
                conPayables.Open()
                cmdVendorInsert.ExecuteNonQuery()
                txtVendorID.Text = cmdVendorID.ExecuteScalar
                conPayables.Close()
                bNewRow = False
                Me.SaveNewData()
            Catch eSql As SqlException
                MessageBox.Show(eSql.Message, "SQL Server error")
            End Try
            Me.SetMaintenanceButtons(True)
        Else
            Me.SetNewValues(cmdVendorUpdate)
            Me.SetOldValues(cmdVendorUpdate)
            Try
                conPayables.Open()
                Dim iRowCount As Integer = _
                    cmdVendorUpdate.ExecuteNonQuery()
                conPayables.Close()
                If iRowCount = 0 Then
                    MessageBox.Show("The row for vendor " & txtName.Text _
                        & " has been changed by another user and can't " _
                        & " be updated.", "Concurrency error")
                    txtVendorID.Text = ""
                    Me.ClearControls()
                    Me.SetMaintenanceButtons(True)
                    Me.SetEntryControls(False)
                Else
                    Me.SetMaintenanceButtons(True)
                    Me.SaveNewData()
                End If
            Catch eSql As SqlException
                MessageBox.Show(esql.Message, "SQL Server error")
            End Try
        End If
        txtVendorID.Focus()
    End If
End Sub
```

Figure 8-6   The code for the Vendor Maintenance program (part 4 of 6)

On page 5 of this listing, you can see the three procedures that are used to manage the old and new values of a vendor row. The SetNewValues procedure is used when a vendor row is inserted or updated. It assigns the values in the form controls to the parameters that will hold the new values. Notice that, like the code you saw in the last chapter, this procedure checks whether either of the controls that contain address information are empty. If so, a null is assigned to the parameter for the address column. Otherwise, the Text property of the control that contains the address is assigned to the parameter.

The SaveNewData procedure is used to store the new or updated data for a vendor in the module-level variables once that data has been written to the database. That's necessary in case the user wants to perform additional operations on the vendor. If these variables don't contain the vendor data that's stored in the database, the concurrency checking that's done by the Update and Delete statements won't work.

The SetOldValues procedure is used when a vendor row is updated or deleted. This procedure assigns the values in the module-level variables to the parameters in the Update or Delete command that provide for concurrency checking. Notice that because the Update and Delete statements check for empty strings in the two parameters that contain the address values, it's not necessary to check for empty strings in the address variables.

The last procedure on this page is executed when the user clicks on the Cancel button. This procedure works just like the one you saw in the last chapter. If the addition of a new row is canceled, it sets the bNewRow variable to False and clears and disables the entry controls. If the update of an existing row is canceled, it calls the FillControls procedure to redisplay the original column values.

A Vendor Maintenance program that uses action queries   Page 5

```
Private Sub SetNewValues(ByVal cmd As SqlCommand)
    With cmd
        .Parameters("@NewName").Value = txtName.Text
        If txtAddressLine1.Text = "" Then
            .Parameters("@NewAddress1").Value = DBNull.Value
        Else
            .Parameters("@NewAddress1").Value = txtAddressLine1.Text
        End If
        If txtAddressLine2.Text = "" Then
            .Parameters("@NewAddress2").Value = DBNull.Value
        Else
            .Parameters("@NewAddress2").Value = txtAddressLine2.Text
        End If
        .Parameters("@NewCity").Value = txtCity.Text
        .Parameters("@NewState").Value = cboStates.SelectedValue
        .Parameters("@NewZipCode").Value = txtZipCode.Text
    End With
End Sub

Private Sub SaveNewData()
    iVendorID = txtVendorID.Text
    sVendorName = txtName.Text
    sAddress1 = txtAddressLine1.Text
    sAddress2 = txtAddressLine2.Text
    sCity = txtCity.Text
    sState = cboStates.SelectedValue
    sZipCode = txtZipCode.Text
End Sub

Private Sub SetOldValues(ByVal cmd As SqlCommand)
    With cmd
        .Parameters("@VendorID").Value = iVendorID
        .Parameters("@OldName").Value = sVendorName
        .Parameters("@OldAddress1").Value = sAddress1
        .Parameters("@OldAddress2").Value = sAddress2
        .Parameters("@OldCity").Value = sCity
        .Parameters("@OldState").Value = sState
        .Parameters("@OldZipCode").Value = sZipCode
    End With
End Sub

Private Sub btnCancel_Click(ByVal sender As System.Object, _
        ByVal e As System.EventArgs) Handles btnCancel.Click
    Me.SetMaintenanceButtons(True)
    If bNewRow Then
        bNewRow = False
        Me.ClearControls()
        Me.SetEntryControls(False)
    Else
        Me.FillControls()
    End If
    txtVendorID.Focus()
End Sub
```

Figure 8-6   The code for the Vendor Maintenance program (part 5 of 6)

The last procedure shown in this listing is executed when the user clicks on the Delete button. This procedure confirms the operation and then calls the SetOldValues procedure to assign values to the parameters used in the Delete command for concurrency checking. Next, it opens the connection, executes the Delete command, and closes the connection. Then, it checks the iRowCount variable to determine if the delete operation was successful. If not, an error message is displayed. In either case, the form is set so that the user can retrieve another vendor.

Now that you've seen the code for this program, you may want to reflect on how it compares to the program in chapter 7 that uses a dataset. Obviously, the program in this chapter requires a lot more code because you have to maintain both the original and the new versions of each row that's retrieved and you have to provide for concurrency checking. In contrast, a data adapter handles versions and concurrency checking automatically. All you have to do is provide for catching and handling concurrency exceptions when they occur. So using a data adapter is a much simpler approach.

Keep in mind, though, that using a data adapter requires additional overhead. If program efficiency is a concern, then, you may want to consider using the technique illustrated by this program instead. You may also need to use this technique if you want to use a method of concurrency checking other than the one that's provided by the data adapter.

A Vendor Maintenance program that uses action queries   **Page 6**

```
    Private Sub btnDelete_Click(ByVal sender As System.Object, _
            ByVal e As System.EventArgs) Handles btnDelete.Click
        Dim iResult As DialogResult _
            = MessageBox.Show("Delete " & txtName.Text & "?", _
              "Confirm Delete", MessageBoxButtons.YesNo, _
              MessageBoxIcon.Question)
        If iResult = DialogResult.Yes Then
            Me.SetOldValues(cmdVendorDelete)
            Try
                conPayables.Open()
                Dim iRowCount As Integer = cmdVendorDelete.ExecuteNonQuery()
                conPayables.Close()
                If iRowCount = 0 Then
                    MessageBox.Show("The row for vendor " & txtName.Text _
                        & " has been changed by another user and can't" _
                        & " be deleted.", "Concurrency error")
                End If
            Catch eSql As SqlException
                MessageBox.Show(eSql.Message, "SQL Server")
            End Try
            txtVendorID.Text = ""
            Me.ClearControls()
            Me.SetMaintenanceButtons(True)
            Me.SetEntryControls(False)
            txtVendorID.Focus()
        End If
    End Sub
End Class
```

Note

* The following procedures have been omitted from this listing:

FillStatesTable	Control_DataChanged
ClearControls	ValidData
SetMaintenanceButtons	btnExit_Click
SetEntryControls	Form1_Closing
txtVendorID_KeyPress	

To see the code for these procedures, please refer to figure 7-11.

Figure 8-6   The code for the Vendor Maintenance program (part 6 of 6)

How to work with stored procedures

Instead of using Select, Insert, Update, and Delete statements that are coded directly into your program, you can use stored procedures that contain the statements you need. A *stored procedure* is a database object that contains one or more SQL statements. In the topics that follow, you'll learn how to work with stored procedures through code as well as using the Data Adapter Configuration Wizard. Keep in mind as you read these topics that they're not meant to teach you how to code stored procedures. They're just meant to give you an idea of how stored procedures work and how you can use them from Visual Basic programs.

An introduction to stored procedures

When you send an SQL statement to a database management system for processing, the DBMS must compile and optimize the query before it executes it. In contrast, because a stored procedure is stored with the database, it only has to be compiled and optimized the first time it's executed. As a result, stored procedures can improve the efficiency of a database application.

Figure 8-7 illustrates how a stored procedure works. At the top of this figure, you can see a Create Procedure statement that creates a stored procedure named SelectVendor. This stored procedure contains a Select statement that retrieves the data for a vendor from the Vendors table based on the Vendor ID. Notice that this stored procedure requires a parameter, which is defined at the beginning of the procedure.

To execute a stored procedure, you use a command object as shown in this figure. Notice that the CommandText property is set to the name of the stored procedure, and the CommandType property is set to CommandType.StoredProcedure. Also notice that a parameter that will contain the value that's passed to the stored procedure is added to the parameters collection of the command. Then, after a value is assigned to the parameter, the connection is opened and the command is executed.

Because the stored procedure in this example contains a Select statement, the ExecuteReader method is used to execute the command and store the result set in a data reader. You can also use the ExecuteNonQuery method to execute a stored procedure that contains an Insert, Update, or Delete statement, and you can use the ExecuteScalar method to execute a stored procedure that returns a single value.

SQL code for creating a stored procedure that retrieves a row

```
CREATE PROCEDURE SelectVendor (@VendorID int)
AS
SELECT VendorID, VendorName, VendorAddress1, VendorAddress2, VendorCity,
    VendorState, VendorZipCode
FROM Vendors
WHERE (VendorID = @VendorID)
```

VB.NET code that creates and executes a command that uses the stored procedure

```
Dim cmdVendorSelect As New SqlCommand()
With cmdVendorSelect
    .Connection = conPayables
    .CommandText = "SelectVendor"
    .CommandType = CommandType.StoredProcedure
End With
cmdVendorSelect.Parameters.Add("@VendorID", SqlDbType.Int)
.
.
cmdVendorSelect.Parameters("@VendorID").Value = txtVendorID.Text
conPayables.Open()
Dim rdrVendor As SqlDataReader = cmdVendorSelect.ExecuteReader()
.
.
```

Concepts

- A *stored procedure* consists of one or more SQL statements that have been compiled and stored with the database.

- Stored procedures can improve database performance because the SQL statements in each procedure are only compiled and optimized the first time they're executed. In contrast, SQL statements that are sent from a Visual Basic program have to be compiled and optimized every time they're executed.

- You can use parameters to pass values from an application to the stored procedure or from the stored procedure to the application. Stored procedures can also pass back a return value, which is typically used to indicate whether or not an error occurred.

How to use stored procedures from Visual Basic

- To use a stored procedure in a Visual Basic application, you set the CommandText property of a command to the name of the stored procedure, and you set the CommandType property to CommandType.StoredProcedure.

- If a stored procedure uses input parameters, you must add parameter objects to the parameters collection just as you do when you use SQL statements directly. You must also add parameter objects for output parameters or a return value returned by the procedure. See figure 8-8 for details.

- To execute a stored procedure, you use the method of the command object that's appropriate for the processing that's done by the procedure. To execute a stored procedure that returns a result set, for example, you use the ExecuteReader method.

Figure 8-7   An introduction to stored procedures

How to work with output parameters and return values

The stored procedure you saw in the last figure used just an input parameter. But stored procedures can also use output parameters, and they can return a return value. Figure 8-8 illustrates how this works.

At the top of this figure, you can see a stored procedure that inserts a new row into the Vendors table. This procedure uses input parameters for each of the required columns in this table. In addition, it uses an output parameter that will return the identity value that's generated for the Vendor ID column. To assign a value to this parameter, the procedure uses a Set statement. As you can see, this statement assigns the value of the @@Identity system function to this parameter.

This procedure also includes a Return statement that passes a return value back to the program. In this case, the procedure simply returns the value of the @@Error system function, which will contain the error number that was generated by the Insert statement. If no error was generated, this function will return a value of zero.

The Visual Basic code shown in this figure illustrates how you can use the output parameter and return value included in this stored procedure. To do that, you add parameter objects to the parameters collection of the command that will execute the stored procedure. Note, however, that if a stored procedure returns a return value, the parameter that receives that value must be the first parameter in the collection. The parameter that will receive the return value of the stored procedure in this figure, for example, is the one named @Error. The one that will receive the new Vendor ID value is named @NewVendorID.

To indicate that a parameter will receive a return value or output from the stored procedure, you set its Direction property as shown here. Then, after the query is executed, you can get the values of the parameters through the parameters collection. In this example, the @Error parameter is checked to see if it has a value of zero, which indicates that no error occurred. In that case, the value of the @NewVendorID parameter is assigned to the Text property of a text box. Otherwise, some other processing is performed.

If you understand how to use commands to execute queries, you shouldn't have any trouble using them with stored procedures. Before you use an existing stored procedure, though, you'll need to find out how it's defined, what parameters it uses, and whether it includes a Return statement. That way, you can define your command objects accordingly.

Of course, you can also code your own stored procedures. You'll learn more about how to do that from the Visual Studio environment in chapter 17. And in the next topic, you'll learn how the Data Adapter Configuration Wizard can create stored procedures for you.

SQL code for creating a stored procedure that returns output parameters and a return value

```
CREATE PROCEDURE InsertVendor
    ( @NewName varchar(50), @NewAddress1 varchar(50),
      @NewAddress2 varchar(50), @NewCity varchar(50),
      @NewState char(2), @NewZipCode varchar(20),
      @NewVendorID int OUTPUT )
AS
INSERT INTO Vendors(VendorName, VendorAddress1, VendorAddress2, VendorCity,
    VendorState, VendorZipCode)
VALUES (@NewName, @NewAddress1, @NewAddress2, @NewCity,
    @NewState, @NewZipCode)
SET @NewVendorID = @@IDENTITY
RETURN @@ERROR
```

VB.NET code that executes the stored procedure

```
Dim cmdVendorInsert As New SqlCommand("InsertVendor", conPayables)
cmdVendorInsert.CommandType = CommandType.StoredProcedure
With cmdVendorInsert.Parameters
    .Add("@Error", SqlDbType.Int)
    .Add("@NewVendorID", SqlDbType.Int)
    .Add("@NewName", SqlDbType.VarChar)
    .Add("@NewAddress1", SqlDbType.VarChar)
    .Add("@NewAddress2", SqlDbType.VarChar)
    .Add("@NewCity", SqlDbType.VarChar)
    .Add("@NewState", SqlDbType.Char)
    .Add("@NewZipCode", SqlDbType.Char)
End With
cmdVendorInsert.Parameters("@Error").Direction _
    = ParameterDirection.ReturnValue
cmdVendorInsert.Parameters("@NewVendorID").Direction _
    = ParameterDirection.Output
    .
    .
    .
conPayables.Open()
cmdVendorInsert.ExecuteNonQuery()
If cmdVendorInsert.Parameters("@Error").Value = 0 Then
    txtVendorID.Text = cmdVendorInsert.Parameters("@NewVendorID").Value
Else
    .
    .
    .
End If
conPayables.Close()
```

Description

- If a stored procedure includes output parameters or a Return statement, you must add parameters to the command that executes the stored procedure. These parameters will receive the values returned by the stored procedure.

- The Direction property of an output parameter must be set to ParameterDirection.Output. The Size property must also be set if the parameter is defined with a string data type.

- The parameter that receives the return value must be the first parameter in the parameters collection, and its Direction property must be set to ParameterDirection.ReturnValue.

Figure 8-8   How to work with output parameters and return values

How to create stored procedures using the Configuration Wizard

You may recall from chapter 3 that when you create a data adapter using the Data Adapter Configuration Wizard, you have three options for how the data adapter will access the database. First, it can use SQL statements as you've seen throughout this book. Second, it can use stored procedures that it creates for you. And third, it can use existing stored procedures.

To see the dialog box that lets you select these options, you can look back at figure 3-3. If you select the Create new stored procedures option from this dialog box, the Configuration Wizard displays a dialog box like the first one shown in figure 8-9. This dialog box lets you enter or build a Select statement. The wizard will use this statement to generate the stored procedures for the data adapter.

After you enter the Select statement and click on the Next button, the second dialog box shown in this figure is displayed. This dialog box lets you name the stored procedures that the wizard will create. As you can see, the wizard can create stored procedures that contain Insert, Update, and Delete statements in addition to the stored procedure that contains the Select statement. If that's not what you want, you can click on the Advanced Options button in the first dialog box and then remove the check mark from the Generate Insert, Update, and Delete statements option in the dialog box that's displayed. You can look back to figure 3-5 to see what this dialog box looks like. You can also use this dialog box to eliminate concurrency checking from the generated code or to eliminate code that refreshes the dataset after an insert or update operation.

Although you'll typically let the wizard create the stored procedures for you based on the options you choose, you can also create them yourself. To do that, just select the No option from the second dialog box in this figure. Then, the wizard will still create the command objects for executing stored procedures with the name you specify, but it won't create the stored procedures themselves.

The Configuration Wizard dialog boxes for creating stored procedures

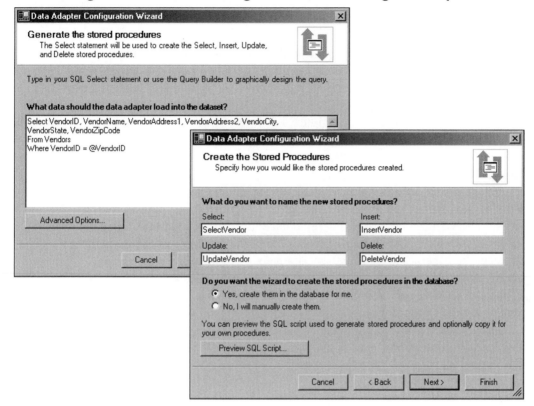

Description

- To create stored procedures that let you select, insert, update, and delete rows using the Data Adapter Configuration Wizard, select the Create new stored procedures option from the Choose a Query Type dialog box. Then, enter or build the Select statement for the query in the first dialog box shown above, and enter names for the procedures in the second dialog box shown above.

- By default, the Configuration Wizard creates the stored procedures with the names you specify and sets the properties for the command objects accordingly. That includes adding parameter objects to the parameters collection for any parameters you specify in the Select statement as well as any parameters that are needed for concurrency checking.

- If you want to create your own stored procedures, you can select the No option from the second dialog box. Then, the wizard sets the command properties but doesn't create the stored procedures.

- If you want to review the code that the wizard generates to create the stored procedures, you can click on the Preview SQL Script button.

Figure 8-9   How to create stored procedures using the Configuration Wizard

How to use existing procedures with the Configuration Wizard

If stored procedures already exist for the operations you want to perform, you can use the Configuration Wizard to identify those procedures and generate command objects for them. Figure 8-10 explains how to do that. The dialog box that's shown here is displayed if you select the Use existing stored procedures option from the first dialog box in figure 3-3. It lets you select the stored procedures to be used for Select, Insert, Update, and Delete operations from drop-down lists. These lists include all of the stored procedures that are defined for the database.

When you select a stored procedure for one of the operations, any parameters used by that stored procedure that receive input from the dataset or store output in the dataset are displayed in the list at the right side of this dialog box. In this figure, for example, you can see some of the parameters that are defined for an update operation. The first six parameters will be used in the Values clause of the Update statement to supply the new values for the row that's being updated. The other parameters will be used in the Where clause to identify the vendor to be updated and to provide for concurrency checking.

Notice that a source column isn't selected for the last parameter that's visible in this dialog box. This is the parameter that will contain the Vendor ID. Although you can't see them here, source columns aren't selected for the parameters that provide for concurrency checking either. Because of that, you have to select the appropriate source columns for this statement to work. If you don't do that from this dialog box, the wizard will display another dialog box indicating that some of the parameter bindings are missing and that values from the dataset won't be used for those parameters. If you continue, you'll need to set the values of these parameters manually or associate them with source columns using the Collection Editor dialog box you saw in figure 7-9. Even if you set the source columns from the wizard dialog box, though, you'll need to set the SourceVersion properties of these parameters from the Collection Editor dialog box. That's because the default version is Current, but you want to use the original version for these parameters.

By the way, you should always select the stored procedure you want to use for the selection operation before you select stored procedures for the other operations. That's because the Select procedure identifies the columns that will be stored in the dataset. If you don't select this procedure first, the wizard won't have access to any source column information.

You should also know that by default, the data adapter maps the source data identified by the Select statement into a table that has the same name as the stored procedure that contains that statement. If you use the Select stored procedure shown in this figure, for example, the data will be stored in a table named SelectVendor. To change how the data is mapped, you can select the TableMappings property of the data adapter and then click on the ellipsis button to display the Table Mappings dialog box. Then, you can change the Dataset table option to the table name you want to use.

The Configuration Wizard dialog box for using existing stored procedures

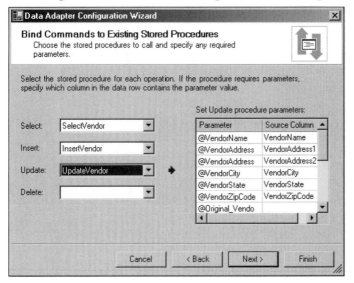

Description

- If you want to create command objects based on existing stored procedures, you can select the Use existing stored procedures option from the Configuration Wizard's Choose a Query Type dialog box. Then, you can select the stored procedures from the dialog box shown above.

- If the stored procedure you choose uses parameters that receive input from the dataset or store output in the dataset, those parameters are displayed in a box to the right of the stored procedure as shown above.

- If a source column isn't provided for a parameter, you can select it from the drop-down list that's available for the parameter. If you don't select a source column, the wizard will display a message indicating that some parameter bindings are missing when you click on the Next or Finish button.

- By default, the wizard will use the current version of the source columns. If that's not what you want, you can use the Collection Editor dialog box as described in figure 7-9 to change the version that's used.

- When you choose a Select procedure, the data columns that are returned are displayed in the box to the right of the procedure.

Note

- When the data adapter uses a stored procedure to retrieve data into a data table, it gives the table the name of the stored procedure. If that's not what you want, you can change the name using the TableMappings property of the data adapter.

Figure 8-10   How to use existing stored procedures with the Configuration Wizard

How to use transactions

A *transaction* is a group of related database operations that you combine into a single logical unit. By combining operations in this way, you can prevent certain types of database errors. Specifically, you can prevent errors that affect the integrity of the data in the database.

How to create and work with transactions

Figure 8-11 presents the methods you use to create and work with transactions. To start a transaction, you use the BeginTransaction method of a connection object. This creates a transaction object that you can then use to work with the transaction.

To use a transaction, you associate it with one or more data commands. To do that, you assign the transaction object to the Transaction property of each command. Note that each of the commands must be associated with the same connection object on which the transaction was started.

After you associate a transaction with a command, any SQL statement you execute using that command becomes part of the transaction. Then, if all of the commands in the transaction execute without error, you can *commit* the transaction. That means that all of the changes that have been made to the database since the beginning of the transaction are made permanent. To commit a transaction, you use the Commit method of the transaction.

In contrast, if any of the commands cause an error, all of the changes made to the database since the beginning of the transaction can be reversed, or *rolled back*. To roll back a transaction, you use the Rollback method of the transaction.

A coding example that uses a transaction

To help you understand when you might use a transaction, take a look at the code in figure 8-11. This code inserts an invoice into the Invoices table and then inserts the line items that make up the invoice into the InvoiceLineItems table. For simplicity, this code specifies the value for each column in a row using a literal. In a production application, of course, these values would be specified using parameters.

Now, consider what might happen if you inserted the invoice and line items without using a transaction. If the statement that inserted the invoice succeeded but one or more of the statements for the line items failed, the Invoices and InvoiceLineItems tables would be out of balance. Specifically, the total of the InvoiceLineItemAmount columns in the InvoiceLineItems table wouldn't equal the InvoiceTotal column in the Invoices table, so the data would be invalid.

To prevent this type of problem, all of the Insert statements can be executed as part of a single transaction as shown in this figure. Then, if all of the statements succeed, the transaction can be committed. Otherwise, the transaction can be rolled back. That way, the tables will always be in balance.

The syntax for creating a transaction object

```
sqlTransaction = sqlConnection.BeginTransaction()
```

Methods for working with transaction objects

Method	Description
Commit	Commits the changes to the database, making them permanent.
Rollback	Reverses the changes made to the database to the beginning of the transaction.

Code that uses a transaction to update related rows

```
Dim sInsertInvoice As String = "Insert Into Invoices " _
    & "(VendorID, InvoiceNumber, InvoiceDate, InvoiceTotal, " _
    & "TermsID, InvoiceDueDate) " _
    & "Values (34, 'Q8839777', '01/15/2003', 4092.59, 3, '02/15/2003')"
Dim cmdInvoice As New SqlCommand(sInsertInvoice, conPayables)
Dim cmdInvoiceID As New SqlCommand("Select @@Identity", conPayables)
Dim cmdLineItem As New SqlCommand()
cmdLineItem.Connection = conPayables
conPayables.Open()
Dim trnInvoice As SqlTransaction = conPayables.BeginTransaction
cmdInvoice.Transaction = trnInvoice
cmdLineItem.Transaction = trnInvoice
cmdInvoiceID.Transaction = trnInvoice
Try
    cmdInvoice.ExecuteNonQuery()
    Dim iInvoiceID As Integer = cmdInvoiceID.ExecuteScalar
    cmdLineItem.CommandText = "Insert Into InvoiceLineItems " _
        & "(InvoiceID, InvoiceSequence, AccountNo, " _
        & "InvoiceLineItemAmount, InvoiceLineItemDescription) " _
        & "Values (" & iInvoiceID & ", 1, 160, 1447.23, 'Disk drive')"
    cmdLineItem.ExecuteNonQuery()
    cmdLineItem.CommandText = "Insert Into InvoiceLineItems " _
    ...
    cmdLineItem.ExecuteNonQuery()
    trnInvoice.Commit()
Catch eSystem As Exception
    trnInvoice.Rollback()
    MessageBox.Show(eSystem.Message, "An error has occurred.")
Finally
    conPayables.Close()
End Try
```

Description

- A *transaction* is a group of SQL statements that are combined into a logical unit. By default, each SQL statement is treated as a separate transaction.

- When you *commit* a transaction, the changes made to the database become a permanent part of the database. Until it's committed, you can undo all of the changes since the beginning of the transaction by *rolling back* the transaction.

- The BeginTransaction method of a connection begins a transaction and returns a transaction object. To associate a transaction with a command, you set the Transaction property of the command to the transaction object.

- If you close a connection while a transaction is pending, the changes are rolled back.

Figure 8-11   How to use transactions

Perspective

In this chapter, you learned the essential skills for working with data commands. As you've seen, when you work with data commands directly, you can perform all of the functions that are typically performed automatically by the data adapter. However, you have more control over how the data is processed when you work with commands directly. In addition, you don't have the overhead of using the data adapter or a dataset. When a program doesn't call for using a dataset, then, using data commands directly is often the most practical solution.

Terms

ordinal
scalar value
aggregate value
action query
stored procedure
transaction
commit a transaction
roll back a transaction

9

How to work with dataset schemas

In chapter 3, you learned that when you generate a dataset from a data adapter, Visual Basic creates a dataset schema file that defines the structure of the dataset. In some cases, though, you won't want to generate the schema file from a data adapter. Then, you can use the techniques in this chapter to create the schema file yourself.

How dataset schemas work

Before you learn the details of working with dataset schemas, you need to understand what a schema is and how it's created. That's what you'll learn in the two topics that follow.

Properties that specify the schema of a dataset

The table at the top of figure 9-1 lists the properties you use to maintain the schema information for a dataset. As you can see, these are properties of the DataTable and DataSet classes. The schema properties for a table include Columns, which refers to a collection that defines the columns of the table; Constraints, which refers to a collection that defines the unique and foreign key constraints of the table; and PrimaryKey, which defines the primary key of the table.

In addition to the table schema, a dataset also has a Tables property, which refers to a collection that defines the tables in the dataset, and a Relations property, which refers to a collection that defines the relationships among those tables. In a moment, you'll see that ADO.NET can generate the schema for the tables in a dataset automatically based on information retrieved from the database. However, it can't generate the relations schema automatically. Because of that, you have to provide this information yourself if your application calls for it. You'll learn three different ways to do that in this chapter.

How to create a dataset schema

The techniques you use to create a dataset schema depend on whether the dataset is typed or untyped. To create a typed dataset, you can either generate it from a data adapter component or you can use the *XML Designer*. In either case, the schema for the dataset is stored in an file within your project that contains an *XML Schema Definition*, or *XSD*. Then, Visual Studio generates the Visual Basic class that represents the typed dataset from this XML file.

You can use three different techniques to create the schema for an untyped dataset. First, you can use the Fill or FillSchema method of a data adapter that you learned about in earlier chapters. Then, the schema is created for you based on information that ADO.NET retrieves from the database. If you want more control over the schema, however, you can create a dataset component at design time and then use the *collection editors* to set its properties. Alternatively, you can write code that creates the schema at runtime. You'll learn how to use both of these techniques later in this chapter.

Properties that specify the schema of a dataset

Object	Property	Description
DataTable	Columns	A collection of DataColumn objects that define the columns in a table.
DataTable	Constraints	A collection of Constraint objects that specify the unique and foreign key constraints for a table.
DataTable	PrimaryKey	An array of columns that make up the primary key for a table.
DataSet	Tables	A collection of DataTable objects that define the tables in the dataset.
DataSet	Relations	A collection of DataRelation objects that define the relationships among the tables in a dataset.

Concepts

- The *schema* for a typed dataset is defined by an XML schema file. This file contains the *XML Schema Definition* (*XSD*) that's used to generate a class file for the typed dataset.

- The class file for a typed dataset includes code that's used to create the tables in the dataset and initialize the columns, constraints, primary keys, and relations based on the schema.

- The XML schema file is used only at design time. At runtime, the program uses the typed dataset class that's generated from the XML schema file.

Two ways to create the schema for a typed dataset

- You can generate the schema for a typed dataset automatically using the Data Adapter Configuration Wizard as described in chapter 3.

- You can create the schema file using the *XML Designer*, which provides a visual interface for defining tables, columns, constraints, and relations.

Three ways to create the schema for an untyped dataset

- You can generate the schema information for an untyped dataset by executing the Fill method of a data adapter. You can also use the FillSchema method of a data adapter to generate the schema information without retrieving data from the data source.

- You can create the schema at design time by adding a DataSet component to the form and setting its properties using the *collection editors*.

- You can create the schema at runtime by writing code that creates the dataset and sets its properties.

Note

- Although ADO.NET can generate table schema information automatically for both typed and untyped datasets, it can't generate relations automatically. Because of that, you must add relations to the schema yourself.

Figure 9-1   How dataset schemas work

How to use the XML Designer

If you don't want to generate a typed dataset from a data adapter but you still want to take advantage of the benefits of a typed dataset, you can create the schema for the dataset using the XML Designer. When you use the XML Designer, a class that defines the typed dataset is generated for you. Then, you can use that dataset just as you would any other typed dataset.

An introduction to the XML Designer

To add an XML schema file and a typed dataset to a project, you select the DataSet template from the Add New Item dialog box. Then, the XML Designer is displayed with an empty design surface, and you can use the techniques you'll learn in the figures that follow to create the schema. In figure 9-2, for example, you can see the schema that's been created for a single table as it's displayed in the XML Designer. This is the schema for the Vendors table that you've seen throughout this book.

Before I go on, I want you to notice two things about the XML Designer. First, when the designer window is open, the XML Schema tab of the Toolbox is available. You can use the items in this tab to create and edit the schema. Second, if you want to see the XML that's generated for the schema, you can click on the XML tab at the bottom of the designer window. Although you can edit this generated code, I don't recommend you do that unless you're familiar with XML.

When you add a typed dataset to a project, three files appear in the Solution Explorer window. (If you can't see all of these files, click on the Show All Files button at the top of the Solution Explorer window.) The file that has an extension of *xsd* is the XML schema file itself. Subordinate to this file is the typed dataset class file (*vb* file extension) and a support file (*xsx* file extension) that keeps track of where the various schema items appear when you view them in the XML Designer. Of these three files, the only one you should work with directly is the xsd file.

The XML Designer

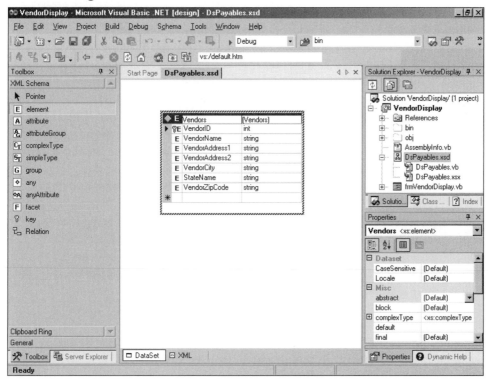

Description

- The XML Designer provides a design surface that you can use to create and edit XML schema files.

- To add an XML schema and a typed dataset to your project, choose the Project→Add New Item command. Then, select DataSet from the available templates, type the name you want to use for the new dataset class, and click OK.

- When you start a new schema, the design surface is empty. Then, you can define the schema by dragging elements from the XML Schema tab of the Toolbox.

- To see the XML code that's generated for the schema, click the XML tab at the bottom of the XML Designer.

Figure 9-2   An introduction to the XML Designer

How to create tables and columns

Figure 9-3 presents the basic techniques for adding a table and columns to a schema. To add a table, you drag the Element icon from the Toolbox to the design surface. This creates an XML *schema element* for a table that has no columns. Then, you can enter a name for the table in the first row of the element, and you can add columns to the table in the rows that follow.

The easiest way to add a column to a table is to click in the name column of the last row in the table element and type a name, then tab to the type column and choose a data type from the drop-down list that appears. When you do that, the letter "E" appears in the first column of that row to indicate that the item is an element. You can also add other types of items to a table element, but that's beyond the scope of this chapter.

After you add a column element, an additional row becomes available at the end of the table where you can add another column. Unfortunately, there's no way to insert a column element between existing columns, and there's no easy way to rearrange the order of column elements once you've created them. So you should create them in the same order that you want them to appear in the table. In most cases, that should be the same order that the columns appear in the Select statement that will be used to retrieve the data that's stored in the table. In addition, you should use the same names that are used in the Select statement. If you don't, you'll have to add table mappings to the data adapter to identify the names of the corresponding columns.

The name and type you specify for each column element are *attributes* of that element. For the purposes of this book, you can think of an attribute as a property. In fact, as the XML Designer creates the typed dataset from the schema, it converts the attributes you specify into properties of the corresponding data columns.

To set other attributes of a column element, you use the Properties window. This figure lists some of the attributes you're most likely to set. Of these attributes, the most interesting is minOccurs. You use this attribute to specify whether or not a column allows nulls. If you set this attribute to 0, it means that the column doesn't have to occur for every row, which is equivalent to saying that the column allows nulls. If the column doesn't allow nulls, you should set this attribute to 1. By default, it's set to 0.

The beginning of an XML schema element for a table

◆ E	Vendors	(Vendors)
E	VendorID	int
E	VendorName	string
✎	VendorAddress1|	
✱		

Common attributes for column elements

Attribute	Description
AutoIncrement	Specifies whether the element is an identity column.
AutoIncrementSeed	The starting value for an identity column.
AutoIncrementStep	The value used as the increment for an identity column.
minOccurs	The minimum number of occurrences allowed for this element. Specify 0 if the column allows nulls. Otherwise, omit or specify 1.
name	The column name.
type	The type of data that's stored in the column. The default is string.

Description

- To create the XML *schema element* for a table, drag the Element icon from the Toolbox to the design surface. A grid that represents the table will appear. The first row of this grid identifies the table and the remaining rows identify the columns.

- To name the table, enter the name into the first column of the first row. The default name will be highlighted when you first create the table, so you can simply type over this name.

- To add a column element to the table, click the first column of the last row in the grid and choose Element from the drop-down list that appears. (The other items in this list let you create other types of schema items.) Then, type a name for the element in the second column and choose a data type for the element from the third column.

- Name and type are two *attributes* that you can specify for a column element. The attributes you specify are used to define the data columns in the dataset class. To set other attributes of a column, use the Properties window.

- If an application requires information from additional tables, use the same techniques to define schema elements for those tables. Then, you can create foreign key constraints and relations using the techniques in figure 9-5.

Note

- You can also create a table element by dragging a table or selected columns from the Server Explorer. Then, the schema for the table is based on schema information retrieved from the database. For more information about working with the Server Explorer, see chapter 17.

Figure 9-3   How to create tables and columns using the XML Designer

How to create a unique constraint

After you create a table and define its columns, you can add unique constraints to the table. To do that, you use the Edit Key dialog box shown in figure 9-4. This dialog box lets you enter a name for the constraint and specify the columns it contains. If you use one of the techniques described in this figure to display this dialog box, the correct columns should already be selected for you. If you need to, however, you can use the Fields list to select other columns.

If the unique constraint column can contain nulls, you can select the Nullable option from this dialog box. Note, however, that a unique constraint that serves as the primary key can't contain nulls. To specify that the constraint you're creating is the primary key, select the Dataset primary key option.

The Edit Key dialog box

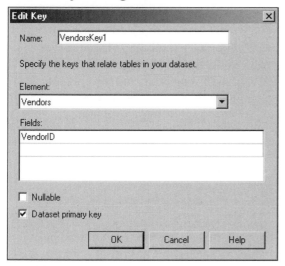

Description

- To add a unique constraint to a table, right-click the row for the column you want to use as the constraint and choose the Add→New Key command to display the Edit Key dialog box. You can also display this dialog box by dragging the Key icon from the Toolbox to the desired key column.

- In the Edit Key dialog box, type the name for the constraint and make sure that the correct element and column are selected.

- To allow nulls in the constraint column, select the Nullable option.

- To define the constraint as the primary key, select the Dataset primary key option.

- To create a constraint that consists of two or more columns, select the columns in the designer window before you display the Edit Key dialog box. Then, the selected columns will appear in the Fields list. Alternatively, you can select additional columns from the drop-down lists in this dialog box.

Figure 9-4   How to create a unique constraint using the XML Designer

How to create a relation

As you learned in chapter 7, if a schema contains two or more tables, you can define the relationships between those tables using the Edit Relation dialog box shown in figure 9-5. In this dialog box, you can select the parent and child tables, the key in the parent table that the relation is based on, and the columns that define the foreign key in the child table. Note that the key you use in the parent table must exist before you can create a relation. If it doesn't, you can use the New button to add it.

When you select a key for the parent table, the key fields for that table are set automatically. Because of that, you can't change the key fields that are listed for this table. In addition, when you select the parent and child tables, the relation name is changed accordingly. However, you can change this name if you don't like the one that's proposed.

In this figure, the Vendors table is the parent table, the Invoices table is the child table, and the VendorID column is the key column for both tables. As a result, you can use this data relation to access all of the invoices for a particular vendor. In addition, you can use it to access the vendor for a specific invoice.

Although a data relation defines the relationship between two tables, it doesn't enforce that relationship itself. To do that, a foreign key constraint is required. Fortunately, when you create a relation using the Edit Relation dialog box, a foreign key constraint is created for you.

In some cases, you may want to create a foreign key constraint without creating a relation object. For example, you may want to enforce referential integrity within a dataset, but you have no need for the navigation features provided by a relation. In that case, you can select the Create foreign key constraint only option from the Edit Relation dialog box.

When you use a table with a foreign key constraint in an application, you must be sure to fill the parent table before you fill the child table. After creating the relation and constraint shown in this figure, for example, you'd have to fill the Vendors table before filling the Invoices table. If you tried to fill the Invoices table first, an exception would occur when the data adapter added the first invoice because the related vendor wouldn't yet exist in the Vendors table.

The three drop-down lists at the bottom of the Edit Relation dialog box let you specify the referential integrity rules for the foreign key constraint. The first two specify what happens if a row in the parent is updated or deleted. I'll have more to say about the rules for these operations in the next topic.

The third rule specifies what happens if changes to the parent table are accepted or rejected using the AcceptChanges or RejectChanges method. The table in this figure lists the available options. If you leave the option at Default, an accept or reject operation on the parent table doesn't affect the data in the child table. That's because the default rule for an accept or reject operation is None. In that case, you have to explicitly accept or reject changes made to the child table, or you have to accept the changes made to the entire dataset. If you want changes to the related rows in the child table to be accepted or rejected along with the changes to the parent table, you can select the Cascade option.

The Edit Relation dialog box

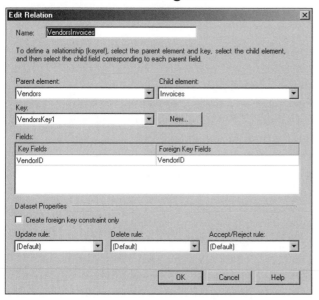

Rules for accept/reject operations

Rule	Description
Default	The default rule (None) is used.
None	The child table is not affected.
Cascade	The operation is cascaded to the child table.

Description

- To add a data relation to an XML schema, right-click the parent or the child table and choose Add→New Relation to display the Edit Relation dialog box. You can also display this dialog box by dragging the Relation icon from the Toolbox or by dragging from the left side of one table to the other table.

- Define the relationship by selecting the parent and child elements, the key in the parent table that the relationship is based on, and the foreign key fields in the child table. If the key isn't defined for the parent table, you can click on the New button to define it. You can also specify a name for the relation instead of using the one that's generated automatically based on the parent and child elements.

- To create a foreign key constraint without creating a relation, select the Create foreign key constraint only option.

- The Update rule and Delete rule options determine how referential integrity is enforced for the relationship. See figure 9-6 for details.

- The Accept/Reject rule option lets you specify what happens when you execute an AcceptChanges or RejectChanges method that affects rows in the parent table.

Figure 9-5   How to create a relation using the XML Designer

How the referential integrity rules affect database operations

In addition to the referential integrity that ADO.NET provides for datasets, relational databases provide referential integrity of their own. Because of that, you'll want to be sure that the dataset rules you choose and the techniques you use to update the database with changes made to a dataset don't conflict with the referential integrity defined by the database. Figure 9-6 presents some guidelines for setting dataset rules and for performing update operations.

The two tables in this figure show the rules that are available for a dataset and for a SQL Server database. Although other database management systems may provide different rules, they should be similar to the ones shown here. To be sure, you'll want to check the documentation for the DBMS you're using. You'll also want to check what rules are set for the particular database you're working with in an application.

If you select the None rule for a dataset, you can delete a row in the parent table without affecting the related rows in the child table. Similarly, if you change the key of a row in the parent table that has related rows in the child table, the child rows are unaffected. In that case, those rows in the child table are orphaned because they no longer have a related row in the parent table. For that to work, though, referential integrity must not be enforced between the two tables in the database. In most cases, that's not what you want.

If you select the Cascade rule, change and delete operations on the parent table are applied to the child table as well. If you define a relationship between a table of invoices and a table of line items, for example, you might want to set the delete rule to Cascade. Then, if you delete an invoice, all of the line items for that invoice will be deleted automatically.

In most cases, you'll set the update and delete rules for a dataset to Cascade only if the rules for the database are set to Cascade as well. Keep in mind, though, that when you update the parent table in the database with changes made to the parent table in the dataset, the child table in the database will be updated automatically by the DBMS. Because of that, you don't need to explicitly perform an update operation on the child table.

The last two dataset rules, SetNull and SetDefault, are ones that you probably won't use often. If you update or delete a row in the parent table when the rule is SetNull, the values of the foreign key columns of all the related rows in the child table are set to Null. For that to work, of course, the foreign key column must allow nulls. If you use SetDefault, the values of the foreign key columns in the related child rows are set to the default value for that column. For this to work, the column must be defined with a default value. In addition, a row with that default key must exist in the parent table in the database. Note that if you use either SetNull or SetDefault, you must be sure to update the child table in the database first. That way, when you update the parent table, no related rows will exist in the child table. Otherwise, an error will occur because the database doesn't have rules that are equivalent to SetNull and SetDefault.

ADO.NET rules for update and delete operations in a dataset

Rule	Description
Default	The default rule (Cascade) is used.
None	The child table is not affected.
Cascade	If the value of the key column of a row in the parent table is changed, the values of the foreign key columns of related rows in the child table are changed. If a row in the parent table is deleted, the related rows in the child table are deleted.
SetNull	The values of the key columns of related rows in the child table are set to null.
SetDefault	The values of the key columns of related rows in the child table are set to their defaults.

SQL Server rules for update and delete operations in a database

Rule	Description
Cascade	If the value of the key column of a row in the parent table is changed, the values of the foreign key columns of related rows in the child table are changed. If a row in the parent table is deleted, the related rows in the child table are deleted.
No Action	The key value of a row in the parent table can't be changed and the row can't be deleted if it has related rows in the child table.

Description

- The Update rule and Delete rule options for a dataset let you specify what happens to the related rows in a child table when the key column of their parent row is changed or when their parent row is deleted.

- When a dataset will be used to update a database, you'll want to set the referential integrity rules for the dataset and perform update operations so that they don't conflict with the rules in the database.

- If you specify None for an update or delete operation on a dataset, the relationship must not be enforced in the database. If it is, an error will occur when the database is updated.

- If you specify Cascade for an update or delete operation on a dataset and the SQL Server rule is also set to Cascade, you only need to update the database with the data in the parent table of the dataset. The child table will be updated automatically by the database.

- If you specify the SetNull rule for an update or delete operation on a dataset, the foreign key columns in the dataset and in the database must allow nulls. Then, when you update the database, you must update the child table first so that there are no rows in the child table related to the row in the parent table to be updated or deleted.

- If you specify the SetDefault rule for an update or delete operation on a dataset, the foreign key columns in the dataset and in the database must be defined with a default value and a row must exist in the parent table with that key value. Then, when you update the database, you must update the child table first.

- If the database rule is set to No Action, an error will occur if you try to update the key value of a row in the parent table or delete a row from the parent table that has related rows in the child table. Since ADO.NET doesn't provide an equivalent rule, you'll need to catch this error or provide for handling this type of situation in code.

Figure 9-6   How the referential integrity rules affect database operations

In some cases, you won't want the user to be able to update or delete a row in a parent table if it has related rows in the child table. For example, you wouldn't want to delete a row from the Vendors table if invoices existed for that vendor in the Invoices table. In SQL Server, this is handled by the No Action rule. This rule causes an error to be thrown if an update or delete operation isn't allowed. Unfortunately, ADO.NET doesn't provide an equivalent rule. Because of that, you'll need to provide for this situation in your program code. To do that, you can catch the error that's thrown by SQL Server, which is the technique that's used by the maintenance programs in this book. Or you can provide program logic that checks for related rows before performing an update or delete operation.

How to create an instance of a custom typed dataset

After you create a dataset schema and the typed dataset class, you'll need to create an instance of that class in your program. To do that, you can use one of the techniques shown in figure 9-7. If you want to use the dataset at design time, you can create a component from the dataset class by using the Add Dataset dialog box shown in this figure. Then, the component will appear in the Component Designer tray and you can use it just as you would any other dataset component. In particular, you can bind controls to it.

You can also create an instance of a typed dataset using code. To do that, you declare a variable that specifies the dataset class as its type. The statement shown in this figure, for example, creates a dataset from the dataset class named DsPayables. When you create a dataset instance that way, you should realize that the dataset isn't available until runtime. Because of that, if you want to bind controls to the dataset, you have to do that at runtime too.

By the way, you should know that you can also use the techniques shown in this figure to create an instance of a typed dataset that you generate from a data adapter created using the Data Adapter Configuration Wizard. In most cases, though, you'll create an instance of the dataset at the same time you generate the dataset, as you saw in chapter 3.

The Add Dataset dialog box

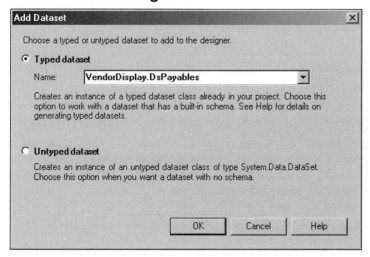

A statement that creates an instance of a custom typed dataset

```
Dim dsPayables As New DsPayables()
```

Description

- To create a dataset component from a custom typed dataset, drag the DataSet component from the Data tab of the Toolbox to a form to display the Add Dataset dialog box. Then, select the typed dataset class you want to use from the drop-down list and click OK. The dataset is added to the Component Designer tray and you can bind controls to it.

- You can also create an instance of a custom typed dataset by coding a Dim statement like the one shown above that names the dataset class. When you use this technique, the dataset isn't available until runtime, so you can't bind controls at design time.

Note

- You can also use the Add Dataset dialog box to create an instance of a typed dataset that you generate from a data adapter.

Figure 9-7   How to create an instance of a custom typed dataset

A Vendor Display form that uses a custom typed dataset

Figure 9-8 presents the specifications for a simple Vendor Display program that uses a custom typed dataset. As you can see, the design of the Vendor Display form is similar to the design of the Vendor Display form that was presented back in chapter 4. The only difference is that this form lets the user select the vendor to be displayed from a combo box, and the program in chapter 4 used navigation buttons.

As you can see in this figure, the schema used to create the custom typed dataset is the same schema you saw in figure 9-2. It consists of a single table named Vendors, with columns for the vendor's ID, name, and address information. The VendorID column is the primary key.

This application uses a component instance of the typed dataset so that the form controls can be bound to the Vendors table at design time. The binding properties are shown in the table in this figure. As you can see, the data source for the combo box is the Vendors table in the dataset, and the vendor name will be displayed in the combo box list. In addition, the Text properties of each of the text boxes are bound to individual columns in the Vendors table.

The design of the Vendor Display form

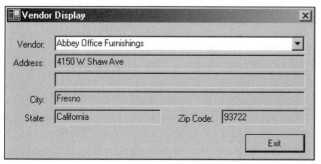

The XML schema for the DsPayables dataset

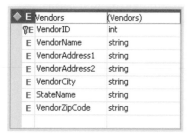

Binding properties for the Vendor Display form

Control	Property	Value
cboVendors	DataSource	DsPayables1.Vendors
	DisplayMember	VendorName
txtAddressLine1	Text (DataBindings)	DsPayables1 - Vendors.VendorAddress1
txtAddressLine2	Text (DataBindings)	DsPayables1 - Vendors.VendorAddress2
txtCity	Text (DataBindings)	DsPayables1 - Vendors.VendorCity
txtState	Text (DataBindings)	DsPayables1 - Vendors.StateName
txtZipCode	Text (DataBindings)	DsPayables1 - Vendors.VendorZipCode

Description

- This version of the Vendor Display program uses a typed dataset class named DsPayables that's created using the XML Designer. This dataset contains the Vendors table shown above.

- A dataset component named DsPayables1 is created from the DsPayables dataset class, and the form controls are bound to columns in this dataset at design time.

- The program will create connection, command, and data adapter objects in code, and then use the data adapter to fill the Vendors table.

Figure 9-8   A Vendor Display form that uses a custom typed dataset

The code for the Vendor Display program

The code for the Vendor Display program is shown in figure 9-9. Because most of the details of this program are handled by the typed dataset and by the data binding that's specified at design time, the actual code is fairly simple. It begins by defining a global BindingManagerBase variable named bmbVendors that will be used to manage the application's bound controls. Then, the Load procedure for the form calls a procedure named FillVendorsTable. This procedure creates the connection, command, and data adapter objects and then fills the Vendors table. The Load procedure also sets the bmbVendors variable to the BindingContext property of the form so it can be used to manage the controls that are bound to the Vendors table.

Before I go on, you should notice that the statement that fills the Vendors table names that table. In other words, it's coded like the statements you saw in chapter 6 that were used to fill an untyped dataset. You may remember from that chapter that the table name is used to identify the table mapping for the source data. That's necessary when you create your own typed dataset too because the table mappings aren't defined automatically like they are when you use the Configuration Wizard to create a typed dataset. You should realize, however, that since you're working with a typed dataset, you can refer to the table through a property of the dataset instead of using the table name. For example, you could use the following statement to fill the Vendors table:

```
daVendors.Fill(DsPayables1.Vendors)
```

The technique you use is a matter of preference.

When the user selects a vendor from the combo box, the SelectedIndexChanged procedure sets the Position property of the binding manager base to the SelectedIndex property of the combo box. That positions the Vendors table at the selected vendor, which causes the data for that vendor to be displayed on the form. Since you've seen this code in several of the programs presented earlier in this book, you shouldn't have any trouble understanding how it works.

A Vendor Display program that uses a custom typed dataset

```
Imports System.Data.SqlClient
Public Class Form1
    Inherits System.Windows.Forms.Form

    Dim bmbVendors As BindingManagerBase

    Private Sub Form1_Load(ByVal sender As System.Object, _
            ByVal e As System.EventArgs) Handles MyBase.Load
        Me.FillVendorsTable()
        bmbVendors = Me.BindingContext(DsPayables1, "Vendors")
    End Sub

    Public Sub FillVendorsTable()
        Dim sPayablesConnection As String _
            = "server=Doug\VSdotNET;" _
            & "database=Payables;" _
            & "integrated security=SSPI;" _
            & "workstation id=DOUG"
        Dim conPayables As New SqlConnection(sPayablesConnection)

        Dim sVendorSelect As String _
            = "Select VendorID, VendorName, VendorAddress1, " _
            & "VendorAddress2, VendorCity, StateName, VendorZipCode " _
            & "From Vendors Join States On VendorState = StateCode " _
            & "Order By VendorName"
        Dim cmdVendors As New SqlCommand(sVendorSelect, conPayables)
        Dim daVendors As New SqlDataAdapter(cmdVendors)
        Try
            daVendors.Fill(DsPayables1, "Vendors")
        Catch eSql As SqlException
            MessageBox.Show(eSql.Message, "SQL Server error")
        End Try
    End Sub

    Private Sub cboVendors_SelectedIndexChanged _
            (ByVal sender As System.Object, ByVal e As System.EventArgs) _
            Handles cboVendors.SelectedIndexChanged
        bmbVendors.Position = cboVendors.SelectedIndex
    End Sub

    Private Sub btnExit_Click(ByVal sender As System.Object, _
            ByVal e As System.EventArgs) Handles btnExit.Click
        Me.Close()
    End Sub

End Class
```

Figure 9-9   The code for the Vendor Display program

How to use the collection editors

In the previous topics, you learned how to use the XML Designer to create the schema for a typed dataset class, and you learned how to create an instance of that class that you can bind controls to. Even if you don't create a typed dataset, though, you can create a dataset component and bind controls to it. To do that, instead of using the XML Designer, you use the *collection editors* that you'll learn about in the topics that follow. As you'll see, these editors let you work with the four types of schema collections: tables, columns, constraints, and relations.

How to create an instance of an untyped dataset component

Before you can use the collection editors, you must create an instance of an untyped dataset component. To do that, you use the Add Dataset dialog box you saw in figure 9-7. Instead of selecting a typed dataset from this dialog box, though, you select the Untyped dataset option. Then, an untyped dataset component is added to the Component Designer tray.

How to use the Tables Collection Editor

To add tables to an untyped dataset component, you use the Tables Collection Editor dialog box shown in figure 9-10. To add a table, you just click the Add button and then set the various properties for the table. The property you're most likely to change is the TableName property. This property specifies the actual name of the data table.

Notice that a table also has a Name property. This property specifies the name of the DataTable variable that's declared in the generated code. Since you don't usually need to refer to this variable directly in your code, you can usually leave the Name property at its default setting.

The Tables Collection Editor dialog box

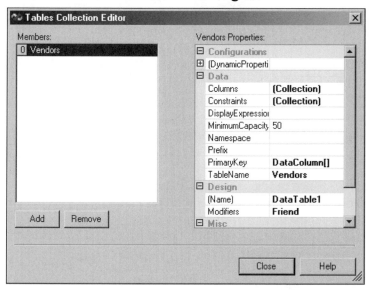

How to create an instance of an untyped dataset component

- To create an instance of an untyped dataset component, drag the DataSet component from the Data tab of the Toolbox to a form to display the Add Dataset dialog box shown in figure 9-7. Then, choose the Untyped dataset option and click OK.

How to add a table to an untyped dataset component

- To add a table to an untyped dataset component, you use the Tables Collection Editor dialog box. To display this dialog box, select the component and then click on the ellipsis that appears when you select the Tables property in the Properties window.

- To add a table to the dataset, click the Add button. Then, change the TableName property to the name you want to use for the table.

- After you add a table to the dataset, you can add columns to the table as described in figure 9-11 and you can add constraints as described in figure 9-12.

- To remove a table from the dataset, highlight the table in the Members list and click the Remove button. To modify an existing table, highlight it and then change its properties.

Figure 9-10 How to use the Tables Collection Editor

How to use the Columns Collection Editor

After you create a table, you can add columns to it using the Columns Collection Editor dialog box shown in figure 9-11. From this dialog box, you click on the Add button to add a column. Note that because the Columns Collection Editor doesn't provide an easy way to change the order of the columns once you've created them, you should add them in the order they'll appear in the Select statement that's used to fill the table. Even though the data adapter matches up columns in the data source with columns in the data table by name, not by position, it still makes sense to keep the columns in order.

To assign a name to a column, you set the ColumnName property. In addition, you may need to set some of the other properties listed in this figure. In particular, you'll want to set the DataType property to the appropriate type. In addition, you may need to set the AllowDBNull property to False for any column that doesn't allow nulls. And, if the column is an identity column, you may need to set the AutoIncrement property to True so its value is generated automatically.

Whether or not you set some of these properties depends on the type of application you're developing. For example, if you're developing a simple display program like the ones in this chapter, you don't need to worry about setting any of the properties shown here except for ColumnName and DataType. That's because these properties only need to provide for existing data, not new data that's entered by the user.

You should also realize that, just as when you use the XML Designer to design a table, you should give the columns the same names as the columns in the Select statement that will be used to fill the table. If you don't, you'll have to define table mappings for the data adapter to map the source columns to the data columns.

Another property you should make note of is the Unique property. This property determines whether or not the values in the column must be unique. If you set this property to True, a unique constraint is created. You can also create a unique constraint using the Constraints Collection Editor as shown in the next figure.

The Columns Collection Editor dialog box

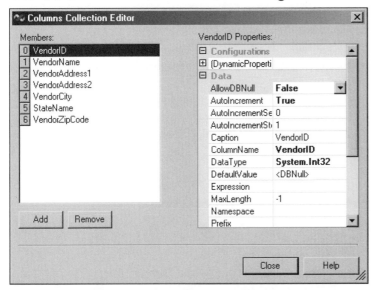

Common properties of the DataColumn class

Property	Description
AllowDBNull	A Boolean value that indicates whether the column can contain nulls. The default is True.
AutoIncrement	A Boolean value that indicates whether the column is an identity column.
AutoIncrementSeed	The starting value for an identity column.
AutoIncrementStep	The value used as the increment for an identity column.
ColumnName	The name of the column.
DataType	The type of data that's stored in the column. The default is string.
DefaultValue	The default value for the column in a new row.
MaxLength	The maximum length of a text column. The default is -1.
ReadOnly	A Boolean value that indicates whether the value of the column can be changed.
Unique	A Boolean value that indicates whether the column's values must be unique. If you set this property to True, a unique constraint is created on the column.

Description

- To add columns to a data table, you use the Columns Collection Editor dialog box. To display this dialog box, click the ellipsis that appears when you select the Columns property in the Tables Collection Editor dialog box.

- To create a column, click the Add button and set the properties for the column. At the least, you should set the ColumnName property. You may also want to change other properties, such as DataType, AllowDBNull, and MaxLength.

- To remove a column, highlight it in the Members list and then click on the Remove button. To modify an existing column, select it and then change its properties.

Figure 9-11   How to use the Columns Collection Editor

How to use the Constraints Collection Editor

Figure 9-12 presents the Constraints Collection Editor dialog box, which you use to add constraints to a data table. When you click the Add button to add a constraint, a menu appears that lists the two types of constraints you can add to a table: unique constraints and foreign key constraints. If you select the Unique Constraint option, the second dialog box shown in this figure is displayed. This dialog box lets you specify a name for the constraint and select the column or columns that must be unique. You can also select the Primary key option from this dialog box to indicate that the constraint should serve as the table's primary key.

By the way, you may notice that the properties in the Constraints Collection Editor dialog box are grayed out. That's because you can't change these properties directly. Instead, you change them from the Unique Constraint dialog box. To display this dialog box for an existing constraint, just highlight the constraint and click on the Edit button.

When you select the Foreign Key Constraint option, the Foreign Key Constraint dialog box appears. Although this dialog box isn't shown in the figure, it's identical to the Relation dialog box that's described in the next figure. The only difference between using these two dialog boxes is that you can't create a relation when you use the Foreign Key Constraint dialog box. In contrast, you can create both a relation and a foreign key constraint using the Relation dialog box.

The Constraints Collection Editor and Unique Constraint dialog boxes

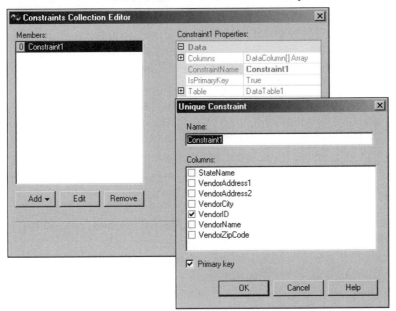

Description

- To add a unique constraint or a foreign key constraint to a schema, you use the Constraints Collection Editor dialog box. To display this dialog box, click the ellipsis that appears when you select the Constraints property in the Tables Collection Editor dialog box.

- To add a constraint, click the Add button and select Unique Constraint or Foreign Key Constraint from the menu that's displayed.

- If you select the Unique Constraint option, the Unique Constraint dialog box is displayed. To create the constraint, select the columns to be included and change the name if you'd like. To indicate that the constraint is the primary key, select the Primary key option.

- If you select the Foreign Key Constraint option, the Foreign Key Constraint dialog box is displayed. This dialog box is identical to the Relation dialog box (shown in figure 9-13). When you use the Foreign Key Constraint dialog box, though, only a foreign key constraint is created. To create a relation, you must use the Relation dialog box.

- To change a constraint, highlight it in the Members list and then click the Edit button to display the appropriate dialog box. To remove a constraint, highlight it and click the Remove button.

Figure 9-12   How to use the Constraints Collection Editor

How to use the Relations Collection Editor

To define the relationships between the tables in a dataset, you use the Relations Collection Editor dialog box shown in figure 9-13. To add a new data relation, you click the Add button to display the Relation dialog box shown in this figure. This dialog box is similar to the Edit Relation dialog box you saw in figure 9-5 that you use to define a relation using the XML Designer, so you shouldn't have any trouble understanding how it works. Note, however, that when you use the Relation dialog box, you don't have to create a unique constraint in the parent table before you define the relation. Instead, both the unique constraint and the foreign key constraint are created automatically if they don't already exist. The unique constraint that's created isn't defined as the primary key for the table, however. So if you want to define this constraint as the primary key, you'll need to create it before you define the relation, or you'll need to modify it after you create the relation.

From the Relation dialog box, you select the parent table and its key columns along with the child table and the foreign key columns. You can also enter a name for the relation. Unlike the Edit Relation dialog box, this dialog box doesn't propose a name based on the selected tables.

The Relation dialog box also lets you specify the referential integrity rules that the dataset will enforce for the relationship. These are the same rules that I presented in figures 9-5 and 9-6, so you can refer back to those figures to see what the available options are. Note, however, that when you use the Relations Collection Editor to create a relation, a Default option isn't available. Instead, the default Update and Delete rules are Cascade and the default Accept/Reject rule is None.

The Relations Collection Editor and Relation dialog boxes

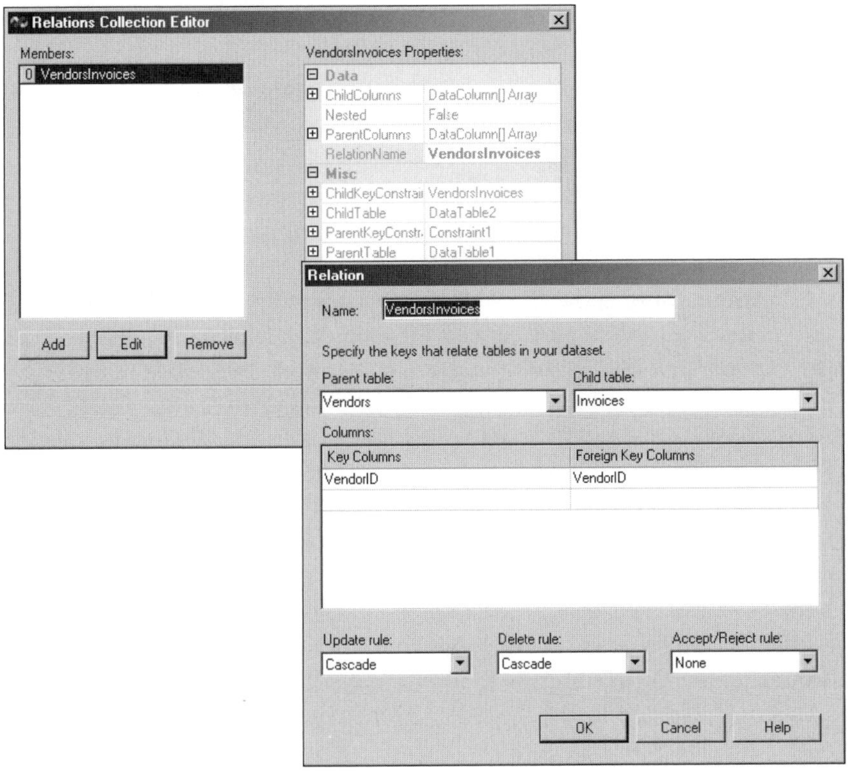

How to create a data relation

- To add a data relation to a schema, you use the Relations Collection Editor dialog box. To display this dialog box, select the dataset component, then click the ellipsis that appears when you select the Relations property in the Properties window.

- To add a relation, click the Add button to display the Relation dialog box. Then, select the parent and child tables and the key columns that define the relation.

- When you add a data relation, unique key and foreign key constraints are created automatically based on the relation if they don't already exist.

- The Update rule and Delete rule options let you specify what happens to the related child rows when a parent row is deleted or the key column of the parent row is updated. The default is Cascade, which causes changes to be cascaded to the child table.

- The Accept/Reject rule option lets you specify what happens when you execute an AcceptChanges or RejectChanges method that affects rows in the parent table. The default is None, which means that the child table isn't affected.

- See figure 9-5 for other Accept/Reject rule options. See figure 9-6 for other Update and Delete rule options and their effect on database update operations.

Figure 9-13   How to use the Relations Collection Editor

A Vendor Display program that uses an untyped dataset component

Figure 9-14 describes another version of the Vendor Display program that you saw earlier in this chapter. Instead of using a custom typed dataset, this version uses an untyped dataset component. The schema information for the dataset was created using the Tables, Columns, and Constraints Collection Editors you saw in the previous topics. The three tables in this figure list the schema definitions.

The most interesting thing about this version of the Vendor Display program is how similar it is to the typed dataset version I presented earlier in this chapter. Like the earlier version, this version of the program uses code to create the connection, command, and data adapter objects. In addition, it uses data binding and a BindingManagerBase object to display the data for a vendor when the user selects that vendor from the drop-down list. In fact, the code for these programs is identical except for the name of the dataset. The only difference between these two programs, then, is the technique that's used to create the schema information for the dataset component.

Although the code you have to write to implement this program is the same regardless of which technique you use, the code that's generated as you define the schema is quite different. In addition, the code that defines the schema in the typed dataset version is located in the class file for the typed dataset that's generated by the XML Designer. In contrast, the code that defines the schema for the untyped dataset version is located in the form class itself. You can see this code in the hidden Windows Form Designer generated code region.

The design of the Vendor Display form

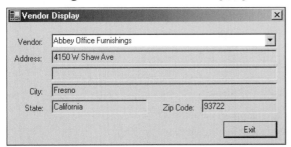

The tables collection of the dsPayables dataset

Name	TableName	PrimaryKey
DataTable1	Vendors	VendorID

The columns collection of the Vendors table

Name	ColumnName	DataType	AllowDBNull	AutoIncrement
DataColumn1	VendorID	System.Int32	False	True
DataColumn2	VendorName	System.String	False	False
DataColumn3	VendorAddress1	System.String	True	False
DataColumn4	VendorAddress2	System.String	True	False
DataColumn5	VendorCity	System.String	False	False
DataColumn6	StateName	System.String	False	False
DataColumn7	VendorZipCode	System.String	False	False

The constraints collection of the Vendors table

ConstraintName	Columns	IsPrimaryKey	Table
Constraint1	VendorID	True	DataTable1

Description

- This version of the Vendor Display program uses an untyped dataset component named dsPayables. The schema for this dataset is created using the collection editor dialog boxes. The dataset contains a single table named Vendors that includes the columns and constraint shown above.

- The data binding for this version of the Vendor Display program is nearly identical to the data binding used in the typed dataset version of the program shown in figure 9-8. The only difference is the name of the dataset.

- The code for this version of the Vendor Display program is also identical to the code for the typed dataset version that was shown in figure 9-9, except for the name of the dataset.

Figure 9-14   A Vendor Display program that uses an untyped dataset component

How to define the schema for a dataset through code

Instead of using the XML Designer or the collection editors to generate schema information for you, you can define the schema yourself using code. When you use this technique, you work directly with the collections of the DataSet, DataTable, DataColumn, and DataRelation classes. As a result, this technique gives you complete control over how the schema is defined.

When you define the schema for a dataset through code, you should realize that the dataset isn't available until runtime. As a result, you can't bind form controls to it at design time. Instead, if you want to use bound controls, you have to bind the controls through code using the techniques you learned in chapter 6.

How to create tables through code

Figure 9-15 presents several techniques you can use to create an untyped dataset and add a table to its tables collection. The first example in this figure declares a dataset variable named dsPayables that holds an instance of the DataSet class and a data table variable named dtVendors that holds an instance of the DataTable class. Notice that the name of the table is passed as an argument to the constructor of the DataTable class. Then, the Add method of the tables collection, which is accessed through the Tables property of the dataset, is used to add the table to that collection.

In the second example, the Vendors table is added to the tables collection without creating a table variable. To do that, the name of the table is passed as an argument to the Add method. Although this technique results in less code, it makes it more difficult to refer to the table later on. That's because, instead of referring to it through the table variable, you have to refer to it through the tables collection like this:

```
dsPayables.Tables("Vendors")
```

If a dataset will contain more than one table, you can use the technique illustrated in the third example in this figure to create the tables and add them to the tables collection. This example starts by declaring variables for the dataset and the two tables it will contain and creating instances of those objects. Then, it uses the AddRange method of the tables collection to add both tables to the dataset at once. The alternative is to code a separate Add method for each table.

Notice that the AddRange method accepts an array of DataTable objects as an argument. You can create the array within this argument using the New keyword as shown in this example. Although this syntax is concise, it's a bit obscure. Alternatively, you can create the array of tables first and then add it to the collection using code like this:

```
Dim dtTables As DataTable() {dtVendors, dtInvoices}
dsPayables.Tables.AddRange(dtTables)
```

The technique you use is a matter of preference.

Two ways to create a data table

```
dataTable = New DataTable()
dataTable = New DataTable(tableName)
```

How to add an existing table to a dataset

```
dataSet.Tables.Add(dataTable)
```

How to add a range of tables to a dataset

```
dataSet.Tables.AddRange(dataTable())
```

How to create a data table and add it to a dataset

```
dataTable = dataSet.Tables.Add(tableName)
```

Code examples

Code that creates a dataset and adds a table to it

```
Dim dsPayables As New DataSet()
Dim dtVendors As New DataTable("Vendors")
dsPayables.Tables.Add(dtVendors)
```

Another way to add a new table to a dataset

```
Dim dsPayables As New DataSet()
dsPayables.Tables.Add("Vendors")
```

How to add tables to a dataset using the AddRange method

```
Dim dsPayables As New DataSet()
Dim dtVendors As New DataTable("Vendors")
Dim dtInvoices As New DataTable("Invoices")
dsPayables.Tables.AddRange(New DataTable() {dtVendors, dtInvoices})
```

Description

- To create a data table, you use the DataTable class. If you don't assign a name to a table when you create it, it's given a default name when it's added to the tables collection of the dataset. The first table is given a name of Table1, the second table is given a name of Table2, and so on.

- You use the Tables property of a dataset to work with the collection of tables in a dataset. To add a table to this collection, you use the Add method. You can specify an existing data table object or the name of a new table on this method. If you specify a table name, this method returns a DataTable object.

- To add a range of tables to the tables collection, you use the AddRange method. On this method, you specify the tables as an array of DataTable objects.

Figure 9-15   How to create tables through code

302   *Section 3   Other database programming skills*

How to create columns through code

Once you've added a table to a dataset, the next step is to define the columns it will contain and add them to the table. To do that, you use the DataColumn class and the columns collection, which you access through the Columns property of the table. Figure 9-16 illustrates how this works.

The first example in this figure declares a variable to hold a data column and creates an instance of the DataColumn class. Because the column name is passed to the constructor of this class, this name will be assigned to the ColumnName property of the column. Then, the next three statements set additional properties of the column. (You can refer back to figure 9-11 for a description of these properties if you need to.) Finally, the last statement uses the Add method of the table's columns collection to add the column to the table. Although it's not shown here, you can assume that the table variable used in this example has been defined previously and that it contains an instance of the Vendors table.

Before I go on, you should notice how the GetType operator is used to assign a data type to the column. Because the DataType property must be set to a type object, you can't just set it to a data type. Instead, you have to use the GetType operator to get a type object for that data type.

The second example also adds a column to the Vendors table. In this example, though, no variables are used to hold the data table or the column that's being added. Instead, the table is referred to through the Tables property of the dataset, and the column is referred to through the Columns property of the table. Because references like these can get lengthy, I recommend you always create variables for tables and columns.

The last example in this figure shows how you can use the AddRange method to add two or more columns at the same time. This method is similar to the AddRange method of the tables collection. It accepts an array of data column objects as an argument.

Three ways to create a data column

```
dataColumn = New DataColumn()
dataColumn = New DataColumn(columnName)
dataColumn = New DataColumn(columnName, dataType)
```

How to add an existing column to a table

```
dataTable.Columns.Add(dataColumn)
```

How to add a range of columns to a table

```
dataTable.Columns.AddRange(dataColumn())
```

Two ways to create a data column and add it to a table

```
dataColumn = dataTable.Columns.Add(columnName)
dataColumn = dataTable.Columns.Add(columnName, dataType)
```

Code examples

Code that creates a column, sets its properties, and adds it to a table

```
Dim dcVendorID As New DataColumn("VendorID")
dcVendorID.AutoIncrement = True
dcVendorID.AllowDBNull = False
dcVendorID.DataType = GetType(System.Int32)
dtVendors.Columns.Add(dcVendorID)
```

Another way to create a column, set its properties, and add it to a table

```
dsPayables.Tables("Vendors").Columns.Add("VendorID")
With dsPayables.Tables("Vendors").Columns("VendorID")
    .AutoIncrement = True
    .AllowDBNull = False
    .DataType = GetType(System.Int32)
End With
```

How to add columns using the AddRange method

```
dtVendors.Columns.AddRange(New DataColumn() {dcVendorID, dcName, _
    dcAddress1, dcAddress2, dcCity, dcState, dcZipCode})
```

Description

- To create a data column, you use the DataColumn class. If you don't assign a name to a column when you create it, it's given a default name when it's added to the columns collection of the table (Column1, Column2, and so on).

- You can also assign a data type when you create a column. To do that, you use the GetType operator to get a type object for a system data type. If you don't assign a data type to a column, it's given a data type of string.

- You use the Columns property of a table to work with the collection of columns in the table. To add a column to this collection, you use the Add method. You can specify an existing column object or a new column name on this method. If you specify a column name, this method returns a DataColumn object.

- To add a range of columns to the columns collection, you use the AddRange method. On this method, you specify the columns as an array of DataColumn objects.

- See figure 9-11 for a list of common data column properties.

Figure 9-16   How to create columns through code

How to create unique constraints through code

Constraints are managed through the constraints collection of the DataTable class. You can add two types of constraints to the constraints collection: unique constraints and foreign key constraints. You'll learn how to work with unique constraints in this topic, and you'll learn how to work with foreign key constraints in the next topic.

Figure 9-17 presents several techniques you can use to create a unique constraint. If you want to assign the constraint to a variable so you can refer to it later, you can use one of the constructors shown at the top of this figure to create an instance of the UniqueConstraint class. The arguments on these constructors let you specify the name of the constraint, the column or columns that make up the constraint, and whether or not the constraint is a primary key. The first code example in this figure illustrates how this works. Here, a unique constraint named Primary Key is created for the VendorID column. Because the isPrimaryKey argument is set the True, the constraint will be defined as the primary key. Then, the second statement in this example uses the Add method of the constraints collection for the Vendors table to add the constraint to this table. To access the constraints collection, it uses the Constraints property of the table.

In most cases, you won't need to refer to a unique constraint once you create it and add it to the table. Because of that, you don't usually need to assign the constraint to a variable. Instead, you can create the constraint and add it to the constraints collection using the Add method of the constraints collection as illustrated in the second example in this figure. The statement in this example creates the same constraint that was created by the two statements in the first example. Notice that to use this technique, you must specify all three arguments of the Add method.

To create a unique constraint that isn't a primary key, you specify False for the isPrimaryKey argument. This is illustrated by the third example in this figure. The statement in this example creates a unique constraint for the VendorName column in the Vendors table.

The fourth example in this figure shows how you create a unique constraint with two columns. To do that, you specify the columns as an array. In this case, the two columns in the dcInvoiceID and dcInvoiceSequence columns are added as the primary key of the dtInvoiceLineItems table.

The last example in this figure shows that you can also create a primary key by setting the data table's PrimaryKey property. The value of this property is an array of DataColumn objects, so you have to assign an array to it even if the primary key consists of a single column. When you set the PrimaryKey property, a UniqueConstraint object is created automatically and added to the table's constraints collection.

Four ways to create a unique constraint

```
constraint = New UniqueConstraint(column|column())
constraint = New UniqueConstraint(column|column(), isPrimaryKey)
constraint = New UniqueConstraint(constraintName, column|column())
constraint = New UniqueConstraint(constraintName, column|column(),
                isPrimaryKey)
```

How to add an existing unique constraint to a table

```
dataTable.Constraints.Add(constraint)
```

How to create a unique constraint and add it to a table

```
constraint = dataTable.Constraints.Add(constraintName, column|column(),
                isPrimaryKey)
```

Common properties of the UniqueConstraint class

Property	Description
Columns	An array of columns that make up the constraint.
ConstraintName	The name of the constraint.
IsPrimaryKey	A Boolean value that indicates whether the constraint is the table's primary key.
Table	The table that the constraint applies to.

Code that creates a primary key with a single column and adds it to a table

```
Dim ucVendors As New UniqueConstraint("PrimaryKey", dcVendorID, True)
dsPayables.Tables("Vendors").Constraints.Add(ucVendors)
```

Another way to create a primary key and add it to a table

```
dtVendors.Constraints.Add("PrimaryKey", dcVendorID, True)
```

Code that creates a unique constraint without creating a primary key

```
dtVendors.Constraints.Add("UniqueConstraint", dcVendorName, False)
```

Code that creates a primary key with two columns

```
dtInvoiceLineItems.Constraints.Add("PrimaryKey", _
    New DataColumn() {dcInvoiceID, dcInvoiceSequence}, True)
```

How to create a primary key using the data table's PrimaryKey property

```
dtVendors.PrimaryKey = New DataColumn() {dcVendorID}
```

Description

- To create a unique constraint, you use the UniqueConstraint class. To access the collection of constraints for a table, you use the Constraints property of the data table.

- To add a unique constraint to a table, you use the Add method of the constraints collection. On this method, you specify the name of the constraint, the columns that make up the constraint, and a Boolean value that specifies whether the constraint is a primary key. Alternatively, you can specify an existing unique constraint object.

- You can also create a primary key for a table by setting the table's PrimaryKey property to an array of columns that make up the key.

Figure 9-17   How to create unique constraints through code

How to create foreign key constraints through code

To create a foreign key constraint for a table, you add a ForeignKeyConstraint object to the table's constraints collection. Figure 9-18 presents the techniques you can use to do that.

Just as with unique constraints, you're not likely to refer to a foreign key constraint once you create it and add it to the table. Because of that, you won't usually assign the constraint to a variable. Instead, you'll create the constraint and add it to the constraints collection in a single statement, as shown in the first example in this figure. This statement creates a foreign key constraint named VendorsInvoices that relates the VendorID column in the Vendors table (the parent table) to the VendorID column in the Invoices table (the child table). This constraint is added to the Invoices table. As in previous examples, the data tables used in this example have been stored in variables named dtVendors and dtInvoices.

The second example in this figure shows how you can specify the referential integrity rules for a foreign key constraint. In this case, a variable is declared to hold the foreign key constraint to make it easier to refer to the DeleteRule, UpdateRule, and AcceptRejectRule properties. Although you might think that you could refer to these properties through the Constraints property of the table, you can't. For example, this code will cause a syntax error:

```
With dtInvoices.Constraints("VendorsInvoices")
    .DeleteRule = Rule.Cascade
    .UpdateRule = Rule.Cascade
    .AcceptRejectRule = AcceptRejectRule.Cascade
End With
```

That's because the Constraints property refers to a collection of Constraint objects, not a collection of ForeignKeyConstraint objects. Although the Constraint class is the base class for the ForeignKeyConstraint (and the UniqueConstraint) class, the Constraint class itself doesn't have a DeleteRule, UpdateRule, or AcceptRejectRule property. As a result, you must use a ForeignKeyConstraint object, not a Constraint object, to access these properties.

Although they're uncommon, you can also create composite foreign keys. To do that, you specify an array of columns for the parent column and child column arguments. Note that the columns you specify for the parent and child tables must match in both number and type.

How to create a foreign key constraint

```
constraint = New ForeignKeyConstraint(parentColumn|parentColumn(),
        childColumn|childColumn())
constraint = New ForeignKeyConstraint(constraintName,
        parentColumn|parentColumn(), childColumn|childColumn())
```

How to add an existing foreign key constraint to a table

```
dataTable.Constraints.Add(constraint)
```

How to create a foreign key constraint and add it to a table

```
constraint = dataTable.Constraints.Add(constraintName,
        parentColumn|parentColumn(), childColumn|childColumn())
```

Common properties of the ForeignKeyConstraint class

Property	Description
Columns	An array of child columns for the constraint.
ConstraintName	The name of the constraint.
RelatedColumns	An array of parent columns for the constraint.
RelatedTable	The parent table for the constraint.
Table	The child table for the constraint.
DeleteRule	The referential integrity rule to apply when a parent row is deleted.
UpdateRule	The referential integrity rule to apply when a parent row is updated.
AcceptRejectRule	The referential integrity rule to apply when changes are accepted or rejected.

Code that creates a foreign key constraint and adds it to a table

```
dtInvoices.Constraints.Add("VendorsInvoices", dtVendors("VendorID"), _
    dtInvoices("VendorID"))
```

Code that creates a foreign key constraint with referential integrity rules

```
Dim fc As New ForeignKeyConstraint("VendorsInvoices", _
    dtVendors("VendorID"), dtInvoices("VendorID"))
fc.DeleteRule = Rule.Cascade
fc.UpdateRule = Rule.Cascade
fc.AcceptRejectRule = AcceptRejectRule.Cascade
dtInvoices.Constraints.Add(fc)
```

Description

- To create a foreign key constraint, you use the ForeignKeyConstraint class. To access the collection of constraints for a table, you use the Constraints property of the data table.

- To add a foreign key constraint to a table, you use the Add method of the constraints collection. On this method, you specify the name of the constraint, the columns in the parent table, and the related columns in the child table. Alternatively, you can specify an existing foreign key constraint object.

- A foreign key constraint must have the same number of parent and child columns and those columns must have matching data types.

Figure 9-18   How to create foreign key constraints through code

How to create data relations through code

Figure 9-19 presents the techniques you can use to create a data relation through code. As you can see, these techniques are similar to the techniques you use to create a foreign key constraint. That makes sense since a relation is typically based on a foreign key constraint.

The easiest way to create a data relation is to use the Add method of the dataset's relations collection, which you access through the Relations property of the dataset. On the Add method, you specify the name of the relation along with the parent and child column or columns. The first example in this figure, for instance, creates a relation named VendorsInvoices that relates the VendorID column in the Vendors table to the VendorID column in the Invoices table.

When you create a data relation, a unique constraint and a foreign key constraint are created automatically if they don't already exist. To access the unique constraint, you can use the ParentKeyConstraint property of the data relation. To access the foreign key constraint, you can use the ChildKeyConstraint property. This is illustrated in the second example in this figure. Here, the ChildKeyConstraint property is used to set the referential integrity rules for the foreign key constraint associated with the data relation.

Although it's not illustrated in this figure, you can also create a data relation without creating unique key or foreign key constraints. To do that, you specify False for the createConstraints argument of the DataRelation constructor or the Add method. You might want to do that if you need to create a relation that lets you navigate a many-to-many relationship rather than a one-to-many relationship.

For example, suppose you have a table of warehouse locations called Warehouses in addition to the Vendors table. A many-to-many relation between the Vendors and Warehouses tables based on the state columns would let you retrieve all of the Vendors that are in the same state as a particular warehouse, or all of the warehouses that are in the same state as a particular vendor. Obviously, you wouldn't want the relation to create a unique constraint for the state column in either table, since you might have more than one vendor and more than one warehouse in the same state.

How to create a data relation

```
dataRelation = New DataRelation(relationName, parentColumn|parentColumn(),
        childColumn|childColumn())
dataRelation = New DataRelation(relationName, parentColumn|parentColumn(),
        childColumn|childColumn(), createConstraints)
```

How to add an existing data relation to a dataset

```
dataSet.Relations.Add(relation)
```

How to create a data relation and add it to a dataset

```
dataRelation = dataSet.Relations.Add(parentColumn|parentColumn(),
        childColumn|childColumn())
dataRelation = dataSet.Relations.Add(relationName, parentColumn|
        parentColumn(), childColumn|childColumn())
dataRelation = dataSet.Relations.Add(relationName, parentColumn|
        parentColumn(), childColumn|childColumn(), createConstraints)
```

Common properties of the DataRelation class

Property	Description
ChildColumns	An array of child columns for the relation.
ChildKeyConstraint	The foreign key constraint for the relation.
ChildTable	The child table for the relation.
DataSet	The dataset for the relation.
ParentColumns	An array of parent columns for the relation.
ParentKeyConstraint	The unique constraint for the relation.
ParentTable	The parent table for the relation.
RelationName	The name of the relation.

Code that creates a data relation

```
dsPayables.Relations.Add("VendorsInvoices", dtVendors("VendorID"), _
    dtInvoices("VendorID"))
```

Code that creates a data relation with referential integrity rules

```
Dim dr As New DataRelation("VendorsInvoices", dtVendors("VendorID"), _
    dtInvoices("VendorID"))
dr.ChildKeyConstraint.DeleteRule = Rule.Cascade
dr.ChildKeyConstraint.UpdateRule = Rule.Cascade
dr.ChildKeyConstraint.AcceptRejectRule = AcceptRejectRule.Cascade
dsPayables.Relations.Add(dr)
```

Description

- To create a data relation, you use the DataRelation class. To access the collection of data relations for a dataset, you use the Relations property of the dataset.

- To add a relation to a dataset, you use the Add method of the relations collection. On this method, you can specify the name of the relation, the columns in the parent table, the related columns in the child table, and a Boolean value that indicates whether constraints should be created (the default is True). Alternatively, you can specify an existing data relation object.

Figure 9-19   How to create data relations through code

A Vendor Display program that uses an untyped dataset created through code

Figure 9-20 presets the Visual Basic code for another version of the Vendor Display program. This version uses an untyped dataset whose schema is created in code. Because of that, the schema information isn't available at design time, so the program must bind the form controls to the dataset through code at runtime.

At the top of the listing, you can see a series of Dim statements that declare variables for the Payables dataset, the Vendors table, and each of the columns in this table. These variables are declared at the module level so they're available to all of the procedures in the form class. As you can see, the table and column names are passed as arguments to the constructors so that they don't have to be set later on.

When the form is first displayed, the Load procedure begins by calling the CreateVendorSchema procedure. This procedure starts by setting the DataType property of the VendorID column. Since all of the other columns contain string values, it's not necessary to specify their data types. It's also not necessary to set any of the other column properties since this program won't let the user change any of the data that's displayed.

To add the columns to the Vendors table, this procedure uses the AddRange method of the columns collection. Then, it uses the add method of the constraints collection to create a primary key constraint and add it to the table. And it uses the Add method of the tables collection to add the table to the Payables dataset. This code is similar to code you've seen in previous figures, so you shouldn't have any trouble understanding it.

The Load procedure also calls the FillVendorsTable procedure. This procedure creates the connection, command, and data adapter objects and then fills the Vendors table. It's almost identical to the code you saw in the typed dataset version of this program in figure 9-9. The only difference is that the Fill method of the data adapter specifies the data table variable as an argument.

The code for the Vendor Display program

Page 1

```vbnet
Imports System.Data.SqlClient
Public Class Form1
    Inherits System.Windows.Forms.Form

    Dim dsPayables As New DataSet()
    Dim dtVendors As New DataTable("Vendors")
    Dim dcVendorID As New DataColumn("VendorID")
    Dim dcName As New DataColumn("VendorName")
    Dim dcAddress1 As New DataColumn("VendorAddress1")
    Dim dcAddress2 As New DataColumn("VendorAddress2")
    Dim dcCity As New DataColumn("VendorCity")
    Dim dcState As New DataColumn("StateName")
    Dim dcZipCode As New DataColumn("VendorZipCode")
    Dim bmbVendors As BindingManagerBase

    Private Sub Form1_Load(ByVal sender As System.Object, _
            ByVal e As System.EventArgs) Handles MyBase.Load
        Me.CreateVendorSchema()
        Me.FillVendorsTable()
        Me.BindControls()
        bmbVendors = Me.BindingContext(dsPayables, "Vendors")
    End Sub

    Public Sub CreateVendorSchema()
        dcVendorID.DataType = GetType(System.Int32)
        dtVendors.Columns.AddRange(New DataColumn() {dcVendorID, dcName, _
            dcAddress1, dcAddress2, dcCity, dcState, dcZipCode})
        dtVendors.Constraints.Add("PK", dcVendorID, True)
        dsPayables.Tables.Add(dtVendors)
    End Sub

    Public Sub FillVendorsTable()
        Dim sPayablesConnection As String _
            = "server=Doug\VSdotNET;" _
            & "database=Payables;" _
            & "integrated security=SSPI;" _
            & "workstation id=DOUG"
        Dim conPayables As New SqlConnection(sPayablesConnection)

        Dim sVendorSelect As String _
            = "Select VendorID, VendorName, VendorAddress1, " _
            & "VendorAddress2, VendorCity, StateName, VendorZipCode " _
            & "From Vendors Join States On VendorState = StateCode " _
            & "Order By VendorName"
        Dim cmdVendors As New SqlCommand(sVendorSelect, conPayables)
        Dim daVendors As New SqlDataAdapter(cmdVendors)
        Try
            daVendors.Fill(dtVendors)
        Catch eSql As SqlException
            MessageBox.Show(eSql.Message, "SQL Server error")
        End Try
    End Sub
```

Figure 9-20 A Vendor Display program that uses an untyped dataset (part 1 of 2)

To bind the controls to the dataset, the Load procedure calls the BindControls procedure. This procedure binds the Vendors combo box by setting its DataSource and DisplayMember properties. Then, it binds the text boxes by adding a Binding object to the each of the text box's data bindings collections. If you're not sure how this code works, you can refer to figure 6-6 for the details. Briefly, though, the Add method here identifies the control property to be bound and the table column to which it's bound.

Notice that the column name for each data binding is provided through the ColumnName property of the DataColumn object. You could also code these names as string literals like this:

```
txtAddressLine1.DataBindings.Add("Text", dtVendors, _
    "VendorAddress1")
```

However, using the ColumnName property of the DataColumn objects is less errorprone because you don't have to worry about misspelling the column names. In addition, if you decide to change a column name later on, you don't have to remember to change it in two places.

The code for the Vendor display program   **Page 2**

```
Private Sub BindControls()
    cboVendors.DataSource = dtVendors
    cboVendors.DisplayMember = dcName.ColumnName
    txtAddressLine1.DataBindings.Add("Text", dtVendors, _
        dcAddress1.ColumnName)
    txtAddressLine2.DataBindings.Add("Text", dtVendors, _
        dcAddress2.ColumnName)
    txtCity.DataBindings.Add("Text", dtVendors, dcCity.ColumnName)
    txtState.DataBindings.Add("Text", dtVendors, dcState.ColumnName)
    txtZipCode.DataBindings.Add("Text", dtVendors, dcZipCode.ColumnName)
End Sub

Private Sub cboVendors_SelectedIndexChanged _
        (ByVal sender As System.Object, ByVal e As System.EventArgs) _
        Handles cboVendors.SelectedIndexChanged
    bmbVendors.Position = cboVendors.SelectedIndex
End Sub

Private Sub btnExit_Click(ByVal sender As System.Object, _
        ByVal e As System.EventArgs) Handles btnExit.Click
    Me.Close()
End Sub

End Class
```

Figure 9-20   A Vendor Display program that uses an untyped dataset (part 2 of 2)

Perspective

In this chapter, you've learned three different techniques for creating dataset schemas. Which technique should you use in your applications? Frankly, the answer depends mostly on personal preference. If you like the benefits of working with typed datasets, you should use the XML Designer to create a typed dataset class. If you like the flexibility of untyped datasets but don't want to code the schema by hand, you should use an untyped dataset component and create the schema using the collection editors. And if you like the control afforded by writing every line of your application's code yourself, you should use an untyped dataset and create the schema through code.

Terms

schema
XML Designer
XML Schema Definition (XSD)
schema element
attribute
collection editor

10

How to develop and use database classes

Up to now, you've developed programs that have consisted of a form class and, in some cases, a dataset class. However, a program can also include additional classes. In particular, a program can contain database classes that handle the database operations for the program.

In this chapter, you'll learn how to develop database classes and how to use them in a Windows application. But first, you'll learn about the architecture that you use when you develop these types of applications. You'll also learn about two different ways you can package database classes and two different ways you can distribute them.

An introduction to multi-layered application design

The topics that follow introduce you to the concepts of multi-layered application design. First, you'll learn how the classes that make up an application can be divided into two or more layers. Then, you'll learn how the classes in a multi-layered application can be packaged so they can be deployed onto separate computers.

The architecture of a three-tiered application

Figure 10-1 shows how you can design database applications using a *multi-layered architecture*, also called a *multi-tiered architecture*. In a multi-layered application, software elements that perform different functions are separated into two or more layers, or tiers. A three-tiered application architecture like the one shown in this figure, for example, consists of a presentation layer, a middle layer, and a database layer. In actual practice, the middle layer is sometimes eliminated and its functions split between the database and presentation layers. On the other hand, some application designs further develop the middle layer into additional layers.

The *presentation layer* handles the details of the application's user interface. For a Windows application, this consists of the form classes that display the user interface. For a web application, the presentation layer consists of the HTML files that display the application's pages.

The *database layer* is responsible for all database access required by the application. The database classes in this layer typically include methods that connect to the database and retrieve, insert, add, and delete information from the database. Then, the other layers can call these methods to access the database, leaving the details of database access to the database classes. In this chapter, I'll focus on how you develop and use this type of class.

The *middle layer* provides an interface between the database layer and the presentation layer. This layer can consist of dataset classes and classes that represent business entities (for example, Vendors and Invoices). It may also consist of classes that implement business rules, such as customer discounts or credit approvals.

In a traditional client/server application, the presentation and middle layers are implemented on the client computer and the database itself is implemented on a database server. Although the database classes are a part of the database layer, they are usually implemented on the client computer along with the classes in the presentation and middle layers.

In a *distributed application,* however, the classes of the middle or database layer (or of both layers) are implemented on server computers rather than on the clients. For example, the database classes might be implemented on a database server. Alternatively, the database classes and the middle layer classes might be implemented on a separate application server.

The architecture of a three-tiered application

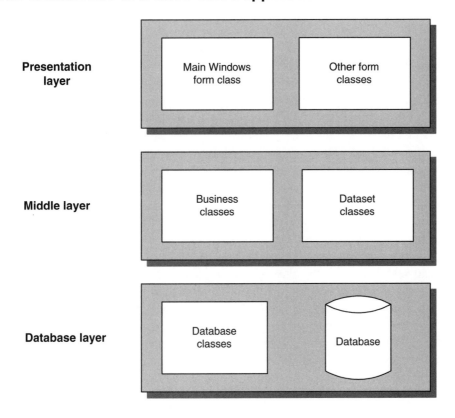

Description

- To simplify development and maintenance, many applications use a *three-tiered architecture* to separate the application's user interface, business rules, and database processing.

- The *presentation layer* controls the application's user interface. For a Windows forms application, the user interface consists of the various forms that make up the application and the Visual Basic code that implements the forms.

- The *database layer* consists of the database itself as well as the database classes that work directly with the database.

- The *middle layer*, sometimes called the *business rules layer*, provides an interface between the presentation layer and the database layer. At the least, it contains the dataset classes that provide data to the presentation layer. It may also contain business classes that represent business entities or that implement business rules.

- In many cases, all three of the application tiers run on a single computer. However, it's possible for each layer to run on a separate computer. If two or more layers run on different computers, the application is called a *distributed application* (see figure 10-3 for more details).

Figure 10-1   The architecture of a three-tiered application

Two ways to package database classes

Figure 10-2 illustrates two basic ways you can develop and package the database classes for an application. The easiest way is to simply add the class files to the project that contains the form classes. Then, when you build the project, all of the class files are compiled into a single executable assembly.

The advantage of this method is its simplicity. Because the class files are all stored together in the same project, you can code, test, and debug them together. If you discover that one of the database methods isn't working right, you can change it and then build and test the project again. If your database class needs an additional method, you can simply add the new method to the database class, write code in the form class to call the new method, and recompile the project.

The disadvantage of storing all the classes in a single project is that you can't easily share the database classes with other projects. Although you could copy the class into each project that needed it, you'd have to update the copy in each project any time a change was required.

The alternative to storing all the classes in a single project is to implement the database classes as a separate *class library*. Then, the class library can be used by any application that needs access to the classes it contains. In addition, if you need to update a database class, you only need to change the class in one place. Because class libraries are built as separate assemblies, any changes you make to them are automatically available to any applications that use them.

The disadvantage of storing database classes in a class library is that it makes the application more complicated to develop. Although the code for a class file is the same whether you include it in the project that contains the form classes or in a separate class library, testing and debugging the class library is more complicated. Also, if you change one of the members in a class library, you must retest every application that uses it.

Although it's not illustrated in this figure, you should also realize that you can implement database classes as components. A *component* is a special type of class that's designed to work with Visual Basic's visual design features. Throughout this book, for example, you've learned how to work with many of the ADO.NET components. If you implement a database class as a component, you can add it to the Toolbox. Then, you can drag and drop it onto the design surface so it appears in the Component Designer tray, and you can set its properties at design time. Because database components are significantly more complicated to develop than simple database classes, however, none of the database classes in this book are implemented as components.

Database classes implemented within a project

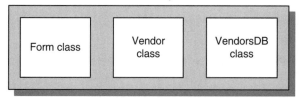

VendorMaintenance assembly

| Form class | Vendor class | VendorsDB class |

Database classes implemented in a class library

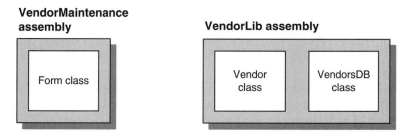

VendorMaintenance assembly

| Form class |

VendorLib assembly

| Vendor class | VendorsDB class |

Discussion

- You can create database classes by simply adding class files to the project that contains the form classes for the application. Then, when the project is compiled, the classes become part of the same assembly.

- When you store all of the classes for an application in the same project, you can develop the form and database classes simultaneously. To use the database classes in another project, however, you have to copy them to those projects. Then, you have to update all the copies any time a change is required.

- If you store the database classes in a separate *class library* project, the classes are compiled into their own assembly. Then, you can include a reference to that assembly in each application that needs to use the database classes.

- When you modify a class in a class library, the changes are immediately available to all the applications that use it.

- Classes in a class library are more difficult to work with because they must be developed independently of the application's form classes.

Figure 10-2   Two ways to package database classes

Two ways to create a distributed database application

If you code your database classes in class libraries as described in the previous topic, the class library must reside on each computer that needs to use it. In contrast, when you develop a distributed application, the database classes can reside on a server so that they're available to any application that has access to that server. Because the processing done by a distributed application is distributed over two or more computers, it's referred to as *distributed processing*.

Figure 10-3 shows the two basic techniques .NET provides for implementing distributed processing: .NET Remoting and XML web services. Although the details of using .NET Remoting and XML web services are beyond the scope of this book, you should at least have a general idea of how they work.

To understand how *.NET Remoting* works, you need to realize that every .NET application runs in a separate *application domain*. Application domains are managed by the .NET Common Language Runtime (CLR) and are protected and isolated from one another. That way, an application that fails doesn't affect applications running in other domains.

Normally, all of the assemblies that make up an application run in the same application domain. However, you can develop database classes so that they run in a separate application domain. To do that, you implement the classes as *remotable components*. Then, you can use .NET Remoting to enable the application domains so they can communicate with one another. That works whether the application domains are on the same computer, on two computers connected to a local area network, or on two computers connected via the Internet.

An alternative to .NET Remoting is to use *XML web services* for your database classes. Simply put, a web service is a class that resides on a web server and can be accessed via the Internet. Web services rely on an industry standard protocol called *SOAP* (*Simple Object Access Protocol*), which is based on XML. Because web services are based on industry standard protocols, they aren't tied to Microsoft's proprietary technology. As a result, you can access them with applications written in any language and running on any operating system.

Whether you choose to use .NET Remoting or XML web services, implementing database classes as distributed objects is not a trivial task. You must consider many factors, including security and authentication, performance, and reliability. Still, the basic design of an application's database classes will be much the same whether you implement them as simple class files, as class libraries, as remotable components, or as web services.

Database classes implemented as a remotable component

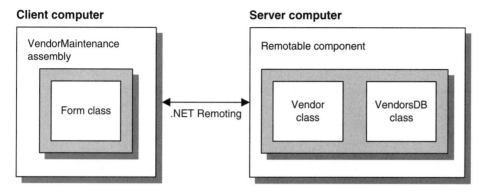

Database classes implemented as an XML web service

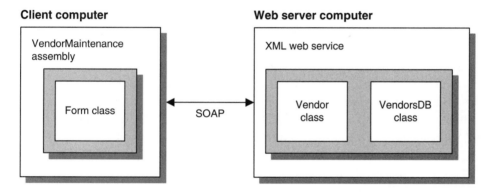

Discussion

- In a distributed application, parts of the application run on different computers, possibly (but not necessarily) in different physical locations. Typically, form classes run on client computers and database classes run on a database server or an application server.

- With *.NET Remoting*, you implement your classes as *remotable components* that can be accessed regardless of whether they're on the same computer, on different computers connected to the same local area network, or on different computers connected via the Internet.

- An alternative to .NET Remoting is to implement the database classes of an application as *XML web services*. An XML web service uses an industry-standard protocol called *SOAP* (*Simple Object Access Protocol*) to allow applications to communicate via the Internet.

- Web services are hosted on a web server and can be accessed from any computer that has a connection to the Internet.

Figure 10-3   Two ways to create a distributed database application

A Vendor Maintenance program that uses database classes

The remaining topics of this chapter present a program that illustrates how you can use database classes. This program is yet another version of the Vendor Maintenance program you've seen throughout this book. Although the database classes it uses are relatively simple, it should give you an idea of how you can design and code applications that use database classes.

The design of the Vendor Maintenance program

Figure 10-4 presents the design of the Vendor Maintenance program. As you can see, the form for this program is almost identical to the form you saw back in chapter 4. The only difference is that the form for this program doesn't include an Update Database button. That's because, unlike the program in chapter 4, this program retrieves a single vendor at a time. To do that, the user selects the vendor from the Vendors combo box, which is loaded when the program starts. Then, when the user changes the data for the vendor and clicks the Update button, the database is updated immediately. Similarly, if the user adds a new vendor and clicks on the Update button, the vendor is immediately added to the database. And if the user selects a vendor and clicks on the Delete button, the vendor is immediately deleted from the database.

Four classes are used to implement this program as indicated in the class diagram in this figure. This diagram uses a simplified version of a standard diagram notation called *Uniform Modeling Language,* or *UML*. In this type of diagram, each class is represented by a box that names the class and lists its members. The symbols that appear before each member indicate the visibility of the members. Private members are preceded by a minus sign, public members by a plus sign, and protected members by a pound sign (#). In addition, an arrow from one class to another indicates that the first class inherits the second class.

The class named frmVendorMaintenance in this diagram is a standard form class that provides the application's user interface. The class named Vendor is a business class that represents a single vendor. It has properties that correspond to the columns in the Vendors database table. Finally, the PayablesDB and VendorsDB classes are the application's database classes. They provide methods that can be used to access the database.

From the class diagram in this figure, you can see that the VendorsDB class inherits the PayablesDB class. The PayablesDB class includes methods that provide connection information. This class is designed to be used as a base class for other database classes, such as VendorsDB, that actually provide access to the database. By placing the connection methods in a base class, you can be sure that any class that inherits that class will use the same database connection. If you're unclear about how class inheritance works, don't worry. It will become clear when you see the actual code for the PayablesDB and VendorsDB classes.

The design of the Vendor Maintenance form

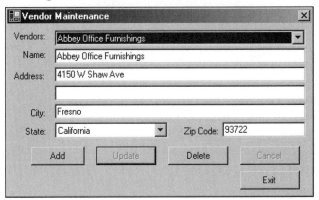

The class diagram for the Vendor Maintenance program

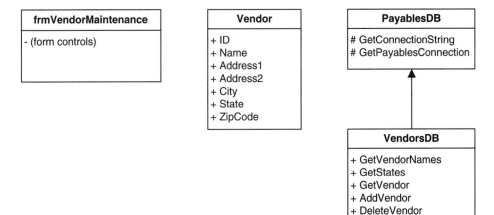

Description

- The operation of the Vendor Maintenance program is similar to other versions of this program presented in earlier chapters. Like the versions in chapters 4, 5, and 6, it lets the user select a vendor from a combo box. Like the versions in chapters 7 and 8, it updates the database each time the user adds, updates, or deletes a row.

- This program is implemented using the four classes in the class diagram shown above. This diagram shows the members that make up each class. The symbol that precedes each member indicates its visibility as follows: - for a private member, + for a public member, and # for a protected member.

- The arrow from the VendorsDB class to the PayablesDB class indicates that the VendorsDB class inherits the PayablesDB class. Because the two members of the PayablesDB class are protected, they can be used only within that class or by the VendorsDB class.

Figure 10-4 The design of the Vendor Maintenance program

The design of the Vendor class

Figure 10-5 presents the design of the Vendor class. As I mentioned earlier, this class represents a single occurrence of a vendor, and its properties correspond to the columns in the Vendors table of the Payables database. Note that because the Vendor Maintenance program updates only the vendor's name and address information, the Vendor class only includes properties for the columns needed to do that. If you were implementing a class that could be used by other applications, however, you would want to include properties for all of the columns in the table that you want the user to have access to.

The code for the Vendor class

Figure 10-5 also shows the code for the Vendor class. As you can see, each property is implemented as a public variable. Because of that, no data validation is performed before values are assigned to these variables.

However, the Vendors table in the Payables database does have validation requirements. For example, a vendor name, city, state, and zip code are required. In addition, the state value must be a valid two-character code. In a production program, then, you might want to add data validation routines to the Vendor class to ensure that invalid data doesn't find its way into the Vendors table.

One way to add validation code to this class would be to add a constructor that accepts the data for a vendor as arguments. Then, the constructor could validate each argument and throw an exception if an invalid value was provided. Another way to validate the data would be to code a property procedure for each property. Then, the set procedure within each property procedure could validate the value of the property.

The design of the Vendor class

Property	Description
ID	The vendor's ID. This value is generated automatically by the database when a vendor is added, so it can be null for a vendor that has not yet been added to the database.
Name	The vendor's name.
Address1	The first line of the vendor's address.
Address2	The second line of the vendor's address.
City	The vendor's city.
State	The vendor's two-character state code.
ZipCode	The vendor's zip code.

The Visual Basic code for the Vendor class

```
Public Class Vendor
    Public ID As Integer
    Public Name As String
    Public Address1 As String
    Public Address2 As String
    Public City As String
    Public State As String
    Public ZipCode As String
End Class
```

Description

- The Vendor class represents a single vendor in the Vendors table. For simplicity, it only includes properties for the columns used by the Vendor Maintenance program. The other columns have default values or don't require values.

- For simplicity, the Vendor class doesn't provide for data validation. Instead, each property is defined as a public variable that can be set to any value that's appropriate for its data type. In a production application, the Vendor class would probably validate each property by including validation code within a property procedure.

Figure 10-5   The Vendor class

The design of the PayablesDB class

Figure 10-6 presents the design of the PayablesDB class. This class provides basic connection functions for the Payables database. It includes the two methods listed in the table at the top of this figure. The GetPayablesConnection method returns a SqlConnection object that can be used to establish a connection to the Payables database. The GetConnectionString method gets the connection string that's used by the GetPayablesConnection method to create the connection.

The code for the PayablesDB class

Figure 10-6 also presents the code for the PayablesDB class. The first thing you should notice is that both methods of this class are protected. That means that they can only be used by the class itself or by classes that inherit the class.

The code for the PayablesDB class is straightforward. The GetPayablesConnection method simply calls the GetConnectionString method to get a connection string. Then, it creates a new SqlConnection object using that string and returns it to the procedure that executed the method.

The GetConnectionString method gets the connection string from an XML file named csPayables.xml. You can see the contents of this file in this figure. If you aren't familiar with XML, this file and the code in the GetConnectionString method that reads it might be a little confusing. So I'll explain it briefly. If you want to learn more about working with XML files, though, you can get our book, *Murach's Beginning Visual Basic .NET*.

The XML file shown in this figure contains a single XML element named Connection. This element contains the complete connection string, which is highlighted in this listing. To get the connection string from this element, the GetConnectionString method uses an XmlTextReader object. As you can see, this object specifies the name of the XML file. (When this object is created, it will look for the XML file in the bin folder for the solution by default. If the file is in a different folder, you'll need to specify its location as well as its name.) Then, the ReadElementString method of the XmlTextReader is used to get the value of the element named Connection. This value is then returned to the procedure that called the GetConnectionString method, which in this case is the GetPayablesConnection method.

The design of the PayablesDB class

Method	Description
GetPayablesConnection	Returns a SqlConnection object that can be used to access the Payables database.
GetConnectionString	Returns a connection string that can be used to connect to the Payables database.

The Visual Basic code for the PayablesDB class

```vb
Imports System.Data.SqlClient
Imports System.Xml

Public Class PayablesDB

    Protected Shared Function GetPayablesConnection() As SqlConnection
        Return New SqlConnection(GetConnectionString)
    End Function

    Protected Shared Function GetConnectionString() As String
        Dim XmlReader As New XmlTextReader("csPayables.xml")
        Return XmlReader.ReadElementString("Connection")
    End Function

End Class
```

The csPayables.xml file

```xml
<?xml version="1.0" encoding="utf-8" ?>
<Connection>data source=DOUG\VSdotNET;initial catalog=Payables;integrated
security=SSPI;persist security info=False;packet size=4096
</Connection>
```

Description

- The PayablesDB class provides the basic functions needed to connect to the Payables database. Other classes can inherit this class so the connection information doesn't have to be duplicated in each class.

- The GetPayablesConnection method returns a SqlConnection object that can be used to connect to the Payables database. This method uses the GetConnectionString method to get the actual connection string used to create the SqlConnection object.

- The GetConnectionString method returns a connection string that's retrieved from an XML file named csPayables.xml. By placing the connection string in a separate file, it can be used by more than one program. In addition, if it needs to be modified, it can be changed in one location rather than in each program that uses it.

- To read the contents of the XML file, the GetConnectionString method uses an XmlTextReader. The ReadElementString method of this object retrieves the content of an XML element named Connection, which contains the connection string.

- The methods in this class don't perform any error checking. As a result, an exception will be thrown if the XML configuration file can't be found or doesn't contain a valid Connection element.

Figure 10-6   The PayablesDB class

The design of the VendorsDB class

The main database processing for the Vendor Maintenance program is done by the VendorsDB class. The design of this class is presented in figure 10-7. As you can see, it provides six methods for working with the data in the Payables database. Notice that all of these methods are shared methods. Because of that, you can execute them without having to create an instance of the VendorsDB class.

The GetVendorNames method returns an untyped dataset that contains the ID and name of every vendor in the Vendors table. As you'll see, the Vendor Maintenance program uses this dataset to populate the Vendors combo box.

The GetStates method returns an untyped dataset that contains the two-character state code and the complete name of each state in the States table. This method is used by the Vendor Maintenance program to populate the States combo box.

The GetVendor method retrieves a specific vendor from the Vendors table. It accepts a Vendor ID as an argument and returns a Vendor object. If no vendor is found in the Vendors table with the specified Vendor ID, the Vendor object is set to Nothing.

The AddVendor method adds a vendor to the Vendors table. To do that, it accepts a Vendor object that contains the data for the new vendor as an argument. Note that because the VendorID column is an identity column that's set by SQL Server when the vendor is added to the database, the AddVendor method ignores the ID property of the Vendor object. However, the value that's assigned to the VendorID column by SQL Server is passed back as the return value of the AddVendor method.

The DeleteVendor method deletes a vendor from the Vendors table. Although I could have designed this method to accept just the ID of the vendor to be deleted, it accepts a Vendor object instead. That way, the method can provide for concurrency checking. If any columns in the row to be deleted have been changed since being retrieved or the row has already been deleted, the row isn't deleted and the DeleteVendor method returns a value of False. Otherwise, it returns a value of True.

The UpdateVendor method updates a vendor in the Vendors table. It accepts two vendor objects named NewVendor and OldVendor as arguments. The OldVendor object is used to identify the vendor row to be updated and to provide for concurrency checking. If the values in the row to be updated haven't changed since it was retrieved and the row hasn't been deleted, the data in the NewVendor object is used to update the row. Like the DeleteVendor method, the UpdateVendor method returns a Boolean value that indicates whether or not the operation succeeded.

The GetVendorNames method

```
Public Shared Function GetVendorNames() As DataSet
```

Returns an untyped DataSet object that contains the Vendor IDs and names of all the vendors in the Vendors table.

The GetStates method

```
Public Shared Function GetStates() As DataSet
```

Returns an untyped DataSet object containing the state codes and state names of all the states in the States table.

The GetVendor method

```
Public Shared Function GetVendor(ByVal VendorID As Integer) As Vendor
```

Returns a Vendor object for the specified Vendor ID. If the vendor doesn't exist, this method returns Nothing.

The AddVendor method

```
Public Shared Function AddVendor(ByVal Vendor As Vendor) As Integer
```

Adds the vendor in the specified Vendor object to the database and returns the Vendor ID value assigned to the new vendor row.

The DeleteVendor method

```
Public Shared Function DeleteVendor(ByVal Vendor As Vendor) As Boolean
```

Deletes the vendor in the specified Vendor object from the database. Returns True if the vendor is successfully deleted. Returns False if a concurrency error occurs.

The UpdateVendor method

```
Public Shared Function UpdateVendor(ByVal NewVendor As Vendor, _
    ByVal OldVendor As Vendor) As Boolean
```

Updates the vendor in the specified OldVendor object with the data in the specified NewVendor object. Returns True if the vendor is successfully updated. Returns False if a concurrency error occurs.

Description

- The VendorsDB class contains the methods that are used to perform the main database processing of the Vendor Maintenance program. The methods in this class are executed from the form class to provide the data that's displayed on the form and to respond to the user's requests.

- This class inherits the PayablesDB class. That way, it can use the GetPayablesConnection method of that class each time it needs to connect to the Payables database.

Figure 10-7   The design of the VendorsDB class

The code for the VendorsDB class

Figure 10-8 presents the code for the VendorsDB class. To start, you should notice the Inherits statement at the beginning of the class. This statement indicates that the VendorsDB class inherits the PayablesDB class. That way, it can use the GetPayablesConnection method in that class to get a connection object for the Payables database. As you can see by the highlighted text in this figure, each of the methods in the VendorsDB class executes this method.

The GetVendorNames method creates a connection object using the GetPayablesConnection method. Then, it creates a data adapter using that connection and a Select statement that retrieves the VendorID and VendorName columns. Next, it creates and fills a dataset with a table named VendorNames based on that data adapter. Finally, it passes the dataset back as its return value.

The GetStates method is similar. It creates and fills a dataset with a table named States. This table contains the StateCode and StateName columns for each row in the States table. Then, it passes the dataset back as its return value.

The GetVendor method accepts a Vendor ID as an argument and then retrieves the vendor with that ID. To do that, the Select statement that retrieves the vendor includes a parameter for the VendorID column, and the value that's assigned to the VendorID argument is assigned to that parameter. Notice that this method uses a data reader to retrieve the vendor row. Then, if a row with the specified value is found, the values in that row are assigned to the properties of a Vendor object that's declared at the beginning of this procedure. Otherwise, Nothing is assigned to the Vendor object. In either case, the method passes the Vendor object back as its return value.

The AddVendor method, shown on page 2 of this listing, receives a Vendor object as an argument and then uses that object to add a vendor row to the Vendors table. To do that, it assigns the values in the Vendor object to the parameters that are included in the Values clause of the Insert statement. Then, after it executes the Insert statement, it executes a Select statement that retrieves the identity value of the new row and passes that value back as its return value.

The DeleteVendor method also accepts a Vendor object as its argument and constructs a Delete statement using the values in this object. Notice that this statement includes concurrency checking. If the Delete statement is successful, this method passes a value of True back as its return value. Otherwise, it returns a value of False.

Like the DeleteVendor method, the UpdateVendor method, shown on page 3 of this listing, provides for concurrency checking. To do that, it accepts two Vendor objects as arguments. The first one contains the new values for the row, and the second one contains the original values that are used for concurrency checking. If the Update statement is successful, this method returns a value of True. Otherwise, it returns a value of False.

Before I go on, you should notice that none of the methods in this class check for errors. Because of that, any error that occurs will be passed up to the calling procedure. In a production application, however, these methods would probably return error codes to the calling procedure so they could be handled

The code for the VendorsDB class   Page 1

```
Imports System.Data.SqlClient
Public Class VendorsDB
    Inherits PayablesDB

    Public Shared Function GetVendorNames() As DataSet
        Dim sSqlCommand = "Select VendorID, VendorName " _
            & "From Vendors Order By VendorName"
        Dim conPayables As SqlConnection = GetPayablesConnection()
        Dim daVendors As New SqlDataAdapter(sSqlCommand, conPayables)
        Dim dsVendors As New DataSet()
        daVendors.Fill(dsVendors, "VendorNames")
        Return dsVendors
    End Function

    Public Shared Function GetStates() As DataSet
        Dim sSqlCommand = "Select StateCode, StateName " _
            & "From States Order By StateName"
        Dim conPayables As SqlConnection = GetPayablesConnection()
        Dim daStates As New SqlDataAdapter(sSqlCommand, conPayables)
        Dim dsStates As New DataSet()
        daStates.Fill(dsStates, "States")
        Return dsStates
    End Function

    Public Shared Function GetVendor(ByVal VendorID As Integer) As Vendor
        Dim Vendor As New Vendor()
        Dim drVendor As SqlDataReader
        Dim conPayables As SqlConnection = GetPayablesConnection()
        Dim sSqlCommand = "Select VendorID, VendorName, VendorAddress1, " _
            & "VendorAddress2, VendorCity, VendorState, VendorZipCode " _
            & "From Vendors Where VendorID = @VendorID"
        Dim cmdVendors As New SqlCommand(sSqlCommand, conPayables)
        cmdVendors.Parameters.Add("@VendorID", VendorID)
        conPayables.Open()
        drVendor = cmdVendors.ExecuteReader(CommandBehavior.SingleRow)
        If drVendor.Read Then
            Vendor.ID = drVendor("VendorID")
            Vendor.Name = drVendor("VendorName")
            Vendor.Address1 = drVendor("VendorAddress1").ToString
            Vendor.Address2 = drVendor("VendorAddress2").ToString
            Vendor.City = drVendor("VendorCity")
            Vendor.State = drVendor("VendorState")
            Vendor.ZipCode = drVendor("VendorZipCode")
        Else
            Vendor = Nothing
        End If
        conPayables.Close()
        Return Vendor
    End Function
```

Figure 10-8   The code for the VendorsDB class (part 1 of 3)

The code for the VendorsDB class

```
Public Shared Function AddVendor(ByVal Vendor As Vendor) As Integer
    Dim conPayables As SqlConnection = GetPayablesConnection()
    Dim sSqlCommand As String _
        = "Insert Into Vendors (VendorName, VendorAddress1, " _
        & "VendorAddress2, VendorCity, VendorState, VendorZipCode) " _
        & "Values (@VendorName, @VendorAddress1, " _
        & "@VendorAddress2, @VendorCity, @VendorState, @VendorZipCode)"
    conPayables.Open()
    Dim cmdVendors As New SqlCommand(sSqlCommand, conPayables)
    With cmdVendors.Parameters
        .Add("@VendorName", Vendor.Name)
        If Vendor.Address1 = "" Then
            .Add("@VendorAddress1", DBNull.Value)
        Else
            .Add("@VendorAddress1", Vendor.Address1)
        End If
        If Vendor.Address2 = "" Then
            .Add("@VendorAddress2", DBNull.Value)
        Else
            .Add("@VendorAddress2", Vendor.Address2)
        End If
        .Add("@VendorCity", Vendor.City)
        .Add("@VendorState", Vendor.State)
        .Add("@VendorZipCode", Vendor.ZipCode)
    End With
    cmdVendors.ExecuteNonQuery()
    cmdVendors.CommandText = "Select @@Identity"
    AddVendor = cmdVendors.ExecuteScalar()
    conPayables.Close()
End Function

Public Shared Function DeleteVendor(ByVal Vendor As Vendor) As Boolean
    Dim conPayables As SqlConnection = GetPayablesConnection()
    Dim sSqlCommand As String _
        = "Delete From Vendors " _
        & "Where VendorID = @VendorID And VendorName = @VendorName " _
        & "And (VendorAddress1 = @VendorAddress1 " _
        & "Or (@VendorAddress1 = '' And VendorAddress1 Is Null)) " _
        & "And (VendorAddress2 = @VendorAddress2 " _
        & "Or (@VendorAddress2 = '' And VendorAddress2 Is Null)) " _
        & "And VendorCity = @VendorCity And VendorState = @VendorState " _
        & "And VendorZipCode = @VendorZipCode "
    Dim cmdVendors As New SqlCommand(sSqlCommand, conPayables)
    With cmdVendors.Parameters
        .Add("@VendorID", Vendor.ID)
        .Add("@VendorName", Vendor.Name)
        .Add("@VendorAddress1", Vendor.Address1)
        .Add("@VendorAddress2", Vendor.Address2)
        .Add("@VendorCity", Vendor.City)
        .Add("@VendorState", Vendor.State)
        .Add("@VendorZipCode", Vendor.ZipCode)
    End With
    conPayables.Open()
    If cmdVendors.ExecuteNonQuery() > 0 Then
        DeleteVendor = True
    Else
        DeleteVendor = False
    End If
    conPayables.Close()
End Function
```

Figure 10-8   The code for the VendorsDB class (part 2 of 3)

The code for the VendorsDB class **Page 3**

```
Public Shared Function UpdateVendor(ByVal NewVendor As Vendor, _
        ByVal OldVendor As Vendor) As Boolean
    Dim conPayables As SqlConnection = GetPayablesConnection()
    Dim sSqlCommand As String _
        = "Update Vendors " _
        & "Set VendorName = @NewVendorName, " _
        & "VendorAddress1 = @NewVendorAddress1, " _
        & "VendorAddress2 = @NewVendorAddress2, " _
        & "VendorCity = @NewVendorCity, " _
        & "VendorState = @NewVendorState, " _
        & "VendorZipCode = @NewVendorZipCode " _
        & "Where VendorID = @OldVendorID " _
        & "And VendorName = @OldVendorName " _
        & "And (VendorAddress1 = @OldVendorAddress1 " _
        & "Or (@OldVendorAddress1 = '' And VendorAddress1 Is Null)) " _
        & "And (VendorAddress2 = @OldVendorAddress2 " _
        & "Or (@OldVendorAddress2 = '' And VendorAddress2 Is Null)) " _
        & "And VendorCity = @OldVendorCity " _
        & "And VendorState = @OldVendorState " _
        & "And VendorZipCode = @OldVendorZipCode"
    conPayables.Open()
    Dim cmdVendors As New SqlCommand(sSqlCommand, conPayables)
    With cmdVendors.Parameters
        .Add("@NewVendorID", NewVendor.ID)
        .Add("@NewVendorName", NewVendor.Name)
        If NewVendor.Address1 = "" Then
            .Add("@NewVendorAddress1", DBNull.Value)
        Else
            .Add("@NewVendorAddress1", NewVendor.Address1)
        End If
        If NewVendor.Address2 = "" Then
            .Add("@NewVendorAddress2", DBNull.Value)
        Else
            .Add("@NewVendorAddress2", NewVendor.Address2)
        End If
        .Add("@NewVendorCity", NewVendor.City)
        .Add("@NewVendorState", NewVendor.State)
        .Add("@NewVendorZipCode", NewVendor.ZipCode)
        .Add("@OldVendorID", OldVendor.ID)
        .Add("@OldVendorName", OldVendor.Name)
        .Add("@OldVendorAddress1", OldVendor.Address1)
        .Add("@OldVendorAddress2", OldVendor.Address2)
        .Add("@OldVendorCity", OldVendor.City)
        .Add("@OldVendorState", OldVendor.State)
        .Add("@OldVendorZipCode", OldVendor.ZipCode)
    End With
    If cmdVendors.ExecuteNonQuery() > 0 Then
        UpdateVendor = True
    Else
        UpdateVendor = False
    End If
    conPayables.Close()
End Function

End Class
```

Figure 10-8   The code for the VendorsDB class (part 3 of 3)

accordingly. I left this code out of the Vendor Maintenance program so you can focus on how the database classes are used. If you want to see one way to provide for exceptions in database classes, you can look at the ASP.NET application that's presented in chapter 13.

The code for the Vendor Maintenance form

Figure 10-9 presents the code for the Vendor Maintenance form. As you'll see, this code is similar in a lot of ways to the other Vendor Maintenance programs you've seen in this book. The biggest difference is that all of the database processing is done by the database classes. Because of that, I'll focus mainly on the use of those classes. The statements that use those classes are highlighted in this figure.

At the beginning of this class, a variable named Vendor is declared with a data type of Vendor. This variable will be used throughout the form class to work with vendors in the Vendors table of the Payables database.

When the form is first loaded, the Load procedure populates both the States and Vendors combo boxes. To populate the States combo box, this procedure calls the GetStates method of the VendorsDB class and assigns the resulting dataset to a local variable. Then, it binds the combo box to this dataset by setting its DataSource, DisplayMember, and ValueMember properties.

To populate the Vendors combo box, the Load procedure calls the RefreshVendors procedure. This procedure uses the GetVendorNames method of the VendorsDB class to get a dataset that contains a VendorNames table. Then, the Vendors combo box is bound to this dataset. This code is placed in a separate procedure because the Vendors combo box will be updated any time the user adds, modifies, or deletes a vendor. This procedure will also be called if the program detects that a vendor no longer exists.

Next, the Load procedure calls the ShowVendor procedure. Notice that the SelectedValue property of the Vendors combo box, which contains the Vendor ID of the vendor that's currently selected, is passed as an argument to this procedure. Then, this procedure executes the GetVendor method of the VendorsDB class to get a Vendor object for the specified vendor. This object is assigned to the Vendor variable that was declared at the module level. Then, this object is tested to determine if the vendor was found. If not, a message is displayed and the RefreshVendors procedure is called to update the list of vendors in the Vendors combo box. Otherwise, the properties of the Vendor object are assigned to the form controls so their values are displayed on the form.

The code for the Vendor Maintenance form   **Page 1**

```
Public Class frmVendorMaintenance
    Inherits System.Windows.Forms.Form

    Dim bLoading As Boolean
    Dim bNewVendor As Boolean
    Dim Vendor As Vendor

    Private Sub Form1_Load(ByVal sender As System.Object, _
            ByVal e As System.EventArgs) Handles MyBase.Load
        Dim dsStates As DataSet
        dsStates = VendorsDB.GetStates()
        cboStates.DataSource = dsStates
        cboStates.DisplayMember = "States.StateName"
        cboStates.ValueMember = "States.StateCode"
        bLoading = True
        Me.RefreshVendors()
        Me.ShowVendor(cboVendors.SelectedValue)
        Me.SetMaintenanceButtons(True)
        bLoading = False
    End Sub

    Private Sub RefreshVendors()
        Dim dsVendors As DataSet
        dsVendors = VendorsDB.GetVendorNames()
        cboVendors.DataSource = dsVendors
        cboVendors.DisplayMember = "VendorNames.VendorName"
        cboVendors.ValueMember = "VendorNames.VendorID"
    End Sub

    Private Sub ShowVendor(ByVal VendorID As String)
        Vendor = VendorsDB.GetVendor(VendorID)
        If Vendor Is Nothing Then
            MessageBox.Show("Another user has deleted that vendor.", _
                "Database error", MessageBoxButtons.OK, MessageBoxIcon.Hand)
            Me.RefreshVendors()
        Else
            txtName.Text = Vendor.Name
            txtAddressLine1.Text = Vendor.Address1
            txtAddressLine2.Text = Vendor.Address2
            txtCity.Text = Vendor.City
            cboStates.SelectedValue = Vendor.State
            txtZipCode.Text = Vendor.ZipCode
            Me.SetMaintenanceButtons(True)
            txtName.Focus()
        End If
    End Sub

    Private Sub SetMaintenanceButtons(ByVal bAddDeleteMode As Boolean)
        btnAdd.Enabled = bAddDeleteMode
        btnUpdate.Enabled = Not bAddDeleteMode
        btnDelete.Enabled = bAddDeleteMode
        btnCancel.Enabled = Not bAddDeleteMode
    End Sub
```

Figure 10-9   The code for the Vendor Maintenance form (part 1 of 4)

When the user selects a vendor from the Vendors combo box, the SelectedIndexChanged procedure is called. This procedure simply calls the ShowVendor procedure to get the selected vendor and display its information on the form.

When the user clicks the Update button, the processing that's done depends on whether a vendor is being added or updated. If a vendor is being added, the Update procedure assigns the values in the form controls to the properties of the Vendor object. Then, it executes the AddVendor method of the VendorsDB class to add the vendor specified by this object to the database. Next, it calls the RefreshVendors procedure so that the new vendor is included in the Vendors combo box. It also assigns the return value from the AddVendor method, which is the Vendor ID value that's generated for the new vendor, to the SelectedValue property of the Vendors combo box so that the new vendor is selected.

If an existing vendor is being updated, the Update procedure starts by declaring a new Vendor object named NewVendor. You can see this code starting at the top of page 3 of this listing. Then, the values in the form controls are assigned to the properties of this object, and the UpdateVendor method of the VendorsDB class is executed to update the vendor. If a concurrency error occurs, an error message is displayed. Next, the RefreshVendors procedure is called to refresh the Vendors combo box. This is done in case the user changed the vendor's name or another user changed the vendor's name or deleted the vendor resulting in a concurrency error. Then, the SelectedValue property of the Vendors combo box is set to the VendorID property of the Vendor object so that the vendor that was updated is selected.

When the user clicks on the Delete button to delete a vendor, the Delete procedure shown at the top of page 4 of this listing is executed. This procedure confirms the delete operation and then executes the DeleteVendor method of the VendorsDB class. If the delete operation is successful, the RefreshVendors procedure is called to refresh the Vendors combo box so that the deleted vendor isn't included. Otherwise, an error message is displayed and the ShowVendor procedure is called to redisplay the vendor data.

If the user clicks on the Cancel button to cancel an add or update operation, the Click event procedure for this button is executed. This procedure assigns the properties of the Vendor object to the form controls. If a new vendor was being added, that causes the data for the previously selected vendor to be displayed. If an existing vendor was being updated, that causes the original data for that vendor to be displayed.

Now that you've seen the complete code for this program, you should have a good feel for how you can use database classes. Although the classes used in the Vendor Maintenance program are relatively simple, you can probably think of ways they could be enhanced. I've already mentioned that you'd want to include all of the columns of the Vendors table in the Vendor class, and you'd want to include data validation in that class. I also mentioned that you'd probably want to add error handling code the VendorsDB class. In addition, you might need to add additional methods to this class to provide for selecting different information from the Vendors table. Even though the classes presented in this chapter don't include these enhancements, they should give you a good start toward developing professional database classes of your own.

The code for the Vendor Maintenance form   **Page 2**

```
Private Sub cboVendors_SelectedIndexChanged _
        (ByVal sender As System.Object, ByVal e As System.EventArgs) _
        Handles cboVendors.SelectedIndexChanged
    If not bLoading Then
        Me.ShowVendor(cboVendors.SelectedValue)
    End If
End Sub

Private Sub Control_DataChanged(ByVal sender As System.Object, _
        ByVal e As System.EventArgs) Handles txtName.TextChanged, _
        txtAddressLine1.TextChanged, txtAddressLine2.TextChanged, _
        txtCity.TextChanged, txtZipCode.TextChanged, _
        cboStates.SelectedIndexChanged
    If not bLoading Then
        Me.SetMaintenanceButtons(False)
    End If
End Sub

Private Sub btnAdd_Click(ByVal sender As System.Object, _
        ByVal e As System.EventArgs) Handles btnAdd.Click
    Me.SetMaintenanceButtons(False)
    txtName.Text = ""
    txtAddressLine1.Text = ""
    txtAddressLine2.Text = ""
    txtCity.Text = ""
    cboStates.SelectedIndex = 0
    txtZipCode.Text = ""
    txtName.Focus()
    bNewVendor = True
End Sub

Private Sub btnUpdate_Click(ByVal sender As System.Object, _
        ByVal e As System.EventArgs) Handles btnUpdate.Click
    If ValidData() Then
        If bNewVendor Then
            Dim iVendorID As Integer
            Vendor.Name = txtName.Text
            Vendor.Address1 = txtAddressLine1.Text
            Vendor.Address2 = txtAddressLine2.Text
            Vendor.City = txtCity.Text
            Vendor.State = cboStates.SelectedValue
            Vendor.ZipCode = txtZipCode.Text
            iVendorID = VendorsDB.AddVendor(Vendor)
            Me.RefreshVendors()
            cboVendors.SelectedValue = iVendorID
            bNewVendor = False
```

Figure 10-9   The code for the Vendor Maintenance form (part 2 of 4)

The code for the Vendor Maintenance form   **Page 3**

```
            Else
                Dim NewVendor As New Vendor()
                NewVendor.Name = txtName.Text
                NewVendor.Address1 = txtAddressLine1.Text
                NewVendor.Address2 = txtAddressLine2.Text
                NewVendor.City = txtCity.Text
                NewVendor.State = cboStates.SelectedValue
                NewVendor.ZipCode = txtZipCode.Text
                If Not VendorsDB.UpdateVendor(NewVendor, Vendor) Then
                    MessageBox.Show("Another user has updated or deleted " _
                        & "that vendor.", "Database error", _
                        MessageBoxButtons.OK, MessageBoxIcon.Hand)
                End If
                Me.RefreshVendors()
                cboVendors.SelectedValue = Vendor.ID
            End If
            Me.SetMaintenanceButtons(True)
            cboVendors.Focus()
        End If
    End Sub

    Private Function ValidData() As Boolean
        Dim sErrorMessage As String
        If txtName.Text = "" Then
            sErrorMessage = "Name required."
            txtName.Focus()
        ElseIf txtCity.Text = "" Then
            sErrorMessage = "City required."
            txtCity.Focus()
        ElseIf txtZipCode.Text = "" Then
            sErrorMessage = "Zip code required."
            txtZipCode.Focus()
        End If
        If sErrorMessage = "" Then
            ValidData = True
        Else
            ValidData = False
            MessageBox.Show(sErrorMessage, "Data entry error", _
                MessageBoxButtons.OK, MessageBoxIcon.Error)
        End If
    End Function
```

Figure 10-9   The code for the Vendor Maintenance form (part 3 of 4)

The code for the Vendor Maintenance form   **Page 4**

```
Private Sub btnDelete_Click(ByVal sender As System.Object, _
        ByVal e As System.EventArgs) Handles btnDelete.Click
    Me.SetMaintenanceButtons(True)
    cboVendors.Focus()
    Dim iResult As DialogResult _
        = MessageBox.Show("Delete " & cboVendors.Text & "?", _
          "Confirm Delete", MessageBoxButtons.YesNo, _
          MessageBoxIcon.Question)
    If iResult = DialogResult.Yes Then
        If VendorsDB.DeleteVendor(Vendor) Then
            Me.RefreshVendors()
            cboVendors.Focus()
        Else
            MessageBox.Show("Another user has updated or deleted " _
                & "that vendor.", "Database error", _
                  MessageBoxButtons.OK, MessageBoxIcon.Hand)
            Me.ShowVendor(Vendor.ID)
        End If
    End If
End Sub

Private Sub btnCancel_Click(ByVal sender As System.Object, _
        ByVal e As System.EventArgs) Handles btnCancel.Click
    txtName.Text = Vendor.Name
    txtAddressLine1.Text = Vendor.Address1
    txtAddressLine2.Text = Vendor.Address2
    txtCity.Text = Vendor.City
    cboStates.SelectedValue = Vendor.State
    txtZipCode.Text = Vendor.ZipCode
    Me.SetMaintenanceButtons(True)
End Sub

Private Sub btnExit_Click(ByVal sender As System.Object, _
    ByVal e As System.EventArgs) Handles btnExit.Click
    Me.Close()
End Sub

Private Sub Form1_Closing(ByVal sender As Object, _
        ByVal e As System.ComponentModel.CancelEventArgs) _
        Handles MyBase.Closing
    If btnUpdate.Enabled Then
        Dim iResult As DialogResult _
            = MessageBox.Show("You have made changes that have not " _
            & "been saved to the database. " & ControlChars.CrLf _
            & "If you continue, these changes will be lost." _
            & ControlChars.CrLf & "Continue?", "Confirm Exit", _
              MessageBoxButtons.YesNo, MessageBoxIcon.Question)
        If iResult = DialogResult.No Then
            e.Cancel = True
        End If
    End If
End Sub

End Class
```

Figure 10-9   The code for the Vendor Maintenance form (part 4 of 4)

Perspective

The goal of this chapter has been to introduce you to the concept of creating and using database classes that handle the database processing of an application. As you've learned, there are several benefits to placing the database processing code in separate classes. In particular, those classes can be shared among all the applications that access the same database.

On the other hand, you've also seen that using separate database classes adds complexity to your programs. That's because, in addition to developing the code for each class, you have to design and develop the interfaces between the classes. In addition, you should realize that you can't use the ADO.NET components that are available from the Toolbox when you create your own classes. That's because classes don't provide the support that's required for these components.

So whether or not you implement database classes depends on the requirements of the application you're developing. In the next section of this book, for example, you'll learn that database classes are especially useful for developing web applications with ASP.NET. In fact, the application examples presented in those chapters use a database class very similar to the one that was presented here.

Terms

multi-layered architecture
multi-tiered architecture
three-tiered architecture
presentation layer
database layer
middle layer
business rules layer
distributed application
class library
component
distributed processing
.NET Remoting
remotable components
application domain
XML web services
SOAP (Simple Object Access Protocol)
UML (Uniform Modeling Language)

11

A complete order entry application

Throughout this book, you've seen examples of applications that demonstrate specific elements of ADO.NET programming. However, those examples have all been simplified so that you can focus on learning the database programming skills. Now that you've learned those skills, you're ready to see how they all fit together in a comprehensive, real-world application. To help you do that, this chapter presents the code for a complete order entry application that's significantly more complicated than any of the examples you've seen so far.

Before you study the information presented in this chapter, you may want to download the order entry application from our web site and run it to see it in action. That way, you'll have a better idea of how it works. You'll find complete instructions for downloading and installing this application and the other applications presented in this book in appendix A.

The specifications and design for the Order Entry application

The Order Entry application accepts and processes telephone orders for a publishing company. The user can enter orders for new or existing customers and, if necessary, change an existing customer's name and address. The user can also display customer sales history information. The following topics present the specifications and design for this application.

The specifications for the Order Entry application

Figure 11-1 shows the main form for the Order Entry application with the Customer tab of the Enter Orders form displayed. Before I describe the process of entering orders, I want to describe the Order Options dialog box, also shown in this figure. It lets the user set the sales tax rate and the shipping charges that the Order Entry application applies to each order. This information is saved in the application's database, so the user will need to work with this form only when the tax rate or shipping charges change.

To enter an order, the user works with the Enter Orders form. As you can see, this form has a tab control with three tabs, labeled Customer, Products, and Payment. Before accepting an order, the user must complete the information on all three of these tabs. To move from one tab to another, the user can click the tabs themselves or click the Next>> and <<Prev buttons in the lower right corner of each tab.

To begin an order, the user enters a customer ID number in the text box and then clicks the Get Customer button. If the user doesn't know the customer's ID, he can click the Find Customer button to display the Find Customer form shown at the top of figure 11-2. With this dialog box, the user can search for a customer using all or part of the customer's last name and, optionally, state.

If the customer hasn't ordered before, the user can click the New Customer button to display the New Customer form shown in figure 11-2. This form lets the user enter the information for a new customer. This form is also displayed when the user clicks the Modify Customer button to modify the information for an existing customer.

To enter the products for an order, the user works with the Products tab of the Enter Orders form shown in figure 11-3. Then, to complete the order, the user enters the payment information in the Payment tab shown in figure 11-4. If the order is accepted, a confirmation dialog box like the one shown in this figure is displayed and the controls in all three of the tabs are cleared so the user can begin another order. If the user omits required information, however, the order isn't posted. Instead, an error message is displayed so the user can correct the error.

Figure 11-5 shows the Customer Details form, which displays history information about a specific customer. This form has a tab control with three tabs, labeled Products, Invoices, and Open Items. Each of these tabs contains a data grid control that displays information for the customer.

The main form and the Customer tab of the Enter Orders form

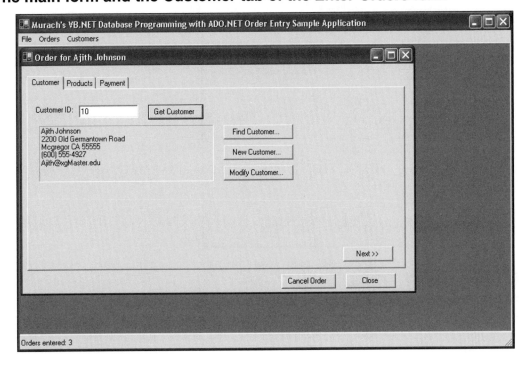

The Order Options dialog box

Description

- The Order Entry application is an MDI application that lets users enter phone orders for a publishing company.

- The Enter Orders form, accessed via the Orders→Enter Orders menu command, lets you enter customer orders. This form includes a tab control with three tabs that let you enter the customer information, product information, and payment details.

- The Order Options dialog box, accessed via the Orders→Set Order Options menu command, lets you set the sales tax rate and the amount charged for shipping and handling. These values apply to every order that's entered.

Figure 11-1   The main form, the Customer tab of the Enter Orders form, and the Order Options dialog box

The Find Customer form

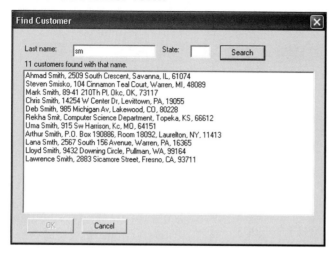

The New Customer form

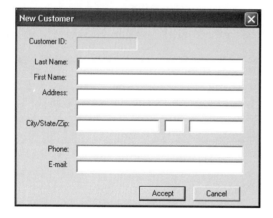

Three ways the user can enter customer information for an order

- Enter the customer's ID number in the Customer ID text box of the Enter Orders form, then press Enter or click the Get Customer button.

- Click the Find Customer button to display the Find Customer form. Then, search for a customer based on all or part of the customer's last name and an optional state code.

- Click the New Customer button to display the New Customer form. Then, enter the information for the new customer and click the Accept button.

Note

- You can also modify an existing customer by selecting a customer and then clicking the Modify Customer button to display a maintenance form that's similar to the New Customer form.

Figure 11-2   The forms for entering customer information

The Products tab of the Enter Orders form

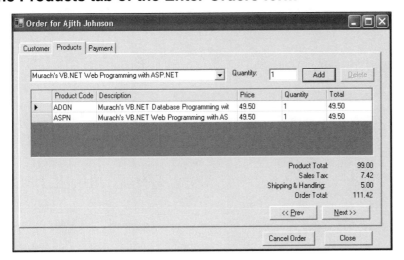

Description

- To enter line items, select a product from the combo box, type the quantity into the text box, and click Add.

- To edit or delete a line item, click the row selector to the left of the line item in the data grid to select it. This selects the product in the combo box, sets the quantity to the current amount, changes the Add button to an Update button, and enables the Delete button. You can then change the quantity and click the Update button or delete the line item.

- You can't change the product for a line item. If you select the wrong product, you must delete the line item and then add one for the correct product.

- As you enter line items, the order totals beneath the line items grid are updated.

Figure 11-3   The form for entering line item information

The Payment tab of the Enter Orders form

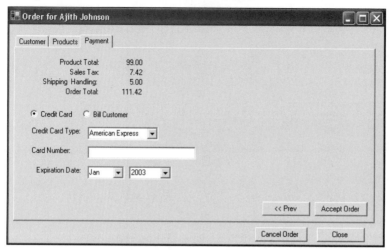

An order confirmation dialog box

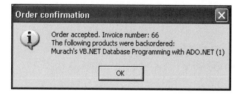

Description

- To complete an order, enter the customer's credit card information or check the Bill Customer option, and then click the Accept Order button.

- If the order is accepted, a confirmation dialog box displays the invoice number and informs you if any products had to be backordered.

- You can cancel the current order at any time by clicking the Cancel Order button. This clears all the order fields and returns you to the Customer tab.

- If you try to close the Enter Orders form after selecting a customer, a dialog box is displayed indicating that you must cancel or finish the order before closing the form.

Figure 11-4   The forms for entering payment information and confirming an order

The Products tab of the Customer Details form

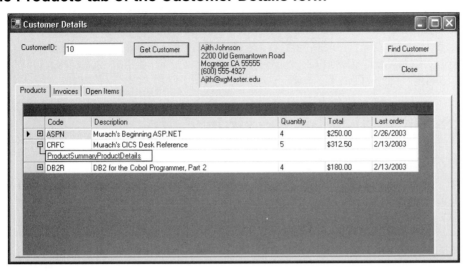

Description

- The Customer Details form displays history information for a selected customer. To display this form, choose one of the commands on the Customers menu:

  Customers➔Products   Brings up the form with the Products tab selected
  Customers➔Invoices   Brings up the form with the Invoices tab selected
  Customers➔Open Items   Brings up the form with the Open Items tab selected

- You can select the customer to display either by entering a customer ID number and clicking the Get Customer button or by clicking the Find Customer button, which displays the Find Customer form shown in figure 11-2.

- The Products tab displays all the products the customer has ordered. The table that contains the product information is the parent table in a relationship with the table that contains the invoice information, and you can use this relationship to drill down to see specific invoices for each product.

- The Invoices tab displays all the invoices for the customer. The table that contains the invoice information is the parent table to the tables that contain the line item, back order, and payment data, and you can use these relationships to drill down to see line item, backorder, and payment history information for an invoice.

- The Open Items tab displays a summary of all unpaid invoices for the customer.

- Table styles are used in the data grid in each tab to customize the grid for each table it displays.

Figure 11-5   The Customer Details form

Because the Order Entry application is a Multiple Document Interface (MDI) application, the user can work with more than one order at a time if necessary. In addition, the user can display two or more Customer Details forms at the same time to display sales history for different customers. The user can also display a Customer Details form for a customer while entering an order for that customer.

The database design for the Order Entry application

The Order Entry application uses a SQL Server 2000 database named Murach to store the data for customers, products, and orders. Figure 11-6 shows a database diagram for the Murach database. As you can see, this database consists of nine tables, eight of which are interrelated. The only table that isn't related to the other tables is the Order Options table, which is used to store the sales tax rate and shipping charges that are applied to each order.

The Customers table stores the name and address of each of the company's customers. In addition, it tracks the date of the customer's first and most recent purchase and the total sales for the customer. Its primary key column, CustomerID, is an identity column that's generated by the database.

The Products table contains the details for each product the company sells. Its primary key column, ProductCode, holds a string value. The other columns store the product's description, price, on-hand quantity, and quantity backordered, as well as month-to-date, year-to-date, and lifetime sales totals.

When a user enters an order for a customer, rows are added to several of the other tables in the database. For every order, a row is written to the Invoices table. For each product ordered, a row is written to the InvoiceLineItems table, assuming that the requested quantity of the product is available. Then, the on-hand quantity for the product in the Products table is reduced accordingly.

If there isn't enough inventory available to fill the order for a product, a row is written to the Backorders table. Then, the QuantityBackordered column in the Products table is increased and the totals in the Invoices row are adjusted. Note that an order can result in both a backorder and a line item being written. For example, if a user orders seven copies of a book and only five are available, the application creates a line item for five copies and a backorder for two.

Notice that the primary key for the InvoiceLineItems table is a composite key consisting of the InvoiceID and the ProductCode. As a result, each invoice can have only one line item for each product.

Because this application is written to handle phone-in orders, it provides only two payment options: the customer can pay by credit card or be billed for the order. If the customer pays for the order by credit card, a row is written to the Payments table. Otherwise, a row is written to the OpenItems table.

The tables and relationships in the Murach database

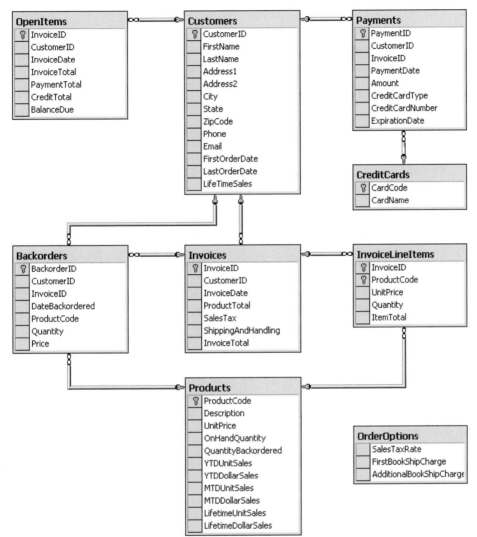

Description

- The Order Entry application uses a SQL Server 2000 database named Murach.
- The main table for this application is the Customers table, which contains one row for each customer. Each customer can have one or more rows in the OpenItems, Invoices, Backorders, and Payments tables. Each row in the Invoices table is related to one or more rows in the InvoiceLineItems table, the Backorders table, or both. And each row in the Backorders and InvoiceLineItems tables is related to one row in the Products table.
- The OrderOptions table contains a single row that stores the sales tax rate and shipping charges used by the application.
- The CreditCards table associates the credit card type in the Payments table with a card name. It's used to load the combo box in the Payments tab of the Enter Orders form.

Figure 11-6   The database design for the Order Entry application

The design of the Order Entry application's classes

The Order Entry application is implemented using a three-tiered design, as shown by the class diagram in figure 11-7. The five form classes provide the user interface for the application. The four business classes provide the middle layer. And the three database classes are responsible for the application's database access.

Actually, the OrderOptions class works as both a business class and a database class. As a business class, it exposes properties that represent the sales tax rate and shipping charges for the application. However, because its database access is simple and not related to any other database processing required by the application, I decided to implement the database processing directly in the OrderOptions class rather than as a separate database class. You'll often find examples of hybrid classes like this in production applications.

Notice that most of the form classes expose properties that can be accessed by the other classes, including other form classes. This is a common programming technique for MDI applications. It lets the forms in the application communicate with each other by sharing common objects. For example, the application's main form exposes an OrdersEntered property that maintains a count of the total number of orders entered during the session. It uses this property to display a count of the orders in its status bar. Then, the Enter Orders form increments this property each time it posts an order.

Although they're not shown in the class diagram, the Order Entry application also uses five typed dataset classes to store information retrieved from the Murach database as follows:

- The dsCreditCards dataset is used to hold data from the CreditCards table. It's filled by the main form and made available to the rest of the application via the CreditCards property.

- The dsProducts dataset is used to hold information from the Products table. It too is filled by the main form and made available to the rest of the application via a property named Products.

- The dsCustomers dataset is used to hold data from the Customers table. It's used by the Find Customer form to search for customers using the customer's last name and state.

- The dsCustomerDetails dataset is a complicated dataset that has seven tables and four data relations. This dataset is used by the Customer Details form.

- The dsOrder dataset is used to hold data in a LineItems table that's used by the Order class.

I created all of these datasets except dsOrder by generating them from data adapters that I created using the Data Adapter Configuration Wizard. The dsOrder dataset is a custom typed dataset that I created using the XML Designer.

The class diagram for the Order Entry application

Form classes

frmMain
- (form controls) + OrdersEntered As Integer + StatusBar As StatusBar + Products As dsProducts + CreditCards As   dsCreditCards

frmEnterOrders
- (form controls) + Customer As Customer + Order As Order

frmFindCustomer
- (form controls) + Customer As Customer

frmCustomer
- (form controls) + Customer As Customer + NewCustomer As Boolean

frmCustomerDetails
- (form controls)

Business classes

Order
+ InvoiceID As Integer + OrderDate As Date + LineItems As LineItemsTable + BackOrders As LineItemsTable + ProductTotal As Decimal + SalesTax As Decimal + ShippingAndHandling As Decimal + InvoiceTotal As Decimal + PaidByCreditCard As Boolean + CreditCardType As String + CardNumber As String + CardExpirationDate As Date + SetExpirationDate(Month, Year)

Customer
+ CustomerID As Integer + LastName As String + FirstName As String + Address1 As String + Address2 As String + City As String + State As String + ZipCode As String + Phone As String + Email As String + FullName As String + FormattedAddress As String

Product
+ ProductCode As String + Description As String + UnitPrice As Decimal + OnHandQuantity As Integer + QuantityBackOrdered As Integer + YTDUnitSales As Integer + YTDDollarSales As Decimal + MTDUnitSales As Integer + MTDDollarSales As Decimal + LifetimeUnitSales As Integer + LifetimeDollarSales As Decimal

OrderOptions
+ SalesTaxRate As Decimal + FirstBookShipCharge As Decimal + AdditionalBookShipCharge   As Decimal + GetOrderOptions() + UpdateOrderOptions()

Database classes

MurachDB

+ GetConnection() As
    SqlConnection
+ GetConnectionString()
    As String

CustomerDB

+ GetCustomer(CustID) As
    Customer
+ InsertCustomer(Customer)
    As Integer
+ UpdateCustomer(NewCustomer,
    OldCustomer) As Boolean

OrderDB
+ WriteOrder(Order, Customer)   As Boolean

Figure 11-7   The design of the Order Entry application's classes

The code for the Order Entry application

The topics that follow present the Visual Basic code for the Order Entry application. Because most of this code is straightforward, I'll just highlight some of its features. Keep in mind, however, that to fully understand all of this code, you'll need to download the application and examine it in Visual Studio. That way, you can review the components and property settings for each of the forms.

The code for the standard module

The Order Entry application uses the standard module shown in figure 11-8. As you can see, this module starts the application by displaying the main form within a Try...Catch statement. That way, it can catch any errors that aren't otherwise handled by the application.

The code for the forms

The code for the Order Entry application's main form, presented in figure 11-9, should be easy to understand. When the form is loaded, it retrieves the order options, fills the product and credit card datasets, and displays the Enter Orders form. Most of the remaining procedures handle the Click events for the menu commands by displaying the appropriate form. Notice that if the user chooses one of the commands on the Customers menu, the appropriate tab is selected before the Customer Details form is displayed. Also notice that the procedure for the Closing event of the form displays a confirmation message before exiting if any child forms are open within this form.

The most complicated form in this application is the Enter Orders form. Its code is presented in figure 11-10. Although you should be able to figure out how this form works by studying its code, I'll point out a few highlights. First, notice that the form declares two public variables: Customer and Order. These variables represent the customer and order information for the current order and are declared as public so that other classes can access them.

Second, notice how the Load procedure initializes the form. For example, it binds the line item data grid to the LineItems property of the Order variable (Me.Order.LineItems). If you look ahead to the code for the Order class in figure 11-15, you'll see that the LineItems property refers to the LineItems table in the dsOrder dataset. The Load procedure also binds the credit card combo box to a table in the credit card dataset exposed by the main form (frmMain.Credit-Cards.CreditCards). Finally, it manually loads the months of the year into the cboExpirationMonth combo box and the current year plus the next nine years into the cboExpirationYear combo box.

Third, take a look the btnAddUpdateLineItem_Click procedure on page 2 of this listing. This code starts by checking to see if a line item already exists for the selected product. If not, a new line item is created. This procedure also checks the Text property of the button (see page 3). If it's "Add," it means that a line item isn't selected in the table, and the quantity entered by the user is added to the line item quantity. If it isn't "Add," it means the value is "Update," and the quantity entered by the user replaces the previous line item quantity.

Fourth, look at the code for the btnAccept_Click procedure on page 4 of this listing. This code validates the data entered by the user by calling the ValidCustomer, ValidLineItems, and ValidPayment functions. If the data is valid, it calls the WriteOrder method of the OrderDB class, passing the Order and Customer objects as arguments.

Finally, notice how the last procedure in the Enter Orders form, shown on page 6 of this listing, handles the Closing event. If the user has selected a customer for the order, this procedure won't let the user close the form. Instead, it displays a message indicating that the order must be finished or canceled before the form can be closed.

The code for the Find Customer form (figure 11-11) and the Customer form (figure 11-12) isn't difficult to understand, so I won't describe it here. However, the code for the Customer Details form shown in figure 11-13 requires some explanation. This form uses a total of seven data adapter components that retrieve transaction details for the customer selected by the user. The Select statements used by five of these data adapters are shown in part 2 of this figure. The remaining two Select statements simply select rows from the Payments and OpenItems tables, so I didn't include them in this figure.

The seven data adapters are used to fill seven tables in the DsCustomerDetails1 dataset. Note that because three of the data adapters (daProductHistory, daProductDetails, and daInvoiceLineItems) retrieve data from the InvoiceLineItems table, two of them have to map the source data to tables with different names. As you can see in this figure, the data retrieved by the daProductHistory data adapter is mapped to a table named ProductHistory, and the data retrieved by the daProductDetails data adapter is mapped to a table named ProductDetails. These tables must all be stored in the same dataset because relationships are defined between them that let the user drill down in the data grids to display more detailed information.

The last form in the Order Entry application is the Order Options form. The code for this form is presented in figure 11-14. If you review this code, you shouldn't have any trouble understanding how it works.

The code for the business classes

Figure 11-15 presents the code for the Order class. This class stores information about an order. It also contains properties that calculate totals related to the order and a method that sets the expiration date for a credit card.

Figure 11-16 presents the code for the Customer and Product classes. The Customer class stores information about a customer. It also contains properties that format the customer's name and address. The Products class simply stores information about a product.

Figure 11-17 presents the code for the OrderOptions class. This class stores information about the sales tax and shipping charges that are applied to all orders. As I mentioned earlier, this class also provides access to the OrderOptions table in the Murach database. To do that, it includes two methods. The GetOrderOptions method retrieves data from the OrderOptions table, and the UpdateOrderOptions method updates this table with changes made using the Order Options dialog box you saw in figure 11-1.

The code for the database classes

Figure 11-17 also presents the code for the MurachDB class. This class contains methods that retrieve the connection string for the Murach database from an XML file and create an SqlConnection object to connect to this database. This class is nearly identical to the PayablesDB class you saw in chapter 10, so you shouldn't have any trouble understanding how it works. You should know, however, that if you download the Order Entry application from our web site, you'll need to change the connection string in the XML file so it's appropriate for your system. This file is stored in the project's Bin folder, so you can open and modify it directly from Visual Studio.

The CustomerDB class, shown in figure 11-18, provides methods that retrieve, insert, and update customer rows. These methods are also straightforward, so I won't describe them here.

The OrderDB class, shown in figure 11-19, is typical of a database class that updates the data in two or more related tables. Here, a single method called WriteOrder is responsible for updating the tables in the Murach database to reflect an order. As you can see, all of these updates are performed as a part of a single transaction. That way, if any of the updates fail, the updates that have already been done are rolled back. Notice here that, unlike the code you saw in chapter 8 that uses a transaction, all of the tables are updated using the same command object. This is a common coding technique that's used when several tables are being updated within a single transaction.

Although the code for the OrderDB class is long, it's straightforward so you shouldn't have any trouble understanding it. The only complicated portions of the code deal with handling backorders. In particular, if a line item triggers a backorder, the AdjustInvoiceTotal procedure is called to update the Invoice row so that the customer isn't charged for the products that are backordered. You can see this procedure on page 4 of this listing.

Perspective

Our goal for presenting the Order Entry application is to show you how the database programming elements you've learned in the first ten chapters of this book can be integrated into an actual business application. Keep in mind, however, that this application doesn't provide for all real-world issues. For example, a real-world application would have to validate credit card numbers entered by the user. In addition, if a business sold more than a few dozen products, it wouldn't be efficient to bind the Products combo box used in the Enter Orders form to the entire Products table. Nevertheless, this application is a good starting point for any data entry application that you develop.

modOrderEntry.vb

```
Imports System.Data.SqlClient
Module modOrderEntry
    Private frmMain As New frmMain()

    Public Sub Main()
        Try
            Application.Run(frmMain)
        Catch eSql As SqlException
            Dim sMessage As String
            sMessage = "A serious database error has occurred." & ControlChars.CrLf
            sMessage &= "Error number: " & eSql.Number & ControlChars.CrLf
            sMessage &= eSql.Message
            MessageBox.Show(sMessage, "Database error", MessageBoxButtons.OK, _
                MessageBoxIcon.Exclamation)
        Catch e As Exception
            Dim sMessage As String
            sMessage = "A serious error has occurred." & ControlChars.CrLf
            sMessage &= "Source: " & e.Source & ControlChars.CrLf
            sMessage &= e.Message
            MessageBox.Show(sMessage, "Application error", MessageBoxButtons.OK, _
                MessageBoxIcon.Exclamation)
        End Try
    End Sub

End Module
```

Notes

- The Order Entry application uses a standard module for its start-up processing to provide standardized error handling.

- The standard module uses the Run method of the Application object to display the application's main form (frmMain). The Run method is called within a Try…Catch block so that any unhandled exceptions will be caught by the standard module.

- To use a standard module in this way, you must set the application's Startup Object to Sub Main. You can do that via the application's Properties dialog box, which you can access by right-clicking the project in the Solution Explorer and choosing the Properties command.

Figure 11-8   The code for the standard module

frmMain.vb   **Page 1**

```vb
Imports System.Data.SqlClient
Public Class frmMain
    Inherits System.Windows.Forms.Form

    Public Shared OrdersEntered As Integer
    Public Shared StatusBar As StatusBar
    Public Shared Products As dsProducts
    Public Shared CreditCards As dsCreditCards

    Private Sub frmMain_Load(ByVal sender As System.Object, _
            ByVal e As System.EventArgs) Handles MyBase.Load
        OrderOptions.GetOrderOptions()
        Me.FillDataSets()
        OrdersEntered = 0
        StatusBar = Me.StatusBar1
        Products = Me.DsProducts1
        CreditCards = Me.DsCreditCards1
        Dim frmEnterOrders As New frmEnterOrders()
        frmEnterOrders.MdiParent = Me
        frmEnterOrders.Show()
    End Sub

    Private Sub FillDataSets()
        conMurach.ConnectionString = MurachDB.GetConnectionString
        conMurach.Open()
        daProducts.Fill(DsProducts1)
        daCreditCards.Fill(DsCreditCards1)
        conMurach.Close()
    End Sub

    Private Sub mnuEnterOrders_Click(ByVal sender As System.Object, _
            ByVal e As System.EventArgs) Handles mnuEnterOrders.Click
        Dim frmEnterOrders As New frmEnterOrders()
        frmEnterOrders.MdiParent = Me
        frmEnterOrders.Show()
    End Sub

    Private Sub mnuSetOrderOptions_Click(ByVal sender As System.Object, _
            ByVal e As System.EventArgs) Handles mnuSetOrderOptions.Click
        Dim frmOrderOptions As New frmOrderOptions()
        frmOrderOptions.ShowDialog()
    End Sub

    Private Sub mnuCustomerProducts_Click(ByVal sender As System.Object, _
            ByVal e As System.EventArgs) Handles mnuCustomerProducts.Click
        Dim frmCustomerDetails As New frmCustomerDetails()
        frmCustomerDetails.MdiParent = Me
        frmCustomerDetails.TabControl1.SelectedIndex = 0
        frmCustomerDetails.Show()
    End Sub

    Private Sub mnuCustomerInvoices_Click(ByVal sender As System.Object, _
            ByVal e As System.EventArgs) Handles mnuCustomerInvoices.Click
        Dim frmCustomerDetails As New frmCustomerDetails()
        frmCustomerDetails.MdiParent = Me
        frmCustomerDetails.TabControl1.SelectedIndex = 1
        frmCustomerDetails.Show()
    End Sub
```

Figure 11-9   The code for the main form (part 1 of 2)

frmMain.vb   **Page 2**

```
    Private Sub mnuCustomerOpenItems_Click(ByVal sender As System.Object, _
            ByVal e As System.EventArgs) Handles mnuCustomerOpenItems.Click
        Dim frmCustomerDetails As New frmCustomerDetails()
        frmCustomerDetails.MdiParent = Me
        frmCustomerDetails.TabControll.SelectedIndex = 2
        frmCustomerDetails.Show()
    End Sub

    Private Sub mnuExit_Click(ByVal sender As System.Object, _
            ByVal e As System.EventArgs) Handles mnuExit.Click
        Me.Close()
    End Sub

    Private Sub frmMain_Closing(ByVal sender As Object, _
            ByVal e As System.ComponentModel.CancelEventArgs) Handles MyBase.Closing
        If Me.MdiChildren.Length <> 0 Then
            If MessageBox.Show("Are you sure you want to exit?", "About to exit", _
                    MessageBoxButtons.YesNo, MessageBoxIcon.Question) _
                        = DialogResult.No Then
                e.Cancel = True
            End If
        End If
    End Sub

End Class
```

The components used by the main form

Component	Description
mnuMain	The menu for the main form. The menu component has three menus: File, Orders, and Customers. The File menu has one command: Exit. The Orders menu has two commands: Enter Orders and Set Order Options. And the Customers menu has three commands: Products, Invoices, and Open Items.
conMurach	A connection to the Murach database. Generated by the Data Adapter Configuration Wizard.
daCreditCards	A data adapter that retrieves all the rows from the CreditCards table. Generated by the Data Adapter Configuration Wizard.
DsCreditCards1	A dataset generated from the daCreditCards data adapter.
daProducts	A data adapter that retrieves all the rows from the Products table. Generated by the Data Adapter Configuration Wizard.
DsProducts1	A dataset generated from the daProducts data adapter.

The Select statement for the daCreditCards data adapter

```
SELECT CardCode, CardName FROM CreditCards
```

The Select statement for the daProducts data adapter

```
SELECT ProductCode, Description, UnitPrice FROM Products
```

Figure 11-9   The code for the main form (part 2 of 2)

frmEnterOrders.vb   **Page 1**

```vb
Imports System.Data.SqlClient
Public Class frmEnterOrders
    Inherits System.Windows.Forms.Form
    Public Customer As New Customer()
    Public Order As New Order()
    Dim OrderDB As New OrderDB()

    Private Sub frmEnterOrders_Load(ByVal sender As System.Object, _
            ByVal e As System.EventArgs) Handles MyBase.Load
        Me.Text = "Enter Orders"
        btnModifyCustomer.Enabled = False
        dgLineItems.DataSource = Me.Order.LineItems
        cboProducts.DataSource = frmMain.Products.Products
        cboProducts.DisplayMember = "Description"
        cboProducts.ValueMember = "ProductCode"
        btnDeleteLineItem.Enabled = False
        rdoCreditCard.Checked = True
        cboCreditCards.DataSource = frmMain.CreditCards.CreditCards
        cboCreditCards.DisplayMember = "CardName"
        cboCreditCards.ValueMember = "CardCode"
        cboExpirationMonth.Items.AddRange(New String() {"Jan", "Feb", "Mar", "Apr", _
            "May", "Jun", "Jul", "Aug", "Sep", "Oct", "Nov", "Dec"})
        Dim iYear As Integer
        For iYear = Today.Year To Today.Year + 9
            cboExpirationYear.Items.Add(iYear)
        Next
        cboExpirationMonth.SelectedIndex = 0
        cboExpirationYear.SelectedIndex = 0
    End Sub

    Private Sub btnGetCustomer_Click(ByVal sender As System.Object, _
            ByVal e As System.EventArgs) Handles btnGetCustomer.Click
        If IsNumeric(txtCustomerID.Text) Then
            Customer = CustomerDB.GetCustomer(txtCustomerID.Text)
        Else
            MessageBox.Show("You must enter a numeric Customer ID.", _
                "Data entry error", MessageBoxButtons.OK, MessageBoxIcon.Hand)
        End If
        If Customer.CustomerID = 0 Then
            lblAddress.Text = ""
            Me.Text = "Enter Orders"
            btnModifyCustomer.Enabled = False
        Else
            lblAddress.Text = Customer.FormattedAddress
            Me.Text = "Order for " & Me.Customer.FullName
            btnModifyCustomer.Enabled = True
        End If
    End Sub

    Private Sub btnFindCustomer_Click(ByVal sender As System.Object, _
            ByVal e As System.EventArgs) Handles btnFindCustomer.Click
        Dim frmFindCustomer As New frmFindCustomer()
        frmFindCustomer.Customer = Me.Customer
        frmFindCustomer.ShowDialog()
        If Me.Customer.CustomerID <> 0 Then
            lblAddress.Text = Me.Customer.FormattedAddress
            txtCustomerID.Text = Me.Customer.CustomerID
            Me.Text = "Order for " & Me.Customer.FullName
            btnModifyCustomer.Enabled = True
        End If
    End Sub
```

Figure 11-10   The code for the Enter Orders form (part 1 of 6)

frmEnterOrders.vb   **Page 2**

```vb
Private Sub btnNewCustomer_Click(ByVal sender As System.Object, _
        ByVal e As System.EventArgs) Handles btnNewCustomer.Click
    Dim frmCustomer As New frmCustomer()
    frmCustomer.Customer = Me.Customer
    frmCustomer.NewCustomer = True
    frmCustomer.ShowDialog()
    If Me.Customer.CustomerID <> 0 Then
        txtCustomerID.Text = ""
        Me.Customer = frmCustomer.Customer
        lblAddress.Text = Me.Customer.FormattedAddress
        Me.Text = "Order for " & Me.Customer.FullName
        btnModifyCustomer.Enabled = True
    End If
End Sub

Private Sub btnModifyCustomer_Click(ByVal sender As System.Object, _
        ByVal e As System.EventArgs) Handles btnModifyCustomer.Click
    Dim frmCustomer As New frmCustomer()
    frmCustomer.Customer = Me.Customer
    frmCustomer.NewCustomer = False
    frmCustomer.ShowDialog()
    Me.Customer = frmCustomer.Customer
    lblAddress.Text = Me.Customer.FormattedAddress
    Me.Text = "Order for " & Me.Customer.FullName
End Sub

Private Sub btnNext1_Click(ByVal sender As System.Object, _
        ByVal e As System.EventArgs) Handles btnNext1.Click
    TabControl1.SelectedTab = tabProducts
    cboProducts.Focus()
End Sub

Private Sub cboProducts_SelectedIndexChanged(ByVal sender As Object, _
        ByVal e As System.EventArgs) Handles cboProducts.SelectedIndexChanged
    If dgLineItems.CurrentRowIndex > -1 Then
        btnAddUpdateLineItem.Text = "Add"
        btnDeleteLineItem.Enabled = False
        dgLineItems.UnSelect(dgLineItems.CurrentRowIndex)
    End If
End Sub

Private Sub btnAddUpdateLineItem_Click(ByVal sender As System.Object, _
        ByVal e As System.EventArgs) Handles btnAddUpdateLineItem.Click
    Dim li As dsOrder.LineItemsRow
    Dim NewLineItem As Boolean
    li = Me.Order.LineItems.FindByProductCode(cboProducts.SelectedValue)
    If li Is Nothing Then
        NewLineItem = True
        li = Me.Order.LineItems.NewLineItemsRow
        li.Quantity = 0
    Else
        NewLineItem = False
    End If
    Dim Product As dsProducts.ProductsRow
    Product = frmMain.Products.Products.FindByProductCode(cboProducts.SelectedValue)
    li.ProductCode = Product.ProductCode
    li.Description = Product.Description
    If Not IsNumeric(txtQuantity.Text) Then
        txtQuantity.Text = 0
    End If
```

Figure 11-10   The code for the Enter Orders form (part 2 of 6)

```vb
        If btnAddUpdateLineItem.Text = "Add" Then
            li.Quantity += txtQuantity.Text
        Else
            li.Quantity = txtQuantity.Text
        End If
        li.Price = Product.UnitPrice
        li.Total = Product.UnitPrice * li.Quantity
        If NewLineItem Then
            Me.Order.LineItems.AddLineItemsRow(li)
        End If
        btnAddUpdateLineItem.Text = "Add"
        btnDeleteLineItem.Enabled = False
        Me.UpdateProductTotals()
    End Sub

    Private Sub UpdateProductTotals()
        lblProductTotal.Text = FormatNumber(Me.Order.ProductTotal, 2)
        lblProductTotal2.Text = FormatNumber(Me.Order.ProductTotal, 2)
        lblSandH.Text = FormatNumber(Me.Order.ShippingAndHandling, 2)
        lblSandH2.Text = FormatNumber(Me.Order.ShippingAndHandling, 2)
        lblSalesTax.Text = FormatNumber(Me.Order.SalesTax, 2)
        lblSalesTax2.Text = FormatNumber(Me.Order.SalesTax, 2)
        lblOrderTotal.Text = FormatNumber(Me.Order.InvoiceTotal, 2)
        lblOrderTotal2.Text = FormatNumber(Me.Order.InvoiceTotal, 2)
    End Sub

    Private Sub btnDeleteLineItem_Click(ByVal sender As System.Object, _
            ByVal e As System.EventArgs) Handles btnDeleteLineItem.Click
        Dim iRow As Integer
        iRow = dgLineItems.CurrentCell.RowNumber
        Me.Order.LineItems.Rows(iRow).Delete()
        txtQuantity.Text = 1
        btnAddUpdateLineItem.Text = "Add"
        btnDeleteLineItem.Enabled = False
        Me.UpdateProductTotals()
    End Sub

    Private Sub dgLineItems_CurrentCellChanged(ByVal sender As Object, _
            ByVal e As System.EventArgs) Handles dgLineItems.CurrentCellChanged, _
            dgLineItems.Click
        If Me.Order.LineItems.Rows.Count > 0 Then
            Dim iRow As Integer
            iRow = dgLineItems.CurrentCell.RowNumber
            cboProducts.SelectedValue = Me.Order.LineItems(iRow).ProductCode
            txtQuantity.Text = Me.Order.LineItems(iRow).Quantity
            btnAddUpdateLineItem.Text = "Update"
            btnDeleteLineItem.Enabled = True
            dgLineItems.Select(iRow)
        End If
    End Sub

    Private Sub btnPrev1_Click(ByVal sender As System.Object, _
            ByVal e As System.EventArgs) Handles btnPrev1.Click
        TabControl1.SelectedTab = tabCustomer
        txtCustomerID.Focus()
    End Sub
```

Figure 11-10   The code for the Enter Orders form (part 3 of 6)

frmEnterOrders.vb   **Page 4**

```
    Private Sub btnNext2_Click(ByVal sender As System.Object, _
            ByVal e As System.EventArgs) Handles btnNext2.Click
        TabControl1.SelectedTab = tabPayment
        cboCreditCards.Focus()
    End Sub

    Private Sub rdoCreditCard_CheckedChanged(ByVal sender As System.Object, _
            ByVal e As System.EventArgs) Handles rdoCreditCard.CheckedChanged
        If rdoCreditCard.Checked Then
            cboCreditCards.Enabled = True
            txtCardNumber.Enabled = True
            cboExpirationMonth.Enabled = True
            cboExpirationYear.Enabled = True
        Else
            cboCreditCards.Enabled = False
            txtCardNumber.Enabled = False
            cboExpirationMonth.Enabled = False
            cboExpirationYear.Enabled = False
            cboCreditCards.SelectedIndex = -1
            txtCardNumber.Text = ""
            cboExpirationMonth.SelectedIndex = 0
            cboExpirationYear.SelectedIndex = 0
        End If
    End Sub

    Private Sub btnPrev2_Click(ByVal sender As System.Object, _
            ByVal e As System.EventArgs) Handles btnPrev2.Click
        TabControl1.SelectedTab = tabProducts
        txtCustomerID.Focus()
    End Sub

    Private Sub btnAccept_Click(ByVal sender As System.Object, _
            ByVal e As System.EventArgs) Handles btnAccept.Click
        Order.PaidByCreditCard = rdoCreditCard.Checked
        If Me.ValidCustomer() Then
            If Me.ValidLineItems Then
                If Me.ValidPayment Then
                    If rdoCreditCard.Checked Then
                        Order.CreditCardType = cboCreditCards.SelectedValue
                        Order.CardNumber = txtCardNumber.Text
                        Order.SetExpirationDate(cboExpirationMonth.SelectedItem, _
                            cboExpirationYear.SelectedItem)
                    End If
                    If OrderDB.WriteOrder(Order, Customer) Then
                        Me.DisplayConfirmation()
                        frmMain.OrdersEntered += 1
                        frmMain.StatusBar.Text = "Orders entered: " _
                                                & frmMain.OrdersEntered
                    End If
                    Customer = New Customer()
                    Order = New Order()
                    dgLineItems.DataSource = Order.LineItems
                    Me.ClearAllControls()
                    TabControl1.SelectedTab = tabCustomer
                End If
            End If
        End If
    End Sub
```

Figure 11-10   The code for the Enter Orders form (part 4 of 6)

frmEnterOrders.vb   **Page 5**

```vb
Private Function ValidCustomer() As Boolean
    If Customer.CustomerID = 0 Then
        MessageBox.Show("You must select a customer or create a new customer.", _
            "Data entry error", MessageBoxButtons.OK, MessageBoxIcon.Hand)
        TabControl1.SelectedTab = tabCustomer
        txtCustomerID.Focus()
        Return False
    Else
        Return True
    End If
End Function

Private Function ValidLineItems() As Boolean
    If Order.LineItems.Count = 0 Then
        MessageBox.Show("You must order at least one product.", _
            "Data entry error", MessageBoxButtons.OK, MessageBoxIcon.Hand)
        TabControl1.SelectedTab = tabProducts
        cboProducts.Focus()
        Return False
    Else
        Return True
    End If
End Function

Private Function ValidPayment() As Boolean
    ValidPayment = True
    Dim sMessage As String
    If rdoCreditCard.Checked Then
        If cboCreditCards.SelectedIndex = -1 Then
            ValidPayment = False
            sMessage = "You must select a credit card."
            cboCreditCards.Focus()
        ElseIf txtCardNumber.Text = "" Then
            ValidPayment = False
            sMessage = "You must enter a card number."
            txtCardNumber.Focus()
        ElseIf cboExpirationMonth.SelectedIndex = -1 Then
            ValidPayment = False
            sMessage = "You must select an expiration month."
            cboExpirationMonth.Focus()
        ElseIf cboExpirationYear.SelectedIndex = -1 Then
            ValidPayment = False
            sMessage = "You must select an expiration year."
            cboExpirationYear.Focus()
        End If
        If Not ValidPayment Then
            MessageBox.Show(sMessage, "Data entry error", MessageBoxButtons.OK, _
                MessageBoxIcon.Hand)
        End If
    End If
End Function

Private Sub DisplayConfirmation()
    Dim sMessage As String
    sMessage = "Order accepted. Invoice number: " & Order.InvoiceID
```

Figure 11-10   The code for the Enter Orders form (part 5 of 6)

frmEnterOrders.vb   **Page 6**

```vb
        If Order.BackOrders.Count > 0 Then
            sMessage &= ControlChars.CrLf
            sMessage &= "The following products were backordered:" _
                    & ControlChars.CrLf
            Dim bo As dsOrder.LineItemsRow
            For Each bo In Order.BackOrders
                sMessage &= bo.Description & " (" & bo.Quantity & ")" _
                        & ControlChars.CrLf
            Next
        End If
        MessageBox.Show(sMessage, "Order confirmation", MessageBoxButtons.OK, _
            MessageBoxIcon.Information)
    End Sub

    Private Sub ClearAllControls()
        txtCustomerID.Text = ""
        btnModifyCustomer.Enabled = False
        lblAddress.Text = ""
        cboProducts.SelectedIndex = 0
        txtQuantity.Text = 1
        btnAddUpdateLineItem.Text = "Add"
        lblProductTotal.Text = ""
        lblProductTotal2.Text = ""
        lblSandH.Text = ""
        lblSandH2.Text = ""
        lblSalesTax.Text = ""
        lblSalesTax2.Text = ""
        lblOrderTotal.Text = ""
        lblOrderTotal2.Text = ""
        rdoCreditCard.Checked = True
        cboCreditCards.SelectedIndex = -1
        txtCardNumber.Text = ""
        cboExpirationMonth.SelectedIndex = 0
        cboExpirationYear.SelectedIndex = 0
        Me.Text = "Enter Orders"
        TabControl1.SelectedTab = tabCustomer
        txtCustomerID.Focus()
    End Sub

    Private Sub btnCancel_Click(ByVal sender As System.Object, _
            ByVal e As System.EventArgs) Handles btnCancel.Click
        Me.ClearAllControls()
        Customer = New Customer()
        Order = New Order()
        dgLineItems.DataSource = Order.LineItems
    End Sub

    Private Sub btnClose_Click(ByVal sender As System.Object, _
            ByVal e As System.EventArgs) Handles btnClose.Click
        Me.Close()
    End Sub

    Private Sub frmEnterOrders_Closing(ByVal sender As Object, _
            ByVal e As System.ComponentModel.CancelEventArgs) Handles MyBase.Closing
        If Customer.CustomerID > 0 Then
            MessageBox.Show("You must first finish or cancel this order.", _
                "About to close", MessageBoxButtons.OK, MessageBoxIcon.Hand)
            e.Cancel = True
        End If
    End Sub
End Class
```

Figure 11-10   The code for the Enter Orders form (part 6 of 6)

frmFindCustomer.vb **Page 1**

```vb
Public Class frmFindCustomer
    Inherits System.Windows.Forms.Form

    Public Customer As Customer

    Private Sub btnSearch_Click(ByVal sender As System.Object, _
            ByVal e As System.EventArgs) Handles btnSearch.Click
        conMurach.ConnectionString = MurachDB.GetConnectionString
        DsCustomers1.Customers.Clear()
        daMurach.SelectCommand.Parameters("@LastName").Value = txtLastName.Text & "%"
        daMurach.SelectCommand.Parameters("@State").Value = txtState.Text & "%"
        daMurach.Fill(DsCustomers1)
        Select Case DsCustomers1.Customers.Rows.Count
            Case 0
                lblMessage.Text = "No customers found with that name."
            Case 1
                lblMessage.Text = "One customer found with that name."
            Case Is > 1
                lblMessage.Text = DsCustomers1.Customers.Rows.Count _
                    & " customers found with that name."
        End Select
        lstCustomers.Items.Clear()
        Dim cr As dsCustomers.CustomersRow
        For Each cr In DsCustomers1.Customers.Rows
            Dim s As String
            s = cr.FirstName & " " & cr.LastName & ", "
            If cr.Address1 <> "" Then
                s &= cr.Address1 & ", "
            End If
            If cr.Address2 <> "" Then
                s &= cr.Address2 & ", "
            End If
            s &= cr.City & ", " & cr.State & ", " & cr.ZipCode
            lstCustomers.Items.Add(s)
        Next
        btnOK.Enabled = False
    End Sub

    Private Sub lstCustomers_SelectedIndexChanged(ByVal sender As System.Object, _
            ByVal e As System.EventArgs) Handles lstCustomers.SelectedIndexChanged
        btnOK.Enabled = True
    End Sub

    Private Sub btnOK_Click(ByVal sender As System.Object, _
            ByVal e As System.EventArgs) Handles btnOK.Click
        Me.SelectCustomer()
    End Sub

    Private Sub lstCustomers_DoubleClick(ByVal sender As Object, _
            ByVal e As System.EventArgs) Handles lstCustomers.DoubleClick
        Me.SelectCustomer()
    End Sub
```

Figure 11-11   The code for the Find Customer form (part 1 of 2)

frmFindCustomer.vb   **Page 2**

```vb
    Public Sub SelectCustomer()
        Dim cr As dsCustomers.CustomersRow
        cr = DsCustomers1.Customers.Rows(lstCustomers.SelectedIndex)
        Customer.CustomerID = cr.CustomerID
        Customer.FirstName = cr.FirstName
        Customer.LastName = cr.LastName
        Customer.Address1 = cr.Address1
        Customer.Address2 = cr.Address2
        Customer.City = cr.City
        Customer.State = cr.State
        Customer.ZipCode = cr.ZipCode
        Customer.Phone = cr.Phone
        Customer.EMail = cr.Email
        Me.Close()
    End Sub

    Private Sub btnCancel_Click(ByVal sender As System.Object, _
            ByVal e As System.EventArgs) Handles btnCancel.Click
        Me.Close()
    End Sub

End Class
```

The components used by the Find Customer form

Component	Description
conMurach	A connection to the Murach database. Generated by the Data Adapter Configuration Wizard.
daMurach	A data adapter that retrieves selected rows from the Customers table. Generated by the Data Adapter Configuration Wizard.
DsCustomers1	A dataset generated from the daMurach data adapter.

The Select statement for the daMurach data adapter

```sql
SELECT CustomerID, FirstName, LastName, Address1, Address2,
        City, State, ZipCode, Phone, Email
FROM Customers
WHERE (LastName LIKE @LastName) AND (State LIKE @State)
```

Notes

- The Find Customer form is displayed when the user clicks the Find Customer button in either the Enter Orders form or the Customer Details form.

- The btnSearch_Click procedure uses a parameterized query to retrieve customers based on the last name and state. The Like clause is used in the Select statement so the user can search based on just a portion of the last name or state code.

Figure 11-11   The code for the Find Customer form (part 2 of 2)

frmCustomer.vb   **Page 1**

```
Imports System.Data.SqlClient
Public Class frmCustomer
    Inherits System.Windows.Forms.Form
    Public Customer As Customer
    Public NewCustomer As Boolean

    Private Sub frmCustomer_Load(ByVal sender As System.Object, _
            ByVal e As System.EventArgs) Handles MyBase.Load
        If Me.NewCustomer Then
            Me.Text = "New Customer"
            Me.ClearEntryFields()
        Else
            Me.Text = "Modify Customer"
            Me.SetEntryFields()
        End If
    End Sub

    Private Sub ClearEntryFields()
        txtLastName.Text = ""
        txtFirstName.Text = ""
        txtAddress1.Text = ""
        txtAddress2.Text = ""
        txtCity.Text = ""
        txtState.Text = ""
        txtZipCode.Text = ""
        txtPhone.Text = ""
        txtEmail.Text = ""
    End Sub

    Private Sub SetEntryFields()
        lblCustomerID.Text = Customer.CustomerID
        txtLastName.Text = Customer.LastName
        txtFirstName.Text = Customer.FirstName
        txtAddress1.Text = Customer.Address1
        txtAddress2.Text = Customer.Address2
        txtCity.Text = Customer.City
        txtState.Text = Customer.State
        txtZipCode.Text = Customer.ZipCode
        txtPhone.Text = Customer.Phone
        txtEmail.Text = Customer.EMail
    End Sub

    Private Sub btnAccept_Click(ByVal sender As System.Object, _
            ByVal e As System.EventArgs) Handles btnAccept.Click
        If ValidData() Then
            If Me.NewCustomer Then
                Me.SetCustomerFields(Customer)
                Customer.CustomerID = CustomerDB.InsertCustomer(Customer)
                Me.Close()
            Else
                Dim NewCustomer As New Customer()
                Me.SetCustomerFields(NewCustomer)
                NewCustomer.CustomerID = lblCustomerID.Text
                Dim sMsg As String
                If CustomerDB.UpdateCustomer(NewCustomer, Customer) Then
                    Customer = NewCustomer
                    Me.Close()
                End If
            End If
        End If
    End Sub
```

Figure 11-12   The code for the Customer form (part 1 of 2)

frmCustomer.vb   **Page 2**

```
Private Function ValidData() As Boolean
    ValidData = True
    Dim sMessage As String
    If txtLastName.Text = "" Then
        ValidData = False
        sMessage = "You must enter a last name."
        txtLastName.Focus()
    ElseIf txtFirstName.Text = "" Then
        ValidData = False
        sMessage = "You must enter a first name."
        txtFirstName.Focus()
    ElseIf txtCity.Text = "" Then
        ValidData = False
        txtCity.Focus()
        sMessage = "You must enter a city."
    ElseIf txtState.Text = "" Then
        ValidData = False
        sMessage = "You must enter a state."
        txtState.Focus()
    ElseIf txtZipCode.Text = "" Then
        ValidData = False
        sMessage = "You must enter a zip code."
        txtZipCode.Focus()
    End If
    If Not ValidData Then
        MessageBox.Show(sMessage, "Data entry error", _
            MessageBoxButtons.OK, MessageBoxIcon.Exclamation)
    End If
End Function

Private Sub SetCustomerFields(ByVal Cust As Customer)
    Cust.LastName = txtLastName.Text
    Cust.FirstName = txtFirstName.Text
    Cust.Address1 = txtAddress1.Text
    Cust.Address2 = txtAddress2.Text
    Cust.City = txtCity.Text
    Cust.State = txtState.Text
    Cust.ZipCode = txtZipCode.Text
    Cust.Phone = txtPhone.Text
    Cust.EMail = txtEmail.Text
End Sub

Private Sub btnCancel_Click(ByVal sender As System.Object, _
        ByVal e As System.EventArgs) Handles btnCancel.Click
    Me.Close()
End Sub

End Class
```

Notes

- The Customer form is displayed when the user clicks the New Customer button or the Modify Customer button in the Enter Orders form. It lets the user enter data for a new customer or edit data for an existing customer.

- The Customer form doesn't use any data components. Instead, it uses methods of the CustomerDB class to insert or update the customer row.

Figure 11-12   The code for the Customer form (part 2 of 2)

frmCustomerDetails.vb

```vb
Imports System.Data.SqlClient
Public Class frmCustomerDetails
    Inherits System.Windows.Forms.Form

    Dim Customer As New Customer()

    Private Sub frmCustomerDetails_Load(ByVal sender As System.Object, _
            ByVal e As System.EventArgs) Handles MyBase.Load
        txtCustomerID.Focus()
    End Sub

    Private Sub btnGetCustomer_Click(ByVal sender As System.Object, _
            ByVal e As System.EventArgs) Handles btnGetCustomer.Click
        If IsNumeric(txtCustomerID.Text) Then
            Customer = CustomerDB.GetCustomer(txtCustomerID.Text)
            Me.ShowCustomerHistory()
        Else
            MessageBox.Show("You must enter a numeric Customer ID.", _
                "Data entry error", MessageBoxButtons.OK, MessageBoxIcon.Hand)
        End If
        lblAddress.Text = Customer.FormattedAddress
    End Sub

    Private Sub ShowCustomerHistory()
        conMurach.ConnectionString = MurachDB.GetConnectionString
        daProductHistory.SelectCommand.Parameters("@CustomerID").Value _
            = Customer.CustomerID
        daProductDetails.SelectCommand.Parameters("@CustomerID").Value _
            = Customer.CustomerID
        daInvoices.SelectCommand.Parameters("@CustomerID").Value _
            = Customer.CustomerID
        daInvoiceLineItems.SelectCommand.Parameters("@CustomerID").Value _
            = Customer.CustomerID
        daBackorders.SelectCommand.Parameters("@CustomerID").Value _
            = Customer.CustomerID
        daPayments.SelectCommand.Parameters("@CustomerID").Value _
            = Customer.CustomerID
        daOpenItems.SelectCommand.Parameters("@CustomerID").Value _
            = Customer.CustomerID
        DsCustomerDetails1.Clear()
        Try
            daProductHistory.Fill(DsCustomerDetails1)
            daProductDetails.Fill(DsCustomerDetails1)
            daInvoices.Fill(DsCustomerDetails1)
            daInvoiceLineItems.Fill(DsCustomerDetails1)
            daBackorders.Fill(DsCustomerDetails1)
            daPayments.Fill(DsCustomerDetails1)
            daOpenItems.Fill(DsCustomerDetails1)
        Catch e As SqlException
            MessageBox.Show(e.Message)
        End Try
        Dim dBalanceDue As Decimal
        Dim OpenItem As dsCustomerDetails.OpenItemsRow
        For Each OpenItem In DsCustomerDetails1.OpenItems
            dBalanceDue += OpenItem.BalanceDue
        Next
        lblBalanceDue.Text = FormatCurrency(dBalanceDue)
    End Sub
```

Figure 11-13   The code for the Customer Details form (part 1 of 2)

frmCustomerDetails.vb   **Page 2**

```
    Private Sub btnFind_Click(ByVal sender As System.Object, _
            ByVal e As System.EventArgs) Handles btnFind.Click
        Dim frmFindCustomer As New frmFindCustomer()
        frmFindCustomer.Customer = Me.Customer
        frmFindCustomer.ShowDialog()
        If Me.Customer.CustomerID <> 0 Then
            lblAddress.Text = Me.Customer.FormattedAddress
            txtCustomerID.Text = Me.Customer.CustomerID
            Me.ShowCustomerHistory()
        End If
    End Sub

    Private Sub btnClose_Click(ByVal sender As System.Object, _
            ByVal e As System.EventArgs) Handles btnClose.Click
        Me.Close()
    End Sub

End Class
```

The Select statements for the data adapters

daProductHistory (maps to ProductHistory table)

```
SELECT InvoiceLineItems.ProductCode AS Code, MAX(Products.Description) AS Description,
    SUM(InvoiceLineItems.Quantity) AS Quantity, SUM(InvoiceLineItems.ItemTotal) AS Total,
    MAX(Invoices.InvoiceDate) AS Date
FROM InvoiceLineItems
    INNER JOIN Products ON InvoiceLineItems.ProductCode = Products.ProductCode
    INNER JOIN Invoices ON InvoiceLineItems.InvoiceID = Invoices.InvoiceID
WHERE (Invoices.CustomerID = @CustomerID) GROUP BY InvoiceLineItems.ProductCode
```

daProductDetails (maps to ProductDetails table)

```
SELECT InvoiceLineItems.ProductCode AS Code, Products.Description AS Description,
    InvoiceLineItems.InvoiceID AS InvoiceID, Invoices.CustomerID AS CustomerID,
    Invoices.InvoiceDate AS InvoiceDate, InvoiceLineItems.Quantity AS Quantity,
    Invoices.InvoiceID AS Expr1, Products.ProductCode
FROM InvoiceLineItems
    INNER JOIN Products ON InvoiceLineItems.ProductCode = Products.ProductCode
    INNER JOIN Invoices ON InvoiceLineItems.InvoiceID = Invoices.InvoiceID
WHERE (Invoices.CustomerID = @CustomerID)
```

daInvoices

```
SELECT InvoiceID, InvoiceDate, ProductTotal, SalesTax, ShippingAndHandling, InvoiceTotal
FROM Invoices WHERE (CustomerID = @CustomerID)
```

daInvoiceLineItems

```
SELECT InvoiceLineItems.InvoiceID, InvoiceLineItems.ProductCode, Products.Description,
    InvoiceLineItems.UnitPrice, InvoiceLineItems.Quantity, InvoiceLineItems.ItemTotal,
    Invoices.CustomerID, Invoices.InvoiceID AS Expr1, Products.ProductCode AS Expr2
FROM InvoiceLineItems
    INNER JOIN Products ON InvoiceLineItems.ProductCode = Products.ProductCode
    INNER JOIN Invoices ON InvoiceLineItems.InvoiceID = Invoices.InvoiceID
WHERE (Invoices.CustomerID = @CustomerID)
```

daBackOrders

```
SELECT Backorders.BackorderID, Backorders.InvoiceID, Backorders.DateBackordered,
    Backorders.ProductCode, Products.Description, Backorders.Quantity, Backorders.Price,
    Products.ProductCode AS Expr1
FROM Backorders
    INNER JOIN Products ON Backorders.ProductCode = Products.ProductCode
WHERE (Backorders.CustomerID = @CustomerID)
```

Figure 11-13   The code for the Customer Details form (part 2 of 2)

frmOrderOptions.vb

```vb
Public Class frmOrderOptions
    Inherits System.Windows.Forms.Form

    Private Sub frmOrderOptions_Load(ByVal sender As System.Object, _
            ByVal e As System.EventArgs) Handles MyBase.Load
        OrderOptions.GetOrderOptions()
        txtTaxRate.Text = FormatNumber(OrderOptions.SalesTaxRate, 4)
        txtFirstBook.Text = FormatNumber(OrderOptions.FirstBookShipCharge, 2)
        txtAdditionalBook.Text = FormatNumber _
            (OrderOptions.AdditionalBookShipCharge, 2)
    End Sub

    Private Sub btnOK_Click(ByVal sender As System.Object, _
            ByVal e As System.EventArgs) Handles btnOK.Click
        If ValidData() Then
            OrderOptions.SalesTaxRate = txtTaxRate.Text
            OrderOptions.FirstBookShipCharge = txtFirstBook.Text
            OrderOptions.AdditionalBookShipCharge = txtAdditionalBook.Text
            OrderOptions.UpdateOrderOptions()
            Me.Close()
        End If
    End Sub

    Private Function ValidData() As Boolean
        ValidData = True
        Dim sMessage As String
        If Not IsNumeric(txtTaxRate.Text) Then
            ValidData = False
            sMessage = "Sales tax rate must be numeric."
            txtTaxRate.Focus()
        ElseIf Not IsNumeric(txtFirstBook.Text) Then
            ValidData = False
            sMessage = "First book amount must be numeric."
            txtFirstBook.Focus()
        ElseIf Not IsNumeric(txtAdditionalBook.Text) Then
            ValidData = False
            sMessage = "Additional book amount must be numeric."
            txtAdditionalBook.Focus()
        End If
        If Not ValidData Then
            MessageBox.Show(sMessage, "Data entry error", _
                MessageBoxButtons.OK, MessageBoxIcon.Exclamation)
        End If
    End Function

    Private Sub btnCancel_Click(ByVal sender As System.Object, _
            ByVal e As System.EventArgs) Handles btnCancel.Click
        Me.Close()
    End Sub

End Class
```

Figure 11-14   The code for the Order Options form

Order.vb

```
Public Class Order
    Public InvoiceID As Integer

    Public ReadOnly Property OrderDate() As Date
        Get
            Return Today()
        End Get
    End Property

    Public LineItems As New dsOrder.LineItemsDataTable()
    Public BackOrders As New dsOrder.LineItemsDataTable()

    Public ReadOnly Property ProductTotal() As Decimal
        Get
            Dim li As dsOrder.LineItemsRow
            Dim dProductTotal As Decimal
            For Each li In Me.LineItems.Rows
                dProductTotal += li.Total
            Next
            Return dProductTotal
        End Get
    End Property

    Public ReadOnly Property SalesTax() As Decimal
        Get
            Return Math.Round(Me.ProductTotal * OrderOptions.SalesTaxRate, 2)
        End Get
    End Property

    Public ReadOnly Property ShippingAndHandling() As Decimal
        Get
            Dim dSandH As Decimal
            Dim li As dsOrder.LineItemsRow
            Dim iQuantity As Integer
            For Each li In Me.LineItems.Rows
                iQuantity += li.Quantity
            Next
            If iQuantity > 0 Then
                dSandH = OrderOptions.FirstBookShipCharge
                dSandH += (iQuantity - 1) * OrderOptions.AdditionalBookShipCharge
            Else
                dSandH = 0
            End If
            Return dSandH
        End Get
    End Property

    Public ReadOnly Property InvoiceTotal() As Decimal
        Get
            Return Me.ProductTotal + Me.SalesTax + Me.ShippingAndHandling
        End Get
    End Property

    Public PaidByCreditCard As Boolean
    Public CreditCardType As String
    Public CardNumber As String
    Public CardExpirationDate As Date

    Public Sub SetExpirationDate(ByVal Month As String, ByVal Year As Integer)
        CardExpirationDate = DateTime.Parse(Month & " 1, " & Year)
    End Sub
End Class
```

Figure 11-15   The code for the Order class

Customer.vb

```
Public Class Customer

    Public CustomerID As Integer
    Public LastName As String
    Public FirstName As String
    Public Address1 As String
    Public Address2 As String
    Public City As String
    Public State As String
    Public ZipCode As String
    Public Phone As String
    Public EMail As String

    Public ReadOnly Property FullName() As String
        Get
            Return Me.FirstName & " " & Me.LastName
        End Get
    End Property

    Public ReadOnly Property FormattedAddress() As String
        Get
            Dim s As String
            s = Me.FirstName & " " & Me.LastName & ControlChars.CrLf
            If Me.Address1 <> "" Then
                s &= Me.Address1 & ControlChars.CrLf
            End If
            If Me.Address2 <> "" Then
                s &= Me.Address2 & ControlChars.CrLf
            End If
            s &= Me.City & " " & Me.State & " " & Me.ZipCode & ControlChars.CrLf
            If Me.Phone <> "" Then
                s &= Me.Phone & ControlChars.CrLf
            End If
            If Me.EMail <> "" Then
                s &= Me.EMail & ControlChars.CrLf
            End If
            Return s
        End Get
    End Property

End Class
```

The Product.vb class

```
Public Class Product
    Public ProductCode As String
    Public Description As String
    Public UnitPrice As Decimal
    Public OnHandQuantity As Integer
    Public QuantityBackOrdered As Integer
    Public YTDUnitSales As Integer
    Public YTDDollarSales As Decimal
    Public MTDUnitSales As Integer
    Public MTDDollarSales As Decimal
    Public LifetimeUnitSales As Integer
    Public LifetimeDollarSales As Decimal
End Class
```

Figure 11-16   The code for the Customer and Product classes

The OrderOptions class

```
Imports System.Data.SqlClient
Public Class OrderOptions
    Public Shared SalesTaxRate As Decimal
    Public Shared FirstBookShipCharge As Decimal
    Public Shared AdditionalBookShipCharge As Decimal

    Public Shared Sub GetOrderOptions()
        Dim conMurach As SqlConnection = MurachDB.GetConnection
        Dim sSelectCommand As String
        sSelectCommand = "SELECT SalesTaxRate, FirstBookShipCharge, " _
            & "AdditionalBookShipCharge FROM OrderOptions"
        Dim cmdMurach As New SqlCommand(sSelectCommand, conMurach)
        Dim rdrMurach As SqlDataReader
        Try
            conMurach.Open()
            rdrMurach = cmdMurach.ExecuteReader(CommandBehavior.SingleRow)
            rdrMurach.Read()
            OrderOptions.SalesTaxRate = rdrMurach.Item(0)
            OrderOptions.FirstBookShipCharge = rdrMurach.Item(1)
            OrderOptions.AdditionalBookShipCharge = rdrMurach.Item(2)
            conMurach.Close()
        Catch e As SqlException
            MessageBox.Show("Could not read invoice settings.", _
                "Database error", MessageBoxButtons.OK, _
                MessageBoxIcon.Exclamation)
        End Try
    End Sub

    Public Shared Sub UpdateOrderOptions()
        Dim conMurach As SqlConnection = MurachDB.GetConnection
        Dim sUpdateCommand As String
        sUpdateCommand = "UPDATE OrderOptions " _
            & "SET SalesTaxRate = @SalesTaxRate, " _
            & "FirstBookShipCharge = @FirstBookShipCharge, " _
            & "AdditionalBookShipCharge = @AdditionalBookShipCharge"
        Dim cmdMurach As New SqlCommand(sUpdateCommand, conMurach)
        cmdMurach.Parameters.Add("@SalesTaxRate", OrderOptions.SalesTaxRate)
        cmdMurach.Parameters.Add("@FirstBookShipCharge", _
            OrderOptions.FirstBookShipCharge)
        cmdMurach.Parameters.Add("@AdditionalBookShipCharge", _
            OrderOptions.AdditionalBookShipCharge)
        conMurach.Open()
        cmdMurach.ExecuteNonQuery()
        conMurach.Close()
    End Sub
End Class
```

MurachDB.vb

```
Imports System.Data.SqlClient
Imports System.Xml
Public Class MurachDB
    Public Shared Function GetConnection() As SqlConnection
        Return New SqlConnection(GetConnectionString)
    End Function

    Public Shared Function GetConnectionString() As String
        Dim XmlReader As New XmlTextReader("csMurach.xml")
        Return XmlReader.ReadElementString("Connection")
    End Function
End Class
```

Figure 11-17   The code for the OrderOptions and MurachDB classes

CustomerDB.vb   **Page 1**

```vb
Imports System.Data.SqlClient
Public Class CustomerDB

    Public Shared Function GetCustomer(ByVal CustID As Integer) As Customer
        Dim Customer As New Customer()
        Dim conMurach As SqlConnection = MurachDB.GetConnection()
        Dim sSelectCommand As String
        sSelectCommand = "SELECT CustomerID, LastName, FirstName, Address1, " _
            & "Address2, City, State, ZipCode, Phone, Email " _
            & "FROM Customers " _
            & "WHERE CustomerID = @CustomerID"
        Dim cmdMurach As New SqlCommand(sSelectCommand, conMurach)
        cmdMurach.Parameters.Add("@CustomerID", CustID)
        Dim rdrMurach As SqlDataReader
        conMurach.Open()
        rdrMurach = cmdMurach.ExecuteReader(CommandBehavior.SingleRow)
        If rdrMurach.Read() Then
            Customer.CustomerID = rdrMurach.Item("CustomerID")
            Customer.LastName = rdrMurach.Item("LastName")
            Customer.FirstName = rdrMurach.Item("FirstName")
            Customer.Address1 = rdrMurach.Item("Address1")
            Customer.Address2 = rdrMurach.Item("Address2")
            Customer.City = rdrMurach.Item("City")
            Customer.State = rdrMurach.Item("State")
            Customer.ZipCode = rdrMurach.Item("ZipCode")
            Customer.Phone = rdrMurach.Item("Phone")
            Customer.EMail = rdrMurach.Item("Email")
        Else
            MessageBox.Show("Could not find that customer.", "Customer not found", _
                MessageBoxButtons.OK, MessageBoxIcon.Exclamation)
        End If
        conMurach.Close()
        Return Customer
    End Function

    Public Shared Function InsertCustomer(ByVal Customer As Customer) As Integer
        Dim conMurach As SqlConnection
        conMurach = MurachDB.GetConnection
        Dim sInsertCommand As String
        sInsertCommand = "INSERT INTO Customers " _
            & "(LastName, FirstName, Address1, Address2, City, " _
            & "State, ZipCode, Phone, Email, FirstOrderDate, LastOrderDate) " _
            & "VALUES (@LastName, @FirstName, @Address1, @Address2, @City, " _
            & "@State, @ZipCode, @Phone, @Email, @FirstOrderDate, @LastOrderDate) "
        Dim cmdMurach As New SqlCommand(sInsertCommand, conMurach)
        With cmdMurach.Parameters
            .Add("@LastName", Customer.LastName)
            .Add("@FirstName", Customer.FirstName)
            .Add("@Address1", Customer.Address1)
            .Add("@Address2", Customer.Address2)
            .Add("@City", Customer.City)
            .Add("@State", Customer.State)
            .Add("@ZipCode", Customer.ZipCode)
            .Add("@Phone", Customer.Phone)
            .Add("@Email", Customer.EMail)
            .Add("@FirstOrderDate", Today())
            .Add("@LastOrderDate", Today())
        End With
        conMurach.Open()
        cmdMurach.ExecuteNonQuery()
        cmdMurach.CommandText = "SELECT @@IDENTITY"
        Customer.CustomerID = cmdMurach.ExecuteScalar
```

Figure 11-18   The code for the CustomerDB class (part 1 of 2)

CustomerDB.vb   **Page 2**

```
        conMurach.Close()
        Return Customer.CustomerID
    End Function

    Public Shared Function UpdateCustomer(ByVal NewCustomer, ByVal OldCustomer) As Boolean
        Dim bUpdate As Boolean = True
        Dim conMurach As SqlConnection
        conMurach = MurachDB.GetConnection
        Dim sUpdateCommand As String
        sUpdateCommand = "UPDATE Customers " _
            & "SET LastName = @LastName, " _
            & "FirstName = @FirstName, " _
            & "Address1 = @Address1, " _
            & "Address2 = @Address2, " _
            & "City = @City, " _
            & "State = @State, " _
            & "ZipCode = @ZipCode, " _
            & "Phone = @Phone, " _
            & "Email = @Email " _
            & "WHERE CustomerID = @CustomerID " _
            & "AND LastName = @OldLastName " _
            & "AND FirstName = @OldFirstName " _
            & "AND Address1 = @OldAddress1 " _
            & "AND Address2 = @OldAddress2 " _
            & "AND City = @OldCity " _
            & "AND State = @OldState " _
            & "AND ZipCode = @OldZipCode " _
            & "AND Phone = @OldPhone " _
            & "AND Email = @OldEmail"
        Dim cmdMurach As New SqlCommand(sUpdateCommand, conMurach)
        With cmdMurach.Parameters
            .Add("@CustomerID", OldCustomer.CustomerID)
            .Add("@LastName", NewCustomer.LastName)
            .Add("@FirstName", NewCustomer.FirstName)
            .Add("@Address1", NewCustomer.Address1)
            .Add("@Address2", NewCustomer.Address2)
            .Add("@City", NewCustomer.City)
            .Add("@State", NewCustomer.State)
            .Add("@ZipCode", NewCustomer.ZipCode)
            .Add("@Phone", NewCustomer.Phone)
            .Add("@Email", NewCustomer.Email)
            .Add("@OldLastName", OldCustomer.LastName)
            .Add("@OldFirstName", OldCustomer.FirstName)
            .Add("@OldAddress1", OldCustomer.Address1)
            .Add("@OldAddress2", OldCustomer.Address2)
            .Add("@OldCity", OldCustomer.City)
            .Add("@OldState", OldCustomer.State)
            .Add("@OldZipCode", OldCustomer.ZipCode)
            .Add("@OldPhone", OldCustomer.Phone)
            .Add("@OldEmail", OldCustomer.EMail)
        End With
        conMurach.Open()
        If cmdMurach.ExecuteNonQuery() = 0 Then
            MessageBox.Show("Another user has modified or deleted that customer. " _
                & "Please try again.", "Concurrency error", MessageBoxButtons.OK, _
                MessageBoxIcon.Warning)
            bUpdate = False
        End If
        conMurach.Close()
        Return bUpdate
    End Function
End Class
```

Figure 11-18   The code for the CustomerDB class (part 2 of 2)

OrderDB.vb   **Page 1**

```
Imports System.Data.SqlClient
Public Class OrderDB
    Dim conMurach As SqlConnection
    Dim cmdOrder As New SqlCommand()
    Dim trnOrder As SqlTransaction
    Dim BackOrder As Boolean

    Dim Order As Order
    Dim Customer As Customer

    Public Function WriteOrder(ByRef Order As Order, ByVal Customer As Customer) _
            As Boolean
        Me.Order = Order
        Me.Customer = Customer
        conMurach = MurachDB.GetConnection
        conMurach.Open()
        trnOrder = conMurach.BeginTransaction(IsolationLevel.RepeatableRead)
        cmdOrder.Connection = conMurach
        cmdOrder.Transaction = trnOrder
        Try
            Me.InsertInvoice()
            BackOrder = False
            Dim li As dsOrder.LineItemsRow
            For Each li In Order.LineItems.Rows
                Me.ProcessLineItem(li)
            Next
            If BackOrder Then
                Me.AdjustInvoiceTotal()
            End If
            If Order.PaidByCreditCard Then
                Me.InsertPayment()
            Else
                Me.InsertOpenItem()
            End If
            Me.UpdateCustomer()
            trnOrder.Commit()
            conMurach.Close()
            Return True
        Catch eSql As SqlException
            trnOrder.Rollback()
            Dim sMessage As String
            sMessage = "A database error has occurred. The order was not posted." _
                    & ControlChars.CrLf
            sMessage &= "Error number: " & eSql.Number & ControlChars.CrLf
            sMessage &= eSql.Message
            MessageBox.Show(sMessage, "Database error", MessageBoxButtons.OK, _
                MessageBoxIcon.Exclamation)
            Return False
        End Try
    End Function
End Function
```

Note

* The BeginTransaction method in the WriteOrder procedure includes an isolation level
  argument of IsolationLevel.RepeatableRead. This argument ensures that all the rows
  affected by the transaction are locked until the transaction ends. For more information on
  isolation levels, see the online help topic on the BeginTransaction method.

Figure 11-19   The code for the OrderDB class (part 1 of 5)

OrderDB.vb   **Page 2**

```
Private Sub InsertInvoice()
    Dim sCommand As String
    sCommand = "INSERT INTO Invoices " _
        & "(CustomerID, InvoiceDate, ProductTotal, " _
        & "SalesTax, ShippingAndHandling, InvoiceTotal) " _
        & "VALUES (@CustomerID, @InvoiceDate, @ProductTotal, " _
        & "@SalesTax, @ShippingAndHandling, @InvoiceTotal)"
    cmdOrder.CommandText = sCommand
    With cmdOrder.Parameters
        .Clear()
        .Add("@CustomerID", Customer.CustomerID)
        .Add("@InvoiceDate", Order.OrderDate)
        .Add("@ProductTotal", Order.ProductTotal)
        .Add("@SalesTax", Order.SalesTax)
        .Add("@ShippingAndHandling", Order.ShippingAndHandling)
        .Add("@InvoiceTotal", Order.InvoiceTotal)
    End With
    cmdOrder.ExecuteNonQuery()
    cmdOrder.CommandText = "SELECT @@IDENTITY"
    Order.InvoiceID = cmdOrder.ExecuteScalar
End Sub

Private Sub ProcessLineItem(ByVal li As dsOrder.LineItemsRow)
    Dim iBackOrderQuantity As Integer = 0
    Dim Product As Product = Me.GetProduct(li.ProductCode)
    If li.Quantity > Product.OnHandQuantity Then
        iBackOrderQuantity = li.Quantity - Product.OnHandQuantity
        li.Quantity = Product.OnHandQuantity
        li.Total = li.Price * li.Quantity
    End If
    If li.Quantity > 0 Then
        Me.InsertLineItem(li)
    End If
    If iBackOrderQuantity > 0 Then
        BackOrder = True
        Me.InsertBackOrder(li, iBackOrderQuantity)
        Dim bo As dsOrder.LineItemsRow
        bo = Order.BackOrders.NewLineItemsRow
        bo.ProductCode = li.ProductCode
        bo.Description = li.Description
        bo.Quantity = iBackOrderQuantity
        Order.BackOrders.AddLineItemsRow(bo)
    End If
    Me.UpdateProduct(li.ProductCode, li.Quantity, iBackOrderQuantity)
End Sub

Private Function GetProduct(ByVal ProductCode As String) As Product
    Dim Product As New Product()
    Product.ProductCode = ProductCode
    Dim sCommand As String
    sCommand = "SELECT OnHandQuantity, QuantityBackOrdered, " _
        & "YTDUnitSales, YTDDollarSales, " _
        & "MTDUnitSales, MTDDollarSales, " _
        & "LifetimeUnitSales, LifetimeDollarSales " _
        & "FROM Products " _
        & "WHERE ProductCode = @ProductCode"
    cmdOrder.CommandText = sCommand
```

Figure 11-19   The code for the OrderDB class (part 2 of 5)

OrderDB.vb

```vb
        With cmdOrder.Parameters
            .Clear()
            .Add("@ProductCode", Product.ProductCode)
        End With
        Dim rdrOrder As SqlDataReader
        rdrOrder = cmdOrder.ExecuteReader
        rdrOrder.Read()
        Product.OnHandQuantity = rdrOrder("OnHandQuantity")
        Product.QuantityBackOrdered = rdrOrder("QuantityBackOrdered")
        Product.YTDUnitSales = rdrOrder("YTDUnitSales")
        Product.YTDDollarSales = rdrOrder("YTDDollarSales")
        Product.MTDUnitSales = rdrOrder("MTDUnitSales")
        Product.MTDDollarSales = rdrOrder("MTDDollarSales")
        Product.LifetimeUnitSales = rdrOrder("LifetimeUnitSales")
        Product.LifetimeDollarSales = rdrOrder("LifetimeDollarSales")
        rdrOrder.Close()
        Return Product
    End Function

    Private Sub InsertLineItem(ByVal li As dsOrder.LineItemsRow)
        Dim sCommand As String
        sCommand = "INSERT INTO InvoiceLineItems " _
            & "(InvoiceID, ProductCode, UnitPrice, Quantity, ItemTotal) " _
            & "VALUES (@InvoiceID, @ProductCode, @UnitPrice, @Quantity, @ItemTotal)"
        cmdOrder.CommandText = sCommand
        With cmdOrder.Parameters
            .Clear()
            .Add("@InvoiceID", Order.InvoiceID)
            .Add("@ProductCode", li.ProductCode)
            .Add("@UnitPrice", li.Price)
            .Add("@Quantity", li.Quantity)
            .Add("@ItemTotal", li.Total)
        End With
        cmdOrder.ExecuteNonQuery()
    End Sub

    Private Sub InsertBackOrder(ByVal li As dsOrder.LineItemsRow, _
            ByVal iBackOrderQuantity As Integer)
        Dim sCommand As String
        sCommand = "INSERT INTO BackOrders " _
            & "(CustomerID, InvoiceID, DateBackOrdered, ProductCode, Quantity, Price) " _
            & "VALUES (@CustomerID, @InvoiceID, @DateBackOrdered, @ProductCode, " _
            & "@Quantity, @Price)"
        cmdOrder.CommandText = sCommand
        With cmdOrder.Parameters
            .Clear()
            .Add("@CustomerID", Customer.CustomerID)
            .Add("@InvoiceID", Order.InvoiceID)
            .Add("@DateBackOrdered", Order.OrderDate)
            .Add("@ProductCode", li.ProductCode)
            .Add("@Quantity", iBackOrderQuantity)
            .Add("@Price", li.Price)
        End With
        cmdOrder.ExecuteNonQuery()
    End Sub
```

Figure 11-19   The code for the OrderDB class (part 3 of 5)

OrderDB.vb   **Page 4**

```
    Private Sub UpdateProduct(ByVal ProductCode As String, ByVal Quantity As Integer, _
        ByVal BackOrderQuantity As Integer)
        Dim sCommand As String
        sCommand = "UPDATE Products   " _
            & "SET OnHandQuantity = OnHandQuantity - @Quantity, " _
            & "QuantityBackOrdered = QuantityBackOrdered + @BackOrderQuantity " _
            & "WHERE ProductCode = @ProductCode"
        cmdOrder.CommandText = sCommand
        With cmdOrder.Parameters
            .Clear()
            .Add("@Quantity", Quantity)
            .Add("@BackOrderQuantity", BackOrderQuantity)
            .Add("@ProductCode", ProductCode)
        End With
        cmdOrder.ExecuteNonQuery()
    End Sub

    Private Sub AdjustInvoiceTotal()
        Dim sCommand As String
        sCommand = "UPDATE Invoices   " _
            & "SET ProductTotal = @ProductTotal, " _
            & "SalesTax = @SalesTax, " _
            & "ShippingAndHandling = @ShippingAndHandling, " _
            & "InvoiceTotal = @InvoiceTotal " _
            & "WHERE InvoiceID = @InvoiceID"
        cmdOrder.CommandText = sCommand
        With cmdOrder.Parameters
            .Clear()
            .Add("@ProductTotal", Order.ProductTotal)
            .Add("@SalesTax", Order.SalesTax)
            .Add("@ShippingAndHandling", Order.ShippingAndHandling)
            .Add("@InvoiceTotal", Order.InvoiceTotal)
            .Add("@InvoiceID", Order.InvoiceID)
        End With
        cmdOrder.ExecuteNonQuery()
    End Sub

    Private Sub InsertPayment()
        Dim sCommand As String
        sCommand = "INSERT INTO Payments " _
            & "(CustomerID, InvoiceID, PaymentDate, Amount, " _
            & "CreditCardType, CreditCardNumber, ExpirationDate) " _
            & "VALUES (@CustomerID, @InvoiceID, @PaymentDate, @Amount, " _
            & "@CreditCardType, @CreditCardNumber, @ExpirationDate)"
        cmdOrder.CommandText = sCommand
        With cmdOrder.Parameters
            .Clear()
            .Add("@CustomerID", Customer.CustomerID)
            .Add("@InvoiceID", Order.InvoiceID)
            .Add("@PaymentDate", Order.OrderDate)
            .Add("@Amount", Order.InvoiceTotal)
            .Add("@CreditCardType", Order.CreditCardType)
            .Add("@CreditCardNumber", Order.CardNumber)
            .Add("@ExpirationDate", Order.CardExpirationDate)
        End With
        cmdOrder.ExecuteNonQuery()
    End Sub
```

Figure 11-19   The code for the OrderDB class (part 4 of 5)

```vb
    Private Sub InsertOpenItem()
        Dim sCommand As String
        sCommand = "INSERT INTO OpenItems " _
            & "(InvoiceID, CustomerID, InvoiceDate, InvoiceTotal) " _
            & "VALUES (@InvoiceID, @CustomerID, @InvoiceDate, @InvoiceTotal) "
        cmdOrder.CommandText = sCommand
        With cmdOrder.Parameters
            .Clear()
            .Add("@InvoiceID", Order.InvoiceID)
            .Add("@CustomerID", Customer.CustomerID)
            .Add("@InvoiceDate", Order.OrderDate)
            .Add("@InvoiceTotal", Order.InvoiceTotal)
        End With
        cmdOrder.ExecuteNonQuery()
    End Sub

    Private Sub UpdateCustomer()
        Dim sCommand As String
        sCommand = "UPDATE Customers  " _
            & "SET LastOrderDate = @LastOrderDate, " _
            & "LifeTimeSales = LifeTimeSales + @InvoiceTotal " _
            & "WHERE CustomerID = @CustomerID"
        cmdOrder.CommandText = sCommand
        With cmdOrder.Parameters
            .Clear()
            .Add("@LastOrderDate", Order.OrderDate)
            .Add("@InvoiceTotal", Order.InvoiceTotal)
            .Add("@CustomerID", Customer.CustomerID)
        End With
        cmdOrder.ExecuteNonQuery()
    End Sub

End Class
```

Figure 11-19   The code for the OrderDB class (part 5 of 5)

Section 4

Database programming with ASP.NET

In the first three sections of this book, you've learned how to use ADO.NET from Windows applications. But you can also use ADO.NET from web applications. The three chapters in this section present the basic skills you need to do that.

In chapter 12, you'll learn some of the concepts related to developing web applications, and you'll learn how to create a simple web page that uses bound controls. In chapter 13, you'll learn three programming techniques that you'll use frequently as you develop web applications that use ADO.NET. And in chapter 14, you'll learn how to use two Web Server controls that are specifically designed for working with databases.

Keep in mind as you read these chapters that they're not meant to teach you everything you need to know to develop web applications or for using ADO.NET within web applications. They're just meant to introduce you to some of the complexities of developing web applications that use ADO.NET. Complete coverage of ASP.NET will be available in our upcoming book, *Murach's VB.NET Web Programming with ASP.NET*.

12

An introduction to database programming with ASP.NET

In this chapter, you'll learn the basic techniques for accessing data from an ASP.NET web application. To do that, you can use the same database classes that you use to access data from a Windows application. However, the nature of web programming often dictates that you use these classes differently than you would in a Windows application. You'll see why that is as you read this chapter and the two that follow.

An introduction to web applications

Before you can develop web applications, you need to understand how they work. In particular, you need to understand how the communication between the client and the server works and how the server processes web applications. In addition, you need to understand the files that make up an ASP.NET application. That's what you'll learn in the topics that follow.

How a web browser communicates with a web server

Figure 12-1 illustrates the basic communication between a *web browser* running on a client computer and a *web server*. To start, the user enters the *URL* (*Universal Resource Locator*) for a *web page* into the browser or clicks on a link in another web page that refers to the page. Then, the web browser uses *HTTP* (*HyperText Transfer Protocol*) to send an *HTTP request* to the web server. This request includes information such as the name and address of the web page that's being requested and the address of the browser that's making the request.

When the web server receives the request from the browser, it's processed by special web server software. For an ASP.NET web application, that software must be Microsoft's *Internet Information Services* (or *IIS*). Once IIS processes the request, it sends an *HTTP response* back to the browser. This response includes the *HTML* (*HyperText Markup Language*) that describes the page the user requested. The browser then formats and displays the HTML content. This entire process is called a *round trip*.

Although web applications are commonly run over the Internet, they can also be run from a local server. In that case, the clients and the server are connected via an *intranet*. Because an intranet uses the same protocols as the Internet, a web application runs the same whether it's accessed over the Internet or over an intranet.

You can also run the web browser and the web server software on the same computer so that one computer functions as both the client and the server. A single-computer setup like this is commonly used for application development. In fact, that's how I developed the web applications in this book.

Before I go on, you should realize that there are two different types of web pages: static web pages and dynamic web pages. A *static web page* consists of an HTML document that contains static information. In other words, the information doesn't change. In contrast, a *dynamic web page* contains information that can change each time it's viewed. To create a dynamic web page, you use ASP.NET.

A browser requesting a web page from a web server

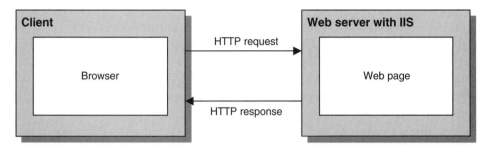

Description

- The user interface for a web application is implemented as a series of *web pages* that are displayed on a client computer using a *web browser*, such as Internet Explorer or Netscape Navigator.

- The application runs on the server computer under the control of *web server* software. For ASP.NET web applications, that software is Microsoft's *Internet Information Services*, or *IIS*. The web server must also have Microsoft's .NET Framework installed.

- A web browser requests a page from a web server by sending the server an *HTTP request*. *HTTP*, or *HyperText Transfer Protocol*, is the communications protocol used to exchange information between web browsers and web servers.

- A user can initiate an HTTP request by entering a web address, or *URL* (*Universal Resource Locator*), into the browser's address area. Alternatively, the user can click on a hyperlink that refers to the web page.

- A web server replies to an HTTP request by sending an *HTTP response* back to the browser. The HTTP response contains the HTML that defines the web page to be displayed. *HTML*, or *HyperText Markup Language*, is a standardized set of markup tags used to format web pages.

- The process that begins with the user requesting a web page and ends with the server sending a response back to the client is called a *round trip*.

- An HTTP request can be for a *static web page*, which is an HTML document that is the same each time it's viewed. The request can also be for a *dynamic web page* that's created by an ASP.NET web application.

- The term *web server* can refer to both (1) the computer that stores the software, HTML documents, and web applications that can be requested by the user and (2) the server software like IIS that manages HTTP requests and responses.

Figure 12-1   How a web browser communicates with a web server

How a web server processes web applications

Figure 12-2 presents an expanded view of how a web server processes a web application. As you can see, HTTP requests from a browser are processed by IIS. Then, if IIS determines that the request is for a dynamic web page rather than a static web page, it passes the request on to ASP.NET for processing. ASP.NET, in turn, executes the application that creates the requested page and then passes the page back to IIS so that IIS can send a response to the browser.

To determine if the request is for a static page or a dynamic page, IIS looks up the extension of the requested page in a list of *application mappings*. These mappings indicate what program a file extension is associated with. For example, a static web page typically has an extension of *htm* or *html*. In contrast, a dynamic page created by an ASP.NET application has an extension of *aspx*.

When the application is executed, it generates the requested page as an HTML document. The exact content of the document depends on the information that was entered by the user. For example, suppose an application lets the user select a vendor and then displays information for that vendor. To do that, the application would use ADO.NET to query the database to obtain the information for the requested vendor. Then, the application would generate a page that contains that information. You'll see an application like this later in this chapter.

A browser requesting a web page from a web application

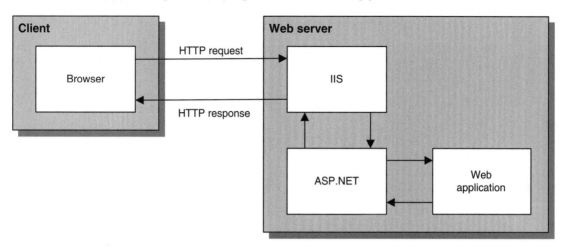

Description

- When IIS receives a request for a web page that's part of a web application, it passes it on to ASP.NET for processing. *ASP.NET* is Microsoft's environment for developing and executing web applications.

- When ASP.NET receives a request for a web application, it locates and executes the application to generate the HTML that represents the page. The page is then sent back to IIS, which sends it back to the browser to be displayed.

- To determine how a request should be processed, IIS looks up the extension of the requested file in a list of *application mappings*. If the extension is *aspx*, the request is passed on to ASP.NET. If the extension isn't found, the requested file is simply returned to the browser without any additional processing.

- A web application can use ADO.NET to access the data in a database just as a Windows application can. Although a web application uses the same ADO.NET classes as a Windows application, the nature of web programming affects the way you use the ADO.NET classes.

Figure 12-2   How a web server processes web applications

The source files that make up an ASP.NET application

A web application consists of one or more *web forms*. Each web form defines a web page that can be displayed in a web browser. To design a web form, you add controls to it just as you do to design a Windows form. You'll learn more about that in the topics that follow.

As you design a web form, Visual Basic generates the appropriate HTML for the form. This HTML, which includes HTML tags and special ASP.NET tags that define the elements that make up the page, is stored in a file with the aspx extension. As you know, it's this extension that tells IIS that the file should be processed by ASP.NET.

Figure 12-3 shows how the aspx files are combined with the other source files in an application to create an ASP.NET application. To start, you should know that each web form has an associated aspx.vb file. This file contains the Visual Basic code that provides the functionality for the form. For example, this file can contain event handlers that respond to user events on the form. This file is sometimes called the *code-behind file* because it provides the Visual Basic code for the page defined by the aspx file.

Although you can place the Visual Basic code in a separate file as indicated in this figure, you can also include it in the aspx file along with the HTML. However, storing the Visual Basic code and the HTML in separate files can simplify application development because it lets you separate the presentation elements for a page from its logic elements. In fact, it's not uncommon to have HTML designers work on the aspx files while Visual Basic programmers work on the corresponding Visual Basic files.

Like Windows applications, web applications can also include additional class files. For example, you could include a database class that handles all of the database processing for an application or a business class that represents a business object. You'll see a program that uses classes like these in the next chapter.

When you build a web application, all of the files that contain Visual Basic code are compiled into a single assembly. Unlike a Windows application that compiles into an exe assembly, though, a web application compiles into a dll assembly. That assembly is stored on the web server, along with the aspx files that define the web pages. Then, when a user requests a page, ASP.NET compiles the aspx file for that page and the assembly for the application into a single dll assembly. It then executes that assembly to generate the page.

How an ASP.NET application is compiled

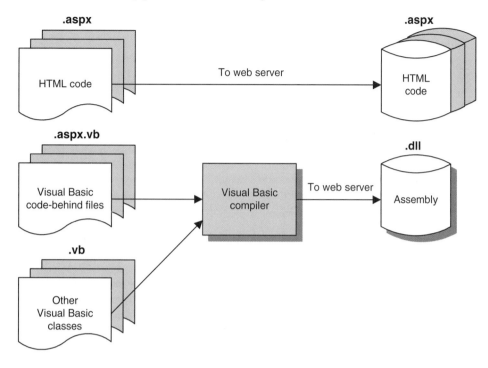

Description

- The .aspx files contain HTML tags along with special ASP.NET tags. Together, these tags determine the appearance of the ASP.NET pages.

- The .aspx.vb files, often called *code-behind files*, provide the code that's associated with the pages. This code includes event handlers that are called when the user interacts with the controls on a page.

- An ASP.NET application may also include other Visual Basic classes, such as business or database classes.

- You use the Visual Basic compiler to build the files that contain Visual Basic code into an assembly, which is stored in a dll file on the web server.

- The .aspx files are also stored on the server. Then, when ASP.NET receives a request for a page, the page and the dll file that was created from the Visual Basic code are compiled into a single assembly, which is then executed.

Figure 12-3   The source files that make up an ASP.NET application

An introduction to ASP.NET programming

In general, you create a web application using techniques that are similar to the techniques you use to create a Windows application. In the topics that follow, I'll introduce you to those techniques.

How to create a web application

Figure 12-4 shows the New Project dialog box for creating a web application. It looks much the same as the dialog box for a Windows application, except that the project location must be on the IIS server. If you're developing a web application that will reside on your own computer, that location is http://localhost as shown in this figure. If the application will reside on another web server, you'll need to find out the address of that server.

To complete the entry for the server location, you enter the name of the folder where you want the project stored. In this example, the folder is named VendorDisplay. Then, when you finish the application, all of the files for the project except the solution file will be stored in that folder under the appropriate folder for the web server. If, for example, you're running IIS on your own PC, the project files will be stored in

```
C:\Inetpub\wwwroot\VendorDisplay
```

because Inetpub\wwwroot is the folder structure that's created when you install IIS.

What happens to the solution file? It's stored in the default folder for Visual Studio projects. That's why you should make sure that this default folder is set the way you want it before you create a new web application. Note that this folder isn't identified by the dialog box in this figure.

When you create a web application, a web form named WebForm1 is automatically added to it. Then, you can use the Visual Basic IDE to design the form, as you'll see in the next figure.

The New Project dialog box for a web application

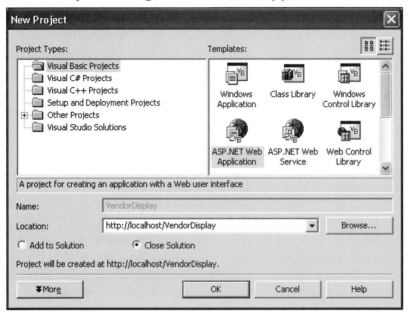

Description

- To create a web application, select the ASP.NET Web Application template from the New Project dialog box. Then, select the IIS server where the project will reside and enter the name of the directory where you want the project stored.

- Visual Basic creates a directory with the name you specify in the \Inetpub\wwwroot directory of the IIS server and stores all the project files in that directory.

- Visual Basic also creates a directory with the name you specify in the default directory for Visual Studio and stores the solution file there. If you want to store the solution in a different directory, change the default directory before you create the project or copy the solution to another directory after you create the project.

- By default, an ASP.NET web application consists of a single web form named WebForm1. This form appears in the Solution Explorer with the aspx extension.

Figure 12-4   How to create a web application

How to use the Web Form Designer

Figure 12-5 shows the *Web Form Designer* that you use to design a web form. When you first start a new project, it consists of a single, blank web form. Then, you can use the Toolbox to add controls to a web form just as you do for a Windows form. You can use the Properties window to set the properties for the form or its controls. And you can use the Solution Explorer to manage the files in the project.

The ASP.NET Server controls you can use on a web form are available from the Web Forms and HTML tabs of the Toolbox. The controls you're most likely to use as you develop a web application are the *Web Server controls* in the Web Forms tab. These controls are new to .NET and provide functionality that wasn't available with traditional HTML elements. In addition, you can work with them using properties, methods, and events just like other .NET objects.

The controls in the HTML tab provide access to the traditional HTML elements. These controls, called *HTML Server controls*, can be processed on either the client or the server. In contrast, the Web Server controls can only be processed on the server. So you may want to use the HTML Server controls whenever it's appropriate to perform client-side processing. Remember, though, that these controls don't provide the same functionality as the Web Server controls. Because of that, I'll focus on the Web Server controls in this chapter, since they're the ones you're most likely to use.

In addition to the Web Server controls and HTML Server controls, you can use the *validation controls* in the Web Forms tab of the Toolbox to validate the data on the form. You can use these controls to validate data in either Web Server or HTML Server controls. Because the form shown in this figure will be used only to display information, it doesn't require any validation controls. In the next chapter, though, you'll see a form that does.

You can also use the items in the Data tab of the Toolbox to add ADO.NET components to a form. The form in this figure, for example, uses a connection, two data adapters, and two datasets. You'll see how these components are used later in this chapter.

When you use the Web Form Designer to design a form, it generates the required HTML for you. Although this is fine for simple applications, you'll often find that you need to modify the generated HTML. To do that, you can click on the HTML tab at the bottom of the designer window to display the HTML and then modify it any way you'd like. You can also modify the HTML in an aspx file using any text editor.

A web form displayed in the Web Form Designer window

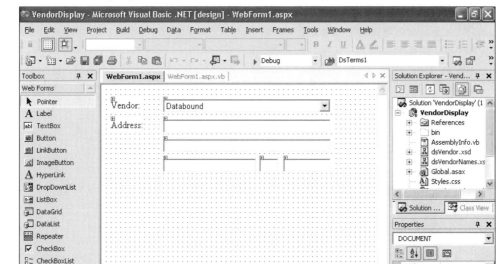

Description

- To design web forms, you use the *Web Form Designer*. This designer lets you add controls and components from the Toolbox. Then, you can set the properties for the page and controls in the Properties window.

- The *Web Server controls* in the Web Forms tab of the Toolbox let you create web forms with controls that work much like their Windows counterparts. The Web Server controls have properties, methods, and events just like other .NET objects.

- The *HTML Server controls* in the HTML tab of the Toolbox map directly to traditional HTML elements.

- You can also use the *validation controls* that are available from the Web Forms tab of the Toolbox to perform common validation checks on Web Server or HTML Server controls, and you can use the components in the Data tab to create ADO.NET components.

- The Web Form Designer generates the HTML that will be used to display the web form. You can view and edit this HTML by clicking the HTML tab at the bottom of the Web Form Designer window.

- The Web Form Designer works in one of two layout modes. *Grid layout mode* lets you position elements on the page by dragging them. *Flow layout mode* uses traditional HTML formatting where the browser determines the exact position of each element.

Figure 12-5   How to use the Web Form Designer

Common properties for web pages and controls

Figure 12-6 presents the properties for web pages and Web Server controls that you're most likely to use as you develop web forms. For a web page, for example, you can use the IsPostBack property to determine when a page is being loaded for the first time and when it's being *posted* back to the server. You can use this property to perform initialization code when the page is first loaded.

The PageLayout property of a web page determines how the form is displayed in the Web Form Designer window. By default, it's displayed in *grid layout mode*. This is the layout mode you saw in the previous figure, and it's the mode you'll typically use to design web forms. With this layout, you can position controls exactly where you want them on the form using *absolute positioning*.

You can also display a form in *flow layout mode*. In this mode, controls are positioned relative to one another. Because of that, the position of the controls can change when the page is displayed depending on the size of the browser window and the resolution of the display. In most cases, you'll want to use grid layout so the position of the controls doesn't change. One exception is if you want users to be able to access the page from older browsers that don't support absolute positioning. Another exception is if you need to position two or more validation controls on the same line. You'll see an example of that in the next chapter.

Most of the properties shown here for Web Server controls provide functionality that's similar to that of Windows controls. For example, you can use the ID property to name a control, and you can use the Text property to determine what's displayed in the control. However, the AutoPostBack, EnableViewState, and CausesValidation properties are unique to Web Server controls.

The AutoPostBack property lets you determine if the page is posted back to the server when the user changes the value of the control. Note that this property is only available with certain controls, such as the check box, drop-down list, and radio button controls. Also note that this property isn't available with the button controls. That's because these controls are almost always used to post a page back to the server, so that's how they're designed by default.

Each time an HTTP request is sent to the server, the code for the web page is restarted from the beginning. That's because the program ends as soon as the HTML for a page is generated. Otherwise, the program would be idle while it waited for the user to perform another action, which would be a waste of the server's resources. The drawback to this is that the values in the web page aren't maintained between executions. In other words, web applications are *stateless*.

Fortunately, Web Server controls can retain their own data, called a *view state*. To do that, the EnableViewState property of the control must be set to True, which is the default. In addition, ASP.NET provides other techniques for maintaining the state of a web application. You'll learn about one of those techniques in chapter 13. For more information about other techniques, see the online help topic, "Introduction to Web Forms State Management."

Common web page properties

Property	Description
IsPostBack	Gets a Boolean value that indicates whether the page is being posted back from the client (True) or is being loaded for the first time (False).
PageLayout	The layout that's displayed in the Web Form Designer window. The possible values are GridLayout and FlowLayout. GridLayout is the default.
Title	The text that's displayed in the title bar of the browser when the web page is displayed.

Common Web Server control properties

Property	Description
AutoPostBack	Determines whether the page is posted back to the server when the value of the control changes. Available with controls such as a check box, drop-down list, radio button, or text box. The default value is False.
CausesValidation	Determines whether page validation occurs when you click on the button, link button, or image button. The default value is True.
EnableViewState	Determines whether the control maintains its view state across HTTP requests. The default value is True.
Enabled	Determines whether the control is functional. The default value is True.
ID	The name that's used to refer to the control.
Text	The text that's displayed in the control.
Visible	Determines whether a control is displayed or hidden.

Description

- The IsPostBack property is often used in the Load procedure of a form to determine whether or not the form is being loaded for the first time during a user's session.

- If the user clicks on a button control whose CausesValidation property is set to True, the data validation that's specified in each of the validation controls on the page is done and the appropriate error messages are displayed.

- By default, Web Server controls retain their *view state* across HTTP requests. That means that all of the property values a control contains are maintained when a page is posted to the server and sent back to the client. If that's not what you want, you can set the control's EnableViewState property to False.

Figure 12-6   Common properties for web pages and controls

The CausesValidation property determines whether the validation controls on the form are activated when the user clicks on any of the button controls (button, link button, or image button). This allows you to check for valid data before the form is posted back to the server. Because this is a technique you'll use regularly, the next topic describes it in more detail.

How to use the validation controls

Figure 12-7 summarizes the validation controls you can use with web forms and presents some of the most important properties for these controls. For example, if you want to be sure that the user enters a value into a control, you can use a required field validator control. If you want to compare the value a user enters into a control with a constant value or a property of another control, you can use a compare validator control. And if you want to make sure that the user enters a value within a given range, you can use a range validator control. You can also use two or more validation controls to validate the data in a single server control.

Each validation control you use is associated with a specific control on the form through its ControlToValidate property. Then, when the user clicks on a button whose CausesValidation property is set to True, all of the controls that have validation controls associated with them are validated. If the data they contain is valid, the page is posted to the server. Otherwise, the appropriate error messages are displayed.

When an error occurs, the Display property of the validation control determines how the message in the ErrorMessage property is displayed. The possible values for the Display property are Static, which lets you allocate space for the error message in the page layout; Dynamic, which causes space to be added for displaying the error message when an error occurs; and None. If you choose None, you can use a validation summary control to display a list of the error messages in a predefined location.

A summary of the validation controls

Name	Description
RequiredFieldValidator	Checks that an entry has been made.
CompareValidator	Compares an entry against a constant value or a property of another control.
RangeValidator	Checks that an entry is within a specified range. If the control is left blank, the range validation is not performed.
RegularExpressionValidator	Checks that an entry matches a pattern, such as a telephone number or an email address, that's defined by a regular expression.
CustomValidator	Checks an entry using validation code that you write yourself.
ValidationSummary	Displays a summary of error messages from the other validation controls.

Common validation control properties

Property	Description
ControlToValidate	The ID of the control to be validated.
Display	Determines how an error message is displayed. Specify Static to allocate space for the message in the page layout, Dynamic to have the space allocated when an error occurs, or None to display the errors in a validation summary control.
ErrorMessage	The message that's displayed when the validation fails.
Text	The text that's displayed for the control in design view. If you leave this property blank, the ID property is displayed.

Additional properties of the CompareValidator control

Property	Description
ControlToCompare	The name of the control whose value you want to use in the comparison.
Operator	An operator that identifies the comparison to be performed.
Type	The data type of the values you want to compare.
ValueToCompare	The value you want to use in the comparison.

Additional properties of the RangeValidator control

Property	Description
MinimumValue	The minimum value that's allowed for the control being validated.
MaximumValue	The maximum value that's allowed for the control being validated.
Type	The data type of the values to be compared.

Description

- You can use validation controls to test user input and produce error messages. The validation is performed when the user clicks on a button control whose CausesValidation property is set to True.
- Each validation control is associated with a specific Web Server or HTML Server control. You can associate one or more validation controls with a single server control.
- The validation controls work by running client-side script. Then, if the validation fails, the page isn't posted back to the server. (If the client doesn't support scripts, the validation is performed on the server.)

Figure 12-7   How to use the validation controls

How to bind Web Server controls

Because of the nature of web programming, data binding for ASP.NET applications is different than for Windows applications. Specifically, ASP.NET data binding is based on *data binding expressions*. The topics that follow explain how to use data binding expressions to bind a property of a Web Server control to a data source.

How to bind a Web Server control to multiple rows of a data source

List controls, such as drop-down lists and list boxes, can be bound to multiple rows of a data source by setting the properties shown in figure 12-8. As you can see, the properties you use to bind these controls are similar to the properties you use to bind a Windows combo box or list box control. Because of that, you shouldn't have any trouble understanding how these properties work.

The DataSource and DataMember properties of a list control identify the dataset and data table that contain the data to be displayed in the list. Note that the value that's assigned to the DataSource property is enclosed in <%# and %> characters, which identifies it as a data binding expression. You'll learn more about how you can code data binding expressions later in this chapter. When you set the DataSource property of a list control using the Properties window, however, the data binding expression is generated for you.

The DataTextField property identifies the column to be displayed in the list, and the DataValueField property identifies the column whose value is returned when the user makes a selection. That makes it possible to display data from one column and retrieve the corresponding data from another. For example, you can display Vendor names in a drop-down list, but return the VendorID value for the selected vendor.

The DataTextFormatString property lets you specify the format for numeric values displayed in the list. You can use many of the standard numeric formatting codes within the format specification. For more information, see the online help topic for this property.

In contrast to a Windows form, a web form doesn't have a binding manager to manage the bound controls on the form. Because of that, the controls aren't automatically bound to the data source when the program is run. Instead, you have to use the DataBind method of a control to bind it to the data source specified in its binding properties. The first statement shown in this figure, for example, binds the control in the first example. The second statement shows how you can bind all of the controls on a page at once. To do that, you execute the Bind method of the page. As you can see, you can use the Me keyword to refer to the page in much the same way that you can use the Me keyword within a form to refer to that form.

You should also realize that you have to rebind a control each time its data source changes. If a row is added to a data table that a drop-down list is bound to, for example, the new row won't appear in the list until it's rebound to the table.

The properties for binding a drop-down list, list box, radio button list, or check box list control to a data source

Property	Description
DataSource	The name of a data source, such as a dataset.
DataMember	A member associated with the data source, such as a data table. If the data source contains only one bindable member, you don't need to set this property.
DataTextField	The column in the data member whose value is displayed in the list.
DataValueField	The column in the data member whose value is stored in the list.
DataTextFormatString	The format of the items displayed in the list.

The HTML for a bound drop-down list control

```
<asp:dropdownlist id=ddlVendors runat="server"
    DataSource="<%# DsPayables1 %>"
    DataMember="VendorNames"
    DataValueField="VendorID"
    DataTextField="VendorName"
    Width="280px"
    AutoPostBack="True" />
```

A statement that binds the control

```
ddlVendors.DataBind()
```

A statement that binds all the controls on a page

```
Me.DataBind()
```

Description

- The data binding properties for drop-down list, list box, radio button list, and check box list Web controls are similar to the data binding properties for the equivalent Windows controls.

- The HTML that's generated for a list control includes attributes that correspond to the data binding properties. The DataSource attribute is coded as a *data binding expression*. For more information, see figure 12-10.

- Because web forms don't have a binding manager like Windows forms, you must bind the controls to the data source as the program executes. You must do that any time the data source changes.

- To bind a control to its data source, you use the DataBind method of the control. To bind all of the controls on a page at once, you use the DataBind method of the page class.

Figure 12-8   How to bind a Web Server control to multiple rows of a data source

How to bind a Web Server control to a single column of a data source

You can also bind some of the Web Server controls, including the text box control, to a single column of a data source. One way to do that is to use the DataBindings dialog box shown in figure 12-9. This dialog box generates a data binding expression based on the selections you make.

When you first display this dialog box, the Text property is selected in the Bindable Properties list. In most cases, that's what you'll want. If you want to bind to a different property, though, just select that property from the list.

Next, you select the column that the control will be bound to from the list of columns in the available data tables. Notice that the columns are listed under the default view for the table. As you know, the default view provides a way of filtering the rows in the table so that only the row or rows you specify are available. That can be important when you're working with bound controls on a web form because they can only be bound to a table or view that contains a single row.

Like the drop-down list you learned about in the last topic, you have to use the DataBind method of a text box control to bind it to its data source as the program executes, and you have to rebind the control each time its data source changes. In the Vendor Display form that's presented later in this chapter, for example, you'll see how the text boxes that display the vendor data are rebound each time the user selects a different vendor.

The DataBindings dialog box for a text box

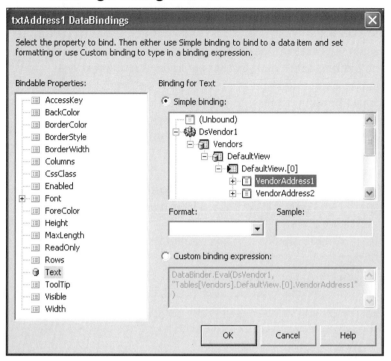

Description

- To bind a text box to a data source, you use the DataBindings dialog box to create a data binding expression. To display the DataBindings dialog box, select the control you want to bind, select the DataBindings property in the Properties window, then click on the ellipsis that appears for the property.

- By default, the Text property is selected in the list of bindable properties. If that's not what you want, you can select any of the other properties in the list.

- To bind the control to a column in a dataset, expand the dataset in the Simple binding list until you can see a list of the columns and then select the column. Notice that the columns are listed under the default view for the dataset.

- You can also format the value that's displayed in the text box by selecting an option from the Format combo box.

- After you create a data binding expression for a property, the property is displayed in the Properties window with a database symbol like the one shown next to the Text property above.

- Because web forms don't have a binding manager, you can't bind a control to the current row. Instead, you have to filter the table that's involved in the binding so it contains a single row, or you have to fill the table with a single row. Then, you can use the DataBind method of the control to bind it to a column in that row.

- You can use the same technique to bind other Web Server controls to a data source.

Figure 12-9   How to bind a Web Server control to a single column of a data source

How to create custom data binding expressions

When you use the DataBindings dialog box as shown in the previous figure, a data binding expression is generated for you. In fact, if you look back at that figure, you can see the binding expression that was generated in the text box below the Custom binding expression option. In some cases, though, you won't be able to create the exact binding expression you need using this technique. Then, you can create a custom binding expression as described in figure 12-10.

One way to create a custom data binding expression is to use the Custom binding expression option in the DataBindings dialog box. When you select this option, the associated text box is enabled so you can enter the binding expression you want to use. Another way to create a custom binding expression is to enter it directly into the HTML code for the page. The three examples in this figure illustrate how this works.

The code in the first example binds a text box named txtCity to the VendorCity column of the Vendors table. To do that, it uses the Eval method of the DataBinder class. The DataBinder class is most useful for binding controls to data columns as shown in this example. Because code like this is added to the HTML automatically when you generate a data binding expression from the DataBindings dialog box, you may never need to create an expression like this yourself.

You should also notice in this example and in the other examples in this figure that the data binding expression is enclosed in <%# and %> characters. Like the DataBinder.Eval method, these characters are added automatically when you generate a data binding expression from the DataBindings dialog box. They're also added automatically when you enter a custom data binding expression in this dialog box. If you enter a binding expression directly into the HTML code, however, you'll need to be sure to enclose it within these characters.

The second and third examples illustrate how to bind a control to a data source other than a data column. In the second example, the Text property of a text box control is bound to the Value property of the item selected from a drop-down list. That way, the text box will show the value returned from the drop-down list for the selected item.

In the third example, the Text property of the text box is bound to a property of a business class named Vendor. This class contains the data for a single vendor. If you read chapter 10 and understand how to work with database classes, you shouldn't have any trouble understanding how this binding expression works.

The HTML for a text box control that's bound to a column in a dataset

```
<asp:TextBox id="txtCity"
    Text='<%# DataBinder.Eval(DsPayables1, "Vendors.Rows(0).VendorCity") %>' >
</asp:TextBox>
```

The HTML for a text box control that's bound to the value of another control

```
<asp:TextBox id="txtVendorID"
    Text='<%# ddlVendors.SelectedItem.Value %>'>
</asp:TextBox>
```

The HTML for a text box control that's bound to a property of a class named Vendor

```
<asp:TextBox id="txtVendorID"
    Text='<%# Vendor.Address1 %>'>
</asp:TextBox>
```

Description

- To create your own custom binding expression for a control, you can select the Custom binding expression option from the DataBindings dialog box and then enter the expression in the text box.

- You can also enter the code that's required to bind a property of a control to a data source directly into the HTML attribute for that property. When you use this technique, you must enclose the expression in <%# and %> characters. These characters are added for you when you use the DataBindings dialog box.

- A data binding expression that binds a property of a control to a data column typically includes a call to the Eval method of the DataBinder class. This method simplifies the code that's required for data binding.

- You can also bind a control to a data source other than a data column. For example, you can bind a control to a property of another control or to a property of a class.

- Data binding expressions are evaluated when you execute the DataBind method for the control that contains the expression or when you execute the DataBind method for the entire page.

Figure 12-10   How to create custom data binding expressions

A Vendor Display program

Now that you've learned the basics of ASP.NET web programming, the next two topics present a simple Vendor Display program that retrieves vendor data from a database and displays it on a web page. Since you've already seen several Windows versions of this program, I don't think you'll have any trouble understanding how it works.

The design and property settings for the Vendor Display form

Figure 12-11 presents the design and property settings for the Vendor Display form. At the top of the form is a drop-down list that displays the names of all the vendors in the Vendors table. When the user selects a vendor from this list, the program retrieves the corresponding vendor information from the database and displays it in the text box controls.

To provide the data for the form, this program uses two data adapters. The Select statements for those data adapters are shown in this figure. The first one, named daVendorNames, will be used to retrieve the data that's displayed in the drop-down list. The second data adapter, named daVendor, will be used to retrieve the data for a single vendor. To do that, it includes a parameter that will be set to the VendorID value for the vendor.

The data that's retrieved by the daVendorNames data adapter is stored in a dataset named DsVendorNames1. Then, the drop-down list is bound to this dataset, as you can see from the properties shown in this figure. Notice that the DataTextField property is set to the VendorName column so that the data from this column will be displayed in the list. In contrast, the DataValueField property is set to the VendorID column. That way, when the user selects a vendor from the drop-down list, the program will be able to get the VendorID value of the selected vendor.

The data that's retrieved by the daVendor data adapter is stored in a dataset named DsVendor1. Although it's not shown in this figure, each of the text boxes on the form is bound to a column in this dataset. The binding expressions for these text boxes were created using the DataBindings dialog box.

At this point, you may be wondering why the two tables used by this program are stored in separate datasets. The answer is that both data adapters retrieve data from the Vendors table, which means that, by default, both of the data tables are created with the name "Vendors." Since you can't have two tables with the same name in the same dataset, the simplest solution was to store them in separate datasets. You should realize, however, that if you changed the table mappings for one of the data adapters so that the table was given a different name, you could store both of the tables in a single dataset. To change the table mappings, you use the Table Mappings dialog box that's displayed when you select the data adapter and then click on the ellipsis that appears for the TableMappings property.

The Vendor Display form

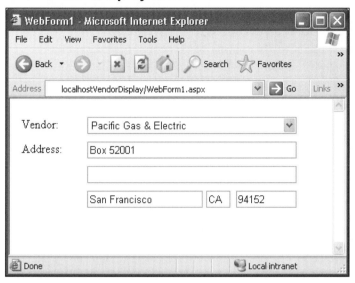

The Select statements for the two data adapters used by the form

Data adapter	Select statement
daVendorNames	`Select VendorID, VendorName From Vendors` `Order By VendorName`

daVendor	`Select VendorID, VendorName, VendorAddress1,`
	`    VendorAddress2, VendorCity, VendorState, VendorZipCode`
	`From Vendors`
	`Where VendorID = @VendorID`

The data binding properties for the drop-down list

Property	Value
DataSource	DsVendorNames1
DataMember	Vendors
DataTextField	VendorName
DataValueField	VendorID

Description

- The Vendor Display form displays information for the vendor that's selected from the drop-down list at the top of the form. To do that, it uses two data adapters.

- The first data adapter retrieves the vendor IDs and names. This data is stored in a dataset named DsVendorNames1, and the drop-down list is bound to this dataset.

- The second data adapter retrieves the data for one vendor based on the value in the @VendorID parameter. This data is stored in a dataset named DsVendor1, and each of the text boxes is bound to a column in this one-row dataset.

Figure 12-11   The design and property settings for the Vendor Display form

The code for the Vendor Display program

Figure 12-12 presents the code for the Vendor Display program. To start, you should notice the declarations near the beginning of this code. Although a web form has a Web Form Designer Generated Code section that's similar to the Generated Code section for a Windows form, the declarations for web controls and other components aren't hidden in this section as they are for Windows forms. For the most part, though, you can ignore these declarations.

The declarations are followed by three procedures. The first one handles the Load event of the page. It fills the DsVendorNames1 dataset, binds the drop-down list control to this dataset, and then calls the ShowVendor procedure to display the information for the first vendor. Note, however, that this is only done if the IsPostBack property of the page is False. In other words, it's only done the first time the page is loaded. This works because this dataset isn't needed after the page is loaded for the first time. That's because the data it contains is stored in the drop-down list, which maintains its view state from one execution to the next.

Remember that the program ends each time a page is generated, and it's restarted each time a page is posted back to the server. As a result, the Load procedure is executed for each round trip. For efficiency, you don't want to reload the drop-down list each time the Page Load procedure is executed. That's why the If logic is used to check the IsPostBack property.

The ShowVendor procedure that's called from the Load procedure starts by getting the data for the selected vendor. To do that, the first statement sets the parameter of the query to the value of the item selected from the drop-down list. Since the DataValueField property of the drop-down list is set to the VendorID column, this means that the vendor ID is used as the parameter. Then, the second statement fills the DsVendor1 dataset with the row for this vendor. After that, the text boxes in the form are bound to the values in this row. When this procedure ends, the program ends, and the page is sent back to the browser so the user can view the data for the vendor and then select another vendor.

The SelectedIndexChanged procedure is executed after the Page Load procedure each time the user selects a vendor from the drop-down list, provided that the page is posted back to the server. For that to happen, the AutoPostBack property of the drop-down list must be set to True. This procedure simply calls the ShowVendor procedure to display the selected vendor.

An ASP.NET Vendor Display program

```
Imports System.Data.SqlClient
Public Class WebForm1
    Inherits System.Web.UI.Page
    Protected WithEvents ddlVendors As System.Web.UI.WebControls.DropDownList
    Protected WithEvents Label1 As System.Web.UI.WebControls.Label
    Protected WithEvents Label2 As System.Web.UI.WebControls.Label
    Protected WithEvents txtAddress1 As System.Web.UI.WebControls.TextBox
    Protected WithEvents txtAddress2 As System.Web.UI.WebControls.TextBox
    Protected WithEvents txtCity As System.Web.UI.WebControls.TextBox
    Protected WithEvents txtState As System.Web.UI.WebControls.TextBox
    Protected WithEvents txtZipCode As System.Web.UI.WebControls.TextBox
    Protected WithEvents daVendorNames As _
        System.Data.SqlClient.SqlDataAdapter
    Protected WithEvents daVendor As System.Data.SqlClient.SqlDataAdapter
    Protected WithEvents DsVendor1 As VendorDisplay.dsVendor
    Protected WithEvents DsVendorNames1 As VendorDisplay.dsVendorNames
    Protected WithEvents SqlSelectCommand1 As _
        System.Data.SqlClient.SqlCommand
    Protected WithEvents SqlSelectCommand2 As _
        System.Data.SqlClient.SqlCommand
    Protected WithEvents SqlConnection1 As _
        System.Data.SqlClient.SqlConnection

    Private Sub Page_Load(ByVal sender As System.Object, _
            ByVal e As System.EventArgs) Handles MyBase.Load
        'Put user code to initialize the page here
        If Not IsPostBack Then
            daVendorNames.Fill(DsVendorNames1)
            ddlVendors.DataBind()
            If DsVendorNames1.Vendors.Rows.Count > 0 Then
                Me.ShowVendor(ddlVendors.SelectedItem.Value)
            End If
        End If
    End Sub

    Private Sub ShowVendor(ByVal VendorID As Integer)
        daVendor.SelectCommand.Parameters("@VendorID").Value = VendorID
        daVendor.Fill(DsVendor1)
        txtAddress1.DataBind()
        txtAddress2.DataBind()
        txtCity.DataBind()
        txtState.DataBind()
        txtZipCode.DataBind()
    End Sub

    Private Sub ddlVendors_SelectedIndexChanged _
            (ByVal sender As System.Object, _
            ByVal e As System.EventArgs) _
            Handles ddlVendors.SelectedIndexChanged
        Me.ShowVendor(ddlVendors.SelectedItem.Value)
    End Sub

End Class
```

Figure 12-12   The code for the Vendor Display program

Perspective

Now that you've read this chapter, you should have a basic understanding of how web applications work, and you should have a general feel for what's involved in developing simple database applications for the web. As you might guess, though, there's a lot more to developing web applications than what's presented here. So in the next chapter, you'll learn about some additional complexities that ASP.NET brings to database programming.

Terms

web page
web browser
web server
IIS (Internet Information Services)
HTTP request
HTTP (HyperText Transfer Protocol)
URL (Universal Resource Locator)
HTTP response
HTML (HyperText Markup Language)
round trip
intranet
static web page
dynamic web page
ASP.NET
application mappings
web form
code-behind file
Web Form Designer
Web Server control
HTML Server control
validation control
grid layout mode
absolute positioning
flow layout mode
stateless application
view state
data binding expression

13

Programming techniques for ASP.NET database applications

In this chapter, you'll learn three ASP.NET programming techniques that are especially important for database programming. First, you'll learn how to use connection pooling, which lets two or more users share connections to a database. Second, you'll learn how to use ASP.NET's caching feature, which lets you save objects in server memory so they can be accessed across sessions. And third, you'll learn how to maintain the state of each user session for an application. Although caching and state management aren't specific to database applications, as you read this chapter, you'll see how they can be critical to developing efficient database applications.

How to use connection pooling and caching

Connection pooling and caching provide more efficient ways for ASP.NET web applications to access database data. Connection pooling makes the process of connecting to ADO.NET data sources more efficient. And caching improves database efficiency by making it unnecessary to connect to a database so often.

How connection pooling works

Figure 13-1 illustrates how *connection pooling* works. The basic idea behind connection pooling is that a pool of database connections is available to two or more users of a database. When a user attempts to connect to the database, ADO.NET checks to see if an existing connection can be retrieved from a *connection pool*. If so, that connection is used and the user doesn't have to wait for a new connection to be created. When the user is finished with the connection, the connection is returned to the pool so that other users can use it.

ADO.NET creates a separate connection pool for each unique database connection string. In this figure, for example, you can see that separate connection pools are used for two databases named Payables and Orders. Keep in mind, though, that two or more connection pools can exist for the same database if different connection strings are used to connect to it. For example, if a large number of users use an application, the name of the application can be included in the connection string. Then, a separate connection pool is created for that application.

Each connection pool contains a limited number of connections. Because of that, if a large number of users attempt to access the database using the same connection string, it's likely that some users will have to wait for a connection to become available. Part of the trick to tuning the performance of ASP.NET database applications, then, is setting the size of the connection pool. If the connection pool is too large, valuable server memory will be wasted on unused connections. However, if the connection pool is too small, users will frequently be forced to wait for database connections to become available.

Although connection pooling is provided by the ADO.NET data providers, you can control some of the aspects of connection pooling for a SQL Server database. You'll see how to do that in the next figure. Because the OLE DB data provider manages connection pooling automatically, you don't have any control over how it works.

Two connection pools that access different databases

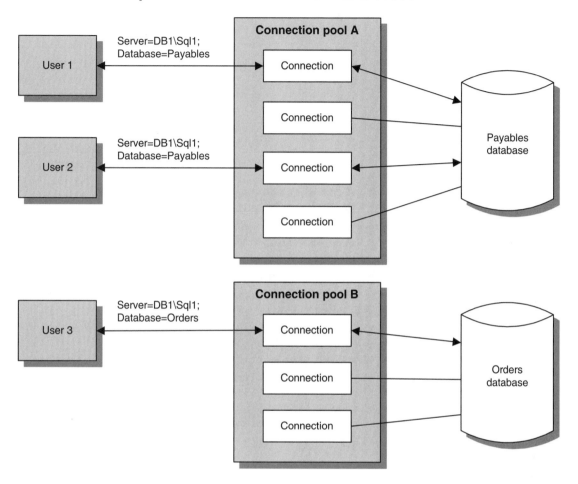

Description

- A *connection pool* consists of zero or more open connections to a database. When a program requests a connection to that database, an open connection is assigned to it if one is available.

- If a program requests a connection and one isn't available in the pool, a new connection is created unless the maximum number of the connections for the pool are already in use. In that case, the program must wait for a connection to become available.

- When a program closes a connection, the connection is returned to the connection pool so that it can be used by another program.

- The connection string determines which connection pool is used. Each application that uses the same connection string uses connections in the same connection pool.

- If an application opens a connection and a connection pool isn't already available for the specified connection string, a new pool is created.

- *Connection pooling* improves the performance of database operations because the programs that use the database typically don't have to wait for a connection to be established.

Figure 13-1   How connection pooling works

Connection string settings that affect connection pooling

To influence the behavior of the connection pools used by the SQL Server data provider, you can use the connection string settings shown in figure 13-2. To change the minimum or maximum number of connections in a pool, for example, you use the Min Pool Size and Max Pool Size settings. Because the minimum number of connections in a pool by default is zero, you'll almost always want to change this value. Similarly, you'll want to change the default maximum number of connections in a pool unless a large number of users will use the same pool.

The first example in this figure shows a connection string that includes these two settings. Here, the Min Pool Size setting specifies that the pool should contain at least 10 connections, and the Max Pool Size setting indicates that the pool can contain a maximum of 20 connections. As a result, this pool will initially be created with 10 connections, and it will expand to as many as 20 connections if necessary. When 20 connections are in use, any additional users will have to wait until an existing connection becomes available.

The second example shows how to create a connection string that doesn't participate in connection pooling. To do that, you set the Pooling setting to False. Although this is uncommon, you might want to opt out of connection pooling if an application is only run occasionally or if it has unique connection requirements.

SQL Server connection string settings for managing connection pools

Setting	Description
Pooling	Indicates whether the connection should be obtained from the appropriate connection pool. The default is True.
Min Pool Size	The minimum number of connections to maintain in the pool. The default is 0.
Max Pool Size	The maximum number of connections to maintain in the pool. The default is 100.
Connection Lifetime	The number of seconds a connection should be allowed to exist before it's destroyed and recreated. The default setting is 0, which causes the connection to last indefinitely.

A connection string that specifies the size of the pool

```
server=DB1\Sql1;database=Payables;integrated security=SSPI;
Min Pool Size=10;Max Pool Size=20
```

A connection string that doesn't participate in pooling

```
server=DB1\Sql1;database=Payables;integrated security=SSPI;Pooling=False
```

Description

- The SQL Server data provider for ADO.NET provides for connection pooling automatically. However, you can control how connection pooling works by specifying values within a connection string.

- The Connection Timeout value you specify in a connection string determines how long an application should wait for a connection. The default is 15 seconds. If a connection can't be obtained within the specified number of seconds, an error is generated.

Note

- The OLE DB data provider manages connection pooling automatically, so you don't need to manage it yourself.

Figure 13-2   Connection string settings that affect connection pooling

How to use a configuration file to store connection information

To be sure that each user of an application uses the same connection string and, therefore, draws connections from the same pool, you should store the connection string in a central location rather than hard coding it into each program. Then, each page that needs the connection string can access it from that location. In addition, if you later need to change the connection string, you can change it in just one place and be assured that the pages will continue to use identical connection strings.

Figure 13-3 shows how you can store a connection string in a configuration file. In the example in this figure, the connection string is stored in the web.config file that's generated by Visual Studio when you create an ASP.NET web project. Although this file is an XML file, you shouldn't have trouble editing it to add a connection string entry even if you aren't familiar with the details of XML syntax.

To edit the web.config file, just double-click on it in the Solution Explorer to display it in the Code Editor window. Then, add an <appSettings> section as shown in this figure. This section should consist of an <add> element that includes a key attribute with the name you want to use for the setting and a value attribute that specifies the value of the setting. In this example, the key is given the name ConnectionString and the value is the actual content of the connection string.

After you add the connection string to the web.config file, you can access it from your program by using the AppSettings property of the ConfigurationSettings class. On this property, you name the setting you want to access. The code shown in this figure, for example, retrieves the setting named ConnectionString and assigns it to a string variable. Then, you can use this variable to create a connection.

Because each application has its own web.config file, any connection string you add to it can only be accessed by that application. If you want two or more applications to use the same connection string, you can define it in the global configuration file. This configuration file, named machine.config, is stored in a central location where it's available to any application that runs on the server. You use the same technique to access this file that you use to access the web.config file. Then, if the setting you specify isn't found in the web.config file, it's retrieved from the machine.config file.

A web.config file with a connection string entry

```
<?xml version="1.0" encoding="utf-8" ?>
<configuration>

    <appSettings>
        <add key="ConnectionString"
            value="server=DB1\Sql1;database=Payables;integrated security=SSPI" />
    </appSettings>

    <system.web>
    .
    .
    .
    </system.web>

</configuration>
```

Code that retrieves the connection string from the web.config file

```
Dim sPayablesConnection As String
sPayablesConnection = ConfigurationSettings.AppSettings("ConnectionString")
```

Description

- When you create an ASP.NET web application, Visual Studio generates a web.config file that stores application settings in an XML format. This file appears in the Solution Explorer, and you can edit it by double-clicking on it.

- To store a connection string in the web.config file, you must add an <appSettings> section. This section should appear after the <configuration> tag and before the <system.web> tag.

- To create a configuration element, code an <add> tag within the <appSettings> section. Within this tag, define two attributes: a key attribute that specifies the name you want to use for the element and a value attribute that specifies the contents of the connection string.

- You can use the AppSettings property of the ConfigurationSettings class within the application to access the elements in the <appSettings> section of the web.config file.

- You can also store connection information in the <appSettings> section of the machine.config file that's stored in the Config folder subordinate to the .NET Framework installation folder. That way, the connection information is available to any application that runs on that machine.

- When you use the AppSettings property to get connection information, it looks first in the web.config file for the application. If the <appSettings> section or the element you specify isn't found in this file, it looks in the machine.config file.

Figure 13-3   How to use a configuration file to store connection information

How to cache data objects

In the previous chapter, you saw a Vendor Display program that lets the user select a vendor from a drop-down list and then uses a parameterized query to retrieve the selected vendor. You may recall that this program used two datasets. The first one was filled the first time the application was executed, and it provided the data for the Vendors drop-down list. The second one consisted of a single row for the vendor selected by the user.

Another way to implement this application is to retrieve all of the vendors into a single table the first time the application is executed. Then, you can bind the drop-down list to this table, and you can retrieve a row from this table when the user selects a vendor from the drop-down list. That's reasonable because the Vendors table is small and doesn't change often. The problem with this scenario is that each time the application ends, the dataset that contains the Vendors table is lost. To avoid that, however, you can store the dataset in server memory in the *application cache*. Figure 13-4 illustrates how the application cache works.

To start, you should realize that ASP.NET maintains a single cache for each application. Because of that, two or more users running the same application can access the same cache. As you can imagine, that can improve the efficiency of database operations.

To work with an application cache, you use the Cache class. You can see some of the common properties and methods of this class at the top of this figure. To add an object to the cache, for example, you use the Insert method as illustrated in the first example. As you can see, this method accepts two arguments. The first one is a string that contains the name of the object, and the second one is the object itself. In this case, the dsPayables1 dataset is added to the cache with a name of dsPayables.

After you place an object in the cache, it remains there even after the application that created the cached object ends. After the application that added the dsPayables1 dataset to the cache ends, for example, the page that's generated is sent back to the browser. Then, when the user selects another vendor, the application can use a statement like the second one shown in this figure to retrieve the dataset from the cache and process the user request. Here, the Item property (the default) is used to retrieve the object named dsPayables.

When you add an object to the cache, it remains there until you delete it or until ASP.NET deletes it. This brings up an important point: ASP.NET can remove objects from the cache at any time to free up memory for other objects. As a result, adding an object to the cache doesn't guarantee that the object will be there the next time you need it. Before you retrieve an object from the cache, then, you should always check if it exists. To do that, you can use code like that shown in the third example. Here, an If statement tests if the dsPayables object is equal to Nothing. If it is, it means that the object doesn't exist. In that case, a procedure is called to create the dataset, and the dataset is added to the cache. Otherwise, the dataset is retrieved from the cache.

Before I go on, you should realize that you can store any type of object in the cache, including simple variables and arrays. However, the cache is particularly useful for storing data between executions of an application.

Common properties and methods of the Cache class

Property	Description
Item(key)	Gets the value of the cache object with the specified key, or adds an object with the specified key.
Count	Gets the number of objects in the cache.

Method	Description
Insert(key, value)	Inserts or replaces the cache object with the specified key with the specified value. See online help for information about overloads that provide greater control over cached objects.
Remove(key)	Removes the object with the specified key from the cache.

A statement that adds a dataset to the cache

```
Cache.Insert("dsPayables", dsPayables1)
```

A statement that retrieves the dataset from the cache

```
dsPayables1 = Cache("dsPayables")
```

Code that retrieves a dataset from the cache or creates a new dataset

```
If Cache("dsPayables") Is Nothing Then
    Me.FillPayablesDataSet()
    Cache.Insert("dsPayables", dsPayables1)
Else
    dsPayables1 = Cache("dsPayables")
End If
```

A statement that removes the dataset from the cache

```
Cache.Remove("dsPayables")
```

Description

- ASP.NET provides an *application cache* that you can use to store objects in server memory. Because the objects remain in memory until they're explicitly deleted or until ASP.NET deletes them, they can be accessed across sessions.

- The objects in the cache can also be accessed by two or more users running the same application. Because ASP.NET provides a separate cache for each application, the objects in the cache can't be shared between applications.

- You can add, modify, and delete cache objects using the properties and methods of the Cache class. To access the cache, use the Cache property of the web page.

- ASP.NET can remove an object from the cache at any time to make room for other objects. As a result, your applications should check to see if an object is available from the cache before trying to use it. Then, if the object isn't available, it can be recreated.

- Because the cache is available to all the pages in an application, you should carefully coordinate the contents of the cache and the names used for the cache objects.

- To avoid repeated database access, it's common to store datasets in the cache. However, the cached dataset must be removed or refreshed whenever the underlying database tables are updated so it doesn't contain outdated data.

Figure 13-4   How to cache data objects

A Vendor Display program that uses caching

Figure 13-5 presents the specifications for a Vendor Display program that uses caching. To the user, this program operates just like the Vendor Display program you saw in the previous chapter. Internally, however, the operation of this program is much different. To start, all of the controls are unbound and all of the ADO.NET objects are created in code. In addition, the Connection object is created using a connection string that's included in the <appSettings> section of the web.config file. The dataset object is created from a custom typed dataset named dsPayables that was created using the XML Designer. And, so that the dsPayables dataset doesn't have to be created each time the program is executed, the dataset is kept in the application's cache.

The code for the Vendor Display program

Figure 13-6 presents the code for the Vendor Display program. It starts by declaring a variable named dsPayables1 to hold the dataset for the program.

The procedure for the Load event of the page starts by calling the GetPayablesDataSet procedure. Notice that this procedure is executed regardless of whether the page is being posted back to the server. That's because each time this program is executed, it needs to get the Payables dataset.

If you look at the code for the GetPayablesDataSet procedure, you'll see that it's identical to the code you saw in figure 13-4 that checks if the dataset already exists in the cache. If so, the dataset is retrieved and assigned to the dsPayables1 variable. If not, the FillPayablesDataSet procedure is called to fill the dataset, and the dataset is added to the cache.

The FillPayablesDataSet procedure creates the connection, command, and data adapter objects and then fills the dataset. Notice that the connection string that's used to create the connection is retrieved from the web.config file using the AppSettings property of the ConfigurationSettings class. Also notice that the Select statement issued by the command doesn't include a Where clause, which means that all of the rows in the Vendors table are retrieved.

If the page isn't being posted back from the server, the Load procedure continues by calling the FillVendorDropDownList procedure. This procedure adds an item to the drop-down list for each row in the Vendors table. To do that, it creates a ListItem object that specifies the text that's displayed along with the value for the item. Although I could have bound this control to the Vendors table, I thought it was interesting to show how to use the ListItem object, since the Windows list controls don't provide an equivalent feature.

After the list is loaded, the procedure checks if the list contains at least one item. If so, the DisplayVendor procedure is called to display the information for the first vendor. This procedure, shown on page 2 of this listing, is also called when the user selects a vendor from the drop-down list to display the information for that vendor. It uses the FindByVendorID method of the Vendors table to locate the specified vendor and then set the Text properties of the text boxes to the appropriate values. If you've read chapter 5, you shouldn't have any trouble understanding how this works.

The Vendor Display form

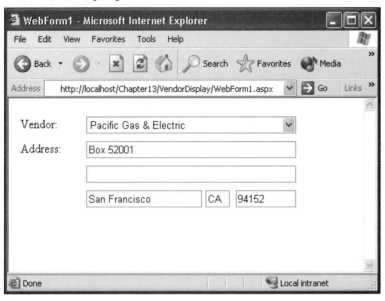

The schema for the Vendors table

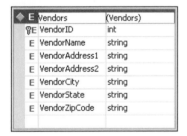

Description

- The Vendor Display program displays address information for the vendor the user selects from the drop-down list at the top of the form.

- The program uses a custom typed dataset named dsPayables that has one table named Vendors. The XML Designer was used to create this typed dataset.

- The dataset will be maintained in the application cache, and the database will be accessed only when the dataset is not available in the cache.

- An <appSettings> section with a configuration element named ConnectionString is included in the web.config file. The program will use the connection information in this element to connect to the Payables database.

Figure 13-5   A Vendor Display program that uses caching

A Vendor Display program that uses caching   **Page 1**

```
Imports System.Data.SqlClient
Public Class WebForm1
    Inherits System.Web.UI.Page
    Protected WithEvents ddlVendors As System.Web.UI.WebControls.DropDownList
    Protected WithEvents Label1 As System.Web.UI.WebControls.Label
    Protected WithEvents Label2 As System.Web.UI.WebControls.Label
    Protected WithEvents txtAddress1 As System.Web.UI.WebControls.TextBox
    Protected WithEvents txtAddress2 As System.Web.UI.WebControls.TextBox
    Protected WithEvents txtCity As System.Web.UI.WebControls.TextBox
    Protected WithEvents txtState As System.Web.UI.WebControls.TextBox
    Protected WithEvents txtZipCode As System.Web.UI.WebControls.TextBox

    Dim dsPayables1 As New dsPayables()

    Private Sub Page_Load(ByVal sender As System.Object, _
            ByVal e As System.EventArgs) Handles MyBase.Load
        'Put user code to initialize the page here
        Me.GetPayablesDataSet()
        If Not IsPostBack Then
            Me.FillVendorDropDownList()
        End If
    End Sub

    Public Sub GetPayablesDataSet()
        If Cache("dsPayables") Is Nothing Then
            Me.FillPayablesDataSet()
            Cache.Insert("dsPayables", dsPayables1)
        Else
            dsPayables1 = Cache("dsPayables")
        End If
    End Sub

    Public Sub FillPayablesDataSet()
        Dim sPayablesConnection As String _
            = ConfigurationSettings.AppSettings("ConnectionString")
        Dim conPayables As New SqlConnection(sPayablesConnection)
        Dim sVendorSelect As String _
            = "Select VendorID, VendorName, VendorAddress1, " _
            & "VendorAddress2, VendorCity, VendorState, VendorZipCode " _
            & "From Vendors " _
            & "Order By VendorName"
        Dim cmdVendors As New SqlCommand(sVendorSelect, conPayables)
        Dim daVendors As New SqlDataAdapter(cmdVendors)
        daVendors.Fill(dsPayables1.Vendors)
    End Sub

    Public Sub FillVendorDropDownList()
        Dim Vendor As dsPayables.VendorsRow
        For Each Vendor In dsPayables1.Vendors
            ddlVendors.Items.Add(New ListItem(Vendor.VendorName, _
                Vendor.VendorID))
        Next
        If ddlVendors.Items.Count > 0 Then
            Me.DisplayVendor(ddlVendors.Items(0).Value)
        End If
    End Sub
```

Figure 13-6   The code for the Vendor Display program (part 1 of 2)

A Vendor Display program that uses caching   **Page 2**

```
Private Sub ddlVendors_SelectedIndexChanged _
        (ByVal sender As System.Object, ByVal e As System.EventArgs) _
        Handles ddlVendors.SelectedIndexChanged
    Me.DisplayVendor(ddlVendors.SelectedItem.Value)
End Sub

Public Sub DisplayVendor(ByVal VendorID As Integer)
    Dim VendorsRow As dsPayables.VendorsRow
    VendorsRow = dsPayables1.Vendors.FindByVendorID(VendorID)
    If VendorsRow.IsVendorAddress1Null Then
        txtAddress1.Text = ""
    Else
        txtAddress1.Text = VendorsRow.VendorAddress1
    End If
    If VendorsRow.IsVendorAddress2Null Then
        txtAddress2.Text = ""
    Else
        txtAddress2.Text = VendorsRow.VendorAddress2
    End If
    txtCity.Text = VendorsRow.VendorCity
    txtState.Text = VendorsRow.VendorState
    txtZipCode.Text = VendorsRow.VendorZipCode
End Sub

End Class
```

Figure 13-6   The code for the Vendor Display program (part 2 of 2)

How to maintain session state

In all but the simplest of web applications, you need to keep track of the state of a user session between round trips. In a typical database maintenance program, for example, the user can add, update, or delete rows. So how does the web application keep track of which function the user is performing? By maintaining session state.

Why session state is difficult to track in web applications

Figure 13-7 shows why the state of a user session is difficult to track in a web application. In the first diagram, you can see that a browser on a client requests a page from a web server. After the server processes the request and returns the page to the browser, it drops the connection. Then, if the browser makes additional requests, the web server has no way to associate the browser with its previous requests. In other words, HTTP doesn't maintain the state of the session. Because of that, it's known as a *stateless protocol*.

How ASP.NET tracks sessions

The second diagram in figure 13-7 shows how ASP.NET keeps track of sessions. To do that, it creates a *session state object* for each session. This object contains a session ID that uniquely identifies the session. This session ID is passed back to the browser along with the HTTP response. Then, if the browser makes another request, the session ID is included in that request so ASP.NET can identify the session.

By default, ASP.NET uses a *cookie* to store the session ID on the client machine. Cookies are an extension of the basic HTTP protocol that let a server store small amounts of information on the client. When the browser sends a request to a server, it automatically sends the server's cookies along with the request.

If cookies have been disabled within a browser, this type of session tracking won't work. In that case, ASP.NET uses a technique known as *URL encoding* to pass the session ID between the client and the server. With this technique, the session ID is added on to the end of the URL that identifies each web page in the application.

Why session state is difficult to track in web applications

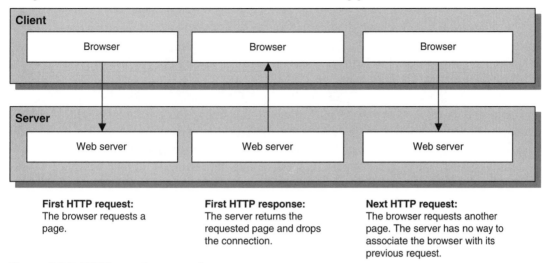

First HTTP request:
The browser requests a page.

First HTTP response:
The server returns the requested page and drops the connection.

Next HTTP request:
The browser requests another page. The server has no way to associate the browser with its previous request.

How ASP.NET tracks sessions

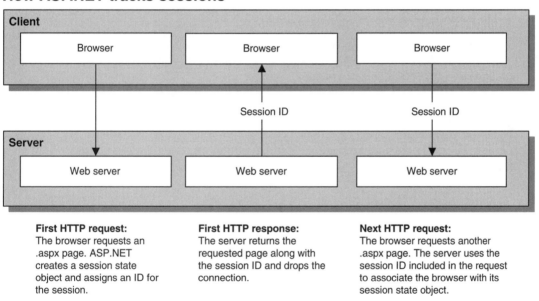

First HTTP request:
The browser requests an .aspx page. ASP.NET creates a session state object and assigns an ID for the session.

First HTTP response:
The server returns the requested page along with the session ID and drops the connection.

Next HTTP request:
The browser requests another .aspx page. The server uses the session ID included in the request to associate the browser with its session state object.

Description

- HTTP is a *stateless protocol*. That means that once a browser makes a request and receives a response, the connection to the server is dropped.

- ASP.NET uses *session tracking* to track the *state* of each user session for an application. To do that, it creates a *session state object* from the HttpSessionState class.

- The session state object includes a session ID that's sent back to the browser as a *cookie*. Then, the browser automatically returns the session ID cookie to the server with each request so the server can associate the browser with an existing session state object.

- If a browser doesn't support cookies, ASP.NET encodes the session ID in the URL for each page of the application.

Figure 13-7   How session tracking works

How to use the session state object

Figure 13-8 shows how you can use the session state object to maintain the state of a session. To do that, you use the properties and methods of this object, which is created from the HttpSessionState class. To access this object, you use the Session property of the page.

The session state object holds a collection of items that consist of the item name and its value. One way to add an item to this collection is to use the Add method of the session state object. On this method, you code the name of the item and its value as illustrated by the first example in this figure. Here, an object named Vendor is assigned to a session state item named OldVendor. If the OldVendor item doesn't exist when this statement is executed, it will be created. Otherwise, its value will be updated.

Another way to add an item to the session state collection is to use the Item property as illustrated in the second example. (As with many other objects you've seen in this book, Item is the default property, so you can omit it as shown here.) Just as when you use the Add method, if the item already exists, it's updated when the assignment statement is executed. Otherwise, it's added to the collection.

You can also use the Item property to retrieve an item from the session state collection as shown in the third example. Here, the value of the OldVendor item is retrieved and assigned to the OldVendor variable.

Because the session state object uses valuable server memory, you should avoid using it to store large objects. If you do use it to store large objects, however, you should remove the objects as soon as you're done with them. To do that, you use the Remove method as illustrated in the last example in this figure.

Common properties and methods of the HttpSessionState class

Property	Description
SessionID	The unique ID of the session.
Item(name)	Gets or sets the value of the session state item with the specified name. You can also access items by index.
Count	Gets the number of items in the session state collection.

Method	Description
Add(name, value)	Adds an item to the session state collection.
Clear	Removes all items from the session state collection.
Remove(name)	Removes the item with the specified name from the session state collection.

A statement that adds or updates a session state item

```
Session.Add("OldVendor", Vendor)
```

Another way to add or update a session state item

```
Session("OldVendor") = Vendor
```

A statement that retrieves the value of a session state item

```
OldVendor = Session("OldVendor")
```

A statement that removes a session state item

```
Session.Remove("OldVendor")
```

Description

- You can use the session state object that ASP.NET creates for a session to store and retrieve items across executions of an application. To access the session state object, you use the Session property of the page.

- Session state objects are maintained in server memory. As a result, you should avoid storing large items in session state.

Figure 13-8   How to use the session state object

A Vendor Maintenance program that maintains session state

Figure 13-9 presents the specifications for a Vendor Maintenance program that uses the session state object. The operation of this application is similar to the Windows versions of this application that you saw in chapters 4, 5, and 6. The main differences are that before the data for a vendor is displayed, the user must click on the Get Vendor button. In addition, if the user clicks on the Cancel button to cancel out of an add or update operation or on the Delete button to delete a vendor, the controls are cleared until another vendor is selected. To help the user navigate through the application, messages are displayed at the bottom of the page to indicate what actions can be performed.

Although it isn't apparent from this figure, validation controls are associated with several of the input controls on the Vendor Maintenance form. For example, a required field validator control is associated with the Name text box, and both a required field validator control and a regular expression validator control are associated with the zip code text box. As a result, the program doesn't have to provide code that validates the user's input. When an entry is invalid, the validation control causes an error message to be displayed, as shown for the city and zip code controls in this figure.

To simplify the development of this application, I created a database class named VendorsDB that provides all of the application's database processing. In addition, I created a Vendor class that represents a single vendor. These classes are much like the classes you saw in chapter 10, so you shouldn't have any trouble understanding how they work. In a moment, though, you'll see the complete code for these classes as well as for the form class.

For this program to work, it saves two items in the session state object. First, it saves an enumeration that indicates whether the user is currently entering a new user or working with an existing user. Then, if the user clicks the Update button, the program can use this enumeration to determine what processing needs to be done.

The second item that's stored in the session state object is a Vendor object named OldVendor. This object contains the original data for a vendor that's retrieved from the Vendors table. If the user updates or deletes the vendor, this object can then be used to provide for concurrency checking.

The form for the Vendor Maintenance program

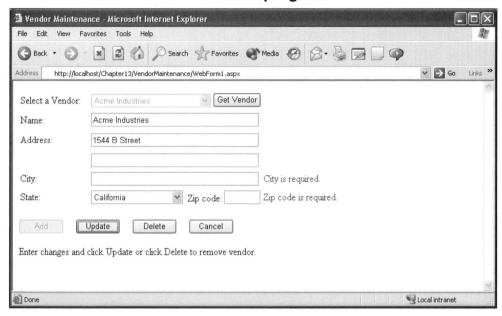

Description

- The Vendor Maintenance program lets users add, update, and delete rows in the Vendors table of the Payables database.

- To display the information for an existing vendor, the user selects the vendor from the drop-down list and clicks the Get Vendor button. Then, the user can enter changes and click the Update or Delete button to update or delete the vendor.

- To add a new vendor, the user clicks the Add button. Then, the controls on the page are cleared so the user can enter the data for the new vendor. To save the new vendor, the user clicks the Update button.

- The user can also click the Cancel button to clear the controls without adding, updating, or deleting the vendor.

- This program uses required field validator controls for the name, city, state, and zip code controls to ensure that the user enters values in those controls. In addition, a regular expression validator control is used for the zip code text box to ensure that the zip code expression is valid. Flow layout is used to align these controls on the form.

- The message that's displayed at the bottom of the page changes as the program executes to instruct the user how to proceed.

- This program uses two classes in addition to the form class. The VendorsDB class provides all of the database processing for the program, and the Vendor class represents a single vendor in the Vendors table.

- This program maintains two items in the session state object. EditMode is an enumeration that's used to determine whether the user is adding or modifying a vendor when the Update button is clicked. OldVendor is a Vendor object with the original values for a vendor that are used for concurrency checking during an update or delete operation.

Figure 13-9   A Vendor Maintenance program that maintains session state

The code for the Vendor Maintenance program

Figure 13-10 presents the code for the Vendor Maintenance program. This program starts by defining two enumerations. The first one, DisplayMode, is used by the SetDisplayMode procedure to determine which form controls are enabled and which are disabled. As you can see, this enumeration provides for three possible display modes: SelectVendor, AddVendor, and EditVendor. You'll see how this enumeration is used when I describe the SetDisplayMode procedure in a few moments.

The second enumeration, EditMode, is the one that will be stored in the session state object. You'll see how this enumeration is used when I describe the procedure for the Click event of the Update button.

The first time the page is loaded, the Load procedure calls three procedures. The first two, FillVendorDropDown and FillStatesDropDown, populate the two drop-down lists on the form. The third, SetDisplayMode, enables and disables controls on the form depending on the DisplayMode value that's passed to it.

The FillVendorDropDown procedure executes the GetVendors method of the VendorsDB class, which returns a data reader that contains the VendorID and VendorName columns for all of the rows in the Vendors table. Then, the procedure reads through these rows and adds a list item to the Vendors drop-down list for each one. Note that I could also have written the GetVendors method so it returns a dataset rather than a data reader. Then, I could have bound the Vendors drop-down list to this dataset. However, using a data reader is slightly more efficient because the data is only read once: as the rows are loaded into the list. In contrast, using a dataset requires reading the data twice: once to populate the data table and a second time to load the drop-down list.

A Vendor Maintenance program that maintains session state   Page 1

```
Public Class WebForm1
    Inherits System.Web.UI.Page
    Protected WithEvents ddlVendors As System.Web.UI.WebControls.DropDownList
    Protected WithEvents btnEdit As System.Web.UI.WebControls.Button
    Protected WithEvents txtName As System.Web.UI.WebControls.TextBox
    Protected WithEvents txtAddress1 As System.Web.UI.WebControls.TextBox
    Protected WithEvents txtAddress2 As System.Web.UI.WebControls.TextBox
    Protected WithEvents txtCity As System.Web.UI.WebControls.TextBox
    Protected WithEvents ddlStates As System.Web.UI.WebControls.DropDownList
    Protected WithEvents txtZipCode As System.Web.UI.WebControls.TextBox
    Protected WithEvents btnAdd As System.Web.UI.WebControls.Button
    Protected WithEvents btnUpdate As System.Web.UI.WebControls.Button
    Protected WithEvents btnDelete As System.Web.UI.WebControls.Button
    Protected WithEvents btnCancel As System.Web.UI.WebControls.Button
    Protected WithEvents lblMessage As System.Web.UI.WebControls.Label
    Protected WithEvents RequiredFieldValidator1 As _
        System.Web.UI.WebControls.RequiredFieldValidator
    Protected WithEvents RequiredFieldValidator2 As _
        System.Web.UI.WebControls.RequiredFieldValidator
    Protected WithEvents RequiredFieldValidator3 As _
        System.Web.UI.WebControls.RequiredFieldValidator
    Protected WithEvents RequiredFieldValidator4 As _
        System.Web.UI.WebControls.RequiredFieldValidator
    Protected WithEvents RegularExpressionValidator1 As _
        System.Web.UI.WebControls.RegularExpressionValidator

    Private Enum DisplayMode
        SelectVendor
        AddVendor
        EditVendor
    End Enum

    Private Enum EditMode
        Add
        Update
    End Enum

    Private Sub Page_Load(ByVal sender As System.Object, _
            ByVal e As System.EventArgs) Handles MyBase.Load
        'Put user code to initialize the page here
        If Not IsPostBack Then
            Me.FillVendorDropDown()
            Me.FillStatesDropDown()
            Me.SetDisplayMode(DisplayMode.SelectVendor)
        End If
    End Sub

    Private Sub FillVendorDropDown()
        Dim drVendors As SqlDataReader
        drVendors = VendorsDB.GetVendors()
        ddlVendors.Items.Clear()
        Do While drVendors.Read()
            ddlVendors.Items.Add(New ListItem(drVendors("VendorName"), _
                drVendors("VendorID")))
        Loop
    End Sub
```

Figure 13-10   The code for the Vendor Maintenance program (part 1 of 4)

The FillStatesDropDown procedure is similar. It executes the GetStates method of the VendorsDB class, which returns a data reader that contains the StateName and StateCode columns for each state in the States table. Then, it uses a data reader to retrieve the row for each state and add it to the States drop-down list. Notice that before the first state is added to this list, a row that consists of empty text and value strings is added. As you'll see later in this program, that will make it easy to clear this drop-down list when that's necessary.

The SetDisplayMode procedure accepts a DisplayMode as an argument and uses a Select Case structure to determine what controls should be enabled or disabled based on the value of that argument. It also sets the text of the label that's displayed at the bottom of the page that tells the user how to proceed. Notice that the message is appended to any text that's already in the label. That's because this program also uses this label to display the result of an add, update, or delete operation.

If the display mode is SelectVendor, the form is set up so the user can select a vendor or click the Add button to add a new vendor. In that case, the Update, Delete, and Cancel buttons as well as the input controls are disabled. If the display mode is AddVendor, the form is set up so the user can enter data for a new vendor. In that case, the Update and Cancel buttons and the input controls are enabled and the vendor drop-down list and Add and Delete buttons are disabled. Finally, if the display mode is EditVendor, the form is set up so the user can edit or delete an existing vendor. In that case, the Update, Delete, and Cancel buttons and the input controls are enabled and the vendor drop-down list and Add button are disabled.

To enable or disable the input controls, the SetDisplayMode procedure calls the SetInputControls procedure. This procedure accepts a Boolean argument that determines whether the controls are enabled or disabled.

A Vendor Maintenance program that maintains session state   Page 2

```
Private Sub FillStatesDropDown()
    Dim drStates As SqlDataReader
    drStates = VendorsDB.GetStates()
    ddlStates.Items.Clear()
    ddlStates.Items.Add(New ListItem("", ""))
    Do While drStates.Read()
        ddlStates.Items.Add(New ListItem(drStates("StateName"), _
            drStates("StateCode")))
    Loop
End Sub

Private Sub SetDisplayMode(ByVal DisplayMode As DisplayMode)
    Select Case DisplayMode
        Case DisplayMode.SelectVendor
            ddlVendors.Enabled = True
            btnAdd.Enabled = True
            btnUpdate.Enabled = False
            btnDelete.Enabled = False
            btnCancel.Enabled = False
            Me.SetInputControls(False)
            lblMessage.Text &= "Select a vendor and click Get Vendor " _
                            & "or click Add to create a new vendor."
        Case DisplayMode.AddVendor
            ddlVendors.Enabled = False
            btnAdd.Enabled = False
            btnUpdate.Enabled = True
            btnDelete.Enabled = False
            btnCancel.Enabled = True
            Me.SetInputControls(True)
            lblMessage.Text &= "Enter vendor data and click Update " _
                            & "to add the vendor."
        Case DisplayMode.EditVendor
            ddlVendors.Enabled = False
            btnAdd.Enabled = False
            btnUpdate.Enabled = True
            btnDelete.Enabled = True
            btnCancel.Enabled = True
            Me.SetInputControls(True)
            lblMessage.Text &= "Enter changes and click Update " _
                            & "or click Delete to remove vendor."
    End Select
End Sub

Public Sub SetInputControls(ByVal EnableMode As Boolean)
    txtName.Enabled = EnableMode
    txtAddress1.Enabled = EnableMode
    txtAddress2.Enabled = EnableMode
    txtCity.Enabled = EnableMode
    ddlStates.Enabled = EnableMode
    txtZipCode.Enabled = EnableMode
End Sub
```

Figure 13-10   The code for the Vendor Maintenance program (part 2 of 4)

When the user clicks the Get Vendor button, the GetVendor procedure is executed. This procedure calls the ShowVendor procedure to display the selected vendor. To do that, it passes the Value property of the selected item. Then, it sets the EditMode session state item to EditMode.Update. That way, if the user clicks the Update button, the program will be able to determine that the user was editing an existing vendor rather than adding a new vendor.

The ShowVendor procedure executes the GetVendor method of the VendorsDB class to get a Vendor object that contains the data for the selected vendor. Next, it sets the input controls to the appropriate values for that vendor. It also calls the SetDisplayMode procedure to enable and disable the appropriate controls. Finally, it sets the OldVendor session state item to the vendor that's currently displayed.

If the user clicks the Add button, the Add procedure calls the ClearVendorControls procedure to clear the input controls. Notice that to clear the States drop-down list, this procedure sets the SelectedIndex property of the control to 0. This works because the first item in the list is empty. The Add procedure also calls the SetDisplayMode procedure to enable and disable the appropriate controls, and it sets the EditMode session state item to EditMode.Add.

The code that's executed when the user clicks on the Cancel button is similar. It calls the ClearVendorControls procedure to clear the input controls and the SetDisplayMode procedure to enable and disable the appropriate controls. However, it's not necessary to set the EditMode session state item. That's because this item isn't used again until the user selects another vendor or clicks on the Add button, in which case this item is set to the appropriate value.

A Vendor Maintenance program that maintains session state   Page 3

```
Private Sub btnGetVendor_Click(ByVal sender As System.Object, _
        ByVal e As System.EventArgs) Handles btnGetVendor.Click
    Me.ShowVendor(ddlVendors.SelectedItem.Value)
    Session("EditMode") = EditMode.Update
End Sub

Private Sub ShowVendor(ByVal VendorID As String)
    Dim Vendor As Vendor = VendorsDB.GetVendor(VendorID)
    txtName.Text = Vendor.Name
    txtAddress1.Text = Vendor.Address1
    txtAddress2.Text = Vendor.Address2
    txtCity.Text = Vendor.City
    ddlStates.SelectedItem.Selected = False
    ddlStates.Items.FindByValue(Vendor.State).Selected = True
    txtZipCode.Text = Vendor.ZipCode
    Me.SetDisplayMode(DisplayMode.EditVendor)
    Session("OldVendor") = Vendor
End Sub

Private Sub btnAdd_Click(ByVal sender As System.Object, _
        ByVal e As System.EventArgs) Handles btnAdd.Click
    Me.ClearVendorControls()
    Me.SetDisplayMode(DisplayMode.AddVendor)
    Session("EditMode") = EditMode.Add
End Sub

Private Sub ClearVendorControls()
    txtName.Text = ""
    txtAddress1.Text = ""
    txtAddress2.Text = ""
    txtCity.Text = ""
    ddlStates.SelectedIndex = 0
    txtZipCode.Text = ""
End Sub

Private Sub btnCancel_Click(ByVal sender As System.Object, _
        ByVal e As System.EventArgs) Handles btnCancel.Click
    Me.ClearVendorControls()
    Me.SetDisplayMode(DisplayMode.SelectVendor)
End Sub
```

Figure 13-10   The code for the Vendor Maintenance program (part 3 of 4)

If the user clicks the Update button, the Update procedure starts by creating a Vendor object from the Vendor class and setting its properties to the values entered by the user. Then, it checks the EditMode session state item to determine whether a new vendor is being added or an existing vendor is being updated. If a new vendor is being added, the procedure executes the AddVendor method of the VendorsDB class to add the vendor. Notice that this method is executed within a Select Case statement. That's because the value that's returned by this method is an enumeration value that indicates whether or not the operation was successful. In this case, the possible values are DBResult.Success and DBResult.DatabaseError. The Update procedure uses this value to display an appropriate message in the label at the bottom of the page.

If an update operation is being performed, the Update procedure creates a Vendor object named OldVendor and assigns to it the value of the OldVendor session state item. Then, it executes the UpdateVendor method of the VendorsDB class to update the vendor. As you'll see in a moment, this method uses the OldVendor object to perform concurrency checking. Like the AddVendor method, the UpdateVendor method returns a value from the DBResult enumeration. In this case, though, the value can also indicate a concurrency error, so the Update procedure must provide for this error.

The Update procedure ends by calling the ClearVendorControls, FillVendorDropDown, and SetDisplayMode procedures. It calls the FillVendorDropDown procedure so that if the user added a vendor, that vendor will appear in the Vendors drop-down list. Also, if the user changed the name of an existing vendor, that new name will appear in the list.

The last procedure of this program is the one that's executed when the user clicks the Delete button. This procedure starts by getting the OldVendor item from the session state collection and assigning it to a Vendor object named OldVendor. Then, it executes the DeleteVendor method of the VendorsDB class to delete the vendor. This method provides for concurrency checking and returns a DBResult value that indicates the result of the operation. The Delete procedure uses this return value to display an appropriate message. This procedure also calls the ClearVendorControls, FillVendorDropDown, and SetDisplayMode procedures to prepare the form for the next operation.

A Vendor Maintenance program that maintains session state   Page 4

```vb
Private Sub btnUpdate_Click(ByVal sender As System.Object, _
        ByVal e As System.EventArgs) Handles btnUpdate.Click
    Dim Vendor As New Vendor()
    Vendor.ID = ddlVendors.SelectedItem.Value
    Vendor.Name = txtName.Text
    Vendor.Address1 = txtAddress1.Text
    Vendor.Address2 = txtAddress2.Text
    Vendor.City = txtCity.Text
    Vendor.State = ddlStates.SelectedItem.Value
    Vendor.ZipCode = txtZipCode.Text
    If Session("EditMode") = EditMode.Add Then
        Select Case VendorsDB.AddVendor(Vendor)
            Case VendorsDB.DBResult.Success
                lblMessage.Text = "Vendor added. "
            Case VendorsDB.DBResult.DatabaseError
                lblMessage.Text = "A database error occurred. "
        End Select
    ElseIf Session("EditMode") = EditMode.Update Then
        Dim OldVendor As Vendor = Session("OldVendor")
        Select Case VendorsDB.UpdateVendor(Vendor, OldVendor)
            Case VendorsDB.DBResult.Success
                lblMessage.Text = "Vendor updated. "
            Case VendorsDB.DBResult.ConcurrencyError
                lblMessage.Text = _
                    "Another user has updated or deleted that vendor. " _
                    & "Please try again. "
            Case VendorsDB.DBResult.DatabaseError
                lblMessage.Text = "A database error occurred. "
        End Select
    End If
    Me.ClearVendorControls()
    Me.FillVendorDropDown()
    Me.SetDisplayMode(DisplayMode.SelectVendor)
End Sub

Private Sub btnDelete_Click(ByVal sender As System.Object, _
        ByVal e As System.EventArgs) Handles btnDelete.Click
    Dim OldVendor As Vendor = Session("OldVendor")
    Select Case VendorsDB.DeleteVendor(OldVendor)
        Case VendorsDB.DBResult.Success
            lblMessage.Text = "Vendor deleted. "
        Case VendorsDB.DBResult.ConcurrencyError
            lblMessage.Text = "Another user has updated or deleted " _
                            & "that vendor. Please try again. "
        Case VendorsDB.DBResult.DatabaseError
            lblMessage.Text = "A database error has occurred. "
    End Select
    Me.ClearVendorControls()
    Me.FillVendorDropDown()
    Me.SetDisplayMode(DisplayMode.SelectVendor)
End Sub

End Class
```

Figure 13-10   The code for the Vendor Maintenance program (part 4 of 4)

The code for the database classes

Figure 13-11 presents the code for the VendorsDB and Vendor classes used by the Vendor Maintenance program. These classes are similar to the VendorsDB and Vendor classes you saw in chapter 10. Because they don't require any database programming techniques that you haven't already seen, you shouldn't have any difficulty understanding how they work. So I'll just describe them briefly here.

The VendorsDB class starts by declaring an enumeration named DBResult. As you'll see in a moment, this enumeration is used to indicate the result of an add, update, or delete operation. You've already seen how this result is used by the Vendor Maintenance form.

The GetPayablesConnection method retrieves a connection string from the web.config file and returns a database connection object. This method is used by the other methods in the VendorsDB class to get a connection to the Payables database. To be sure that it's not accessed from outside the class, this method is defined as a Private function.

The GetVendors method gets the VendorID and VendorName columns for all the rows in the Vendors table. Those rows are stored in a data reader that's returned to the calling procedure. In this case, the calling procedure is the FillVendorDropDown procedure of the Vendor Maintenance form, which loads the vendors into the drop-down list.

The GetStates method also returns a data reader. In this case, the data reader contains all of the state codes and state names from the States table. This data reader is then used by the Vendor Maintenance form to load the States drop-down list.

The GetVendor method retrieves a vendor from the Vendors table based on the VendorID that's passed to it. To do that, it uses a parameterized query and a data reader. After the vendor data is retrieved into the data reader, the data is read and stored in a Vendor object, which is passed back to the Vendor Maintenance form.

The AddVendor method, shown at the top of page 2 of this listing, accepts a Vendor object as an argument. Then, it uses the data in that object to add the vendor to the Vendors table. When it's done, it returns a DBResult value to indicate whether the vendor was added successfully.

The UpdateVendor method accepts two Vendor objects as arguments. The first one contains the updated vendor data and the second one contains the original vendor data. As you can see, the original vendor data is used for concurrency checking. The DBResult value that's returned by this method indicates whether the operation was successful, a concurrency error occurred, or some other type of database error occurred (see page 3).

The DeleteVendor method, which begins on page 3 of this listing, accepts a Vendor object as an argument and deletes the specified vendor from the Vendors table. Like the UpdateVendor method, this method provides for concurrency checking and returns a DBResult value that indicates whether the vendor was successfully deleted.

The code for the VendorsDB class   **Page 1**

```vb
Imports System.Data.SqlClient
Public Class VendorsDB

    Public Enum DBResult
        Success
        ConcurrencyError
        DatabaseError
    End Enum

    Private Shared Function GetPayablesConnection() As SqlConnection
        Dim sConnectionString As String _
            = ConfigurationSettings.AppSettings("ConnectionString")
        Return New SqlConnection(sConnectionString)
    End Function

    Public Shared Function GetVendors() As SqlDataReader
        Dim drVendors As SqlDataReader
        Dim conPayables As SqlConnection = GetPayablesConnection()
        Dim sSqlCommand As String = "Select VendorID, VendorName " _
            & "From Vendors Order By VendorName"
        Dim cmdVendors As New SqlCommand(sSqlCommand, conPayables)
        conPayables.Open()
        drVendors = cmdVendors.ExecuteReader(CommandBehavior.CloseConnection)
        Return drVendors
    End Function

    Public Shared Function GetStates() As SqlDataReader
        Dim drStates As SqlDataReader
        Dim conPayables As SqlConnection = GetPayablesConnection()
        Dim sSqlCommand As String = "Select StateName, StateCode " _
            & "From States Order By StateName"
        Dim cmdVendors As New SqlCommand(sSqlCommand, conPayables)
        conPayables.Open()
        drStates = cmdVendors.ExecuteReader(CommandBehavior.CloseConnection)
        Return drStates
    End Function

    Public Shared Function GetVendor(ByVal VendorID As Integer) As Vendor
        Dim Vendor As New Vendor()
        Dim drVendor As SqlDataReader
        Dim conPayables As SqlConnection = GetPayablesConnection()
        Dim sSqlCommand As String
        sSqlCommand = "Select VendorID, VendorName, VendorAddress1, " _
            & "VendorAddress2, VendorCity, VendorState, VendorZipCode " _
            & "From Vendors Where VendorID=@VendorID"
        conPayables.Open()
        Dim cmdVendors As New SqlCommand(sSqlCommand, conPayables)
        cmdVendors.Parameters.Add("@VendorID", VendorID)
        drVendor = cmdVendors.ExecuteReader(CommandBehavior.SingleRow)
        If drVendor.Read Then
            Vendor.ID = drVendor("VendorID").ToString
            Vendor.Name = drVendor("VendorName").ToString
            Vendor.Address1 = drVendor("VendorAddress1").ToString
            Vendor.Address2 = drVendor("VendorAddress2").ToString
            Vendor.City = drVendor("VendorCity").ToString
            Vendor.State = drVendor("VendorState").ToString
            Vendor.ZipCode = drVendor("VendorZipCode").ToString
        End If
        conPayables.Close()
        Return Vendor
    End Function
```

Figure 13-11   The code for the database classes (part 1 of 4)

The code for the VendorsDB class

```vb
Public Shared Function AddVendor(ByVal Vendor As Vendor) As Integer
    Dim conPayables As SqlConnection = GetPayablesConnection()
    Dim sSqlCommand As String _
        = "Insert Into Vendors (VendorName, VendorAddress1, " _
        & "VendorAddress2, VendorCity, VendorState, VendorZipCode) " _
        & "Values (@VendorName, @VendorAddress1, " _
        & "@VendorAddress2, @VendorCity, @VendorState, @VendorZipCode)"
    conPayables.Open()
    Dim cmdVendors As New SqlCommand(sSqlCommand, conPayables)
    With cmdVendors.Parameters
        .Add("@VendorName", Vendor.Name)
        If Vendor.Address1 = "" Then
            .Add("@VendorAddress1", DBNull.Value)
        Else
            .Add("@VendorAddress1", Vendor.Address1)
        End If
        If Vendor.Address2 = "" Then
            .Add("@VendorAddress2", DBNull.Value)
        Else
            .Add("@VendorAddress2", Vendor.Address2)
        End If
        .Add("@VendorCity", Vendor.City)
        .Add("@VendorState", Vendor.State)
        .Add("@VendorZipCode", Vendor.ZipCode)
    End With
    Try
        If cmdVendors.ExecuteNonQuery() > 0 Then
            AddVendor = DBResult.Success
        End If
    Catch e As SqlException
        AddVendor = DBResult.DatabaseError
    End Try
    conPayables.Close()
End Function

Public Shared Function UpdateVendor(ByVal NewVendor As Vendor, _
        ByVal OldVendor As Vendor) As DBResult
    Dim conPayables As SqlConnection = GetPayablesConnection()
    Dim sSqlCommand As String _
        = "Update Vendors " _
        & "Set VendorName = @NewVendorName, " _
        & "VendorAddress1 = @NewVendorAddress1, " _
        & "VendorAddress2 = @NewVendorAddress2, " _
        & "VendorCity = @NewVendorCity, " _
        & "VendorState = @NewVendorState, " _
        & "VendorZipCode = @NewVendorZipCode " _
        & "Where VendorID = @OldVendorID " _
        & "And VendorName = @OldVendorName " _
        & "And (VendorAddress1 = @OldVendorAddress1 " _
        & "Or (@OldVendorAddress1 = ''And VendorAddress1 Is Null)) " _
        & "And (VendorAddress2 = @OldVendorAddress2 " _
        & "Or (@OldVendorAddress2 = ''And VendorAddress2 Is Null)) " _
        & "And VendorCity = @OldVendorCity " _
        & "And VendorState = @OldVendorState " _
        & "And VendorZipCode = @OldVendorZipCode"
    conPayables.Open()
    Dim cmdVendors As New SqlCommand(sSqlCommand, conPayables)
```

Figure 13-11   The code for the database classes (part 2 of 4)

The code for the VendorsDB class   Page 3

```
    With cmdVendors.Parameters
        .Add("@NewVendorID", NewVendor.ID)
        .Add("@NewVendorName", NewVendor.Name)
        If NewVendor.Address1 = "" Then
            .Add("@NewVendorAddress1", DBNull.Value)
        Else
            .Add("@NewVendorAddress1", NewVendor.Address1)
        End If
        If NewVendor.Address2 = "" Then
            .Add("@NewVendorAddress2", DBNull.Value)
        Else
            .Add("@NewVendorAddress2", NewVendor.Address2)
        End If
        .Add("@NewVendorCity", NewVendor.City)
        .Add("@NewVendorState", NewVendor.State)
        .Add("@NewVendorZipCode", NewVendor.ZipCode)
        .Add("@OldVendorID", OldVendor.ID)
        .Add("@OldVendorName", OldVendor.Name)
        .Add("@OldVendorAddress1", OldVendor.Address1)
        .Add("@OldVendorAddress2", OldVendor.Address2)
        .Add("@OldVendorCity", OldVendor.City)
        .Add("@OldVendorState", OldVendor.State)
        .Add("@OldVendorZipCode", OldVendor.ZipCode)
    End With
    Try
        If cmdVendors.ExecuteNonQuery() > 0 Then
            UpdateVendor = DBResult.Success
        Else
            UpdateVendor = DBResult.ConcurrencyError
        End If
    Catch e As SqlException
        UpdateVendor = DBResult.DatabaseError
    End Try
    conPayables.Close()
End Function

Public Shared Function DeleteVendor(ByVal Vendor As Vendor) As DBResult
    Dim conPayables As SqlConnection = GetPayablesConnection()
    Dim sSqlCommand As String _
        = "Delete From Vendors " _
        & "Where VendorID = @VendorID And VendorName = @VendorName " _
        & "And (VendorAddress1 = @VendorAddress1 " _
        & "Or (@VendorAddress1 = ''And VendorAddress1 Is Null)) " _
        & "And (VendorAddress2 = @VendorAddress2 " _
        & "Or (@VendorAddress2 = ''And VendorAddress2 Is Null)) " _
        & "And VendorCity = @VendorCity And VendorState = @VendorState " _
        & "And VendorZipCode = @VendorZipCode "
    conPayables.Open()
    Dim cmdVendors As New SqlCommand(sSqlCommand, conPayables)
    With cmdVendors.Parameters
        .Add("@VendorID", Vendor.ID)
        .Add("@VendorName", Vendor.Name)
        .Add("@VendorAddress1", Vendor.Address1)
        .Add("@VendorAddress2", Vendor.Address2)
        .Add("@VendorCity", Vendor.City)
        .Add("@VendorState", Vendor.State)
        .Add("@VendorZipCode", Vendor.ZipCode)
    End With
```

Figure 13-11   The code for the database classes (part 3 of 4)

On the last page of this listing, you can see the code for the Vendor class. This class is identical to the one you saw in chapter 10. It defines a public variable for each column in the Vendors table that's used by the Vendor Maintenance program. Although I could have defined a property procedure for each column that validated the data the user enters before setting the property value, that wasn't necessary for this program. That's because the form includes validation controls that validate the data before it's posted back to the server. In some cases, though, you'll find it necessary to include property procedures that include additional validation code.

The code for the VendorsDB class   Page 4

```
    Try
        If cmdVendors.ExecuteNonQuery() > 0 Then
            DeleteVendor = DBResult.Success
        Else
            DeleteVendor = DBResult.ConcurrencyError
        End If
    Catch e As SQLException
        DeleteVendor = DBResult.DatabaseError
    End Try
    conPayables.Close()
    End Function

End Class
```

The code for the Vendor class

```
Public Class Vendor
    Public ID As Integer
    Public Name As String
    Public Address1 As String
    Public Address2 As String
    Public City As String
    Public State As String
    Public ZipCode As String
End Class
```

Figure 13-11   The code for the database classes (part 4 of 4)

Perspective

In this chapter, you've learned how to use three ASP.NET programming techniques: connection pooling, caching, and session tracking. As you develop ASP.NET database applications, you'll find caching and session tracking to be invaluable. On the other hand, connection pooling will probably be handled by the database administrator in all but the smallest shops. That's particularly true if connection strings are stored in the global configuration file. Because of that, you may never have the opportunity to use the techniques for managing a connection pool that were presented in this chapter. Even so, you should now understand how connection pools work, and you should be able to manage one if the need ever arises.

Terms

connection pooling
connection pool
application cache
stateless protocol
session tracking
state
session state object
cookie
URL encoding

14

How to use the DataList and DataGrid controls

In this chapter, you'll learn how to use two ASP.NET web controls that are designed specifically for working with the data in a data source such as a dataset. The DataList control displays data from a data source in a list, and the DataGrid control displays data in a grid with columns and rows. As you'll see, you can customize the content, appearance, and operation of these controls in a variety of ways.

How to use the DataList control

A data list control displays a list of items from a bound data source such as dataset. In the topics that follow, you'll learn the basic techniques for working with data list controls. Keep in mind, though, that there's a lot more you can do with data list controls than what's presented here.

An introduction to the data list control

Figure 14-1 shows the interface for a simple web application that uses a data list control. To use this application, the user selects a vendor from the drop-down list at the top of the page. Then, all of the invoices for that vendor are displayed in a data list. Notice that the data list provides one row for each invoice in the data source. In addition, it provides a row of headings that identify the data in the list.

Although this data list appears to have four columns, you should realize that it actually has only one. Then, within that column, a *template* is used to define the information that the column contains. As you'll see later in this chapter, you can define several templates for a data list control, including the ones that define the items in the list and the one that defines the header that's displayed at the top of the list. You can also format a data list and its templates so they look the way you want them to using one of the techniques you'll learn in this chapter.

Below the browser screen, this figure shows how the same data list control appears in the Designer window. As you can see, all of the data in the control except for the header text is bound to a data source. In the topics that follow, you'll learn how to create a data list like this one.

An Invoice Display program that uses a data list control

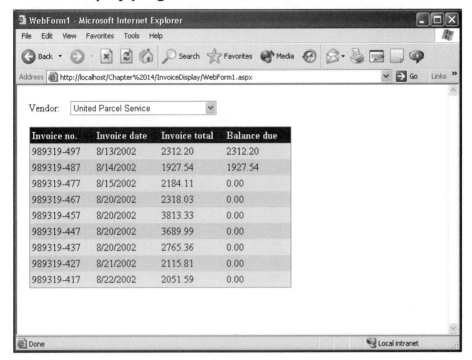

The data list control in the Designer window

Invoice no.	Invoice date	Invoice total	Balance due
Databound	Databound	Databound	Databound
Databound	Databound	Databound	Databound
Databound	Databound	Databound	Databound
Databound	Databound	Databound	Databound
Databound	Databound	Databound	Databound

Description

- The DataList control displays a list of items from the data source that it's bound to. Typically, a data list is bound to a data table or a data view, but it can also be bound to a data reader or an array as well as other data sources.

- Each row of a data list consists of a single column. To define the information that's displayed in that column, you use templates. See figure 14-3 for details.

- You can also apply formatting to a data list control to change its appearance. See figure 14-5 for details.

- The data list control is typically used for simple display operations. However, it can also be used for more complex display operations as well as for edit operations. For more information, see online help.

Figure 14-1   An introduction to the data list control

How to create and bind a data list control

The data list control is a Web Server control that appears in the Web Forms tab of the Toolbox. When you first add a data list control to a form, it appears as shown in figure 14-2. Notice that the message that's displayed in this control indicates that an Item template is required. As you'll learn in the next topic, this is the template that defines the items that are displayed in the data list.

To specify the source of data for a data list control, you set the DataSource and DataMember properties. Typically, you'll set the DataSource property to the name of a dataset, and you'll set the DataMember property to the name of a table within that dataset. Then, you bind the data list control to its data source at runtime using the DataBind method of the control or the page.

A data list control before templates and formatting are applied

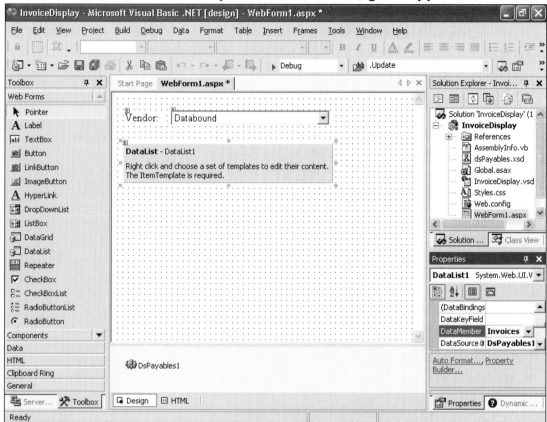

Properties and methods for binding a data list control

Property	Description
DataSource	The name of the data source, such as a dataset.
DataMember	A member associated with the data source, such as a data table. If the data source contains only one bindable member, you don't need to set this property.

Method	Description
DataBind	Binds the control to its data source. This method must be executed each time the data source changes.

Description

- To create a data list control, drag it from the Web Forms tab of the Toolbox to the form. The control will initially appear as shown above.

- To specify the data source for a data list control, set its DataSource and DataMember properties.

- To bind the data list control to its data source at runtime, execute the DataBind method.

Figure 14-2   How to create and bind a data list control

How to define the templates for a data list control

To define the information that's displayed in a data list, you add controls to its templates. Figure 14-3 shows you how to create the templates for a data list control. As the table at the top of this figure indicates, you can create seven different templates. The only one that's required is the Item template, which defines how each item in the data source is displayed. Depending on the requirements of your application, you may need to use one or more of the other templates as well. For example, you'll typically use a Header template to create headings that are displayed in the first row of the data list.

To create a template, you use the commands in the Edit Template menu that's displayed when you right-click the data list control and choose Edit Template. When you choose a command from this menu, the control is placed in *template-editing mode* and the templates you selected are displayed. If you select the Item Templates command, for example, the four item templates shown in this figure are displayed. And if you select the Header and Footer command, the Header and Footer templates shown here are displayed.

To add controls to a template, you can simply drag them from the Toolbox. In the Item template in this figure, you can see that I've added four label controls. Note that the controls shown here are already bound to columns in the data source, which is why they appear with the ID property within brackets. When you first add a control, however, the Text property is displayed. This is illustrated by the Header template shown in this figure, which also includes four label controls. In this case, the Text property of each control has been changed to specify the text that will be displayed in the header row of the data list.

When you add controls to two or more templates, you typically want the controls in each template to be aligned. To do that, you simply set the Width properties of the corresponding controls to the same value. In this illustration, for example, I set the Width property of each control to 100 pixels.

Although you can easily set the width of each control, there isn't an easy way to align the data within each control. If you look back at the form in figure 14-1, for example, you can see that all of the data is aligned on the left. However, numeric data is typically easier to read if it's aligned on the right. One way to change the alignment is to change the HTML that's generated for a control, but that's beyond the scope of this book.

Before I go on, you should realize that you use templates to define the content of a data list control and not its appearance. For example, you use the AlternatingItem template to display different content for every other row in a data list, not to shade or highlight every other row in some way. Although you can use some of the properties of a data grid control to define styles for the templates, that's usually easier to do using the formatting features you'll learn about later.

You can use the other two item templates that are available for a data list control, SelectedItem and EditItem, to provide for the user selecting and editing items in the list. Because these functions are easier to implement using a data grid control, however, I won't show you how to use those templates here.

The templates for a data list control

Template	Description
Header	Displayed before the first item in the data source.
Footer	Displayed after the last item in the data source.
Item	Displayed for each item in the data source.
AlternatingItem	Displayed for alternating items in the data source.
SelectedItem	Displayed for the selected item in the data source.
EditItem	Displayed when an item is edited.
Separator	Displayed between items.

The item templates

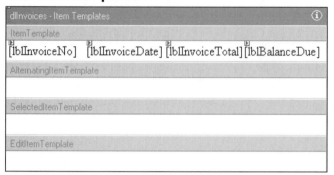

The Header and Footer templates

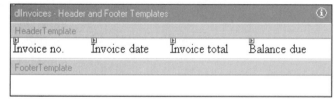

Description

- The *templates* you define for a data list control specify what content to display and what controls to use to display it. At the least, you must create an Item template that defines the items from the data source that you want to display.

- To create a template, right-click the data list control, choose Edit Template, then choose a command from the menu that appears. The control is displayed in *template-editing mode*.

- To add a control to a template, drag it from the Toolbox. Then, use the Properties window to set its properties. To bind the control to an item in the data source, use the DataBindings property. See figure 14-4 for details.

- To line up the controls in two or more templates, set each control's Width property to the same value.

- To return to normal display mode, right-click the control and choose the End Template Editing command. Before you do that, though, you should set the binding properties for the controls that are to be bound to the data source.

Figure 14-3   How to define the templates for a data list control

How to bind the controls within a template

After you add controls to a template, you can bind them to the data source using the DataBindings dialog box shown in figure 14-4. This is similar to the DataBindings dialog box you saw back in chapter 12. In this case, though, the Simple binding list includes Container and DataItem groups that contain the columns you bind the controls to.

To understand how this works, you need to realize that each control in a data list has a Container property that refers to the DataListItem object that contains it. The DataListItem object, in turn, has a DataItem property that refers to a DataItem object that represents a row in the data list. You can then use the DataItem object to bind a control to a column in the data source.

In addition to specifying the data bindings, you can use the DataBindings dialog box to specify the format of the data that's displayed. In this figure, for example, you can see the format that's selected for the InvoiceTotal column. This format will cause the invoice totals to be displayed as decimal values with two decimal places. Note that you can select a standard format from the Format list, or you can enter a custom format string into the Format box. For additional information about the format strings you can use, search online help for "format strings."

The DataBindings dialog box for a control in a template

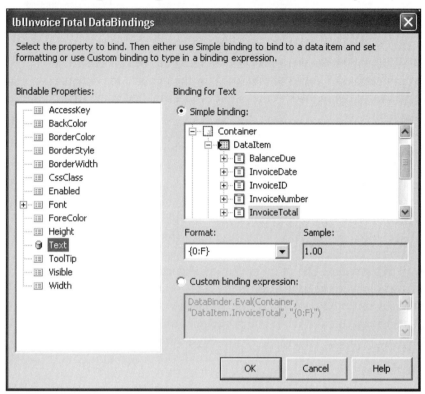

Description

- To bind a control in a template for a data list control, display the control in template-editing mode as described in figure 14-3. Then, select the control and click the ellipsis next to (DataBindings) in the Properties window to display the DataBindings dialog box.

- By default, the Text property is selected in the list of bindable properties. If that's not what you want, you can select any of the other properties in the list.

- To use simple binding to bind the control to an item in the data source, choose the Simple binding option, expand the Container and DataItem groups, and then select the data item.

- The Container object that's referred to in the binding expression is a DataListItem object, and DataItem is a property of that object that you can use to set a data item associated with the object. Because a data list control includes a DataItem object for each row in the data source, each object is bound to a different row.

- To format the value that's displayed, select a format from the Format combo box or enter any valid format string into this combo box.

- You can also use the Custom binding expression option to create your own custom binding expression. See chapter 12 for details.

Figure 14-4   How to bind the controls within a template

How to format a data list control

To format a data list control, you can use one of the techniques presented in figure 14-5. The easiest way to apply formatting is to use the Auto Format dialog box. This dialog box lets you select one of 13 predefined schemes that use different combinations of colors and borders for the items in the data list. The data list you saw in figure 14-1, for example, was formatted using the Professional 1 scheme.

Another way to format a data list control is to use the Format page of the Properties dialog box shown in this figure. This dialog box lets you set the colors, fonts, alignment, and other formatting options for the data list and each of its templates. Note that you can use this dialog box to customize an Auto Format scheme or to design your own scheme.

The Auto Format and Properties dialog boxes provide convenient ways to format a data list control. However, you can also apply formatting directly from the Properties window. To do that, you use the properties in the Appearance and Style sections of this window. The properties in the Appearance section apply to the data list as a whole, and the properties in the Style section apply to the templates that make up the data list. To set the properties for the Item template, for example, you can expand the ItemStyle group, and to set the properties for the Header template, you can expand the HeaderStyle group.

The Auto Format dialog box

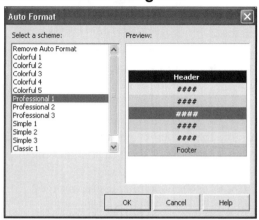

The Format page of the Properties dialog box

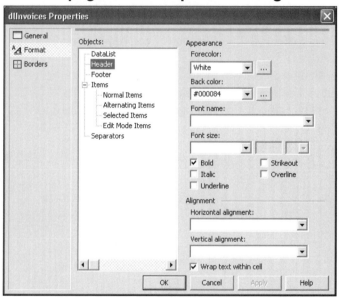

Three ways to format a data list control

- The easiest way to format the contents of a data list control is to use one of the built-in schemes. To apply a scheme, right-click the control and choose the Auto Format command. Then, choose the scheme you want to use.

- To manually set the formatting for a data list control, right-click the control and choose the Property Builder command. Then, click the Format tab and set the properties for the data list and its templates.

- You can also format a data list control and its templates from the Properties window. To display the formatting properties for a template, expand the style property for that template. To display the formatting properties for the Item template, for example, use the ItemStyle property.

Figure 14-5   How to format a data list control

The specifications for an Invoice Display program

Now that you've learned the basic techniques for creating and using a data list control, this topic and the next present a simple program that uses a data list to display invoices for a selected vendor. You saw the user interface for this program back in figure 14-1. Now, figure 14-6 presents some additional specifications for this program.

At the top of this figure, you can see the schema for the dataset used by this program. It includes two tables: a Vendors table that's used to populate the drop-down list at the top of the form, and an Invoices table that's used to populate the data list. Note that I used the XML Designer to create this schema.

This figure also shows the property settings for the Vendors drop-down list and the Invoices data list and its controls. As you can see, the drop-down list is bound to the Vendors table. Since you learned how to use the drop-down list in chapter 12, you shouldn't have any trouble understanding how it works. Notice, however, that the AutoPostBack property of this control is set to True so that the form is posted to the server whenever the user selects a vendor. In addition, the EnableViewState property is set to True so that the control will retain its values between round trips.

The data list is bound to the Invoices table. In addition, each of the controls in the Item template is bound to a column in the Invoices table through the DataItem property of the Container object. Formatting has also been applied to three of the columns.

The schema for the dsPayables dataset

◆ E	Vendors	(Vendors)
E	VendorID	int
E	VendorName	string

◆ E	Invoices	(Invoices)
E	InvoiceID	int
E	VendorID	int
E	InvoiceNumber	string
E	InvoiceDate	date
E	InvoiceTotal	decimal
E	BalanceDue	decimal

The properties for the Vendors drop-down list

Property	Description
AutoPostBack	True
DataSource	DsPayables1
DataMember	Vendors
DataTextField	VendorName
DataValueField	VendorID
EnableViewState	True

The properties for the Invoices data list

Property	Description
DataSource	DsPayables1
DataMember	Invoices

The data binding properties for the controls in the Item template

Control	Simple Binding	Format
lblInvoiceNo	Container, DataItem.InvoiceNumber	
lblInvoiceDate	Container, DataItem.InvoiceDate	{0:d}
lblInvoiceTotal	Container, DataItem.InvoiceTotal	{0:F}
lblBalanceDue	Container, DataItem.BalanceDue	{0:F}

Description

- The Invoice Display program lets the user select a vendor from a drop-down list and then displays the invoices for that vendor in a data list control.

- This program uses a custom dataset that was created using the XML Designer. It includes a Vendors table, which is used as the data source for the drop-down list, and an Invoices table, which is used as the data source for the data list.

- The data list control uses two templates: an Item template and a Header template. The Item template contains label controls that are bound to the InvoiceNumber, InvoiceDate, InvoiceTotal, and BalanceDue columns. The Header template contains labels that identify these columns. All the columns have a width of 100.

- The Professional 1 format has been applied to the data list control.

Figure 14-6   The specifications for an Invoice Display program

The code for the Invoice Display program

Figure 14-7 presents the code for the Invoice Display program. As you can see, most of this code is used to define the ADO.NET objects used by the program and to fill the dataset. Because of that, you shouldn't have any trouble understanding how it works.

The first time the program is executed, the Load procedure starts by calling the FillVendorsTable procedure to retrieve all the vendor IDs and names from the Vendors table in the Payables database. Then, it binds the drop-down list to its data source, which is the Vendors table in the DsPayables1 dataset that was created from the custom dataset class.

Next, the Load procedure calls the GetVendorInvoices procedure to get the invoices for the selected vendor. In this case, the user hasn't selected a vendor yet, so the first vendor in the list is selected by default. The VendorID value for that vendor is passed to the GetVendorInvoices procedure so it can be used to retrieve the data for that vendor. Finally, after the invoices are loaded into the Invoices table, the Load procedure binds the data list control to this table.

The last procedure in this program is executed when the user selects a vendor from the drop-down list. It simply calls the GetVendorInvoices procedure to get the invoices for the selected vendor and then rebinds the data list control to the Invoices table so the correct invoices are displayed.

An Invoice Display program that uses a data list control

```
Imports System.Data.SqlClient
Public Class WebForm1
    Inherits System.Web.UI.Page
    Protected WithEvents Label1 As System.Web.UI.WebControls.Label
    Protected WithEvents ddlVendors As System.Web.UI.WebControls.DropDownList
    Protected WithEvents dlInvoices As System.Web.UI.WebControls.DataList
    Protected WithEvents DsPayables1 As InvoiceDisplay.dsPayables

    Private Sub Page_Load(ByVal sender As System.Object, _
            ByVal e As System.EventArgs) Handles MyBase.Load
        'Put user code to initialize the page here
        If Not IsPostBack Then
            Me.FillVendorsTable()
            ddlVendors.DataBind()
            Me.GetVendorInvoices(ddlVendors.SelectedItem.Value)
            dlInvoices.DataBind()
        End If
    End Sub

    Private Sub FillVendorsTable()
        Dim conPayables As SqlConnection = GetPayablesConnection()
        Dim sVendorSelect As String _
            = "Select VendorID, VendorName " _
            & "From Vendors " _
            & "Order By VendorName"
        Dim cmdVendors As New SqlCommand(sVendorSelect, conPayables)
        Dim daVendors As New SqlDataAdapter(cmdVendors)
        daVendors.Fill(DsPayables1.Vendors)
    End Sub

    Private Function GetPayablesConnection() As SqlConnection
        Return New SqlConnection _
            (ConfigurationSettings.AppSettings("ConnectionString"))
    End Function

    Private Sub GetVendorInvoices(ByVal VendorID As Integer)
        Dim conPayables As SqlConnection = GetPayablesConnection()
        Dim sInvoiceSelect As String _
            = "Select InvoiceID, VendorID, InvoiceNumber, " _
            & "InvoiceDate, InvoiceTotal, " _
            & "InvoiceTotal - PaymentTotal - CreditTotal As BalanceDue " _
            & "From Invoices " _
            & "Where VendorID = @VendorID " _
            & "Order By InvoiceDate"
        Dim cmdInvoices As New SqlCommand(sInvoiceSelect, conPayables)
        cmdInvoices.Parameters.Add("@VendorID", VendorID)
        Dim daInvoices As New SqlDataAdapter(cmdInvoices)
        daInvoices.Fill(DsPayables1.Invoices)
    End Sub

    Private Sub ddlVendors_SelectedIndexChanged _
            (ByVal sender As System.Object, ByVal e As System.EventArgs) _
            Handles ddlVendors.SelectedIndexChanged
        Me.GetVendorInvoices(ddlVendors.SelectedItem.Value)
        dlInvoices.DataBind()
    End Sub

End Class
```

Figure 14-7   The code for the Invoice Display program

How to use the DataGrid control

Like the data list control, the data grid control lets you display information from multiple rows of a data source. As you'll learn in the next few topics, however, the data grid control also provides a convenient way for letting users select and edit data. As a result, the data grid lends itself especially well to applications that let users maintain the data in small tables.

An introduction to the data grid control

Figure 14-8 presents the web page for a program that lets the user maintain the data in a Terms table. This table is part of the Payables database you've worked with throughout this book. It consists of just three columns: TermsID, TermsDescription, and TermsDueDays. The TermsID column is an identity column that serves as the primary key for the table. This column is also included as a foreign key in both the Vendors and Invoices tables. In the Vendors table, it's used to identify the default payment terms for a vendor. In the Invoices table, it's used to identify the actual terms for an invoice.

Like the Windows data grid control, the web data grid control displays the data from a data source in a row and column format. Unlike the Windows data grid control, however, you can't just type directly into a cell in a web data grid control to change the data it contains. Instead, you have to use Edit buttons that you add to the control to make the cells in a row available for editing. Similarly, you have to add Delete buttons to a data grid control to provide for deleting rows. You'll learn how to create and work with these buttons later in this chapter.

Note that the data grid control doesn't provide for adding new rows. Because of that, you have to provide for adding rows yourself. The form shown in this figure, for example, includes a button control that the user can click to add a new, blank row to the data grid. You'll see how this works later in this chapter when I present the code for this program.

Another way to provide for adding a row to a data grid is to include a set of input controls where the user can enter the data for the new row along with an Add button. Then, when the user clicks the Add button, the program can add the new row to the data source and then rebind the data grid control so it displays that row. Although I won't present the code for this technique in this chapter, you shouldn't have any trouble figuring out how to implement it.

By the way, you can format a data grid control using the same three techniques you use to format a data list control. To format the control in this figure, for example, I applied the Simple 1 scheme using the Auto Format dialog box. Because you already know how to use these techniques, I won't present them again here.

A Terms Maintenance program that uses a data grid control

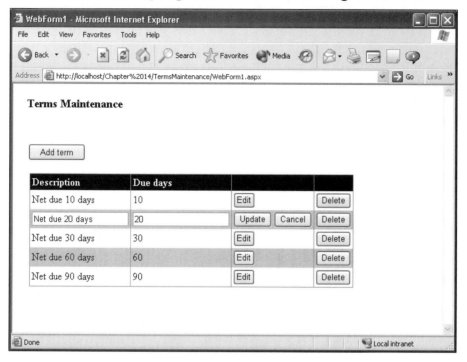

The data grid control in the Designer window

Description	Due days		
abc	0	Edit	Delete
abc	1	Edit	Delete
abc	2	Edit	Delete
abc	3	Edit	Delete
abc	4	Edit	Delete

Description

- A web data grid control can display bound data in a row and column format. In addition, it can include button columns that let you select, edit, and delete data in the data source.

- A data grid control doesn't provide for adding new rows. Because of that, you have to provide for this function using other techniques.

- You can use the AutoFormat command, the Format tab of the Properties dialog box, or the Properties window to apply formatting to a data grid control just as you can for a data list control.

Figure 14-8   An introduction to the data grid control

How to create and bind a data grid control

Figure 14-9 shows you how to create and bind a data grid control. When you first add a data grid control to a form, it consists of three columns. Then, when you bind the control to a data source, each column in the data source appears as a column in the control. In this figure, for example, you can see that the data grid includes a column for each of the columns in the Terms table.

As with other ASP.NET controls, you specify the data source for a data grid control using the DataSource and DataMember properties, and you bind the control using the DataBind method. In addition, you can use the DataKeyField property to specify a column from the data source that you want to use to create a collection of key values for the control. Then, the key value for each row in the data source is stored in the collection, and you can use the collection to get the key value for a row in the data grid.

In this figure, for example, you can see that I set the DataKeyField property to the TermsID column. That way, I can use the index of a row in the grid to get the key value for that row. This is similar to using the DataValueField property of a drop-down list control to get the value of a selected row, except it lets you get the key value of any row in the data grid. You'll see how this feature is used in the Terms Maintenance program later in this chapter.

A data grid control after it's bound to a data source

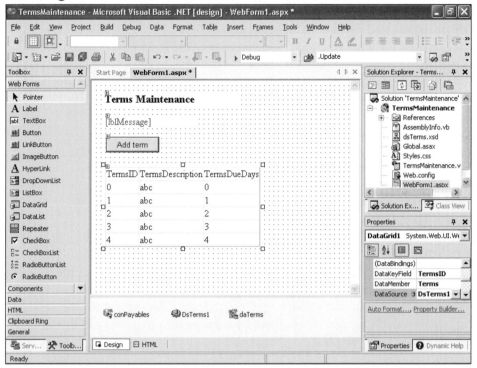

Properties and methods for binding a data grid control

Property	Description
DataSource	The name of the data source, such as a dataset.
DataMember	A member associated with the data source, such as a data table. If the data source contains only one bindable member, you don't need to set this property.
DataKeyField	The name of a column that's used to build a DataKeys collection.

Method	Description
DataBind	Binds the control to its data source. This method must be executed each time the data source changes.

Description

- To create a data grid control, drag it from the Web Forms tab of the Toolbox to the form. By default, the control will contain three columns.

- To specify the data source for a data grid control, set its DataSource and DataMember properties. Then, the data grid will reflect the columns in the data source as shown above.

- To bind the data grid to the data source at runtime, execute the DataBind method.

- The DataKeys collection is a collection of key values specified by the DataKeyField property. You can use this collection to retrieve a key value for a specific row in the data grid. To access this collection, use the DataKeys property of the data grid.

Figure 14-9   How to create and bind a data grid control

How to define the data columns

By default, a data grid control displays one column for each column in the data source. If that's not what you want, you can change the columns that are displayed using the Columns page of the Properties dialog box shown in figure 14-10. You can also use this dialog box to change the text that's displayed in the header for a column or to specify the formatting for a column.

When you first display the Columns page of this dialog box, the Create columns automatically at run time option is selected. This option causes a column to be added to the data grid for each column in the data source. Then, any additional columns you select are displayed after those columns. Since that's usually not what you want, you should deselect this option and select the columns you want to display manually.

To add a column to the data grid, you simply select it from the list of columns in the Data Fields group and click on the Add button (>). As you select columns, they'll appear in the Selected columns list. Then, you can use the buttons to the right of this list to change the order that the columns appear in the data grid or to delete a column from the data grid. You can also change the text that's displayed above a column by changing the Header text property, and you can specify the format of the data in a column by entering a format string in the Data formatting expression text box.

The Columns page of the Properties dialog box with the data fields displayed

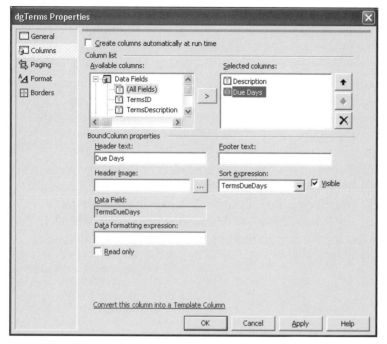

Description

- By default, a data grid control includes one column for each field in its data source. To modify or delete data columns, you use the Columns page of the Properties dialog box. To display this dialog box, right-click the data grid control and choose the Property Builder command. Then, click the Columns tab at the left side of the dialog box.

- To define the columns in a data grid, remove the check mark from the Create columns automatically at run time check box.

- To add a bound column, expand the Data Fields group in the Available columns list. Then, select a field and click on the Add button (>). You can also add all the columns by selecting the All Fields option. The fields you select appear in the Selected columns list.

- To change the order of the columns in the data grid, use the up and down arrows to the right of the Selected columns list. To delete a column from the data grid, select the column in the Selected columns list and then click on the Delete (X) button.

- To change the text that's displayed above a column, enter the text in the Header text box. The default is the name of the bound column.

- To format the value that's displayed, enter a format string in the Data formatting expression text box. For more information about format strings, search online help for "format strings."

- For more information about the other options that are available from this dialog box, click the Help button.

Figure 14-10   How to define the data columns

How to create button columns

You also use the Columns page of the Properties dialog box to create button columns. To do that, you select the type of button you want to add from the Button Column group as shown in figure 14-11. When you click the Add button, a column with the button you selected appears in the Selected columns list.

You can also set properties for each button column you add. In this figure, for example, you can see the properties for an Edit, Update, Cancel column. This is a column like the third one in the data grid shown in figure 14-8 that can display either an Edit button or Update and Cancel buttons. For this type of column, you can set the Edit text, Update text, and Cancel text properties to specify the text that's displayed on the buttons. For a Select or Delete button, a single Text property is available that lets you set the text for that button. In most cases, you'll leave these properties at their defaults. You can also change the Header text property for any button column to display text in its column header, and you can determine the appearance of the button by selecting a Button type option.

The Columns page of the Properties dialog box with the button columns displayed

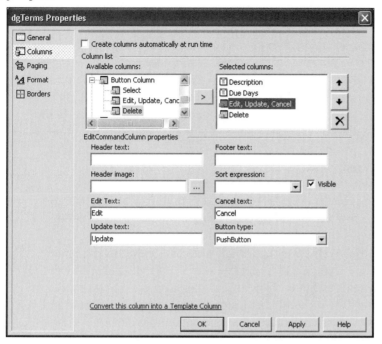

Description

- To add a button column, display the Columns tab of the Properties dialog box and expand the Button Column group. Then, select the type of button column you want to add and click the Add button (>). The columns you select are displayed in the Selected columns list.

- You can use the buttons to the right of the Selected columns list to change the order of the columns in the data grid or to delete columns from the grid.

- To display text at the top of the button column, enter the text in the Header text box.

- The Button type property determines the type of button that's displayed in the grid. The options are PushButton and LinkButton.

- The properties that are available change depending on the type of button column that's selected. For an Edit, Update, Cancel column, the Edit text, Update text, and Cancel text properties determine the text that's displayed on the corresponding button. See figure 14-12 for information on how these buttons work.

- For a Select or Delete column, the Text property determines the text that's displayed on the button.

Figure 14-11   How to create button columns

How to work with button columns

To work with the button columns in a data grid, you use the data grid events listed in figure 14-12. As you can see, the five events listed here correspond to the five possible buttons. When the user clicks on one of these buttons, the program should respond to the appropriate event. The exception is the SelectedIndexChanged event, which is fired when the user clicks on a Select button. In that case, that row is automatically selected and highlighted using the formatting specified by the SelectedItemStyle properties for the data grid. In the first data grid in this figure, for example, the third row is selected. If you want to perform any additional processing when a row is selected, you can respond to the SelectedIndexChanged event.

To illustrate how you use the events for the Edit, Update, and Cancel buttons, suppose the user clicks the Edit button in the third row of the data grid shown here. Then, the program should respond to the EditCommand event of the data grid by displaying the row in *edit mode*. In this mode, the data columns are displayed as text boxes so the user can change the data they contain, and the Edit button is replaced by Update and Cancel buttons. This is illustrated by the second data grid shown in this figure. Note that to display a row in edit mode, the program simply sets the EditItemIndex property to the appropriate row and rebinds the control. The rest is taken care of by the data grid control.

While a row is in edit mode, the user can click on either the Update or Cancel button. If he clicks on the Update button, the program should respond to the UpdateCommand event by saving the changes to the data source, exiting from edit mode, and then rebinding the control. To exit from edit mode, you set the EditItemIndex property of the data grid to -1. Similarly, if the user clicks the Cancel button, the program should respond to the CancelCommand event by exiting from edit mode and rebinding the control as shown in the coding example in this figure. However, it should not save any changes to the data source.

If the user clicks a Delete button, the DeleteCommand event is raised. The procedure that handles this event should delete the row from the data source and then call the DataBind method to update the data grid so the deleted row is no longer displayed.

Data grid events for working with buttons

Button	Event	Response
Edit	EditCommand	Place the row in edit mode and then rebind the control.
Update	UpdateCommand	Update the data source, exit from edit mode, and rebind the control.
Cancel	CancelCommand	Exit from edit mode and then rebind the control to display the original data.
Delete	DeleteCommand	Delete the row from the data source and then rebind the control.
Select	SelectedIndexChanged	No response is required.

A data grid with a row selected

Description	Due days			
Net due 10 days	10	Select	Edit	Delete
Net due 20 days	20	Select	Edit	Delete
Net due 30 days	**30**	Select	Edit	Delete
Net due 60 days	60	Select	Edit	Delete
Net due 90 days	90	Select	Edit	Delete

A data grid with a row in edit mode

Description	Due days				
Net due 10 days	10	Select	Edit		Delete
Net due 20 days	20	Select	Edit		Delete
Net due 30 days	30	Select	Update	Cancel	Delete
Net due 60 days	60	Select	Edit		Delete
Net due 90 days	90	Select	Edit		Delete

An event handler for the CancelCommand event

```
Private Sub dgTerms_CancelCommand(ByVal sender As System.Object, _
        ByVal e As System.Web.UI.WebControls.DataGridCommandEventArgs) _
        Handles dgTerms.CancelCommand
    dgTerms.EditItemIndex = -1
    dgTerms.DataBind()
End Sub
```

Description

- If the user clicks an Edit, Update, Cancel, Delete, or Select button, the data grid events listed above are fired and the program should respond to them as indicated.

- To place a row in *edit mode*, set the EditItemIndex property of the data grid to the index of that row. Then, the bound columns become text boxes so the user can enter changes, and the Edit button is replaced by Update and Cancel buttons.

- To exit from edit mode, set the EditItemIndex property to -1 to indicate that no rows are being edited.

- If the user clicks a Select button, the SelectedIndex property of the data grid is automatically set to the selected row and the row is displayed with the formatting specified by the SelectedItemStyle properties.

Figure 14-12   How to work with button columns

The specifications for a Terms Maintenance program

Figure 14-13 presents the specifications for the Terms Maintenance program you first saw in figure 14-8. This program lets the user edit or delete rows in the Terms table using a data grid control. In addition, the user can click on the Add term button to add a new row to this table.

Unlike the Invoice Display program presented earlier in this chapter, the ADO.NET components for the Terms Maintenance program were created using the Data Adapter Configuration Wizard. The Select statement for the data adapter is shown in this figure. As you can see, it simply selects the TermsID, TermsDescription, and TermsDueDays columns from all the rows in the Terms table and sorts the rows by TermsID. A dataset named dsTerms was generated from this data adapter, and a dataset component named DsTerms1 was added to the form.

This figure also shows the properties that were used to bind the data grid control to the Terms table. Notice that the DataKeyField is set to the TermsID column so that the values in this column can be used to get the key value for a row. In addition, the first two columns of the data grid are bound to the TermsDescription and TermsDueDays columns of the Terms table.

Although it isn't apparent in this figure, a label control is included on this form above the Add term button. (You can look back to figure 14-9 to see this label.) This label is used to display error messages if the program detects invalid data. Note that this label and the Add term button are placed above the data grid control so that they'll always be visible on the page. In contrast, if these controls were placed below the data grid, the user may not be able to see them depending on the size of the browser window and the number of rows in the data grid.

The form for the Terms Maintenance program

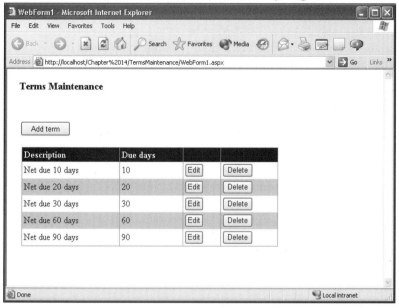

The Select statement for the data adapter

```
Select TermsID, TermsDescription, TermsDueDays
From Terms Order By TermsID
```

The data binding properties for the Terms data grid

Property	Value
DataSource	DsTerms1
DataMember	Terms
DataKeyField	TermsID

Description

- The Terms Maintenance program lets the user modify or delete rows in the Terms table of the Payables database using a data grid control.

- To add a new row to the Terms table, the user clicks the Add term button. Then, a new row is added at the bottom of the grid and that row is placed in edit mode.

- This form uses ADO.NET components created by the Data Adapter Configuration Wizard to retrieve the Terms table from the Payables database and to update the Terms table when the user enters changes.

- The data grid control is bound to the Terms table of the dataset. Then, the first two columns are bound to the TermsDescription and TermsDueDays columns of that table.

- The Simple 1 format has been applied to the data grid control.

- A label control that will be used to display error messages is included above the Add term button.

Figure 14-13   The specifications for a Terms Maintenance program

The code for the Terms Maintenance program

Figure 14-14 presents the code for the Terms Maintenance program. As you'll see, most of this code responds to the events that occur on the buttons of the data grid control.

The Load procedure for the page is responsible for managing the dataset used by this program. When this procedure is run for the first time, it fills the Terms table in the dataset and then binds the data grid control to this table. Then, it places the dataset in the session state object so it can be retrieved later. When the Load procedure is run after the first time, it simply retrieves the dataset from the session state object.

If the user clicks on the Add term button, the Click event procedure for this button starts by adding a blank row to the Terms table. Then, it sets the EditItemIndex property of the data grid to the index of the newly created row, which is equal to the Count property of the Rows collection of the Terms table minus 1. That places the new row in edit mode. Finally, it binds the data grid and sets a session state item named AddMode to True to indicate that the user is adding a row.

If the user clicks on an Edit button, the procedure for the EditCommand event is executed. This procedure starts by checking the AddMode session state item to see if a new row is being added. If so, that row must be deleted and the AddMode session state item must be changed to False before another row can be edited. Another way to handle this would be to ask the user if the new row should be saved before the next row is edited. In either case, the EditItemIndex of the data grid is set to the index of the row that contains the Edit button that was clicked, so that row is placed in edit mode. To get the index of that row, the procedure uses the Item property of the e argument that's passed to it to get the Item object. Then, the ItemIndex property of the Item object gets the index of that object. Finally, the Edit procedure calls the DataBind method to rebind the data grid.

A Terms Maintenance program that uses a data grid control   Page 1

```
Imports System.Data.SqlClient
Public Class WebForm1
    Inherits System.Web.UI.Page
    Protected WithEvents daTerms As System.Data.SqlClient.SqlDataAdapter
    Protected WithEvents conPayables As System.Data.SqlClient.SqlConnection
    Protected WithEvents DsTerms1 As TermsMaintenance.DsTerms
    Protected WithEvents SqlSelectCommand1 As System.Data.SqlClient.SqlCommand
    Protected WithEvents SqlInsertCommand1 As System.Data.SqlClient.SqlCommand
    Protected WithEvents SqlUpdateCommand1 As System.Data.SqlClient.SqlCommand
    Protected WithEvents SqlDeleteCommand1 As System.Data.SqlClient.SqlCommand
    Protected WithEvents lblMessage As System.Web.UI.WebControls.Label
    Protected WithEvents btnAdd As System.Web.UI.WebControls.Button
    Protected WithEvents dgTerms As System.Web.UI.WebControls.DataGrid

    Private Sub Page_Load(ByVal sender As System.Object, _
            ByVal e As System.EventArgs) Handles MyBase.Load
        'Put user code to initialize the page here
        If Not IsPostBack Then
            daTerms.Fill(DsTerms1.Terms)
            dgTerms.DataBind()
            Session("DsPayables1") = DsTerms1
        Else
            DsTerms1 = Session("DsPayables1")
        End If
    End Sub

    Private Sub btnAdd_Click(ByVal sender As System.Object, _
            ByVal e As System.EventArgs) Handles btnAdd.Click
        DsTerms1.Terms.AddTermsRow("", 0)
        dgTerms.EditItemIndex = DsTerms1.Terms.Rows.Count - 1
        dgTerms.DataBind()
        Session("AddMode") = True
    End Sub

    Private Sub dgTerms_EditCommand(ByVal sender As System.Object, _
            ByVal e As System.Web.UI.WebControls.DataGridCommandEventArgs) _
            Handles dgTerms.EditCommand
        If Session("AddMode") = True Then
            DsTerms1.Terms.Rows(DsTerms1.Terms.Count - 1).Delete()
            Session("AddMode") = False
        End If
        dgTerms.EditItemIndex = e.Item.ItemIndex
        dgTerms.DataBind()
    End Sub
```

Figure 14-14   The code for the Terms Maintenance program (part 1 of 3)

The most complicated procedure in this application is the one that's executed when the user clicks the Update button. This procedure starts by declaring three variables. The first one will hold a row in the Terms table, and the other two will hold the data for the TermsDescription and TermsDueDays columns of that row. Then, the next two statements retrieve the data for those columns from the two text box controls in the data grid. To do that, they use the Item property of the e argument that's passed to the procedure to refer to the row in the data grid that's being updated. Then, they use the Cells property to refer to the collection of cells within the row. Because the collection of cells is zero-based, the first cell has an index value of zero, the second cell has an index value of 1, and so on.

Although it's not discussed in this chapter, each cell can have one or more controls. To refer to a specific control within a cell, you have to use the Controls collection. Like the Cells collection, the Controls collection is zero-based. So to refer to the first control in the first cell, you use an expression like this:

```
e.Item.Cells(0).Controls(0)
```

You can see this expression in the first of the two assignment statements in this procedure. Finally, the procedure uses the CType function to cast the resulting control to a text box so that its Text property can be assigned to the appropriate variable.

After the values have been extracted from the text boxes, the procedure calls the ValidData procedure to validate the input data. If invalid data is detected, the Text property of the message label on the page is set to an error message so that message will be displayed when the page is sent back to the browser. Otherwise, the procedure uses the DataKeys property of the data grid to get the key of the row that's being edited. This works because the data grid's DataKeyField property specifies TermsID, which is the primary key of the Terms table. Then, the FindByTermsID method is used to retrieve the row from the table, the new values are applied to that row, and the UpdateDatabase procedure is called to update the database with the changes. The rest of the procedure sets the EditItemIndex property to -1 to exit from edit mode, rebinds the data grid, saves the updated dataset in the session state object, and changes the AddMode session state item to False in case a row was being added to the dataset.

The UpdateDatabase procedure executes an Update method to update the Terms table defined by the Terms data adapter. This statement is coded within a Try...Catch statement so that any exceptions that occur during the update can be handled by the procedure. In this case, the first exception that's handled is a concurrency exception. If a concurrency exception occurs, the procedure assigns an error message to the message label, clears and reloads the Terms table so that it contains the updated data, and rebinds the data grid.

The second exception this procedure handles is SQL Server exception number 547. This exception occurs if you try to delete a row from the Terms table when related rows exist in the Vendors or Invoices table and the relationships between these tables are enforced by foreign key constraints that don't allow cascading deletes. If this exception occurs, the procedure displays an appropriate error message, rejects the changes to the dataset, and rebinds the data grid. If some other SQL Server exception occurs, the Throw statement causes the error to be treated as unhandled.

A Terms Maintenance program that uses a data grid control Page 2

```
Private Sub dgTerms_UpdateCommand(ByVal source As System.Object, _
        ByVal e As System.Web.UI.WebControls.DataGridCommandEventArgs) _
        Handles dgTerms.UpdateCommand
    Dim TermsRow As DsTerms.TermsRow
    Dim sTermsDescription As String
    Dim sTermsDueDays As String
    sTermsDescription = CType(e.Item.Cells(0).Controls(0), TextBox).Text
    sTermsDueDays = CType(e.Item.Cells(1).Controls(0), TextBox).Text
    If ValidData(sTermsDescription, sTermsDueDays) Then
        Dim iTermsID As Integer = dgTerms.DataKeys(e.Item.ItemIndex)
        TermsRow = DsTerms1.Terms.FindByTermsID(iTermsID)
        TermsRow.TermsDescription = sTermsDescription
        TermsRow.TermsDueDays = sTermsDueDays
        Me.UpdateDatabase()
        dgTerms.EditItemIndex = -1
        dgTerms.DataBind()
        Session("DsPayables1") = DsTerms1
        Session("AddMode") = False
    End If
End Sub

Private Function ValidData(ByVal Description As String, _
        ByVal DueDays As String) As Boolean
    ValidData = True
    If Description = "" Then
        ValidData = False
        lblMessage.Text = "Description is required."
    ElseIf DueDays = "" Then
        ValidData = False
        lblMessage.Text = "Due days is required."
    ElseIf IsNumeric(DueDays) = False Then
        ValidData = False
        lblMessage.Text = "Due days must be numeric."
    End If
End Function

Public Sub UpdateDatabase()
    Try
        daTerms.Update(DsTerms1)
    Catch e As DBConcurrencyException
        lblMessage.Text = "Another user has updated or deleted that " _
            & "row. Please try again."
        DsTerms1.Terms.Clear()
        daTerms.Fill(DsTerms1.Terms)
        dgTerms.DataBind()
    Catch e As SqlException
        If e.Number = 547 Then
            lblMessage.Text = "Could not delete term because it is " _
                & "used by active vendors or invoices."
            DsTerms1.RejectChanges()
            dgTerms.DataBind()
        Else
            Throw e
        End If
    End Try
End Sub
```

Figure 14-14   The code for the Terms Maintenance program (part 2 of 3)

If the user clicks on the Cancel button while a row is being added or changed, the CancelCommand procedure is executed. This procedure starts by checking the AddMode session state item to determine if a row was being added. If so, the procedure deletes the row and sets the AddMode item to False. Then, it sets the EditItemIndex property of the data grid to -1 to exit from edit mode, and it rebinds the data grid.

The DeleteCommand procedure is executed if the user clicks on the Delete button for a row. This procedure also checks the AddMode session state item to determine if a row is being added. If so, it must then determine if the Delete button that was clicked is in the new row or another row. If it's not in the new row, the procedure deletes the new row. In either case, it sets the AddMode session state item to False.

Next, the DeleteCommand procedure uses the DataKeys property to get the key for the row to be deleted. Then, it uses the FindByTermsID method to retrieve that row from the Terms table. Finally, it calls the UpdateDatabase procedure to update the database, it rebinds the data grid, and it saves the updated dataset in the session state object.

A Terms Maintenance program that uses a data grid control   Page 3

```
Private Sub dgTerms_CancelCommand(ByVal source As System.Object, _
        ByVal e As System.Web.UI.WebControls.DataGridCommandEventArgs) _
        Handles dgTerms.CancelCommand
    If Session("AddMode") = True Then
        DsTerms1.Terms.Rows(DsTerms1.Terms.Count - 1).Delete()
        Session("AddMode") = False
    End If
    dgTerms.EditItemIndex = -1
    dgTerms.DataBind()
End Sub

Private Sub dgTerms_DeleteCommand(ByVal source As System.Object, _
        ByVal e As System.Web.UI.WebControls.DataGridCommandEventArgs) _
        Handles dgTerms.DeleteCommand
    If Session("AddMode") Then
        If e.Item.ItemIndex <> DsTerms1.Terms.Count - 1 Then
            DsTerms1.Terms.Rows(DsTerms1.Terms.Count - 1).Delete()
        End If
        Session("AddMode") = False
    End If
    Dim TermsID As Integer
    TermsID = dgTerms.DataKeys(e.Item.ItemIndex)
    DsTerms1.Terms.FindByTermsID(TermsID).Delete()
    Me.UpdateDatabase()
    dgTerms.DataBind()
    Session("DsPayables1") = DsTerms1
End Sub

End Class
```

Figure 14-14   The code for the Terms maintenance program (part 3 of 3)

Perspective

With the techniques you've learned in this chapter, you can create relatively sophisticated ASP.NET database applications. However, you should realize that you can do a lot more with the data list and data grid controls than what's presented in this chapter. For example, by editing the HTML for a data grid control directly, you can create command buttons in addition to the Select, Edit, Update, and Cancel buttons that are available from the Properties dialog box. You can also use command buttons in a data list control to include additional functionality. But even without these skills, the database programming techniques you've learned in this chapter, combined with what you learned in chapters 12 and 13, should get you well on your way to developing professional ASP.NET database applications.

Terms

template
template-editing mode
edit mode

Section 5

Related skills

In the last three chapters of this book, you'll learn some additional skills related to database programming with ADO.NET. First, in chapter 15, you'll learn how to use ADO.NET to work with XML files. In case you're not familiar with XML, this chapter starts by introducing you to its basic structure. Then, it presents some common techniques for transferring XML data to and from a dataset.

In chapter 16, you'll learn how to use the Crystal Reports program that's included with Visual Studio .NET. This program can help you create professional-looking reports quickly and easily. Because this program doesn't come with the Standard Edition of Visual Basic .NET, however, you'll need to have Visual Studio .NET to use it.

In chapter 17, you'll learn how to use the Server Explorer to work with the objects in a database. That includes using the designers that come with Visual Studio to define and work with tables, views, and stored procedures. When you finish this chapter, you'll have all the skills you need to develop database programs efficiently and effectively.

15

How to work with XML data

XML is one of the most talked about features of the .NET Framework. In fact, much of ADO.NET is based on XML. Fortunately, most of ADO.NET's reliance on XML is internal and doesn't affect you as a programmer. However, XML does occasionally become apparent, particularly when you work with datasets. In chapter 9, for example, you learned how to use the XML Designer to generate the XML schema for a dataset. The truth is that XML lies just beneath the surface whenever you work with ADO.NET datasets.

In this chapter, you'll learn the basics of how XML represents data and dataset schemas. Then, you'll learn how to use the methods of the DataSet class that are designed to work with XML data. Because this isn't an XML book, however, you won't learn everything you can do with XML in an ADO.NET application. But you will learn enough to have a good basis for learning more about XML if you ever need to do that.

An introduction to XML

The topics that follow introduce you to the basics of XML. Here, you'll learn what XML is, how it's used, and the rules you must follow to create a simple XML file. You'll also learn about the language that ADO.NET uses to create an XML schema. And you'll learn about four ways that you can use XML with ADO.NET.

What XML is and how it is used

XML, the *Extensible Markup Language*, provides a standardized way of structuring text information by using *tags* that identify each data element. In some ways, XML is similar to HTML, the markup language that's used to format documents on the World Wide Web. So if you're familiar with HTML, you'll have no trouble learning how to create *XML documents*.

Figure 15-1 shows a simple XML document that contains information about two vendors. In the next two figures, you'll learn how the tags in this XML document work. But even without knowing those details, you can pick out the data for these vendors in the XML document.

By the way, this XML document and the documents you'll see in the next two figures are typical of documents that you would create from scratch. The XML that ADO.NET generates for the data in a dataset, however, is slightly different. You'll see an example of XML like that later in this chapter. You'll also learn how you can control the XML ADO.NET generates.

XML was designed as a way to represent information so it can be exchanged between dissimilar systems or applications. The .NET Framework uses XML internally for many different purposes. In particular, ADO.NET relies extensively on XML. If you understand how data and dataset schemas are represented in XML, then, you'll have a better understanding of how XML is used behind the scenes.

The data for two vendors

Column	First vendor	Second vendor
ID	1	9
Name	U.S. Postal Service	Pacific Gas and Electric
Address1	Attn: Supt. Window Services	Box 52001
Address2	PO Box 7005	
City	Madison	San Francisco
State	WI	CA
ZipCode	53707	94152

The same data stored in an XML document

```
<?xml version="1.0" encoding="utf-8" ?>
<!--Vendor information--><Vendors>
  <Vendor ID=1>
    <Name>U.S. Postal Service</Name>
    <Address1>Attn: Supt. Window Services</Address1>
    <Address2>PO Box 7005</Address2>
    <City>Madison</City>
    <State>WI</State>
    <ZipCode>53707</ZipCode>
  </Vendor>
  <Vendor ID=9>
    <Name>Pacific Gas and Electric</Name>
    <Address1>Box 52001</Address1>
    <City>San Francisco</City>
    <State>CA</State>
    <ZipCode>94152</ZipCode>
  </Vendor>
</Vendors>
```

Description

- *XML*, the *Extensible Markup Language*, provides a method of structuring information in a text file using special *tags*. A file that contains XML is known as an *XML document*.

- The XML document in this figure contains information for two vendors. Each vendor has an *attribute* called ID and *elements* that provide name and address information. You'll learn more about attributes and elements in the next two figures.

- XML's main use is for exchanging information between different systems, especially via the Internet.

- Many .NET classes, particularly the ADO.NET and web classes, use XML internally to store or exchange information.

- The ADO.NET DataSet class includes methods that let you save a dataset in XML format and load a dataset from an XML file. In addition, the .NET Framework provides many other classes that are designed specifically for working with XML data.

Figure 15-1   What XML is and how it is used

XML tags, declarations, and comments

Figure 15-2 shows how XML uses tags to structure the data in an XML document. As you can see, each XML tag begins with the character < and ends with the character >, so the first line in the XML document in this figure contains a complete XML tag. Similarly, the next three lines also contain complete tags. In contrast, the fifth line contains two tags, <Name> and </Name>, with a text value in between. You'll see how this works in a moment.

The first tag in any XML document is an *XML declaration.* This declaration identifies the document as an XML document and indicates which XML version the document conforms to. In this example, the document conforms to XML version 1.0. In addition, the declaration usually identifies the character set that's being used for the document. In this example, the character set is UTF-8, the most common one used for XML documents in English-speaking countries.

An XML document can also contain *comments*. These are tags that begin with <!-- and end with -->. Between the tags, you can type anything you want. For instance, the second line in this figure is a comment that indicates what type of information is contained in the XML document. It's often a good idea to include similar comments in your own XML documents.

XML elements

Elements are the building blocks of XML. Each element in an XML document represents a single data item and is identified by two tags: a *start tag* and an *end tag*. The start tag marks the beginning of the element and provides the element's name. The end tag marks the end of the element and repeats the name, prefixed by a slash. For example, <Name> is the start tag for an element named Name, and </Name> is the corresponding end tag.

It's important to realize that XML doesn't provide a predefined set of element names the way HTML does. Instead, the element names are created so that they describe the contents of each element. Note that XML names are case-sensitive, so <Name> and <name> are not the same.

A complete element consists of the element's start tag, its end tag, and the *content* between the tags. For example, <City>Madison</City> indicates that the content of the City element is *Madison.* And <Address1>Attn: Supt. Window Services</Address1> indicates that the content of the Address1 element is *Attn: Supt. Window Services.*

Besides content, elements can contain other elements, known as *child elements*. This lets you add structure to a *parent element.* For example, a parent Vendor element can have child elements that provide details about each vendor, such as the vendor's name and address. In this figure, for example, you can see that the start tag, end tag, and values for the Name, Address1, Address2, City, State, and ZipCode elements are contained between the start and end tags for the Vendor element. As a result, these elements are children of the Vendor element, and the Vendor element is the parent of each of these elements.

A Vendor element and its child elements

```
<?xml version="1.0"? encoding="utf-8" ?>
<!--Vendor information-->
<Vendors>
   <Vendor ID=1>
      <Name>U.S. Postal Service</Name>
      <Address1>Attn: Supt. Window Services</Address1>
      <Address2>PO Box 7005</Address2>
      <City>Madison</City>
      <State>WI</State>
      <ZipCode>53707</ZipCode>
   </Vendor>
</Vendors>
```

Vendor element

Name element

City element

A Vendor element with an additional level of child elements

```
<?xml version="1.0"? encoding="utf-8" ?>
<!--Vendor information-->
<Vendors>
   <Vendor ID=1>
      <Name>U.S. Postal Service</Name>
      <StreetAddress>
         <Address1>Attn: Supt. Window Services</Address1>
         <Address2>PO Box 7005</Address2>
         <City>Madison</City>
         <State>WI</State>
         <ZipCode>53707</ZipCode>
      </StreetAddress>
   </Vendor>
</Vendors>
```

XML tags, declarations, and comments

- Each XML tag begins with < and ends with >.

- The first line in an XML document is an *XML declaration* that indicates which version of the XML standard is being used for the document. In addition, the declaration usually identifies the standard character set that's being used (UTF-8 in this example).

- An XML document can include comments that clarify the information it contains. *XML comments* begin with the sequence <!-- and end with -->.

Elements

- An *element* is a unit of XML data that begins with a *start tag* and ends with an *end tag*. The start tag provides the name of the element and contains any attributes assigned to the element (see figure 15-3 for details on attributes). The end tag repeats the name, prefixed with a slash (/). You can use any name you want for an XML element.

- The *content* for an element is coded within the element's start and end tags.

- Elements can contain other elements. An element that's contained within another element is a *child element*. An element that contains other child elements is a *parent element*.

- A child element can itself have child elements. In that case, the element is both a child and a parent.

- The highest-level parent element in an XML document is known as the *root element*. An XML document can have only one root element.

Figure 15-2   XML tags, declarations, comments, and elements

The XML in figure 15-2 also shows that a child element can itself be a parent element to additional child elements. For example, the second XML document in this figure shows how an element named StreetAddress can be used to contain the address elements. As a result, the StreetAddress element is a child of the Vendor element and the parent of the Address1, Address2, City, State, and ZipCode elements.

Although figure 15-2 doesn't show it, you should also realize that an element can contain more than one occurrence of a child element. The Vendors element in the XML document you saw in figure 15-1, for example, contained two occurrences of the Vendor element.

The highest-level parent element in an XML document is known as the *root element*, and an XML document can have only one root element. In the examples in figures 15-1 and 15-2, the root element is Vendors. For XML documents that contain repeating information, it's common to use a plural name for the root element to indicate that it contains multiple child elements.

XML attributes

As shown in figure 15-3, *attributes* are a concise way to provide data for XML elements. In the Vendors XML document, for example, each Vendor element has an ID attribute that provides an identifying number for the vendor. Thus, <Vendor ID=1> contains an attribute named ID whose value is 1.

Here again, XML doesn't provide a set of predefined attributes. Instead, attributes are created as they're needed using names that describe the content of the attributes. If an element has more than one attribute, the attributes can be listed in any order, but they must be separated from each other by one or more spaces. In addition, each attribute can appear only once within an element.

In many cases, either elements or attributes can be used to represent a data item. In the Vendors document, for example, I could have used a child element named ID rather than an attribute to represent each vendor's ID. Likewise, I could have used an attribute named Name rather than a child element for the vendor's name.

Because attributes are more concise than child elements, designers are often tempted to use attributes rather than child elements. However, an element with more than a few attributes soon becomes unwieldy. As a result, most designers limit their use of attributes to certain types of information, such as identifiers like vendor ID numbers, product codes, and so on.

An XML document

```
<?xml version="1.0"? encoding="utf-8" ?>
<!--Vendor information-->
<Vendors>
   <Vendor ID=1>──────────────────────────────────── ID attribute
     <Name>U.S. Postal Service</Name>
     <Address1>Attn: Supt. Window Services</Address1>
     <Address2>PO Box 7005</Address2>
     <City>Madison</City>
     <State>WI</State>
     <ZipCode>53707</ZipCode>
   </Vendor>
</Vendors>
```

Description

- A start tag for an element can include one or more *attributes*. An attribute consists of an attribute name, an equal sign, and a literal value.

- If an element has more than one attribute, the order in which the attributes appear doesn't matter, but the attributes must be separated by one or more spaces.

Differences between attributes and child elements

- The data for an element can be represented using child elements, attributes, or a combination of elements and attributes. The choice of whether to implement a data item as an attribute or as a separate child element is often a matter of preference.

- Two advantages of attributes are that they can appear in any order and they are more concise because they don't require end tags.

- Two advantages of child elements are that they are easier for people to read and they are more convenient for long string values.

Figure 15-3   XML attributes

An introduction to the XML Schema Definition language

I've been using the term "schema" in this book since chapter 3. Now, I want you to realize that a schema actually defines the structure that an XML document must adhere to for the document to be considered valid. To specify the schema for an XML document, you use a *schema language*. Two schema languages are supported by the XML standards: *Document Type Definition*, or *DTD*, and *XML Schema Definition*. XML Schema Definition is also known as *XSD*, but is usually referred to as *XML Schema*. ADO.NET is designed to work with XML Schema, and figure 15-4 presents an introduction to it.

The schema presented in this figure defines a document that contains information about vendors. This schema is for a dataset named DsPayables that contains the Vendors table that you've worked with throughout this book. It indicates that a document based on this schema can contain one or more Vendors elements, each of which must contain a specific sequence of elements that specify the name and address of the vendor.

Although you can create an XML schema manually by typing the correct XSD language elements, it's easier to let Visual Studio generate the schema for you. You learned two ways to do that in this book. In chapter 9, you learned how to use the XML Designer to generate the schema as you drag elements from the Toolbox. And in chapter 3, you learned how to generate the schema from a data adapter that you create using the Data Adapter Configuration Wizard. That's how I created the schema shown in this figure.

When you generate a schema from a data adapter or use the XML Designer to create a schema, Visual Studio creates a typed dataset from the schema. However, the schema for an untyped dataset can also be represented using XSD. To generate an XML schema for an untyped dataset or to read an XML schema into an untyped dataset, you can use the methods of the DataSet class that you'll learn about later in this chapter.

An XML Schema Definition

```
<?xml version="1.0" encoding="utf-8" ?>
<xs:schema id="DsPayables" targetNamespace="http://tempuri.org/DsPayables.xsd"
elementFormDefault="qualified" attributeFormDefault="qualified"
xmlns="http://tempuri.org/DsPayables.xsd"
xmlns:mstns="http://tempuri.org/DsPayables.xsd"
xmlns:xs="http://www.w3.org/2001/XMLSchema" xmlns:msdata="urn:schemas-microsoft-
com:xml-msdata">
   <xs:element name="DsPayables" msdata:IsDataSet="true">
     <xs:complexType>
       <xs:choice maxOccurs="unbounded">
         <xs:element name="Vendors">
           <xs:complexType>
             <xs:sequence>
               <xs:element name="VendorID" type="xs:int" minOccurs="1" />
               <xs:element name="VendorName" type="xs:string" minOccurs="0" />
               <xs:element name="VendorAddress1" type="xs:string" minOccurs="0" />
               <xs:element name="VendorAddress2" type="xs:string" minOccurs="0" />
               <xs:element name="VendorCity" type="xs:string" minOccurs="0" />
               <xs:element name="VendorState" type="xs:string" minOccurs="0" />
               <xs:element name="VendorZipCode" type="xs:string" minOccurs="0" />
             </xs:sequence>
           </xs:complexType>
         </xs:element>
       </xs:choice>
     </xs:complexType>
     <xs:key name="DsPayablesKey1" msdata:PrimaryKey="true">
       <xs:selector xpath=".//mstns:Vendors" />
       <xs:field xpath="mstns:VendorID" />
     </xs:key>
   </xs:element>
</xs:schema>
```

XML Schema Definition language elements

Element	Description
Schema	The parent element for the schema.
Element	Declares elements that can occur in the document.
Choice	Declares a list of elements, only one of which can occur in the document.
ComplexType	Declares a type that is made up of one or more simple elements.
Sequence	Declares a sequence of items that must occur in the specified order.
Key	Declares a key field.

Description

- ADO.NET is designed to work with the *XML Schema Definition* (*XSD*) language. This language uses the elements listed above to define the structure of an XML document.
- To create the schema for a dataset, you can generate a typed dataset from a data adapter as you learned in chapter 3, or you can use the XML Schema Designer to create a custom typed dataset as you learned in chapter 9. You can also type the XSD language elements directly into a text editor.

Figure 15-4   An introduction to the XML Schema Definition language

Four ways to use XML with ADO.NET

Figure 15-5 summarizes four ways you can use ADO.NET to work with XML data. First, you can use properties and methods of the ADO.NET classes to read XML data or schema information into a dataset or to write XML data or schema information to an XML file. You'll learn how to use these properties and methods in the remaining topics of this chapter.

One of the standard ways of processing an XML document in .NET is with the XmlDocument class. This class represents an XML document in memory and provides methods that let you navigate through the document. Beyond that, though, ADO.NET provides an XmlDataDocument class that combines an XML document with a dataset. This class is designed to let you process the data in a dataset using both ADO.NET and XML programming techniques.

To do that, an *XML data document* inherits the XmlDocument class. That means that it can use any of the properties and methods defined by that class. In addition, an XML data document has a DataSet property that exposes a standard ADO.NET dataset that's linked to the underlying XML document. The XML data document automatically synchronizes any changes made to the XML document or the dataset, so you can use either one to access the data. For example, you can use a data adapter to fill the dataset associated with the XML data document with data from a database. Then, you can process the data in the dataset as an XML document.

Another way to work with XML data in an ADO.NET application is to retrieve the data using SQL Server 2000's Select For XML statement. The For XML clause tells SQL Server to return the results of the Select statement in XML format. To execute a Select For XML statement, you use the ExecuteXmlReader method of an SqlCommand object. This method returns an XmlReader object that you can use to access the data.

Unfortunately, the SqlCommand object doesn't fully support all of the XML features provided by SQL Server 2000. To use all of these features, you have to use the SqlXml data provider. Although this data provider doesn't currently come with ADO.NET, you can download it for free from Microsoft's web site. Then, you can use the command, parameter, and data adapter classes it provides to work directly with XML data from SQL Server 2000.

XML features of the ADO.NET classes

- The DataSet class contains methods that let you write the contents of a dataset to an XML file, get XML data from a dataset, and load a dataset from an XML file.

- The DataSet class also contains methods that let you read an XML schema into a dataset, get the XML schema from a dataset, and write the XML schema for a dataset to an XML file.

- The DataSet, DataTable, DataColumn, and DataRelation classes contain properties that affect the XML output that's generated for a dataset.

- You can use the properties and methods for working with XML with both typed and untyped datasets.

The XmlDataDocument class

- An *XML data document* is a combination of a dataset and an XML document.

- You can fill an XML data document from a database, process it as if it were an XML document, and then update the database from the data document.

- You can also fill an XML data document from an XML file, process it as if it were a dataset, and then write the contents to an XML file.

- For more information on using XML data documents, search the online help for *XmlDataDocument*.

The Select For XML statement

- SQL Server 2000 lets you use the For XML clause on a Select statement to retrieve data in XML format. For example:

  SELECT VendorID, VendorName FROM Vendors FOR XML AUTO, ELEMENTS

  returns XML that contains a parent element for each vendor in the Vendors table and child elements for the VendorID and VendorName columns.

- To issue a Select For XML statement, you use the ExecuteXmlReader method of a SqlCommand object. This method returns an XmlReader object that you can use to process the XML.

- For more information on retrieving data in XML format, search the online help for *ExecuteXmlReader*.

The SqlXml data provider

- The SqlXml data provider provides better support for retrieving XML data from a SQL Server 2000 database than the standard SQL Server data provider.

- The SqlXml data provider includes three classes. The SqlXmlCommand class represents a SQL XML command. The SqlXmlParameter class represents a parameter. And the SqlXmlAdapter class lets you fill a dataset or update a database using a SqlXmlCommand object.

- The SqlXml data provider isn't included with the initial release of the .NET Framework. However, you can download it for free from Microsoft's web site. To do that, go to www.microsoft.com and search for *SqlXML*.

Figure 15-5   Four ways to use XML with ADO.NET

How to transfer XML data to and from a dataset

ADO.NET provides several properties and methods that let you work with XML data using a dataset. You'll learn how to use these properties and methods in the remaining topics of this chapter.

How to use the XML methods of the DataSet class

Figure 15-6 presents the methods of the DataSet class that you can use to work with XML data. To read data from an XML file into a dataset, for example, you can use the ReadXml method. Then, you can process the data using any of the dataset programming techniques you've learned in this book. That includes binding form controls to the data, filtering the data using views, and adding, updating, and deleting data rows. When you're done, you can use the WriteXml method to write the data back out to an XML file.

The ReadXml and WriteXml methods are often used to convert data that's retrieved from a database to XML or vice versa. To illustrate, take a look at the first code example in this figure. The first statement in this example uses the Fill method of a data adapter to load data into a dataset. Then, the second statement uses the WriteXml method to write the data back out in XML format.

Note that if you use the WriteXml method as shown in this example, the resulting XML file won't include schema information. If you want to include an XML Schema Definition in the XML file, you have to include the XmlWriteMode.WriteSchema argument on the WriteXml method as shown in the second example. When you use the WriteXml method in this way, the XML file includes both the schema and the data. In that case, the schema appears as a separate element immediately after the root element, but before any data elements. If you want the file to include just the schema, you use the WriteXmlSchema method instead.

The third example shows how to read the contents of an XML file into a dataset. Here, a file named Payables.xml is read into a dataset named DsPayables1. Note that you can use this method regardless of whether the XML file includes schema information. If it does include schema information, the ReadXml method uses this information to create the schema for the dataset. Otherwise, the ReadXml method creates the schema based on the XML data in the file.

You can also use the GetXml method to retrieve XML data from a dataset as a string value. And you can use the GetXmlSchema method to retrieve the XML schema from a dataset as a string value. These methods are useful if you want to view the XML while you're testing an application. Otherwise, you're more likely to use the Write methods.

Methods of the DataSet class for working with XML data

Method	Description
GetXml	Gets a string that contains the XML data for a dataset.
GetXmlSchema	Gets a string that contains the XML schema for a dataset.
ReadXml	Reads XML data from a file or stream into a dataset. The schema is inferred from the data if it isn't included in the file or stream.
ReadXmlSchema	Reads an XML schema from a file or stream into a dataset.
WriteXml	Writes XML data from a dataset to a stream or file.
WriteXmlSchema	Writes an XML schema from a dataset to a stream or file.

XmlWriteMode enumeration members

Member	Description
WriteSchema	Includes the XML schema in the output.
IgnoreSchema	Doesn't include the XML schema in the output. This is the default.
DiffGram	Includes the original and current versions of the rows in the output.

Code that fills a dataset and then writes the data to an XML file

```
daVendors.Fill(DsPayables1)
DsPayables1.WriteXml("C:\Payables.xml")
```

Code that writes XML data and schema information to a file

```
DsPayables1.WriteXml("C:\Payables.xml", XmlWriteMode.WriteSchema)
```

Code that loads a dataset from an XML file

```
DsPayables1.ReadXml("C:\Payables.xml")
```

Description

- The DataSet class includes methods that let you work with XML data. You can use these methods to save the contents of a dataset in XML format or to load a dataset from an XML file rather than from a database.

- The GetXml and GetXmlSchema methods are useful if you want to view the XML for a dataset. If you want to save the XML for a dataset to a file, use the WriteXml and WriteXmlSchema methods.

- The WriteXml, WriteXmlSchema, ReadXml, and ReadXmlSchema methods are over-loaded to provide different ways of specifying the file to be written or read. You can specify the file name and path as a string, or you can specify a Stream, a TextWriter, or an XmlWriter object.

- You can specify one of the three values of the XmlWriteMode enumeration as a second argument on the WriteXml method to indicate what's included in the output. See figure 15-9 for more information on the DiffGram option.

- You can use the properties described in figure 15-7 to influence the XML that's generated when you use the Get and Write methods.

Figure 15-6   How to use the XML methods of the DataSet class

How to control the format of XML output

When you use one of the Write or Get methods shown in figure 15-6, ADO.NET generates XML output based on the data in the dataset and the information in the dataset class. By default, each row of each table is written as a separate element, and each column is represented as a child element. The dataset name, table names, and column names are used for the names of the elements.

If you're writing the dataset to an XML file so that you can read it back into a dataset later on, this default XML format is fine. If the XML file will be processed by another application, however, you may need to alter the XML output based on the format that the application expects. For example, the application may expect different element names than the defaults, and it may expect some of the columns to be represented as attributes rather than elements.

Figure 15-7 presents some properties you can use to control the XML that's generated. To control the names of the elements that are generated, you use the DataSetName, TableName, and ColumnName properties of the appropriate object. To indicate whether the data in a child table is nested within the data in its parent table, you use the Nested property of the DataRelation object that defines the relationship between the two tables. You'll learn more about how this works in the next topic.

The ColumnMapping property lets you control how a column is rendered in the XML output. To set this property, you use the members of the MappingType enumeration shown in this figure. To see how this property works, look at the coding example shown here. This example uses a dataset named DsVendors1 that contains a table named Vendors with a row for a single vendor. The first three lines of code retrieve the XML for the row using the GetXml method and display it in a message box. Then, the statements within the With statement set the ColumnMapping properties of four of the columns. It sets the ColumnMapping property of the VendorID column so it's created as an attribute rather than as an element, and it sets the ColumnMapping properties of the other columns so they're hidden. Then, it retrieves and displays the XML again. If you compare the XML output shown in the two message boxes, you can see how these properties affect the XML that's generated for the dataset.

Properties that affect the XML that's generated for a dataset

Class	Property	Description
DataSet	DataSetName	Provides the name of the root element.
DataTable	TableName	Provides the name of the table element.
DataColumn	ColumnName	Provides the name of the element or attribute for the column.
DataColumn	ColumnMapping	Specifies how the column should be rendered in the XML output.
DataRelation	Nested	Specifies whether the data in a child table should be nested within the data in the parent table. See figure 15-8 for more information.

Common MappingType enumeration members

Member	Description
Attribute	Maps the column to an XML attribute.
Element	Maps the column to an XML element.
Hidden	Hides the column so it doesn't appear in the XML output.

Code that displays two variations of the XML for a dataset

```
Dim sXml As String
sXml = DsVendors1.GetXml
MessageBox.Show(sXml, "Vendor with elements")
With DsVendors1.Vendors
    .VendorIDColumn.ColumnMapping = MappingType.Attribute
    .VendorAddress1Column.ColumnMapping = MappingType.Hidden
    .VendorAddress2Column.ColumnMapping = MappingType.Hidden
    .VendorStateColumn.ColumnMapping = MappingType.Hidden
    .VendorZipCodeColumn.ColumnMapping = MappingType.Hidden
End With
sXml = DsVendors1.GetXml
MessageBox.Show(sXml, "Vendor with an attribute and hidden columns")
```

The resulting dialog boxes

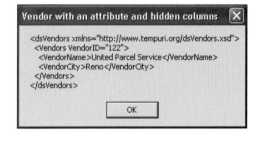

Description

- You can use the properties shown above to influence how the XML is generated when you use the GetXml, GetXmlSchema, WriteXml, or WriteXmlSchema methods.
- These properties don't affect the schema of the dataset within the application.

Figure 15-7   How to control the format of XML output

How to nest data in XML output

The Nested property of the DataRelation class lets you control how the XML data for parent and child rows is generated. The examples shown in figure 15-8 should help you understand how this works. These examples show nested and unnested XML for a dataset that has two tables named Invoice and LineItem. The Invoice table has two invoices. The invoice with ID 101 has one line item, and the invoice with ID 102 has two line items.

If you nest the XML output, the LineItem elements appear nested within their corresponding Invoice elements as illustrated by the first example. To generate nested XML like this, you set the Nested property of the DataRelation object to True. Before you do that, of course, you have to define a data relation between the two tables.

If you don't define a data relation between two related tables or you leave the Nested property of the data relation at its default setting of False, the data in the tables is unnested as shown in the second example. Here, all of the LineItem elements follow the Invoice elements.

The technique you use depends on what the XML data will be used for. If it will be read back into a dataset, you'll usually create unnested XML. That way, the XML file will more closely correspond to the dataset's relational tables. On the other hand, if the XML data will be processed by an XML application, you'll usually create nested XML. That's because XML applications typically expect the data to be organized hierarchically, with child elements nested within their parent elements.

By the way, as you look at the unnested XML, you may wonder why there aren't separate start and end tags for the two Invoice elements. That's because these elements don't contain any content or any child elements. As a result, the slash at the end of each tag marks the end of the element.

Nested XML

```
<Invoices>
    <Invoice ID="101" VendorID="80">
        <LineItem InvoiceID="101" Sequence="1">
            <ItemAmount>92.50</ItemAmount>
            <ItemDescription>Media</ItemDescription>
        </LineItem>
    </Invoice>
    <Invoice ID="102" VendorID="65">
        <LineItem InvoiceID="102" Sequence="1">
            <ItemAmount>425.21</ItemAmount>
            <ItemDescription>Printer</ItemDescription>
        </LineItem>
        <LineItem InvoiceID="102" Sequence="2">
            <ItemAmount>52.75</ItemAmount>
            <ItemDescription>Toner Cartridges</ItemDescription>
        </LineItem>
    </Invoice>
</Invoices>
```

Unnested XML

```
<Invoices>
    <Invoice ID="101" VendorID="80" />
    <Invoice ID="102" VendorID="65" />
    <LineItem InvoiceID="101" Sequence="1">
        <ItemAmount>92.50</ItemAmount>
        <ItemDescription>Media</ItemDescription>
    </LineItem>
    <LineItem InvoiceID="102" Sequence="1">
        <ItemAmount>425.21</ItemAmount>
        <ItemDescription>Printer</ItemDescription>
    </LineItem>
    <LineItem InvoiceID="102" Sequence="2">
        <ItemAmount>52.75</ItemAmount>
        <ItemDescription>Toner Cartridges</ItemDescription>
    </LineItem>
</Invoices>
```

Code that sets the Nested property

```
DsInvoices1.Relations("InvoiceLineItem").Nested = True
```

Description

- You can use the Nested property of the DataRelation class to nest child data within its parent data when you use the GetXml or WriteXml method. By default, the data isn't nested.

- Before you can set the Nested property, you must define a data relation between the two tables involved in the relationship. See chapter 9 for more information.

Figure 15-8   How to nest data in XML output

How to use DiffGrams

In chapter 5, you learned that ADO.NET maintains one or more versions of each row in a data table. Rows that existed when the table was loaded have both an original version and a current version. If the row hasn't changed, these versions are identical. If the row has been changed, however, the current version contains the modified data and the original version contains the original data. In addition, a row that's been added to the table has a current version but no original version. And a row that's been deleted has an original version but no current version.

Normally, the WriteXml method writes only the current version of each row to the XML file. However, you can write both versions by specifying XmlWriteMode.DiffGram on the WriteXml method as shown in figure 15-9. An XML file like this that contains both current and original row versions is called a *DiffGram*.

If you study the XML output shown in this figure, you can see the two versions of the vendor row. Here, the difference between the current and original versions is the value of the VendorName column. In the current version, it's UPS. In the original version, it's United Parcel Service.

In most cases, you won't need to use a DiffGram. Instead, after you update the data in the database, you'll write the current version of each row to an XML file if you need to save it in that format. If you think you may need to recreate the dataset with both versions later on, though, you can save it as a DiffGram before you update the database. You may also save a dataset as a DiffGram to send it to another application for processing.

A DiffGram for a table that contains a single row

```
<?xml version="1.0" standalone="yes"?>
<diffgr:diffgram xmlns:msdata="urn:schemas-microsoft-com:xml-msdata"
xmlns:diffgr="urn:schemas-microsoft-com:xml-diffgram-v1">
  <DsPayables xmlns="http://www.tempuri.org/DsPayables.xsd">
    <Vendors diffgr:id="Vendors1" msdata:rowOrder="0"
        diffgr:hasChanges="modified">
    <VendorID>122</VendorID>
    <VendorName>UPS</VendorName>
    <VendorAddress1>P.O. Box 505820</VendorAddress1>
    <VendorCity>Reno</VendorCity>
    <VendorState>NV</VendorState>
    <VendorZipCode>88905</VendorZipCode>
    </Vendors>
  </DsPayables>
  <diffgr:before>
    <Vendors diffgr:id="Vendors1" msdata:rowOrder="0"
        xmlns="http://www.tempuri.org/DsPayables.xsd">
    <VendorID>122</VendorID>
    <VendorName>United Parcel Service</VendorName>
    <VendorAddress1>P.O. Box 505820</VendorAddress1>
    <VendorCity>Reno</VendorCity>
    <VendorState>NV</VendorState>
    <VendorZipCode>88905</VendorZipCode>
    </Vendors>
  </diffgr:before>
</diffgr:diffgram>
```

Current Vendor element

Original Vendor element

Code that writes an XML file in DiffGram format

```
DsPayables1.WriteXml("C:\PayablesDiff.xml", XmlWriteMode.DiffGram)
```

Description

- A *DiffGram* is an XML document that contains both the current and original versions of the rows in a dataset. To create a DiffGram, specify XmlWriteMode.DiffGram as the second argument on a WriteXml method.

- You should save a dataset to a DiffGram before you execute the Update method of the dataset. Otherwise, the values in the current and original versions will be identical.

- When you use the ReadXml method to load a dataset from an XML file in DiffGram format, the appropriate row versions are created automatically.

Figure 15-9   How to use DiffGrams

Perspective

In this chapter, you learned the basic concepts and techniques for working with XML files and for exchanging data between XML files and ADO.NET datasets. Keep in mind, though, that there's much more to working with XML data than this short chapter has presented. In particular, the .NET Framework includes classes that are designed specifically for working with XML data. You can learn about some of these classes in chapter 14 of our companion book, *Murach's Beginning Visual Basic .NET.*

Terms

XML (Extensible Markup Language)
tag
XML document
attribute
element
XML declaration
XML comment
start tag
end tag
content
child element
parent element
root element
schema language
Document Type Definition (DTD)
XML Schema Definition (XSD)
XML Schema
XML data document
DiffGram

16

How to use
Crystal Reports
to develop reports

Crystal Reports is a report-preparation program that's included as part of the Visual Studio development environment. You can use it to create professional reports for business applications. Then, you can view and print those reports from within your applications.

An introduction to Crystal Reports

Before you learn how to create a Crystal report, you need to be familiar with the elements that make up a report and the two models you can use to provide data to a report. That's what you'll learn in the two topics that follow. Then, you'll learn how to start a Crystal report.

The three elements of a Crystal report

Figure 16-1 presents a Visual Basic application that contains a Crystal report. This report is made up of three elements. The Crystal Report file is a typed component that contains the definition of the report. You'll learn how to create files like this throughout this chapter. The Crystal Report Viewer control provides the area where the report is displayed. As you can see in this figure, you place the Crystal Report Viewer control on a form just as you would any other control. The data source provides the data that's displayed in the report. In this case, the data source is a typed dataset. As you'll learn in a moment, though, you can use data sources other than a dataset to provide data to a Crystal report.

The two models for providing data to a report

Figure 16-1 also describes two ways you can provide the data for a Crystal report. The easiest way is to "pull" it directly from a database. When you use the *pull model*, all of the information that's needed to connect to the database and retrieve the data is stored in the report file. In addition, Crystal Reports handles all of the data access for you, so no program code is required. To access the database, Crystal Reports uses the OLE DB or ODBC driver you specify.

Instead of storing the information for accessing and retrieving data in the report file, you can define the data to be retrieved and provide the code for retrieving it within your program. Then, you can "push" the retrieved data into the report. You can use this *push model* with ADO.NET datasets like the ones you've learned about throughout this book. You can also use it with *recordsets* that you create by retrieving data using either an OLE DB or ODBC driver.

Since this book is about ADO.NET, this chapter will focus mainly on how you create reports using ADO.NET datasets as the data source. However, the basic techniques for creating a report are the same regardless of how the data is provided. So you shouldn't have any trouble using other data sources if you need to.

An application with a report created using Crystal Reports

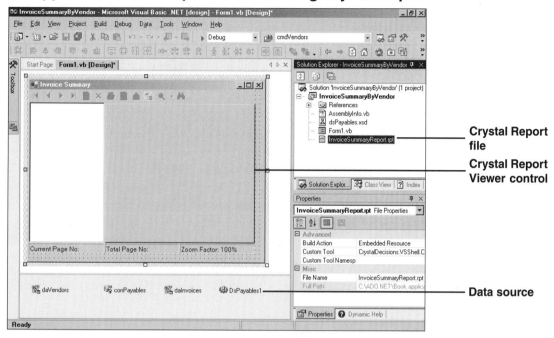

Crystal Report file

Crystal Report Viewer control

Data source

Two models for providing data to a report

Model	Drivers	Description
Pull	OLE DB ODBC	Data is "pulled" directly from the database. Information about connecting to the database and the data to be retrieved is stored in the report file, and the data access is handled automatically by Crystal Reports.
Push	ADO.NET OLE DB ODBC	A dataset or recordset is defined within the application, and the application must provide the code for retrieving the data. The data is then "pushed" into the report.

Description

- Crystal Reports is a report writing tool that has been integrated into the Visual Studio environment. To create a report using Crystal Reports, you need three elements: a Crystal Report file, a Crystal Report Viewer control, and a data source.

- A Crystal Report file is a typed component that contains the definition of a report. A Crystal Report Viewer control provides the area on a form where the report is displayed. To display a report within this control, you bind the control to the report file.

- The *pull model* for retrieving data lets Crystal Reports talk directly to the database. Because this model doesn't require any code, it's the easiest to use.

- The *push model* requires that the program retrieve the data into a dataset or a *recordset* before it's used by Crystal Reports. This model lets you control access to the data from within the application. Before you can create a report using this model, you must create the dataset or the connection used by the recordset.

Figure 16-1   An introduction to Crystal Reports

How to start a Crystal report

You can use the Add New Item dialog box to add a Crystal Report file to a project. When you do that, the Crystal Report Gallery dialog box shown in figure 16-2 is displayed. As you can see, this dialog box lets you create a report by using the *Report Expert*, by starting from a blank report, or by starting from an existing report. In most cases, you'll use the Report Expert to develop the basic design of a report. Then, you'll use the Crystal Report Designer to modify that design so the report looks just the way you want it to. You'll learn how to use both the Report Expert and the Crystal Report Designer in this chapter.

When you select the Report Expert option, you can select from a variety of Experts. The table in this figure summarizes the types of reports you can create with each Expert. In this chapter, I'll focus on the Standard Report Expert since this is the one you'll use most often.

The Crystal Report Gallery dialog box

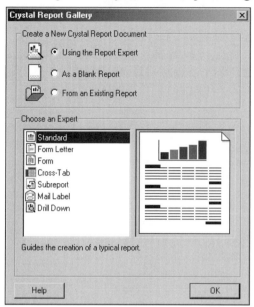

The Report Experts

Expert	Description
Standard	Creates a report with both detail and summary lines.
Form Letter	Creates a letter that combines text and data.
Form	Creates a report for use with preprinted forms.
Cross-Tab	Creates a report that cross-tabulates data.
Subreport	Creates a report with a subreport.
Mail Label	Creates mailing labels or other reports that require multiple columns.
Drill Down	Creates a report that lets you hide or display the details of summarized data.

Description

- To add a new Crystal Report file to a project, Select Project→Add New Item to display the Add New Item dialog box. Then, select the Crystal Report template, enter a name for the file, and click Open to display the Crystal Report Gallery dialog box.

- To use a *Report Expert*, select the Using the Report Expert option and then select the Expert you want to use.

- To start a new report based on an existing report, select the From an Existing Report option and use the resulting dialog box to choose the file for the existing report.

- To start a custom report, select the As a Blank Report option. This opens an unformatted report with placeholders for the most basic report information.

- You can also add an existing report file to a project by selecting Project→Add Existing Item and then locating and selecting the file.

Figure 16-2   How to start a Crystal report

How to use the Standard Report Expert

After you select the Report Expert you want to use, you will be led through a series of pages that will help you design your report. The topics that follow show you how to use the pages for the Standard Report Expert. The report I'll create is an Invoice Summary report that lists all the invoices with a balance due, grouped by vendor.

How to select the tables for a report

If you're going to use a dataset as the source of data for a report, you must create that dataset before you create the report using the Report Expert. To create the Invoice Summary report, for example, you'll need to create a dataset that defines the data from the Vendors and Invoices tables that will be used by the report. Then, as you can see in figure 16-3, the Data page of the Standard Report Expert dialog box lets you select the tables you want to use from that dataset. Here, both the Invoices and Vendors tables have been selected.

Notice that the Data page also lets you select from external data sources, including those that have OLE DB or ODBC drivers. OLE DB can be used with ADO, which was the predecessor to ADO.NET, and ODBC can be used with RDO, which was the predecessor to ADO. In addition, you can select from connections that are defined within the project. These connections can be used by ADO or RDO to retrieve data from OLE DB or ODBC data sources into a recordset that can be pushed into the report.

The Data tab of the Standard Report Expert

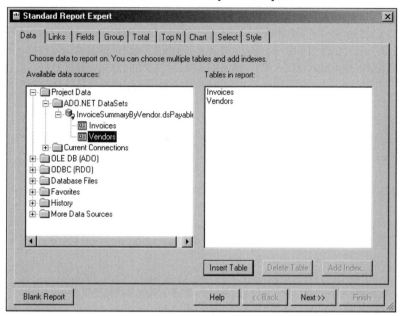

Description

- The Data tab of the Standard Report Expert lets you select the data source for the report.

- To use the push model with an ADO.NET dataset, expand the Project Data node, the ADO.NET DataSets node, and the dataset node you want to use. Then, select each table you want to use and click on the Insert Table button.

- To use the push model with an ADO or RDO recordset, expand the Project Data node, the Current Connections node, and the connection node you want to use. Then, insert each recordset you want to use.

- To use the pull model, click on the plus sign to the left of the OLE DB (ADO) or ODBC (RDO) folder and respond to the dialog boxes that are displayed to choose a driver and create a database connection. Then, expand the nodes for the database to display its tables and insert the tables you want to use.

Figure 16-3   How to select the tables for a report

How to link tables

If you select two or more tables for a report, the Expert displays the Links page shown at the top of figure 16-4. By default, the Expert creates a link if it finds columns with the same names in two tables. A link indicates how the tables are related. The Links page in this figure, for example, indicates that the Invoices and Vendors tables are related by the VendorID column in each table.

Because the Expert doesn't create links between columns with different names, you'll need to do that yourself. If you've defined a relationship between two tables in the dataset that contains them, you can create a link by selecting the By Key option from the Link Tables group and then clicking the Auto-Link button. Otherwise, you can create a link by dragging a column in one table to the related column in the other table.

To work with a link, you can click it to select it and then use the available buttons. To change how a link is defined, for example, you can click the Link Options button. Then, the dialog box that's displayed lets you select the type of join that's used as well as the operator that's used to relate the two tables. In most cases, you'll use the default, which is to use an inner join with the equal operator.

How to select fields

To select the fields you want to appear on a report, you use the Fields page of the Expert, also shown in figure 16-4. The Available Fields list on this page lists the columns in the tables you selected for the report. To add a column, you just select it and click the Add button. Or, you can add all of the columns in all of the tables at once by clicking the Add All button. The columns you've selected appear in the Fields to Display list. Then, you can remove any columns you don't want to include by using the Remove button.

Since the order of the fields in the Fields to Display list is the order in which the fields will appear on the report, you need to be sure these fields are in the proper sequence. To adjust the position of a field, you can highlight it and click the up or down arrow button above the Fields to Display list.

By default, the field name for a field you select is used as the column heading for that field in the report. If that's not what you want, you can modify the name shown in the Column Heading text box. In this figure, for example, "Due date" will be used as the column heading for the InvoiceDueDate field.

The Expert also lets you add fields to a report that are calculated from other fields in the tables you've selected. To create a calculated field, or *formula field*, you click the Formula button in the Fields tab. Then, you use the Formula Editor to create the field, as you'll see in the next topic.

The Links and Fields tabs of the Standard Report Expert

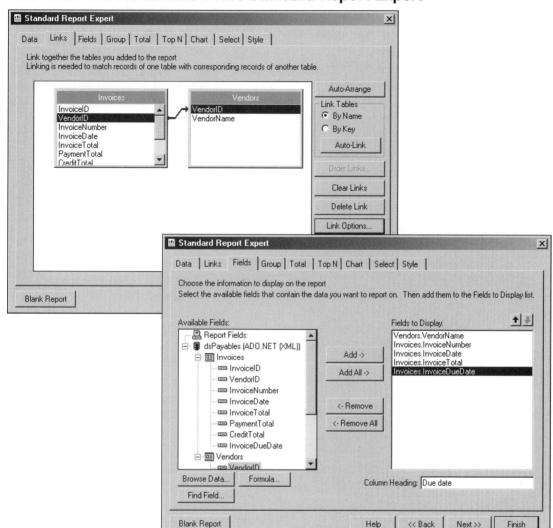

Description

- The Expert creates links automatically if it finds columns with the same name in two tables. If a relationship is defined between two tables, you can create a link from the Links page by selecting the By Key option and then clicking on Auto-Link. Or, you can create a link manually by dragging from one table to another. To modify a link, select it and then use the available buttons.

- To add a field to the report, highlight it in the Available Fields list of the Fields tab and click the Add button, or click the Add All button to add all the fields from the data source.

- To change the column heading used for a field, highlight the field in the Fields to Display list and enter the new heading in the Column Heading text box. To change the sequence of the selected fields, use the up and down buttons above the Fields to Display list.

- To create a calculated field, click on the Formula button. See figure 16-5 for details.

Figure 16-4   How to link tables and select fields

How to create a formula field

If you click the Formula button on the Fields page, the Expert displays a dialog box that asks you to provide a name for the formula field. Note that Crystal Reports precedes the field name you specify with an at sign (@) to distinguish it from a field in the data source. Then, it displays the *Formula Editor* window shown in figure 16-5. In this example, a field named @BalanceDue is created by subtracting the PaymentTotal and CreditTotal columns from the InvoiceTotal column.

To create an expression like this, you can double-click on a report field, a field in the data source, a function, or an operator in the lists that are provided to add it to the expression in the Formula Text window. You can also type directly into this window if you need to. For example, you might need to add parentheses to clarify complicated expressions.

When you're done creating an expression, you might want to check it to be sure its syntax is correct. To do that, just click the Check button in the toolbar. Then, to save the field and close the Formula Editor window, click the Save and close button. When you do, you're returned to the Fields page of the Expert, and you can add the new field to the report.

If you scroll through the functions and operators that are available from the Formula Editor window, you'll see that Crystal Reports provides rich sets of both. As a result, you should be able to create whatever calculated fields you need. If, for example, you want to create fields that print the invoice amounts in four different columns of the report depending on how old each invoice is (called an *aged* report), you can use an If statement like this for the first field:

```
if {Invoices.InvoiceDate} in Aged0To30Days then
    {Invoices.InvoiceTotal} else 0
```

Then, the value of the field is the invoice total if the invoice date is aged from 0 to 30 days when compared with the current date. Otherwise, the value is zero. Later on, you can format this field so a zero value isn't printed.

To create a formula field like this, you can find the If..Then..Else structure in the Control Structures folder of the Operators list, the In keyword in the Ranges folder of the Operators list, and the Aged0To30Days function in the Date Ranges folder of the Functions list. For the other three columns of the report, you can use the same basic code with these functions: Aged31To60Days, Aged61To90Days, and Over90Days.

The Formula Editor

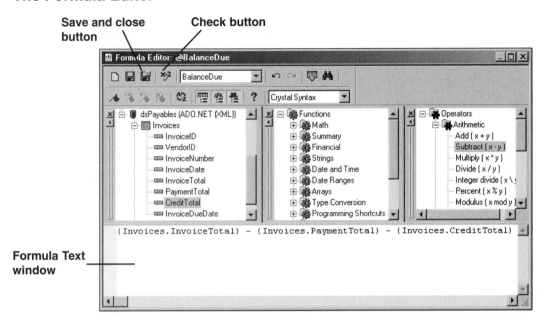

Save and close button   **Check button**

Formula Text window

Description

- When you click on the Formula button in the Fields tab, a dialog box is displayed that asks you to enter a name for the new calculated field, or *formula field*. After you enter the name and click the OK button, the *Formula Editor* is displayed.

- To build the expression for a calculated field, double-click on a field, function, or operator in the available lists to add it to the Formula Text window. You can also type directly into the Formula Text window.

- To check the syntax of an expression, click the Check toolbar button.

- To save the calculated field and return to the Fields tab of the Report Expert, click the Save and close toolbar button. The formula field will appear in the Available Fields list so you can add it to the report.

Figure 16-5   How to create a formula field

How to group data

After you select the fields for the report, you can group the report by one or more fields so you can print totals for each group. To do that, you add the fields to the Group By list in the Group page of the Expert as shown at the top of figure 16-6. Here, the report will be grouped by the VendorName column so that the invoices for each vendor will appear in a group.

You can also use the Group page to determine how the groups will be sorted. The options are to sort in ascending order, descending order, the original order specified in the Select statement, or a specified order. If you select the specified order option, additional controls become available that let you specify the order you want to use.

If you add more than one field to the Group Fields list, the report is grouped and sorted by each of the fields. If, for example, a sales report is sorted by salesperson number within branch number, the report can print group totals for each salesperson as well as group totals for each branch. As you'll see in the next topic, however, you don't have to include group totals for each field that you're grouping by.

You can also sort and group based on date fields or Boolean fields. Then, you can use a drop-down Break list that's available for these fields to choose when you want group totals prepared. For a date field, you can choose from items like Weekly, For Each Month, and For Each Quarter. For a Boolean field, you can choose from items like On Change to Yes, On Change to No, and On Every Yes.

How to summarize data

The Total page of the Expert, also shown in figure 16-6, includes one tab for each field you've chosen to group by. Then, you can choose the fields that you want to print group totals for in each group. When the tab for each group field is first displayed, the Summarized Fields list includes all of the numeric fields included in the report. If that's not what you want, you can add or remove fields from this list.

By default, the sum function is used to total each of the fields in the Summarized Fields list. However, Crystal Reports provides a variety of summary functions that you can choose. To use a different function, just select it from the Summary Type combo box. You can also select the Percentage of option to display the percentage that each group is of the total, and you can select the Add Grand Totals option to print grand totals for each field that has group totals.

The Group and Total tabs of the Standard Report Expert

Description

- To group the rows in a report by one or more fields, highlight the fields in the Available Fields list of the Group page and click the Add button to add them to the Group By list. To determine how a field is sorted, select an option from the Sort Order combo box.

- By default, the Report Expert summarizes all numeric fields on the report. If that's not what you want, you can use the Total page to add and remove summary fields. This page contains one tab for each group in the report.

- You can also use the Total page to change the type of summary that's performed for each field and to determine whether grand totals are included for the field.

Figure 16-6   How to group and summarize data

How to sort report groups

If a report is grouped by one or more fields and includes summary data for one or more fields, you can use the Top N page of the Expert shown in figure 16-7 to sort the groups by the summary fields. In this figure, for example, you can see that the VendorName groups will be sorted by the sum of the invoice totals for those groups in ascending sequence. In other words, the vendors with the smallest group totals will appear first in the report. Note that this sorting overrides the sorting you specify on the Group tab. Also note that, like the Total page, this page includes one tab for each group field.

In addition to sorting all of the groups by a summary field, you can sort just the top or bottom number or percent of the groups. If you select one of the top or bottom options, additional controls become available that let you specify the number or percent of groups to sort and how the rows that aren't in those groups will be identified in the report. Then, the rows that aren't included in the top or bottom groups are sorted by the fields specified in the Group tab. If this sounds confusing, you may want to try it to see how it works. It's probably not a feature you'll use often, though.

How to add a chart

A Crystal report can also include charts. To add a chart, just select one of the chart types from the Type tab of the Chart page shown in figure 16-7. Then, select the placement and layout of the chart and the data to be charted from the Data tab, and specify the text and format of the titles to be used in the chart from the Text tab. If you take a few minutes to experiment with this feature, you'll see that you can quickly and easily create charts that make the data in your reports easy to understand.

The Top N tab of the Standard Report Expert

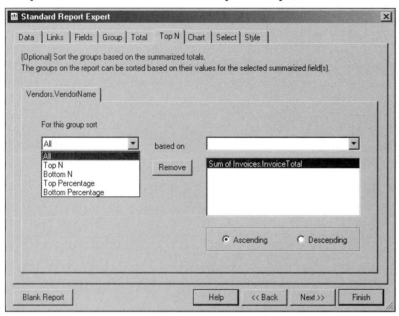

The Chart tab of the Standard Report Expert

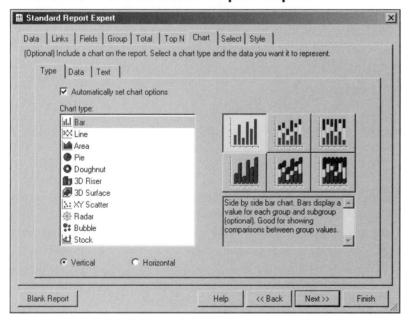

Description

- If you selected group and summary fields, you can use the Top N page to sort the groups by the summary fields.

- To include a chart in the report, select a chart type from the Type tab of the Chart page and then set the appropriate options on the Data and Text tabs.

Figure 16-7   How to sort report groups and add a chart

How to filter the report data

The Select page of the Expert, shown at the top of figure 16-8, lets you filter the data that's included in a report. To do that, you create one or more conditional expressions that are based on a field in the report or data source. Then, only the rows that satisfy those conditions are included in the report. In this figure, for example, you can see that the Invoice Summary report will include only those invoices whose BalanceDue value is greater than zero. In other words, the report won't include data for invoices that have already been paid.

If you create more than one select field, all of the conditions must be satisfied before a row is included in the report. If, for example, you added a state column to the report, you could select rows for just the vendors in a specific state. Then, the report would include only the unpaid invoices for vendors in that state. If necessary, you can modify the way the selection conditions work after the Expert creates the initial version of the report. For instance, you can change an *and* relationship between the conditions to an *or* relationship.

If you use an ADO.NET dataset as the source of data for a report, you should filter the data when it's retrieved from the database rather than as the report is created. That way, the amount of data that's passed from the server to the client is reduced, making the program more efficient. On the other hand, if you're using the pull model with OLE DB or ODBC to create a report, you must specify the filter criteria as part of the report definition since the report will retrieve the data directly from the data source.

How to select a report style

The last page of the Standard Report Expert lets you add a title to the report and choose a style to format the report. Although the report image to the right of the Style list gives you a rough idea of what the report will look like when it's displayed using the selected style, you usually have to experiment with the various styles to find the ones that you like the best. However, you can easily change the style after you finish using the Expert.

To end the Expert and display the report in design view, click on the Finish button. Then, as you'll learn later in this chapter, you can use the Crystal Report Designer to modify the report so it looks just the way you want it to. Before you learn how to modify a report generated by the Expert, though, I want to show you how to use the Crystal Report Viewer control to view and work with a report.

The Select tab of the Standard Report Expert

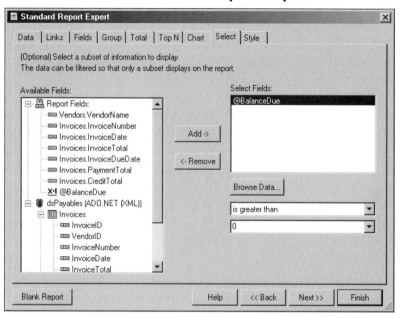

The Style tab of the Standard Report Expert

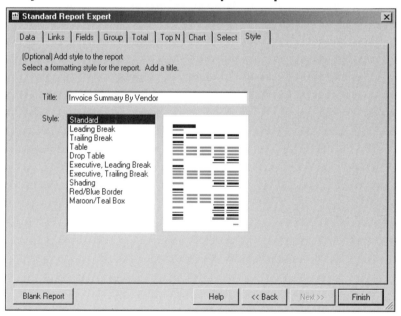

Description

- To filter the rows included in the report, choose the fields that the filter is based on from the Select page and then enter the selection criteria for each field.

- Enter the Title for the report on the Style page and select a report style. To preview a style, click on it in the Style list.

Figure 16-8   How to filter the report data and select a report style

How to use the Crystal Report Viewer control

To display a report in a Visual Basic application, you add a Crystal Report Viewer control to a form and bind the control to the report. Then, you can use the controls that are built into the viewer control to work with the report. You can also customize the viewer control so it provides just the features you want, and you can work with it in code.

How to bind a viewer control to a report

The Crystal Report Viewer control is available from both the Windows Forms and Web Forms tabs of the Toolbox, so you can add a report to either a Windows or a web form. Figure 16-9 shows a viewer control after it's added to a Windows form. After you add a control, you'll want to resize it so its size is appropriate for the data it will display. Unfortunately, there's no way to see how the data will appear in the control until you run the program. So you may have to adjust the size of the control several times before you get it just right.

After you add a viewer control to a form, you have to specify the report that it will display. The technique you use to do that depends on whether you're using the push or the pull model. The examples in this figure show you how to use both of these models.

To use the push model, you start by creating an instance of the report. Then, you fill the dataset with the data that's used by the report, and you use the SetDataSource method of the report to bind the report to that dataset. Finally, you set the ReportSource property of the Crystal Report Viewer control to the report.

To use the pull model, you simply set the ReportSource property of the viewer control so it points to the report file. You can do that either in code as shown here or from the Properties window. Note that even if the report is included as a file in the project that uses it, the ReportSource property must specify the full path to the report file.

A Windows form with a Crystal Report Viewer control

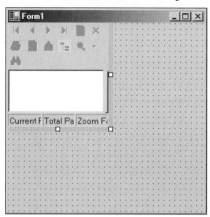

Code that binds a viewer control to a report that pushes data

```
Private Sub Form1_Load(ByVal sender As System.Object, _
        ByVal e As System.EventArgs) Handles MyBase.Load
    Dim rptInvoices As New InvoiceSummaryReport()
    daVendors.Fill(DsPayables1)
    daInvoices.Fill(DsPayables1)
    rptInvoices.SetDataSource(DsPayables1)
    crInvoicesViewer.ReportSource = rptInvoices
End Sub
```

Code that binds a viewer control to a report that pulls data

```
Private Sub Form1_Load(ByVal sender As Object, _
        ByVal e As System.EventArgs) Handles MyBase.Load
    crInvoicesViewer.ReportSource = _
        "C:\Reports\InvoiceSummaryByVendor\InvoiceSummaryReport.rpt"
End Sub
```

Description

- To add a Crystal Report Viewer control to a Windows or web form, drag it from the Windows Forms or Web Forms tab of the Toolbox. Then, move and resize the control as appropriate. The size of the control determines the size of the window that will be used to display the report.

- Before you can bind a viewer control to a report that uses an ADO.NET dataset, you must fill the dataset and create an instance of the report class. Then, you use the SetDataSource method of the report to set its data source to the dataset, and you set the ReportSource property of the viewer to the report object.

- To bind a viewer control to a report that pulls data, set its ReportSource property to the name and location of the report file. You can do that at design time or at runtime.

Note

- You can also use an untyped component to work with a report. To do that, you use the ReportDocument class. See online help for more information.

Figure 16-9   How to bind a viewer control to a report

How to work with a report viewer using its built-in controls

Figure 16-10 shows how a report appears in a report viewer control at runtime. Here, the Invoice Summary report that I created in the previous topics using the Standard Report Expert is displayed. As you can see, the report itself is displayed in the *Report pane*. You can use the scroll bars in this pane to scroll up and down or side to side in a page, and you can use the page controls in the toolbar to move from one page to the next. If the report includes group fields, you can also move directly to a group by clicking on that group in the *Group tree*. The Invoice Summary report, for example, is grouped by vendor name, so the vendor names are listed in the Group tree, and you can click on a vendor name to display the invoices for that vendor.

By default, the Report pane consists of a single tab named MainReport that lists all of the groups in the report. If you want to, however, you can create separate tabs for specific groups. To do that, just locate the group in the Report pane and then double-click on the group name. A separate tab will be created that contains just the data for that group.

The report viewer also provides a variety of other tools that you can use to work with a report. For example, you can use the Print toolbar button to display the standard Print dialog box so you can print the report. You can use the Zoom toolbar button to change the magnification of the report. And you can use the Search Text toolbar button to search for the text you specify within the report. If you experiment with these buttons, you shouldn't have any trouble figuring out how they work.

The report viewer with the Invoice Summary report displayed

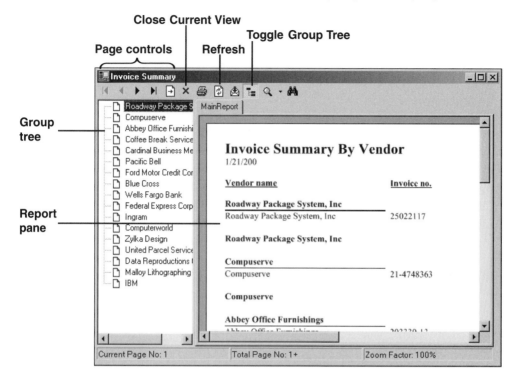

Description

- After you bind a report viewer to a report, you can build and run the application to display the report in the viewer as shown above.

- If a report includes grouping, the grouping fields are displayed in the *Group tree* at the left side of the viewer. To hide or display the Group tree, click on the Toggle Group Tree toolbar button. To navigate to a particular group, click on it in the Group tree.

- To create a view of the report for a single group, double-click on the group name in the *Report pane*. The group will be displayed in a separate tab of the Report pane. To close this tab, click on the Close Current View toolbar button.

- To requery the data source so that it reflects any changes made to the data since it was retrieved, click the Refresh toolbar button. This will also close any group views that you've opened.

- To navigate through the pages of a report, use the page controls at the left side of the toolbar.

- You can use the other toolbar buttons to print the report, export the report to another application, zoom in or out, or locate text within the report.

Note

- You can set properties of the viewer control to determine whether some of the toolbar buttons are available. See figure 16-11 for details.

Figure 16-10   How to work with a report viewer using its built-in controls

How to customize a report viewer

Because an interface like the one shown in the previous figure may be overwhelming to the average user, you may want to customize the report viewer control so it provides just the features the user needs. To do that, you use the properties listed in figure 16-11. Most of these properties determine which buttons are included on the toolbar. You can also omit the toolbar altogether by setting the DisplayToolbar property to False. And you can hide the Group tree by setting the DisplayGroupTree property to False.

In addition to the properties that control the features that are available from a report viewer control, you can set properties that control the data that's included in the report. You're already familiar with the ReportSource property. Although you can set this property at design time when you use the pull model, you have to set it at runtime when you use the push model as you saw in figure 16-9.

The SelectionFormula property lets you specify a conditional expression that's used to filter the data in the report. Although you can set this property at design time, it's typically set at runtime to respond to selections made by the user. For example, suppose the form that contains the report viewer for the Invoice Summary report also contains a combo box that lets the user select a specific vendor. Then, the report could list just the invoices for that vendor by setting the SelectionFormula property as shown in the code example in this figure. Note that the condition you specify for this property is used in addition to any filter conditions you specify when you create the report.

Common properties of a report viewer

Property	Description
DisplayGroupTree	Determines whether the Group tree is displayed.
DisplayToolbar	Determines whether the toolbar is displayed.
ShowCloseButton	Determines whether the Close Current View button is included on the toolbar.
ShowExportButton	Determines whether the Export Report button is included on the toolbar.
ShowGotoButton	Determines whether the Goto Page button is included on the toolbar.
ShowGroupTreeButton	Determines whether the Toggle Group Tree button is included on the toolbar.
ShowPageNavigationButtons	Determines whether the page navigation buttons are included on the toolbar.
ShowPrintButton	Determines whether the Print Report button is included on the toolbar.
ShowRefreshButton	Determines whether the Refresh button is included on the toolbar.
ShowTextSearchButton	Determines whether the Search Text button is included on the toolbar.
ShowZoomButton	Determines whether the Zoom button is included on the toolbar.
ReportSource	The report to be displayed in the viewer. You typically set this property at runtime as shown in figure 16-9.
SelectionFormula	A formula that's used to filter the rows in the report. This formula is used in addition to any filter conditions you specify within the report.

Code that changes the selection formula

```
Private Sub cboVendors_SelectedIndexChanged(ByVal sender As System.Object, _
    ByVal e As System.EventArgs) Handles cboVendors.SelectedIndexChanged
  crInvoiceViewer.SelectionFormula _
      = "{Invoices.VendorID} = " & cboVendors.SelectedValue
End Sub
```

Description

- You can set any of the properties shown above except for the last two to either True or False to indicate whether the associated feature is available. These properties are typically set at design time.

- Although you can set the SelectionFormula property at design time, it's more common to set it at runtime based on selections made by the user. Any report fields referred to within the selection formula must be enclosed in braces as shown above.

- The report viewer provides many other properties that you can use to change the appearance of the report viewer, including properties that let you change the foreground color, the background color, and the text font. For a complete list of properties, see online help.

Figure 16-11   How to customize a report viewer

How to work with a report viewer using its methods

If you customize a report viewer control by hiding the toolbar or removing toolbar buttons, you can add your own controls and code to provide for the functions the user needs. That way, you can design the user interface so it's consistent with other applications. To work with a report viewer in code, you use the methods listed in figure 16-12.

To let the user move from one page of a report to another, for example, you can add your own navigation buttons along with code like that shown in this figure. As you can see, this code executes the ShowFirstPage, ShowPreviousPage, ShowNextPage, or ShowLastPage method depending on which button the user clicks. Similarly, you can add a Print button and then use the PrintReport method to display the Print dialog box when the user clicks that button.

Common methods of a report viewer

Method	Description
CloseView	Closes the current view tab.
ExportReport	Displays the Export Report dialog box so that the user can export the report.
GetCurrentPageNumber	Gets the current page number of the report that's displayed in the viewer.
PrintReport	Displays the Print dialog box so the user can print the report.
RefreshReport	Refreshes the data used by the report by requerying the data source.
SearchForText	Searches the report for the specified text and returns a Boolean value that indicates whether the text was found.
ShowFirstPage	Shows the first page of the report.
ShowGroupTree	Displays the Group tree.
ShowLastPage	Shows the last page of the report.
ShowNextPage	Shows the next page of the report.
ShowNthPage	Shows the specified page of the report. If the page number you specify is beyond the end of the report, the last page is shown.
ShowPreviousPage	Shows the previous page of the report.
Zoom	Changes the magnification percent for the report. You can also specify a value of 1 on this method to display the entire width of the page. And you can specify a value of 2 to display the entire page.

A procedure that uses form buttons to provide for navigation

```
Private Sub NavigationButtons_Click(ByVal sender As System.Object, _
        ByVal e As System.EventArgs) Handles btnFirst.Click, _
        btnPrevious.Click, btnNext.Click, btnLast.Click
    Select Case sender.name
        Case "btnFirst"
            crInvoicesViewer.ShowFirstPage()
        Case "btnPrevious"
            crInvoicesViewer.ShowPreviousPage()
        Case "btnNext"
            crInvoicesViewer.ShowNextPage()
        Case "btnLast"
            crInvoicesViewer.ShowLastPage()
    End Select
End Sub
```

Description

- If you hide the toolbar on a report viewer or you remove some of the toolbar buttons, you can use some of the methods of the report viewer to provide the same functionality.

Figure 16-12   How to work with a report viewer using its methods

How to use the Crystal Report Designer

After you create a report using a Report Expert, you'll probably want to modify it so it works just the way you want it to. To modify a report, you use the *Crystal Report Designer*. You can also use the Designer to create a report from scratch if you choose to do that.

An overview of the Crystal Report Designer

Figure 16-13 shows the Invoice Summary program that was created earlier in this chapter using the Standard Report Expert as it appears in the Crystal Report Designer. As you can see, the Crystal Report Designer includes a *Field Explorer window* and a *Report Designer window*. The Field Explorer window lists all of the fields that are available to the report. Note that the fields that are already included in the report have a check mark next to them. To add a field to the report, you can simply drag it from the Field Explorer window to the Report Designer window.

To modify the layout of a report, you work in the Report Designer window. From this window, you can move and size a field using the mouse, you can change the font and alignment of a field using the toolbar buttons, and you can apply special formatting using the Format Editor dialog box. You can also format the sections of a report from this window.

Each report includes at least five sections: report header and report footer sections that appear at the beginning and end of the report; page header and page footer sections that appear at the top and bottom of each page; and a details section that contains the fields from the data source as well as other fields you've created for the report. In addition, a report includes a group header and a group footer section for each group you define. You'll learn more about working with these sections in the next figure.

To make other changes to a report, you can use the commands in the menu that's displayed when you right-click on any section or field in the report. For example, if you want to add additional tables or datasets to a report or change the links between the tables you've selected, you can use the Add/Remove Database command in the Database submenu. This displays a Database Expert dialog box with the Data and Links pages you saw earlier in this chapter. Similarly, you can use commands in the Report submenu to change the selection criteria, grouping, and sorting for a report. And you can use the commands in the Insert submenu to add groups, totals, special fields, and charts. You can also use the buttons in the toolbar to perform some of these functions. The best way to find out what's available is to spend some time experimenting.

The Invoice Summary report in the Crystal Report Designer

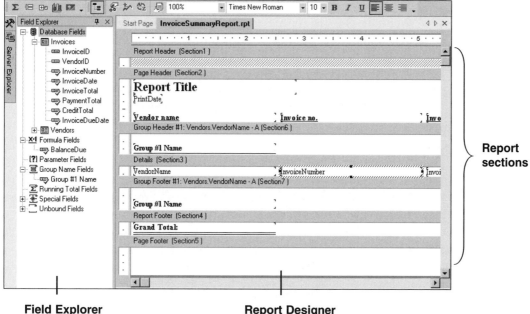

Field Explorer   **Report Designer**

Description

- To modify the design of a report, you use the *Crystal Report Designer*. To open the designer for a report, double-click on the report file in the Solution Explorer.

- The Crystal Report Designer includes a *Field Explorer* that lists the fields that are available to the report; a *Report Designer* that you can use to work with the layout of a report; and toolbars that provide access to the most useful functions.

- Each report consists of five or more sections. The details section contains the data from each row in the data source, the report header and footer sections appear at the beginning and end of the report, and the page header and footer sections appear at the top and bottom of each page. Additional sections are included for each group you define.

- To add a field to a report, drag it from the Field Explorer to the Report Designer. The fields that are already included in the report have a check mark next to them in the Field Explorer. For more information on using the Field Explorer, see figure 16-15.

- To change the format of a report object, select it and use the toolbar buttons or right-click on it and select Format to display the Format Editor dialog box. You can also position and size an object using the mouse, and you can delete it by pressing the Delete key.

- To format the sections of a report, right-click in the Report Designer and select Format Section from the menu that's displayed. For details, see figure 16-14. You can also change the height of a section by dragging its bottom border.

- To change other aspects of a report, use the shortcut menu that's displayed when you right-click in the Report Designer.

- You can also design a new report that you create from scratch using these techniques.

Figure 16-13   An overview of the Crystal Report Designer

How to work with report sections

Figure 16-14 shows the Section Expert dialog box that's displayed when you select the Format Section command from the shortcut menu for any section. As you can see, this dialog box lists all of the sections in the report. Then, you can select a section and change any of the available options. For example, if you want to print each group of a report on a separate page, you can select the New Page Before option for the group header section or the New Page After option for the group footer section. This is particularly useful for printing on preprinted forms like invoices.

Another option you may want to use is Underlay Following Sections. This option lets you print a section underneath the sections that follow it. In other words, the two sections are layered on each other, with the sections that follow being the top layer. This option is particularly useful for printing group information on just the first detail line of the group. For example, instead of printing the vendor name in each detail line of the Invoice Summary report, you can omit the vendor name from this section and select the Underlay Following Sections option for the group header section as shown in this figure. Then, the vendor name in the group header section will print in the first detail line of the group. You'll see how that looks later in this chapter.

The Section Expert

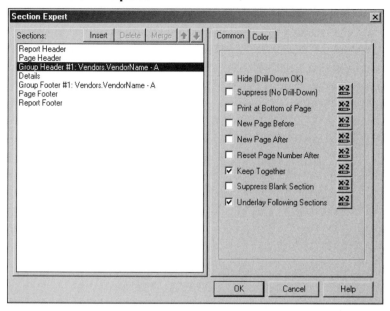

Options for formatting sections

Option	Description
Hide (Drill-Down OK)	Hides the section but makes it available for drill-down.
Suppress (No Drill-Down)	Suppresses printing of the section.
Print at Bottom of Page	The value for each group is only printed at the bottom of the page. This option is typically used with preprinted forms such as invoices where a single group prints on each page.
New Page Before	The section starts printing on a new page. Only available for a group section or the details section.
New Page After	The section that follows this section is printed on a new page.
Reset Page Number After	Resets the page number to 1 for the following page.
Keep Together	All lines for the section are kept together on the current page if they will fit or on multiple pages if they won't.
Suppress Blank Section	Suppresses printing of the section if it's blank.
Underlay Following Sections	The section is printed underneath the objects in the following sections.
Format With Multiple Columns	Displays the Layout Tab, which lets you format the report in multiple columns. This option is only available for the details section.
Reserve Minimum Page Footer	Minimizes the space that's reserved for the page footer section.

Description

- To format the sections of a report, you use the Section Expert. To display the Section Expert dialog box, right-click in the Report Designer and select Format Section.

Figure 16-14   How to work with report sections

How to work with fields in the Field Explorer

Figure 16-15 presents some information about working with fields in the Field Explorer. As you know, you can drag any field from this window to the Report Designer window to add the field to the report. You can also use the shortcut menus for field groups and individual fields to work with the fields as summarized in this figure. For example, you can create a new formula field by right-clicking on the Formula Fields group and selecting the New command.

In addition to the database fields, formula fields, and group fields you're already familiar with, you can also create parameter fields and running total fields. If you create a *parameter field*, the user will be prompted for the value of the parameter when the report is opened. Then, you can use that value within the report. For example, you might use it within the SelectionFormula property of the report to filter the data that's included in the report.

You can use a *running total field* to keep a running total of another field in the report. In this figure, for example, a running total field is being created to count the number of invoices for each vendor group. You'll see how this field is used in the custom Invoice Summary report in the next figure.

The fields in the Special Fields group let you add common report information like page number and print date to a report. Note, however, that if you use a Report Expert to create a report, some of these fields may be added by default. When you use the Standard Report Expert, for example, a print date field is added below the report title and a page number field is added at the right side of the page footer.

The dialog box for creating a running total field

Toggle Field View

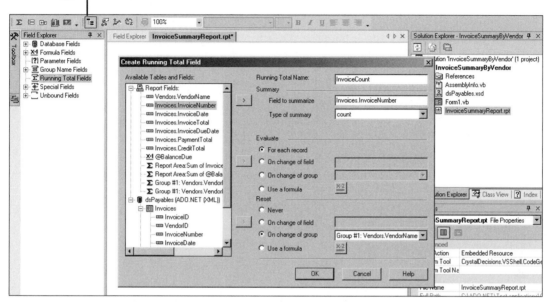

Field types

Type	Description
Database	The fields that are available from the database. You can add and remove fields and specify filter criteria using the Database Expert and the Select Expert.
Formula	Fields that are calculated from other fields in the report or database. You can create new fields and edit existing fields using the Formula Editor.
Parameter	Fields that prompt the user for values when the report is opened. You can create new fields and edit existing fields.
Group Name	The fields that are used for grouping in the report. You can add and delete groups and change grouping criteria using the Top N Expert and the Select Expert.
Running Total	Fields that are used to keep running totals of other fields in the report. You can create new fields and edit existing fields.
SQL Expression	Fields that query the database directly. You can create new fields and edit existing fields using the SQL Expression Editor. Only available with pulled data.
Special	Predefined fields such as print date and page number.
Unbound	Fields that contain expressions that aren't dependent on the data source.

Description

- You can use the Field Explorer to modify existing fields and to create new ones. To hide or show the Field Explorer, use the Toggle Field View toolbar button.
- To work with a field or field type, right-click on it and then select the appropriate item from the menu that's displayed.

Figure 16-15   How to work with fields in the Field Explorer

A custom Invoice Summary report

Figure 16-16 presents the design of the Invoice Summary report after I customized it using the Crystal Report Designer. If you compare this with the design in figure 16-13, you'll notice several differences. To start, I sized, positioned, and formatted many of the fields so they appear just the way I want them to. In addition, I changed the height of some of the sections so that the lines are spaced out appropriately.

Next, I removed the VendorName field from the details section of the report so that it doesn't print for every invoice for a vendor. Instead, I want it to print on just the first invoice. To accomplish that, I selected the Underlay Following Sections option for the group header section, which contains the vendor name.

I also added a running total field to the report to count the number of invoices for each vendor. You saw the definition of this field in the previous figure. Then, I placed this field in the group footer section, followed by another formula field. This formula field contains the following expression:

```
IIF ({#InvoiceCount} = 1,"invoice for a total of:",
"invoices for a total of:")
```

This expression determines the text that's displayed after the invoice count depending on the number of invoices. Note that when you create a running total field or specify one in building an expression, Crystal Reports precedes the field name you specify with a pound sign (#) to distinguish it from a field in the data source.

You can see the result of these changes in the report shown in the report viewer in this figure. If you compare this report to the one back in figure 16-10, I think you'll see that the customized report has a more appealing format and is much easier to read.

The design of a custom Invoice Summary report

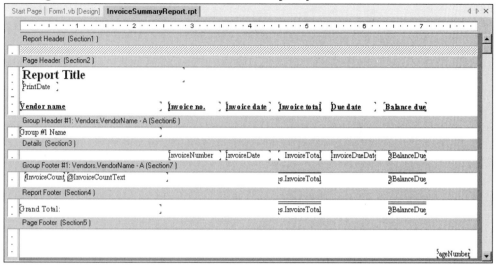

The report in a report viewer

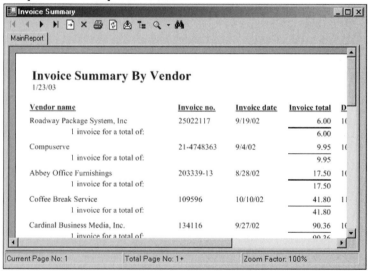

Changes made to customize this report

- The vendor name field has been removed from the details section of the report, and the Underlay Following Sections property of the group header section has been selected so that the vendor name field in that section will print on the first detail line for each vendor.

- A running total field has been added to count the number of invoices for each vendor. The settings for this field are shown in figure 16-15.

- An additional formula field has been added so that the correct text is displayed after the invoice count. This formula uses an IIf function to test the InvoiceCount field.

- The heights of some of the sections have been changed and several of the fields have been sized, positioned, and formatted.

Figure 16-16   A custom Invoice Summary report

Perspective

Although this chapter has introduced you to the primary features of Crystal Reports, it will take some experimentation before you become comfortable with using it. In particular, you'll want to try using some of the other Report Experts to see what they can do. You'll also want to experiment with the Report Designer to see what features are available for customizing a report. You may even want to try creating a report from scratch to see what's involved in doing that. If you do, I think you'll agree that it makes sense to use one of the Report Experts to start most reports.

Terms

pull model
push model
recordset
Report Expert
formula field
Formula Editor
Group tree
Report pane
Crystal Report Designer
Field Explorer
Report Designer
parameter field
running total field

17

How to use
the Server Explorer

The Server Explorer is a convenient tool for performing common database tasks. You can use it to create and modify the databases, tables, and other database objects that you need to test your applications. You can also use it to add connection, data adapter, and command objects to your forms. In this chapter, you'll learn how to take advantage of this powerful tool.

If you're using the Standard Edition of Visual Basic .NET rather than one of the editions of Visual Studio .NET, you should know that you can't perform all of the tasks presented in this chapter. Specifically, you can't use the Server Explorer to create or modify any database objects. However, you can still view the objects that are available, and you can still create connection, data adapter, and command objects.

An introduction to the Server Explorer

Chances are, you've already used the Server Explorer at least to look at the list of objects in a database. In case you aren't familiar with the Server Explorer, though, I'll begin this chapter by showing you the basic techniques for using it. Then, I'll describe how you use it to create a new database.

How to use the Server Explorer

Figure 17-1 presents an overview of the Server Explorer. At the top level, the Server Explorer consists of two nodes: Data Connections and Servers. The Data Connections node lists all of the databases that you've created a connection to. That includes the connections you've created using the Data Adapter Configuration Wizard.

The Servers node lists all of the database servers that are available to you. (This node isn't available if you're using the Standard Edition of VB.NET.) By default, only available instances of SQL Server are listed under this node. Depending on the type of database you're using, however, you may be able to add it to the Servers node using the Connect to Server button at the top of the Server Explorer window. But even if you can't do that, you can still work with the database by creating a connection to it. In fact, you can use all of the skills you'll learn in this chapter by working with the database objects listed under a data connection if a server isn't available. In this chapter, though, I'll assume you're working with a SQL Server database.

To work with the objects in a database, you expand the nodes until you can see the objects you need. In this figure, for example, you can see the five categories of objects in the Payables database. You can further expand these nodes to display the objects they contain. If you expand the Tables node, for example, you'll see the six tables in the Payables database. Then, you can expand the nodes for those tables to display the columns they contain.

To use the Server Explorer, you right-click on an object to display its shortcut menu. In this figure, for example, you can see the shortcut menu for the server that contains the Payables database. In this chapter, I'll present the commands you'll use most often as you develop database applications.

How to create a new database

Figure 17-1 also describes how you create a new database. If you're creating a new SQL Server database, you can do that using either the New Database command shown in this figure or the Create New SQL Server Database command that's displayed when you right-click on the Data Connections node. In either case, the Create Database dialog box is displayed, which lets you enter the database name and security information. If you display this dialog box from the Data Connections node, you'll also need to enter the name of the server.

The Server Explorer window

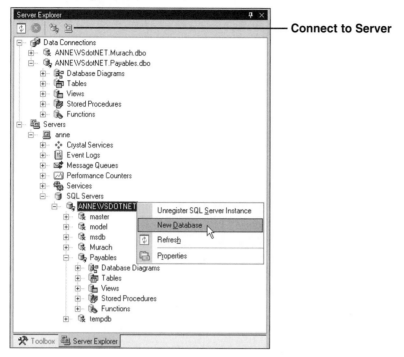

How to work with servers and connections

- The *Server Explorer* is a graphical tool for viewing, creating, and modifying the databases you have access to. You can use it to work with both the data connections you create for your applications and the databases themselves.

- The Server Explorer has two top-level nodes. The Data Connections node lists existing connections and the Servers node lists all of the servers currently available for use. You can work with the objects in a database from either of these nodes (the Servers node isn't available with the Standard Edition of VB.NET).

- If you're using SQL Server, the servers and databases that are available automatically appear under the Servers node. If you're using another server, you may be able to use the Connect to Server button to connect to a database so it appears under the Servers node.

- To work with the objects in a database, you use the shortcut menus that are displayed when you right-click on an object.

How to create a new database

- To create a new database, right-click on the node for the server under the SQL Servers node and select New Database. Then, enter the database name and security information in the Create Database dialog box that's displayed.

- You can also create a new SQL Server database by right-clicking on the Data Connections node and selecting Create New SQL Server Database. In that case, you must also specify the name of the server in the Create Database dialog box.

Figure 17-1   An introduction to the Server Explorer

How to work with tables

After you create a database, you're ready to design the tables it contains. Then, later on, you can use the same skills to modify the table if you need to.

How to define the columns of a table

Figure 17-2 presents the *Table Designer* window for the Invoices table in the Payables database. This window lets you work with the design of a new or existing table. As you can see, each column in the table is listed in the column grid. This grid includes the column name, the data type for the column, the length of the column, and whether or not the column allows nulls.

In addition to the properties in the column grid, you can set the additional column properties that appear at the bottom of the Table Designer window. For example, you can set the default value for a column or define it as an identity column. The properties that are available for each column change depending on the properties in the column grid.

You can also set the primary key for a table from this window. To do that, just click on the box to the left of the key column to select it and then click on the Set Primary Key toolbar button. If the key consists of two or more columns, you can select them by dragging over several boxes or holding the Ctrl key down while you click. When you set the primary key, a key icon appears to the left of the key column(s) as shown in this figure.

You can also display the Property Pages dialog box from this window. To do that, just click on the Relationships, Manage Indexes and Keys, or Manage Check Constraints toolbar button to display the related tab in that dialog box. You'll see how to use each of these tabs in the topics that follow.

The Table Designer window

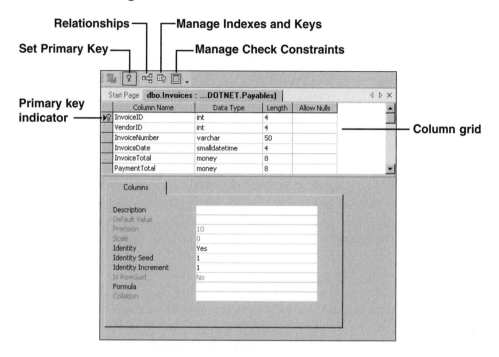

How to edit the design of an existing table

- Right-click the table in the Server Explorer and select the Design Table command to display the table in the *Table Designer* window.

How to create a new table

- Right-click the Tables node for the database and select the New Table command to display the Table Designer window.

How to work in the Table Designer window

- Use the column grid to set the basic attributes for each column, including column name, data type, length, and whether or not the column accepts nulls. To set other column attributes, click in the column and then set the options that appear in the bottom of the window.

- To set the primary key, click on the box to the left of the key column or select multiple columns by dragging over the boxes or using the Ctrl key as you click on them. Then, click on the Set Primary Key toolbar button. A key icon appears in the key columns.

- To work with table relationships, indexes and keys, or check constraints, click the corresponding toolbar button.

- When you close the Table Designer window, you will be asked whether you want to save the changes you've made. If you're creating a new table, you'll also be prompted to enter a name for the table.

Figure 17-2   How to define the columns of a table

How to define relationships

Figure 17-3 shows the Relationships tab of the Property Pages dialog box. You use this tab to define how the tables in the database are related. In this figure, for example, you can see the relationship that's defined between the Invoices and Vendors tables. Notice that the Enforce relationship for INSERTs and UPDATEs option is selected so the referential integrity between these two tables will be maintained. In other words, this relationship defines a foreign key constraint. If this option weren't selected, SQL Server would recognize but not enforce the relationship. In most cases, then, you'll want to be sure this option is selected.

Also notice that the Cascade Update and Cascade Delete options aren't selected. That means that primary keys in the Vendors table can't be changed if related rows exist in the Invoices table, and a row can't be deleted from the Vendors table if related rows exist in the Invoices table. In some cases, that's what you want. In other cases, though, you'll want to cascade update and delete operations to the foreign key table.

To create a new relationship, you click on the New button. Then, you select the primary key and foreign key tables and the columns in each table that are related. When you do, SQL Server will generate an appropriate relationship name for you, so you won't usually change this name. It will also select the first three options. I've already described the third option, which enforces the referential integrity between tables. The first option causes existing data to be checked to be sure that it satisfies the relationship.

The second option causes the relationship to be enforced when the database is replicated. *Replication* is a technique that's used to create multiple copies of the same database in different locations. By using this replication option, SQL Server can keep the various copies of a database synchronized. In most cases, though, you'll be working with test databases, so you won't need to worry about this option.

The Relationships tab of the Property Pages dialog box

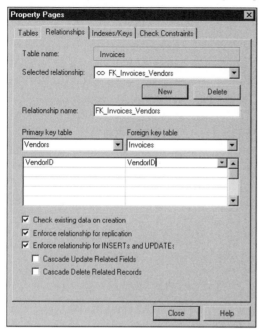

Description

- The Relationships tab of the Property Pages dialog box lets you create and modify the relationships between tables. To display this tab, click the Relationships toolbar button in the Table Designer window.

- To view or modify an existing relationship, choose the relationship from the Selected relationship drop-down list. The name and definition of the relationship are displayed in the dialog box.

- To add a new relationship, click the New button. Then, select the primary key and foreign key tables and the columns in each table that define the relationship.

- By default, SQL Server checks existing data when you add a new relationship to be sure it satisfies the relationship. If that's not what you want, you can remove the check mark from the Check existing data on creation option.

- To enforce the relationship for insert and update operations, select the Enforce relationship for INSERTs and UPDATEs option. This is the default.

- To cascade update or delete operations from the primary key to the foreign key table, select the Cascade Update Related Fields or Cascade Delete Related Records option.

- To enforce the relationship when the database is *replicated*, select the Enforce the relationship for replication option. This is the default.

- To save the new or modified relationship, close the Property Pages dialog box and then close the Table Designer. You will be asked to confirm the changes.

- To delete a relationship, select the relationship and then click the Delete button.

Figure 17-3   How to define relationships

How to define keys and indexes

Figure 17-4 presents the Indexes/Keys tab for the Invoices table. You use this tab to modify and delete existing indexes and keys and to add new indexes and keys.

An index provides for locating one or more rows directly. Without an index, the server has to scan each row of the table to locate the right ones, which is much slower. By indexing a column, you'll speed performance not only when you're searching for rows based on a search condition, but when you're joining data between tables as well. However, since maintaining an index requires some system overhead, you should index only those columns that are commonly used in search conditions and joins.

You can create two types of indexes: clustered and nonclustered. A *clustered index* defines the order in which the rows of a table are stored. Because of that, each table can have only one clustered index. By default, SQL Server creates a clustered index based on the table's primary key. A *nonclustered index* is a separate structure that has pointers to direct the system to a specific row, similar to the way the index of a book has page numbers that direct you to a specific subject. In SQL Server, one table can have up to 249 nonclustered indexes.

When you select an index from the Indexes/Keys tab of the Property Pages dialog box, the Type box indicates whether the index is for a primary key, in which case it's the clustered index; a unique key, in which case it's a nonclustered index; or some other nonclustered index. This tab also lists the name of the index, the columns that make up the index, and other options related to the index.

To create a new index for a table, you click on the New button, enter a name for the index, then select the columns you want to include in the index and specify the sort order for each column. If you want to create a unique key, select the Create UNIQUE option. The Constraint option that's subordinate to that option is selected by default, which means that SQL Server will create a unique key constraint along with the index. If you want to create an index that enforces the uniqueness of its values without using a unique key constraint, however, you can do that by selecting the Index option. In most cases, though, you'll want to enforce uniqueness by using a unique key constraint.

By default, the index will be nonclustered. If the table doesn't have a primary key, however, you can select the Create as CLUSTERED option to create a clustered index. You can also use some of the other options in this dialog box to tune an index for optimum performance. In most cases, though, the default values for these options are acceptable.

The Indexes/Keys tab of the Property Pages dialog box

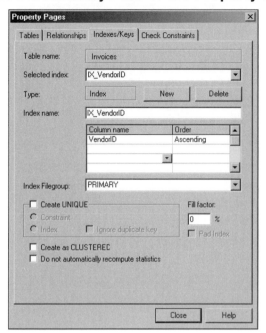

Description

- To display the Indexes/Keys tab of the Property Pages dialog box, click the Manage Indexes and Keys toolbar button in the Table Designer window.

- To view an existing index, choose the index from the Selected index drop-down list. The index name and definition appear in the dialog box.

- To define a new index, click the New button, enter the name you want to use for the index, and select the column name and sort order for each column in the index.

- To create a unique key and an index that's based on that key, select the Create UNIQUE check box and the Constraint option. To create a unique index without creating a unique key, select the Create UNIQUE check box and the Index option.

- To create a *clustered index*, select the Create as CLUSTERED option. A clustered index determines the sequence in which the rows in the table are stored. A clustered index is created automatically based on the table's primary key, so you usually won't select this option.

- The other options in this dialog box are used for performance tuning. In most cases, the default values for these options are acceptable.

- To delete an index, select the index and then click the Delete button.

Figure 17-4   How to define keys and indexes

How to define check constraints

Figure 17-5 presents the Check Constraints tab of the Property Pages dialog box. You use this tab to modify or delete existing check constraints for a table or to add new constraints. In this figure, for example, you can see a check constraint for the Invoices table. This constraint specifies that the InvoiceTotal column must be greater than or equal to zero. Although this constraint refers to a single column in the Invoices table, you should know that a constraint can refer to any number of columns.

The options that are available from this tab are similar to the options you saw in the Relationships tab. The first one determines if existing data is checked when a new constraint is created. The second one determines if constraints are enforced when the database is replicated. And the third one determines if constraints are enforced when rows are inserted or updated. In most cases, you'll select all three of these options. If you want to temporarily disable a constraint during testing, however, you can do that by removing one or more of these check marks.

The Check Constraints tab of the Property Pages dialog box

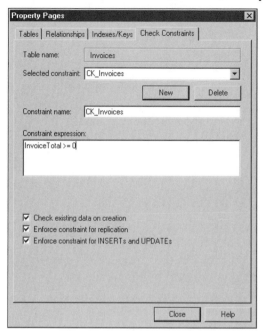

Description

- To display the Check Constraints tab of the Property Pages dialog box, click the Manage Check Constraints toolbar button in the Table Designer window.

- To view or modify an existing constraint, choose the constraint from the Selected constraint drop-down list. The constraint name and expression are displayed in the dialog box.

- To define a new constraint, click the New button, enter the name you want to use for the constraint, and enter a conditional expression in the Constraint expression box. The expression you specify can refer to one or more columns in the table.

- By default, SQL Server checks existing data when you add a new check constraint to be sure it satisfies the constraint. If that's not what you want, you can remove the check mark from the Check existing data on creation option.

- To enforce the constraint for insert and update operations, select the Enforce constraint for INSERTs and UPDATEs option. This is the default.

- To enforce the constraint when the database is replicated, select the Enforce constraint for replication option. This is the default.

- To delete a constraint, select the constraint and then click the Delete button.

Figure 17-5   How to define check constraints

How to work with the data in a table

You can also use the Server Explorer to retrieve and edit the data in a table. To do that, you use the results pane of the *Query Designer window* shown in figure 17-6. Here, you can see the data in the Vendors table.

By default, all of the data in the table you select is displayed in the results pane. If you want to restrict the data that's displayed, however, you can display the other panes of the Query Designer window and then use them to modify the generated Select statement. These panes are identical to the panes of the Query Builder that you saw in figure 3-4. To display them, you can use the appropriate toolbar buttons. Then, after you modify the query, you can click the Run toolbar button to display the new results in the results pane.

You can also use the results pane to insert, update, and delete rows from a table. To update the data in a row, just move to the columns you want to change and begin typing. As soon as you move to another row, the changes are saved in the database. To insert a new row, navigate to the end of the result set and enter the data in the row that has an asterisk in the row selector. In this figure, for example, you can see that I started to enter the data for a new row. When I did that, a pencil appeared in the row selector and another row was added at the end of the result set for the next new row. Finally, to delete a row, just click on its row selector to select it and then press the Delete key.

As you can see, the results pane provides a quick and easy way to modify the data in a table without having to write Insert, Update, or Delete statements. That can come in handy when you're testing a new database. You should realize, however, that to insert a row, it must include all of the required columns. The only columns that can be omitted are identity columns, columns with default values, and columns that allow null values. In addition, to update or delete an existing row, the Query Designer must be able to uniquely identify that row. In most cases, that means that the primary key must be included in the result set.

Because the results are editable, the Server Explorer must constantly check them for changes, which requires a significant amount of server resources. For this reason, if you keep the results pane open for more than a few minutes, the system will automatically clear the results pane. If you need to continue working with the result set, just click the Run toolbar button.

The data in the Vendors table

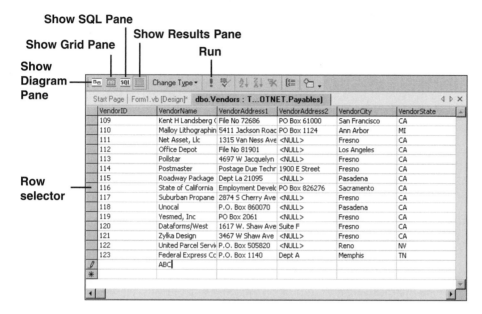

How to retrieve data

- To retrieve data from a table, right-click the table in the Server Explorer and select the Retrieve Data from Table command to open the results pane of the *Query Designer*.

- The data that's displayed is the result of a Select statement that returns all of the rows and columns from the table.

- To modify the Select statement, use the buttons in the toolbar to display the diagram, grid, and SQL panes like the ones you saw in the Query Builder window in figure 3-4. After making the changes, click the Run toolbar button to display the new results.

How to edit the data in the results pane

- To add a row to the table, scroll to the bottom of the table, click in the last row (the one with an asterisk in the row selector) and enter the data for each required column.

- To change the value of one or more columns in a row, click in the columns and enter the changes. A pencil appears in the row selector to indicate that it has been modified. To save the changes, move to another row.

- To cancel a change to the current column, press the Esc key. To cancel all the changes to a row, move to a column that hasn't been modified and then press the Esc key.

- To delete a row, click its row selector and then press the Delete key. To delete two or more rows, drag over their row selectors and then press the Delete key.

- You can also use the shortcut menu that's displayed when you right-click in the results pane to work with the data in that pane.

- Some restrictions may apply to queries that can be used to insert, update, and delete rows. For more information, see online help.

Figure 17-6   How to work with the data in a table

How to diagram a database

After you create a database and the tables it contains, you can diagram its structure using the *Database Designer*. This graphical tool makes it easy to document the relationships between the tables in the database. Although you can also use the Database Designer to design the tables of a database, you're more likely to use the skills you've already learned to do that. So I won't show you how to do that in this chapter.

Figure 17-7 presents a database diagram for the Payables database. Because this database is small, I included all of the tables in a single diagram. For a larger database, though, you may want to create several diagrams that each contains a subset of the tables in the database.

To create a diagram like the one in this figure, you select the tables you want to include from the Add Table dialog box that's displayed when you first start the diagram. If you've already defined relationships between those tables, they'll appear as links like the ones shown in this figure. These links have endpoints that indicate the kind of relationship that exists between the tables. In this figure, all of the relationships are one-to-many, so a key appears on the "one" side of the link and an infinity symbol (∞) appears on the "many" side.

You can also add tables to a diagram by clicking the Add Table toolbar button to redisplay the Add Table dialog box. Or, you can add all the tables related to a table in the diagram by selecting the table and clicking the Add Related Tables toolbar button. To remove a table from the diagram, select the table and click the Remove Table from Diagram toolbar button.

A database diagram for the Payables database

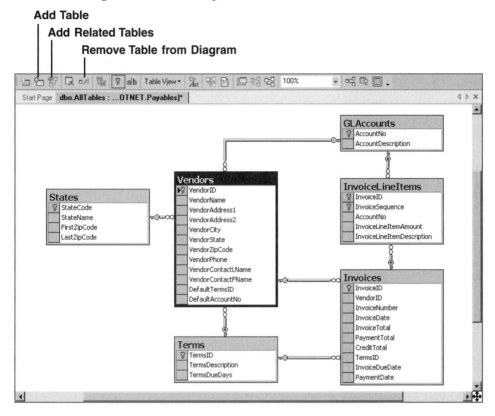

Add Table
Add Related Tables
Remove Table from Diagram

Description

- A *database diagram* illustrates the relationships between some or all of the tables in a database. To create and work with database diagrams, you use the *Database Designer*.

- To modify an existing diagram, right-click on it in the Server Explorer and select the Design Database Diagram command.

- To create a new diagram, right-click the Database Diagrams node for the database and select the New Diagram command. Then, select the tables you want to include in the diagram from the Add Table dialog box that's displayed.

- If relationships exist between two tables in the diagram, they appear as links where the endpoints of the links indicate the type of relationship. A key indicates the "one" side of a relationship, and the infinity symbol (∞) indicates the "many" side of a relationship.

- To add a table to a diagram, click the Add Table toolbar button and select the table from the Add Table dialog box. To add all the tables that are related to a table in the diagram, select the table and click the Add Related Tables toolbar button. To remove a table from the diagram, select the table and click the Remove Table from Diagram toolbar button.

- You can also work with the design of individual tables and the relationships between them using the Database Designer. For more information, see online help.

Figure 17-7   How to diagram a database

How to work with other database objects

In addition to tables, you can also use the Server Explorer to work with other database objects. In particular, you can use it to work with views and stored procedures. After I show you how to do that, I'll summarize the other objects you can work with using the Server Explorer. Then, you can experiment on your own if you ever need to use these objects.

How to create and modify a view

A *view* is a Select statement that's stored with the database. Because views are stored as part of the database, they can be managed independently of the applications that use them. Views can be used to restrict the data that a user is allowed to access or to present data in a form that's easy for the user to understand. In some databases, users may be allowed to access data only through views.

Figure 17-8 shows you how to create and modify a view. To do that, you use the *View Designer*. As you can see in this figure, the View Designer consists of four panes just like the Query Builder you learned about in chapter 3 and the Query Designer you learned about earlier in this chapter. You can use these panes to create the Select statement that's stored in the view.

To select the tables to be included in the view, you use the Add Table dialog box that's displayed when you first start a new view. You can also redisplay this dialog box at any time by clicking the Add Table toolbar button. When you display this dialog box, you'll notice that it lets you add other views as well as tables to the new view. In other words, you can base a new view on one or more existing views.

How to work with the data in a view

You can also retrieve and work with the data in a view from the View Designer window as described in figure 17-8. If you're already in the View Designer window, you can simply click the Run toolbar button to display the results in the results pane. Otherwise, you can use the Retrieve Data from View command from the Server Explorer to display just the results pane.

After you retrieve the data from a view, you can use the results pane to insert, update, and delete rows just as you can when you're working with the Query Designer. In general, though, I don't recommend you do that because it's prone to errors, particularly if the view contains data from two or more tables. Instead, you should use the Query Designer to work directly with the data in a single table.

Once you create a view, you can use it in your Visual Basic projects almost anywhere you can use a table. For example, you can add a view to the Query

A view that retrieves data from two tables

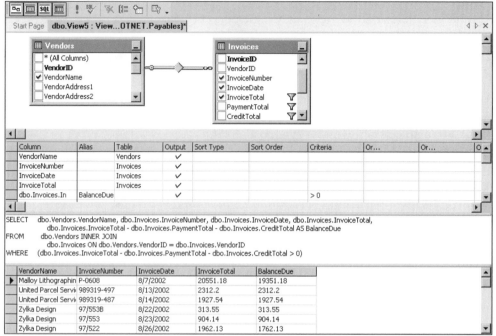

How to create and modify a view

- A *view* is a SQL Select statement that's stored within a database. To create and work with views, you use the *View Designer*.

- To edit an existing view, right-click on it in the Server Explorer and select the Design View command.

- To create a new view, right-click the Views node for the database and select the New View command. Then, select the tables, views, and functions you want to include in the view from the Add Table dialog box that's displayed.

- The View Designer is similar to the Query Builder that was presented in chapter 3. It consists of a diagram pane, a grid pane, a SQL pane, and a results pane.

- You can use the buttons in the toolbar to hide and show the panes, run the query, check the syntax of the query, and add tables to the diagram pane.

How to work with the data in a view

- To retrieve data from a view, open and run it as described above. Or, right-click the view in the Server Explorer and select the Retrieve Data from View command to display the data in the results pane. Then, you can work with it as described in figure 17-6.

- You can also use a view in place of a table in most queries.

Figure 17-8   How to create and work with views

Builder when you build the Select statement associated with a data adapter. You can also refer to a view from almost any SQL statement you create in code. In general, though, you'll use views only in Select statements.

How to create and modify a stored procedure

As you learned in chapter 8, a stored procedure is a set of SQL statements that can be pre-compiled and saved as an executable object in the database. By using stored procedures, you can avoid coding SQL queries within your program. This provides a performance advantage and simplifies the use of the database. In this topic, you won't learn how to code stored procedures in detail, but you will learn how to create and modify them.

Figure 17-9 presents the *Code and Text Editor window* you use to create and modify stored procedures. When you create a new procedure, a skeleton like the one shown in the example at the top of this figure is displayed. You can use this skeleton to help you create the stored procedure.

To name the stored procedure, for example, you can replace the generated name on the Create Procedure clause. Note that the name is prefixed with the owner of the new procedure, in this case, dbo. Since dbo is the default owner of a database, you can omit it if you want to and it will be assumed.

The next six lines of code consist of characters that begin with a comment (/*), an open parenthesis that encloses any parameters required by the procedure, skeleton definitions for two parameters, a close parenthesis, and characters that end the comment (*/). If the procedure won't use any parameters, you can delete all of these lines. Otherwise, you'll need to delete the comment characters and replace the skeleton definitions with the actual definitions as shown in the second example in this figure. Here, the procedure is defined with a single input parameter named @BalanceDue.

Next, you enter the SQL statements that make up the stored procedure following the As keyword. You can type the statements directly into this window, or you can use the Query Designer window to design a query and insert it into this window. When you're done, each statement is enclosed in a box as shown in the second example in this figure. Here, the stored procedure contains a Select statement that will retrieve vendor and invoice information depending on the value of the @BalanceDue parameter.

By default, the server returns a count of the number of rows that are affected by a query. If you don't use that value in your program, it's simply discarded. If you don't want the server to generate this value, though, you can remove the comment characters from the next line of code to set the NoCount option on.

The last generated line of code is a Return statement, which ends the procedure. You can also use this statement to return a value to the calling program, as you saw in chapter 8. If you don't specify a value on this statement, however, zero is returned.

The skeleton for a new stored procedure

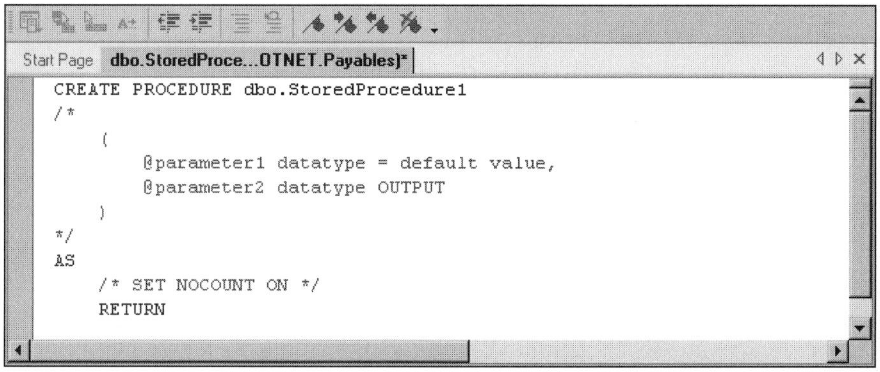

```
CREATE PROCEDURE dbo.StoredProcedure1
/*
    (
        @parameter1 datatype = default value,
        @parameter2 datatype OUTPUT
    )
*/
AS
    /* SET NOCOUNT ON */
    RETURN
```

A stored procedure that retrieves vendors by balance due

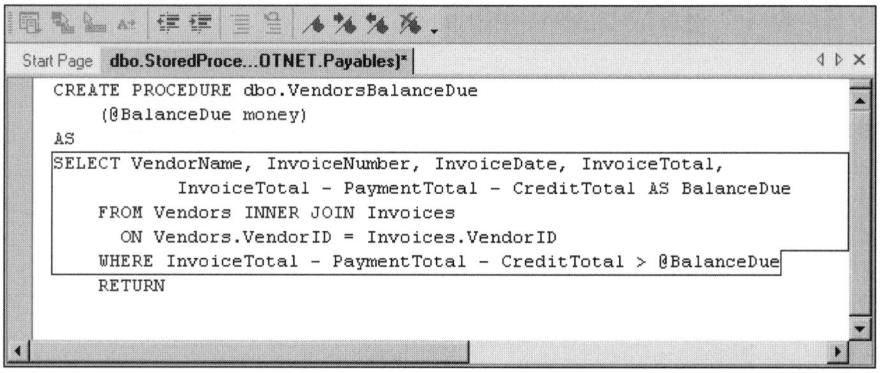

```
CREATE PROCEDURE dbo.VendorsBalanceDue
    (@BalanceDue money)
AS
SELECT VendorName, InvoiceNumber, InvoiceDate, InvoiceTotal,
        InvoiceTotal - PaymentTotal - CreditTotal AS BalanceDue
    FROM Vendors INNER JOIN Invoices
      ON Vendors.VendorID = Invoices.VendorID
    WHERE InvoiceTotal - PaymentTotal - CreditTotal > @BalanceDue
    RETURN
```

Description

- To edit an existing stored procedure, right-click on it in the Server Explorer and then select Edit Stored Procedure. The stored procedure is displayed in the *Code and Text Editor window*, and each SQL statement within the procedure is enclosed in a box.

- You can edit an existing SQL statement directly in the Code and Text Editor window, or you can display the statement in the Query Designer by right-clicking in the box that contains it and selecting Design SQL Block.

- To create a new stored procedure, right-click the Stored Procedures node for the database and select New Stored Procedure. The Code and Text Editor window is displayed with skeleton statements for the stored procedure.

- To change the name of the stored procedure, edit the Create Procedure clause. If the procedure requires parameters, you can define them using the skeleton parameters as a guide. If you replace the skeleton parameters, be sure to delete the /* and */ characters that comment them out.

- You enter the SQL statements to be executed by a stored procedure following the As keyword. You can enter a statement directly into the Code and Text Editor window, or you can right-click in this window where you want the statement inserted and select Insert SQL to create the statement using the Query Designer.

Figure 17-9   How to create and modify a stored procedure

How to execute a stored procedure

The Server Explorer also lets you test a stored procedure so you can be sure it works before you use it in an application. Figure 17-10 shows you how to do that. Here, you can see the dialog box and output that are displayed for the stored procedure you saw in the previous figure. The dialog box is displayed because the procedure includes an input parameter, and it needs a value for that parameter to execute the query it contains. If you execute a procedure that doesn't have any input parameters, this dialog box isn't displayed.

After you provide the values for any input parameters, the output created by the procedure is displayed in the Output window. For the query shown here, the output includes a result set, a row count, and a return value. If a procedure has output parameters, they're also displayed in the Output window.

Other SQL Server database objects

In addition to stored procedures, SQL Server also provides for two other types of executable objects: functions and triggers. You can create and work with these objects using the Server Explorer in much the same way that you create and work with stored procedures. (You won't have access to these objects if you're using the Standard Edition of VB.NET.) Since you're not likely to work directly with these objects as an application programmer, however, I won't show you how to do that here. Instead, I'll just describe their general use.

A *function* is a special type of procedure that always returns a value. Like a stored procedure, a function can accept input parameters. However, a function differs from a stored procedure in three ways. First, you typically execute a function from within other SQL code. Second, a function can return a single value. Third, the value that a function returns can be of any data type, including the table data type. A function that returns a single, scalar value is called a *scalar-valued function*. A function that returns an entire table is called a *table-valued function*.

A database *trigger* is a special type of procedure that's executed (or *fired*) automatically when rows are inserted, updated, or deleted from a table or view. Unlike a stored procedure, you can't fire a trigger directly and a trigger can't accept or return parameters or return values.

Triggers are used most often to validate data before a row is added or updated. However, they can also be used to maintain referential integrity between related tables. In that case, they provide flexibility that's not available with foreign key constraints.

The dialog box that lets you enter parameter values

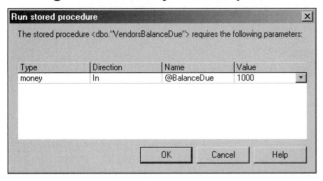

The results of the stored procedure are displayed in the Output window

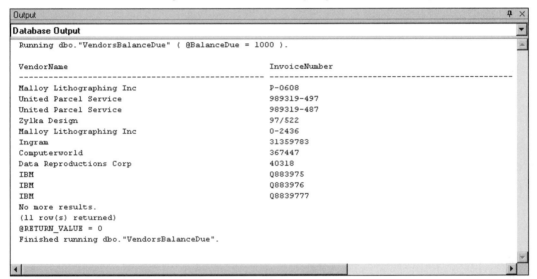

Description

- To execute a stored procedure, right-click on it in the Server Explorer and select the Run Stored Procedure command.

- If the procedure has input parameters, the Run stored procedure dialog box is displayed. Enter the value for each parameter in this dialog box and click the OK button to execute the procedure.

- The output from the procedure is displayed in the Output window. This output includes the result set, the row count (unless NoCount is specified), the return value, and any output parameters.

Figure 17-10   How to execute a stored procedure

How to work with ADO.NET objects

Up to now, you've created the ADO.NET objects you use in your projects by dragging components from the Toolbox or by defining the objects you need in code. But you can also create and work with some of these objects using the Server Explorer. You'll learn how to do that in the topics that follow.

How to work with data connections

When you use the Data Adapter Configuration Wizard, the data connection that's created is listed in the Data Connections node of the Server Explorer. But you can also add a data connection or modify an existing connection from the Server Explorer. Figure 17-11 shows you how.

To add or modify a connection, you use the Data Link Properties dialog box shown in this figure. This dialog box is identical to the dialog box that's displayed when you use the Data Adapter Configuration Wizard, so you should already know how to use it. Remember, though, that by default, the SQL Server data provider will be used. If that's not what you want, you can click on the Provider tab and select a different provider.

Regardless of how you create a data connection, once it's created, you can use it to add connection components to your forms. To do that, just drag the data connection from the Server Explorer to a form. The connection will appear in the Component Designer tray, and you can use it just as you would any other connection.

Before I go on, you should realize that Visual Studio maintains the data connections you create until you explicitly delete them. That way, you don't have to redefine a connection each time you use it. If you no longer need a data connection, however, you can delete it by right-clicking on the connection and selecting Delete Connection.

The Data Link Properties dialog box

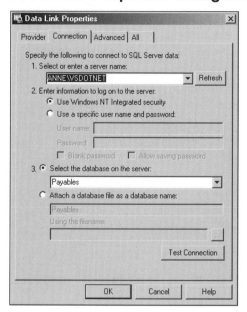

How to create a new database connection

- Right-click on the Data Connections node in the Server Explorer and select Add Connection to display the Data Link Properties dialog box. You can also display this dialog box by clicking the Connect to Database toolbar button.

- Select the server, enter the security information, and select the database. To connect to a database other than SQL Server, click the Provider tab and select the provider for that database.

- To verify that the connection information is correct, click the Test Connection button. To create the new connection, click OK.

How to modify or delete a database connection

- To edit the properties of an existing connection, right-click the connection and select Modify Connection to display the Data Link Properties dialog box.

- To delete a connection, right-click the connection and select Delete Connection.

How to add a Connection object to your project

- Drag the connection from the Server Explorer to a form to add a connection object to that form.

Figure 17-11   How to work with data connections

How to create other ADO.NET objects

You can also use the Server Explorer to add data adapter and command objects to a form. To do that, just drag a table, a view, or selected columns from one or more tables or views to the form. Then, Visual Studio generates one data adapter for each table or view, along with the commands that contain the Select, Insert, Update, and Delete statements for each data adapter and a connection if one doesn't already exist.

To illustrate, take a look at figure 17-12. Here, you can see that columns are selected from both the Vendors and Invoices tables. When I dragged these columns to the form, two data adapters were created: one for the Vendors table and one for the Invoices table. In addition, a connection object was created for the Payables database based on the existing data connection.

As you can see, this is a quick and easy way to add ADO.NET objects to your forms. Keep in mind, however, that most of the queries you create will include some type of filter criteria, and there's no way to specify that criteria when you use this technique. Instead, you have to modify the query after it's generated. Because of that, you're likely to use this technique only for the simplest forms.

If you're using stored procedures in an application, you can also use the Server Explorer to add command objects that will execute those procedures. To do that, just drag the stored procedures from the Server Explorer to the form. If the form doesn't already include a connection to the database that contains the stored procedures, a connection is added as well.

In addition to dragging objects from the Server Explorer to the Form Designer window, you can also drag them to many of the other designer windows. If you're creating a dataset schema using the XML Designer as described in chapter 9, for example, you can drag a table, view, or selected columns to this window to create a table element. Or if you're creating a view using the View Designer as described earlier in this chapter, you can drag a table, view, or selected columns to the diagram pane to add a table to that pane. This is just one more way that Visual Studio makes it easy to work with the data in a database.

ADO.NET objects created by dragging columns from two tables

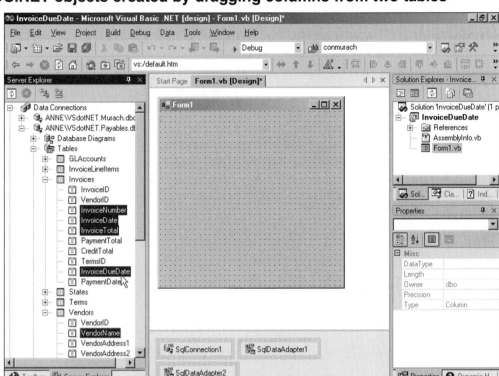

How to create a data adapter object

- To add a data adapter for all the columns in a table or view, drag the table or view from the Server Explorer to a form. If you haven't already created a connection object, one is added automatically.

- To add a data adapter for selected columns in a table or view, select the columns and then drag them to a form.

- You can also drag columns from more than one table or view. Then a separate data adapter is created for each table. If you want to create a data adapter based on a join between tables, define the join in a view and then drag the view to the form.

- You can also drag a table, view, or columns to other designers like the XML Designer and the View Designer.

How to create a command object

- Drag a stored procedure to a form to create a command object that you can use to execute that stored procedure. If you haven't already created a connection object, one is added automatically.

- Select, Insert, Update, and Delete command objects are also created automatically when you create a data adapter object by dragging a table, view, or columns to a form.

Figure 17-12   How to create other ADO.NET objects

Perspective

In this chapter, you've learned how to use the Server Explorer to work with the objects in a database. If you take a few minutes to experiment with this tool, I think you'll quickly recognize its usefulness. In particular, it provides an easy-to-use interface for designing new tables and for reviewing the design of existing tables. In addition, it makes it easy to work with the data in a database as you test your database applications.

You probably realize, though, that there's much more to learn about database features like views, stored procedures, functions, and triggers. So if you want to expand your knowledge of these and other SQL features, I recommend you get our book, *Murach's SQL for SQL Server*. Since the use of SQL is so essential to effective database programming, this book will help raise your skill to another level.

Terms

Server Explorer
Table Designer
replication
clustered index
nonclustered index
Query Designer
database diagram
Database Designer
view
View Designer
Code and Text Editor window
function
scalar-valued function
table-valued function
trigger

Appendix A

How to install and use the software and downloadable files for this book

To develop the database applications presented in this book, you need to have Visual Studio .NET or the Standard Edition of Visual Basic .NET installed on your system. In addition, if you're going to access databases that are stored on your own PC rather than on a remote server, you need to install MSDE (Microsoft SQL Server 2000 Desktop Engine). And if you're going to develop web applications using a web server on your own PC, you need to install IIS. This appendix describes how to install these products. It also describes the files for this book that are available for download from our web site and tells you how you can use them.

How to use the downloadable files

Throughout this book, you'll see complete applications that illustrate the material presented in each chapter. To help you understand how they work, you can download the source code and data for these applications from our web site. Then, you can open and run them in Visual Studio. These files come in a single download, as summarized in figure A-1. This figure also describes how you download, install, and use these files.

When you download the single install file and execute it, it will install all of the files for this book in the Murach\ADO.NET folder on your C drive. Within this folder, you'll find a folder named Book applications that contains the source code for all the Windows applications in this book. The source code is organized in folders by applications within chapters. For example, the source files for the Vendor Maintenance application in chapter 3 are stored in C:\Murach\ADO.NET\Book applications\Chapter 3\VendorMaintenance. You can then use Visual Studio to open and run these applications. Before you run an application, though, be sure to change any connection strings it uses so they're appropriate for your database. Otherwise, a runtime error will occur.

You may also need to prepare your system for using the databases that come with this book. That's the case if you want to use these databases on your own PC rather than using databases that have been installed on a remote server. Then, you'll need to install MSDE on your system, and you'll need to attach the databases for this book to MSDE. You can learn how to do that in figure A-3. As you'll see there, the databases and the files needed to attach them are found in a folder named Databases that's subordinate to the Murach\ADO.NET folder.

You may also need to prepare your system for developing and running web applications. That's the case if these applications will be deployed to a web server on your own PC. Then, you need to install IIS on your system as described in figure A-4. In addition, to use the web applications that come with this book, you'll need to copy the project files for these applications to the appropriate folder and then configure the applications for use with IIS. The procedure for doing that is presented in figure A-5.

Because not everyone needs to have MSDE and IIS installed on their PCs, I'll start by showing you how to install Visual Studio or Visual Basic. Note in this figure, however, that if you're going to install all the software components, you should install IIS first.

What the downloadable application file for this book contains

- The source code for all of the applications presented in the book
- The Payables and Murach databases used by these applications
- A batch file that uses a SQL script to install the databases as required

How to download and install the files for this book

- Go to www.murach.com, and go to the page for *Murach's VB.NET Database Programming with ADO.NET*.
- Click on the link for "FREE download of the book applications." Then, download "All book files." This will download one file named adon_allfiles.exe to your C drive.
- Use the Windows Explorer to find the downloaded file on your C drive. Then, double-click on this file and respond to the dialog boxes that follow. This installs the files in folders that start with C:\Murach\ADO.NET.

How to use the source code for the applications

- The source code for the applications presented in this book can be found in chapter folders in the C:\Murach\ADO.NET\Book applications folder. You can view this source code by opening the project or solution in the appropriate folder. Before you can run any of these applications, you'll need to change the connection strings they use so they're appropriate for the database you're using.

How to prepare your system for using the databases

- If you're going to use the databases that come with this book on your own PC, you'll need to install MSDE and then attach the databases to MSDE as described in figure A-3.

How to prepare your system for developing web applications

- If you're going to be developing or running web applications on a web server on your own PC, you'll need to install IIS as described in figure A-4.
- Before you can open the web applications that come with this book, you'll need to copy the project files for these applications to IIS and then configure the application for use with IIS as described in figure A-5.

The order of software installation

1. Install IIS.
2. Install Visual Studio .NET or Visual Basic .NET.
3. Install MSDE.

Note

- If you're using Windows XP Home Edition, IIS is *not* available, so you won't be able to create or run web applications using your PC alone. You'll need a separate web server.

Figure A-1   How to use the downloadable files for this book

How to install the .NET Framework and Visual Studio .NET

If you've installed Windows applications before, you shouldn't have any trouble installing Visual Studio .NET. You simply insert the first Visual Studio CD, and the setup program starts automatically. This setup program will lead you through the steps for installing Visual Studio as summarized in figure A-2.

The first step of the installation procedure for Visual Studio .NET (or the Standard Edition of Visual Basic .NET) is to update the Windows components. During this step, the components of the .NET Framework will be installed on your system. The second step is to install Visual Studio itself. Although you will have a variety of options for what's actually installed, it's safest to just accept the defaults unless you're familiar with the various components and know exactly what you need. The final step is to apply any updates that have become available since the product was released. Note that if you don't do that and updates are available, a link will appear on the Visual Studio Start page that you can use to install the updates.

The Visual Studio .NET setup program

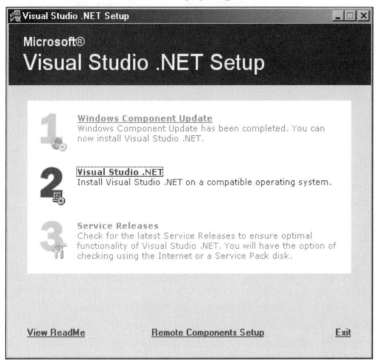

How to install Visual Studio .NET

- To install Visual Studio .NET, insert Disc 1 of the Visual Studio .NET CDs and the setup program will start automatically.

- If the .NET Framework has not been installed on your system, you will need to install it before installing Visual Studio .NET. To do that, click on the Windows Component Update link in the Setup dialog box.

- After the .NET Framework is installed, click on the Visual Studio .NET link and follow the instructions to install Visual Studio .NET. When the Options page is displayed, you can usually just accept the default options unless you have special requirements.

- After you install Visual Studio .NET, click on the Service Releases link to check for and install any updates that are available.

What if you're using Visual Basic .NET

- The setup program for the Standard Edition of Visual Basic .NET is similar to the setup program for Visual Studio .NET, but fewer options are available on the Options page.

Warning

- If you're going to develop the web applications for chapters 12-14 and you're going to use a web server that's on your own PC, you need to install IIS before installing the .NET Framework. See figure A-4 for details.

Figure A-2   How to install the .NET Framework and Visual Studio .NET

How to install MSDE and use it with our databases

MSDE is a desktop version of Microsoft SQL Server that can be used to test database applications. MSDE came with Visual Studio .NET 2002 (and Visual Basic .NET 2002), but it doesn't come with the 2003 versions of Visual Studio .NET and Visual Basic .NET. Instead, you have to download and install MSDE from Microsoft's web site. Figure A-3 describes the procedure for installing MSDE for both the 2002 and 2003 versions of Visual Studio .NET and Visual Basic .NET.

After you install MSDE, you'll notice a server icon near the right side of the Windows taskbar. If you double-click on this icon, the SQL Server Service Manager dialog box shown at the top of this figure is displayed. You can use this dialog box to start, continue, pause, or stop the SQL Server engine. By default, SQL Server is started each time you start your PC. If that's not what you want, you can remove the check mark from the Auto-start option in this dialog box. Then, you can start SQL Server whenever you need it using this dialog box.

Although you don't need to know much about how MSDE works to use it, you should know that when you run the setup program, it creates a copy of SQL Server with the same name as your computer appended with VSdotNET. For example, the copy of SQL Server on my system is named ANNE\VSdotNET as you can see in the dialog box in this figure. After this server is installed and started, you can add databases to it. Then, you can create connections to those databases for use in your Visual Basic programs.

If you want to use the databases that are available with the download for this book, you can do that without much trouble. Once you've installed the downloaded file, you can use the Windows Explorer to find and run the batch file named DB_Attach.bat in the C:\Murach\ADO.NET\Databases folder. This batch file runs a SQL Server script named DB_Attach.sql that attaches the databases to the copy of SQL Server running on your computer.

Note, however, that if the copy of SQL Server on your system has a name other than the computer name appended with VSdotNET, the batch file we provide won't work. But you can easily change it so it will work. To do that, just open the file in a text editor, such as NotePad. When you do, you'll see a single command with this server specification:

```
%COMPUTERNAME%\VSdotNET
```

Then, you can just change this specification to the name of your server.

The SQL Server Service Manager

How to install and use MSDE

- If you're using Visual Studio .NET 2002, use Windows Explorer to navigate to this folder: C:\Program Files\Microsoft Visual Studio .NET\Setup\MSDE. Then, double-click on the Setup.exe file to run it and install MSDE. When you're done, restart your PC. (If you didn't select the option to install MSDE when you installed Visual Studio .NET 2002, you can install it directly from Disk 3 of the distribution CDs. You'll find the setup program for MSDE in the Program Files\Microsoft Visual Studio .NET\Setup\MSDE folder.)

- If you're using Visual Studio .NET 2003, use Windows Explorer to navigate to this folder: C:\Program Files\Microsoft Visual Studio .NET 2003\Setup\MSDE. Then, double-click on the msde_readme.htm document to display it in your browser. Click the link in that document to go to the Microsoft web site, and follow the directions on the page that's displayed to download and install MSDE. When you're done, restart your PC.

- After you install MSDE, SQL Server will start automatically each time you start your PC. An icon will appear near the right side of the Windows taskbar to indicate that this service is running. To manage this service, double-click the icon or select the Start➔Programs➔MSDE➔Service Manager command to display the dialog box shown above.

- The setup program creates a copy of SQL Server with your computer name appended with VSdotNET. You can use this server name to define connections to the databases you add to this server, as shown throughout this book.

How to attach the databases for this book to MSDE

- If you're going to use the Payables and Murach databases used by the programs in this book on your own PC, you need to attach them to MSDE. To do that, you can use the batch file and SQL script that are downloaded and installed along with the other files for this book.

- To attach the databases to MSDE, use the Windows Explorer to navigate to the C:\Murach\ADO.NET\Databases folder, and double-click on the DB_Attach.bat file to run it.

Figure A-3   How to install MSDE and use it with our databases

How to install IIS

If you're going to develop web applications that use databases as described in chapters 12-14, you'll need access to a web server running IIS. If you don't have access to a web server, you can install IIS on your own PC...*unless* you're using Windows XP Home Edition. In that case, IIS isn't available to you, and you'll have to have access to a separate web server. Figure A-4 shows you how to install IIS.

To start, you display the Add/Remove Programs dialog box and then click on the Add/Remove Windows Components link as shown in this figure. When you do, the Windows Components Wizard starts and the second dialog box shown in this figure is displayed. This dialog box lists all the available Windows components. The components that are currently installed have a check mark in front of them. To install another component (in this case, IIS), just check it, click on the Next button, and complete the dialog boxes that are displayed.

As I mentioned earlier, if you're going to use IIS, you should install it before you install the .NET Framework or Visual Studio .NET. If you install Visual Studio first, you'll need to reinstall it after installing IIS. And if you install the .NET Framework first, you'll need to repair it after installing IIS. To do that, you can execute the command shown in this figure. This command runs an executable file named dotnetfx.exe that can be found on one of the Visual Studio .NET installation CDs.

The dialog boxes for installing IIS

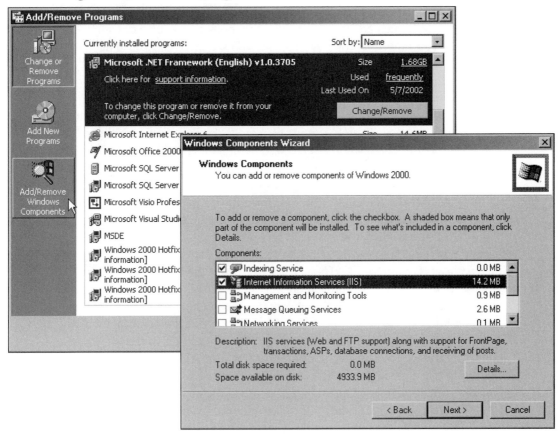

Description

- To install IIS, display the Windows Control Panel, and double-click on the Add/Remove Programs icon to display the Add/Remove Programs dialog box. Then, click on Add/Remove Windows Components to display the Windows Components Wizard, select Internet Information Services (IIS) from the list of components that are displayed, and click on the Next button to complete the installation.

When to install IIS

- IIS should be installed prior to installing the .NET Framework and Visual Studio .NET.

- If you install IIS after installing the .NET Framework, you will need to repair the Framework. To do that, insert the Visual Studio .NET Windows Component Update CD. Then, click on the Start button in the Windows taskbar, choose the Run command, and enter this command:

```
<CD Drive>:\dotNetFramework\dotnetfx.exe /t:c:\temp /c:"msiexec.exe /fvecms
c:\temp\netfx.msi"
```

- If you install IIS after installing Visual Studio .NET, you will need to reinstall Visual Studio. To do that, use the Add/Remove Programs dialog box.

Figure A-4   How to install IIS

How to use the downloaded web applications

Before you can open and run the web applications that you've downloaded for this book, you'll need to copy them to the web server. Then, you'll need to configure them for use with IIS. If IIS is installed on your own system, you can do that by using the procedure in figure A-5.

When you install IIS on your system, it creates a folder named Inetpub on your C drive. Within this folder is a folder named wwwroot. This is where all of your web applications and services must be stored. To start, then, you'll need to copy the chapter folders that contain the web applications to this folder. You'll find the chapter folders in the C:\Murach\ADO.NET\Book applications\IIS files folder that's created when you install the files for this book.

After you copy the folders to IIS, you'll need to configure each application for use by IIS. To do that, you use the Internet Information Services program shown in this figure. When you first start this program, it will list the available web servers in the left side of its window. In most cases, this list will include just the web server on your PC. Then, you can expand the node for this server and then expand the node for the default web site to display the IIS applications.

Next, locate the chapter folder that contains the application you want to use, and expand it to display the application folder. Notice that it's displayed with a folder icon rather than an IIS icon like most of the other items in the list. In this figure, for example, you can see the folder for the VendorDisplay application. To configure this application for IIS, display its properties as described in this figure, and then click on the Create button in the Directory tab. When you do, you'll notice that the icon for the application changes from a folder icon to an IIS icon. To complete the configuration, click on the OK button in the Properties dialog box.

The Internet Information Services and the properties for an IIS application

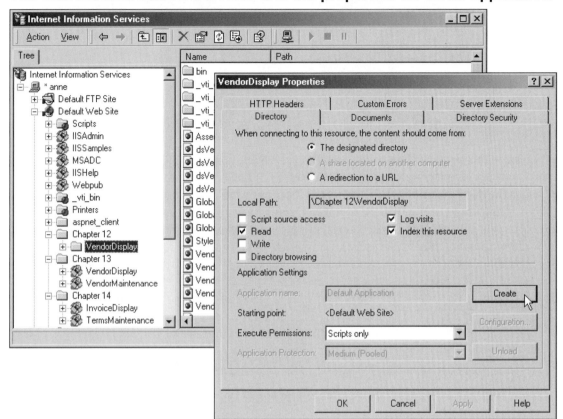

How to use the downloaded web applications

1. Use the Windows Explorer to navigate to the C:\Murach\ADO.NET\Book applications\IIS files folder. Then, copy the chapter folder for the application you want to use to the C:\Inetpub\wwwroot folder.

2. In Windows XP, start the Internet Information Services program using the Start→Programs→Administrative Tools→Internet Information Services command. In Windows 2000, use the Start→Programs→Administrative Tools→ Internet Services Manager command.

3. Expand the server node (anne in the window shown above) and the Default Web Site node to display the available applications. Then, expand the chapter folder you just copied so you can see the folder for the application you want to use. Right-click on that folder and select the Properties command from the menu that's displayed to display the Properties dialog box for that folder.

4. Display the Directory tab and then click on the Create button to configure the application for use with IIS. The icon in the Internet Information Services window will change from a folder to an IIS application icon like those shown above. Click on the OK button to accept the property changes, then close the Internet Information Services program.

Figure A-5   How to use the downloaded web applications for this book

Appendix B

Coding and syntax conventions

Throughout this book, you've learned how to use Visual Basic .NET and ADO.NET classes, methods, properties, and events, as well as SQL Server statements. In most cases, we've shown you only minimal syntax because when you work with Visual Studio, many of the coding details are taken care of for you by the Intellisense feature. However, this appendix summarizes the coding rules you have to follow and the syntax conventions that are used in the syntax summaries in the figures in case you ever have a question about them.

Coding rules and guidelines for VB.NET

General coding rules

1. Use spaces to separate the words and operators in each statement.

2. Indentation and capitalization have no effect on the operation of a statement.

Comments

1. Type an apostrophe followed by the comment.

2. A comment can be coded to the right of a statement or on a line with no statement.

3. A comment can't be coded to the right of a continuation character.

Continuations

To code a statement on more than one line so it's easier to read, type a space followed by an underscore (the continuation character) at the end of the first line. Then, type a return and continue the statement on the next line.

Coding recommendations

1. Use indentation and extra spaces to align statements and clauses within statements.

2. Use blank lines before and after groups of related statements.

Syntax conventions

`Boldfaced element`	Indicates that the element must be entered exactly as shown.
`Regular-font element`	Indicates that the element is provided by the programmer.
`[option]`	Indicates an option that may be coded but isn't required.
`[option|option]`	Indicates a set of alternative options, one of which may be coded.
`{option|option}`	Indicates a set of alternative options, one of which must be coded.
`...`	Indicates that the preceding option may be repeated multiple times.
`option`	Indicates the default value for an option.

A VB.NET coding example

Syntax: `dataAdapter.Update(dataSet[.dataTable])`

Example: `SqlDataAdapter1.Update(DsVendors1)`

A SQL coding example

Syntax:

```
Select column-list
From table-1
    [Inner] Join table-2
    On table-1.column-1 {=|<|>|<=|>=|<>} table-2.column-2
[Where selection-criteria]
[Order By column-1 [Asc|Desc] [, column-2 [Asc|Desc]]...]
```

Example:

```
Select VendorName, InvoiceNumber, InvoiceDate, InvoiceTotal
From Vendors Join Invoices
    On Vendors.VendorID = Invoices.VendorID
Order By VendorName, InvoiceTotal Desc
```

Index

S

W

X

Z

For more on Murach products, visit us at
www.murach.com

To get announcements and special offers on our books, please sign up for our emailing or postal mailing list via our web site or by contacting us by email, phone, fax, or mail.

For professional programmers

Murach's VB.NET Database Programming with ADO.NET	$49.50
Murach's Beginning Visual Basic .NET	49.50
Murach's SQL for SQL Server	49.50
Murach's Visual Basic 6	45.00
Murach's Beginning Java 2	$49.50
Murach's Java Servlets and JSP	49.50
Murach's OS/390 and z/OS JCL	$62.50
Murach's Structured COBOL	62.50
Murach's CICS for the COBOL Programmer	54.00
Murach's CICS Desk Reference	49.50
DB2 for the COBOL Programmer, Part 1 (Second Edition)	45.00
DB2 for the COBOL Programmer, Part 2 (Second Edition)	45.00

Coming soon

Murach's ASP.NET Web Programming

Prices and availability are subject to change. Please visit our web site or call for current information.

Our unlimited guarantee...when you order directly from us

You must be satisfied with our books. If they aren't better than any other programming books you've ever used...both for training and reference....you can send them back for a full refund. No questions asked!

Your opinions count

If you have any comments on this book, I'm eager to get them. Thanks for your feedback!

Mike Murach

To comment by

Email:	murachbooks@murach.com
Web:	www.murach.com
Postal mail:	Mike Murach & Associates, Inc.
	2560 West Shaw Lane, Suite 101
	Fresno, California 93711-2765

To order now,

Web: www.murach.com

Call toll-free:
1-800-221-5528
(Weekdays, 8 am to 5 pm Pacific Time)

Fax: 1-559-440-0963

Mike Murach & Associates, Inc.
Professional programming books

What software you need for this book

- Any version of Microsoft Visual Studio .NET or the Standard Edition of Microsoft Visual Basic .NET (see the Introduction for more details).
- If you're going to use databases on your own PC, you need to install MSDE (Microsoft SQL Server 2000 Desktop Engine), which comes with both Visual Studio and Visual Basic 2002. For Visual Studio or Visual Basic 2003, you'll need to download the files for installing MSDE from the Microsoft web site.
- If you're going to use a web server that's on your own PC, you need to install IIS, which comes with Windows 2000 or XP (except the XP Home Edition).
- If you haven't installed these products yet, please read appendix A in this book. *It will probably save you some time.*

The downloadable files for this book

- Complete source code and data for the applications presented in this book
- Descriptions and data for practice exercises and new projects that you can develop on your own, along with additional instructional aids like chapter summaries and learning objectives
- Files that make it easy for you to set up the databases if you're going to use your own PC as a database server (these are incorporated into both of the downloads listed above)

How to download the application files

- Go to www.murach.com, and go to the page for *Murach's VB.NET Database Programming with ADO.NET*.
- Click on the link for "Free download of the book applications." Then, download "All book files." This will download one file named adon_allfiles.exe to your C drive.
- Use the Windows Explorer to find the downloaded file (adon_allfiles.exe). Then, double-click on it and respond to the dialog boxes that follow. This installs the application files and databases in folders that start with C:\Murach\ADO.NET.
- From that point on, you can find the applications and data in folders like C:\Murach\ADO.NET\Book applications\Chapter 03 and C:\Murach\ADO.NET\Databases.
- Go to appendix A for instructions on how to set up the databases and web applications if you're going to have them reside on your own PC.

www.murach.com